THE MIDDLE EAST

THE MIDDLE EAST

A Guide to Politics, Economics, Society, and Culture

Volume One

Barry Rubin, Editor

M.E.Sharpe
Armonk, New York
London, England

Pages 399–401 reprinted by permission from *The Massachusetts Review*, Volume 42, Number 4, Winter 2001.
Pages 402–408 reprinted by permission from *Middle East Quarterly*, Volume 14, Number 3, Summer 2007.

Library of Congress Cataloging-in-Publication Data

The Middle East: a guide to politics, economics, society, and culture / Barry Rubin, editor.
p. cm.
Includes bibliographical references and index.
ISBN 978-0-7656-8094-5 (hardcover : alk. paper)
1. Middle East. 2. Middle East—Politics and government. 3. Middle East—Economic conditions.
4. Middle East—Social conditions. I. Rubin, Barry M.

DS44.M497 2012
956—dc22 2011016602

Printed in the United States of America

The paper used in this publication meets the minimum requirements of
American National Standard for Information Sciences
Permanence of Paper for Printed Library Materials,
ANSI Z 39.48-1984.

IBT (c) 10 9 8 7 6 5 4 3 2 1

Contents

Editor

Barry Rubin
Global Research in International Affairs (GLORIA) Center at the Interdisciplinary Center, Israel

Contributors

Yeru Aharoni
Global Research in International Affairs (GLORIA) Center at the Interdisciplinary Center, Israel

Ibrahim Al-Marashi
California State University San Marcos

Patrick Clawson
Washington Institute for Near East Policy, Washington, D.C.

Shmuel Duvdevani
Department of Film and Television, Faculty of the Arts, Tel Aviv University, Israel

Charles Paul Freund
Freelance writer and editor

Hillel Frisch
Begin-Sadat Center for Strategic Studies (BESA) and Department of Political Studies, Bar-Ilan University, Israel

Nissim Gal
Department of Art History, University of Haifa, Israel

Leora Garten
Global Research in International Affairs (GLORIA) Center at the Interdisciplinary Center, Israel

Najib Ghadbian
Department of Political Science and Middle East Studies at the University of Arkansas

Eytan Gilboa
Center for International Communication, Bar-Ilan University, Israel, and Visiting Professor at the Annenberg School for Communication, University of Southern California

Liora Hendelman-Ba'avur
The Center for Iranian Studies, Tel Aviv University, Israel

Haim Koren
Israeli Defense College

Anna Melman
Global Research in International Affairs (GLORIA) Center at the Interdisciplinary Center, Israel

Rasool Nafisi
Department of Arts and Sciences, Strayer University, Virginia

Dr. Alexandra Nocke
Freelance researcher in cultural studies and exhibition curator

Nimrod Raphaeli
Middle East Media Research Institute (MEMRI), Washington, D.C.

Keren Ribo
Formerly of the Global Research in International Affairs (GLORIA) Center at the Interdisciplinary Center, Israel

Kathleen Ridolfo
Leader Development and Education for Sustained Peace (LDESP), Naval Postgraduate School, California

Judith Colp Rubin
Journalist and independent scholar

Dr. Brent E. Sasley
Department of Political Science, University of Texas at Arlington

Peter Theroux
Author

Preface

The Middle East is an area of great importance globally, yet misperceptions abound. Events have made it a region of special interest to the West and so the search for understanding gains momentum. This publication is intended to clarify the region's complex history and issues.

In developing this project, we set out to explore seven significant themes that are usually not found in other sources. While many books focus on political history and conflicts, this two-volume work deals specifically with culture, religion, women, economics, governance, and media, as well as the role that the region's modern history has played in shaping its society and worldview. Our hope is that this collection will provide a new and different perspective, and at the same time shed light on a number of interesting issues.

There are differences in the structure of the constituent sections due to the nature of the materials presented. Thus, in discussing religions, there are separate sections devoted to each one, while governance is organized according to country and type of regime. There are three main cultural areas in the region: Arabic, Persian, and Israeli, corresponding to the Arabic, Farsi, and Hebrew languages. Most books, songs, newspapers, films, and other cultural products circulate mainly within these linguistic areas and are products of their traditions. The intent here is not to present a comprehensive portrayal of the region but to explore some specific, often neglected topics. We hope you find these materials useful.

Barry Rubin

THE MIDDLE EAST

Part I

Politics of Governing in the Middle East

Brent E. Sasley

Middle Eastern Governance

An Introduction

These pages examine how Middle Eastern states govern themselves and why they have the specific governmental systems they do. Of necessity this analysis leaves out some elements and some details; whole volumes are written on single countries alone. The focus, therefore, is on introducing readers to the major factors influencing the politics of governing in the Middle East, including historical developments, identity politics, regional conflict, and domestic struggles over power.

The Middle East here is defined as the Arab countries of North Africa (Morocco, Algeria, Tunisia, and Libya), Egypt, the countries of the Arabian Peninsula and the Gulf (Saudi Arabia, Yemen, the United Arab Emirates, Oman, Qatar, Bahrain, and Kuwait), Iraq, Iran, Syria, Jordan, Israel, Turkey, and the Palestinian areas (though for reasons of space the latter two and North Africa are not included in this discussion). Though others have used different understandings of "Middle East" to include some of the African countries bordering on the above-mentioned states, Afghanistan, and the southern republics of the former Soviet Union, there is good reason for keeping to the countries listed above.

This is because the Middle East is not just a geographic but also a political-cultural-historical area as well. Many or all of the countries listed above have shared similar cultural features (e.g., Arab ethnicity and culture), similar historical experiences (e.g., colonialism), and certainly share in a regional political dynamic that includes a variety of specific issues, such as the Arab-Israeli conflict, inter-Muslim disputes, the influx of oil wealth, and relations with the West.

Like other countries elsewhere in the world, Middle Eastern states are a product of their historical development. They have all shared some common elements (including the points mentioned above), though each has of course had its own particular trajectory. Israel, for example, has had a considerably different developmental experience because it is the only Jewish country in the region (though with a significant Arab minority) and has followed Western models of development. Iran, too, has its own particularities given its long history and the fact that it is predominantly Persian in language (Farsi) and ethnicity. And dependent primarily on oil revenues, the oil states of the Gulf have a different social contract with their citizens than non-oil states like Egypt or Jordan do, with the state providing for all of the citizens' needs in return for political quiescence.

Common Features

It is useful to begin with the commonalities that tie regional states together. This helps demonstrate why we should study this region as a whole. These similarities include the recent establishment of most of the regional states; similar instruments of governance; authoritarianism; a continuing state of political uncertainty; the close relationship between the state and the regime; and the governments' concerns over their own security.

First, any study of Middle Eastern governing systems must acknowledge the recentness of most states in the region. Aside from Turkey, Iran, Egypt, Yemen, and Morocco—which have venerable histories as geographically centralized political entities, though with borders that have shifted over the years—Middle Eastern states are recent creations, formed in the interwar period. Many gained independence only after World War II. Therefore, the governing systems of the region have undergone dramatic changes in a very short period of time.

Second, in terms of the instruments used to support the Arab regimes (who form the bulk of the regional states), there is no difference between the radical-nationalist states (those countries governed by a president and structured around specific ideological goals, such as Egypt, Syria, and Iraq under Saddam Hussein) and the monarchies (those countries ruled by a king, such as the Gulf states, Jordan, and Morocco)—and in fact, both share many similarities with the theocratic regime in Iran. All are heavily bureaucratized, all rely to some degree on narrow societal groups to fill the top positions in government and the state, all rely on a series of coercive agencies to enforce their will, and all repress their citizens in order to remain in power and prevent any threat to their positions.

Third, there is the persistence of authoritarianism in the region. Democracies or genuine democratic processes have been established in every other region of the world, yet in the Middle East, even where such processes have been created, they have largely been cosmetic, without giving any real power to the populations. For example, elections have been held in which citizens have voted for representatives to their parliaments and the presidencies, but these elections are tightly controlled: candidates are first vetted by the regime, information from candidates not endorsed by the regime is strictly limited, and parliaments have little direct role in policymaking. What rights have been given are tightly constrained by the state.

Fourth, at the same time, Middle Eastern governing systems are all in a state of political uncertainty in that they are reacting to constant pressure for change from both internal and external sources. None have achieved the widespread legitimacy among their citizens—defined as voluntary acceptance of the state's right to make decisions for them—that populations in Western countries bestow on their states. This raises questions about the long-term existence of current forms of government in the region. As each of the case studies that follow makes clear, the governing systems of the region's countries are at a crossroads as a result of changes in the regional system and within their own countries. This makes it a particularly propitious time to examine the politics of governing in the region. However, it is not clear which direction these changes will take. Can the existing systems survive or will they be decisively challenged by either radical religious or democratic movements? In some countries there have been movements toward greater political openness—for example, in Kuwait and Bahrain—but such reforms are fragile in that the regimes can and have overturned these changes. In this context, any conclusions drawn from such reforms can only be preliminary and are subject to change.

Fifth, in all of the Middle Eastern states except Israel, Turkey, and Lebanon, the difference between the state as a set of governing institutions and the regime as the particular individuals and groups who govern it is negligible. State institutions have been made or created to serve the interests of the regime: the latter inserts its closest supporters into positions of decision-making authority of the state, tying these to the furtherance of the regime's specific interests and needs. The state and regime become fused together.

Sixth, in all the regimes of the region, with the exception of Israel, Turkey, and Lebanon, the top priority is regime security, which is not necessarily the same as national security. That is, these regimes are concerned first and foremost with their continued dominance of the country, access to political and economic power, and even survival itself as the overwhelming factor shaping policy. This concern for their security has prompted these regimes to fashion a set of instruments such as concentration of executive power, expansive coercive agencies, control of information, and so on to protect themselves from external and, especially, internal threats and maintain their grip on power. This more than anything has shaped the contemporary politics, economics, and society in these states. This control is no longer absolute, if it ever was; challenges to the regimes' control have arisen from domestic groups organized to represent citizens' needs, especially Islamist movements such as the Muslim Brotherhood in Egypt and Jordan, which promote Islamic ideas and norms play a greater role in politics and society, and uncoordinated but broad-based movements calling for more political and civil rights. But central control remains powerfully embedded in their governing systems.

Arab Regimes

Because almost all of the regional states are considered, by themselves and by others, as Arab countries (they identify themselves as Arab, Arabic is the national language, they are members of the Arab League), we focus mostly on these states. Only Israel, Turkey, and Iran are non-Arab states, in that the majority populations in them are Jewish, Turkish, and Persian (though Israel has a sizable and Iran a smaller Arab minority). Any discussion of the Arab world is general. The states differ in many ways, including size, population, relationship to external powers, and wealth. Careful attention should be paid to discussing the Arab world so that abstract yet false generalizations are not imposed across the board. Still, the Arab world as a whole shares a number of similarities that make it possible to study it as a coherent area while recognizing the range of distinctness that also characterizes this region. These similarities include a history of colonial penetration, authoritarianism, and similar instruments of governance. The case study sections provide some examples of how these similarities coexist with differences that stem from each country's individual historical experience.

For example, one major common thread tying all the Arab regimes together is rule by a single strongman-dictator, who uses power via a system of repression and coercion. Both monarchies and republics, despite their different systems, operate in the same manner. In some cases, such as Saudi Arabia, the strongman is closely supported by a group of ethnic, tribal, familial, or religious kin and other loyalists, such that it is acceptable to speak of a regime in the sense of being composed of a large number of people; in other cases, such as Iraq under Saddam Hussein, there was a single leader who makes use of supporters' advice, but just as often ignored it. But in all cases, the regime is centered on the ruler. In fact, the existence of this strongman has been the critical variable in understanding the stability of the Arab regimes since the 1970s.

It may be tempting to explain this by the fact of culture—the "Arab character," historic tribalism, or Islam—but this would be misleading. Although culture is certainly relevant, the historical circumstances of the development of states in the Middle East point to a number of factors that help explain the persistence of authoritarianism. These include: political economy, external support in the form of great power patronage—which did not press for reform of the authoritarian system because of broader strategic concerns—ideology, fear of domestic challenges to their rule, and the concerted efforts of governments to maintain themselves in power.

Monarchies in the Middle East

Monarchies are governmental systems in which decision-making authority is centered in an individual who is like the "father" of the country and utilizes the trappings of royalty to represent himself to the people; power is kept in the royal family from one generation to the next, typically although not always from father to son. It is appropriate to begin a survey of the politics of governing in the Middle East with a discussion on monarchies. Beginning the discussion in this way helps us to better understand the developments that have swept the governing systems of the region since World War II—in some cases, completely changing these systems—as many of the states of the region were monarchies at the time of independence from the colonial powers. In fact, only in the British mandate of Palestine and where the French imposed a more direct form of colonial control (Lebanon, Syria) did monarchy not prevail.

There are today eight monarchies in the Middle East: Morocco, Jordan, and the six monarchies of the Gulf area—Saudi Arabia, Kuwait, Bahrain, Qatar, the United Arab Emirates (UAE), and Oman. Among the eight, there are some nominal differences in how they refer to their ruler. Kuwait and Qatar are emirates (ruled by emirs), Bahrain was an emirate until 2002 and has since then re-formed into a kingdom with a king, Oman is a sultanate (ruled by a sultan), and the UAE is a federation of seven smaller emirates, each with its own emir. These semantic differences are insignificant in that all of these rulers are actual kings in form if not in name. In addition, five former monarchies have since been overthrown in revolutions and converted to republican-presidential systems: Egypt (1952), Iraq (1958), Yemen (1962), Libya (1969), and Iran (1979).

The monarchies differ in the size of the royal family and its role in government. The Saudi Arabian and Kuwaiti royal families are large compared to other monarchies (with Saudi Arabia's numbering six or seven thousand), and family members fill the key political and administrative positions in the state. On the other hand, Jordan and Morocco have small royal families and rely for their inner circle of advisors on personnel from other key social groups.

In the context of similarities between Arab regimes, it is important to note that in the three main republican states there are also elements of dynastic rule. In Syria, Bashar al-Assad replaced his father Hafez al-Assad as president when the latter died in 2000. In Iraq, President Saddam Hussein was believed to be grooming his son Qusay to succeed him before he fell, while in Egypt, it is believed that before his fall in 2011, President Hosni Mubarak was preparing his son Gamal to follow him into office. In all cases, the sons were given positions of power within the ruling party's institutions as well as within the military and state apparatus. This was in order to give them experience with governing and generate familiarity with other members of the regime.

At any rate, all the surviving monarchies in the region share a set of common characteristics. Most particular is the same governmental structure: an individual leader who wields absolute or significant decision-making authority surrounded by members of his ethnic, tribal, or familial group in key positions of political and military power, or nonrelated senior civil servants, politicians, or military officers who have an interest in the perpetuation of the system so as to retain their positions of power and wealth.

They also differ from the republican regimes, which have tended to be more radical and anti-Western, usually siding with the Soviet bloc during the Cold War. For the republican regimes, radical pan-Arabist ideology (the belief in a single Arab nation across the Middle East that should be incorporated into a single political union) and a desire to change the status quo drove attempts to eliminate the remaining monarchies and seek hegemony in the region. In contrast, the monarchies generally turned toward the United States and the West for financial and military aid to secure them from threats from their republican neighbors.

Explaining Monarchy in the Middle East

For some observers, the predominance of monarchy as a form of Middle Eastern governance can be traced to the cultural characteristics of the region—primarily in the form of the "Arab character" or Islam. In other words, monarchy is part of a long tradition in the Arab-Islamic world. However, this approach has two flaws: First, monarchies are not unique to the Muslim world—after all, the kingly tradition has been found in various European, Native American, African, and Asian cultures. The uniqueness of Arab monarchy *today* cannot be explained by reference to ancient Arab kingdoms, since monarchy was a historical pattern throughout the world. Second, historical investigation reveals that the factors that do explain monarchy in the region incorporate cultural configurations to some extent, but also include the contemporary role of external powers, oil, inter-Muslim conflicts, and sheer political skill by ambitious leaders. The more critical question for the purposes of this discussion, then, is why does monarchy *persist* in the Middle East while it has virtually disappeared from the rest of the world?

Arab culture is closely identified with tribalism and patterns of interaction stemming from it. Tribalism refers to the organization of individuals into social and political units tied together by family and broader kinship patterns, typically governed by a single male ruler or family. These organizational patterns have been the predominant form of polity in the region since before the advent of Islam in the early seventh century C.E. Some scholars have made the argument that the patriarchy practiced in tribal society engendered obedience to central authority, and that the onset of monarchy merely meant a transfer of loyalty from the tribal leader to the king. However, tribal societies are characterized by decentralized authority, with each tribe laying claim to a tract of land and fiercely protecting its territory. The independence of tribes is also noteworthy: in the Gulf area, for example, tribal independence was ferociously defended by tribes who did not wish to submit to a stronger, centralized authority.

Cooperation between tribes was the dominant form of political structure until they were conquered by an expanding central government beginning in the first half of the twentieth century. In some Gulf states, tribal restlessness continued well into the 1970s. The gradual expansion of a king's authority against tribal resistance in this area indicates that monarchy is not a longtime tradition in the region but rather a conditional situation. Moreover, six of the eight current monarchies (excluding Oman and Morocco, both of which have monarchical forms of government stretching back centuries) were formed in only the 1910s, 1920s, and 1930s—with the UAE as late as 1971. Up to then, the most important tribal leaders ruled only with the explicit cooperation and support of other tribes. Without this backing, these leaders could not maintain an independent power such as today's kings do.

Islam is also sometimes considered to be conducive to monarchy because of its emphasis on submission to God and to the traditions of its founder, Muhammad, as well as its ostensible lack of democratic thought. But in fact, Islam does not identify monarchy as the best form of government. On one hand, in theological terms it emphasized a caliphate, leadership based on religion, rather than a sultanate, a purely political monarchy. At the least, the power of the king is supposed to be bound by religious obligations and laws. At the same time, Islam emphasizes consultation and includes the right of citizens to seek a new leader if the old one was engaged in misrule. It expects citizens to be actively engaged, to provide popular and uncoerced legitimacy, and to ensure that their representatives look after their interests. Certainly, the wide-ranging and absolute power of modern kings is not something Islamic thought has historically identified as the most effective means of governing. The entrenchment of monarchs as the representatives of separate national communities also undermined the Islamic conception of government as representative of the entire Islamic community (the *umma*).

The Shift to *Malik* and the Practice of Kingship

The Middle Eastern–Islamic use of the term "king" (*malik* in Arabic) in its general connotation is itself an early- to mid-twentieth-century phenomenon. The connotation in the pre- and early Islamic period was quite negative. "King" implied the arbitrary and secularist practices associated with the absolutist kings of Europe and thus was regarded with derision, contempt, and as an instrument of the nonbeliever.

By the early twentieth century, however, this attitude began to shift toward greater acceptance and adoption of the term, in the fullest sense of the word as historically used by the kings of Europe. First, as smaller political entities began to assert their autonomy from the Ottoman Empire, they used malik to refer to themselves as rulers over a small area and not necessarily in complete independence from the central imperial authority. For example, Sharif Hussein of the Hijaz, in what is today Saudi Arabia, insisted on being a king.

Second, with the decline and eventual dismantling of the Ottoman Empire and the creation of republican Turkey in 1923, the Islamic world no longer had any ruler that could compare to the Europeans on this type of imperial scale. Islamic rulers used the term to maintain equality with their European counterparts who were inserting themselves into the Middle East through economic and political control (and who by this point had essentially ceased to be kingdoms in the traditional sense of the term). Thus, the adoption of malik was a way of gaining domestic and international stature and sovereignty.

Sharif Hussein was the first to take the title, as King of the Hijaz in 1916. (The Hijaz is the narrow strip of land along the western coast of present-day Saudi Arabia, which contains the holy cities of Mecca and Medina.) His son Faisal also took the title of king in Syria in 1920 and Iraq in 1921, after being driven out of Syria by the French. In Egypt, Sultan Fu'ad declared himself king in March 1922, after Britain granted Egypt formal independence. In 1926, after conquering the Hijaz, Ibn Saud declared himself king over the area, and King of Saudi Arabia when in 1932 he consolidated his control over all of the country. In 1946, Emir Abdallah of Jordan became king; in 1951 Idris became King of Libya; and in 1957 the Moroccan ruler also shifted from sultan to king. In all these cases, malik, previously considered a derogatory term, became associated with power, respect, and control.

As Arab monarchs came to embrace the concept and practice of kingship, they expanded their kingdoms both in territory and of political authority. They did so through a series of instruments that enhanced their influence and control over a given (and expanding) geographic area. These included British support and the facilitation of the monarchy, the use of patronage to buy loyalty, the presentation of the king as the symbolic father of the people, and the use of religion, ostensible democratic structures, and oil wealth.

British Facilitation of Monarchy

Not all Europeans sought to establish monarchies in the Middle East. In Libya, Italy was willing to work with a monarchy (after an attempt at decentralization) in order to strengthen its own control, but the French in their mandatory territories avoided monarchy altogether, preferring instead a republican system. Britain was the primary external facilitator of Middle Eastern monarchies. The British did not always start out intending to raise one Arab ruler to kingship over his rivals. (In what became Saudi Arabia, for example, they were careful to support both Ibn Saud of the Najd and Sharif Hussein of the Hijaz in the early twentieth century even though they were fierce rivals.) But they eventually did so because they believed this type of indirect rule was the best method for looking after their interests in the region, as compared to France, which preferred direct rule. In addition, Britain was simply exporting its own historical tradition of political organization. Because Britain was the major external controlling or interfering power in the area, it ended up having the greatest outside effect on the region's developing governing structures. The British controlled or dominated in Egypt, Jordan, Palestine, Iraq, Saudi Arabia, and the smaller Gulf states, and with the sole exception of Palestine—then Israel—all of its territories became monarchies in the course of the twentieth century.

Britain's primary interests in the Middle East were strategic: to enhance and protect its international commercial and security interests as the world's preeminent power, and to guard the Middle Eastern route to India, often referred to by the British as "the jewel in the crown" of the British

Empire because it represented the main achievement of British colonialism. It did this in three main ways. First, in the early twentieth century Britain provided local rulers with an umbrella security guarantee against external powers, to prevent the latter from invading areas of British influence. In the coastal Gulf states, Britain signed a series of pacts from the 1920s to mid-century with the strongest families to protect their commercial ships from pirates. In Bahrain, the leading al-Khalifa family decided in the eighteenth century to make Bahrain a British protectorate, to prevent the Iranians (known then as the Persians) from capturing it. In Saudi Arabia in the 1930s and 1940s, Britain helped Ibn Saud against other Arabian tribes loyal to the Ottoman Empire, notably the Rashidis.

Second, Britain used a combination of financial, economic, diplomatic, and military aid to support local leaders who were expanding their own spheres of control. With this British support, these leaders, such as the Saudis, the al-Sabah in Kuwait, and the al-Khalifa in Bahrain, were elevated in power over other competing families, tribes, and clans. British aid came mostly in the form of weapons (guns and ammunition) and financial subsidies. These subventions were critical to the strengthening and development of the early monarchs. They allowed these rulers to avoid having to heavily tax their own subjects and allied tribes, which might breed discontent or resentment, and gave these leaders the capacity to lure other tribes to them with the offer of British financial aid.

Third, by drawing the borders of the Arab states (either on their own or in consultation with local Arab leaders), the British also succeeded in defining the boundaries of the monarchies. This helped by curtailing the areas beyond which the budding monarchs could not expand, thus shifting their concerns to internal consolidation. But more importantly, it gave the monarchs a stake in the survival of their kingdoms, with a physical investment to protect, and motivated them to enhance their rule at the expense of both external and internal competitors.

British facilitation of monarchy was nowhere more evident than in the promises London made to Sharif Hussein of the Hijaz. At the beginning of World War I, the British perceived that Hussein was an important Arab figure who could lead a revolt against the Ottoman Empire, Britain's enemy in the war. In return for his support, the British promised Hussein that the Arabs would be granted independence, and that he would be given a position of some control over these territories (though these latter elements were much more vague).

However, Hussein's own regional ambitions to reconstitute the caliphate under his rule soon became a liability to the British, by threatening their own influence and control. The rise of Ibn Saud in central Arabia offered the British an alternate leader they could support. Although they stopped providing the same levels of support to Hussein that they had during the war (and in fact, these levels kept up to a considerable degree in the immediate years after the war), the British still felt they owed a debt to Hussein and that, moreover, it would be useful to keep him dependent on them.

The British therefore made Hussein's sons monarchs in their own right—Abdullah in Jordan and Faisal in Iraq. In doing so, the British expanded the number of kingdoms in the region through artificial means, establishing monarchies in places where there was no history of monarchy. At the same time, because Abdullah and Faisal were outsiders to their kingdoms, with no attachment to the local populace, the British had to provide all of the military and most of the financial support just so that the two could survive. In Jordan especially, British support was vital for the survival of the monarchy. Tiny, landlocked, with few natural resources, and characterized by tribal social structures unused to centralized authority, Jordan needed British economic and military aid to keep the monarchy in power and facilitate the social engineering that brought together the various Bedouin tribes of the country in accepting the monarchy's legitimacy. British officers trained and led the Jordanian military (the Arab Legion), continuing to do so into the mid-twentieth century.

British backing was critical for all of the monarchies that Britain supported. Of course, British support (both direct and inadvertent) for emergent Middle Eastern monarchies was not the only reason for their development and maintenance. In fact, once British aid was removed, some monarchies continued and thrived while others did not.

Patronage

The use of patronage (the dispensation of money, arms, political positions, and so on, in return for loyalty) as a form of politics was a key element in the creation and maintenance of Middle Eastern monarchies. The two social groups most relevant in this context are merchants and, especially, tribes. It is no coincidence that the Yemeni monarchy is the only one of the Gulf monarchies that has been overthrown; it was also the only one that did not succeed in suppressing the tribes and ensuring their loyalty, through patronage, to the regime.

The merchants were those families or clans (sometimes tribes) who controlled a particular trade route or specific commercial enterprise, such as pearling in the coastal Gulf states. They thus wielded significant economic and political power. But the dominant social structure of the Middle East has been that of tribes. Under this system, tribes (bound together by blood and intermarriage, and tied into a loose political framework with a sense of distinctiveness and shared traditions) controlled their own area for settlement, grazing, and wandering, and cooperated with each other on various matters when it was deemed necessary, such as trade or resolution of intertribal conflicts. They resisted any loss of this autonomy under a more centralized authority.

However, both merchants and tribes were willing to provide loyalty and support to a strong leader, provided their positions and independence were not compromised. Merchants could provide revenue, while tribes could supply soldiers for war and conquest. As the key social groups in society, both could also provide legitimacy. Such support was critical for emerging strongmen who wished to transform themselves into monarchs—they needed the revenue and troops to finance and staff their expansion and consolidation. The trick for rulers was to ensure that these groups were kept happy; tribes especially were very jealous of their independence and fought fiercely to retain it. In Oman, for example, a tribal revolt against the sultan lasted from 1964 to 1975, and was overcome only with great difficulty.

Patronage was used to buy the support of merchants, especially in the Gulf states, and of tribes, especially in Saudi Arabia, Jordan, and Morocco. In the late nineteenth and early twentieth centuries, before the borders of the contemporary states had been set, patronage took the form of subsidies (which many of the rulers themselves received from the British), reduced taxes and tributes, a stake in the continuation of the strongman's rule through political consultation, or placement over a primary trade route or commercial enterprise.

As the state began to emerge in territorial, political, and bureaucratic form, and the strongman was transformed into the king, other forms of patronage were utilized. These included cooptation of religion, employment in the burgeoning bureaucracy, prominent positions within the state machinery and politics, and—in an effort to go over the heads of the leading merchants and tribes directly to the citizens—provision of social services such as health care.

Although the importance of religious leaders to society varied across the different states, all monarchies sought to bring them under state control by offering political and financial inducements. The practice of religion for the most part was made a function of the state bureaucracy. This meant that the state paid the salaries of religious leaders, providing a direct form of subsidy in return for supporting the state itself. At the same time, the kings gave these leaders funding for their own educational and religious purposes, such as the building of mosques and religious schools.

The monarchies also provided employment as a direct form of patronage to their citizens. Primarily this was done by expanding the state bureaucracy, which opened up thousands of jobs and directly provided wages to the citizens. Wealthier members of society (particularly the merchants and tribal leaders) were given access to government aid to conduct their businesses. This came in the form of contracts, licenses, and land leases. In both cases, the population was given direct payments in return for supporting the monarchy's existence and for acceptance of its right to make decisions on behalf of the population.

Regimes also incorporated leading families and key social groups into bureaucratic and political positions, giving them some involvement in the conduct of state business and a feeling that they were being consulted by the rulers in the affairs of state. In Jordan, for example, the Bedouin—

who today are the most loyal supporters of the monarchy—were gradually brought into the civil service in the mid- to late 1920s, replacing the Palestinians and Syrian nationalists who had staffed these positions when the state was first created in 1922. Bedouin (also known as "East Bankers") were also purposefully recruited into the military and other security agencies, giving them room for social mobility, income to replace that lost as the state took control over the area's economic activity, and a direct stake in the maintenance of the monarchy's security. The incorporation of the Bedouin into the military also allowed the ruling Hashemite family to avoid the military coups that plagued several other erstwhile monarchies, such as Egypt and Iraq.

Finally, as the states became more institutionalized, the monarchs were able to use growing and stable revenue to tie the citizens directly to them. They did this by providing a plethora of social services, including health care, education, housing, food, energy, and pensions. The oil monarchies were better able to provide these things because they had more income from oil exports, but even the non-oil states expended government resources to offer them.

The Monarch as the Father Figure of Society

Patronage alone could not suffice to ensure the continuation of the monarchies. After all, any other type of government could do the same, provided it had the necessary funds. To further underscore their legitimacy, the regimes legitimized themselves by emphasizing the importance and significance of the ruler and his family to the state, holding themselves up as symbols of national pride, strength, and indeed the very essence of the state. Monarchies were much more successful at this than the republican regimes, which could only ask for loyalty to an abstract system or idea; in contrast, monarchies are embodied in the physical person of the king and his family. Such symbolism was aided by the long rule of individual kings.

King Hussein of Jordan, who ruled from 1953 until his death from cancer in February 1999, best exemplifies this symbolism. Hussein was widely loved by the Jordanian population; in fact, many Jordanians had known no other ruler their entire lives. Hussein purposely cultivated this fatherly image in a number of ways, including his constant attention to the key tribal groups in society and a personal touch that brought him into direct contact with ordinary Jordanian citizens. For example, he would often visit Jordanian families to help mourn a loss or celebrate an achievement of one of their members. He also met regularly with petitioners who sought his help in resolving a given problem. Other Gulf monarchs have acted similarly, touring their countries to hear in person petitions and complaints of citizens. Hussein personally guided Jordan through many of its key formative crises, including the loss of the West Bank (1967), civil war (1970, during which Hussein ordered the army to destroy the Palestine Liberation Organization), the ceding of Jordanian aspirations over the West Bank (1988), the Gulf War (1991), and the peace treaty with Israel (1994).

King Hassan II in Morocco (who ruled from 1961 until his death also in 1999) is another example. In the conflict with Algeria and over the Western Sahara (where Morocco has made claims against Spain and Algeria), the king promoted himself as the symbol of resistance to external aggression and interference and, in the case of Western Sahara, the defender of national honor. Sultan Qaboos of Oman, who took power in 1970 and continues to rule today, has done the same. Widely seen as a hero who would make life better for Oman and Omanis, Qaboos encouraged this sentiment over his long reign by presenting himself as the modernizer and savior of Oman.

The creation of hereditary monarchies—in which succession remains within the royal family—went a considerable way toward entrenching the monarchy as the symbol of the state and its national community. Efforts by republican states could not duplicate the results. In part this is a reflection of the sheer size of many of the Middle Eastern royal families. In such cases, the families are presented as the symbolic unifying element for the country. But hereditary succession also ensures that the kingly authority is maintained and the ideas represented by the king and his family perpetuated.

Such arrangements are helped by the fact that most of the monarchical dynasties have been the dominant family in the area for hundreds of years. The Alaouite family in Morocco has been the ruling family since it first united the country in 1664. In Bahrain, the al-Khalifa family has been dominant since the late eighteenth century, while the al-Sabah in Kuwait have been the leading family since the 1750s. In Qatar, the al-Thani family has ruled since the nineteenth century. In Oman, the current ruler's family, the al-Said, stretches back to the leadership of the Ibadi imamate in the 1700s. The House of Saud constructed the first Saudi state in the 1750s. In the UAE, by tacit agreement the president of the federation comes from the al-Nahyan clan of Abu Dhabi (whose claim to authority stretches back to the second half of the eighteenth century), while the prime minister comes from the al-Maktum clan of Dubai. And in Jordan, the most artificial of the contemporary monarchies, the royal family traces its descent to the ruler of the Hijaz at the beginning of the twentieth century and through him back to the family of Muhammad himself.

The historical pattern thus indicates that the formation of monarchies in the region has not been a deterministic cultural process but rather an accidental political one. The particular form of government that monarchy represents was chosen because it was the easiest way for an ambitious leader to consolidate and centralize authority in his (and his family's) hands over a wider area than had previously been the case when the king was only a leader of a single tribe. The creation of monarchy also helped destroy other power centers and potential challengers to the king's authority, and provided the citizens with a single locus toward which they could direct their loyalty.

Three Types of Middle Eastern Monarchies

There are three types of Middle Eastern monarchies in existence today: Islamic monarchies, which depend heavily on religious or divine mandates to rule; constitutional monarchies, in which rules are guided by a set of written or customary norms and the king's position is more ceremonial; and oil monarchies, which rely on oil revenue to generate legitimacy. These are, of course, ideal types; in reality there is overlap between the categories, and some kings rely on a combination of factors inherent in each class to rule. But these categories are still useful to help us better understand their basis for rule.

Islamic Monarchies

Although all the monarchies in the Middle East define Islam as the religion of the state and use shariah (Islamic law as established through the Koran and the sayings and traditions of Muhammad) as a basis for their legal structures, some monarchies rely more heavily and explicitly on Islam as a legitimating factor for their rule than others. Islamic monarchies exist in Jordan, Morocco, and Saudi Arabia. The former two base the monarch's claim to rule on his ancestral connection to Muhammad, the founder of Islam. Saudi Arabia's monarchy bases its legitimacy on its role as guardian of the Islamic holy sites (Mecca and Medina) and the practice of what it considers the most pure form of Islam, Wahhabism.

The only two monarchies not overthrown by revolutionaries or reinforced by oil wealth are Jordan and Morocco. It is no coincidence that both claim their legitimacy from religious mandate. The ruling Hashemite family of Jordan traces its lineage to Muhammad, who was a member of the House of Hashim of the Quraysh tribe, in what is now Saudi Arabia. Since the beginning of the thirteenth century, the Hashemites were the governors of the Hijaz, ruling with the title *sharif*, which referred to a descendent of the Prophet. This position is what convinced the British to turn to Sharif Hussein—great-great-grandfather of Jordan's current King Abdullah—for leadership of the Arab Revolt against the Ottoman Empire during World War I. The Hashemites were thus the symbolic and most visible leaders of the Arab national movement, and Hashemite sons were installed as kings in Syria, Iraq, and Jordan.

The line of the current king of Morocco, Muhammad VI, also traces back to the founder of Islam through Muhammad's daughter Fatima. The king's official title is also Commander of the Faithful (Amir al-Mu'minin). Like the Hashemites, the Moroccan kings have used their sharifian status to endow their monarchy with divine mandate. This has been further enhanced in Moroccan legal texts, which have provided religious authorization and support for the kings. King Hassan II, who ruled from 1961 to 1999, was also active in ensuring that his rule was legitimated through ostensibly Islamic political acts, such as the use of *bay'a* (allegiance) to promote his absolute authority. This was to emphasize the duty of Moroccans, as Muslims, to provide unity and consensus to the ruler so that he could—as an Islamic ruler—better meet the population's needs and fit with the traditional Islamic understanding of leadership.

Although the Saudi kings do not trace their ancestry to Muhammad, they do rely heavily on Islam as the basis for their continuing authority. This is done in two ways. First, in the mid-1980s the Saudi king took as an official title the Custodian of the Two Holy Mosques (in response to Iranian claims that monarchy and Islam did not fit together). The holiest sites in Islam, the cities of Mecca and Medina, are also the objective of the annual hajj, the pilgrimage that is the duty of all Muslims. This gives the Saudi monarchy a powerful legitimacy.

Second, the Saudi state itself is the direct result of an alliance begun in 1745 in central Arabia between Muhammad ibn Saud, a local tribal leader, and Muhammad ibn Abd al-Wahhab, a religious reformer. Wahhabism was heralded as a return to the pure form of Islam practiced during the era of the Prophet and his immediate successors. It provided a powerful appeal—out of religious zeal, opportunism, and sheer fear—to the people of Arabia as the Saudi state expanded in the early twentieth century. This fusion of political and religious authority in Saudi Arabia is unique among the region's monarchies, and so is discussed as a separate case below.

Constitutional Monarchies

There are no true constitutional monarchies in the Middle East in the European sense of the term, referring to a ceremonial monarchy only. All monarchies in the region are absolutist in that they retain ultimate and final decision-making authority. However, officially, there are four current constitutional monarchies: Jordan, Morocco, Kuwait, and Bahrain. In addition, so-called constitutional monarchies of the same type existed in Egypt, Iraq, and Libya until the radical-nationalist movements overthrew them in 1952, 1958, and 1969 respectively, and in Iran (from 1905 until the year of the Islamic Revolution in 1979).

In all Middle Eastern constitutional monarchies, the kings did not accept a set of constitutional rules and regulations out of a belief in their inherent value; none wanted their rule to be constrained in any way. They accepted such restrictions out of necessity or pressure from European states or powerful local groups. The General Syrian Congress, for example, tried to construct a true constitutional monarchy by proclaiming Faisal king of Syria in March 1920, but limiting his power through the imposition of rules and consultative mechanisms. The kings also believed constitutional monarchy was a reflection of progress and modernity, which they considered necessary to maintain in order to obtain support from foreign powers and legitimacy from domestic groups.

In short, no king took constitutional monarchy seriously. Because of this, the current monarchies listed here are better represented in one of the other two categories. This category is more noteworthy for the fact that the constitutional monarchies are better known for being overthrown than anything else.

Oil Monarchies

The main difference between the oil and other types of monarchies is that the former possess massive oil reserves that have generated significant revenue for them and allowed these regimes to buy high levels of legitimacy for themselves, as well as pay for a vast system of suppression, entrenchment, and patronage. The oil monarchies are all concentrated in the Gulf area: Saudi Arabia, Kuwait, Oman, Bahrain, Qatar, and the UAE. They all started out as either local tribal authorities or city-states that gradually extended their authority in the surrounding areas, and then used income from oil to buy support from their populations by tying them to the central government and creating central state institutions.

The oil-producing monarchies are rentier states. Such countries rely on rents that accrue to the state by virtue of its location, in terms of its geopolitical position or its possession of natural resources. Rents are not earned as the result of domestic economic productivity, but rather are simply a reward for the accident of historical and geographic development. A rentier state is one where rents are the predominant source of government income, and the bulk of the population is engaged in receiving the benefits of these rents, rather than contributing to their production.

In the Gulf region, oil provides these states with their rents. Oil exploration in the area began in the 1930s (oil was first discovered in Bahrain in 1932) and by the 1950s had become a major source of income for the regimes. But it was not until the 1970s that oil revenue dramatically increased: oil prices tripled from under $3 per barrel in mid-1973 to almost $12 per barrel by the end of the year as a consequence of the 1973 Arab-Israeli War between Syria and Egypt on one side and Israel on the other. Subsequently, Arab oil-producing states sought to punish Western countries it felt were too supportive of Israel, particularly the United States and the Netherlands, by cutting oil production and initiating embargoes against them for a short period of time.

Later, as a result of the panic engendered by the overthrow of the shah in the Iranian Revolution of 1979 and the decline in Iranian oil production, oil prices rose again from about $13 to $34 per barrel. As a result, revenue from oil exports shot up from 1972 to 1980 (in constant 2005 U.S. dollars) among the Arab oil producers of the Organization of the Petroleum Exporting Countries (OPEC), the main world body of oil-producing states: in Kuwait revenues rose from $10.3 to $38.4 billion; in Qatar, from $1.7 to $11 billion; in Saudi Arabia, from $17.2 to $213.6 billion; and in the UAE, from $3.9 to $38.5 billion.

Today, the bulk of the export base and source of government revenue of the oil monarchies come from the sale of oil. Oil exports account for 60 percent of export receipts and 60 percent of government revenues in Bahrain; 70 percent of total exports and 75 percent of government revenue in the UAE; 90–95 percent of revenue from exports and 80 percent of government income in Kuwait; 85 percent of export earnings (including natural gas) and 70–80 percent of government revenue in Qatar; over 70 percent of total exports and about 70 percent of government earnings in Oman; and 85–95 percent of export earnings and 75 percent of government income in Saudi Arabia.

The influx of oil wealth has given the oil monarchies a dominant role in society and the economy as well as the tools to control their populations to a greater degree than their republican counterparts. Iraq had a similar experience with the rise in oil prices, but its costly suppression of a Kurdish rebellion in the 1970s and its war with Iran in the 1980s siphoned off much of this revenue and placed it in a different category from the smaller oil producers. With the generation of oil wealth, kings in the Gulf became independent of tribal or commercial support: they had enough money on their own, and they could use that money to fund their own militaries and, especially, to pay for the loyalty and support of the citizens and elites through social services and patronage. It also meant that the kings no longer had to mediate through tribal, religious, or merchants: the provision of social services tied citizens directly to the regime without having to go through these others.

This process also had the effect of reducing the direct coercion and violence that marked the republican regimes, such as Syria and Iraq. Given the citizenry's reliance on and acceptance of state financial support, there was less need for repression as a tool of control. This became for the monarchies such a critical part of their rule, that even when the world price of oil declined in the mid-1980s, the kings preferred to engage in deficit spending or draw down their foreign reserves, rather than cut back on the services they provided to their societies.

These services include: free health care and education through the university level; large pensions for the elderly, widows, and the disabled; no income tax; heavy subsidies for services such as electricity, water, and housing; subsidies on food staples such as bread, rice, and flour; and, of course, very cheap gas. The state also plays the central role in the economy; employees depend on the regime for jobs, as do businesses for licenses and contracts. At the same time, the influx of oil wealth has weakened the capacity of other social groups—such as tribes and merchants—to act as an independent power center from the king. For many elites in these areas, pearling, trade, and British subventions were the key sources of income until the exploitation of oil. Oil wealth allowed the strongest families (those that came to form the monarchy) to be independent of these elites for military, financial, and political support.

The end result is that all citizens have a stake in the continuation of the system and its stability, and are less willing to undermine the regimes by trying to change the system. Even when, during the 1990s, there were increasing demands for political liberalization, only extremist or fringe groups called for an overhaul of the system (that is, the end of the monarchy); most demands focused only on greater political participation or economic liberalizations.

Saudi Arabia: The Fusion of Political and Religious Authority

Saudi Arabia is unique among the Middle Eastern monarchies because it relies heavily on oil wealth to ensure its tacit social contract, but it also relies heavily on religion as a legitimating factor. It is further unique in that nowhere else were political and religious authority integrated so closely together, to form the basis for state expansion and consolidation. This fusion did not take place in the other Gulf monarchies, where secular authority prevailed and Islam was used only as a façade for the temporal regimes to claim the right to rule. In the coastal Gulf states, the kings descended from local sheikhs who cemented their authority over small areas with their military skill and commercial capacities.

Saudi Arabia was founded on three elements: political unification, tribal support, and religious endorsement. The authority of the royal family increased in conjunction with the development of the state and the creation and expansion of the oil industry. This has meant that the monarchy is responsible for creation of the state, its technological modernization, the generation of oil wealth, and its provision of services to Saudi society. At the same time, the close collaboration between political and religious leaders has provided for further identification of the House of Saud with the sociocultural foundations of society. The regime, therefore, is identified with both societal and state development.

The Saudi state began in the 1750s, when a tribal strongman, Muhammad ibn Saud, allied himself with an Islamic religious reformer, Muhammad ibn Abd al-Wahhab. In return for supporting their call for a stricter interpretation of Islam, and pushing for conversion to it of his subjects, the Wahhabis recognized Muhammad ibn Saud as an imam, or religious leader, and this arrangement continued under succeeding Saudi rulers and *ulama* (Islamic scholar-clerics). It was reinforced by successive intermarriages between the House of Saud and the families of leading Islamic scholars. This prototype of the Saudi state later collapsed when Muhammad Ali of Egypt invaded the Arabian Peninsula in 1811–1818, and over the next century and a half, the Saudis tried to reconstruct their state but could never make it last. In 1902, Abd al-Aziz ibn Saud began a new campaign to unify the peninsula under Saudi control, which finally ended in success in 1932.

The creation and expansion of the Saudi state was not driven by religion, but Wahhabi revivalist fervor did play a critical role. At the core of this process were the much-feared Ikhwan, fervent religious warriors, whose military successes brought tribes fearful of it to Ibn Saud, expanding his territorial reach and political authority and legitimacy (in addition to Ibn Saud's adept politicking among the tribes and the British). Once the kingdom was united in 1932, Ibn Saud relied heavily on the ulama for administrative service, since the nascent state lacked qualified people trained in modern governance of such a large entity. Ulama participation in government also provided further legitimacy and credibility to the regime. As the bureaucratization of the state advanced, the clerics were incorporated into the state through positions in the state machinery, state salaries, a consultative role in the king's decision-making process, the authority to oversee religious matters within the state and interpret shariah according to their strict version, and funding to carry out religious activities both within the state and beyond its borders (for example, the construction of mosques in other Islamic countries in Africa, the Balkans, and Central Asia).

Saudi political authority has also been purposely based on Islam as religion. The Koran is identified as the country's constitution, while shariah is the foundation for all laws in the country (though some secular codes have been introduced, particularly in commercial affairs). This has allowed the Saudi kings to set themselves up as the highest authority, subject only to Islamic law and thus beyond the demands of the citizens. In order to retain Islam as the key legitimating factor for their absolutist rule, the monarchy has also created a series of institutions to underline its claim to religious-political authority. A religious police force (the *mutawwa'in*), part of the Committee for the Propagation of Virtue and Prevention of Vice, a government agency, enforces the social laws of shariah. Non-Muslim worship is forbidden, and only Muslims can be citizens of the kingdom.

The Basic Law, promulgated in 1992, best exemplifies the fusion of political and religious authority in Saudi Arabia. In addition to using the Koran as the source of legal authority, the law stipulates that the king shall be a direct heir to Abd al-Aziz al-Saud, as either his son or grandson. The Saudi monarchy is thus explicitly founded on Islamic as well as temporal authority.

Why Do Monarchies Persist in the Middle East?

Why have monarchies disappeared from virtually the entire rest of the world—confined to symbolic and ceremonial purposes at best—but not the Middle East? And why do Middle Eastern monarchies retain such power over their citizens? It is important to consider these questions so that the difference between secular, presidential regimes and monarchies, despite their shared authoritarianism, is more clearly understood.

The eight contemporary Middle Eastern monarchies have survived both regional (radical-nationalism) and global (the end of the Cold War in 1991) changes that have swept away their counterparts elsewhere in the Middle East and in other regions of the world. Although there is some disagreement among scholars regarding the specific reasons for this, several factors are relevant: the monarchy as symbol, American support during the Cold War, less tolerance for radical-nationalist regimes, the influx of oil wealth, the sheer skill and adaptability of the kings themselves, and the government's openness to political and social change.

Symbols of the State

First, the monarchs have presented themselves as the symbols of the state and the national populace. Loyalty has converged on the monarchy itself, as representative of a particular national triumph or symbol. In Morocco, the king is the heir to the independence movement and the founder of Islam; in Jordan he is also the heir to the Hashemite legacy; and in Saudi Arabia kings are direct descendants of the kingdom's founder and the symbol of Wahhabism. Moreover, because they have stayed in power for so long, the royal families have become identified in the minds of their citizens as representative of the country. Aside from the Islamist opposition, mainstream opponents to the monarchies do not demand an end to the monarchy itself, but rather a more open system to allow citizens a greater say in decision making alongside the king.

U.S. Support During the Cold War

Second, most Middle Eastern monarchs had direct American support during the Cold War, as the United States sought to keep Soviet influence out of the Middle East. American military and economic aid allowed the regimes to protect themselves from external enemies and meet internal challenges. This continued the tradition of outside powers propping up the regimes, as the British did in the early years of the monarchies' development and then independence.

Decreased Tolerance for Radical-Nationalist Regimes

Third, although radical-nationalism entailed a serious threat to the monarchies—such that some of them seemed ripe for collapse in the 1950s and 1960s—that threat ended by the late 1960s and 1970s. The heavy defeat inflicted by Israel on the radical-nationalist regimes of Syria and Egypt in 1967 helped discredit their populist, adventurous call for dramatic change in the region. The monarchies were then identified as more stable and less volatile, and therefore less likely to bring disaster down on their states.

Influx of Oil Wealth

Fourth, as discussed above, the accumulation of massive amounts of oil wealth ensured the loyalty of citizens, as the monarchies traded social services for political quiescence and societal acceptance. By providing cheap or free housing, electricity, gas, foodstuffs, education, health care, and other services, the regimes tied the population directly to their own existence.

Leadership Skills

Fifth, most of the individual monarchs themselves were quite successful at state and nation building, engendering the loyalty of the population and key social groups. The kings became quite skilled at mediating among their society's various and conflicting elements, helping to resolve tensions, earn loyalty, and present themselves as above these divisions and thus the true representative of the state. Particularly when it came to smaller minorities, the king was seen as the protector and thus earned the staunch loyalty of that group.

In Jordan, for example, East Bankers are a pillar of support for the Hashemite monarchy in the face of a majority Palestinian population that has not always viewed its own interests as compatible with those of the East Bankers. In Saudi Arabia it was religious elites, while in Kuwait the al-Sabah family ruled with the support of the merchants. Thus, diverse populations made up of various sectarian, linguistic, or ethnic groups can coexist more easily, because they are not competing for political power but rather subject to the same source of political power, the king. The monarchies also successfully combined technological development with traditional or religious styles of governing. Citizens reaped the benefits of economic advancement but did not necessarily have to endure the radical social change that often comes with it. They had, in other words, the best of both worlds, which the monarchs facilitated and made possible.

Openness to Political and Social Change

Finally, the oil monarchs have been more open to political and social change than the republican regimes (a notable exception is Saudi Arabia, though even there have been signs of minor change). They have, for example, allowed for some political liberalizations through elections and some greater freedom of the press. They have also been more progressive in family law than much of the rest of the Arab world, for example by expanding the status of women to participate in politics. This has given their citizens an opportunity to feel as though they have more say in the political process, if not the actual decision-making process, and thus removed some points of contention that could be used to generate greater opposition to the regimes.

Throughout the world, states in the early stages of formation and consolidation have historically gone through a period of centralized authority in the form of a monarchy of some kind. Middle Eastern states are no different, and most arose in the context of the development of the state and independence from colonial powers. The question centers on whether or not monarchies will soon disappear in the Middle East, as part of the same general historical development evident elsewhere. The answer is unclear at this point. The monarchies have faced serious challenges in the past, which they have dealt with through a successful combination of repression and change. It remains to be seen if they can continue such a balancing act as new challenges and threats arise.

References and Further Reading

Beblawi, Hazem, and Luciani Giacomo, eds. *The Rentier State.* London: Croom Helm, 1987.

Gause, F. Gregory, III. *Oil Monarchies: Domestic and Security Challenges in the Arab Gulf States.* New York: Council on Foreign Relations Press, 1994.

Herb, Michael. *All in the Family: Absolutism, Revolution, and Democracy in the Middle Eastern Monarchies.* Albany: SUNY Press, 1999.

Kostiner, Joseph. *The Making of Saudi Arabia, 1916–1936: From Chieftaincy to Monarchical State.* New York: Oxford University Press, 1993.

———, ed. *Middle East Monarchies: The Challenge of Modernity.* Boulder, CO: Lynne Rienner, 2000.

Salame, Ghassan, ed. *The Foundations of the Arab State.* London: Croom Helm, 1987.

Zahlan, Rosemary Said. *The Making of the Modern Gulf States: Kuwait, Bahrain, Qatar, the United Arab Emirates, and Oman.* London: Unwin Hyman, 1989.

The Rise of the Radical-Nationalist Regimes

A new era in Arab and Middle East politics began on July 23, 1952. A group of mid-ranking military officers calling themselves the Free Officers staged a coup in Egypt that ushered in the era of radical-nationalism, a movement to enact major social and political change both within the Arab states and in the Middle East as a whole, including the overthrow of the old elites and an end to Western influence. This era lasted throughout the 1950s and 1960s as coup-revolutions led by similar forces followed throughout the Arab world: in Iraq (1958), North Yemen (1962), Syria (1963), Algeria (1965), and South Yemen and Libya (1969). In all of these, the old order of parliamentary monarchies and traditional ruling elites—many beholden to or supported by foreign powers—was replaced by ostensible republics led by military officers committed to Arab nationalism, populism, and radical change in social, economic, and foreign policy. They all eventually became as authoritarian as the regimes they had overthrown.

The radical-nationalists criticized the monarchies, including the ones that survived the revolutions that swept the region such as Jordan and the Gulf states, for being too conservative in their promotion of social change, too subservient to Western interests, and for not doing enough in the promotion of the pan-Arab cause, especially the cause of Palestine (that is, promoting the idea of a Palestinian-Arab state at the expense of Israel). The major radical-nationalist states (Egypt, Syria, and Iraq) sought to undermine each other and the monarchies by calling on one another's populations to withdraw support from their governments. In fact, the accusations and recriminations that flew back and forth through the radio waves across the region eventually spiraled out of control into the June 1967 Arab-Israeli War, when Israel inflicted a crushing defeat on Egypt, Syria, and Jordan, and captured the Sinai Peninsula and Gaza Strip, Golan Heights, and West Bank.

The disappointment and disillusionment with the radical-nationalists that overtook the region in the aftermath of the 1967 war profoundly reduced the appeal of radical-nationalism. In the early 1970s, new leaders came to power who stabilized their systems, reduced their revolutionary activities, and proceeded instead to institutionalize and cement their rule, notably Anwar Sadat in Egypt and Hafez al-Assad in Syria. But while the resulting regimes were more cautious in action, the basic approach toward their societies and in their foreign policies remained the same.

Background: The Failure of Parliamentarianism

The old order that predominated in much of the Arab world, between the end of World War I and the advent of radical-nationalism, is sometimes referred to by scholars as a system of liberal parliamentarianism. This is because the governing systems of the region were dominated by a monarch (in British-controlled areas) or by European administrators (in French-run mandates) who were ostensibly advised and constrained by a legislature that reflected the will and demands of the populations.

Certainly parliaments did exist, but they were not liberal in the sense of contributing to policy-making; they usually functioned as rubber stamps for royal or European decisions. Where they did exist as an independent power source and acted to limit the power of the kings or the European agents, they were often dissolved, remade, or ignored—all on the authority granted to the kings or Europeans on legitimate constitutional and legal grounds.

There was much corruption and misrule in these systems. Political power and control over the economy were shared by the royal houses (particularly in Egypt, Iraq, and Libya) and the notables who lived in the urban areas—the landowning elites who owned much of the production of agricultural goods. These elites were subject to the interventions of the British and French, but otherwise they dominated the political processes in their countries. The monarchs and the notables ensured that their (and their families' and close supporters') interests took precedence over the interests of the state or the population in general. Although the economies did not suffer terrible lapses, unemployment, immobile standards of living, and burgeoning populations combined to generate widespread dissatisfaction with the regimes. The expansion of public education during this period also led to an increase in politically conscious citizens, who were better able to articulate and make demands on their governments.

The elites also blocked popular participation. In Egypt, for example, the Wafd Party was originally created during World War I as a voice of the popular will, but by the 1940s it had become a regular part of the established political system, unable to effect genuine change. Iraq was even less participatory, with politicians coming from a limited pool of elites and political activity strictly circumscribed by the regime. For the most part the elites in all these countries also came from the Sunni population, so that in some places the revolutions that came later in the 1950s and 1960s also heralded an end to Sunni domination, particularly in Syria, where the minority Alawites—a heterodox Islamic sect—seized power.

Though the revolutionaries were motivated at first by these social and economic concerns, the old regimes' reliance on European powers was also an important consideration. This was manifested in two ways. First, the monarchies (and those elites who benefited from them) depended on the Europeans, especially the British, to protect them from both domestic and external threats. This was an affront to national pride. None of the Arab states had a military capable (or large) enough for national defense; in addition, the Europeans preferred to trust in their own armed forces, or at least to lead the Arab armies. Because the French and British had constructed the regional states to serve their own strategic and economic interests, they retained a stake in the system they had created and therefore saw no choice but to remain heavily involved in maintaining these systems—and those who governed them. In Egypt, for example, the British often vetoed the nomination of prime ministers they considered opposed to their continuing domination. In 1955, Britain prompted Iraq into the Western-sponsored Baghdad Pact, a regional agreement with Pakistan, Iran, Iraq, and Turkey against the Soviet Union, despite the opposition of most Iraqis.

Second, European state and private interests dominated the regional economies, even holding much of the national debts. Since the beginning of the nineteenth century Europe had directed much of the economic development of the region according to European needs. Egyptian cotton production, for instance, was geared toward the British market, where the cotton was used as raw material for manufacturing. Because there was little encouragement of domestic industrialization, the regimes depended on the Europeans for continued access to global markets and finances, as well as financial subsidies. Thus, many of the benefits from economic production accrued to the Europeans and to the elites who were tied to them—and not to the populations at large. Middle Eastern elites therefore continued to support the European presence.

The parliamentary regimes thus ensured a disconnect between themselves and the citizenry. Paradoxically, the intent of the constitutional regimes to generate legitimacy by pretending their rule depended on popular support and participation ended up undermining these regimes by revealing that the citizenry had no real role in policymaking, and that the parliaments had no independent capacity to influence decision making. By the time the radical-nationalists overthrew the old order, most of the populations were ready for a change in politics. They believed the rhetoric of the revolutionaries that promised drastic changes, including more equitable distribution of economic wealth and greater popular participation in politics.

Finally, the parliamentary regimes had "lost" Palestine as a result of the 1947–1949 Arab-Israeli War. After its creation in 1948, Israel defeated the Arab armies and succeeded in surviving and preventing the establishment of an independent Arab state in the whole of Palestine (to which Jordan and Egypt also contributed, by retaining control over the West Bank and Gaza Strip, respectively). This had a double effect: First, by virtue of their loss, the regimes had undermined the Arab cause by not being able to prevent the establishment of what the Arab leaders and their populations considered to be a foreign implant injected by imperialist powers under the influence of Zionist agents into the Arab region in order to disrupt Arab unity. Second, the defeat undermined the regimes' already tenuous credibility with the military, many of whose officers were increasingly discontented about being used to put down domestic protests against the Arab governments in support of a regime they did not believe in.

Memoirs of Arab officers at the time recount their unhappiness at being thrown into the first Arab-Israeli War with little preparation or proper capabilities, which they argued contributed to their defeat. This had a profound psychological effect on many of these officers. The leader of the Free Officers coup in Egypt, Gamal Abdel Nasser, served as an officer in Palestine during the war; he reported afterward that the loss of Palestine was a key factor in his determination to replace the Egyptian monarchy with a government more attuned to the population and better able to meet the country's proper foreign policy priorities.

A similar pattern was evident across the region: military officers were now willing to become involved in politics (that is, overthrow the old regimes) because they did not believe any other group was capable enough. The regimes completely ignored or missed these growing ideological trends, and thus did not try to address them. Furthermore, some of the militaries (such as in Syria) also included a significant number of minorities, who chafed under the marginalization imposed on them by the ruling elites. This gave them an added incentive to overthrow the old system and help install a new one that they believed would enhance their political and economic status.

This was a critical development, since military officers spearheaded all of the revolutions and ensured their success; there were two reasons why this was the case. First, coup-plotters could only succeed if they had the backing of the military, or at least significant segments of it. Without that power, they would be defenseless against retaliation. And flowing from the first point, if the regimes that were overthrown did retain considerable support among the armed forces, they would be able to prevent the revolutionaries from achieving their goals, since the military could physically block the would-be plotters. In short, the military was the only social group with the resources to act on its dissatisfaction. The notables, of course, had significant resources, but they were content with the status quo and so did not desire to change anything.

Thus, the liberal parliamentarian regimes failed to meet their citizens' expectations, particularly among the constitutional monarchies. The regimes were never able to foster the necessary national legitimacy required to sustain them, or to generate enough loyalty among their citizens, since they relied only on foreign powers and a small economic and political elite. As the regimes did not expand their support base, and social and economic problems multiplied, they could not continue to support themselves; hence, they were ripe for overthrow.

The Free Officers in Egypt and the Onset of Radical-Nationalism

Egypt set both the tone and the framework for the radical-nationalist revolutions in the rest of the Arab world. It did so through its adoption of the tenets of radical-nationalism, the manner in which it came to power, and the manner in which the revolution unfolded.

The clandestine Free Officers movement was formed in 1949, though Nasser only became its leader in 1950. It was made up of nine mid-level officers who opposed the misrule of the king and were outraged by the disgrace of their defeat in Palestine. They resolved to overthrow the corrupt and tired monarchy, led at the time by King Farouk, and install a revolutionary regime committed to economic development and social justice.

On July 23, 1952, the Free Officers deposed the king and installed Ali Maher, a longtime politician, as prime minister in order to demonstrate stability. A Revolutionary Command Council (RCC), led by Nasser, was set up to supervise implementation of the revolution. Though the revolutionaries had always intended for change to be a top-down process, their populist rhetoric had distracted much of the population from understanding that they were less interested in procedural change (that is, how politics was conducted) and more interested in substantive change (specific domestic and foreign policies). Given that the Free Officers were the first of the revolutionary regimes to come to power, as well as the influence Nasser came to have on similar movements in other Arab countries, the increasing authoritarianism in Egypt set the example for the same development in other states where radical-nationalist military officers took power.

The Free Officers quickly entrenched their rule by eliminating all other rival power sources, such as political parties and wealthy elites, so that in the end the governing system of Egypt was changed in tone and makeup but not in substance. Building on this, Nasser then eliminated all challenges to his personal rule by removing his rivals from power and engineering the concentration of decision-making authority in his person. He entrenched in Egypt a presidential system that was for all intents and purposes as authoritarian as any of the absolutist monarchies.

First, the prime minister, Ali Maher, clashed with the RCC over plans for land reform; he insisted on increasing the maximum allotment of land allowed per owner once the larger estates were broken up, opposing the smaller allotment favored by the RCC. He was forced to resign and the RCC took effective control of the country. Other developments quickly followed: The RCC abolished the constitution in December 1952, banned political parties in January 1953, and replaced the monarchy with a republic in June 1953. In addition, in its determination to prevent any return to the old order, the RCC banned anyone who had held public office between 1946 and 1952 from entering politics.

The shift to complete control by Nasser soon followed. By the end of 1956 he had seized ultimate power, disbanding the RCC and putting his close friend, Abd al-Hakim Amr, in charge of the military in order to secure its loyalty. His personal example was later followed in Iraq, Syria, and Libya, as Saddam Hussein, Hafez al-Assad, and Muammar Qaddafi all concentrated power in their hands after their revolutions, to an extent greater even than in Egypt.

Domestic Policies

The radical-nationalist states truly were revolutionary in two senses. First, in the domestic arena, they engaged in a series of changes that swept away the older systems. This included a commitment to socialist development through nationalized industrialization (at least in the beginning), more equal distribution of wealth and property, wider educational opportunities (e.g., more schools), and expansion of the state machinery by increasing the size of the civil service and developing its capacity to govern the country.

Second, in foreign affairs, the radical-nationalist states orchestrated first an independent position between the American-led West and the Soviet-led East; their experiences under colonialism had instilled in them a distrust of any dependence on foreign powers. But under the conditions of the Cold War, the radical-nationalists drifted into the Soviet camp and adopted a clearer anti-Western policy (though they were never under the control of Moscow). In the Middle East this encouraged divisions in the Arab-Israeli conflict, too, as the Soviets came to back the radical states most opposed to Israel, while the United States backed Israel against them.

The regimes also shared in common the fact that most of their proclaimed goals were not met: though foreign influence was largely dissipated, few segments of the populations obtained more material wealth, economies were still underdeveloped, and a new class of former revolutionaries now became the wealthy elite. This included a class of businesspeople who had benefited first from the nationalizations and then from the limited economic liberalization that took place in the 1970s; they took the place of the former landed aristocracy connected to the foreigners. Finally, the appeal of pan-Arabism began to wane with the Israeli victory in the 1967 Arab-Israeli War (though pan-Arabism never completely disappeared and even today retains a strong attraction for some groups and a powerful rationale for some Arab regimes, such as in Syria).

Arab Socialism

The coup leaders in Iraq, Syria, Egypt, Algeria, and Libya mostly came from rural middle- or lower-middle-class backgrounds. Although they never engaged in class-based politics, their backgrounds did engender in them a general shared outlook on the best way to deal with the state's problems. Their thinking on these issues took time to coalesce, but once it did they concentrated on socialist development and a redistribution of wealth and resources that would lead, they assumed, to greater social justice and economic equality. These initiatives also had the political goal of reducing the power of the old notables.

The term "Arab socialism" was first used by Michel Aflaq of Syria, one of the founders of the Baath Party. The promoters of Arab socialism intended it, like Soviet communism, to ensure state control over the economy. The Arab version differed in that the former allowed for a greater role for private property than the latter. But traditional Marxism was also considered ill-suited to the Arab world because of its universalist and atheist underpinnings. "Arab" socialism was designed to illustrate that the Arabs could form their own brand of socialism, reflecting Arab needs and identity. It was, as Nasser and Baath leaders described it, to be a system in which class distinctions did not exist and society was governed by social justice and equality.

The new leaders believed that because the Arab states had to industrialize and develop rapidly in order to meet the revolutionary goals set out by the regimes and strengthen the states vis-à-vis external powers and Israel, state control over economic development would be the most appropriate and effective method of achieving these goals. Previously, Arab governments had participated in their countries' economies, including ownership of some key industries such as railways and the setting of food prices or import licenses. But this had been limited, and government expenditures in the economy were much lower in the Arab world at the time than in places like Britain and the United States.

The leaders did not consider capitalism to be a viable option, because it connoted Western dominance and socioeconomic inequality. This stemmed directly from the belief that the Western capitalist powers had been responsible for keeping the Arabs economically underdeveloped. It was the capitalists who had helped drive colonialism in the first place, they argued, based on the objective of economic dominance of the region in order to profit from its natural resources. Capitalism also automatically carried with it the stigma of being under imperialist influence, particularly as the old elites had worked with the European capitalists and benefited from their system, and so was further discredited as a viable system for the Arabs.

More practically, a capitalist system required substantial economic changes and financial and human capital, all of which were lacking in the Arab world at the time. It would require the creation of a large, wealthier class; a set of skilled workers that was missing due to a lack of relevant educational systems; and resources that were either absent from the region or were more cheaply obtained from the industrialized states. In addition, given the influence that communism had on some of the revolutionaries, some of the new leaders believed that a socialist system would entail quicker economic results. Finally, some of these same leaders were concerned that the creation of the necessary class structures that drove capitalist development might lead to a contest for political power, as had happened elsewhere.

For all intents and purposes, Arab socialism translated into limited attempts at state-led industrialization, though there still were some elements of private capital involved in the economy even after the radical-nationalists came to power. The state had to be involved because of the massive funding needed, the importance of developing key industries such as transportation and heavy manufacturing, and the sensitivity of these industries (that is, the necessity of keeping them under national, rather than foreign, control), particularly transportation and communication.

The most important manifestations of this policy were land reform (see below) and, particularly as the regimes moved into the Soviet orbit in the 1950s and 1960s, the nationalization of major industries and financial sectors. Again, Egypt began the trend with its nationalization of the Suez Canal Company in 1956. Though this was also partly a political maneuver in response to American pressure to join the Western camp during the Cold War, it was followed by the nationalization later that year of Egypt's European-owned banks; in the next year nationalization was extended to other banks and other financial services and economic enterprises, such as insurance firms and labor unions. In 1961 another wave of nationalization swept the economy, putting even hotels and department stores under state control.

Other radical-nationalist regimes followed suit. By 1965, most of Syria's economic activity, including banking and foreign trade, was under state control. During the same period, Iraq also nationalized its major industries and financial services, though full nationalization of the oil industry was not completed until the early 1970s. Algeria's own oil and gas industries were nationalized at the end of the 1960s and start of the 1970s. In addition, the radical-nationalists publicly committed to providing employment for university graduates, as well as price controls and subsidies for staple items (such as basic foodstuffs).

Land Reform

The other major development fostered by Arab socialism was land reform. Agriculture had long been a mainstay of most of the Arab states. Indeed, the Fertile Crescent (stretching from Egypt to Iraq and back through Syria and Lebanon) was so named because of its rich land and agricultural capacity. But over the course of the establishment and consolidation of the Arab states (a process that occurred as well in the rest of the world), a small elite of wealthy landowners came to control much of the land, leaving the peasants and poorer classes with few tangible material assets.

In part, the regimes used land reform to break the power of the notables and garner support from the peasantry, by breaking up larger estates and redistributing them to landless peasants and small landowners. In Egypt, for example, by 1952 about 1 percent of the population owned 70 percent of the arable land, while in Iraq at the time of the revolution about 2 percent of the population owned 68 percent of the land.

But land reform was also seen as a socioeconomic imperative necessary for achieving social justice and economic development, to which the radical-nationalists were committed. Though the radical regimes did make land reform a critical part of their policy platforms early in their tenures, many of the reforms were reversed in the 1970s and 1980s during a move away from agricultural activity and the subsequent shift to *infitah* (economic opening). In addition, in many cases, the state retained ownership of most of the land taken for redistribution, to be used for its own wealth generation and as a reward for loyalty.

Land reform edicts were promulgated in Egypt in September 1952 and were the strictest of all the radical land reforms. The maximum holding of land per person was set at 200 *feddans* (one feddan equals slightly more than one acre), with an extra 100 feddans allowed for each dependent. Later revisions decreased the maximum allotment to 100 feddans per owner and 50 feddans per dependent. In keeping with the general tenets of Arab socialism, Egyptian land reform also included the formation of agricultural cooperatives, in which families were grouped together to work a specific piece of land and share equipment and other means of production and export.

Syrian land reform began in 1958, in the framework of Syria's union with Egypt into the United Arab Republic (see below). But the revolutionary coup in Syria on March 8, 1963 (led by the Baath Party), reinforced the desire for land reform. The radical-nationalist regime pursued redistribution of land more aggressively, setting a ceiling on the amount of land allowed per family at about 617 acres. It appears that the rural middle classes, from which the regime drew considerable support, benefited most from this restructuring.

Iraqi land reform began in the same year as the 1958 revolution, and a ceiling of 1,800 total acres was set. Land redistribution continued throughout the 1970s, as these ceilings were reduced and the reforms were applied throughout the entire country more aggressively. As in Egypt, agricultural cooperatives were also introduced, though they largely failed in their implementation: productivity and revenues did not increase substantially.

Although an important policy plank in the beginning, agriculture as the critical element in economic activity quickly declined when the revolutionaries began to focus on industrialization and development. Still, land reform was pursued quite vigorously in its time, and although it was never fully implemented, it did succeed in all of the radical-nationalist states in breaking the power of the old notables.

Foreign Policy

The radical-nationalist regimes had a clear foreign policy platform though not a means for achieving it. They all wanted complete independence from foreign powers. This program, which in fact was a major motivating factor for their decision to overthrow the monarchies, included expelling Western influence to the maximum extent possible and uniting the Arab world into one political entity (or at least a close union). In the case of the former, this led to a distinct anti-Western policy and somewhat inadvertently to closer ties with the Soviet Union.

Anti-Westernism

In general, by the late 1950s the radical-nationalists pursued a foreign policy underlined by an anti-Westernism that, in the context of the Cold War, helped push these states into the Soviet camp. This anti-Western position was a natural outgrowth of the radicals' Arab nationalism, though it was not assumed at the beginning of the revolutions. Egypt, for example, understood the need for American aid to finance its development and wanted to continue working with the United States, despite its oppositional rhetoric.

In reality, what became an anti-Western position had begun as a concerted effort at nonalignment. The Free Officers in Egypt wanted to chart an independent course between the two superpowers in the context of the emerging Cold War. This would, they presumed, allow the regional states the maximum leeway to look after their own interests, something they had not been able to do since the onset of colonialism in the region. But Western, particularly American, resistance to nonalignment, and the willingness of the Soviet Union to supply large-scale aid and advanced arms, pushed the radical-nationalists toward the Soviet bloc.

Since it was the Western powers that had invaded and repressed the Middle East and retained or sought to obtain influence over their domestic and foreign affairs for their own interests, it could be expected that they would bear the brunt of Arab frustration and resentment at the lack of independence and development. The Western powers, particularly Britain and France, had been responsible for preventing the Arabs from achieving independence or, once it was granted, continuing to interfere in Arab affairs. Their actions even after formal independence proved to the radical-nationalists that these powers intended to continue to dominate the region for their own economic and political purposes. With the coming of the Cold War to the region, America's efforts (beginning in the mid-1950s) to subsume local states' concerns to its own struggle against the Soviet Union seemed to many to be a continuation of British and French policy. Nonalignment was not enough for the United States—Washington wanted the Arab states to explicitly join the Western camp, and consistently asked or demanded that they come out publicly and explicitly against Soviet communism.

In addition, the revolutionaries were committed to wholesale change in the regional order. They pursued a policy of pan-Arabism, calling for unity among the Arab states under a common radical-nationalist agenda. This would of course mean the end of the monarchies. This prompted the monarchies to turn to the West for military protection and financial aid and to strengthen their existing ties with Britain, as in the case of the smaller Gulf states. The revolutionaries thus perceived Western powers as hindering their efforts at regional control. The radical-nationalists moved, therefore, to demand the end of Western involvement in Middle Eastern affairs. At the same time, consistent Soviet rhetoric against Western imperialism, Soviet support for "liberation" movements, and the lack of a historical or contemporary presence in the Middle East also channeled revolutionary anger at Western inference.

At first, the point was to remove Western military bases and economic and political influence, but not to sever all ties completely. Nasser, especially, in the early 1950s was willing to establish a working relationship with the United States. He recognized the need for U.S. financial aid to underwrite the growth of the Egyptian economy, particularly the completion of the Aswan Dam in order to generate electricity for many rural areas of Egypt that lacked access to energy. He also believed that only the United States could pressure Britain to withdraw from Egypt and the region. In addition, the United

States did not have a history of colonialism in the region, and the anti-imperialist rhetoric of American officials since the promulgation of Woodrow Wilson's Fourteen Points during the First World War convinced many Arabs that the United States would protect their new independence.

But Washington and Cairo could not agree on the role of the United States and other Western countries in the region, the relevance of the Cold War to Middle Eastern affairs, and orientation of the Arab states in this context. For his part, Nasser had his own regional ambitions: he wanted Egypt to be the primary state in the Middle East, at the head of a pan-Arab union of some kind, and he wanted to be its leader. In his frequent radio broadcasts in the 1950s and 1960s, he regularly called for the establishment of this type of entity. He also called for the destruction of Israel and the overthrow of the monarchies. The United States could not support such a position. Though its close relationship with Israel did not develop until after 1967, Washington was committed to the existence of the Jewish state and could not accept its annihilation on political, moral, or practical grounds. It also could not sever its support for the pro-Western oil monarchies and Jordan and Lebanon, which were increasingly calling on the United States for protection against the radical-nationalists.

In addition, the United States perceived that a Middle East controlled by Nasser threatened to undermine the stability of oil supplies, upset the superpower balance, and contribute to instability and insecurity in neighboring areas. Nasser's growing authoritarianism was also a cause for concern. Finally, his belligerent rhetoric—for example, name-calling of pro-Western Arab leaders and demands for war against Israel—led to a personal dislike for him among some American policymakers, particularly President Lyndon Johnson. All of these factors made U.S. leaders less sympathetic to Nasser's and Egypt's own interests.

On the other hand, the United States subordinated regional policy to its larger Cold War policy. Washington's highest priority was to prevent the expansion of communist influence, and it wanted the Arab states to actively reject the Soviet Union and to allow only Western involvement in the region. To achieve this, the United States demanded that local states be in complete agreement with U.S. policy and actively support it. This was not something Nasser could do, given his own objectives of Egyptian regional dominance and the Free Officers' intention of reducing their commitment to Western states, not enhancing it.

A series of events coincided to prompt Nasser, in light of his own personal agenda and the desire to rid the region of Western interference, to conclude that the United States was not necessarily better than Britain, and that the only way to avoid dependence on it was to foster ties with the Soviet Union. Three developments in particular are relevant.

First, the United States in 1953 actively supported a coup against the elected nationalist prime minister in Iran, Mohammed Mossadegh, when he threatened British oil interests in the country. The Central Intelligence Agency provided funding and some logistical support to the dissenters. Nasser was unmoved by American efforts to forestall instability in Iran before resorting to the coup, the U.S. refusal at first to back British demands for an oil embargo against the country, its fear of communist expansion, and the fact that Mossadegh's policies failed to resolve Iran's growing economic and social problems. Instead, he viewed American involvement as a continuation of the decades old Western policy of interference in the domestic affairs of local states to protect U.S. interests rather than the interests of the local states.

Second, the creation of the Baghdad Pact (also known at various times as the Middle East Treaty Organization and the Central Treaty Organization) in February 1955 infuriated Nasser. The Pact included Britain, Iraq, Iran, Pakistan, and Turkey, and was designed to defend the region from Soviet encroachment. The United States did not join, but it did participate in the discussions of some of the Pact's committees. Nasser saw the agreement as a signal of Britain's desire to continue to interfere in the region's politics and to dominate the region's security policies. He put heavy pressure on Jordan and Syria to shun the Pact. Washington responded by reducing its aid commitments to Egypt. It believed that since the Pact was framed as an anti-Soviet treaty designed to keep the Middle East free from communist expansion, any leader that did not support it was allowing for Soviet involvement in the region.

Third, the Arab defeat in the 1947–1949 Arab-Israeli War still rankled the Free Officers, and Nasser continued to publicly promote confrontation with Israel. To do so, however, he needed advanced offensive weapons, and his preferred supplier was the United States. But the United States, in addition to its growing dissatisfaction with the lack of Egyptian support for anti-Soviet interests in the region and in keeping with the 1950 American-British-French Tripartite Declaration, refused to sell such arms to the regional states out of concern that this would inflame the Arab-Israeli conflict. Yet the conflict with Israel was a priority for Nasser, and if he could not get the arms from the West he was determined to obtain them elsewhere.

Ties with the Soviet Union

All of these developments pushed the radical-nationalists to turn to the Soviet Union for economic and military support. Much as it did in domestic policy, Egypt led the revolutionary regimes by example when it turned to Moscow in September 1955 for advanced armaments. Czechoslovakia, acting under Moscow's direction, sold $200 million worth of advanced weaponry to Egypt. This deal marked the first real involvement of the Soviet Union in the Middle East and undermined the Western monopoly on arms sales and influence in the region. It also helped solidify the division of the region into pro-American and pro-Soviet camps.

By the following year Moscow had become the chief supplier of military aid to Syria as well. In the 1970s, the Soviet Union also strengthened its relationship with Baathist Iraq, including through arm sales. In July 1956, angry at what it perceived to be Nasser's move into the Soviet camp, Washington withdrew its offer to finance the construction of the Aswan Dam, and by 1965 had discontinued all aid to Egypt. This left the Soviet Union as the only country Egypt and the other radical-nationalists could turn to for military and economic support. After Nasser had nationalized the Suez Canal from British and French companies, intending to use the revenues to pay for the Aswan Dam, the USSR provided its own financing for the dam.

Soviet-radical ties became further entrenched after Egyptian president Anwar Sadat took Egypt into the American camp in the mid-1970s. With the loss of its alliance with the most important Arab state, Moscow worked hard to make sure it did not lose any more influence in the region. It expanded its support of the remaining radical-nationalists, particularly Syria, by increasing its aid and its commitment to provide advanced weaponry. Not until the late 1980s did Moscow begin to reduce the amount of this aid. At that time, Soviet leader Mikhail Gorbachev began to promote a more cooperative rather than conflictual relationship with the United States, and this included reducing support for states actively involved in regional conflict in opposition to American allies.

Pan-Arabism

Pan-Arabism is the belief that there is one Arab nation that has been divided artificially into separate states, but that based on common language, culture, and experience belongs in a single political entity. First taking institutional form in the middle of the nineteenth century, it is a very secular understanding of the Arab nation: pan-Arabism's most prominent thinkers were Christian Arabs, many from Syria, including Constantin Zureiq, Sati al-Husri, and Michel Aflaq (the ideological founder of the Baath Party). Based on the existence of this single nation, pan-Arabism also included shared experiences: victories, such as the successful oil embargo against Western states in the mid-1970s or the skillful performance of the Syrian and Egyptian armies during the first part of the 1973 war with Israel; and defeats, such as the 1948 and 1967 conflicts with Israel. According to Michael Barnett in *Dialogues in Arab Politics* (1998), pan-Arabism in the second half of the twentieth century also entailed a set of regional norms, including a unified stance against Israel, hostility to foreign interference in Arab affairs, and support for the Palestinian cause.

Pan-Arabism manifested itself in several unity projects beginning in the late 1950s. None of them lasted, and most entailed only vague notions of integration without clear policy guidelines. This is because the national interests of the individual Arab states always came to take precedence over a commitment to common policies. At the same time, none of the Arab states ever intended that these unity schemes should undermine their own capacity for independent policymaking or leadership. Egypt's role in such projects provides a good example of the radical-nationalist commitment to pan-Arabism and why it eventually failed.

The most important of the pan-Arab unity projects was the United Arab Republic (UAR), which merged Syria and Egypt and loosely brought North Yemen in as well. The project brought together two of the major radical-nationalist states (Egypt and Syria), and for the time it lasted it did enact a common policy, with an integrated decision-making structure. No other Arab union displayed these same levels of amalgamation.

Despite Nasser's image as the ultimate pan-Arabist, the UAR was formed at the behest of Syria, with Nasser agreeing somewhat reluctantly, believing that he simply could not refuse the offer of unity once it was presented to him. In fact, Nasser's preeminent concern was to maintain independence from the West, as well as Egypt's position as leader of the Arab world; his *Philosophy of the Revolution*, published in 1955, also spoke of the need for Egypt to maintain a leadership position in the Muslim and African world.

Syria was the birthplace of modern pan-Arabism, and this type of Arab nationalism was popular among the entire Syrian population. In addition, the Syrian Baath Party became fearful that an increasingly strong Communist Party, gaining support among the population and garnering more influence in politics, was prepared to take over the country along with the Left in general. It believed that a union with Egypt could forestall such a development. Damascus presented Nasser with the offer of union, and the UAR was officially formed on February 1, 1958. It was designed to merge the two countries into a single state with a common political structure and economy. The experiment ended when a coup in Syria on September 28, 1961, brought a new military government to power that took Syria out of the union.

Other pan-Arab projects followed. In February 1958, in response to the creation of the UAR, the two Hashemite kingdoms of Iraq and Jordan formed the Arab Federation of Iraq and Jordan, to offset the sudden increase in power afforded to Egypt through the UAR. The two countries were not well integrated, and the project lasted only six months; it was dissolved after the Iraqi revolution in July brought to power a radical-nationalist government opposed to the pro-Western monarchy of Jordan.

After the 1969 revolution in Libya, Libyan leader Muammar Qaddafi took up the mantle of pan-Arabism, believing himself to be the heir to Nasser as leader and facilitator of the movement. He coaxed and cajoled Syria and Egypt to join Libya in forming the Federation of Arab Republics, which was officially established in January 1972. Disagreements between the countries on logistics, timetables, and how to confront Israel enervated the Federation. Unity progressed only along symbolic lines, such as the adoption of a common flag, and eventually the project dissolved completely in March 1977. Qaddafi tried again in 1974, pushing for a union between Libya and Tunisia, but the latter balked at the intensive unification programs Qaddafi had in mind.

With the end of pan-Arabism as a viable ideological alternative in the 1970s, unity projects were all but abandoned by the radical-nationalists. Later plans for closer cooperation were discussed and enacted by some of the Arab states, but these reflected concrete security and economic considerations that had little to do with pan-Arabism. For example, in 1981 Saudi Arabia and the other five Gulf monarchies formed the Gulf Cooperation Council—now the Cooperation Council for the Arab States of the Gulf—as a security measure to protect themselves from the consequences of the Iran-Iraq War of the 1980s. In 1989, Algeria, Morocco, Mauritania, Tunisia, and Libya formed the Arab Maghreb Union, which was designed to facilitate closer economic and political cooperation among its members; however, border disputes and national rivalries have undermined its ability to act cohesively.

The most formal, institutionalized expression of the radical-nationalists' pan-Arabism was the Baath Party, *baath* meaning "resurrection" or "renaissance." Established in Syria in the late 1940s, the party symbolized what later became the key tenets of radical-nationalism discussed above: populism, Arab socialism, independence from foreign interference, and pan-Arabism. The party came to power in Syria (in 1963) and in Iraq (in 1963 and then again from 1968 until 2003), but it could never establish itself as a viable transnational framework for all of the Arab states. This is mostly because the party did not have successful branches in other countries, and other states did not subscribe to all of its tenets.

The Syrian and Iraqi branches of the party were bitter rivals. In addition to personal antipathy between Syrian and Iraqi leaders and competition for regional leadership, the Syrian branch in power was composed primarily of military officers, while the Baath regime in Iraq was dominated by civilians, who, beginning in the 1970s, promoted a more aggressive foreign policy agenda than the military branch at a time when radical-nationalism was fading as a determining framework.

Aside from these internal divisions, the party suffered from the same malady that struck all of the radical-nationalist regimes: the promises for social revolution dissolved amid an inability to resolve their countries' economic and social problems and increasing authoritarianism and repression. In the end, like radical-nationalism more generally, the Baath was used by the top leaders in Syria and Iraq, Hafez al-Assad and Saddam Hussein, to promote their centralized rule.

Pan-Arab nationalism was also used by the radicals as an internal tool to protect the regimes. Though many Arab leaders, particularly the Baath, were ideologically committed to it, most of the dictators who led these regimes (perhaps aside from Muammar Qaddafi of Libya) did not intend to subsume their regimes under a new region-wide political entity. The consequences of the UAR for Syria reinforced this belief. The minority nature of many of these regimes also underlined this contradiction. The Baath regime in Syria, for example, was based partly on the support of a minority of the population, the Alawites. Entering into a pan-Arab union would undermine the Alawites' position and put them under the domination of the majority Sunni population of the Middle East. The rhetoric of Arab nationalism thus became divorced from practical policies. The capture by the regimes of the language of Arab nationalism did not leave room for any other interpretation of how it should be promoted. The efforts by the regimes to put their survival and security first underline this point quite clearly.

Inter-Arab Conflict

The other main policy that marked the radical-nationalists' foreign affairs agenda was somewhat paradoxical. Although they believed in pan-Arabism, the radical-nationalists universally found it difficult to completely subsume their sovereignty under a larger supranational entity, and some of them, particularly in Egypt, Syria, and Iraq, believed that they should lead the Arab world whether it was united or not. These two concerns converged into a region-wide conflict among the Arab states, both between the radical-nationalists and others, and among the radical-nationalists themselves. The late Malcolm Kerr, a noted scholar of the region, has referred to this era in Arab politics as the "Arab cold war" (1971).

After the failure of the United Arab Republic and the rise of radical-nationalist regimes in Syria and Iraq, Egypt's position as leader of the Arab world could no longer be presumed. The radicals in Damascus and Baghdad believed that they should be the proper leaders of the revolutionaries, and neither was willing to accept Egypt's perception of itself as the natural principal state in the Arab world. Thus, the failure of the UAR prompted Nasser to engage in even more vehement revolutionary rhetoric, castigating the monarchies, Iraq, and sometimes certain leaders in Syria for their lack of true commitment to the Arab cause. Egypt became, in the words of Mohamed Hassanein Heikal (a close confidante of Nasser's), a "revolution" as opposed to just a state. By this he meant Egypt was to be the vanguard of radical-nationalist revolutions throughout the Arab world. In practice, this led to increasing friction and conflict with other Arab states.

The pan-Arab norms to which all the Arab states publicly committed enhanced these regional rivalries. Under the rhetoric of pan-Arabism, the Arab states, particularly the revolutionaries, accused each other of not being Arab enough, or not doing enough for the Arab cause. Nasser and the other leaders frequently appealed to the populations of the other Arab countries, accusing each other of cowardice or betrayal.

Committed to radical change, in addition to the more standard leadership ambitions that marked the major states in the region (Egypt, Syria, Iraq, and Saudi Arabia), the revolutionary nationalists wanted a complete change in how all of the states of the region were governed. They also demanded a wholesale commitment to Arab unity that would ensure the predominance of the radicals. The Arab world thus became divided; on one side were the revolutionary nationalists (who referred to themselves as the "progressives"): Egypt, Syria, Iraq, the two Yemens, Libya, Algeria, and the Palestine Liberation Organization. On the other side were the pro-Western "conservatives," the monarchies (whom the radicals named "reactionaries"): Saudi Arabia and the Gulf monarchies and Jordan, who depended on Western military and economic support and could not countenance any social revolution that was bound to make their governing systems untenable. (Lebanon, though not a monarchy, was also considered to belong in this latter grouping.)

Although these states engaged in continuous rhetorical subversion of each other, the most dramatic manifestation of this inter-Arab conflict was the North Yemeni civil war from 1962 to 1970. In September 1962, a group of military officers, inspired by Nasserite and pan-Arabist ideas, overthrew North Yemen's ruler, Imam Muhammad al-Badr. The imam rallied support for a counteroffensive. The civil war became a reflection of wider Arab political disputes, between the radical-nationalists and the conservative monarchists: the imam's royalist forces were supported by Saudi Arabia and, to a lesser extent, by Jordan, while the republican faction was actively supported by Egypt. By 1966, Nasser had approximately 70,000 Egyptian troops in the country assisting the republicans.

The end of the civil war in 1970, due to Egypt's exhaustion, combined with a series of other events to undermine radical-nationalism as the dominant ideological and policy framework in the Middle East. By the early 1970s the revolutionary regimes became institutionalized, in the sense that their policymaking became less radical and more cautious, and their guarantees of drastic change faded away as conditions did not improve as promised.

In fact, it could be argued that the radical-nationalists made things worse for their societies in some ways. Internal repression and misrule marked these regimes almost as much as they had the older parliamentarian regimes; repression was far worse and, as the revolutionaries consolidated themselves, far more violent. In 1982, for example, in an effort to stamp out Islamist opposition groups, the Syrian regime attacked the city of Hama, destroying entire neighborhoods and killing some 10,000 inhabitants or more.

In economic terms, the radicals did not improve economic development as much as they had promised. Syria's economic mismanagement created a series of structural problems that continue to affect the state even today. In Iraq, the Baathist regimes, including that of Saddam Hussein, used oil revenues to embark on a successful program of modernization: Iraq in the 1970s and 1980s boasted one of the region's best health-care and education systems. But Saddam's wars against Iran (1980–1988) and against a U.S.-led coalition (in 1991) redirected expenditures away from social services. In addition, Iraq owed about $80 billion in debt by 1990, so that there was little revenue to devote to domestic government activity. In short, prominent internal and regional changes contributed to undermine the radicals' promises and all but ended the revolutions that they had promoted.

References and Further Reading

Ajami, Fouad. *The Arab Predicament: Arab Political Thought and Practice Since 1967*. New York: Cambridge University Press, 1981.

Barnett, Michael N. *Dialogues in Arab Politics: Negotiations in Regional Order.* New York: Columbia University Press, 1998.

Batatu, Hanna. *The Old Social Classes and the Revolutionary Movement of Iraq*. Princeton, NJ: Princeton University Press, 1978.

Brynen, Rex. "Palestine and the Arab State System: Permeability, State Consolidation and the Intifada." *Canadian Journal of Political Science* 24:3 (September 1991): 595–621.

Fromkin, David. *A Peace to End All Peace: The Fall of the Ottoman Empire and the Creation of the Modern Middle East.* New York: Avon Books, 1989.

Hudson, Michael. *Arab Politics: The Search for Legitimacy*. New Haven, CT: Yale University Press, 1977.

Kerr, Malcolm H. *The Arab Cold War: Gamal 'abd al-Nasir and His Rivals, 1958–1970*. 3rd ed. London: Oxford University Press, 1971.

Lesch, David W., ed. *The Middle East and the United States: A Historical and Political Reassessment*. 3rd ed. Boulder, CO: Westview Press, 2003.

The Decline of Radicalism and the Institutionalization of the Nationalist States

By the 1970s, radical-nationalism as both an alternative ideology and a specific policy framework had declined in appeal and viability, though it remained an attractive, if unrealistic, option for many. The radical-nationalist regimes essentially became institutionalized—that is, their domestic and foreign policies became more cautious, their focus shifted from revolutionary ideals to the more mundane task of governing and maintaining their power, they sought to stabilize their countries to prevent a repeat of the previous decades (when instability, coups, and countercoups were the norm), and there was a growing acceptance of the regional interstate system and the status quo (with the notable exceptions of Iraq and Libya). Today, at the beginning of the twenty-first century, there is only one radical-nationalist state left: Syria. But even it is not radical in the sense of the 1950s and 1960s.

Institutionalization was the result of three broad factors. One, the regimes lost the revolutionary legitimacy that had characterized them in their first two decades of existence. Few of their promises had materialized to any significant degree: domestic socioeconomic conditions did not improve to the expected levels, Israel was not defeated, and the West (now represented by the United States) remained a powerful presence in the Middle East. The regimes could no longer rely on these promises to sustain their popularity, and so had to rely on other instruments of governance.

Two, regional conditions were quite different in the 1970s than they had been in the 1950s and 1960s, the heyday of radical-nationalism. Israel's victory in the 1967 war, the American presence in the region, and the failure of pan-Arab unity projects all contributed to a shift in general ideas about radicalism, exposing its limitations and leading to a desire for ideological change.

Three, new leaders emerged in the radical states in the early 1970s, specifically in Egypt and Syria, who purposely shifted policy away from radicalism. These leaders were mostly ruthless strongmen who used force and repression to impose stability and protect their regimes; in the case of Egypt, the new leader Anwar Sadat took the country out of the Soviet camp and into the American camp. The end result of these changes was the decline of radical-nationalism and the convergence of all of the Arab regimes toward the same general ideas of governance, even if their specific systems remained different (i.e., monarchy versus presidential republic).

To better present the story of radicalism's decline, we turn first to a discussion of the military's declining role in decision making. This is important because the sheer power of the military made it a source of instability before the radical revolutions: factionalized armies would use their resources to raise different officers to power. Once the armed forces were made loyal to the regime and challenges were contained, domestic stability enhanced the regime's staying power. This was accompanied by a growing awareness among ruling elites that they benefited enough from the contemporary system that there was little incentive to continue advocating for revolutionary change. Then, increasing repression by the regimes became part of the process of institutionalization.

As mentioned, external forces such as the failure of pan-Arab unity projects and the victory of Israel in the 1967 Arab-Israeli war both served to undermine radical-nationalism, exposing the bankruptcy of its agenda. Following the movement's decline, a series of new leaders came to power, particularly in Egypt and Syria. These leaders believed that only by ignoring or reversing the policies of radical-nationalism could they protect their regimes and strengthen their states. One of the specific policies these leaders pursued was *infitah*, a process of economic liberalization in direct opposition to the Arab socialism that was a major plank of the radical-nationalist agenda.

The Declining Role of the Military

Military officers established all of the radical-nationalist regimes, and the military played the key supporting role for these regimes in the immediate years after the revolutions because it was the only societal group with the requisite resources (though in Syria the military formed only one part of a wider coalition). Yet beginning in the 1970s the military was, in most cases, eased out of direct power, except in Algeria, where the regime of Houari Boumédiènne continued to rely heavily on it. Even though the leaders came from the military in most cases, as an institution the armed forces were removed from a dominant or even major role in decision making. This allowed the regimes to use the military to help maintain domestic stability and protect the regime, and it prevented the military from fomenting dissent or engaging in outright attempts to overthrow the regime. This was most critical for the Syrian regime, since the military participated in all of the numerous coups that had wracked the country since 1949.

Thus, what began as military regimes were eventually civilianized. The leaders, even if they still wore their uniforms, essentially moved out of the military and into the civilian sector. The primary tactic was to make the army content with its own institutional development. This was accomplished through higher wages, advanced weapons systems, prestige, the capacity to play an independent role as an institution in economic life, institutional autonomy, a role suppressing internal threats, the creation of parallel organizations to supervise the military (e.g., in Syria and Iraq), and in some cases, external military campaigns (such as the 1973 Arab-Israeli War).

This is not to say that the military was unimportant to these regimes. In all of the radical-nationalist states the army provided the necessary resources to shield the government from domestic threats. For example, in Syria, the military brutally crushed a rebellion against the regime in 1982, while in Egypt it was used to suppress riots in 1977 and 1986 against government economic policy. In Iraq, the military waged a campaign against rebellious Kurds throughout the 1960s, 1970s, and into the 1980s. It also acted as a means of national socialization, loyalty, and indoctrination to the regime's ideology. But in terms of influence on decision making, the removal of a leadership role from the military contributed to the institutionalization of the radical states. Two examples, from Egypt and Syria, will suffice to explain this trend.

In Egypt, different leaders enacted different policies toward the military, but the intention was always to remove the capacity of the military to play a direct role in governing. In the 1950s Gamal Abdel Nasser placed his close friend, Abd al-Hakim Amir, in charge of the army. Amir kept the armed forces out of politics in return for steadily increasing expenditures on the military, which jumped from 4 percent of gross national product in 1950 to 12 percent in 1965. This is not to say that the military did not penetrate the political decision-making process; indeed, it continued to have an effect on policy through, for example, rampant cronyism. Amir also jealously guarded his position and tried to ensure his own independent power base in the military. And, of course, the military continued to play an "advisory" role to Nasser, since he could not completely ignore the vehicle that had brought him to power. But it is fair to say that the military as institution was less and less used as the main voice in policymaking on major nonsecurity issues.

In the 1970s, Anwar Sadat took a different tack: he reduced the resources available to the military so that it would not have the strength to challenge the regime, cutting government spending and demobilizing hundreds of thousands of troops after the 1973 war with Israel. In the 1980s his successor, Hosni Mubarak, moved back to the Nasser tactic by increasing the military's budget and giving it a greater role in decision making in certain areas (e.g., internal security). But he has continued to limit the military's position in overall decision making, preventing it from exerting any serious influence over policies that he himself wishes to control.

In Syria, the regime pursued a multipronged strategy. First, because the regime itself was based primarily on a single communal group (the Alawites), it placed members of this group in many of the senior officer positions within the military. These individuals provided guarantees of loyalty to their sectarian kin in government, particularly the president, Hafez al-Assad. Second, the military was "Baath-ized"; that is, it was indoctrinated to share the same ideology of the regime, making it less likely to challenge the regime on ideological grounds. Third, the military was professionalized, provided with funding, resources, and a clear foreign policy mission (the confrontation with Israel). This helped keep it separate from the government and content with being focused on its own development.

A final method of control that all of the regimes imposed on their militaries was the creation of parallel security institutions. These organizations were tied directly to the regime itself. In Iraq, for example, the Republican Guard was used as a bulwark against the regular military in case the latter should try to overthrow the Saddam Hussein regime. Baathist officials in both Syria and Iraq were also assigned to military units to ensure their continued ideological convictions and loyalty. In this way, the military was constantly reminded that it was not the only instrument of force in the country, and that it would face serious resistance if it engaged in violence against the regime.

Having said all this, it must still be remembered that the militaries in the Arab states remained powerful actors; despite being out of the daily business of politics and decision making, they maintain a powerful presence within the state. During the widespread demonstrations in Egypt in January 2011, the military first protected the regime by trying to restrict the scope of the protests; but at the same time, it showed that it would not support the regime at any cost. In a public announcement, the army declared it would not fire on the (peaceful) protestors. By doing this, the armed forces undermined the Mubarak regime by letting it know it didn't have free reign to stay in power, thus influencing the outcome of the protests.

A Growing Stake in the Status Quo

The radical regimes gradually lost their will to engage in drastic revolutionary changes, as they had promised and as they had done in the years immediately following the revolutions. This was out of fear of upsetting the system as it had developed; major change could now undermine the regimes themselves. At the same time, although the general populations did not always do as well, the key supporting elites of the regimes did benefit from their support of the new system. Combined with concerns over their lack of legitimacy (given the waning of the revolutions), the radical regimes have also relied on the support of key elites in society. By tying these elites to the regime, in exchange for resources, the regimes have given these groups a reason to see the system continue.

All Middle Eastern countries, including Israel, have had large public sectors. In the radical-nationalist states, the revolutionary platforms made the expansion of the public sector necessary. The social revolution promised by the radicals led to the development of the state machinery for two reasons: First, it was necessary in order to build up the strength of the state. Only a strong state could pursue the promised foreign policies (defeat of Israel and expulsion of foreign influence). Second, social justice could only be carried out by the state, since only the state had the necessary resources.

Thus, the regimes engaged in a rapid expansion of state apparatuses—in other words, bureaucratization. This meant that an increasingly significant segment of the population became dependent on the state for employment, services, and economic activity in general. Like the communist regimes, this led to inefficiency and mismanagement, since the government is committed to keeping state enterprises and state activity going to keep people employed and satisfied. The belief is that dissatisfaction could lead to demands for change or, worse, active challenges to the regime.

The consequence was that the regimes came to rely on the system in order to retain support. Any major reordering of the system could disrupt the benefits the regime and its key supporters accrued, thus putting the regime at risk of losing legitimacy among its main backers. There was, in short, no political will to continue making changes. This was especially evident in the case of economic reform. Structural reforms were necessary to strengthen stagnating economies, but such reforms would have led to severe socioeconomic dislocation (as they have done elsewhere) among most groups in society, including the regimes' supporters. Any move toward serious economic reform would, it was feared, open up space in which groups could operate and make more demands. As well, economic reforms could well lead to demands for political reforms, as groups whose wealth begins to increase might begin demanding greater say in policymaking, in order to ensure their continued gains and to see the state continue to make policy consistent with wealth generation. In this way the radicals' status quo orientation reflected the same outlook of the liberal parliamentary regimes.

In addition to lack of political will to change the status quo, both the regimes and their supporters have been drawn together by the coalescence of a specific type of opposition that has sprung up in all of the radical-nationalist states. Islamist groups—those with social and political action platforms who wish to see Islam become the guiding framework for all economic and political decision making—have become the primary form of opposition and challenge to the regime in all the states. This has engendered in the regimes a powerful resistance to any change, out of the fear that it would give these groups room to operate and further undermine them.

In Egypt the Muslim Brotherhood, founded in 1928, has been struggling for an Islamist state that would replace the regime founded by Nasser. Because it advocates nonviolence, the Brotherhood had splintered at times into smaller groups dedicated to using violence to achieve their goals. Gamaat Islamiya (the Islamic Group) and Egyptian Islamic Jihad have attacked and murdered government officials and tourists in Egypt. In Syria as well, the Muslim Brotherhood has been the main opposition group to the secular regimes dominated by Alawites, who are considered heretics by the Sunni-dominated Brotherhood. The Brotherhood led an insurrection against the regime from the mid-1970s until Assad finally suppressed it in a violent campaign beginning in 1980 and ending in 1982, during which a brutal military assault destroyed parts of the city of Hama and left thousands dead. Finally, in Algeria, the Islamic Salvation Front, founded in 1989, won a majority of seats in the first round of parliamentary elections in December 1991. Fearing that the party would turn Algeria into an Islamist state, the Algerian military seized power and canceled the second round of elections that same month. The Islamists splintered into a series of smaller groups, most of them engaging in an insurgency against the regime that led to the deaths of tens of thousands of civilians.

In all cases, the Islamist opposition represented a direct threat to the elites in power: under an Islamist regime they would lose their position, their wealth would be redistributed, and their very lives might be at stake in any purge of the government and the state and its apparatuses—much as happened in Iran after 1979. In response, the regimes and their supporters have relied on the status quo to fend off these challenges, preferring to avoid any reforms or changes out of the fear that they would lead to the undermining and overthrow of the regimes. Thus, institutionalization of the radical-nationalists has meant a turn away from revolutionary change to status quo–oriented policies designed to prop up the regimes and keep them in power. This has become the major focus of the regimes since the 1970s.

Increasing Domestic Repression

As dominant elites came to enjoy the benefits of the status quo and new leaders emerged to consolidate and institutionalize the revolutions, the biggest concern of radical regimes came to be defined as regime security—that is, threats to their core values, position, power, and wealth. Even their very lives were considered to be at risk—until the 1970s it was not unusual for power to be passed from one leader to the next because the former was killed by the latter, particularly in Syria and Iraq. As such, regimes became increasingly concerned with domestic order and stability.

The radical-nationalist regimes, in order to protect themselves and contain domestic dissent, engaged in a series of actions designed to prevent the formation of any serious opposition. These have included: concentration of power in the executive, little to no freedom of the press (in conjunction with state-run media), no genuine democratic processes and no real popular representation at the political level, modest space for a civil society not directed by the state, few general individual political and economic freedoms, and widespread use of secret police and other domestic intelligence agencies.

The capacity for domestic repression expanded as the state itself bureaucratized. By all measurements—including increase in the number of government ministries, percentage of the population on the government payroll, and government expenditures in the economy—the Arab states (including the monarchies) underwent very rapid and wide-ranging expansion, allowing them to dominate all aspects of civilian life. As the revolutionaries began to entrench themselves and work to ensure that they could not be threatened by other societal forces, they made sure that there was no rival center of power, such as political parties or parliaments, which could challenge their rule. They also created domestic agencies such as secret police, paramilitary units, intelligence units, and even employed the regular army, to forcibly suppress any dissent. This has led to such states often being referred to as *mukhabarat* (intelligence) states, to connote their reliance on these coercive structures to protect the regime.

The development of the radical-nationalist state led to the integration of these coercive agencies with the regimes in power. As these agencies became staffed at the top level with ethnic, tribal, or sectarian kin of the top leader (the president), they gained a direct stake in maintenance of the system. They became status quo–oriented because these agencies and their officers benefited from preventing change, the kind of change that begins with domestic demands for reform. These benefits include power, status, and wealth. The desire to prevent change further undermined the revolutionary radicalism that marked the early days of these regimes.

Repression is manifested in a variety of ways, but all are tied to the simple method of silencing critics and dissenters. Arbitrary detention, disappearances, torture, special security courts, and lack of general capacity to speak, publish, and organize freely are commonly used to this end. This process has continued to today. In its 2009 Annual Survey, Freedom House ranked these regimes in the following way (where 1 is the "most free" and 7 is the "least free"): On political rights Algeria is ranked as a 6; on civil liberties as a 5. Egypt's ranking is the same. Syria is ranked as a 7 in the first category and a 6 in the second. Libya is ranked at 7 for both categories.

At the same time, the growing preference for the status quo undermined the populism that was a major plank of the radicals' platforms. The regimes began to use mass parties as pillars of support rather than genuine vehicles for popular participation in politics. The regimes also placed loyal supporters in key positions of authority within the party, state, and military. In Syria this was done primarily—though not only—through the Alawites, the sectarian kin of President Assad, while in Iraq it was done through Saddam Hussein's tribal connections and with minority Sunnis. Because of this, repression became even more necessary to maintain these narrowly based regimes in power at the expense of the majority of the population.

This is not to say that the regimes were completely successful at containing all dissent and that there were no more coup attempts. Indeed, there were several throughout the 1970s and 1980s. Saddam Hussein, who had created one of the more efficient intelligence and security service structures, had to defeat a series of coup attempts throughout the 1980s. But as a signal of the success of the regimes at protecting themselves and preventing instability from returning, the coups were never successful.

The Failure of Pan-Arabism

As discussed, the various pan-Arab unity projects created by the radical states all failed. A major reason was because of the growth of national state identity, separate from any transnational ideas based on Arab identity. The failure of pan-Arab schemes led to disillusionment among many of the general populations, even in Syria, which has always seen itself as dedicated to a greater Arab nation. As regimes became entrenched, they came to view their own narrow national interests as predominant; their identities as *states* rather than as *Arab states* became their point of reference. The failure of pan-Arabism, one of the primary foreign policy goals of the radical-nationalists, thus undermined their purpose and therefore their legitimacy, forcing them to seek other means of remaining in power (that is, institutionalization), though they continued to use the rhetoric of pan-Arabism to cloak their true desire to avoid any practical application of this ideology.

Examining the failure of the United Arab Republic (UAR)—the 1958–1961 merger of Egypt and Syria—more closely sheds light on a good example of this process. And because the UAR was the most important effort at pan-Arabism—given how long it lasted and because it included two of the major Arab states—its ending demonstrates pan-Arabism's nonfeasibility.

The union was proposed by Syria. Baathists and other key elites were increasingly concerned about the rise of the Communist Party and the Left in general, and that Syria would collapse into factional fighting or perhaps even disintegration. Union with Egypt also fit well with Baathist and popular conceptions of a single Arab nation artificially divided into separate states.

Contrary to Syrian expectations, Egypt's Nasser dominated the union. He was elected as the republic's president, Cairo was made its capital, and Egyptian officials streamed into Syria to take over the governing functions from Syrians. Egyptian ideas and laws were imposed on Syria while Syrian political parties were disbanded and Syrian military officers dismissed. The Syrians felt the Egyptians were treating them as second-class citizens. The Syrian elites that had proposed union as a way of protecting their own interests soon found themselves increasingly on the outside of decision-making. Their resentment of Egyptian control began to intensify, and pan-Arabism soon came to be seen by the Syrians as simply a vehicle for Nasser's personal and Egypt's regional ambitions.

Increasingly unpopular, the UAR was ended after a coup in Syria in September 1961 brought to power a group of military officers opposed to the union, supported by private economic interests fearful of Nasser's socialism. They quickly took Syria out of the union. (As a signal of its continuing commitment to revolution and pan-Arabism, Egypt continued to use the name United Arab Republic until 1971.) The new regime was more traditional and conservative, and reversed many of the changes imposed by the UAR.

Thus the most prominent example of radical-nationalist pan-Arabist policy ended in failure, and no other unity project ever came close in substance. Indeed, a second attempt at union between the two failed in 1963. The important effect this had on radicalism can be observed by the impact the UAR's failure had on Syrians. Though they had long considered themselves the bearers of the pan-Arab banner, many Syrians were so disillusioned that they increasingly accepted the pursuit of distinct national Syrian interests over wider regional Arab interests.

In the short term, the end of the UAR galvanized Nasser into more vitriolic revolutionary rhetoric; in policy terms, this led to the intervention in Yemen and the 1967 Arab-Israeli War. In hindsight, scholars have argued that the failure of the UAR signaled the failure of pan-Arabism in general. Since inter-Arab conflict had for the most part been promoted in the 1950s and 1960s by the radical-nationalists seeking to reorder regional politics, the growing acceptance of state boundaries dividing the Arab world into distinct national-political units meant there was less motivation for the radical Arab leaders to engage in subversion based on pan-Arabism. Because it no longer carried much appeal, it could not be used as a foreign policy tool to undermine one's rivals. Nasser himself epitomized this shift, when by the late 1960s he withdrew Egyptian troops from North Yemen and accepted a reconciliation between the Yemeni parties.

Moreover, by the mid-1970s, what inter-Arab conflict that did exist was based on national interests and border disputes rather than drives to establish either more radical regimes or mergers between the Arab states. Even Saddam Hussein's invasion of Kuwait in August 1990 was based, in addition to concerns over regime security, on a belief that Kuwait was historically part of Iraq as a national unit. There was simply no more appetite among the regimes for actively pushing the pan-Arab agenda. A growing satisfaction with the contemporary state boundaries, combined with attempts to shift these boundaries to strengthen national rather than transnational interests, illustrates a preference for the status quo.

The 1967 Arab-Israeli War

No other regional event did more to undermine radical-nationalism than the 1967 war, in which

Israel, fearing it was about to endure a devastating assault by the Arab states, launched a preemptive strike against and defeated the Egyptian, Syrian, and Jordanian armies. In the process it seized the Gaza Strip and Sinai Peninsula from Egypt, the Golan Heights from Syria, and the West Bank (including the hallowed Old City of Jerusalem) from Jordan. The defeat of Egypt and Syria, the preeminent radical-nationalist regimes, called into question their ideologies and the promises they had made to strengthen the Arabs, defeat Israel, and usher in a new era of Arab superiority. And just as the Israeli victory in 1948 discredited the old regimes based on monarchies and notables, so did the Israeli victory in 1967 expose the radical regimes as weak and incompetent.

The war began as a series of crises that spiraled out of control but that were given impetus by the radical rhetoric emanating from Cairo and the other Arab states. Beginning in the mid-1960s, tensions between Israel and Syria boiled over into direct clashes between the countries' air forces in April 1967. This was followed in May by Israeli threats against the Syrian regime over its support for Palestinian fighters operating across the border. The continuing activities of Palestinian guerilla and terrorist units crossing into Israel from the Syrian and Jordanian borders underscored the interstate tensions.

Throughout this period—indeed, since the establishment of Israel in 1948—Israeli leaders were aware of Arab public declarations calling for Israel's destruction. The formation of the Palestine Liberation Organization (PLO) in 1964 was considered to be one of the means to achieve this. The collective memory of Israeli leaders relied on the historical experience of Jews in Europe and the Middle East, and particularly the Holocaust in the 1940s, prompting them to take these pronouncements seriously. Many Israeli leaders believed that peace with the Arab states was not possible under such conditions; some advocated a more aggressive military policy against the Arab regimes in order to undermine them.

In the context of Israeli threats against the Arabs, the Soviet Union became concerned for the security of its ally Syria. It sent a report to Nasser that Israel was massing troops along the border with Syria in preparation for an invasion. Although the report was exposed as false, it put Nasser in a difficult position: throughout the 1950s and 1960s he had been threatening Israel with attack and promising that a strengthened Arab world would be able to right the wrong of 1948, that is, restore Palestine to the Arabs. As the major leader of the Arab world, Nasser's credibility and prestige, and Egypt's position as the primary Arab state in the confrontation with Israel, were at stake as it became obvious his rhetoric was not matching his actions. Other Arab states began to accuse him of failure and cowardice. The Soviet report, coming when it did, galvanized him into action.

In response, Nasser made three moves in quick succession that made the war inevitable. On May 14 he had large numbers of Egyptian soldiers move into the Sinai; on May 16 he demanded that the UN remove from Sinai its peacekeepers that had been stationed there since the 1956 war; and on May 22 he closed the Straits of Tiran to Israeli shipping. These three actions, but particularly the last, were considered by Israel as a *casus belli*. Evidence of a growing united Arab front put enormous pressure on Israel: the country felt itself internationally isolated, as the United States declined to take action to keep the Straits open; Arab threats provided strong reminders of the Holocaust; and the closure of the Straits had a negative impact on Israel's economy. The government mobilized its military, but given the small size of the population and the fact that the military includes a sizable portion of reservists, it could not remain mobilized for long without undermining the economy. Israel decided that the only way out of these conditions was to attack first. On June 5 its air force struck at Egypt's air force. The war ended six days later with Israel completely victorious.

The defeat of the major radical-nationalist states dented their allure and undermined their promises. Nasser himself reflected this psychological and ideational change: on June 9, even before the end of the war, he offered his resignation to the Egyptian people. Although the public clamored for him to remain as president, he was, according to contemporary observers, never the same after that, having lost the revolutionary fervor that had characterized his previous years. Given Nasser's position as the major radical and pan-Arabist, the undercutting of his prestige affected the credibility of the entire pan-Arabist movement.

The Coming to Power of New Leaders

The process of the decline in radicalism was centered on Egypt and Syria because, in addition to the regional changes that affected all of the radical states, new leaders came to power in these two major countries, directing a near-complete shift away from radicalism. In Egypt, Anwar Sadat came to power on October 15, 1970, and in Syria, Hafez al-Assad seized power in a coup on November 16, 1970. Both presidents sought to reduce adventurism and inject greater pragmatism into their foreign policies, as well as put an end to revolutionary changes in domestic policies. Both were successful, and thus helped mark the end of the radical-nationalist era.

Nasser's pan-Arab policies, regional ambitions, and wild rhetoric had led Egypt into three regional wars: the 1956 Sinai campaign, the 1960s civil war in North Yemen, and the June 1967 Arab-Israeli War. The latter had resulted in a humiliating destruction of the Egyptian military, breaking Nasser's spirit and contributing in no small measure to the end of radical-nationalism as a viable alternative in the region. When Nasser died on September 28, 1970, his supporters chose to raise former vice president Sadat to the presidency and leadership of the country because he was perceived to be easily manipulated and could therefore be expected to serve the Nasserites' interests. However, beginning in October and running into the early 1970s, Sadat began to take power for himself in what was called the Corrective Revolution. By 1971 he had reduced the influence of those who did not actively support him and continued Nasser's tendency to concentrate power in his own hands.

Sadat believed that Nasser's adventurism had been bad for Egypt by leading to military defeat and economic problems. It had also alienated the United States, which Sadat was eager to court in order to obtain American financial support. Nasser had relied on the Soviet Union for economic and military aid, but Sadat perceived that the United States could provide more aid and better weaponry. He also believed that only Washington could pressure Israel into returning the Sinai Peninsula, captured by Israel in the 1967 war.

Consequently, by the mid-1970s Sadat led Egypt into the American camp, becoming the first Arab state to sign a peace treaty with Israel (1979) and becoming America's close regional ally. Finally, Sadat believed that Nasser's socialism had created severe economic problems for Egypt by leading to mismanagement, inefficiency, and stagnation. Instead, Sadat engaged in *infitah*, a process of economic opening in which he exposed the economy to private enterprise and foreign investment. In all of these policies, Sadat moved Egypt away from Nasser's radicalism; in so doing he helped to undermine radical-nationalism.

In Syria, Assad seized power in November 1970, in what he also referred to as a Corrective Revolution. Before that, Syria had been a model of instability, wracked by coups and countercoups that brought various factions to power for short periods of time. On March 8, 1963, a coalition of Baathist military officers and civilians seized power in yet another coup. Over the next seven years the new regime engaged in a series of radical changes in domestic policy and a more active foreign policy.

Assad, as commander of the air force and then defense minister, played a role in the coup and its subsequent policies, but he did not support all of them. Some of the nationalizations and land reforms promulgated by the Baathist regime were later repealed. In addition, the Baathist government engaged in a series of major foreign policy actions, including rabid anti-Western rhetoric, clashes with Israeli forces in the lead-up to the 1967 war, and intervention into Jordan in September 1970 to support PLO fighters against King Hussein. Assad viewed all of these as unnecessary and reckless provocations that undermined Syria's military and political position.

After he seized power, Assad changed the contours of Syrian foreign policy. No longer would ideology determine policy; instead, he concentrated on what he believed was a realistic appraisal of Syria's geopolitical situation and military conditions, and how these could be improved through careful policies. Pan-Arab unity was no longer the determining framework (except primarily for rhetorical purposes); it was now trumped by Syrian national interests.

Assad's chief foreign policy goal was now to regain the Golan Heights from Israel. To do this, Syria shifted from adventurism to pragmatism:

Assad began to mend fences with the conservative monarchies in order to obtain funding for strengthening his military. He also expanded ties with the Soviet Union and engaged in his own limited process of infitah in order to promote economic development and foreign investment. Though infitah was the opposite of Arab socialism, it was perceived as necessary for building up the Syrian economy and consequently the Syrian military.

Sadat's and Assad's single war against Israel in 1973 was a very controlled affair. It was a limited war with a limited purpose—to regain territory seized by Israel in 1967, not the destruction of Israel. Both leaders were acutely aware that they likely could not defeat Israel; Syrian troops ignored certain opportunities in the course of the war to push beyond the Golan for a direct strike at Israel (though other factors, such as Syria's own military capabilities, may also have contributed to these decisions). In the event that the territories could not be taken by force, the war would at least draw superpower attention and increase their standing vis-à-vis the other Arab states and the superpowers.

Saddam Hussein, it should be noted, was the exception to the rule. Of the emerging leaders of the radical-nationalists (he took complete power in July 1979), he engaged in a series of foreign policies that brought devastation to the Iraqi economy and destroyed the Iraqi military, thus undermining any Iraqi chance at regional domination. In 1980 he invaded Iran, leading to an eight-year war that left hundreds of thousands dead or injured; and in 1990 he invaded Kuwait, provoking an American-led coalition that defeated the Iraqi army, broke up Saddam's programs of weapons of mass destruction and sharply limited his own authority within northern and southern Iraq, and set the conditions for the later 2003 U.S.-led invasion that led to his overthrow, capture, and execution.

Infitah

In addition to a shift in radical foreign policy, the new leaders who emerged in the early 1970s engaged in economic activity that undermined and reversed many policies considered the bedrocks of Arab socialism. *Infitah* (literally, "open door") was pursued because socialism was perceived as not contributing to the strengthening of the state. It was associated with failed idealism: deteriorating economic conditions combined with rapid population growth created enormous socioeconomic problems. In addition, there was a demand on the part of the wealthier classes for more consumer products, which put pressure on the regimes to provide them. Arab socialism therefore had to be shunted aside in favor of more rational and practical policies designed to meet concrete policy goals such as building up the economic capacity and the military power of the state.

Egypt set the tone and example of this shift in policy. It began the process under Sadat in the early 1970s (though there already had been some minor moves toward economic liberalization toward the end of Nasser's reign). The need for foreign investment prompted a revival of the private-sector. To this end, Sadat created financial incentives for foreign capital, including in sectors such as banking, which had previously been considered integral to the national interest and therefore off limits to foreigners. Trade was liberalized, the commitment to forgo nationalization was legislated, and the exchange-rate system was left to be guided by the market.

Syria under Assad followed. Some agrarian reforms were reversed. As well, some state controls over trade were removed and private sector activity was allowed in small niches in the economy, such as construction. Finally, foreign firms were encouraged to participate in the Syrian economy.

In truth, the radical-nationalist states fell into a kind of mixed economy, somewhere between capitalism and socialism, as they were unwilling or unable to completely give up their use of the economy as an instrument of governing, particularly in terms of providing patronage or cooptation. At the same time, the economic openings these regimes presided over increased economic disparity, as the rising middle and upper classes were able to take advantage of the changes and accumulate more wealth for themselves, while the bulk of the population remained stuck in the lower classes. Inefficiency and corruption also marred the process. Still, this does not take away from the fact that the radical-nationalists were now pursuing economic policies in opposition to those they had trumpeted at the beginning of their revolutions.

Is Radical-Nationalism Gone Forever?

The above analysis illustrates the reasons behind the waning of radical-nationalism. The combination of policy failure, Israeli military victory, the emergence of elites dependent on the status quo, and the coming to power of leaders very different from those who initiated the revolutions undermined radical-nationalism to the point that it was simply no longer viable. It is unlikely that it can be brought back as a viable policy alternative or ideology in the immediate future. However, some of its underlying tenets have remained, absorbed into the radical Islamist agenda promoted by Iran and groups throughout the region, such as Hezbollah in Lebanon and Hamas in the Palestinian areas.

Pan-Arabist ideas also continue to be discussed and promoted in much of the Arab media, sometimes encouraged by the regimes themselves, which has helped to keep the concept alive. Moreover, the growing discontent increasingly evident among populations throughout the Middle East could well lead to the overthrow of the current regimes—whether through violence or peaceful means—and the emergence of a new generation of secular-radical leaders. Finally, as author Marc Lynch pointed out in his 2006 book *Voices of the New Arab Public: Iraq, Al-Jazeera, and Middle East Politics Today*, the American invasion of Iraq in 2003 and its aftermath have united much of the region's Arab populations in their opposition to the U.S. occupation and the continuing insecurity and instability in Iraq, providing a foundation for common cause. Such a discussion is beyond the scope of this book, but mention should at least be made of its possibility.

The 1990s were full of global and regional changes that seem to have completely removed any possibility of radical-nationalism coming back. At the global level, two events in 1991 led to a complete shift in the international balance of power, leading to structural changes that impacted on politics in every region of the globe. First, the U.S.-led coalition that pushed Iraq out of Kuwait was a war by the West against a former Soviet client. Moscow allowed the United States to put together the coalition, and although it did engage in some efforts at a negotiated end to the crisis, it did not stop the attack.

Second, the Soviet Union itself imploded in December 1991, and with its death the Cold War ended. Instead of a bipolar division of the world into a U.S.-led camp and a Soviet-led camp, there was now a single superpower: the United States. This meant there were no more challengers to American dominance in the world. This changed the balance of power in the Middle East as well. For former Soviet clients like Iraq and Syria, this meant they had no support against their U.S.-backed enemies. Syria, especially, now suffered from a lack of much-needed military and economic aid (for example, spare parts for its tanks and armored vehicles) that undermined its capacity to be a serious contender for regional dominance.

At the regional level, a series of structural changes took place that upset the balance of power that might have benefited any radical-nationalists had they been interested. The Madrid peace conference in 1991 involving Israel and most of the Arab states, the Oslo Accords between Israel and the PLO in 1993, the peace treaty between Israel and Jordan in 1994, and a series of regional conferences designed to facilitate closer regional economic cooperation all indicated a growing acceptance of Israel in the region, at least by the regimes. The onset of a close military relationship between Israel and Turkey, beginning in 1996, also seemed to threaten the radical bloc.

Domestically, all of the radical-nationalist states had engaged in a series of policies that, from the 1970s through the 1990s, weakened their capacity to follow through on these promises. Egypt took itself directly out of the radical-nationalist camp by making peace with Israel in 1979 and becoming a close American ally. Egypt's defection completely undermined the radical front: as the largest and strongest Arab state in the region, no Arab coalition could defeat Israel without Egyptian participation. The Egyptian shift therefore removed the primary foreign policy objective of the radicals.

The Iraqi radical regime has been overthrown and replaced by a democracy, however troubled it may be. The 1990 invasion of Kuwait was followed by an American-led destruction of Iraq's military, the imposition of United Nations sanctions and weapons inspectors, and an eventual U.S.-led invasion in 2003 that ended with the capture and execution of Saddam Hussein himself.

North and South Yemen, both former radical regimes, united in 1990 and formed a semi-democracy. By the twenty-first century it, too, became an ally in the U.S. "war on terrorism." For its part, Algeria was convulsed throughout the 1990s by a vicious civil war between radical Islamist groups and the military that left hundreds of thousands dead and ended only in the early 2000s.

Even Libya, the most enduring of the radical-nationalists because of its late revolution (1969) and the self-perception of its leader Muammar Qaddafi as the heir to Nasser, has moved away from radical-nationalism. Desperate for foreign investment and Western aid to develop its oil industry and promote economic development, Libya has moved away from Arab socialism. At the end of 2003, it agreed to give up its programs of weapons of mass destruction and reintegrate into the world community in exchange for improved relations with the United States and a lifting of harsh economic sanctions.

Finally, though it continues to pay lip service to many of the tenets of radical-nationalism, Syria too has moved away from its former revolutionary zeal and promoted a policy of maintenance of the status quo, particularly in domestic affairs. The successful transition from Hafez al-Assad to his son Bashar, upon the latter's death on June 10, 2000, is evidence of this. Bashar has been supported by most of the same elites who supported his father. Obviously, they too benefit enough from the status quo to the extent that they have been willing to support a relative newcomer to the game of Syrian politics in order to retain their advantages. The institutionalization of the radical regimes that began in the 1970s is thus continuing into the next generation.

Despite all these changes, it would be wrong to assume that some form of radical-nationalism will never be a viable alternative again. The growing strength of radical extremist Islamist groups such as Hezbollah in Lebanon and Hamas in the Palestinian areas, supported by the Islamic Republic of Iran, indicates that radical transnational ideologies demanding wholesale change remain attractive for at least some groups. They are not nationalist in the secular understanding of the 1950s and 1960s, but their Islamist agenda promotes a wholesale change in the governing systems of the region, much as the radical-nationalists did. The Islamists seek an overthrow of the contemporary systems and the installation of a series of national Islamic regimes dedicated to pursuing Islamic "values" (however they are defined) and the basing of all laws and policies on shariah, Islamic law. They are, in this sense, a throwback to the revolutionary regimes of the previous era.

References and Further Reading

Ayubi, Nazih N. *Over-stating the Arab State: Politics and Society in the Middle East.* London: I.B. Tauris, 1995.

Dawisha, Adeed, and I. William Zartman, eds. *Beyond Coercion: The Durability of the Arab State.* London: Croom Helm, 1988.

Ehteshami, Anoushiravan, and Raymond A. Hinnebusch. *Syria and Iran: Middle Powers in a Penetrated Regional System.* London: Routledge, 1997.

Henry, Clement M., and Robert Springborg. *Globalization and the Politics of Development in the Middle East.* Cambridge: Cambridge University Press, 2001.

Hinnebusch, Raymond A., Jr. *Egyptian Politics Under Sadat: The Post-Populist Development of an Authoritarian-Modernizing State,* updated ed. Boulder, CO: Lynne Rienner, 1988.

Maddy-Weitzman, Bruce. *The Crystallization of the Arab State System.* Syracuse, NY: Syracuse University Press, 1993.

Richards, Alan, and John Waterbury. *A Political Economy of the Middle East.* 3rd ed. Boulder, CO: Westview Press, 2008.

Instruments of Governance Among the Arab Regimes

All Arab regimes—monarchies and radical-nationalists—remain in power because they rely on a shared set of policy instruments designed to maintain their positions. Though the specific tactics and methods differ according to national circumstances and governing system (for example, oil monarchies rely more heavily on a social contract that trades resources for political quiescence), the broad tools are the same.

The Arab regimes have historically relied heavily on repression and coercion to stay in power. They supplement these methods with a wide range of nonviolent instruments of legitimacy generation, control, and co-optation. The regimes thus rely on a dual strategy of inclusion plus repression. Citizens are both incorporated into the state and repressed, that is, dissent is kept to a minimum.

The co-optive methods used by Arab regimes include the process of bureaucratization (that is, the expansion of the state machinery), the central role of the state in the economy, exertion of state control over religion, the use of a mass party, a narrow base of support, and cosmetic liberalization designed to deflate pressure for change. Tools of repression include the military and other coercive organizations, such as intelligence agencies, secret police, and special security forces. In addition, regimes turn to foreign policy tools to stay in power. An issue that generates the greatest amount of anger is the Arab-Israeli conflict, which includes the cause of Palestine and the Palestinians.

Bureaucratization

The 1950s heralded a new era in bureaucratization—that is, the growth of state machinery. The radical-nationalists, as they came to power, began to rapidly develop the machinery of state in order to meet their revolutionary promises. As they became institutionalized, bureaucratization continued as a way for the regimes to co-opt and coerce their citizens. The monarchies also engaged in a similar process and for similar reasons (regime security). With the influx of oil money in the 1970s, the oil monarchies were able to expand to a much larger degree and at a much faster rate. As a general process, bureaucratization enabled the Arab regimes to better protect themselves, to build up their states in economic and military terms, and to control their populations more easily—all through greater centralization, the corollary to bureaucratization. The process became so entrenched that bureaucratization continued even while attempts to reduce state involvement in the economic sector, based on *infitah*, were enacted.

The first priority motivating this process was the development of the state, or the process of state building. Most of the Arab states (with the exceptions of Egypt, Morocco, and Yemen) are very new; their creation and/or independence came in the period between the 1930s and the 1960s, and the smaller oil monarchies only became independent in 1971. Thus, swift expansion of the state was seen as necessary in order to strengthen the Arab states so that they could hold their own in regional and global politics. It also dovetailed with a widespread belief that a "modern" developed state was one with a large bureaucracy.

The second motivation for bureaucratization was as a mechanism of control. Not only does expansion of the public sector allow the regimes to co-opt citizens by providing employment, job security, wages, and so on, but it also means they can exert control over the actions of these citizens. By creating overlapping positions, moving civil service members around to different positions, and having all power flow from the leader at the top of the hierarchy, control is reinforced and allows the regime to tacitly threaten the population that lack of obedience could result in a loss of employment, access to capital (graft), or benefits.

The third motivation of bureaucratization was to provide for a rapidly expanding population. For example, Egypt's population more than doubled from 21.8 million in 1950 to 43.8 million in 1980, and grew to 55.6 million in 1990. Algeria's population in 1950 was 8.7 million; again, this more than doubled to 18.8 in 1980, and neared 26 million in 1990. Following the same trend, Libya's population went from 1 million in 1950 to 3 million in 1980 to 4.3 million in 1990. Syria grew from 3.4 million citizens in 1950 to 8.9 million in 1980 and to 12.8 million in 1990. Morocco's population leaped from 8.9 million in 1950 to 19.5 million in 1980 and 24.6 million in 1990. And Saudi Arabia's inhabitants tripled from a mere 3.2 million in 1950 to 9.6 million in 1980, then grew to 16.3 million in 1990.

These burgeoning populations needed to be taken care of, particularly as the populations of the regions have increasingly been younger. The only way to do so was to increase the capacities of the state. This meant that the state had to provide services and jobs for more people. Expansion of the state was a way of meeting these goals: the civil service, the military, and public enterprises were used to provide employment for hundreds of thousands of people. These institutions had to be enlarged in order to do so. In addition, expansion of government (through the creation of more ministries, departments, and agencies) was necessary in order to provide the necessary services, whether medical, professional, educational, and so on.

At the same time, the process of expansion fed upon itself. The combination of a growing population and the efforts by the Arab regimes to build up their states resulted in an expansion of education (particularly postsecondary education; Algeria, for example, had no universities at independence in 1962; by the late 1990s it had eleven). The radical-nationalists had made this a priority, as part of their promise for bettering the lives of society, but the monarchies were no less interested. The state was therefore now producing more and more graduates, particularly in areas of public policy and professional and vocational fields, such as civil service, engineering, and agriculture.

In keeping with their promises and ideas about the purpose of the state (such as, that employing more educated people leads to more development), the regimes had to provide jobs for these graduates within state institutions—even as state institutions became more and more bloated. This was coupled with the general perception that employment in the civil service entailed prestige and status. Thus the state had to expand in order to provide opportunities for the growing numbers of university graduates, regardless of the economic or administrative costs this entailed for the state and its decision making.

Intervention in the Economy

In one sense, all of the Arab regimes have become socialist, including the monarchies. This is because in all the Arab countries, the state has become the primary actor in the economy. Economic development is based on state activity, not just in terms of setting regulations but also in terms of the state acting as a physical presence, through standard economic activity (buying and selling products and services) and the provision of jobs, contracts, and licenses. As well, individual state officials and members of key elites that support the regimes are involved in various economic enterprises on their own. Because of their ties to or membership in the regime, these individuals further the interests of the state in the economy.

The central role of the state in the economy stems from the desire and necessity of the regime to engage in state building alongside continuing centralization of authority. It was one of the most effective ways that the regimes could exert control. In addition, it was the only entity that had the capacity to do so: the private sector was either not large enough or not considered trustworthy, given its presumed focus on its own wealth generation or its close ties to international capital.

The most important manner in which the regimes have used the economy is as a newer form of patronage. Through its expansion, the state has been able to provide employment for its citizens: the number of people working for the government, in the civil service, military, security services, public economic enterprises, and agriculture, has increased dramatically in all of the Arab states. (In Iraq, under Saddam Hussein, a significant portion of the population was also employed as domestic informants and spies.) By tying citizens directly to the state, making them dependent on the state through employment, the regimes have calculated that there will be less demand for change since people are unlikely to undermine the security that comes from having a permanent job. This is why university graduates are all but guaranteed a job once they enter the workforce. This trend is reflected in all sectors.

In Egypt, for example, the number of people working in the bureaucracy and public sector leaped from 350,000 in 1951 to over 1 million in 1965. In Saudi Arabia, the civil service employed only a few hundred people in 1950, but 85,000 in 1970, and 336,000 in 1980. In Iraq, from 1958 to 1967 the number of citizens employed by the state had leaped by a factor of four, to 319,000. By the early 1980s, public-sector employment in Syria represented 20 percent of the total labor force, and in Egypt, 40 percent. By 1990, the Algerian public sector employed 59 percent of the labor force, the Jordanian, 47 percent.

By the early 2000s, the number of employees in the public sector, as a percentage of the total workforce, stood at: 31.3 percent in Algeria, 34.9 percent in Egypt, 36.1 percent in Jordan, and 21.9 percent in Tunisia. Excluding workers in agriculture, the percentages are even higher: 39 percent in Algeria, 70.3 percent in Egypt, 42.1 percent in Jordan, and 28.2 percent in Tunisia. Militaries are also used to absorb labor. The Egyptian army, especially, has been used in this manner. The number of people serving in the military rose from 80,000 in 1955 to 180,000 in 1966. In 2007, out of a population of almost 80 million, 1.1 million people were employed in the Egyptian military. (For the sake of comparison, the United States has a population of 300 million and a military that contains 2.3 million people.)

At the same time that they provide direct employment, the Arab regimes also serve as indirect patrons. Corruption is rampant among the Arab states, in many cases simply because employees feel that their salaries are not enough to support their families. They therefore supplement their official income with private, black-market business. Doing so requires contacts initiated and cultivated through connections made while working for the state. Thus, public employment provides a double function—income and contacts—and makes the population doubly dependent on the state through economic activities.

In addition to being an employer, the state also became the main investor in the economy. By the 1960s it accounted, in most Arab states, for at least 50 percent of total investment. The figure ran as high as 75 percent in countries like Egypt and Iraq. As a percentage of gross domestic product (GDP), government expenditures in 1975 stood at: 56 percent in Algeria, 58 percent in Saudi Arabia, 59 percent in Egypt, 46 percent in Syria, and 51 percent in Iraq.

The state's role as investor is coupled with more direct forms of government-to-population economic activity. In order to keep citizens happy and to at least maintain some semblance of their commitment to either socialism or promises to look after the welfare of the populace, Arab regimes have made effective use of price controls, subsidies on a wide range of items, social services (particularly in the oil states), and other financial transfers directly to citizens. In 2003, direct transfers and subsidies, as a percentage of GDP, stood at: almost 6 percent in Algeria, 9.2 percent in Egypt, and 8.8 percent in Jordan. While at least part of the explanation behind these figures is the commitment to providing benefits based on a value system that believes the state should look after its citizens, the major reason seems to be the desire for control.

This state involvement in the economy, particularly through the large civil service and state subsidies to, and ownership of, various industries and enterprises, has had negative effects on the economy, similar to those experienced in the former communist countries. Inefficiency, waste, mismanagement, and stagnation have been the result. Any real reforms would affect not only key elites but also the wider population, which would generate widespread dissatisfaction and, regimes fear, lead to unrest and challenges. This is why, for instance, when oil prices dropped in the mid-1980s the oil monarchies preferred to engage in deficit spending rather than reduce their expenditures on providing a range of free or low-cost services to their populations.

State-Sanctioned Religion

The historical relevance of Islam for both societies and polities in the Middle East has made it impossible for Arab regimes to ignore its potential as a rival source of power and legitimacy. Regimes have therefore sought to co-opt religion by making Islam's preachers, teachers, and scholars part of the state apparatus. This gives these groups a stake in maintaining the system, as they benefit from it in ways both tangible (through funding for projects such as mosques and education centers, and through wages) and intangible (support for their particular brand of Islam and foreign activities, and allowing them to see to the spiritual needs of the populations). By controlling these groups, regimes attempt to remove the possibility that they will become a source of opposition, while presumably gaining more legitimacy among the population.

As discussed earlier, some of the monarchies rely heavily on their historical-Islamic credentials (Jordan and Morocco) or achieve a partnership with the religious establishment (Saudi Arabia). And while none of the other states, oil monarchies or former radical-nationalists, have sought to adopt an overly Islamist character, they all have sought hegemony over Islam. This control is managed in a number of ways.

First, Islam is incorporated into state structures. This is done through several avenues. The state has become the main employer of Islamic officials. Ministries of Religious Affairs (or a similar government department, such as Saudi Arabia's Ministry of Justice) were created as the formal, official structure within which Islamic clerics must operate. Thus their sermons and writings are supervised by the state so that they do not promote any values or ideas the state does not want heard. Islamic teachers are also under the authority of a Ministry of Education, which gives the regime control over what information and values are passed on to younger generations.

More importantly, regimes have been very successful at removing the Islamic leaders' own sources of power. For example, land or other endowments are now directly under the supervision of a government agency. In addition, because they are supervised, religious leaders no longer have direct, unfettered access to the populations. This access is mediated by the regimes, though often regimes and clerics will agree at least nominally on sermon content. In this context, the regimes now also pay the salaries of the ulama and other religious leaders. This makes them dependent on the state for their own welfare, giving them incentive to work with the regime.

Other incentives come in the form of funding for the building of mosques, educational and spiritual centers, and contracts to build these in foreign countries. The Saudi monarchy in particular has used this as an incentive, and Saudi-funded mosques have been built throughout the Balkans and Central Asia. And, of course, because they are on the government payroll, Islamic officials who do not toe the government line can be dismissed and replaced by more compliant prayer leaders and teachers, while those who cooperate can move up through the government bureaucracy to a higher position and better pay.

Second, most Arab regimes have constitutionally made Islam the official state religion and specified Islam as one of the sources of their judicial and legal systems. By providing this official stamp of approval, the regimes believe they can transfer the loyalty and legitimacy the population feels toward Islam to the regime itself. Even Algeria, whose independence movement was strongly revolutionary and Marxist, and thus less inclined to embrace religion than most Arab states, adopted Islam as the state religion soon after independence.

Basing the state's legal principles on Islam has also allowed the regimes to utilize the ulama for legitimating unpopular decisions. This is done by having these clerics issue *fatwas*—religious rulings that authorize or legitimate decisions on Islamic grounds. In May 1979, for example, Egyptian president Sadat obtained from the highly respected Islamic university al-Azhar a fatwa supporting his widely disliked 1977 trip to Jerusalem.

Third, incorporation of Islamic officials into government structures allowed these individuals to represent Islam in the public sphere and promote their associated ideas and values. Being part of the regime gives their activities official government sanction. It also gives them more leeway to preach and teach than those Islamists who are not incorporated into the regime. The most dramatic expression of this is in Saudi Arabia, where religious police (*mutawwa'in*) are tasked with ensuring that Saudi citizens follow the strict Islamic laws in the country, such as attendance at mosque prayers, obeying the restrictions of the holy month of Ramadan, proper dress, and separation of nonrelated men and women.

Finally, the regimes use as a last resort the tool of outright suppression. Despite the efforts at co-optation, some Islamic groups have avoided working with the regimes and instead directly challenged them, calling for their replacement by a fundamentalist Islamic regime based on Islamic precepts. Here, regimes have utilized force to suppress these challenges. In such cases, Islamist organizations are dissolved and banned, their members jailed, or outright violence breaks out as the regime physically confronts these groups. The Muslim Brotherhood groups in both Egypt and Syria, for example, have consistently faced widespread arrest. This has become more of a concern for the regimes since the 1980s, when a renewed public interest in Islam, partly as a reaction to deteriorating socioeconomic conditions, affected all Muslim countries. Islamist groups not affiliated with the regime have expanded, presenting a fresh approach to public policy as the available space in which to organize and operate has grown.

But even when the regimes have engaged in physical confrontation with radical Islamist groups, they have been careful not to denigrate Islam itself or to seem as though they are attacking religion. The radical groups are accused of not representing real Islam, of wanting to undermine the achievements of the country and the people, so that the population will continue to believe that the regime is in fact looking out for Islam, though it seems that this tactic has become less successful beginning in the 1990s.

The Mass Party

No Middle Eastern state is totalitarian in the same way that the Soviet Union was. But there are no truly independent political parties in the Arab governing systems. (Israel and Turkey are known for a proliferation of such parties. Independent parties are allowed to form in Iran, but the regime vets all candidates and frequently bars dissenting groups from running in elections.) Instead, most Arab regimes have allowed for the existence of some political movements that are under direct or indirect control of the regime, or are so hemmed in by restrictions that they cannot function in any truly independent sense. As a reflection of the differences between the monarchies and the former radical-nationalist regimes, political parties are banned by law in most of the Arab oil monarchies and Libya.

Instead, some of the Arab states have sought to create a mass party to mobilize the general population in support of the regime and enhance its legitimacy. None of these have been successful, and in fact these systems are better described as dominant-party systems, but they deserve mention because it is a common thread among at least some of the former radical-nationalist states.

Mass parties are not used in the oil monarchies since loyalty is formed around the individual ruler and his kingly family. But in systems where the leader must base his legitimacy on popular support, the system itself must be the focus of loyalty. Hence, a mass party serves the purpose of drawing the population together in an organization whose sole purpose is to proclaim the presumed participatory nature of the system and give the masses the feeling that they are connected to the ruling elites. It is a way of mobilizing popular support and exerting control through a hierarchical system that reaches down into local village and town organizations. Party branches in the military are also sometimes used. As well, the parties have affiliated groupings such as youth and sports clubs, women's sections, and so on, to incorporate as much of the population as possible and make them feel part of the system.

In Egypt, the first mass party was created by the Revolutionary Command Council (composed of the leaders of the 1952 coup). The Liberation Rally lasted from 1953 to 1958, but it was largely unsuccessful as it had essentially been a stopgap measure to make up for the council's official ban on political parties. By 1956 the council was disbanded and Nasser had seized complete power. In 1958 he replaced the Liberation Rally with the National Union, and in order to make it a truly mass party he stipulated that all adult Egyptians had to become members. The National Union, too, was unsuccessful at achieving real mass party status and purpose, and was dissolved in 1961. It was replaced in 1962 with the Arab Socialist Union (ASU).

The ASU was more of a mass party in the true sense of the word than its previous incarnations.

Although membership was technically voluntary, in reality one could not advance through any level of government or any professional association or similar organization without ASU membership. Nasser also used it as a personal instrument for consolidating more power in his hands. But it, too, eventually failed to achieve its objectives, never having generated the necessary ideological indoctrination or institutional bonds.

Sadat continued to use the ASU for some years after he came to power in 1970, but lacking Nasser's charisma and personal authority he had to generate legitimacy for himself and his unpopular policies regarding Israel and Islam. He broke up the ASU into individual parties and ushered in a new era of (ostensibly) competitive multipartyism in 1976. In 1978 he created the National Democratic Party, which remains the ruling party under Hosni Mubarak. In the 2005 November–December parliamentary elections, the party won 311 out of 454 seats in the Majlis al-Sha'ab (the People's Council).

A truer form of mass party was the Baath Party, which came to power in Syria (1963) and Iraq (1963, 1968, to 2003), though it only became "mass" after achieving power. In Syria especially it was begun as a populist machine that reflected the ideas of its founders, Michel Aflaq and Salah al-Din al-Bitar: pan-Arab unity, freedom, and socialism. In both countries, the party became indistinguishable from the state and the regime, and by the 1970s it lost its founding ideological purpose and became only a mechanism for control by the top leaders, Hafez al-Assad in Syria and Saddam Hussein in Iraq.

According to the Syrian constitution, only the Baath can hold power. As a result of the March 2003 national elections, the party held 135 out of 250 seats in its own Majlis al-Sha'ab; the April 2007 parliamentary elections gave the Baath 134 seats. (The rest of the seats are occupied by parties that follow the Baathist line.) In Iraq's last free elections before the 2003 invasion, in 2000, the Baath took 165 out of 250 seats in its own Majlis al-Watani (National Assembly); the rest of the seats were filled with token opposition parties approved by the regime.

Tunisia also used a mass party model. The Neo-Destour Party was created in the 1930s before Tunisian independence in 1956. In 1957, Habib Bourguiba seized power and used the Neo-Destour as a mass party in order to consolidate control and concentrate loyalty to him. In 1964, reflecting a short-lived turn to socialism, Bourguiba changed the party to the Socialist Destour. In 1987, when Bourguiba was overthrown in a coup by Zine al-Abidine Ben Ali, the party was renamed the Constitutional Democratic Rally Party. It followed the other mass parties of the Arab world, acting as a mechanism for control without any true loyalty among the population except as a possible vehicle for advancement in society. At the beginning of 2007 it held 152 out of 189 seats in the Majlis al-Nuwaab (Chamber of Deputies). The regime was overthrown in the popular demonstrations of January 2011; it remains to be seen if a new mass party will be formed to replace it.

A Narrow Base of Support

In addition to specific policies, most of the Arab regimes have also sustained themselves by their reliance on key elites within society to support them. These elites are given access to wealth and power and prestige, so that they have a stake in the system and will work to maintain it. But they also are minorities within the wider society; as such they have greater incentive to maintain the system, since otherwise they would then become subject to the revenge of the majorities in the population that they have neglected for so long. These bonds vary according to country and can be based on ethnicity, tribal heritage, religion, and/or family.

The Saudi regime relies on the royal family, which numbers several thousand. The family has permeated several other societal groups through marriage, including powerful tribes, merchant families, and religious leaders. In this way, all of these groups become tied to the regime. But the core decision-making power remains in the hands of the direct descendants of the founder of the Saudi state in 1932, Abd al-Aziz ibn Saud. They occupy the top positions in the civil service, military, and government (both central and regional). In addition, Saudi law states that only the descendants of Ibn Saud can become the kings of the country. Though the royal family itself is riven by factionalism, it is tied together by a common fear that the family as a whole might be overthrown and all would lose their power and privileges. The other monarchies follow the same pattern of minority rule.

But the presidential regimes also rely on a narrow base of support. The Baath regime under Saddam Hussein in Iraq was based on two main groups: the Sunnis, a minority (about 35 percent) among the majority Shi'ites (approximately 60 percent); and tribal kin from the Tikrit area, Saddam's hometown, particularly the al-Bu Nasir. Tribal relatives, who are also Sunni, dominated the government and security services.

The Syrian regime is also a minority regime. The top positions in the military and security services, government, Baath Party, and bureaucracy are dominated by Alawites, a heterodox Islamic sect that many among the Sunni majority do not consider true Muslims. Alawites, which include the Assad family, make up about 12 percent of the population. They are supported by other minority Islamic sects such as Druzes, who do not consider themselves Muslims (3 percent of the population), and Ismailis (1 percent of the population), both of which are also fearful of the dominant Sunni population, which stands at 75 percent of the population. The Alawites have dominated Syria since Assad's coup in 1970. This longevity has entrenched in them a fear that were they to lose power, they would face a backlash from the majority Sunni population, much as Sunnis have from Shi'ites in Iraq since the overthrow of Saddam Hussein in 2003.

Cosmetic Liberalizations

Many Arab states started off, at independence, with some form of democracy. But the development of regional threats, not least from each other, personal and regional ambitions, and the inability of the regimes to meet their publicly declared goals of development (which led to the rise of threatening dissent from within the population) soon led to challenges from domestic elements. This pushed these regimes to become more authoritarian. The concentration of power in a single leader's hands removed the capacity for the populations to have any form of representation, through parliaments, in decision making.

Until the 1980s, most of the Arab states did not worry much about how obvious their authoritarianism was, in the context of matching their democratic rhetoric with reality. Beginning in that decade, Arab regimes began to hear growing calls for reform. In addition, deteriorating economic conditions often sparked unrest that the regimes viewed as threatening. Aside from Islamist groups, which also increased their strength in that decade, these demands were not usually for the overthrow of the regime but rather for a measure of political liberalization that would give the populations greater say in some aspects of decision making.

The regimes began to respond in the 1990s and continued to do so into the 2000s. Some had engaged in electoral processes before then as well, but in quantitative terms (numbers and types of parties and groups allowed to run) the regimes were trying a new tact. However, none of the reforms they engaged in reduced their power to any degree. The purpose of such "cosmetic" liberalizations has thus been to serve as a safety valve, letting out the steam of reform demanded by the populations and Islamist groups. This would, it was calculated, keep the pressure off the regimes and complement their other instruments of control. They were thus used, as a number of observers have categorized them, as "survival strategies." The regimes have focused on parliaments as the best arena in which to control the liberalization efforts. This is because parliaments are designed around the world (superficially or genuinely) to reflect the will of the people. That is, populations elect representatives who sit in the parliament and make laws, supervise the executive, and generally respond to public demands. To use the 2011 political crisis in Egypt again as an example, the Mubarak regime first tried to construct a new government with some limited participation from the people, through new popularly elected representatives to parliament. But the parliament was still to be dominated by the National Democratic Party.

On the face of it, all of the Arab states are liberalizing. Algeria held parliamentary elections in May 2007, Bahrain in October 2010, Egypt in November–December 2010, Jordan in November 2007, Kuwait in May 2009, Morocco in September 2007, Oman in October 2007, Syria in April 2007, Tunisia in October 2009, and Yemen in April 2003 (elections were to be held again in April 2009, but have been postponed to 2011).

In December 2006, the United Arab Emirates held indirect elections through local councils. Qatar has held municipal elections in 2003 and 2007. For its part, Libya does not hold national elections; instead, a General People's Congress is composed of individuals indirectly elected through a series of local committees and congresses. Nor does Saudi Arabia hold parliamentary elections (though it held its first municipal elections from February to April 2005). Members of its Majlis al-Shura (Consultative Council) hold a purely advisory role and are appointed by the regime.

But none of the Arab regimes allow their parliaments to constrain their authority or capacity for decision making. They are filled with loyal parties or individuals who depend on the regime for their own positions, and are constrained with so many restrictions that they become meaningless, used as rubber stamps for executive decisions, or are completely bypassed and ignored in policymaking. In addition, the ruler (whether king or president) retains widespread powers of governance himself, including the (direct or indirect) authority to dissolve parliament, appoint (or dismiss) cabinet members, disallow the formation of new political parties, vet individual candidates for office, gerrymander districts, and control the output from the media, among other powers. Electoral laws are also often changed to favor the ruling party if the regimes note that prior elections resulted in an increase in opposition membership in parliament.

Some scholars have seen national or local elections in the Arab states as signs of emerging political openness. The two-volume study of liberalization and democratization in the Arab world by Rex Brynen, Bahgat Korany, and Paul Noble, *Political Liberalization and Democratization in the Arab World*, analyzed contemporary trends and historical experiences to conclude that despite entrenched autocracy there are still several elements of liberalization, within both the political system and civil society. Some Arab regimes do provide their parliaments with a degree of independence. In Jordan, for example, the Majlis al-Nuwaab (Chamber of Deputies) can amend government-initiated legislation and has in the past even rejected some of the government's proposed laws. But this liberalization may be more relevant and apparent at the local level and among domestic groups in society, rather than at the national level.

The cosmetic nature of national elections is complemented by the electoral power held by the top leaders in the Arab states. In the monarchies, of course, there are no elections for the executive; kings rule by claims to divine or hereditary right. But in the presidential systems, the presidents must run in ostensibly open elections in order to maintain at least the façade of parliamentarianism (though in many cases these are single-candidate elections). But the extremely high vote counts these presidents typically garner provide evidence of the sheer concentration of power in their hands, and none have ever left power willingly. Not only are parliaments refused any genuine capacity for decision making, but presidential candidates running against the leader are so hampered by rules and regulations so as to ensure the incumbent's reelection, that the results are almost comical.

This might be better illustrated with concrete examples. Egypt's president Mubarak received 88.6 percent of the vote in the September 2005 presidential elections; in Algeria, President Abdelaziz Bouteflika garnered 85 percent in the April 2004 elections and 90 percent in the April 2009 elections; Tunisia's Ben Ali polled 94.5 percent in October 2004 and almost 90 percent in October 2009; and Yemen's president Ali Abdullah Saleh won 96.3 percent of the September 1999 presidential elections and 77.17 percent of the vote in September 2006.

Syria and Iraq provide the best examples of how much of a charade these elections are: In Syria, Hafez al-Assad won 99.9 percent of the presidential vote in February 1999, while his son, Bashar, won 97.29 percent in a special yes-no presidential referendum held in 2000 after the death of his father. In May 2007, Bashar again won a referendum on whether or not he would be president for another seven years, with 97.6 percent of the vote. In Iraq, Saddam Hussein polled 99.9 percent in a single-candidate 1995 presidential election; he did even better in October 2002, winning 100 percent of the electorate's votes. Algeria's former president, Muhammed Ahmed ben Bella, was given the honor of being a "guest voter" in that election; he cast his ballot for Saddam.

The Military and Other Coercive Agencies

In the final calculation, the Arab regimes have known that they can rely on outright coercion and repression to maintain their rule. Some, like Iraq, have been more open to using this instrument against their populations, while others, like Jordan, have preferred to use as little physical force as possible. But all of the regimes maintain large militaries and other coercive institutions, such as secret police, security services, and domestic intelligence agencies. In addition, these are often directed against each other as much as against the general population. That is, they are used to watch over each other and balance them out. There has been a proliferation of these organizations not only because of external threats to the regimes (from Israel or each other), but also because of the (real and perceived) existence of subversive threats from within the state itself. This expansion of coercive and security agencies has led many to refer to the Arab states as *mukhabarat* (literally, intelligence) states.

In all Arab regimes the regime's and the army's interests overlap, giving the latter incentive to protect the former. The consequences of a lack of a strong, centralized military are evident in Lebanon, where each sectarian group has its own militia and does not trust the Lebanese Armed Forces. (Since the 1990s, these militias have been partially disbanded, with the exception of Hezbollah, which has fully retained its paramilitary capacities.)

The backing of the military is earned in two ways. First, militaries are kept content by a series of institutional and individual privileges. On the institutional level, regimes have provided enormous resources (primarily funding) to the military. Consider the following jumps in defense spending, as a percentage of gross national product: in Egypt it rose from 3.9 percent in 1950–1951 to 12.2 percent in 1964–1965; in Syria from 4.4 percent in 1953 to 10.2 percent in 1965; in Iraq from 6.6 percent in 1953 to 12.2 percent in 1965; and in Saudi Arabia from 12.3 percent in 1959 to 17.4 percent in 1967.

The end of constant and direct confrontations with Israel has contributed to a decline in military expenditures, though the figures remain relatively high. In the Gulf, Iraqi (until 2003) and Iranian ambitions have helped maintain higher levels of military spending. In the mid-2000s and after, these levels, as a percentage of gross domestic product, hover around the following: Oman at 11.4 percent, followed closely by Qatar and Saudi Arabia at 10 percent. Defense spending stands at 8.6 percent in Jordan, 6.6 percent in Yemen, 5.9 percent in Syria, 5.3 percent in Kuwait, 5 percent in Morocco, 4.5 percent in Bahrain, and 3.9 percent in Libya. By comparison, U.S. military spending is estimated at 4.06 percent of GDP.

The costs of not keeping the military satisfied were evident in Egypt in February 1986, when a minor revolt by lower-ranking officers in the Central Security Forces broke out in protest over low wages. Thus, even when economies experience a decline, good wages continue to be paid (to the officers, at least) and resources provided to the military. The regimes cannot afford to alienate the armed forces, either because they could form their own opposition group or because they might not act to protect the regime in the face of a physical challenge. The Egyptian military's cautious reactions to the 2011 demonstrations again underlined this consideration.

At an individual level, military officers, particularly senior ones, are allowed to pursue their own economic activities. This includes both legal and illegal activity, such as smuggling or involvement in the black market. This is considered to be something like an extra form of payment to supplement the officers' wages. The secondary benefit is that the officers are more likely to oppose any reforms to the system, since these would remove a significant source of income for them. At the same time, individual officers are often given a set of benefits that elevates their standing in society, along with the material advantages. In some cases, such as Saudi Arabia's National Guard (composed of tribes loyal to the regime) and Saddam Hussein's Special Republican Guard, the units are small enough that all members are paid much higher wages than the other coercive forces, also receiving a series of luxury items and privileges such as special housing and cars.

Second, loyalists are placed in many of the top and most sensitive positions. In most cases, these loyalists come from the leader's own family, tribe, ethnic, or sectarian group. In some cases, special forces or units are created, composed solely of these communal groups. Some militaries purposely recruit from the poorer segments of society in order to give these classes the feeling that the regime is providing them with a place to work and advance. This tactic, it is assumed, is likely to help defuse agitation among these classes. But even in such cases, the senior officer corps is always dominated by a specific group loyal to the regime.

That these officers come from the same ethnic group, sect, tribe, or family as the regime ensures a sense of duty and loyalty. Moreover, because the regime is often narrowly based, it provides the officers with incentive to keep the regime in power out of fear of a backlash against that minority group by the majority of the population. Saddam Hussein, for example, often purged his military and security services of those whom he suspected of disloyalty, replacing them not with qualified officers but rather with individuals who displayed devotion to him—particularly tribal kin and other Sunnis. Most senior officers in the Syrian military and other coercive institutions are Alawites, like Hafez and Bashar al-Assad. The Saudi military and intelligence agencies are all controlled by members of the royal family. The flip side to this policy is that other ethnic or sectarian groups are in general prohibited from attaining the top ranks in these organizations. In Jordan, Palestinians are not allowed to rise past the rank of lieutenant-colonel in combat units.

In addition to the regular military, the Arab regimes have established a series of other domestic intelligence agencies, security forces, and paramilitary organizations. These are all created to protect the regime from the military, from any domestic threats, and from each other. The system is purposely designed with overlapping and redundant functions, so that the regime will always be able to ferret out any dissent or challenges to its rule, and to prevent any one group from becoming too powerful. In addition to the sheer number of such organizations, some Arab regimes also have special parallel units, often coming out of the ruling party, that are attached to the military and other security agencies to contribute to direct indoctrination of the regime's ideology. Syria, for example, is known for inserting branches of the Baath into various military commands to watch over the officers.

Saddam Hussein had perhaps one of the more complex systems. In addition to the regular military, there was the Republican Guard, tasked with protecting the regime from the army; the Special Republican Guard, assigned to protect the regime from the Republican Guard; and the Special Security and the Presidential Guard, charged with protecting the regime from the Special Republican Guard.

The Syrian regime is protected not only by the regular army, but also by the Presidential Security Forces (itself made up of four distinct intelligence agencies, with overlapping responsibilities), the Republican Guard, and the Special Forces (in the regular military). Saudi Arabia has its military, the National Guard, and a chain of intelligence agencies, of which not much is known. And Jordan's military contains the Royal Guard (drawn from Bedouin tribes with long-standing loyalty to the monarchy) and the Special Operations Command, both of which are designed to protect the regime against domestic threats, possibly including even the military itself.

Though it has a totally different governing system, the Iranian theocratic government is quite similar to the Arab regimes in its use of domestic intelligence and coercive agencies. In addition to its regular military, it has the Pasdaran (Islamic Revolutionary Guards Corps), tasked with internal security and keeping watch over the military. The Pasdaran have their own air force, army, navy, and intelligence units, in parallel to the armed forces.

The regime is also protected by the Basij, a 9- or 10-million-strong militia loyal to the hard-line clerics in power and that provides both internal security protection and enforcement of Islamic law among the population. More zealous than the Basij is Ansar e-Hezbollah (Helpers of the Party of God), a thug-like group dedicated to ensuring implementation of Islamic rules and regulations. Through their alliances with the regime, these groups assume they are protecting not just the regime but the Islamic Revolution as well, giving them added incentive to engage in their activities. Other coercive agencies include the Ministry of Intelligence and Security, which has its own paramilitary group, and the Law Enforcement Forces, a somewhat shadowy domestic intelligence agency. Finally, the Political-Ideological Directorate, like the Baath Party in Syria, assigns its officers to all military units in order to maintain ideological loyalty and prevent the formation of dissent.

The policy of control and repression has been very effective for all of the Arab regimes as well as Iran. First, the Middle East as a whole has not seen a successful military coup in over thirty years, with the exception of Algeria in 1991 (and non-Arab Turkey's history of military involvement in politics). Even the Algerian case was unique, as the military intervention was not directed against the government but against the Islamists. Second, the region's militaries (in some cases in combination with other security services) have been very effective at putting down domestic challenges to the regimes, which have come primarily from radical Islamist groups. It seems likely that this trend will continue for the near future and that direct physical challenges to the regimes will not succeed in the face of the coercive power the regimes wield.

Foreign Policy and the Arab-Israeli Conflict

Finally, the Arab regimes have become adept at using foreign affairs as a vehicle for generating legitimacy, deflecting domestic criticism and demands for reform, and suppressing the population in the name of a higher (external) objective. The primary foreign policy issue is the Arab-Israeli conflict.

The confrontation with the Arabs' number one enemy (at least until the 1990s) has been the ideal problem on which to concentrate attention. The regimes can argue that they are engaged in the heroic confrontation with Israel. The issue also successfully serves to redirect anger, frustration, and attention away from the regime and onto Israel. It is useful for uniting disparate communal groups under a patriotic banner. This tactic is not as widely used in the 2000s as it once was, but in general the Arab populations continue to view Israel with resentment and continue to advocate active (i.e., military) support for the Palestinian cause while the Arab governments continue to allow the ulama and media to castigate and focus on Israel. Finally, the focus on an Israeli enemy is used to justify repression in the name of a higher goal and to silence critics of the regime by accusing them of being traitors to the Arab cause, since they are charged with distracting attention from the more pressing problem of Israel. Relatedly, the conflict has helped fuel the expansion of coercive agencies, as these are necessary to fend off the Israeli threat and prepare the state for war.

The symbolic and physical importance of Palestine has various facets: the Arab feeling that Israel was implanted by colonial or imperial Western powers; its imposition on a piece of Arab land straddling the lines of communication between Egypt and the Mashrek (eastern portion of the Arab world); the military defeats inflicted by the Jews/Israelis on the Arabs; the refugees (particularly for Lebanon and Jordan); and Palestine's location as the site of the third holiest place in Islam (the Dome of the Rock).

This has been translated into concrete policies designed by the Arab regimes to focus attention on Israel and the Palestinian cause, particularly on regaining Arab land "lost" (in the language used by many Arabs to describe the failure of the Arab regimes to defeat Israel) to Israel in the 1947–1949 Arab-Israeli War and returning Palestinian refugees to the homes that they lost in the context of this and the 1967 war. The populations have not needed any prompting toward these feelings: their support for the Palestinians and their anger at Israel is genuine. One poll of Syrians, Jordanians, Palestinians, and Lebanese conducted at the end of the 1990s found that 45 percent of interviewees felt that the Palestinian question "essentially concerns" the Arab world, while 40.5 percent said it concerned the entire Islamic world. More importantly, 78.9 percent said they believe the "conflict must go on."

All the regimes have had to do is channel these feelings away from themselves. They have done this by allowing for the continuation of anti-Israel propaganda, editorializing, and popular demonstrations and protests. The fact that the Arab regimes have almost complete control over their media (the level of control varies—Egypt is freer than Syria, for example) is an indication that the regimes approve of these activities—or at least implicitly condone them. Frequently, anti-Israel actions have underlying tones of anti-Semitism, which also puts the conflict in starker terms as not just a political dispute but also a pitched battle between different "nations." Even al-Jazeera, the Arab satellite television station that has done much for the cause of freedom of the press and open information in the Arab world, frequently has guests on its various programs who engage in anti-Israel tirades.

Other foreign policy issues have also been utilized by the Arab regimes, depending on the specific country and the specific conditions at any given time. Most of the Arab regimes, in addition to anti-Israel activity such as protests and editorials, also allow for staunch anti-Americanism. The U.S.-led invasions of Afghanistan and Iraq only fueled this sentiment. In addition, some of the Arab regimes have focused on other enemies in order to generate legitimacy and forge a unified stance against an external party despite deep domestic divisions. Saddam Hussein worked hard to promote the war with Iran in the 1980s as part of the long-standing conflict between Arabs and Persians so that the majority Shi'ite population would not sympathize with their co-religionists in Iran.

The protests and popular revolutions that swept through parts of the Arab world in the 2000s, particularly in Tunisia and Egypt in 2011, as well as Iran in 2010, reflect a breakdown of these systems of control. In particular, the grinding poverty and economic stagnation and the growth of young populations have raised questions about whether all, or even any, of these instruments of governance remain effective.

References and Further Reading

Brynen, Rex, Bahgat Korany, and Paul Noble, eds. *Political Liberalization and Democratization in the Arab World.* 2 vols. Boulder, CO: Lynne Rienner, 1995–1998.

Lynch, Marc. *Voices of the New Arab Public: Iraq, Al-Jazeera, and Middle East Politics Today.* New York: Columbia University Press, 2006.

Owen, Roger. *State, Power, and Politics in the Making of the Modern Middle East.* New York: Routledge, 1992.

Posusney, Marsha Pripstein, and Michele Penner Angrist, eds. *Authoritarianism in the Middle East: Regimes and Resistance.* Boulder, CO: Lynne Rienner, 2005.

Richards, Alan. "Democracy in the Arab Region: Getting There from Here." *Middle East Policy* 12:2 (Summer 2005): 28–35.

Rubin, Barry. *The Tragedy of the Middle East.* Cambridge: Cambridge University Press, 2002.

Rubin, Barry, and Thomas A. Keaney, eds. *Armed Forces in the Middle East: Politics and Strategy.* London: Frank Cass, 2002.

Salem, Paul. *Bitter Legacy: Ideology and Politics in the Arab World.* Syracuse, NY: Syracuse University Press, 1994.

Syria

Syria is a good example of a modern Arab authoritarian government for two main reasons. First, it is the quintessential presidential Arab republic, formerly based on radical-nationalism but since the 1970s increasingly institutionalized and status quo oriented. The entire system of politics is set up so that ultimate power flows upward to the president. In addition, though radical-nationalism as an organizing principle has long since declined, Syria retains lingering elements of its former radical domestic and, particularly, foreign policies. For example, although all of the other former radical states, including Algeria, Libya, Egypt, Yemen, and Iraq, have drawn closer to the United States and adopted a less rejectionist role in regional politics, Syria continues to support rejectionism (in particular of the Israeli-Palestinian peace process). It has also aligned itself with the region's two rising radical powers, Hezbollah and Iran, by providing material support (weapons, economic aid, territory for transit) to the former and acting on behalf of the latter's interests in regional disputes.

Second, Syria very successfully utilizes all of the instruments of co-optation and repression examined earlier. After experiencing at least eleven coups or attempted coups in twenty-one years, Syria has enjoyed thirty-seven years of remarkable stability (notwithstanding a major, yet unsuccessful, revolt in 1982 and an attempted coup in 1983–1984), engineered by a minority-based regime dominated by the military and the Baath Party and presided over with ultimate power by, first, Hafez al-Assad, and then his son Bashar.

Governing systems in the Middle East cannot be understood without reference to their historical developments. We will therefore turn to a discussion of the period between independence in 1946 and 1970, when Assad took power. This includes reference to the onset of radical-nationalism in Syria, since this directly laid the groundwork for Assad's decision to overthrow the Baathist government. We will focus on the three main institutions of the Assad regime: the presidency, the Baath Party, and the military. Because Assad was also always careful to enlist the support of societal groups as necessary, his economic reforms are particularly relevant as he engaged them in such a way as to expand the regime's support.

Historical Background: The Era of Instability

A short discussion of Syrian history since independence is necessary here, to provide the backdrop to the later changes that swept the country and ushered in the eras of radical-nationalism and institutionalization. The main theme in this period is instability: the Syrian government was consistently overthrown in a series of coups from 1949 to 1970, many of which involved to some degree the Baath Party. It was not until Hafez al-Assad's Corrective Revolution in November 1970 that the country was finally stabilized.

Syria achieved independence from France in April 1946. Recently carved out of what had always been either a much larger political or administrative entity, the new country was fragmented along sectarian, class, regional, and tribal lines, making it difficult for an opposition encompassing all these elements to come together. This made it easier for the old notables, the ones who had achieved economic wealth and political power under the Ottomans and then the French, to govern once the French left. These were the same notables who dominated politics in all of the Arab states in that period: conservative landowners interested primarily in maintaining their wealth and influence over the country.

The previous decade had seen a boom in the economy and the emergence of a new middle and upper class not tied directly to the landowners but owing their growing power instead to the industrialization, economic liberalizations, and economic growth that marked Syria into the 1950s. A new working class was also born, one that was open to ideas for radical social and political change. As in Egypt, the military was also discontented with its poor performance in the first Arab-Israeli War (1947–1949), which it blamed on the notables' neglect of the military. These developments combined to undermine the notables' hold on power, leading to the formation of a wide variety of opposition groups committed to reform and change.

The new era was heralded by the first of three military coups in 1949. On March 30, the army chief of staff, General Husni al-Zaim (from the minority Kurdish population), seized power from the old notables. There was much support for the takeover among the population and other societal groups, who had tired of the notables' rule and their disregard, and in fact Zaim (who made himself president) did much for the development of Syria during his short tenure. He immediately engaged in a building spree, including hospitals, roads, schools, water projects, and construction of a harbor at Latakia, and expanded the size of the military from 5,000 to 27,000. He also gave women the right to vote and made changes to the criminal and civil codes. Finally, he made overtures to Israel on establishing relations between the two countries.

He was overthrown in the second coup of the year, on August 14. Colonel Muhammed Sami al-Hinnawi restored civilians (the old notables) to government, although he and the military did not withdraw completely from politics, instead remaining to keep watch over the civilians. But Hinnawi did not govern well, and on December 19 Colonel Adib al-Shishakli (another Kurd who had taken part in the first two coups) overthrew him. He, too, returned the notables to power, though like Hinnawi he refused to give up all of his authority. Shishakli soon grew impatient at the inability of civilians to improve the economy and at their defiance of his wishes. On November 28–29, 1951, he arrested the government and took power for himself.

Shishakli's military rule, from 1951 to 1954, was a forerunner of Assad's dictatorship: a military officer at the head of government, use of repression to ensure implementation of his reforms, and a commitment to developing and strengthening Syria. He also banned all political parties and ruled by decree. But the changes that had been ongoing in Syrian society since the days of the French Mandate could not be contained. The emergence of radical movements, with significant support among various segments of the population, threatened Shishakli and eventually led to another coup on February 25, 1954. This was once again conducted by the military, but was actively supported by all of the opposition parties and movements that Shishakli had previously barred from politics.

Again, civilian government was restored. But it proved too difficult for the various parties to cooperate, given their very different agendas. In particular, conservative parties representing the traditional notables, who wanted to maintain much of the economic and social status quo, clashed with leftist parties, who wanted to engage in radical changes and overhaul the existing economic and social systems. The leftists—Nasserites, Communists, and Baathists—also disagreed on the specific contours of policy and often fought each other as much as they fought the conservatives.

In fact, the Baath grew so concerned at rising communist influence that the party approached Egyptian president Gamal Abdel Nasser and proposed a union between Egypt and Syria (though union also fit with its pan-Arab ideology). Syrian political leaders came to view the period of the United Arab Republic (UAR) (1958–1961) as disastrous for Syria. All Syrian political parties, including the Baath, were dissolved; Egyptian officials came to Syria to run most of its affairs; the parliament that incorporated both countries had more seats allotted to Egypt; Nasser became head of the union; Egyptian socialist measures were extended to Syria when the latter was not yet ready for them; Syrian military officers were removed from active command and had their pay levels reduced; and Egyptians in general treated the Syrians as second-class citizens.

The widespread dissatisfaction culminated in another military coup on September 28, 1961, in which the traditionalists and conservatives returned to power to run a series of governments that would fail to achieve much progress in economic development or uniting the country around common ideas. This period has become known as the *infisal* ("secessionist" or "separatist") period because those who took power opposed any reunion with Egypt. Their rule was interrupted several times by direct military interference, and they were widely unpopular. Then, on February 8, 1963, Baathists seized power in Iraq in their own coup. This provided inspiration to leftist Syrians, who, led by the military, then launched their own coup a month later, on March 8. The 1963 coup marked the onset of radical-nationalism in Syria.

The Radical-Nationalist Regime in Syria

The Baathists had to share power with the Nasserites (and some independent army officers as well) in a Revolutionary Command Council, which made all final policy decisions. But whereas the latter were eager to push for immediate reunion with Egypt, the former were less sure this would be good for Syria at that time. A power struggle ensued and the Nasserites attempted a coup on July 18, 1963. The military responded harshly, resulting in total domination by the Baathists.

The new government became increasingly radicalized. In part this was a response to continuous attacks on its credibility and legitimacy by others, particularly Nasser. But it was also due to infighting that continued to wrack the party. The old guard Baathists, primarily urban-based and led by veteran leaders Michel Aflaq and Salah al-Din al-Bitar, were gradually weakened as younger Baathist military officers and rural-based civilians increasingly asserted control. The younger group was much more radical than the older leadership. The two could not cooperate for long in the government, and on February 23, 1966, the radicals, led by the military and a group of civilians, defeated the old guard in a new coup.

The new government was the most radical that Syria had seen yet. The need to consolidate its rule, its ideological bent, and the fact that the urban middle classes were not supporters of the new government anyway prompted the regime to engage in major changes in social and economic policy that centralized economic control in the government's hands, undermining private-sector activity, and not seek compromise to retain popular support. In addition, the new regime was the first in which the armed forces held virtually all of the decision-making power.

Yet the military continued to be factionalized, despite the fact that it was dominated by Alawites, the heterodox Islamic sect considered by many Muslims as heretical, who shared a sense of sectarian loyalty, and despite the fact that it was now part of the Baath Party. Two groups emerged: Salah Jadid led the radical civilian wing of the party (despite being an officer), and Assad became the leader of a second group, considered to be the pragmatic military wing of the party. Jadid and the civilians pushed for sweeping changes in domestic policy (socialism) and foreign policy (aggressiveness), including rapid union with Egypt. Assad's group preferred to dampen down radical changes and engage in a slower building process to strengthen Syria's military and alliances with other Arab states. It also opposed union with Egypt on the grounds that Syria was not ready, and out of fear of being dominated by Nasser again.

The defeat in the 1967 war with Israel brought these divisions into the open. The radicals' foreign policy, including support for Palestinian militants operating against Israel from within Syria, was in part responsible for provoking Israel to attack. The loss of the Golan Heights and the poor performance of the armed forces strengthened the moderate wing of the party. Assad called for putting the revolution on hold in order to concentrate on rebuilding the army and mending ties with the conservative monarchies in order to obtain their financial support (which itself was contingent on the end of Syria's verbal attacks against the monarchies). He also called for some liberalization in the economy in order to stimulate investment and growth. This was, of course, anathema to the socialist revolutionaries under Jadid.

Over the next two years the two factions existed in uneasy alliance, with Assad quietly strengthening his group. The pragmatic officers finally decided to act after the Syrian intervention in Jordan, which the radicals pushed ahead with and which the pragmatists viewed with alarm as another unnecessary provocation. By September 1970 the Jordanian monarchy was engaged in a pitched battle against the Palestine Liberation Organization (PLO), the umbrella organization of Palestinian parties and paramilitary groups, over the PLO's autonomous activities within Jordan. In keeping with its policy of supporting the Palestinians, the Syrian government sent scores of tanks into Jordan to support the PLO against the Jordanian army. When Israel threatened to intervene to protect the monarchy against Syria, Assad, as commander of the air force, refused to provide air cover to the Syrian army. The Jordanian military routed the Syrians, who quickly withdrew.

The Corrective Revolution: Assad Takes Power

Assad decided to act. The intervention in Jordan demonstrated for him the recklessness and sheer incompetence of the radicals. He believed they had already damaged Syria in the 1967 war and feared that they would bring further disaster on the country. But the radicals moved first. On November 12, 1970, they dismissed Assad and some of his close supporters from government. But Assad had built up a wide network of support in the military. The next day, November 13, he arrested Jadid and his supporters, removed the government, and installed loyalists in key positions in the party, government, and military.

Assad moved quickly to secure his new regime. In February 1971 he created a new parliament, the Majlis al-Sha'ab (the People's Council), with 173 seats and engineered the Baath's dominance in it, with 87 seats. The council also nominated Assad for president of the republic. In March 1971 the Baath made him head of the party, and that same month he was elected president in a national referendum.

Assad also broadened his regime's support base. He won grudging acquiescence from the social groups that the previous Baath government had alienated, the urban middle classes, by relaxing some of the harsher political constraints that prevented their freedom of expression, and engaging in some liberalizations of the economy. He also reduced the opposition to his regime among conservative segments of the population by referring less to the secularism of the Baath and putting himself on display as a devout Muslim. In 1974 he prompted Imam Musa al-Sadr, a well-respected imam in Lebanon, to issue a fatwa declaring Alawites to be Muslims, and he had written into the constitution the stipulation that the president must be a Muslim, thus granting himself, as an Alawite, legal recognition.

Assad later referred to his coup as the "corrective" revolution or movement, to indicate that it was not a brand-new regime coming to power but rather a necessary modification and improvement of the previous Baathist government. By this he meant he would continue with many of the former regime's policies (which he did believe in), but that some would be jettisoned or adapted to better serve Syria's needs.

Presidential Dictatorship

Under Assad, Syria became truly authoritarian. Before his coup, Syrian governments had been a mixture of autocracy (rule by elites without popular participation) and pluralism (the unconstrained competition among different interest groups for power), the balance shifting under different governments. But most of the regimes depended on support from a number of diverse groups in society, such as the upper classes, the middle classes, landowners, private industry, religious leaders, and so on, and so had to meet at least some of their demands and open up the political process to their participation. In contrast, Assad made himself the ultimate decision maker and set up a hierarchical system of governance based on the Baath Party, the military, and the Alawites. He thus came to exercise complete control over all facets of Syrian life. No policy was made that did not have his approval.

Assad had learned several lessons from the preceding period of instability. The two most important were that the military had to be defactionalized, otherwise it would continue to interfere in politics; and that neither society nor government could afford to have so many different parties and movements competing in politics, with different policy agendas, since their constant fighting undercut any long-term efforts at stabilizing Syria. He responded by removing the military as an institution, as well as its senior officers, from politics and placing in the top positions loyalists whom he trusted (to some extent) not to make trouble. He also banned all independent and autonomous political activity. The Baath was made the only institutional avenue for social and political life. Other political parties were allowed to exist, but they were vetted and controlled by the Baath. Any hint of dissent was rapidly dealt with through coercion, with participants threatened and forced to end their activities. In this way, Assad excised from Syria the constant bickering between different groups that had been the hallmark of politics there since 1949. This was only possible through a powerful presidency that concentrated all power in his hands.

The three main institutions of Syria—the Baath Party, the presidency, and the armed forces—were all headed by Assad, and since his death in 2000 are today headed by his son Bashar. In the previous era in Syrian politics, presidents were replaced often due to the constant shifts in power among contending parties, or the government's decisions were made by compromise among different factions. In neither case did one person hold the office long enough, and without serious challenge from other groups, to maintain and extend his grip on power.

As head of government, Assad made all final decisions. The March 1973 constitution provided for a set of governing institutions designed to meet the country's stated constitutional commitment to a "democratic," "popular state," and they remain in place as of this writing. This includes a prime minister, a cabinet (Council of Ministers), a parliament (the People's Council), and a series of courts. In reality, these institutions have been used merely as tools to implement both Hafez's and Bashar's own policies, as both retained complete control over them, with all power vested in the president. Under the elder Assad, this power was based on his capacity to pick and choose members of the government. In addition, the constitution created a number of competing offices in the executive that allowed Assad to balance out those who served in these positions, so that they had no capacity to organize themselves as an independent center of power. The powers of the presidency continue to be based on the following.

First, the president of the republic must be nominated by the People's Council for a seven-year term. He is then approved or not in a national referendum, with no opposing candidate. Hafez al-Assad was approved in all of the presidential referendums since 1971 with an approximately 99 percent approval rating. In addition, the president can only be removed from power for crimes of "high treason," which must be activated through the People's Council. In that case, the president would then be tried by the Supreme Constitutional Court, the body that supervises all legislation and policy—of which the president is a member who appoints the other members.

Second, as chief executive Assad had the power to appoint, dismiss, and replace the prime minister, deputy prime minister, the three vice presidents (none of whose powers are clearly defined), cabinet, parliament, military officers, and top civil servants. Most of these positions were shaped so that they balanced each other out. The president is also the commander of the armed forces. In this way, Assad retained absolute discretion over all members of government and the military, ensuring that he could remove those he considered disloyal or a threat and replace them with more compliant partisans. The prime minister, in particular, had been used only as a tool to implement Assad's own policies, while at the same time acting as a useful foil: he could be removed when Assad needed a scapegoat or to assuage elite dissatisfaction.

Third, a unicameral parliament has been and remains only a rubber stamp for the Assads' policies. In 1990 Hafez expanded the People's Council to 250 seats in order to broaden his base of support and make room for groups that he had largely ignored in the past—business, the middle class, and professionals. But the Baath remains the dominant party in the council (see below), which means that through it Assad controlled the legislative agenda: 167 of the 250 seats are reserved for the National Progressive Front, an umbrella organization composed of several small parties and the Baath (which in turn is guaranteed the majority of spots in the front). Parliament cannot initiate legislation; it can only debate and, theoretically anyway, amend legislation sent to it by the executive. In addition, the president becomes the legislative authority of the country when the parliament is not in session (though his laws must then be approved of by the council), and even when it is in session the president can override parliament and legislate his own laws according to the constitution "in case of absolute need relating to national security."

Finally, the regime has put in place a series of very restrictive laws governing all social and political activity. Article 49 of the constitution declares that any organization (unions, social groups, professional syndicates, etc.) must agree to have as its core premise a commitment to socialism and defense of the political system (and thus the regime). There are no independent media outlets: the 2001 Publications Law prohibits the dissemination of "inaccurate" information that calls into question the military, the regime and its policies, or generally undermines the vaguely defined "public interest." Similar to Turkey, other legislation bans the promotion of ideas or publications that criticize the state or the "revolution."

Underlying all these restrictions, both Assads have allowed the state of emergency first declared in March 1963 by the first Baath government to remain in force. This legislation allows the regime to restrict a series of individual freedoms, such as those of assembly and association, and gives the regime the power to arrest, detain, and punish individuals. This is done in the name of the confrontation with Israel, in response to which the regime argues requires national unity. It allows the government to argue that anything that undermines support for the regime will weaken Syria and provide Israel with an opportunity for victory.

In addition to institutional control, Hafez al-Assad used a form of ideational control. He created an extensive cult of personality to prove to Syrians that it was not just the office of the presidency that mattered, but the specific person who occupied it as well. Similar to Saddam Hussein, Assad used his image (or rather, images, since different situations required different appearances) to either convince or dull the population into accepting that he was the father of Syria; that no other leader was capable; and that all loyalty flowed to his very person. Because he lacked the innate personal charisma and popularity of Nasser, Assad's rule was based on explicitly framing and massaging the message that he was the ultimate leader.

Tens of thousands of pictures, banners, posters, busts, and other visuals of the Assads adorn the country. At first they displayed only Hafez's visage. When he began to groom his first son Basil for succession, these images included Basil. When Basil died in a car crash in January 1994 and Bashar became the heir apparent, all three Assads were presented.

Rallies and festivals honoring the Assads were and are attended by thousands. Media extol the greatness of the Assad family, reminding Syrians that without them the country would be nothing. Public events regularly include references to their accomplishments in all fields: Hafez was often referenced as a soldier, teacher, even pharmacist. Lisa Wedeen's 1999 study on politics in contemporary Syria argued that Syrians do not actually buy into these interpretations: the cult has been successful in ensuring that as a person Assad (and to a lesser extent Bashar, though it is reported that he has been somewhat embarrassed by this kind of spectacle) is granted deference and obedience. Wedeen found that dissenting from this country-wide display of admiration and obsequiousness was considered by Syrians as too obvious and thus dangerous.

Pillars of the Regime: The Army-Party Symbiosis

The presidency as an institution could not be enough for the Assad regime to exert the level of control that it does. Two other institutions were critical for governing: the Baath Party and the military. Both were also used as recruitment mechanisms for the lower classes in the rural areas, giving them a sense of satisfaction after years of urban, upper-class domination, and developing in them a greater commitment to the maintenance of these institutions' integrity—and thus the regime. After 1963 the two bodies became increasingly intertwined, and gradually the military began to assert its power in the party. Under Assad the military became dominant, supplanting civilians throughout the government. The interlocking nature of these institutions became so tight that already in 1972 Itamar Rabinovich referred to the entire system as an "army-party symbiosis."

The Baath Party

Officially called the Arab Socialist Baath Party, the Baath (meaning "resurrection" or "renaissance") was formed in 1947, when its first congress was held under the leadership of Michel Aflaq, a Christian Arab, and Salah al-Din al-Bitar, a Sunni Arab. Its founders and original members were genuinely dedicated to its ideology, which was centered on the slogan "unity, freedom, and socialism," where unity meant pan-Arab unification, freedom referred to independence from foreign control, and socialism equaled Arab socialism. For its first three decades the Baath was fervently committed to its ideological program (though the party was often vague in how to translate its ideology into practice); under the Baathist regime from 1963 to 1970 the party was used to actively promote its revolutionary agenda. But under Assad, who preferred pragmatism to radicalism, it became only a vehicle for promoting control.

In its original construction, the Baath was designed to be a populist party, incorporating all elements of society that adhered to its ideology, in particular the lower classes. It set up party offices in a hierarchic organization that stretched down to the local level. Assad was able to use this hierarchy to facilitate his own rule by directly transmitting his preferences through all levels of the party. Until his later years, Assad was also known for letting policy matters be discussed within the party, so long as his own final decisions were not challenged. This supplemented his direct control by maintaining at least some semblance of participatory politics for party members.

At the grassroots level, the party is organized into "Cells" of several individuals. Several Cells are assembled together into a "Group," and several Groups are in turn organized into "Sections." Above the Sections are the Branches, located in the provinces, major cities, and the universities. These also include important local government officials such as mayors or provincial governors, depending on where the Branch is located. In addition, each level had its own "Leadership," something like a miniature board of directors, headed by a "Secretary," who owes his position to leaders above him in the hierarchy. A parallel organization, up to the Branch level, was also put in place within the military.

Outside of its own party structure, the Baath's institutional control, and through it the regime's, is guaranteed by the party offices it has established in all public institutions—including professional syndicates, workers' groups, and the civil service. Most of the members of these institutions' organizing committees are also members of the Baath. In addition, union activity is controlled by the General Federation of Trade Unions, the country's only national trade union. It is also headed by a Baathist.

The Branches elect a Regional Leadership of several hundred members, which in turn selects a ninety-member Central Committee and a twenty-one-member Regional Command or Conference. Made up of civilians and military officers, the Regional Command is the party's highest authority within the country. Technically, the National Command or Conference is made up of different countries' Regional Commands and is designed to be the institutional framework for an eventual pan-Arab entity. But in reality, given that none of the other Arab states have expressed interest in such a union, the Regional Command functions as the Baath's supreme deliberating council.

The Baath's dominance is enhanced by a legal, constitutional, and political framework that confirms Syria's status as a single-party state. According to the constitution, the Baath is the ruling party of state and society. Members of the government must be members of the Baath, or at least approved of by the party. In addition, no other political party, articulating the demands of any societal group, can ever hope to gain enough power to influence decision making. This stipulation is somewhat redundant, since there are several other legal restrictions governing the formation and behavior of political parties in Syria. The whole point of these laws is to ensure the Baath's dominance.

In 1972 Assad established al-Jabha al-Wataniya al-Taqadumiya (the National Progressive Front, or NPF), of which he was, and Bashar is now, chairman. The NPF is guaranteed 167 seats in the 250-seat People's Council. It was designed as an overarching organization to be run by the Baath: any legal political party must be a member of the NPF. Political parties are vetted by the Baath and must conform to its agenda of revolutionism and socialism; in 2010 the NPF was made up of nine officially sanctioned parties, excluding the Baath. Independent candidates may run in elections, but again, the Baath determines their eligibility and they must conform to the same standards as

NPF parties. The result is little to no independent political activity.

Assad ensured that he had double control over the Baath. First, as secretary-general of the party he controlled its agendas and appointments. Second, the Baath has been dominated by the military since 1970. With Assad controlling the military as well, he ensured that nonmilitary members of the Baath had no ability to gain control over the party to challenge him. With the Baath's penetration of Syrian society, Assad thus had complete institutional control over the entire country.

As with the regime in general, the Baath also retains a disproportionate number of minorities, particularly Alawites. The Alawites responded naturally to the Baath because of its emphasis on secularism as the core element of pan-Arabism—that is, language rather than religion as the basis for Arab identity. This removed the issue of religion, a thorny one for the Alawites, who are not considered real Muslims by the majority Sunni population because of their mysterious ways and ideational links to paganism and Christianity. The populist egalitarianism that informed the Baath's ideology (class struggle was rejected by Aflaq and Bitar) was also attractive, as it provided an avenue of advancement that the Alawites would not otherwise have had. The result was, as with the military, that a small minority came to support the regime because its became intimately connected with it.

The Military

The second pillar of the regime is the military. Its importance is evident by the attention Assad gave to it when, beginning in the mid-1990s, he began to prepare the regime for the succession of his son Bashar, slowly purging the top ranks of old-time veterans who had long supported him and replacing them with younger officers said to be closer to Bashar. The purpose was to ensure that the military would remain loyal to his successor.

The military has a long history of involvement in Syrian politics. Beginning in the late 1940s it became radicalized, particularly after 1962, along with much of the population; it also became factionalized along sectarian and ideological lines. Different groups within the military often clashed with each other, seizing power when a particular faction felt strong enough. Civilian groups would seek out affiliated military officers in hopes of using their resources to promote their own agendas or ambitions. Most of the time the military shared power with civilians or worked behind the scenes, influencing decision making. All this made for both bad government and a weak armed forces.

Assad largely removed the military from politics. There have been no military coups since the Corrective Revolution, compared to their abundance in the 1950s and 1960s. Following the pattern of other Arab regimes, Assad accomplished this by material incentives, close watch by the Baath Party and other intelligence agencies, and filling the top positions with sectarian and tribal kin as well as family members. This has ensured the near-absolute loyalty of the military: when Hafez al-Assad died, Bashar was immediately promoted to commander of the armed forces, and he received a delegation from the military pledging its support.

The military's dominance in and inextricable connection to the Baath began in the early 1960s. The military led the 1963 coup that brought the Baath to power, but the Baath itself was dominated by that point by the army. This domination had its roots in the formation of the Military Committee during the UAR period. The committee was a shadowy group of officers led by three Alawites (including Jadid and Assad), all of whom believed in Baathist ideology. Its purpose was to promote the Baath's interests, and the party itself, in the fierce struggles that marked Syrian politics in the 1950s and 1960s. Although it fell apart when Jadid and Assad became the leaders of separate factions in the later 1960s, it did succeed in inserting itself into the party and thus establishing its eventual control.

But it was this deep involvement in politics that, in Assad's view, helped dilute the military's main purpose—acting as a fighting force dedicated to supporting the regime's foreign policies and protecting it from internal challenges. Upon taking control, Assad immediately began to purge the army of (most) non-Baathists in order to cement its identification with a single political movement. This was ensured through the establishment of branches of the party alongside military units, and making senior officers members of the Baath. Tying the party to the military gave Assad a secondary lever of control. To complement this indoctrination, he also provided funding and materiel, relatively generous salaries for senior officers, as well as the permission to engage in their own economic enterprises.

It helped that the military had long been dominated by minority groups, even under French rule (though many Sunnis from the rural lower classes have also joined up). In particular, the Alawites, estimated at 12 percent of the population, have been the principal minority in the armed forces. The military was viewed as an avenue to better living conditions and social mobility, opportunities that would not otherwise be available. But this mass enrollment also motivated the military as a whole to support a regime led by one of its own. Even the lower-class Sunnis had reason to support the Alawite-led regime, since they, too, were dissatisfied with the control the wealthier, urban-based Sunni notables had long exercised over Syria, beginning with independence in 1946.

For the Alawites, there was an extra incentive to protect the regime: given that the regime itself was primarily Alawite, if the regime fell it was expected that all Alawites would suffer a backlash from the more populous Sunnis, who had been out of power since 1970, if not 1963. This is why even where Hafez promoted Sunnis to senior officer position, he also made Alawites deputies to them.

Although the military remains the primary coercive pillar of the regime, it is supplemented by a series of security and intelligence organizations that help maintain a close watch over Syrian society and each other, and that can be used to protect the regime from any direct physical threat. As with the military, Assad installed family members and Alawites at the heads of these organizations. All such institutions are considered to be elite squads: the Republican Guard (the only force allowed to operate within the capital city), the Special Forces, the Struggle Companies, and the Presidential Security Forces (itself composed of four distinct intelligence units—Political Security, General Intelligence, Military Intelligence, and Air Force Intelligence). Until the mid-1980s, there was also a squad called the Defense Companies. It was headed by Assad's brother, Rifaat. When Rifaat attempted to seize power in 1983–1984 and was defeated, the Companies were disbanded and incorporated into the Fourth Armored Division.

Economic Liberalizations

Mention should be made of the economic tools that Assad used to bolster his regime. By the late 1980s, Assad engaged in his own limited process of *infitah* (economic liberalizations). These reforms were prompted by two things: First, by the 1980s, the economy was stagnating. The deterioration was the result of declining oil prices, loss of aid from the oil monarchies, the Soviet Union's decision to dampen down the Arab-Israeli conflict by reducing its support for its clients, poor agricultural output (itself the consequence of a string of bad weather), high defense expenditures, and general structural problems inherent in the state socialism promoted since 1963 that now came to the fore.

Second, Assad perceived the need to broaden the regime's support. Liberalization of the economy would provide some satisfaction to the middle classes and private sector, and, he hoped, obtain their support in return for a chance to take advantage of these reforms.

Thus, political considerations determined the pace and structure of economic reforms. Reducing state control too much would, the regime feared, open too much space for dissidents to operate. The key, Assad felt, was to slowly encourage foreign investment and stimulate private-sector activity. To this end, in the late 1980s, he loosened state control over some industries in order to open up trade to private firms (though he avoided outright privatization). The major change came in May 1991, when Assad unveiled the centerpiece of his infitah strategy, Investment Law No. 10 for 1991. The purpose of the law was to open up agriculture and some industry to foreign and private investment and allow the formation of joint private-public enterprises by reducing taxes on relevant firms, removing tariffs on materials they imported, and allowing them to reinvest their profits outside the country.

Assad's efforts paid off. According to the World Bank, in 1980, the private sector accounted for only 40 percent of gross domestic product (GDP). By 2002, as a result of the controlled liberalizations, it accounted for 61 percent of GDP.

Because the liberalizations did not address the mismanagement and corruption deeply entrenched in the system, the economy continued to suffer. However, the limited reforms did provide new groups with motivation to support the regime, and stimulated the perception that the regime was not moribund and was in fact addressing the country's problems. The middle classes' incentives, now that they were able to pursue wider economic opportunities, were based on recognition that if the regime did not perceive itself to be deriving any benefit from the changes, could still reverse the reforms and reengage in the radical socialism promoted by the 1963–1970 Baathist regime. Thus did Assad succeed, at least for part of the 1990s, in expanding his base of support and ensuring that his son would not have to start from scratch in his own economic reform, and thus risk alienating those with interests in a command economy.

Hereditary Succession in the Republic: Bashar al-Assad Comes to Power

In 2000 the story of Syria's governance system had a new protagonist. On June 10, 2000, Hafez al-Assad died from a heart attack, reportedly during a phone conversation with the president of Lebanon, Émile Lahoud. In order to preserve the regime, Assad's supporters moved quickly to secure the succession of his son Bashar, whom Assad had been grooming for the presidency since the 1994 death of his eldest son and first choice, Basil. Bashar became president on July 17, after being approved in a national referendum on July 10.

It would not be accurate to say that the Syrian regime remains wholly unchanged. Upon assuming the presidency Bashar was hailed as a reformer, representing a new generation of Arab leaders (alongside King Abdallah of Jordan and King Muhammad of Morocco) ready to end the pervasive authoritarianism in their countries. The first year of his tenure was optimistically referred to as the "Damascus Spring," in reference to the Prague Spring at the end of the 1960s, when Czechoslovakia under Alexander Dubček began to engage in a series of political liberalizations.

The Prague Spring came to an end when the Soviet Union invaded the country and put an end to Dubček's government. Similarly, the Damascus Spring ended when Bashar reversed his own early political liberalizations. The difference between the two is that whereas in Czechoslovakia the end of the Prague Spring led to another twenty years of repressive Communist rule, it is not yet clear what the near future holds for Syria. Bashar has shown no indication that he is willing to open up the political or economic system to any great degree, but he has been prepared to allow for some easing of restrictions.

The Damascus Spring was so called because in his first months in office, Bashar eased some of the more constrictive rules governing political activity in the country. First, at the Baath's Ninth Regional Congress in June 2000, Bashar raised hopes of a dramatic shift in power to a younger, presumably more reform-minded generation when he pushed for junior Baath members to be able to compete for membership in the Congress by opening up the electoral process. When, during the Congress, elections were held for the Central Committee and the Regional Command, new candidates won sixty-two seats in the former and twelve seats in the latter. Most of these newcomers were supporters of Bashar, but the process was still considered to be an important change for the better.

Second, 600 political prisoners, jailed under his father, were released. Third, the infamous al-Mazzeh prison was closed. Fourth, some exiled members of the Muslim Brotherhood—an organization responsible for an uprising in 1982 that led to the destruction by the military of parts of Hama and banned in Syria—were allowed to return. Fifth, for the first time a private newspaper was given a license to publish. Sixth, and perhaps most important, groups of Syrians were allowed to gather in their homes to discuss politics, religion, and other social issues. Compared to the salons characteristic of nineteenth-century Enlightenment Europe, these informal groupings were an unheard-of occurrence in the Syria under Hafez, when any open discussion of such topics was considered an invitation for a visit by the security services.

But by February 2001, the regime began to backtrack on its liberalizations. Several leading reformists were arrested and jailed. Two independent members of the People's Council, who had called for the participation of non-Baath political parties in government, had their parliamentary immunity removed and were convicted of trying to change the constitution. Finally, the "salons" were forcibly shut down.

Having shown its citizens that there was a limit to their political freedoms, a few years later the regime began to explore further political reforms. In July 2003 Bashar moved to disentangle the Baath from the state by announcing that promotion in government would be based on merit rather than party membership. In 2004 he declared that party officials would have to retire when they turned sixty. Then, in June 2005, at the Tenth Regional Congress, the party, under Bashar's prompting, voted to narrow the state of emergency from its contemporary expansive understanding to a focus on specified security threats. The Congress also announced that a new law would soon be enacted that would authorize more independent political parties. Finally, the Congress moved to support greater market reforms in the economy (a "social market economy") and end corruption.

None of these changes has yet been implemented as of early 2011. It is not clear if they were simply designed as a veil to cover up the regime's continued authoritarian bent, or if they were genuine efforts to open up Syrian society and politics. Some observers report that Bashar's grip on power is unsteady, and that a group of officers from the military and security services are the real decision makers, or are at least preventing Bashar from engaging in political and economic reforms that they fear will undermine their power and privileges. Others believe that Bashar is biding his time, waiting for his own strength to grow to the point that he can challenge the old guard.

And some believe that he really is as authoritarian as his father was, and that he has no intention of reforming Syria. They note that even where minor changes have been made, there has been no reduction in the regime's authority and control. The "Damascus Declaration," a call for wholesale political reform issued in October 2005 by Syrian opposition groups, including Islamists, Kurds, and secularists, would not have been possible under Hafez al-Assad, but Bashar has not shown as of this writing that he is prepared to agree to its demands; indeed, some of the declaration's signatories have been arrested and imprisoned since it was first promoted. Syria continues to provide the best example of a modern Arab dictatorship, and until Bashar does engage in concrete reforms, we must conclude that the regime in Syria remains overall the same as it did under his father.

References and Further Reading

Hinnebusch, Raymond A. *Authoritarian Power and State Formation in Ba'thist Syria: Army, Party, Peasant.* Boulder, CO: Westview Press, 1990.

———. *Syria: Revolution from Above.* London: Routledge, 2001.

Rabinovich, Itamar. *Syria Under the Ba'th, 1963–1966: The Army-Party Symbiosis.* New York: Halsted Press, 1972.

Wedeen, Lisa. *Ambiguities of Domination: Politics, Rhetoric, and Symbols in Contemporary Syria.* Chicago: University of Chicago Press, 1999.

Lebanon

Lebanon is unique in the Middle East and among the Arab states. It is neither a monarchy nor a radical-nationalist state. It is not completely authoritarian, though it has engaged in harsh repression; yet it is not an open democracy, though most sectarian groups do participate in elections and are represented in parliament. Its governing system is based on confessionalism, a system in which decision-making structures are proportionately allocated according to the size of different sectarian groups in society. This has been the only way the country's competing communal groups have been able to work together. Lebanon has, in general, struggled to make a legitimate democratic process work, but four factors have hampered its ability to do so.

First, there is Lebanon's confessional system, discussed further below, in which elections are essentially sectarian and personal affairs guided not by a genuine competition over ideas but by patron-client relationships. Second, the civil war from 1975 to 1990 tore the country apart and prevented the leadership from engaging in the daily work of government. Third, the establishment of Syrian dominance over the country from 1989 to 2005 led to a reduction in political freedoms and made the country an appendage of Syria. Fourth, the rise of Hezbollah, an Islamist Shi'ite group based in southern Lebanon, which by the 1990s was the strongest group in the country, undermined the capacity of the Lebanese government to control its own territory and population.

In 2005 Lebanon began to move away from its past patterns of governing to a more politically active and democratic system. This was accomplished at the expense of Syrian influence. Hezbollah remains a powerful player in the country, and twice in the late 2000s it engaged in a sustained effort to overthrow the democratically elected and pro-Western government. In the June 2009 parliamentary elections, Hezbollah won 13 out of 120 seats; after extended discussions it was incorporated into the government in November 2009. On January 12, 2011, its ministers resigned from the government, leading to its dissolution and then recognition by a parliamentary majority of its preferred candidate to replace the prime minister.

Since its independence from France in 1943, the most common feature of governance in Lebanon has been the intrusive role of external actors in the country's politics and in the shaping of its governance system. This history includes the French Mandate over Lebanon and the creation of the confessional system; the National Pact—an unwritten agreement that formalized the division of government according to sect; the period between the National Pact and the outbreak of the civil war; the civil war itself; and the Ta'if Accord, a major landmark that changed Lebanon's political framework and overrode the long-standing National Pact. Since the mid-1980s, Hezbollah has come to play a critical role in Lebanon, and since the early 2000s, the Lebanese government's authority has declined as groups either supportive of or opposed to Syria's influence in the country began to confront each other over the future of the country.

The French Creation of Lebanon, Confessionalism, and the Demographic Balance: 1920–1943

Lebanon's political system has, since the early 1920s, been based on confessionalism. This means that government offices and seats in parliament are distributed among sectarian groups according to their demographic weight. It is a delicate balance, and theoretically subject to change according to changes in population growth. But because of the country's deep sectarian divisions and its past civil wars, there is little desire to engage in such exact accounting. The confessional system has therefore twice been frozen into place: once at the creation of the National Pact, an agreement between the major Christian and Sunni groups, from 1943 to 1989; and then, with some modifications, since the signing of the Ta'if Accord, a Saudi-supervised political framework, in 1989.

Lebanon's population politics stems from the manner of its formation. Like most Middle Eastern states, modern Lebanon was an artificial creation of the Europeans, its borders drawn by the French, with different regions incorporated into the same state. And like many of the other regional states, Lebanon was carved out of what had for centuries been part of larger imperial or administrative entities. There had never been an entity with similar borders to the Lebanese state that came into existence with the establishment of the League of Nations Mandate in 1919 and the French declaration of the State of Greater Lebanon on September 1, 1920.

Greater Lebanon was invented to serve the interests of the Maronites, who were concentrated in the Mount Lebanon region. As the largest sect within the Christian community, the Maronites wanted a system that would ensure their dominance. But they also wanted a larger national territory, to expand their economic base and to better protect themselves from what they believed was (Muslim) Syria's desire to absorb their lands into its own country. As a sister Christian community, France acquiesced in their demands, adding Beirut, the coastal areas, and the Bekaa Valley. But in doing so, it set the stage for conflict between the various sects.

In the Mount Lebanon area the Maronites had comprised about 60 percent of the Christian community, which in turn was about 80 percent of the total population. But the addition of the new regions brought many more Muslim inhabitants into the country. It is estimated that in Greater Lebanon the Christians were reduced to only 55 percent of the total population, and the Maronites (though they still made up the single largest communal group) trimmed down to only one-third of the populace. At that time the Sunnis made up the largest sect among Muslims in Lebanon, at about 20 percent of the total population, following by the Shi'ites at 17 percent.

These sectarian divisions did not translate into major political problems at the time because France installed its own governors and administrators over the country. But the Maronites still sought to protect their majority rule through political and constitutional means. From 1922 to 1925 the governor was advised (to the extent that these advisors were actually consulted) by a representative council elected on a confessional basis. Each communal group elected a number of representatives based on its share of the total population. It was, the French concluded, the best way to ensure popular participation in the system. From 1925 to May 1926 the confessional system was abolished as the French governor attempted to impose a nondenominational system. None of the communal groups supported this, and—in order to maintain its control—the French restored the confessional system through the establishment of the Lebanese Republic and a constitution on May 23, 1926.

The next two decades in Lebanon were marked by continuing differences and disagreements between its communal groups. They cooperated in an uneasy coexistence. One of the main issues of contention among them was the country's orientation: the question was whether it would be primarily Arab (in which case Lebanon would move closer to Syria, the option promoted by many Sunnis) or Western (which would mean a deeper relationship with France, which most Maronites favored). Some groups and individuals from across the confessional spectrum also preferred a completely independent Lebanon.

The country's last official census was taken in 1932, when it was determined that the population ratio of Christians to Muslims had slipped to 51:49. The Maronites and the Sunnis were found to be the largest sects. Out of the total population, Maronites were 29 percent, Sunnis 23 percent, Shi'ites 20 percent, Greek Orthodox 10 percent, Druzes 7 percent, and Catholics 6 percent. No government since then has conducted a census, first because the Maronites feared that if the statistics showed a majority Muslim population they would have to cede their dominant position in the government, and then later because most of the groups feared that the country's delicately balanced political system would collapse if different sects began demanding political change based on new demographic information. On the basis of this data, the Maronites and the Sunnis, as the largest sects in the country, agreed to an arrangement called the National Pact, which was designed to freeze in place a particular governing system and thus avoid continuing disputes over it. All of this took place while the country was still under the French Mandate.

The National Pact: 1943

The National Pact structured Lebanese politics from 1943 until 1989, at which time the Ta'if Accord was signed, superseding the Pact. Made possible by the sincere cooperation between the sectarian communities, the National Pact was prompted in part by growing confrontation with France over independence and in part by increasing tensions among the communal groups. It was a clever compromise that allowed Lebanon to have a relatively stable existence, compared to its Arab neighbors, until the onset of the civil war in 1975. This period of stability helped turn Beirut into the "Paris of the Middle East," a financial and luxury center hailed around the world.

After the Vichy government came to power in France, British and Free French forces invaded Lebanon in June 1941 and drove out the Vichy representative. Under heavy Lebanese and British pressure, the French declared Lebanon independent on November 26, 1941. But even the Free French could not bring themselves to give up complete control over Lebanon. A series of confrontations ensued that forced the French, in March 1943, to reinstate the constitution. In the wake of these conflicts, Maronite and Sunni community leaders met in the summer to work out a political-legal arrangement that would help them present a united front against the French, ease the tensions between the sectarian groups, and preempt any future political struggles between them that might turn violent.

The pact was an unwritten agreement between Maronite leader Bishara al-Khuri and the head of the Sunni community, Riyad al-Sulh. They agreed to accept the results of the 1932 census as binding the sectarian division of government offices and parliamentary seats, which gave the Christians a majority of the population, even though it was widely believed that by then Muslims outnumbered Christians. Several factors led to the historic agreement. For their part, the Maronites feared what would happen to them if the Muslims gained control over the government, and so wanted to entrench their "majority" rule. The Sunnis wanted to ensure that Lebanon would remain Arab and independent, and not become tied to France or the West. The National Pact preserved these trade-offs.

The pact entailed a number of elements. First, parliament would be divided among Christians and Muslims (including Druzes) according to a 6:5 ratio, in multiples of eleven. Second, the president of the republic (who would have considerable independent power) and the commander of the armed forces would always be a Maronite; the prime minister would always be a Sunni; and the speaker of the parliament would always be a Shi'ite. (The cabinet and the civil service would also reflect a similar division.) Third, Lebanon would remain an independent country: the Christians would accept its "Arab face" and not try to bring the French in to protect them or bind the country to the West, though it would not cut off ties with the West. In return, the Muslims accepted the 1920 borders of Lebanon and promised not to seek any merger with Syria. And fourth, confessionalism would remain the governing system of Lebanon. On account of this, no further official population counts would take place.

On the basis of the National Pact, parliamentary elections to the Majlis al-Nuwaab (Chamber of Deputies) were held in summer 1943. In September al-Khuri was elected by the legislature as president, and, as per the powers granted to him, he appointed al-Sulh as prime minister. On November 8, the Majlis amended the constitution, removing those articles that dealt with the Mandate and French control over Lebanon—a unilateral declaration of independence that infuriated the French. In response, Paris arrested the government, in turn angering all of the Lebanese communities. They quickly organized to pressure the French into leaving; Britain and the United States lent their support to Lebanese demands. France finally relented, releasing the government on November 22—considered by Lebanon to be its independence day—and ending French rule over Lebanon.

The Calm Before the Storm: 1943–1975

The National Pact remained the political framework of Lebanon for the next thirty-two years, until the outbreak of the civil war between the various sectarian groups in April 1975 (though it was not officially revoked until it was incorporated into the 1989 Ta'if Accord). The system was threatened by political and security crises a number of times, and several communal groups did seek to dissolve the pact. But as a system of governance, the pact held. It thus helped to maintain stability—a troubled and sometimes fragile state of affairs, but stability nonetheless. When compared to its neighbor Syria, the 1943–1975 period in Lebanon was a model of dependability.

This chapter in Lebanon's history was still marked by a series of problems, including increasing authoritarianism among successive presidents in their efforts to shift Lebanon's orientation either toward the West, the Arab world, or independence; a growing discontent with the division of confessional power; and disagreements among the sectarian factions over Lebanon's foreign policy orientation. The influx of Palestinians after 1948 and 1970 exacerbated these problems and helped lead to the outbreak of war.

Even when it fell under Syrian control in the 1990s, Lebanon never experienced the same level of repression that characterized the other Arab states. Political activity itself was channeled through the sectarian parties, making it difficult to engage in independent politicking. Lebanese presidents sought to enhance their own power at the expense of other groups in society, leading to an autocratic presidency that clashed with other elements in the government and the parliament.

But at the same time many personal freedoms were recognized and allowed, and the state did not intrude on citizens' lives to anywhere near the same degree as, for example, in Egypt or Syria. In addition, the National Pact itself encouraged a minimal amount of government activity in everything from education to the economy. The efforts at presidential authoritarianism were relevant more for intragovernmental struggles rather than active dictatorship throughout society. This was because in order to avoid getting drawn into a confessional fight, Lebanese governments simply avoided active involvement in governing. Sectarian groups were left to maintain their own educational systems and, more dangerously, their own militias at the expense of the national army.

This helped the development of Lebanon's economy. Unlike the socialism that came to permeate the other Arab regimes, Lebanon supported an open, capitalist economy. This is what earned it the status of banking capital of the Middle East. The overall development of the economy also put off for a time active discontent with the nature of the confessional system. At least until the 1970s, many sectarian elites could support the system to some degree because they benefited from their high position in it, for example by controlling particular industries or sectors of the economy.

Despite these positive aspects, the system began to unravel by the 1970s for three reasons. First, by that time it had become too obvious to the Lebanese that the demographic balance had completely shifted in favor of the Muslims: by the mid-1970s it is estimated that close to 60 percent of the population was Muslim, with Shi'ites now the largest communal group, at 30 percent. This prompted Muslims to push harder for a change in the governing system, which in turn triggered fear in the Christian population and a vow to resist any such reforms. This was coupled with the rise of secularist factions that demanded the abolition of the confessional system in its entirety.

Second, the agreement to keep Lebanon from aligning too closely with either the West or the Arab world became impossible to keep with the rise of Gamal Abdel Nasser, the president of Egypt in the 1950s and 1960s. The wild excitement that he inspired in Muslim populations around the Middle East led, in Lebanon, to greater encouragement of pan-Arab ideas and threatened to undermine the independence that the National Pact had guaranteed. This alarmed the Maronites as much as the demographic issue, since given their small percentage of the population as a whole in the region, drawing closer to the Arab world would mean the Christians would be dominated by an overwhelming Muslim majority population.

Third, the existence of a few hundred thousand Palestinians (mostly refugees) in the country threatened to upset the demographic balance further. Many of them had fled to Lebanon as a result of the first Arab-Israeli War in 1947–1949, when they were displaced as a result of fighting between the Zionist/Israeli and Arab armies and irregular forces. This problem was solved by not granting the Palestinians Lebanese citizenship. But their very presence within the country stirred among Lebanese Muslims a natural sympathy for the Palestinian cause. Nasser's fiery rhetoric calling for all Arabs to support the Palestinians against Israel encouraged these feelings.

Sympathy became support when elements of the Palestine Liberation Organization (PLO) began, in the late 1960s, to operate against Israel out of sovereign Lebanese territory. This brought Israeli retaliatory raids upon Lebanon. The PLO also began to involve itself in the confessional politics of the country. The government was unable to stop these activities by moving against the Palestinians, because the Muslims, especially the Sunnis, would not condone such action. On November 2, 1969, the government signed the Cairo Agreement with the PLO, its only real option. In it, Lebanon agreed that the PLO would be free to operate against Israel from Lebanese territory, but in return the PLO agreed not to interfere in the domestic affairs of Lebanon (in other words, to avoid upsetting the confessional balance). When the entire leadership of the PLO moved from Jordan to Lebanon, in the wake of the battle between the PLO and the Jordanian military in 1970-71, the Cairo Agreement became more difficult to sustain. It was soon abrogated by the Chamber of Deputies.

Combined, all the above developments led to a widespread dissatisfaction with the governing system of Lebanon and an increasingly powerful desire among many sectarian groups, particularly the Muslims, to change it. Minor skirmishes between the various militias became more common into the 1970s. It was only a matter of time before one of these clashes sparked a wide conflagration across the entire country. This is, in fact, what happened on April 13, 1975.

The Civil War: 1975–1990

There was no Lebanese governing system during the period of the civil war because the state all but collapsed. It was torn apart by open war between the sectarian groups and by direct Syrian and Israeli military intervention. The central government became only a pretense. The Lebanese military broke apart as its soldiers either defected to their respective communities or decided not to report for duty. Parliament ceased to be a legitimate vehicle for popular representation from 1972, the year of the last national elections, until 1992, when elections were finally held again. In this period, the only real authority that existed was in the leadership of the different communal groups.

Discussion of the civil war itself is beyond the scope of this section. It will be enough to note the devastation it wrecked upon the country: over 200,000 casualties, up to 900,000 people displaced, billions of dollars in property and infrastructure damage, the destruction of much of Beirut (and an end to its famed status as a financial hub and place of extravagance), and the emigration of tens of thousands of Lebanese citizens.

It began on April 13, 1975, when unknown gunmen shot dead four members of the Phalange Party (primarily supported by Maronites) in what was believed to be an assassination attempt against the party's founder, Pierre Gemayel. The Phalange retaliated by attacking a busload of Palestinians, killing over twenty. Almost immediately, fighting broke out between the various sects, most of which had begun in the 1960s to form their own militias as a form of protection. As with the PLO, the government was hampered in taking decisive action to end the violence by the very system that created it. Most government and civil service officials and parliamentarians absconded to their communal groups.

The fighting worsened throughout 1975. In January and February 1976, Syria attempted to mediate an end to conflict. An agreement was drawn up on February 14 that included several points later incorporated into the Ta'if Agreement, including equal representation between Christians and Muslims in the Chamber of Deputies and a reduction in the powers of the president. But some of the key Christian and Muslim factions did not support the agreement, and sectarian fighting resumed.

Syrian Intervention

Frustrated by a lack of progress on ending the civil war, anxious to prevent the rise of radicalism in Lebanon—which seemed a distinct possibility given that several leftist and extremist Palestinian groups had formed a bloc and were participating in the fighting—and perhaps perceiving an opportunity to expand Syrian influence, Hafez al-Assad decided to invade Lebanon and put an end to the fighting. His troops entered the country in May 1976 in support of the Christians, since he was more anxious about radical Muslim groups gaining power than he was about Maronite dominance. Syrian forces immediately engaged the Palestinians.

By October a tenuous cease-fire was arranged. The Arab League legitimized the Syrian military presence through the establishment of a 30,000-strong Arab Deterrent Force, of which Syria first supplied over 20,000 of its troops and then the entire contingent. Although the civil war resumed in a matter of months, its first phase saw the onset of Syrian influence and eventual hegemony in Lebanon.

Israeli Intervention

The second phase of the civil war began with Israel's own invasion, the "Litani Operation," on March 15, 1978. Given the inability of the Lebanese government to control the PLO fighters operating across the border, Israel had responded with air strikes, artillery barrages, and small counter-raids. At the beginning of March, however, PLO terrorists crossed into Israel and took a bus hostage. In the ensuing firefight between the PLO and the Israeli military, thirty-three civilians were killed. On March 15, Israel responded in force, seizing Lebanese territory up to the Litani River. Although Israel withdrew later that year, the invasion sparked renewed fighting between Lebanon's sects. In addition, Israel supported in its absence a Christian paramilitary group in southern Lebanon, which fought the PLO.

On June 6, 1982, Israel launched a full-scale invasion of Lebanon in response to continuing PLO attacks and provocations, which dovetailed with the plans of some Israelis (primarily Defense Minister Ariel Sharon) to rewrite the Lebanese political equation and put the Maronites back on top of the country. In between Israel's two incursions, Syrian troops had begun to attack their former allies, the Maronites. At the same time, other communal militias continued to fight for territory and power and to defend themselves against the encroachment of rivals.

These conditions continued until the end of the 1980s. By then the Lebanese were proclaiming their exhaustion with the fighting. Their country was in ruins, two of their neighbors had invaded, and the militias had weakened each other to the point that it was clear none of them would achieve a clear victory over the others. The country's leaders were increasingly searching for a way to end the fighting and, if not resolve all of the outstanding issues, at least work toward removing some of the more contentious issues that had led to the civil war, such as reconstituting power-sharing arrangements. Crucially, the Christians had by that time come to accept that they could no longer dominate the country the way they had in the past—the demographic balance had shifted against them too much for them to reasonably demand the continuation of the old system.

The Ta'if Accord and Syrian Domination: 1989–2005

At the beginning of 1989 a committee of Arab states, including Saudi Arabia, Algeria, and Morocco, began work on formulating a plan to end the civil war. By October, a workable document had been produced. The critical element was a change in the nature of the governing system. Confessionalism remained the basis for the country's political system, notwithstanding an article in the document that stipulated the government must work to abolish sectarianism. But the representation of the various sects in the government, civil service, and Chamber of Deputies was now made equal between Christians and Muslims, instead of the previous inequality in favor of the Christians. On October 22, sixty-two Lebanese parliamentarians came to Ta'if, in Saudi Arabia, to sign the document—now known as the Ta'if Accord but officially called the National Reconciliation Accord. They returned to Lebanon, where the accord was ratified on November 4, creating what has been referred to as the Second Lebanese Republic.

Apart from ending the civil war and bringing a semblance of peace to the country, Ta'if had two consequences in terms of changing the Lebanese political equation. First, as noted above, it changed the balance of political power to a more accurate reflection of the country's varied population. To this end, Ta'if called for equal numbers of Christians and Muslims in a larger, 108-seat parliament (later expanded to 128 seats), and within each religious group a division of seats based on the proportion of each sect. This division of power did not completely mirror the population, otherwise the Shi'ites would have had the largest number of seats and the Christians, now a minority of the overall population, would not have had equal representation.

In August 1990 the government and legislature worked out the following distribution: Christians and Muslims, as a religious grouping, would receive sixty-four seats each. Within the Christian bloc, thirty-four seats went to the Maronites, fourteen to the Greek Orthodox, eight to the Greek Catholics, five to Armenian Orthodox, one to an Armenian Catholic, one to a Protestant, and one seat to be shared by the rest of the Christian sects (which include the tiny Coptic, Chaldean, and Assyrian Christian communities). Within the Muslim bloc, both Sunnis and Shi'ites received twenty-seven seats each, Druzes were given eight seats, and Alawites two. The cabinet was now also to be divided equally among Christians and Muslims. The first post–civil war national elections took place in August–September 1992.

Although the Ta'if Accord left in place the unwritten agreement that the president would be a Maronite, it also removed some of his powers and transferred them primarily to the Sunni prime minister. This was done by giving the prime minister and the cabinet more executive power, but also by removing from the president the sole authority to name and replace the prime minister, which now had to be done in consultation with the legislature. By these means, the Ta'if Accord integrated the National Pact, retaining the confessional system of governance, but reallocating the representation the various sects were allowed in order to more realistically reflect the changed demographic circumstances of the country.

The second main consequence of the accord was its legitimization of Syrian occupation and hegemony in Lebanon. Syria had long believed that Lebanon was a historic part of Syria, and it had never formally accepted Lebanon's independence—it refused, for example, to establish official diplomatic relations with Lebanon, since that would imply recognition of national borders. Thus, although Ta'if was good for Lebanon because it ended the civil war, it led to a long period of quasi authoritarianism, as Syria expanded its own autocratic system to Lebanon, where it was now the dominant power. Repression never rose to the same levels as it did in Syria, and the Lebanese were able to retain some of their previous individual freedoms, but Damascus was careful to ensure that dissent from and criticism of the governments that it supported in Lebanon never went very far. Parliament and government essentially became divided among pro- and anti-Syrians, and given the pervasive nature of Syrian rule, the former group tended to dominate—though this by no means meant that there was no independent or anti-Syrian activity.

Ta'if did this in two ways. First, the document itself prepared the way by referring to the "special relationship" between the two countries. It also called for a Syrian withdrawal of troops within a specified time frame, but the pro-Syrian government that came to power after the accord did not request Syria's departure, making its presence legal. In addition to the accord itself, on May 20, 1991, Syria and Lebanon signed a Treaty of Brotherhood, Cooperation, and Coordination, which called for the two countries to work to achieve the "highest level" of cooperation in political, security, and economic terms, and stated that they share a "common destiny" and interests. Most Lebanese believed that these words were code for Syrian domination over its smaller, weaker neighbor.

Second, the accord and everything it symbolized had the support of both the Arab world and the United States, thus lending tacit agreement to Syria's occupation. For its part, the United States preferred a stable Lebanon to an unstable one. In addition, it agreed to look the other way as Syria extended its power over the country in return for Syria's support against Iraq in the 1991 Gulf War.

Syria accomplished its control in a number of ways. In political terms, its supporters in the Lebanese parliament gerrymandered the electoral districts, shrinking the voting districts for its allies so they did not have to compete for votes with others, and putting Christian districts within larger Muslim districts to dilute the electoral strength of the former. In this way, groups that opposed Syria, such as some Christian sects that then boycotted the election, would be unlikely to win many seats in the Chamber of Deputies. The result was that approximately 90 percent of those who entered the new parliament were pro-Syrian. The parliament then did the same thing before the 1996 national elections. In 1994, it passed a naturalization law that granted Lebanese citizenship to 300,000 foreign residents. Because Syrians made up the bulk of the new citizens, pro-Syrian politicians received a not insignificant boost in polling numbers.

Damascus also directly chose the president and prime minister, and they were confirmed by an obedient parliament. Twice (in 1995 and in 2006) Syria also had the parliament extend the tenure of its handpicked presidents for an additional three years, despite the constitutional ban on presidents serving more than six years. This control over policymaking was Syria's most effective asset in furthering its supremacy over the country.

But there were other forms of domination as well. Syria has played a critical role in the Lebanese economy, giving it extra leverage. It is estimated that a million Syrians are working in Lebanon. This has an impact on the number of unemployed Lebanese, and because the Syrian workers usually send their remittances to their families in Syria, it also results in a loss of capital for Lebanon. Syrian intelligence agents and military officers are closely involved in black market activity in Lebanon, such as smuggling and the narcotics trade, which leads to corruption and a weakening of the formal economy.

Syria also maintained, until 2002, about 30,000 troops in the country, based mainly in the Bekaa Valley (at the height of its intervention in the civil war, in 1976, it had 40,000 soldiers in Lebanon). These troops served as a reminder of the ultimate coercion that the Lebanese faced if they decided to begin to agitate against the Syrian presence. They were supplemented by a gang of Syrian intelligence troops (whose numbers remain unknown), who fanned out across the country to spy on and threaten Lebanese citizens into submission.

Assassinations of outspoken critics of Syria were common, as were their detention, torture, and disappearance. Wiretapping of cabinet ministers was routine. Finally, Lebanon itself had a number of security agencies that, under the direction of Syria, worked to curtail individual freedoms, independent political activity, and independent media activity. These include the Internal Security Forces, the State Security Apparatus, and the Sûreté Générale (General Security Directorate).

In short, despite the continued existence of the confessional structure, Lebanon's governing system between 1989 and 2005 was Syrian-authoritarian; that is, it was controlled by Syria and exhibited elements of the autocracy that marked Syria's governing system, but adapted to the specific conditions of Lebanon. There was still a far greater degree of personal and political freedom in Lebanon than in other Arab countries, provided criticism was not directed against Syria and its control over Lebanon or the security forces. Criticism of the government was even allowed, so long as it remained within reasonable limits (that is, did not begin to advocate wholesale change). This stemmed in part from the long history of these freedoms in the country, and in part from Syria's desire to avoid too much oppression lest it generate international opposition to its presence in the country. But the overall system had become rigid and repressive, and removed the capacity of the Lebanese to determine their own affairs—including choosing their own governments.

The Rise of Hezbollah: 1982–2005

In addition to Syrian control and manipulation, the central Lebanese government and Lebanese sovereignty have been undermined by the presence and role of Hezbollah (Party of God). A Shi'ite-based organization formed out of the 1982 Israeli invasion, the group at first had widespread support and legitimacy within the country because of its fight against the Israeli occupation, which continued in the south from 1985 until 2000, when the Israeli military withdrew from Lebanon. But the withdrawal of Israeli forces undermined the raison d'être of Hezbollah, and the continuation of its military attacks and provocations against Israel (despite United Nations certification of the withdrawal) and its direct move into Lebanese politics angered many Lebanese, though they were unable to take any serious action against it until 2005.

The exact date of Hezbollah's inception is disputed, but it is known that sometime between 1982 and 1985, several Shi'ite groups coalesced to form the party, which announced its existence in February 1985. Alongside the smaller Amal movement, it became the main organization fighting the Israel Defense Forces and the Israel-backed South Lebanon Army in southern Lebanon. It drew for inspiration on the 1979 Islamic Revolution in Shi'ite Iran; indeed, its second objective (after ejecting Israeli forces from Lebanese territory and the destruction of Israel) is the establishment of a fundamentalist Islamic state in Lebanon. Iran is also the major patron of Hezbollah, supplying it with funding, arms, training, and logistical assistance. Hezbollah took, and received, credit for the complete withdrawal of Israeli troops from Lebanon in May 2000.

Because of its confrontation with Israel, Hezbollah garnered widespread support among the Muslim population in Lebanon. But its base is in the Shi'ite community. The Shi'ites in Lebanon have long been marginalized, as the Sunnis and Maronites dominated the country's politics and economy. Even after the Shi'ites surpassed all other communal groups in demographic weight, they remained stuck in an inferior socioeconomic and political position. The rise of Hezbollah was an important symbol for them, representing the growth of Shi'ite military power and, as Hezbollah became more directly involved in Lebanese politics after 2000, political power. Given its control over the country, Syria's logistical and diplomatic support for Hezbollah as a low-cost method of continuing the confrontation with Israel also strengthened the group's standing in Lebanon.

The Ta'if Accord stipulated that all militias in Lebanon would be disbanded and disarmed. But both Hezbollah and Amal were exempt from this requirement on the grounds that they needed weapons to continue to resist Israeli occupation of Lebanese territory. With the dissolution of most of the other sectarian militias, this put Hezbollah, and through it the Shi'ites, in a powerful position not only to resist central Lebanese authority, but also to begin to make its own demands on the government. Hezbollah has participated in all Lebanese parliamentary elections after the civil war, winning a similar number of seats: eight seats in 1992, seven in 1996, and eight in 2000. But in none of these elections did it opt to force its way into the government, preferring to remain apart.

But its biggest electoral win came in the May–June 2005 poll. It took fourteen seats in the Chamber of Deputies, but more importantly it decided for the first time to join the government. It was given two ministries, while its ally Amal took a third ministry. As a member of cabinet, Hezbollah now had a powerful voice in the country's decision making, even apart from its hero status among Shi'ites and the support of Syria. There was little time for it to exercise any influence, however, as events soon overtook all of Lebanon and led to Hezbollah ministers' resignation from the administration. These events, which indicate Lebanon has entered a new era in its politics, are detailed below.

The Murder of Rafik Hariri and the Cedar Revolution: 2005–Present

By 2005 it appeared that Syrian influence in Lebanon was on the wane, but that Hezbollah's position was not. A wide variety of Lebanon's confessional groups had banded together to protest Syria's authoritarian control and Hezbollah's attacks on Israel, which were provoking Israeli retaliatory strikes on the country. This new dynamic began with the assassination of former prime minister Rafik Hariri on February 14, 2005, though it had antecedents in the four years prior, to which we will turn first. In this period, governing was about the growing confrontation between Syria and its supporters in Lebanon and those Lebanese groups that wanted to eject Syria from the country. It continued, beginning in December 2005, in a tense political standoff between the pro-Western government of Fouad Siniora and Hezbollah, culminating at the end of 2009 with an uneasy coalition government led by Hezbollah in one camp and Prime Minister Saad Hariri (the son of Rafik Hariri) in the other, until this government was brought down by Hezbollah's withdrawal of support.

This period was also marked by growing challenges to Syria's control from Lebanese individuals and groups. By 2000, most Lebanese had tired of

Syrian authoritarianism in their country. But their frustration was given impetus by three things: an economic decline, the May 2000 withdrawal of Israel from southern Lebanon (which seemed to remove the major reason for Syrian control and Hezbollah's existence), and the death a month later of Syrian President Hafez al-Assad, which was perceived to herald a decline in repression. Lebanese began to speak more openly about their concerns and to criticize the Syrian presence in their country. Demonstrations against this control sprang up. A reconciliation meeting between Maronite and Druze leaders in August 2000 signaled an increasing willingness of anti-Syrian groups to work together to eradicate Syrian influence.

In June 2001, Syrian leader Bashar al-Assad agreed to redeploy Syrian troops in Lebanon, moving them almost completely out of the capital, Beirut. It is unclear why he agreed to do so: some argue that he was not strong enough to resist the growing demands for removal of Syrian influence, while others suggest he thought that by addressing some of these concerns he could ignore the deeper reasons for the growing dissatisfaction. In any event, demands for their complete removal continued. In April 2002, Syrian forces were redeployed again, and again in September 2004. By February 2005, only 14,000 troops remained in the country—mostly in the Bekaa Valley and around Tripoli in the north.

But troop redeployments and withdrawals were only one aspect of the growing pressure on Syria to give up its control of Lebanon. Other states and the United Nations, too, began to call more forcefully for Syria to release its grip on the country. After the U.S.-led invasion of Iraq in spring 2003, an insurgency began in Iraq against the coalition forces and fellow Iraqis. Syria allowed insurgents and terrorists to cross into Iraq from its territory, thereby assisting indirectly in the attacks on American soldiers. Washington grew angry and began to actively criticize the Syrian occupation of Lebanon, something it had not done since the Ta'if Accord.

Fearful that it might actually begin to lose its control over Lebanon, and in order to illustrate that Syria remained the premier player in Lebanese politics, Bashar al-Assad began to pressure the Lebanese Chamber of Deputies to amend the constitution and extend the tenure of pro-Syria president Émile Lahoud, due to expire in late 2004. There was little attempt at subtlety, as Damascus decided to demonstrate it was in firm control. Lebanese presidents are constitutionally bound to serve only one six-year term. At the end of August, parliament acquiesced, extending Lahoud's presidency by three years.

By 2004, in the wake of Syria's blatant manipulation of the Lebanese parliament and constitution, it was becoming obvious that the Lebanese themselves were demanding the removal of all Syrian influence. France took a lead role in pressing Syria to leave, and began to put together a United Nations Security Council Resolution to give these condemnations international legitimacy and legal weight, eventually co-introducing with the United States Security Council Resolution 1559. On September 2, the Security Council passed Resolution 1559, which called for the "disbanding and disarmament" of all militias in Lebanon, the withdrawal of "all remaining foreign forces" from the country (a clear reference to Syria, since Israel had withdrawn four years earlier), the restoration of full Lebanese control and sovereignty over its national territory, and free and fair elections "without foreign interference or influence."

On February 14, 2005, Rafik Hariri was murdered in a car bombing that killed over 20 others and wounded close to 100. Hariri was a billionaire businessman who had twice been prime minister of Lebanon (1992–1998 and 2000–2004) and was known for his efforts in the country's reconstruction. An erstwhile supporter of Syria, he had, after resigning from government in October 2004, become a staunch critic of its control over Lebanon. It is not yet known with certainty who was behind the assassination, but Syria's guilt is widely presumed in Lebanon. The killing sparked international condemnation. The International Criminal Court established the Special Tribunal for Lebanon, to investigate and prosecute those responsible. Its preliminary report pointed toward Syria as bearing some responsibility, and it was widely reported in January 2011 that the first indictments, handed down on January 17 but not made public, would implicate Hezbollah in the murder.

Hariri's assassination sparked an immediate reaction within Lebanon as well, including anti-

Syrian demonstrations across the country. The response has become known in much of the world as the Cedar Revolution, to reference the symbolic trees of Lebanon. (In the Arab world it is referred to as the Independence Uprising or Revolution.) The pro-Syrian government of Prime Minister Omar Karami resigned under pressure. The pro-Syrian president reappointed him ten days later, but only to act as a caretaker government until new national elections could be held in May–June 2005. When he could not convince opposition leaders to join his cabinet, he was forced to resign again on April 3.

As protests continued, Hezbollah arranged a demonstration in support of Syria on March 8, which was estimated to have included up to several hundred thousand people. In response, the anti-Syria groups organized a rally on March 14, the one-month anniversary of Hariri's murder. By some estimates the rally garnered up to one million protestors. The turnout to both of these rallies prompted both factions to give a new name to their movements: the March 8 Coalition (to retain Syria's presence) and the March 14 Coalition (to expel Syrian influence).

As the protests against Syria continued, scattered violence broke out, particularly in Christian areas. But the pressure on Syria was kept up, and in a historic development, all Syrian troops left Lebanon by the end of April 2005. This did not mean the end of all Syrian influence in the country, since it still retained support among the population and particularly from Hezbollah, and it is unclear how many Syrian intelligence agents remain in Lebanon. But it did remove a major obstacle to reform and political and individual freedom, emboldening anti-Syrian groups even more.

The March 14 Coalition won the May–June 2005 national elections, considered by international monitors to be free and fair (though allegations of vote buying did surface), taking sixty-nine seats in the parliament. Fouad Siniora, a wealthy businessman and close friend of Hariri's, was appointed prime minister on July 19. In a bid for national unity, his cabinet included two Hezbollah representatives (and one from Amal). Though the coalition dominated the cabinet, it did not have the required two-thirds majority in parliament to remove Lahoud from the presidency; a Hezbollah-led faction, which included Amal and the fascist Syrian Social Nationalist Party, received thirty-five seats. The government was left in a state of paralysis for the next year.

The conflict between pro- and anti-Syrian groups intensified in the summer of 2006. On July 12, Hezbollah launched a cross-border raid against Israel, killing three soldiers and kidnapping two. In a move that even Hezbollah leader Hassan Nasrallah admitted was a surprise, Israel responded immediately with a massive aerial bombardment against Hezbollah targets and Lebanese infrastructure, as well as limited ground incursions. Hezbollah responded by firing thousands of rockets and missiles into Israeli territory. By the time the war ended with a cease-fire on August 14, over 1,300 people in Lebanon and Israel had been killed, and almost a million Lebanese and about 300,000 Israelis were displaced from their homes. The damage to Lebanon's infrastructure ran into the billions of dollars, setting back its reconstruction efforts.

The result of the war had a significant impact on Hezbollah. Analysts believe that much of its rocket arsenal was depleted or destroyed. But perhaps more importantly, Hezbollah's previous capacity to maneuver freely in the south was now constrained: for the first time since 1975, the Lebanese military moved into the south to keep Hezbollah away from the border with Israel. In addition, the United Nations Interim Force in Lebanon (UNIFIL), a peacekeeping force put in the south in 1978 to monitor Israel's withdrawal, was strengthened with more troops and a wider mandate. Security Council Resolution 1701 (August 11) authorized UNIFIL "to take all necessary action in areas of deployment of its forces and as it deems within its capabilities, to ensure that its area of operations is not utilized for hostile activities of any kind." Finally, the war and the resultant destruction in parts of Lebanon were widely blamed in the Arab world and in Lebanon itself on Hezbollah. Its actions were considered reckless, manipulative, and without any thought to the impact they might have on the Lebanese population Hezbollah claimed to protect.

In the meantime, a United Nations investigation into the killing of Rafik Hariri was set up under Irish police commissioner Peter FitzGerald. Based on interviews with Lebanese politicians and forensic investigations, the investigation's final report in

March 2005 (the FitzGerald Report) placed blame on Syria for creating an atmosphere in which the murder could take place, and possible complicity, but concluded that it could not reliably accuse any party until the actual assassins were arrested.

The report was the basis for a February 2006 agreement between the UN and the Lebanese government to establish the Special Tribunal for Lebanon to try Hariri's killers. Hezbollah rejected the report's conclusion and refused to support a tribunal, arguing that it was only a vehicle for Western and Israeli interference in Lebanese affairs. The two government factions continued to struggle over this issue until, on November 11, 2006, Hezbollah and Amal resigned from the government. According to the Shi'ites, this meant that any decisions taken by the government would be illegitimate.

Then, on November 21, Pierre Gemayel, a charismatic leader of the Maronite community and a vocal critic of Syria, was shot to death by unknown gunmen, though the killers proclaimed in a statement that they took action because of Gemayel's anti-Syrian politics. That same day the UN sent the draft plan for the tribunal to Beirut for approval. On November 23, several hundred thousand people attended Gemayel's funeral, which morphed into an anti-Syria rally. Two days later, the Siniora cabinet approved the investigation. President Lahoud instantly declared it an unconstitutional decision because there were no Shi'ites in the government due to the resignations of November 11. The speaker of the parliament, Nabih Berri (from Amal), then refused to bring the decision to the chamber for ratification, using the same argument as the president.

Hezbollah then declared it would overturn the government in a series of peaceful protests unless the government gave the Shi'ites effective veto power. Protests began with a large rally, several hundred thousand strong, at the beginning of December 2006. The protests continued through 2007 and 2008. Siniora stood firm, announcing that he had no intention of resigning. Most of the international community, including France and the United States, backed him.

In May 2008, the government—without Shi'ite or pro-Syrian representation by this point—decided to shut down Hezbollah's communications network, arguing that the group was threatening the Lebanese government. Hezbollah leader Hassan Nasrallah proclaimed that the government had declared war on Hezbollah, and on May 7 violent clashes broke out between Hezbollah and its supporters, and those factions that supported the government. By late afternoon on May 9, Hezbollah had routed the government forces, seizing pro-government media buildings and controlling most of Beirut's streets. Fighting continued in and around the capital for a few more days, until on May 11 the Lebanese Army, the country's official military, brokered a cease-fire. The cease-fire did not completely hold, and fighting broke out again in other Lebanese cities. On May 14, the government and the Hezbollah-led opposition reached an agreement to end the violence and rescind the government's decision to shut down Hezbollah's communications.

Negotiations continued for the next week, and on May 21 the factions reached an agreement in which the government was reformed to include both the pro-Western March 14 Coalition and the Hezbollah-led March 8 Coalition. Known as the Doha Agreement, after the city in Qatar where the deal was struck, this accord established a power-sharing arrangement in which the March 14 Coalition received sixteen ministers in the new government and the March 8 Coalition received eleven. Both sides also agreed not to disrupt government decision making, pledging to work together to advance Lebanon's interests. The agreement also included a vaguely worded stipulation that called on independent militias not to take up violence to resolve disputes. Finally, both sides agreed on a compromise candidate for the president, former commander of the Lebanese Armed Forces Michel Suleiman.

The Doha Agreement was widely praised both within Lebanon and by other countries, including the Arab states and Iran, as well as France and the United States. Primarily it was greeted with relief, out of fears that a new civil war had been about to erupt. At the same time, it was widely interpreted as a victory for Hezbollah and pro-Syrian forces, as these were brought into the government without having to give up any of their key demands. In addition, it was unclear what would be done to follow up on the FitzGerald Report.

Predictions of Hezbollah's power were born out on January 12, 2011. The Special Tribunal for Lebanon by then was completing its work, and it was reported that Hezbollah—or at least some agents working for Hezbollah—would be indicted for Hariri's murder. Hezbollah had been vehemently denouncing the Tribunal as a front for American and Israeli pressure on the group and on Lebanon, and stated its refusal to work with the Tribunal or accept its legitimacy. It threatened that if the government accepted the Tribunal, it would bring down the government and work to replace it with a new one. It did so on January 12, as its ministers and allied minister resigned from the government, depriving it of the necessary support required in the Doha Agreement.

The March 14 Coalition worked to obtain a parliamentary majority to support Saad Hariri for prime minister again. Hezbollah vowed it would oppose such a move. Working with the Druze leaders and some Christian leaders, Hezbollah secured enough votes in the parliament to nominate its preferred candidate, billionaire businessman Najib Mikati. Although he has proclaimed that he would be a compromise candidate between the various factions and work to ensure cooperation in government, analysts note that he will be beholden to Hezbollah for his nomination. Hezbollah, it is now argued, holds the key to government in Lebanon.

At the moment the confessional system that guided Lebanese politics since the French Mandate in the 1920s seems to have been superseded by a dual system of orientation: either the end of Syrian influence and weakening of Hebollah, or the maintenance of Syrian influence and dominance of Hezbollah. The balance at the beginning of 2011 appears to be in Hezbollah's favor; it remains the strongest military force in the country, and it has demonstrated its ability to impose its political will on parliament. It remains to be seen whether the March 14 Coalition will successfully fend off Hezbollah's control and end Syrian influence. Beyond this, the March 14 Coalition was originally composed of a diverse range of sectarian groups, including Druze, Christians, and some Muslims, and disputes within it have led to some factional infighting. The Druze faction left the movement in 2009. Sectarian loyalties remain strong, and as the representation of the Shi'ite community, Hezbollah is distrusted by many groups in society. After it secured the nomination of Mikati, Sunnis began demonstrating against the organization, agitating for its removal from government. It is generally feared that the country could fall back into sectarian conflict. No confident predictions can be made, given that the situation in currently in a state of flux.

References and Further Reading

Blanford, Nicholas. *Killing Mr. Lebanon: The Assassination of Rafik Hariri and Its Impact on the Middle East.* London: I.B. Tauris, 2006.

Harel, Amos, and Avi Issacharoff. *34 Days: Israel, Hezbollah, and the War in Lebanon.* New York: Palgrave Macmillan, 2008.

Hudson, Michael. *The Precarious Republic: Political Modernization in Lebanon.* New York: Random House, 1968.

Norton, Augustus Richard. *Amal and the Shi'a: Struggle for the Soul of Lebanon.* Austin: University of Texas Press, 1987.

Iran

Iran is not an Arab country—the majority of its population is ethnically and linguistically Persian, and there is a significant Azeri (ethnic) and Turkic (linguistic) minority. Also, since the 1979 Islamic (or Iranian) Revolution, it has had a very different government from the rest of the Arab world—it is an Islamic theocracy, a system of government in which religious leaders (in this case, Islamic leaders) govern the state based on holy scripture. This makes it unique not just in the Middle East, but in the world. Yet both before and after the revolution, Iran has shared with the Arab regimes a number of instruments of governance. These have all been geared toward repression. The country's governing system is currently managed by hard-line Islamic clerics who, in the name of Islam and the Islamic Revolution, suppress any independent political activity and numerous personal freedoms.

Beginning in 1997, it appeared as though this authoritarianism was on the wane. A reformist president and parliament were elected and both promised to loosen the restrictions on personal liberties, engage in some economic liberalization, and repair Iran's poor relations with the international community. The purpose was not to change the Iranian system, but to give new meaning and impetus to the Islamic Revolution. Still, most Iranians were eager for these changes without a complete overthrow of the system. But soon after the reformists came to power, it became clear that the hard-liners retained virtually all of the power in Iran. They undermined and reversed most of the reforms, to the point that the Iranian population became disillusioned with the reformists. A hard-line nationalist, Mahmoud Ahmadinejad, was elected president in 2005, cementing the absolute control the autocratic clerics had enjoyed in the years immediately after the revolution; he was reelected in the September 2009 presidential elections, though these were heavily disputed by opposition groups within Iran, which came together as the Green Movement. This reformist movement still exists in Iran, but it is weak. The protests it led after the 2009 elections continued for some months, petering out by 2011. Although it has successfully articulated popular dissatisfaction with and dissent from the ruling clerical elite, the movement has not been able to translate this support into political gains within the regime's governing institutions.

The focus in these pages is on Iran after the revolution, with attention paid to the hard-line clerics who came to power during that period as well as the contemporary regime, the reform movement, and the conservative backlash it provoked. It is important, however, to set the stage for the Iranian Revolution in 1979 by looking first at Iran under the shahs.

Iran Under the Shahs

Iran is one of the few countries in the Middle East with a long history as a centralized political entity. Until 1935 it was known as Persia, encompassing the core of a series of ancient and modern empires that stretched into the twentieth century, including the Median, Achaemenian, Parthian, Sassanid, Safavid, and Qajar empires. The beginning of the end of the Iranian imperial era came on February 21, 1941, when a military officer, Colonel Reza Khan, overthrew the government. Over the next five years, Reza Khan concentrated more and more power into his own hands, eventually engineering his appointment as prime minister and then forcing the last Qajar king, Ahmad Shah, to take a "vacation" in Europe. Then, on December 12, 1925, Reza Khan had the parliament crown him as Shah of Iran, ending the Qajar Dynasty. On April 25, 1926, the crown was physically placed on Reza Shah's head, inaugurating the Pahlavi Dynasty—what would become the last monarchical family to rule in Iran.

As shah, Reza Khan was as autocratic as any of the later Arab rulers, including making the parliament a rubber stamp for his decisions. He directed most of his energies at building up Iran, including its armed forces, civil service, and transportation network. He extended central government control throughout the country, using harsh force where necessary to bring unruly tribes under his authority. He also embarked on a campaign of Westernization, developing Iranian legal and educational structures along Western models.

Reza Shah amassed a vast personal fortune through his control over land and other economic activity within the state. Iran also became an oil monarchy much like Saudi Arabia. The shah used all this wealth to co-opt various elites, building up a clientelistic system especially among the big landowning families that entrenched corruption in the government and ignored most of the population. Finally, in a country where religion had long been fused with political authority and was deeply ingrained in popular culture, the shah engaged in a strict policy of secularism. He undermined the independent authority of the ulama (Islamic scholars and jurists), though he was more successful in removing their influence from politics than from society. He banned traditional Islamic dress (veils for women and the fez for men), and the Western legal codes that he introduced took precedence over shariah, or Islamic law.

As a result of these activities, despite the rapid development that marked his years, the shah was disliked by much of the population. Thus he had little support when the British and Soviets moved against him in 1941. With the outbreak of World War II, the shah was required to engage in a delicate balancing act between Britain, the Soviet Union (the two powers that had occupied Iran during the First World War), and Germany. Despite Iran's official claim to neutrality, it appears that the shah was sympathetic to Germany, and there were many Germans working in Iran (some as covert operatives, according to the British). London and Moscow feared that Iran was moving to outright alliance with Germany, which would impede the Allied war effort. On August 16, 1941, they demanded that the shah expel the Germans. Still trying to balance out the Great Powers, the shah played for time. On August 25, the British and Soviets could wait no longer; they invaded, deposed the shah and put his son, Mohammed Reza, on the throne, and occupied the country until 1946.

The new shah lost much of the autocratic authority that his father had held. Occupation resulted in a strengthening of the Pahlavis' domestic opponents, including all those Reza Shah had suppressed (the tribes, the ulama, and the notable-dominated parliament). It was not until the later 1940s that the shah began to regain the control exercised by his father. But by the early 1950s he was constrained by a wave of popular mobilization directed against the Anglo-Iranian Oil Company (AIOC), a massive British-controlled firm that dominated Iran's oil industry. A growing sentiment in Iran demanded that the AIOC be nationalized, as a signal that Iran controlled its own actions without foreign interference and so that all of the profits from oil would go to Iran and not foreign companies.

The shah resisted, not least because of the restraints on his own authority this mobilization was generating. And because he was perceived as having allowed for this foreign domination, the movement's anger and the resultant demonstrations were also directed against him. Under the shah's direction, the government negotiated a new arrangement with the AIOC that was then sent to the parliament for approval. But because the new agreement left control of the oil industry in AIOC's hands, the nationalist parliament rejected it. The shah's prime minister tried to push it through, but he was assassinated. On March 20, 1951, parliament passed a law nationalizing the AIOC. On April 28, the assembly elected Mohammed Mossadegh prime minister. A leader of the nationalist opposition, Mossadegh focused his efforts on nationalization. The shah finally gave in, and on May 1 signed a law nationalizing the AIOC.

The results were swift and negative. The AIOC and Britain supported an oil embargo on Iran, eventually convincing the United States to go along with it. The Iranian economy faltered, causing widespread dissatisfaction among the populace. Protests soon broke out between supporters of the shah and supporters of Mossadegh. The government was paralyzed as the two antagonists undermined each other. Convinced that the turmoil would open the door to a communist takeover, and fearing that instability in Iran would spread throughout the region, the United States became involved in a plot to overthrow Mossadegh. On August 16, the shah dismissed Mossadegh, but the prime minister refused to leave his post. Demonstrations broke out again; they included Central Intelligence Agency–funded groups trying to bring Mossadegh down. On August 19, the shah's forces triumphed in the street battles, and Mossadegh was arrested.

This episode had two important consequences for Iran: First, it marked the beginning of sustained and increasingly close U.S. involvement in the country. Second, it convinced the shah that a strong, authoritarian, repressive government was necessary in order to stabilize Iran and continue its development.

This soon became supplemented with what can only be described as delusions of grandeur, as the shah began to lavish on himself the trappings of the old Persian emperors. In October 1971, for example, he commemorated 2,500 years of Persian monarchy with an extravagant celebration at the ancient city of Persepolis that reportedly cost about $100 million. This was at a time when parts of the country were experiencing the ravaging effects of a drought. Both factors were critical in leading to widespread discontent and even hatred of the shah and his regime. Foreign interference in Iran was a lightning rod for frustration with the government. And as the shah became increasingly autocratic and profligate, spending vast sums on dreams of opulence, he became disconnected from even those elites that originally supported him, including the military.

The Iranian Revolution

Although it is commonly thought that the Iranian Revolution of 1979 was an Islamic Revolution—that is, that it was initiated and led by Islamists—this is not in fact the case. The revolution essentially began in 1977 and took place over the next several years. The Islamists were only one of the groups that conducted the revolution: the shah's policy had alienated and angered a broad spectrum of Iranian society, most of whom participated in the demonstrations and strikes that brought down the regime. Moreover, the revolutionary years were also marked by a struggle between these groups over what would come after the shah's reign—including between moderate and fundamentalist Islamists. It was not until 1982 that the hard-line Islamists were able to seize complete control.

After triumphing over Mossadegh, the shah cracked down hard on those who had opposed him during the early 1950s and those who continued to criticize his regime. Arbitrary detention, torture, and murder became common occurrences as the shah unleashed on the population a newly created secret police, the Sazeman-e Ettela'at va Amniyyat-e Keshvar (Organization for Intelligence and National Security, or SAVAK). Independent political activity was banned, and politics was shaped and guided by the shah. Personal freedoms were limited.

The shah changed tack in the 1960s, combining repression and control of the government with a set of social and economic reforms he referred to as the White Revolution, to indicate that dramatic changes could take place without violence and blood (which would imply a "red" revolution). Land reform, expansion of health services and literacy, and development of the rural areas were the highlights of the White Revolution. But the reforms failed for two reasons: First, they simply were not implemented effectively, and in some cases actually worsened the conditions for Iranians. Many peasants, for example, did not receive enough of the redistributed land to engage even in subsistence farming. They were forced to move to the urban areas, contributing to the rise of slums and urban dissatisfaction. Second, the land reforms threatened the power of the old notables and the ulama, turning them into opponents of the regime. This was particularly important in the case of the ulama, who exercised great influence over the population because of their religious, moral, and spiritual standing. Underlying these failures was the widespread corruption of the elite, of the government, and of the shah himself—all of whom pilfered millions of dollars from the public purse for themselves and their families. A seething and growing anger came to mark the period of the second half of the 1960s and the 1970s.

In what would later prove to be a major factor in the shah's undoing, the religious establishment became one of the key opposition groups. Its hostility to the shah was the result of a number of factors, including a loss of economic power resulting from the White Revolution's land reform, the social and political reforms the shah promoted that undermined the ulama's control over education and offended their sensibilities and beliefs (such as raising the status of women and religious minorities), and the spread of Western influence on Iran, which was perceived as violating Iran's Islamic precepts and primacy in its own country. Most egregious was the shah's decision in 1976 to change the Iranian calendar from an Islamic one (dating from the migration of Muhammad from Mecca to Medina in 622) to a pre-Islamic Iranian one, dating from the imperial period of Cyrus the Great in the sixth century B.C.E.

Though some elements of the ulama did continue to support the shah, a small group of radicals began to actively preach against him and his policies, criticizing the regime on the above points. In 1963, Ayatollah Ruhollah Khomeini became the leader of this faction. He and his followers believed that Iranian society and politics should be guided by strict interpretations of Islam. Khomeini became vocal enough about his opposition that the regime began to perceive him as a serious threat. The shah had him arrested but, following three days of angry protest against the arrest, then released him. But Khomeini continued to agitate against the regime, and in October 1964 he was exiled from the country.

Khomeini continued to circulate his ideas, and in 1970 published a book of his lectures and sermons titled *Velayat-e faghih* (Guardianship of the Jurisprudent). In it he outlined his ideas for a true Islamic government, which included an end to the Iranian monarchy. This system called for a "guardian" as leader of the state, a cleric steeped in Islamic jurisprudence who would guide the implementation of Islamic principles in polity and society. The idea was later incorporated into the Iranian constitution when the Islamists took power.

The shah's legitimacy problems continued. His foreign policies (close alliance with the United States and a working relationship with Israel) and his domestic policies (suppression of political and civil rights and Islam, as well as corruption) had alienated most segments of Iranian society. His purchase of Western arms and the major development projects that he proposed led to an influx of Western technicians, experts, and advisors—about 60,000 of them by 1977—that caused resentment among Iranians, especially Islamists.

His economic policies undercut the *bazaaris* (merchants of the bazaars), and the severe economic problems that struck Iran in the mid-1970s further angered this class. Unemployment and inflation became rampant, and were blamed on the shah's mismanagement of the economy and his continuing diversion of resources to finance his and the top elite's expensive style of living. His shift to a one-party state with the creation of the Resurgence Party in 1975 did not, as the shah had hoped, lead to greater control over political activity but only increased the bitterness of Iranians. Finally, to make matters worse, Jimmy Carter became president of the United States in January 1977. With his concern over human rights paramount in the beginning of his presidency, Carter immediately began to put pressure on the shah to liberalize his regime.

Despite some last-minute efforts on the part of the shah in the late 1970s to reverse many of his most offensive policies (including changing the calendar back to an Islamic one, closing down the Resurgence Party, and avoiding the use of harsh force to quell disturbances), it was too late. Virtually all of Iranian society was estranged by now, and short of engaging in a wholesale change of the regime himself there was no longer anything the shah could do to satisfy his citizens.

Protests began in the spring of 1977. These were primarily liberal in character, composed at first of middle-class intellectuals and professionals who were later followed by university students (many with leftist ideals) and some bazaaris (who were close to the ulama). The intellectuals and professionals who dominated the opposition that year based their demands for change on the language of human rights and were emboldened by the fact that the shah's closest ally, the United States, was pushing a similar agenda. The leader of this movement, Mehdi Bazargan, advocated a constitutional monarchy that left the shah in place but bound him by a series of democratic procedures such as elected parliaments, and that included a major role for Islam in Iranian society.

These protestors coalesced into the National Front. Bazargan had some support among moderate Islamists, but was soon competing with the radicals among the Islamists, whom Khomeini continued to inspire from his exile in Iraq and then, after 1978, in France through tapes smuggled into the country. Khomeini's group soon garnered the support of much of the populace because of its staunch opposition to the shah (Khomeini demanded the abolishment of the monarchy), the credibility of its leader (who had never compromised and worked with the regime), and its focus on social justice. This was tied together by the religious-spiritual appeal of Islam.

In January 1978, the character of the protests shifted. From a liberal alternative they took on a more populist Islamic tone, as the ulama became more involved and, among them, the radicals began to assert themselves more forcefully. That month, in an effort to blunt the force of the opposition, the regime printed in *Ettela'at*, one of Iran's major newspapers, an article that denounced Khomeini as a British agent, questioned his Islamic credentials, and referred to a "dubious past." Religious leaders and students were scandalized and outraged, and at the holy city of Qom protests were violently broken up by security forces, leaving seventy people dead.

The protestors, following Islamic customs, took forty days to mourn those killed by the regime. After that, on February 18, more demonstrations erupted; in Tabriz they became violent and the shah's security forces killed another hundred people. The cycle was repeated on March 29 and May 10. The shah tried to stem the dissent by appointing a new prime minister and making a number of economic reforms. These only made matters worse, especially for the urban workers, who now joined the demonstrations.

In the fall of 1978, the shah declared martial law and forbade protests. But on September 8, in the capital city of Tehran, unarmed protestors continued their activities. In response, the shah unleashed the military, and helicopter gunships and tanks were brought in. Hundreds died on what became known as Black Friday. The shah's harsh repression put the liberals on the defensive, forcing them to endorse Khomeini's position that the monarchy be completely eradicated and depriving them of much independent authority among the protestors.

The economic problems brought out the workers and the bazaaris, who beginning in October led a series of strikes that shut down the economy. The shah did not know how to respond. Already known for his indecisiveness, the shah was by now terminally ill with cancer, and, it was reported, the drugs he was taking to alleviate his pain dulled his capacity for lucid thought. He turned to the last bastion of his regime, the military and security forces. On December 2, again defying a government ban, hundreds of thousands of demonstrators converged in Tehran. The military responded with force, killing an estimated 700 civilians.

The protests did not slacken, and on December 12 some two million people marched through Tehran. At this point, the military abandoned the shah. Tired of protecting a regime many of them did not believe in (much like the Egyptian military in King Farouk's time and in the Mubarak regime in 2011), they did not want to kill unarmed shopkeepers, students, craftsmen, workers, and peasants. They deserted, and it was reported that some fired on their commanding officers.

In a last act of desperation, the shah appointed as prime minister a member of the National Front known for his moderation, Shapour Bakhtiar. Though Khomeini denounced him for serving under the shah, Bakhtiar insisted that Mohammed Reza leave Iran—which he did on January 16, 1979. Thus, 2,500 years of monarchy in Iran came to an end. The revolution and the later establishment of theocratic government marked a new era in Iranian history and governance.

On February 1, Khomeini returned to Iran, where he was greeted at the airport by millions of euphoric supporters whose adulation verged on hero worship and who followed his procession through Tehran. He immediately had Bakhtiar removed (the regime would assassinate him in Paris many years later). The removal of Bakhtiar was the beginning of Khomeini's efforts to seize total control.

The New Constitution

It seems that Khomeini, who had by the end of 1978 become the leader of the revolution, never intended to share power with liberals, leftists, or even moderate Islamists. It also seems that at first he preferred a minimal government that would only implement shariah. But his supporters (mainly former students) wanted a more active government, one dominated by the clerics, and Khomeini eventually fell in with them.

Because the revolution had been the work of virtually all segments of Iranian society, there were several groups jostling for power in government in early 1979. In addition to the hard-line Islamists, there were more liberal Islamists, communists and Marxists, and secular nationalists. The hard-liners therefore worked to ease the other groups out of power. They did this primarily in two ways: first, by dominating all of the new institutions of the state, and second, by crafting a constitution that vested all decision-making power in them.

Under Khomeini's direction, Iranians participated in a simple referendum in March 1979 on whether or not to replace the monarchy with an Islamic republic. Ninety-eight percent voted in favor of the Islamic republic, but it was not clear what exactly such an entity would look like. In June, the liberal-dominated government drafted a constitution that was quite democratic in scope. There was no supreme leader, and the clerics' role was limited to a consultative council.

The draft was submitted to an elected Assembly of Experts, a body dominated by clerics. The assembly completely rewrote the constitution, removing virtually of the democratic elements in it and vesting all power in the ulama. It provided for a *velayat-e faghih* as the supreme leader who was answerable only to God (Khomeini was later made supreme leader for life). All laws had to be based on Islam. Though the constitution created a popularly elected presidency and parliament, they were subject to the Council of Guardians, which was to ensure that all laws and decisions were in line with Islamic principles and regulations. In December, the constitution was submitted to a national referendum and passed.

Elements of the Regime

The contemporary theocratic regime is made up not just of ulama, but also other agencies and groups that benefit from the ulama's domination. They all work together to ensure the continuation of the regime and suppress any challenge that might unravel it. In addition to the ulama, this includes the coercive agencies (such as the military), the *bonyad*s (charitable foundations), and the bazaaris.

The Ulama

The Iranian regime is run by ulama. These Islamic scholars supervise all laws, policies, and decisions so that they remain in line with their interpretation of Islamic principles. They also ensure that the Islamic Revolution remains actively in place; anything that is seen to be undercutting it is considered to be a threat. Their power is enshrined in the constitution: many of the institutions of government, such as the Supreme Leader, the Assembly of Experts, and the Council of Guardians, are their special purview.

The ulama are often considered to be a monolithic group, sharing the same goals and ideas. They do in fact all share a commitment to a stricter form of Islam and to the Islamic Revolution—that is, to maintaining a theocratic Iran. But there are various factions that, despite this shared ultimate objective, differ on the methods of achieving it and disagree on the degree of intensity with which the Revolution needs to be forced onto the people in Iran, as well as on the divisions of power within the government.

Author Nikki Keddie divides the ulama into three broad categories: the Islamic left, which calls for more socialist and populist measures; the Islamic right (or conservatives), who are staunchly opposed to any reduction in clerical authority but also advocate for some private property rights; and the pragmatists, who are willing to engage in political and social change in order to strengthen Iran after years of destabilizing revolution and war. After 1997 some observers have added a fourth category: the reformists, who believe that some of Iran's social and political restrictions should be lifted in order to reinvigorate a belief in the revolution among the population, and whose focus on human rights essentially means a reduction in the all-encompassing nature of Islamic law. In addition, there are what might be called "independent" ulama, who argue that religious authority should be reduced, particularly that of the supreme leader.

These groups often clashed with each other. After 1997, Iranian politics was dominated by a struggle between the reformists and the conservatives. But none of these groups is interested in the complete removal of the ulama from power; their presence, they all believe, is necessary to maintain a true Islamic state.

Military and Coercive Agencies

Although the ulama criticized the shah for his heavy-handed physical repression, they have followed a similar policy. In addition to the regular military, the ulama have at their disposal several paramilitary and intelligence agencies that are used to protect the regime and promote the revolution. The military's job is to protect the country and, if needed, deal with any major internal rebellions. But the purpose of the other coercive agencies is focused solely on internal security.

The most important is the Pasdaran (Islamic Revolutionary Guards Corps). It is a parallel body to the regular military, with its own army, navy, air force, intelligence capabilities, and special forces. It was also given responsibility for Iran's missile program. Khomeini established the Pasdaran in May 1979 because he associated the regular military with the shah's regime and therefore distrusted and feared it.

The Pasdaran functions as both an arm of the regime and as its protector, to stand between it and the military. Its loyalty is to the supreme leader, who is its commander in chief. It is an ideological force, indoctrinated with revolutionary and Islamic ideals, though there have been reports that it widely supported the election of reformist president Mohammad Khatami in 1997. As such, it has participated in attacks on reformist, independent, and liberal newspapers, individuals, and political movements, which it perceives as a threat to the regime. Given that it was created as a tool of the regime, it has played an important role in the export of the revolution. The Pasdaran have trained and advise Hezbollah in Lebanon, and have been linked to other violent acts around the world, particularly in Europe and South America.

The Basij make up a third force. Estimated to have 9 or 10 million members, the Basij is considered to be a branch of the Pasdaran. It began as a supplementary military force during the Iran-Iraq War (1980–1988). The Basij were known for their "human wave" tactics, in which they charged headlong in great numbers over minefields and straight into the gunsights of the Iraqi soldiers. Since the end of the war, the Basij have shifted to domestic activities, in particular enforcing Islamic laws and mores. In the later 1990s and 2000s they were used by the hardline clerics to attack student protestors and media critical of the regime. Their power is centered in the mosques, from which they recruit Iranians of all ages, including youth under eighteen.

Supplementing the Basij is Ansar-e Hezbollah (Helpers of the Party of God). This body is a thuggish vigilante group absolutely dedicated to the Islamic Revolution. They are known for attacking bars and other supposed symbols of Western influence. They have often clashed with students protesting against the regime, using clubs and other weapons to beat the demonstrators.

The Ministry of Intelligence and Security and the Law Enforcement Forces are the other two main coercive agencies. Little is known about them except that they are also loyal to the regime and work to prevent any domestic challenge to it. Finally, the regime created the Political-Ideological Directorate to keep watch on all of the security forces and prevent the coalescence of opposition within them. Typical of all authoritarian regimes, the Iranian regime has needed several coercive agencies to protect itself, even while it fears the power of these agencies. The directorate tries to manage these fears by ensuring keeping these bodies separate, indoctrinated, and under close guard.

Bonyads

When the shah was in power he established a series of economic enterprises that were designed primarily to serve as vehicles for personal wealth generation. With his overthrow, the Islamic regime built on these enterprises to create the *bonyads*, charitable foundations that were used to provide income to the poor and to the families of those who had died in the war with Iraq. They soon became major players in the Iranian economy: according to most estimates, they control about 20 percent of the economy—or even more if the oil sector is excluded.

These large economic foundations control hundreds of smaller firms and industries. The Foundation of the Oppressed, for example, runs about 1,200 companies ranging from amusement parks to housing. They are exempt from taxes and do not pay tariffs on imported foreign goods, giving them a major advantage over private and even other state enterprises. Like the shah before it, the theocratic regime uses the foundations to generate income for its own activities. The bonyads are answerable to the supreme leader only, who channels their income to the Pasdaran and other agencies under his command. The directors of the bonyads are also close and loyal allies of the hard-line ulama more generally. Given their purpose, they have become inefficient entities, wracked with corruption and mismanagement. Most of them are no longer even economically viable; that is, they do not make a profit. Yet because they are considered a tool of the ulama, they remain in place and unchanged.

Bazaaris

The *bazaaris* are a class of economic actors that includes small shopkeepers, craftsmen, retailers, and other similar businesspeople operating in urban centers and in a primarily middle-class setting. They have long been key supporters of the ulama; even under the shah the bazaaris and ulama were closely linked through shared conservative principles, distrust of Westernization, and social ties (especially marriages between the two groups). The bazaaris were critical in undermining the shah in 1978 through paralyzing strikes, which were effective given the weight of their commercial activity in the economy at the time.

They thus formed a key support group for the hard-line ulama in the years immediately following the revolution. But beginning in the 1990s their power has been diluted. Industrialization and economic reform have shifted resources and political power, and university students combined with the popular paramilitary gangs have become a more important element of support for the regime at the expense of the merchants. They are still important for the regime, not least because of historical links, but they increasingly matter less for the regime's ability to exert control.

Organs of Governments

The ulama built a system of governance to maintain themselves in power and facilitate the spread, entrenchment, and enforcement of their hard-line interpretation of Islam. The fundamentalists remain in firm control of Iran, buttressed by hard-line nationalists who are not part of the religious establishment but share its conservative views. The organs of government that they created diffused authority throughout these different agencies and bodies. In addition, intra-elite disputes (based on the above-mentioned categories of ulama as well as other influential bodies and institutions that benefit from keeping the regime in power) have made compromise in governing a necessity.

This has led to a situation in which no one person has ultimate control over government decisions; instead, decisions tend to be made either collectively or through bargaining between various groups. The constitution established all of these bodies, which has made it difficult to shift the weight of their power around. Yet the ulama have always dominated all of these institutions except the presidency and the parliament (though in 2007 they did control the parliament, and the president's office was occupied by a nationalist allied to their cause), and there is no indication that their grip on power is slipping.

Supreme Leader

The *faghih* (the supreme leader or guide who governs under the concept of *velayat-e faghih*) is the ultimate decision maker in the Iranian system of governance. The purpose of the supreme leader is to ensure that government is based properly on Islam, as understood by learned Shi'ite scholars and clerics. The faghih is supposed to be well versed in Islamic law so that he can make the appropriate judgments. As such, he is meant to interpret and implement Islamic law and, in more mundane terms, act as a coordinator or link between the three branches of government (executive, legislature, judiciary). He is elected by the Assembly of Experts, who base their choice on the above criteria. But the Iranian constitution also endows the supreme leader with immense temporal power as well. Khomeini himself was made supreme leader for life at the end of 1979.

The faghih is accountable only to God, so that his rulings cannot be questioned. He controls both the military and the Pasdaran. He can dismiss the elected president, and he appoints the head of the judiciary. In short, his powers give him control over Iranian politics should he choose to exercise it. In the clash between reformists and conservatives after 1997, Khomeini's successor as supreme leader, Ali Khamenei, often overruled the reformist president and parliament's decisions.

Despite these powers it would be a mistake to call the Iranian regime a dictatorship. Even under Khomeini, who died in 1989, power was diffused not only among a variety of government institutions but also through a serious difference of opinion among the ulama themselves. Many respected ulama did not approve of the absolute powers exercised by the supreme leader, forcing Khomeini to shift the emphasis of the faghih to temporal rather than religious authority.

But especially under Khamenei, the supreme leader has not been able to exercise absolute authority. Because he lacks the stature of Khomeini, Khamenei has been considered more often than not a first among equals. Because he shares a fundamentalist interpretation of Islam with many of the other hard-liners in government, there have not been any open disagreements over policy. This could change depending on who is next elected supreme leader, but it is difficult to imagine that the Assembly of Experts would choose someone who does not follow their conservative interpretation.

Assembly of Experts

Different from the elected assembly formed to draw up the Iranian constitution, this eighty-six-member body theoretically has great power in guiding the government and its decisions. Elected every eight years, candidates to the Assembly of Experts are vetted by the Council of Guardians. The assembly then selects the supreme leader and supervises his activities and rulings to make sure they are in line with Islamic laws and principles. Because of this, members of the assembly must be well versed in Islamic jurisprudence. This requirement means that only ulama can be elected to the assembly. Since the assembly chooses the supreme leader, this body helps ensure clerical dominance. Otherwise, the assembly is not involved in the daily operations of government, and much of what it does when there is no supreme leader to elect is vague and ambiguous.

Council of Guardians

Aside from the supreme leader himself, the Council of Guardians wields considerable power in Iranian politics and can exert control over virtually the entire process of governmental decision making. It combines the powers of an upper-house parliament, constitutional court, and electoral commission. Its primary purpose is to ensure that all laws are in line with Islamic principles and the Iranian constitution. Made up of only 12 members, it has powers greater than the elected president and 290-seat parliament.

The council is not popularly elected. Of its twelve members, six are chosen directly by the supreme leader himself. The other six are Islamic lawyers selected by the parliament from a list provided by the head of the judiciary—himself appointed by the faghih. Thus the Council of Guardians acts as one of the main institutional levers of control of the hard-line ulama.

The council reviews all legislation passed by the parliament to make sure that it conforms with Islamic guidelines and laws as well as with the Iranian constitution. Only the ulama on the council can determine whether the laws are compatible with Islam. If a bill does not meet with the council's approval, it is sent back to parliament for revision.

In addition, the council vets all candidates running for president and parliament. In this way, it can control to a great degree whom the public elects to these positions. In the 2004 parliamentary elections, for example, as part of the conservative backlash against the reformist tide that had swept Iranian politics beginning in 1997, the council barred 2,400 candidates from competing on the grounds that they were a danger to the state and to Islam.

Expediency Discernment Council

The constitution provides for the creation of an Expediency Council by the supreme leader in case of disagreement between the parliament and the Council of Guardians. In February 1988, after a series of unresolved disputes between these two bodies, Khomeini established the Expediency Council and charged it with resolving these differences. Made up of representatives from all branches of government, its purpose since then has been to mediate between the two institutions.

In February 2007, a new council was put together with twenty-seven members directly chosen by the supreme leader. The council can also advise the faghih on policy matters. In addition, although it cannot initiate legislation, it can remove some powers from the parliament. In April 2000, for example, it removed from parliament's purview the capacity to investigate any institution directly under control of the supreme leader—including the Pasdaran and the Council of Guardians. Since it is dominated by conservative ulama, this has only served to further entrench their control over decision making.

Presidency

Both the president and the parliament are democratically elected. But they are hemmed in by a series of restrictions placed on them by the unelected ulama, who through the Council of Guardians also have the power to veto candidates. According to the constitution, the president of Iran is the head of government and is the highest authority in the country after the faghih. With the abolishment of the post of prime minister in April 1989, he has theoretically gained more control. He heads the cabinet and sends bills to the parliament for approval, and conducts the regular administrative business of government—such as the appointment of ambassadors, making economic policy, and so on. Since the second half of the 1990s he has also become, by default, the public face of the Iranian regime.

Because he is elected by popular vote, the president's mandate flows from the people. But in a theocratic regime like Iran's, this kind of power is negligible. Governing power stems not from the population but from God (Allah) and from Islam. This has constrained the president in both theoretical and in practical terms, serving to either undermine his authority or force him to comply with the parameters set out by the ulama in the upper bodies of the state. This is not to say that the president does not have influence or any capacity for independent policymaking. He does, but at the same time he is hampered by the welter of government bodies and agencies that also participate in governmental decision making, thus diluting his authority and, since these other bodies are dominated by harder-line ulama, shaping decisions and laws to their preferences.

Parliament

The 290-seat Majlis-e Shura-ye Eslami (Islamic Consultative Assembly) is elected by popular vote. However, its powers are considerably diminished by the existence of the ulama-dominated bodies described above. The Majlis has functioned primarily as a spirited arena for debate and discussion, particularly on social and economic matters. At some points in the past, particularly in the mid- to late 1980s, it did try to exert its legislative power. But it is hampered by the Council of Guardians, which reviews and can veto any legislative agenda the Majlis puts forward. When the reformists swept the parliament in the 2000 elections, their efforts to liberalize the political systems were met with staunch opposition by the fundamentalist Council of Guardians, Assembly of Experts, and Expediency Council, as well as the supreme leader himself. The Majlis's only real power comes from its capacity to confirm or reject presidential nominations for cabinet.

The Reformist Wave and the Conservative Backlash

Beginning with the presidential elections in 1997, Iran experienced a wave of popular demands for change that were reflected in the elections for president and parliament over the next several years. This was the result of two main factors: First, the Iranian population is growing at a rapid rate, and it is especially young—between two-thirds and three-fourths of the population is under thirty. This means that a major proportion of the populace does not remember or was not even born at the time of revolution; its fervor, slogans, and even purpose mean little to this segment of the population. They thus do not see the need for the overbearing nature of clerical government.

Second, Iranians (not only from the under-thirty demographic) have tired of Iran's isolation in the international system, its economic problems, and the suppression of individual freedoms. They believe that the harsh, uncompromising rule of the ulama has prevented Iran from achieving its potential as a great regional power. This widespread dissatisfaction came to a head during the presidential elections on May 23, 1997.

On that day, Mohammad Khatami was elected president with almost 70 percent of the vote. Khatami campaigned on easing some of the political and personal restrictions on society, strengthening the rule of law and expanding civil society, and engaging in a less hostile foreign policy (including with the United States). He forged an alliance with groups dissatisfied with the repressive tactics practiced by the regime, including students, women, residents of Tehran, intellectuals, and youth in general. He also had the support of Islamic liberals, who did not approve of the direct clerical participation in government or the absolute authority exercised by the supreme leader and the Council of Guardians. After his election some supporters formed the Second of Khordad Front (deriving its name from the Iranian date of Khatami's first election) to act as the vehicle for election campaign and political and social reforms.

Khatami was able to meet some of his campaign promises, particularly by lifting restriction on the media, but he was far more successful in foreign policy than in domestic policy. The hard-liners, perceiving a threat to their position, responded almost immediately. In April 1998, Tehran's popular reformist mayor, Gholamhossein Karbaschi, an ally of Khatami, was arrested and removed from office. Similar arrests of cabinet members followed. Student demonstrations in favor of Khatami were broken up by vigilante gangs (Basij, Ansar-e Hezbollah) who were either directly supported by the security forces or allowed to do their work without interference. These groups also raided the independent and critical newspapers and press that Khatami's government had licensed, most of which were eventually closed down. Leading critics of the regime and intellectuals were assassinated.

Still, Khatami was perceived as the vanguard of a reformist wave that would change Iran's governing system. This perception was supported by the February–May 2000 parliamentary elections, in which reformist candidates won about 70 percent of seats in the Majlis. But as with the 1997 presidential elections, the hard-liners struck back almost immediately. Reformists (including students, journalists, politicians, and even some ulama) were arrested, many were beaten, and the Council of Guardians rejected several bills put forward by the Majlis.

The conservative backlash was so heavy that Khatami himself was undecided about running for president again, publicly musing about his lack of power. In the end he decided to run, winning on June 8, 2001, about 78 percent of the vote—more than in the previous election. As in his first term, he was unable to pass many of the reforms he had campaigned on. His major successes came in reducing Iran's international isolation and repairing ties with Europe and some Arab states, particularly Saudi Arabia.

Khatami's reformist movement led to some changes in Iran. Civil liberties have expanded somewhat, though those who utilize them are still subject to harassment and physical violence. The strict observance of conservative Islamic laws regarding social behavior has not been enforced so much since 1997. And an independent (if somewhat curtailed) press continues to exist, despite being under constant regime surveillance.

But overall the reform movement has been a major disappointment to Iranians who supported it. This has led to large-scale desertion of the reformists. This was reflected in the February–May 2004 parliamentary elections, in which thousands of reformist candidates were banned by the Council of Guardians. Turnout was low, at about 51 percent, and conservatives and hard-liners won handily. In the June 2005 presidential elections, a hard-line nationalist won with over 60 percent of vote. Though not a cleric, Mahmoud Ahmadinejad has much support among the Basij and Pasdaran—both of which are close to the fundamentalist ulama and Supreme Leader Khameini himself. This combination of presidential and parliamentary elections has effectively erased any gains the reformists made, giving the regime a relatively one-sided viewpoint from which to make all policy decisions—an outcome not seen since Khomeini's time.

The reform movement failed for two reasons. First, Khatami himself was not interested in overhauling the system. He still believed in the Islamic Revolution and that Islam should remain the guiding framework for Iran. Thus, despite his commitment to easing restrictions, he was not willing to openly challenge the hard-liners. And second, so long as the hard-liners retain control of the most important institutions of the state—the post of supreme leader, the Council of Guardians, the security forces—no president or parliament can ever implement any changes that these bodies do not approve of, despite the level of popular support.

The different preferences between reformers and hard-liners came to the fore again in the June 2009 presidential elections. Ahmadinejad ran for a second term, representing the hard-liner ulama and nationalists. The Council of Guardians approved three other candidates, while rejecting over 400 others. Mir-Hossein Mousavi, a former prime minister, represented for many the reformists and dissenters, and those who in general wanted to see an end to the restrictive policies and laws of the regime. (Khatami later endorsed Mousavi.)

The election was conducted under imbalanced conditions. Mousavi's campaign and his supporters were routinely harassed: campaign offices were burned down, communications were shut down on several occasions, and the results of the election itself were—to many Iranian and outside observers—flagrantly falsified. Some polling stations apparently returned results of over 100 percent turnout. Ahmadinejad received 63 percent of the final tally, while Mousavi took 34 percent (two other candidates received less than 2 percent and 1 percent respectively).

Almost immediately after the election, protests broke out against what were widely perceived as rigged results. At first the demonstrations were peaceful, but they became increasingly more violent: shops and other buildings were damaged, and tires were burned in some streets in Tehran. Although he rejected violent protests, Mousavi did call for civil unrest, and soon crowds of several hundred thousand (by some reports over a million) began to meet regularly in Tehran, despite warnings from the government that such activities were illegal and would be dealt with harshly.

The election took place on June 12; by June 13 the government had begun arresting protestors, including opposition leaders, student leaders, and human rights activists who were accused of being foreign agents and undermining the Iranian government. In a June 26 sermon, the Supreme Leader Khameini was reported to have called for violence and death of those who protested "the Islamic society" and "God." Government crackdowns were accompanied by accusations that the dissenters were working under the control or manipulation of foreign enemies, such as the "Zionists" and the British. Government security forces' violent attacks on protestors soon took the lives of tens of demonstrators. Some of the killings were videotaped and uploaded to the Internet, and viewers around the world watched and then condemned the Iranian regime for its intolerance and viciousness. Those who were arrested were reportedly tortured.

Intermittent protests continued to take place throughout 2009 and 2010, while the government continued to react violently. Some have hailed these developments as the beginning of the end of the Islamic Revolution, or as the beginning of a new era of freedom in Iran. There is no sign that the regime is prepared to loosen its grip on power, but it remains to be seen whether the protests and the widespread support they enjoyed are an interim event in the continuation of Iranian theocracy, or whether they do represent a genuine change.

References and Further Reading

Arjomand, Said Amir. *After Khomeini: Iran Under His Successors.* Oxford: Oxford University Press, 2009.

———. *The Turban for the Crown: The Islamic Revolution in Iran.* New York: Oxford University Press, 1988.

Keddie, Nikki R. *Modern Iran: Roots and Results of Revolution.* Rev. ed. New Haven, CT: Yale University Press, 2003.

Rajaee, Farhang. *Islamism and Modernism: The Changing Discourse in Iran.* Austin: University of Texas Press, 2007.

Ramazani, R.K. *Revolutionary Iran: Challenge and Response in the Middle East.* Baltimore, MD: Johns Hopkins University Press, 1986.

Israel

Like Iran, Israel, too, is unique in the Middle East. First, it is the only Jewish state in the world. Second, it is a true liberal democracy, the only country in the Middle East ranked "free" by Freedom House. Though there are problems with the social and economic aspects of its democracy (particularly regarding the Arab population), it does not utilize repression as a tool of governance; in fact, it might be characterized as a hyper-democracy, with dozens of parties running in national elections, including Arab parties. (As a result of the February 2009 elections, there are twelve parties in the parliament.) Otherwise, it operates much like any Western parliamentary democracy: there is a head of state (the president), a head of government (the prime minister), and a parliament (the unicameral, 120-seat Knesset).

Israeli politics is known for its fractious, boisterous nature, and contemporary politics have become increasingly so. Until the 1990s this was kept under control by the dominance of the Labor Party (until 1977), followed by a brief moment of Likud primacy (1977–1984), and then for most of the 1980s a collaborative effort by both parties. But in the 1990s, Israeli politics became increasingly fragmented as smaller parties began to erode the electoral strength of the two major parties (left-wing Labor and right-wing Likud). In many ways this has inhibited effective policymaking, since Labor and Likud have been unable to put together consecutive governments and thus ensure policy continuity.

Three factors are particularly relevant in explaining the fragmented nature of contemporary governing in Israel: One, the presence of multiple political parties and movements in the Yishuv (the Jewish community in pre-state Palestine) entrenched a multipartyism that since the 1990s has caused instability in coalition government. Two, the inclusion of orthodox parties and religious-Zionist parties in the governing institutions of the state has prevented the creation of a formal constitution and, particularly in the 1980s and 1990s, given the religious parties' (especially the non-Zionists) disproportionate influence in all of Israel's coalition governments. And three, the capture of the West Bank and Gaza Strip in the 1967 Arab-Israeli War shattered the consensus in Israeli society about the proper borders of the country and its relationship to these areas, and led to intense political and policy differences among the major parties. Combined with external pressures (particularly terrorist attacks by radical Palestinian groups on Israeli citizens), this has pushed Israelis to switch their votes from one major party to the next in electoral succession, disrupting the flow of policymaking.

Some observers might add a fourth factor, namely the existence of a large Arab minority (approximately 20 percent) living among the Jewish population. But this is not relevant for the discussion here, since the issues that flow from it do not have an impact on the functioning of Israel's system of governance. It will therefore not be discussed. Others might mention a possible fifth factor: the external threat Israel has faced from regular and irregular Arab armies since its establishment. This has certainly had an impact on the style of governing in Israel—it has, for instance, contributed to a centralization of decision making in foreign and security policy in the prime minister's office. This has led to some inefficiency in governing, but no democracy is completely free of inefficiency. Our discussion is concerned with the main factors that shape and affect Israel's governance system and its policymaking on domestic affairs. As such, it must necessarily leave out any discussion of Israel's security situation (though mention will be made of it where relevant).

The Development of Hyper-Democracy

Israeli politics is pluralistic to the extreme. The electoral system is based on proportional representation in which the entire country functions as a single district and citizens vote for a set party list or list of parties rather than individual candidates. Given this, it has not been uncommon for dozens of parties to compete in general elections, or for over a dozen to make it past the minimum threshold (now 2 percent) necessary for representation in the Knesset. The result has been that no party has ever won a majority of seats (sixty-one) in the Israeli parliament. This pluralism has been historically conditioned by two factors: the international Zionist movement, represented by the World Zionist Organization (WZO), and the existence of several competing Zionist groups that came to Palestine at the end of the nineteenth and beginning of the twentieth centuries.

Israeli institutions have been shaped by the Zionist experience. Zionism is the Jewish national movement that called for a return of the Jews to "Zion"—another name for Jerusalem but taken to refer to what is today Israel (and, for some groups, also Jordan, the West Bank, and the Gaza Strip).

Zionism's commitment to democratic norms was applied for the most practical of reasons. In 1897, the World Zionist Organization was created as an international instrument through which the Zionist movement could coordinate the promotion of its agenda on the world stage. Its membership came from a variety of countries across Europe and Russia, with members usually already formed into specific parties and groups. Each had its own sets and subsets of ideologies and ideas, visions of what Zionism meant for the Jewish people, and concerns reflecting particular national and regional circumstances. It was decided that in order to mobilize and maintain the inclusion of these diverse groups, and to give the WZO as much legitimacy as possible, proportional representation was the most appropriate means of electing delegates to the organization.

The plurality of ideologies and parties represented in the WZO was imitated and expanded on in the Yishuv. During the period from 1882 to 1939, sustained Jewish immigration into Palestine (which was first under the control of the Ottoman Empire and then, after World War I, the British) took place in a series of five waves of *aliyot* (literally, "going up"). For the most part, these new immigrants were politically conscious individuals and groups motivated by the Zionist program of establishing a Jewish homeland in the ancient kingdoms of the Jewish people. Many of these groups had opposing visions of Zionism, including labor/socialist Zionists (themselves divided into strict Marxists and those who advocated a milder form of socialism), right-wing nationalist Zionists, and religious Zionists, among others.

Each group saw itself as having its own individual identity, structure, constituency, and ideas about what a Jewish state should look like. Most of them formed political parties to compete in national and local community elections, but these parties were more like broad movements given their wide-ranging and comprehensive nature. They formed their own autonomous structures, including sports and leisure clubs, youth movements, education systems, and cultural associations. They were well organized, usually with a strict hierarchy that was governed by a party elite and supported by an efficient bureaucracy. In short, as David Horowitz and Moshe Lissak noted in *Origins of the Israeli Polity: Palestine Under the Mandate* (1978), they acted as a series of subcenters operating independently in the larger context of Jewish life in Palestine.

These parties/movements were not willing to give up their independence, not least because this would hamper their ability to pursue their particular vision of Zionism. But they were willing to work together to some degree in community-wide institutions, most of which were formed by the labor Zionists. If they would not completely give up their autonomy, at least they would compromise in decision making for the betterment of the community as a whole.

Most political parties and movements did recognize that inclusion and compromise would benefit them—though some groups chose to remain outside the official community structures, such as the non-Zionist *haredi* (ultra-Orthodox) Agudat Israel and the Communists. Participation gave all groups a chance to be represented at the table and share in the authority that came with elections and other federative arrangements, and to direct the allocation of resources, which ran from the WZO through the national center to their own members. With the creation of Israel in 1948, these bodies were carried over and became state institutions.

Labor Zionism's Creation of Community Institutions

The willingness to compromise was important in that it led to the inculcation of democratic processes among the various parties and was used to govern Israeli politics once the state was established. But the establishment of Israeli governing institutions was the direct result of the efforts of the socialist Zionist movement, which actively worked to create effective structures of governance that at the same time entrenched its own control in these structures. Its control of the Jewish community's political and economic institutions facilitated Israeli democracy through a system of patronage and trade-offs: as the dominant parties in the Jewish community, the socialist Zionists always had a plurality, though not a majority, in the Yishuv's governing structures. They thus maintained their power through the participation of nonsocialist parties that cooperated with them. In return, the nonsocialist parties obtained legitimacy and a share of the political and economic resources that the official structures of the Yishuv could provide them, which in turn could be passed on to their supporters.

The supremacy of the labor movement began near the beginning of Yishuv politics. The onset of sustained and organized Jewish immigration into Palestine in the 1880s brought future socialist leaders to the area (mainly from Russia), particularly during the Second Aliyah (1904–1914). They came with revolutionary ideas about a strong, independent Jewish community with an underlying Jewish working and especially agricultural class that would reclaim its biblical and historical heritage and reestablish a Jewish political entity in Zion. The collectivist-nationalist ideals inherent in their value structures, drawn from the Russian political culture in which they were steeped, enhanced their domination, instilling in the Jews a sense of national commitment and willingness to work under the socialist leadership for ultimate Zionist goals.

To both these ends the workers of the Second Aliyah became the first group in the Yishuv to set up their own political parties and the political institutions that came to govern the Jewish community and later carried over into the state. These consisted of an elected parliament, the Asefet Hanivcharim (National Assembly), and an executive, the Va'ad Leumi (National Council). Twenty different parties competed for seats in the first elections to the National Assembly, in 1920.

The socialist movement also came to control the Yishuv's economic structures. In 1920, two labor parties set up the Histadrut (the General Federation of Hebrew Workers in the Land of Israel). A giant labor federation designed to meet the needs of the independent Jewish economy in Palestine, it also became a primary patronage instrument, as it allocated a wide range of resources and services on the basis of labor priorities.

Socialist Zionists recognized that this willingness to participate in Labor-dominated institutions could only be encouraged by democratic norms of governance—proportional representation, compromise, majority rule, and coalitions—since it gave all groups a chance to both increase their piece of the political and economic pie, and to join the governing coalition. This prompted the labor Zionists to give up some measure of absolute control in return for the legitimacy that accrued to them by widespread participation in the institutions they set up and continued to manage and control.

Effects of Hyper-Democracy on Israeli Politics

The entrenchment of a multiparty system dominated by the labor movement in Yishuv institutions was simply transferred to the State of Israel after its establishment in 1948. Every election in Israel has resulted in ten to fifteen parties being represented in the Knesset. For most of Israel's existence, however, this did not translate into coalition instability; in fact, from 1948 to 1988 Israeli governments were remarkably stable. This was the result in particular of the Labor Party's dominance, which lasted from 1948 to 1977. But beginning in the 1990s, coalition instability did become a problem, as smaller parties began to influence decision making and policy to an unprecedented degree.

A Dominant Party System

Because of the success of the socialist parties in establishing and dominating Yishuv governing institutions that became state institutions after 1948, Israel was a dominant party system from 1948 to 1977. This means that a single party dominates the parliament and thus government through a plurality, but not a majority, of seats in the parliament. The dominant party operates in the center of the political spectrum, drawing support from parties around it that acquiesce in its dominance in exchange for resources, government portfolios, and influence on decision making in matters of considerable importance to them. Israel's Labor Party (known from 1930 until 1968 as Mapai—Mifleget Poalei Eretz Israel, Workers' Party of the Land of Israel) played this role. Its dominant status is captured in the popular observation that in this period elections were not conducted to determine who would lead the country, but rather who would become Labor's coalition partners.

The formation of Mapai in 1930 brought together three of the socialist movements operating at the time in the Yishuv. This gave the party more power by combining its constituent parts' electoral strength and resources. But given the welter of parties in the Jewish community, combined with the highly competitive democratic nature of Israel's politics, no single party could receive an absolute majority of votes to govern on its own. The largest party therefore had to rely on coalition partners in either the National Assembly or, after 1948, in the Knesset in order to form a government.

Because Labor always obtained a plurality, it was in a position to trade concessions for support. In this way it was able to hold on to the major portfolios, including the prime ministry, defense ministry, and foreign ministry, and usually the finance ministry. At the same time, Labor occupied the center of the political continuum. Thus, parties on either side of it would have to cooperate in order to form a government without Labor. This proved impossible, given the often diametrically opposing views these parties had on various issues, leaving Labor as the only possible choice for coalition partner.

In addition, Labor's control of the levers of decision-making authority enabled it to entrench its ideology and agenda in Israeli political institutions. This was facilitated by a lack of qualified career civil servants and administrators at the establishment of the state. Since it was the party in control of government, Labor naturally put its own people and supporters into these open positions, thus embedding its message and objectives directly into policymaking institutions and setting the policy agenda.

The result was that Labor controlled Israeli politics for thirty years. The complete dominance of Labor allowed for overall political stability and the pursuit of Labor policies in both foreign affairs and domestic matters. Not until 1977 did Labor lose its position of prominence, falling to the right wing, nationalist Likud. After that point the Israeli system became a truly competitive system, at least between these two major parties. Even then, though, dramatic shifts occurred primarily only in regard to policy toward the Palestinians. The more significant effect of the decline of the dominant party system and the end of Labor hegemony was the increase in bargaining power of the smaller parties.

Electoral Reform: Direct Election of the Prime Minister

Multipartyism has become entrenched in Israeli politics. For many years individuals, groups, and even some politicians have been arguing that the system has been counterproductive, because it has led to bargaining for government office that weakens the major parties and gives the smaller parties, and their narrowly focused demands, too much weight in government. The system, they argue, needs reform. But the only electoral reform ever enacted was the 1992 law allowing for the direct election of the prime minister in separate elections from the Knesset. It was later repealed, in 2001, after Ariel Sharon was directly elected prime minister.

As long as Israel was a dominant-party system, coalition bargaining was not a major problem. For Labor, the combination of a large plurality of Knesset seats and its position in the middle of the political spectrum ensured that it could relatively easily form a coalition government without being subject to unreasonable demands from potential coalition partners. This was because these parties could not threaten to move to another coalition.

Two developments undermined this process of coalition bargaining and raised questions about the disproportionate power of smaller parties. First, the elections in May 1977 signaled the end of Labor dominance and the rise of Likud. Likud took forty-three seats to Labor's thirty-two. This was the first time Labor did not win a plurality of seats. Labor's decline was the result of a number of factors, including the lingering trauma of the 1973 Yom Kippur War, the increasing loss of confidence in a party/movement that had ruled Israel in the pre- and post-state eras since the 1930s, economic and demographic-social problems, changes in the electorate, clashes among members of the ruling coalition, personal and factional clashes within Labor, the loss of Labor votes to the new Democratic Movement for Change, and the rise of Likud as a viable alternative.

The sudden existence of this alternative to Labor meant in political terms that the Labor Party was not the only possible core coalition partner. This gave the smaller parties, particularly the religious parties, greater bargaining power. They could now choose between the two major parties, forcing each to outbid the other in offers of resources and ministries.

Second, the unwillingness of Labor and Likud to cooperate, especially after 1993, meant that they had to rely on the smaller parties in order to form a government. Had they been willing to work together, they would not have needed any other party to form a government. Their combined strength in terms of seats was: seventy-five after the 1977 elections, ninety-five in 1981, eighty-five in 1984, seventy-nine in 1988, and seventy-six in 1992. In each case, the two parties had well above the sixty-one seats needed for a majority in the Knesset.

There were moments of cooperation. Beginning during the period that led to the 1967 war and ending in 1970, Likud was brought into the government to present a united front in the face of the crisis. In 1984, the two parties formed a National Unity Government based on rotating prime ministers. And from 1988 to 1990 they cooperated again, with Likud as the senior partner in the coalition.

But over the years, the intense debates over Israeli policy toward the West Bank and Gaza (WBG) led to a pronounced inability to cooperate because of the dichotomous difference in opinion on this issue. These fundamental disagreements were sparked not only by the capture of these territories in the 1967 war but also by the Yitzhak Rabin Labor government's signing of the Oslo Accords in 1993, which laid the groundwork for an independent Palestinian state there. The unwillingness to give in to the other side forced the two parties to seek out the support of the smaller parties in order to form coalitions.

The power of the smaller parties to determine government and, increasingly in the 1980s, the demands of the religious parties convinced Labor and Likud leaders that some reform of the electoral system was necessary to strengthen the larger parties and stabilize coalition government. The two parties cooperated to change the electoral system on April 14, 1992. In the past, like any parliamentary system, the electorate voted for its preferred party and the party with the greatest number of seats formed the coalition, with its head becoming prime minister. The new electoral law provided for a double vote. Citizens would now cast one ballot for their preferred party and one for prime minister. It was believed that this would increase the authority of the prime minister and free him/her from the constraints and pressures of having to bargain with the smaller parties. Since the people and not the parliament directly elected the prime minister, it was hoped that this would remove some of the negotiating power of the smaller parties. The law took effect in 1996, and was used in three direct elections: May 29, 1996, May 17, 1999, and February 6, 2001 (a special election for the prime minister only).

However, the law had the opposite effect of what its proponents had hoped for: instead of strengthening the prime minister's position the law ended up weakening it. This was because citizens were now able to split their vote. Previously, they would have to consider voting for the party whose leader they wished to see become prime minister. Now, they could vote for the person they wanted to be prime minister, but then cast their second vote for the party they felt best reflected their needs and ideas. This system thus increased fragmentation in Israeli politics, and in both the 1996 and 1999 elections the party that won set a record for receiving the smallest number of seats any winning party had ever had: thirty-four seats for Labor in 1996 and twenty-six seats for a Labor-led alliance in 1999. In both elections the two biggest parties also received the smallest total amount of seats they had ever won since 1977. In light of this, Labor and Likud cooperated again (on March 7, 2001) to repeal the direct election law and restore the previous electoral rules (with some minor changes).

The decline of the two largest parties has continued, however. In the January 28, 2003, elections Likud received thirty-eight Knesset seats to a Labor-led alliance's nineteen; in the March 28, 2006, poll the same Labor coalition again received nineteen seats and Likud dropped to twelve—its lowest total since 1977. In the 2009 elections Likud increased its share to twenty-seven seats, while Labor dropped to thirteen. In part, the low number of seats for both parties in the last two elections is because of the formation of a centrist party, Kadima, to which several Likud and Labor parliamentarians defected. (Kadima received twenty-nine seats in 2006 and twenty-eight seats in 2009.) Then, in a move that took observers and politicians by surprise, the leader of the Labor Party, Ehud Barak, announced on January 17, 2011, that he and four other Labor parliamentarians were leaving the party and establishing a new one (*Atzmaut*—Independence). This brought Labor to its lowest point in its history, at seven seats. Immediately analysts began eulogizing the party, remarking on a historical end to the party that created Israel. All this highlights the fluid nature of Israeli politics and the shifting demands of citizens for change.

The Inclusion of Religion into State Institutions

There are several religious parties that operate in Israeli politics, and they are all Orthodox (*dati* in Hebrew) or haredi. Though all of them have supported various governments led by Labor or Likud and most have been willing to serve in the cabinet, only one truly supports Zionist efforts to establish and maintain the State of Israel. Mafdal (Miflaga Datit Leumit—National Religious Party, or NRP) is the only religious Zionist party in the Israeli political constellation. Where other religious parties believe that the return of the Jews to Zion should be left to God, through the appearance of the Messiah, Mafdal believes that God acts through human agency and that the secular Zionist efforts to create a Jewish state reflect the will of God.

Given their support for the secular Zionist efforts, Mafdal has been willing to serve in any Israel government. In fact, it was a key partner, in one form or another, of all Labor goverments during the years of Labor dominance. Since then it has been part of most government coalitions. Beginning in the 1984 election, other religious parties also came to play a critical role in supporting government coalitions, particularly Shas (Shomrei Torah Sephardim—Sephardi Torah Guardians), a party that represents haredi, Mizrachi (Jews from Spain and the Middle East), and religiously traditional elements of Jewish-Israeli society. Reflecting the changes that have been occurring in the Israeli party system since the 1990s, Mafdal was dissolved in November 2008, bringing an end to one of the oldest political parties in Zionist and Israeli history, and incorporated into a new party that combined secular right-wing nationalism and religious Zionism.

The religious parties wield a disproportionate influence in government. This power stems from the commitment made to them by the country's secular leaders, in particular Israel's founding father David Ben-Gurion, at the inception of the state: in return for their support (which provided legitimacy for the Zionist efforts and presented a united Jewish front to the international community), the secular Zionists gave the Orthodox leadership control over several aspects of social life in the new Jewish state.

The basis of this exchange is what is called the "status quo agreement" that Ben-Gurion made with the Orthodox leaders in 1947, before the state was established. In return for their support for the creation of Israel, Ben-Gurion agreed that Orthodox Judaism would be the guiding framework for social life among Jews in Israel. The Orthodox would remain in charge of marriage, divorce, conversion, burial, and other personal status issues for Jews (Christians and Muslims have their own religious authorities). It was called the status quo agreement because it enshrined the arrangement that had existed under the British Mandate of Palestine, when the religious communities had been given control over their own "internal" affairs, which included social matters.

The pact was also reflected in Israel's Declaration of Independence, which asserted that the Zionists put their trust in the "Rock of Israel," a euphemism for God (Ben-Gurion managed to keep direct reference to God out of the Declaration), as a key pillar of the establishment and maintenance of the Jewish state. In later years, the arrangement was further entrenched in Israel's system of governance, including the observance in government institutions of strict Jewish dietary laws and the closing down of all public buildings, offices, and public transportation on the Sabbath (Friday evening to Saturday evening).

Effects of Religious Participation on Israeli Politics

The haredi monopoly on many elements of Jewish social life has a profound impact on Israel's governing system. It means that no decisions on any of these matters can be made without the input of the rabbis of the religious parties—each of which has its own individual rabbi who acts as the party's spiritual guide and whose pronouncements determine the political decisions of the party. At times this has caused problems for the government, such as the controversy over who is defined as a Jew—the haredi insist it must be someone who is Jewish according to Orthodox Jewish law or has been converted by Orthodox standards, while the Conservative and Reform denominations resist such a categorization.

But the status quo agreement also prompted the religious parties to become more involved in Israeli political life, since they now had a stake in the system. Aside from the NRP, none of the religious parties actively support the state or consider themselves Zionists, as they believe that a Jewish state can only be created by God, not humans. But despite this, their indispensable role as potential participants in coalition governments gives them a weight that their electoral votes do not match. This dilutes the nonreligious authority that the state is supposed to wield and is demonstrated in two issues: the separation of Orthodox communities from "regular" life within the state and the religious parties' unwillingness to sanction a written constitution.

Separate Religious Communities

Except for the Mafdal and its followers, Orthodox Jewish communities exist apart from the rest of Israeli society. Because they do not support the Zionist effort, driven as it is by human hands and not divine will, they are unwilling to participate fully in Israeli political, social, and economic life. Whereas most Israeli citizens (Arab Israelis excepted) are required to serve in the Israel Defense Forces, most members of these communities do not. (Their exemption stems from the Status Quo Agreement, in which a small number of haredi students would be allowed to continue studying in *yeshivot*, where they study Jewish texts and commentaries, instead of serving in the army. The numbers have gradually increased so that there is today a near-blanket exemption for all haredi, though small numbers do serve in strictly Orthodox units.) They also run their own educational systems, funded by the public purse but over which the state has little or no control: the curriculum is devised solely by the religious leaders, which means that the focus of training and learning is on Judaism, Jewish law, and so on.

This self-enforced disconnection has had two effects on Israeli governing. First, it has led to a groundswell of anger and resentment toward the non-Zionist Orthodox communities (about 10 percent of the Jewish population) among the secular and non-Orthodox majority, causing friction between the haredi and especially the staunch secularists. This in turn has troubled policymaking, leading to confrontations between Orthodox political parties and secular parties on relevant issues.

Second, it has led to a situation in which a community in Israel does not support the purpose of the state or even its very existence, but garners significant state resources to sustain itself. The growing political strength of the religious parties in the 1980s and 1990s exacerbated this, as the haredi parties—especially Shas—were seen as cynically insisting on more and more resources to support their communities from an entity they opposed. This contributed to the growing anger and frustration among the Israeli populace and has led at times to a backlash against the religious parties. It helped prompt the two major parties to collaborate in National Unity Governments in the 1980s and to pass the law for direct prime ministerial elections.

An Unwritten Constitution

It is not, of course, only the fault of the religious parties that Israel does not have a written constitution. The lack of one stems from a stalemate between the religious parties and the secular leaders in which the Orthodox parties insist that any document must enshrine their hegemony among the Jewish population and base Israel's political framework on *halacha* (Jewish law). The nonreligious parties balk at these provisions, yet are unwilling to confront the Orthodox communities on this issue, despite the calls for a written constitution by a growing number of citizens, legal practitioners and jurists, and others. In addition, there are some disagreements among the secular parties over what to include in such a document.

The result has been a situation similar to the situation in Britain, where there is no legal document setting out the main principles and framework of the country. In Israel's case, it is instead governed by a series of Basic Laws that set out the structure of the system, the nature of government, and the parameters of governing. As of 2011 there are eleven Basic Laws: the President, the Knesset, the Government, the Judiciary, the Israel Defense Forces, Jerusalem, Israel Lands, the State Comptroller, the State Economy, Human Dignity and Liberty, and Freedom of Occupation.

The lack of a written constitution has two consequences for governing in Israel. First, it means that there is no resolution to the issue of the role of religion in Israeli political and social life. This has, as mentioned above, caused at best an uneasy waiting period and at worst friction between Orthodox groups on the one hand, and secular non-Orthodox groups on the other. It also means that the secular authorities must be attentive to the demands of the religious parties.

Second, the lack of a written document gives more power to the judiciary, especially to the Supreme Court, which also sits as the High Court of Justice. The purpose of this body is to make sure that legislation and government policies are in line with "constitutional" principles and regulations. Since Israel does not have a constitution but rather the Basic Laws, the Court has greater latitude to interpret the laws and thus constrain or guide Israel's policymaking. This is considered to be a hindrance to democratic development, since unelected judges end up telling elected officials what kinds of policies they can and cannot make.

The 1967 War and the Debate Over Israeli Territory and Identity

The final factor that has had a major impact on contemporary Israeli governing is Israeli control over the West Bank and, until the withdrawal of all Jewish settlers and soldiers in August 2005, the Gaza Strip. The capture of these territories in the June 1967 Arab-Israeli War (known in Israel as the Six-Day War) raised a series of questions about the identity of Israel and which political party best represented that identity. These questions have not been answered as of yet, and it does not seem likely that they will be at any time in the near future.

The events that led up to the 1967 war have been discussed above, in the section on the decline of radical-nationalism What is important here is the impact the capture of the WBG had on the Israeli population and on the nature of governing in Israel. The conquest of the West Bank and Gaza removed what had long been the generally approved status quo regarding Israel's boundaries and, closely tied to them, its identity. Before 1967, only smaller groups on the right (including Herut, the forerunner of Likud) promoted a Greater Israel that would include all of Mandatory Palestine (and for a time Jordan as well), arguing that these were essential pieces of Jewish-Israeli identity. Labor did not support this vision, but contented itself with the boundaries of the state as they emerged from the 1947–1949 Arab-Israeli War (called the War of Independence in Israel). Labor's hegemony removed any debate on this issue. In addition, it was simply not thought practical to assume that Israel could ever take these lands away from the Arab states holding them.

In the event, Israel did seize the West Bank from Jordan and Gaza from Egypt. Where they had previously been blocked by the Jordanians, Israelis now had open access to the historical and biblical heartland of the ancient Jewish kingdoms in the West Bank—the place where the Jewish people were founded and where God had, according to the Bible, promised them a home.

Equally important, the capture of eastern Jerusalem put into Israeli hands for the first time the Old City, which had also been under Jordanian control after 1949, and which held the holiest site in Judaism and Jewish identity—the Western Wall, a piece of the wall surrounding the Holy Temple that was the center of the Jewish religion and identity until it was destroyed by the Romans in 70 C.E. The outpouring of emotion followed a widespread fear for its survival that had gripped the country in the days leading up to the war. These sensations affected the Labor government as well; by the end of the month it formally incorporated all of Jerusalem under its sovereignty.

Effects of the 1967 War on Israeli Politics

Although the end of Labor hegemony did not come for a decade after the Six-Day War, the spectacular military victory for which the Labor government was able to take credit paradoxically helped undermine its dominant position in the Israeli political system. It did this by raising questions about the proper borders of Israel and the role of land in what it meant to be a Jewish state. Likud was well positioned by that time to provide answers to these questions that resonated among most Israelis.

Nationalist sentiments attached to what was considered by most Israelis to be the historical Land of Israel (the place where Jews had once lived) were aroused across the political spectrum, making concrete what had previously been considered to be only an abstract idea—namely, the concept of Jewish sovereignty over the Jews' ancient territory. This made Herut/Likud relevant to a national discourse, since this is what it had advocated for many years. What had seemed to be unrealistic was now suddenly plausible. It helped that, in the lead-up to the war, Herut had been brought into the government to present a united front and meet popular and elite pressure for a government that included as much of the political spectrum as possible. This brought a legitimacy to Herut and its leader, Menachem Begin, that they otherwise would not have had.

Consequently, the Israeli political system changed from a dominant-party system to a truly competitive one. This contest lasted throughout the 1980s: in the 1981 election Likud obtained forty-eight Knesset seats to Labor's forty-seven; in 1984 Labor took forty-four seats to Likud's forty-one; and in the 1988 poll Likud garnered forty mandates and Labor thirty-nine. Questions about what to do with the WBG, and whether they were integral elements of a Jewish state, dominated these electoral campaigns, though they were by no means the only relevant issues for voters.

By 1992, though it seemed as if Labor was returning to its previous stature, in fact it was the beginning of the decline of the major parties to a degree unprecedented even in 1977. Labor received forty-four Knesset seats and Likud only thirty-two. Labor prime minister Yitzhak Rabin used his strong mandate to engage in a peace process with the Palestine Liberation Organization (PLO). In September 1993 he signed the Oslo Accords, a framework agreement that laid the groundwork for an independent Palestinian state in the WBG.

This marked a "revolution" in Israeli foreign policy: since the PLO's creation in 1964, every Israeli government had viewed it as a terrorist organization committed to Israel's annihilation, either through force of arms or through the "right of return"—the PLO claim that the hundreds of thousands of Palestinians who became refugees as a result of the 1947–1949 war (and their descendants) had the right to return to their homes inside Israel. (Absent a separate Palestinian state, such a return would upset the demographic balance and undermine the purpose of Israel as a Jewish state.)

In addition, no Israeli government until then had ever seriously considered the possibility of an independent state in the WBG. The most Labor had been willing to do was to give up *some* of the territories to an entity that would be federated with Jordan, while the most Likud was prepared to do was grant the Palestinians autonomy within a framework of overall Israeli sovereignty.

The Oslo Accords caused a political firestorm in Israel. Likud, the right wing, and some religious parties denounced it. By 1995, however, Israel did in fact withdraw from some parts of the West Bank. This had the unintended effect of removing Israeli military and intelligence capabilities from the very areas from which Palestinian terrorism and violence would come. Then, in an atmosphere of increasing vitriol and violence promoted by some of the religious authorities in the West Bank and tolerated by all the parties, Rabin was assassinated in November 1995 by a zealous right-wing religious Jew who believed Rabin was committing grave sins against the Jewish people. The mid-1990s also saw a spate of terrorist activities carried out primarily by the Palestinian Islamist group Hamas. A campaign of bus bombings terrorized the Israeli public, killing almost sixty civilians. In May 1996, Likud leader Benjamin Netanyahu was elected prime minister even though Likud only garnered thirty-two parliamentary seats (in alliance with two other parties) to Labor's thirty-four seats.

This was the beginning of a consistent switching off between the two main parties on the part of Israeli voters. Though the public based its decisions on what it perceived to be Israel's needs in response to the ups and downs of the relationship with the Palestinians, the result was that Israeli governments never had time to pursue a consistent foreign or domestic policy, either in regard to the peace process or in regard to economic and social policy. Indeed, elections were held in 1999 and, for prime minister only, in 2001—in both cases before the Knesset's or prime minister's mandate was officially over. By the second half of the 1990s, Israelis were tiring of the focus on the Palestinians and foreign policy and wanted their governments to concentrate on fixing what had by then become severe internal social, economic, and political problems.

In the 1999 prime ministerial and parliamentary elections, Labor leader Ehud Barak beat Netanyahu by about twelve percentage points, while his Labor-led alliance took twenty-six mandates to Likud's nineteen. In the special elections for prime minister in 2001, Likud leader Ariel Sharon was then voted in, defeating Barak by an almost 25 percent margin. In the 2003 general poll, Likud won thirty-eight seats, and Labor, allied with a dovish religious party, only nineteen. In the March 2006 parliamentary election a new party, Kadima, formed by former Likud head Sharon, won twenty-nine seats, followed by Labor with nineteen and Likud with twelve. Finally, in the February 2009 elections, Kadima won twenty-eight seats, Likud twenty-seven, and Labor thirteen. Likud was asked by the president to form the government, because it had the support of more parties in the Knesset (totaling thirty-eight seats, plus Likud's own twenty-seven for a total of sixty-five, a majority) than Kadima or Labor.

The Decline of Labor and Likud

The seesaw victories of Labor and Likud illustrate two things. First, Israeli policymaking has been disrupted since the second half of the 1990s not only by coalition instability (resulting in part from the split-ticket voting law that was in effect for the elections in 1996 and 1999) but also by the stark differences in policy toward the WBG and the Palestinians. It seems as though by the end of the 1990s the Israeli public had tired of the two major parties, believing that they had nothing new to offer. By the 1990s, even though they remained the largest parties, Labor and Likud were in decline as the primary vehicles for political participation.

The parties' decaying was exemplified by the March 2006 and February 2009 elections. Kadima's plurality stemmed from the fact that it was a brand-new party, located in the center of the political spectrum and encompassing figures from both Labor and Likud. Ariel Sharon's sole purpose in setting up Kadima to run in elections was to serve as a centrist platform that could engage in territorial withdrawals from the West Bank (though not necessarily all of the West Bank). Labor was seen as bankrupt and untrustworthy, and Likud had shifted further to the right and was no longer willing to consider major territorial withdrawals, at least not for the immediate future. Though it did not do as well as was first assumed, Kadima won twenty-nine mandates in 2006—an impressive showing for a first-time party. It is, moreover, the first time that a party received a larger mandate than both Labor and Likud.

As mentioned above, Likud earned twelve mandates in 2006, rising to twenty-seven in 2009. Labor won the same number of seats in 2006 as it had in 2003 (nineteen), dropping to thirteen in 2009, and then to eight in 2011. Another new party was formed for the 2006 election, drawing votes away from Labor: Gil (Pensioners Party). This party was established by a group of elderly Israelis who campaigned solely on bettering the standard of living for Israeli senior citizens and, to a lesser extent, for the population as a whole. It won seven seats. It did not pass the minimum threshold of votes in the 2009 elections, in part due to the continued popularity of Kadima and a resurgence of Likud. Finally, Shas won twelve seats in 2006 (the same as Likud) and eleven in 2009, while Yisrael Beitenu (Israel Is Our Home), a right-wing nationalist party accused by many of racism against Israeli Arabs, won eleven seats in 2006 and, in what was widely viewed as a resurgence not just of the Likud but of a preference for right-wing policies more generally, fifteen in 2009, making it the third largest party.

The results indicate that Israelis no longer feel that the former dominant parties, Labor and Likud, can meet their needs. This seems to stem from a combination of factors, including a weariness with old-time parties and old ideas, a desire to try new approaches with the Palestinians, and a greater focus on domestic issues rather than foreign policy. At the same time, Israeli voter participation rates have been dropping into the 2000s, reflecting the disillusionment with the old parties and what is seen as the gratuitous bickering among the parties more concerned with their own position and status than meeting the needs of their constituents.

The combination of these considerations with the extreme multipartyism of Israeli politics and the contentious rôle of religion in politics has led to a fractious system of governance. This has, beginning in the 1990s, inhibited many, though not all, aspects of policymaking. The 2006–2009 government in Israel, led by Kadima head Ehud Olmert, did not fulfill its complete mandate: after a seemingly inept military confrontation with the Lebanese terrorist organization Hezbollah in July and August 2006, combined with ongoing investigations into corruption, Olmert's government collapsed under increasing pressure. The current government, led by Benjamin Netanyahu of Likud, has already engendered frustration among many Israelis with its support for continued building of settlements in the West Bank. It also clashed with the Barack Obama Administration over settlements, though by 2011 the two governments appear to have moved beyond this to a somewhat tense but working relationship. Netanyahu's intransigence has been mirrored by the Palestinian leadership, and combined with domestic American support for Israel has made it harder for Washington to push harder for Israeli concessions in the peace process. As of 2011, the events in the Arab world (the popular demonstrations against the authoritarian regimes) distracted the Obama Administration from the peace process and redirected attention from it to a concern for overall regional stability in light of the advent of new governments in Tunisia and Egypt.

Whether the trends identified above will continue, or whether they can be arrested by the development of new electoral laws or new political parties, cannot be known at this writing. The shrinking of Labor indicates that trends toward dissolution of the old parties and the party system will continue. But Israeli politics has, since the 1990s, been in a state of near constant flux, and it is not inconceivable that Labor will be reconstituted by new leaders, though it is unlikely it will ever achieve its former powerful position, at least in the near future. And Likud remains the strongest party on the right; if it can fend off Kadma's appeal to voters, it, too, will remain at the apex of the political system.

References and Further Reading

Arian, Asher. *The Second Republic: Politics in Israel.* 2nd ed. Washington, DC: CQ Press, 2004.

Halpern, Ben, and Jehuda Reinharz. *Zionism and the Creation of a New Society.* New York: Oxford University Press, 1998.

Heller, Mark A. *Continuity and Change in Israeli Security Policy,* Adelphi Paper 335. London: International Institute for Strategic Studies, 2000.

Horowitz, Dan, and Moshe Lissak. *Origins of the Israeli Polity: Palestine Under the Mandate,* trans. Charles Hoffman. Chicago: University of Chicago Press, 1978.

Kimmerling, Baruch. *The Invention and Decline of Israeliness: State, Society, and the Military.* Berkeley: University of California Press, 2001.

Medding, Peter Y. *Mapai in Israel: Political Organisation and Government in a New Society.* Cambridge, UK: Cambridge University Press, 1972.

Sachar, Howard M. *A History of Israel: From the Rise of Zionism to Our Time.* 2nd ed. New York: Alfred A. Knopf, 2003.

Iraq

Of all the states in the Middle East, Iraq is the only one that in recent years has had a total change of regime—not just in terms of a particular individual or party but a wholesale switch from authoritarianism to democracy. This was accomplished only by large-scale external force—a U.S.-led invasion in 2003 that overthrew the Baathist regime of Saddam Hussein and has ushered in a governing system unprecedented in Iraqi history. Two implications can be drawn from this: First, Iraq may serve as a model for other authoritarian regimes in the region, not necessarily in the complete overhaul of its political system but rather as a political prototype for other autocracies to examine and, perhaps one day, follow. Second, the change in regime was carried out through violence. Contrary to the first implication, this does not bode well for the end of authoritarianism in the region.

Given the recentness of the U.S. invasion and the establishment of a functioning democracy (if not yet a fully functioning system of governance), it is difficult to discuss contemporary Iraqi politics. Like the situation in Lebanon and Israel, Iraqi politics is in flux. Instead, we will focus on the development of the Iraqi governing system between the establishment of the British Mandate and the rule of Saddam Hussein, Iraq's dictator until his overthrow and capture in 2003. The key element in this process was repression, as in the other Arab regimes—in fact, the Iraqi and Syrian regimes shared many similarities in the way they governed, including a Baath Party–dominated political system, an invasive cult of personality, and support structures at the top of which sat a narrow communal group. There are two additional twists to the Iraqi story: First, though the Iraqi regime may not have been the most repressive in the Middle East, under Saddam it was the cruelest. And second, Iraqi society is sharply divided in both ethnic and religious terms. Both elements helped condition Iraqi politics in the second half of the twentieth century and had profound effects on bargaining and disagreements within the new Iraqi democracy after the U.S. invasion in 2003.

From Monarchy to Revolution

Like most other countries in the Middle East, modern Iraq was created in the aftermath of World War I. There were two key developments in postwar Iraq: the establishment of the state itself, and its organization as a constitutional monarchy (but one in which the king retained significant, if not ultimate, control). Both had profound implications for the future politics of the country. A tertiary development was the rise of nationalism, both pan-Arab and Iraqi, which resisted British influence and created the conditions that eventually helped lead to the 1958 revolution.

As a country, Iraq did not exist before 1920. Under the Ottoman Empire, modern Iraq was divided into three administrative units, or *vilayets:* Mosul in the north, Baghdad in the center, and Basra in the south. These also roughly corresponded to the concentration of ethnic/religious groupings in the area. The Kurds, who are Sunni Muslims, are ethnically non-Arab and live mostly in Mosul province. The Sunni Arab population is concentrated in the middle of the country, in Baghdad province. The Shi'ites, ethnically Arab but considered a deviant form of Islam by the regionally dominant Sunnis, are mainly clustered in Basra in the south. In addition, much of Iraqi society was tribally based (particularly in the south), and so was more loyal to a particular tribe or clan than to the nascent state. The tribes were hostile to attempts by any central government to exert control over them.

British plans to unite the regions into one country stirred widespread opposition. Kurds were apprehensive about a potential Arab hegemony over them, and almost immediately engaged in a series of rebellions to obtain autonomy or secession from Iraq that continues even today, under the American-installed democratic system. The Shi'ites feared Sunni domination, and indeed were marginalized under a governing system presided over by a long-standing Sunni elite, particularly after 1958. This marginalization contributed to a willingness to rebel against Saddam's central government in the wake of the 1991 Gulf War. The political tensions and ethnic/sectarian violence stemming from the formation of the country have had profound implications for Iraq today, as the country struggles to forge a national identity and political structure that overarches these three different identities.

There also existed a significant group of nationalists who were angry at the thought of British rule. Still, Britain pushed ahead, and at the San Remo Conference in April 1920, the Allied victors of World War I granted Britain the mandate for Iraq, though the country's final borders were not set for a few years more.

Because of these divisions, general opposition within the new country to British rule, and a desire to reduce as much of the direct costs of maintaining control as possible, London sought to strengthen a central government under the Iraqis themselves. Britain could then assume an indirect rule over the country, through treaties of defense and cooperation, financial and military support, and making sure the new leaders were dependent on Britain for their positions. This led to the second major development, the construction of the Iraqi monarchy.

As in Jordan and the small Gulf states, Britain chose monarchy as the governing system at least in part because it fit with British sentiments and reflected its own form of governance. The British had an available and willing candidate in Faisal ibn Hussein. Faisal was the son of Sharif Hussein, the ruler of the Hijaz and a longtime British client in the Arabian Peninsula. Hussein had agreed to support the Arab Revolt against the Ottoman Empire in the war, in exchange for British support for Arab independence once the war ended.

This did not happen. The British might have felt that installing Faisal as ruler of Iraq could go some way toward fulfilling the debt they owed Hussein. Faisal had tried to make himself ruler of Syria in 1920; the Syrian National Congress, the nationalist parliament, elected him king in March. But the French, who were granted the mandate over Syria, did not intend for a British-affiliated king to rule over their possession (which in any case was to be governed along the lines of the French republic). When Faisal refused to step down, the French invaded and at the end of July defeated the would-be king, forcing him into exile in Britain.

In addition, Faisal had international and regional credibility as an Arab leader of stature. In particular, as a member of the Hashemite family he was a direct descendent of Muhammad, the founder of Islam, and so had obvious Islamic integrity as well. This would, the British hoped, help reduce the perception that Faisal was simply a British lackey. At the same time, he was considered moderate enough that he would follow the British line in foreign policy and protect British economic and strategic interests within the country.

So the British brought Faisal to Iraq in 1921 and constructed a constitutional monarchy with him on the throne. National legitimacy was established through the careful orchestration of a referendum on the question on Faisal's kingship. A bicameral parliament was also written into the constitution, as was an independent judiciary. But despite these trappings of democracy, the governing system was authoritarian to the extent that Faisal did what he could to impose his own wishes on the governments that served under him.

In addition, politics centered around the struggle among a few elites who were not interested in opening up the system to the population at large except to mobilize them to vote for the narrow-based political parties that competed in elections. But even these political parties were little more than vehicles for representation of personal, familial, or tribal preferences; they were not national parties in the truly democratic sense of the term. The closed nature of the system alienated much of Iraqi society, opening the door by the 1940s for the rise of parties dedicated to a particular ideology, including Communists and Baathists. Politics came to be about the struggle for power between three main groups who served as the country's elite, in addition to the monarchy.

The first group was composed of the tribal sheikhs who were supported by Britain and owned much of the land in the countryside. The second group comprised mainly Iraqi officers, who came with Faisal to the new Iraq when he was made king. These were referred to as Sharifian officers, because they had participated with Sharif Hussein in the Arab Revolt. Both groups became the monarchy's natural allies and strongest supporters. The third group was made up of the old notables, the Sunni-dominated class that had ruled much of the Arab world under the Ottoman Empire and filled much of the civil service. After the 1958 revolution and particularly after Saddam Hussein consolidated power in 1979, the first two groups lost much of their influence.

Independence and Military Involvement in Politics

Britain was determined to rule Iraq indirectly. This led it to create a series of treaties with the new country that outlined Iraq's commitment to British interests and dependence on Britain for survival, both of the state itself and of its governing elites. The 1930 Anglo-Iraqi Treaty promised Iraq full sovereignty within two years, while granting Britain extensive military rights within the country, including two air bases, the right to train the Iraqi army, and use of all of Iraq's communications systems in case of need. On October 3, 1932, Iraq was welcomed as a member of the League of Nations as one of the first Arab countries to achieve independence from the colonial powers. This independence was nominal, and British control or influence remained in one form or another until 1958.

In September 1933 King Faisal died. He had been a powerful influence for compromise among the contending elites, and his contacts with the tribes, the religious establishment, and the ex-Ottoman elite had ensured their support (however qualified) for the new regime established in 1932. His death removed one plank of stability in Iraq. Faisal's death also coincided with the rise in the importance of the military to the regime.

During the 1930s, the army became increasingly critical to the survival of the regime. First, the regime had made the building up of the army a major priority. There were a number of reasons for this, including the recognition that ex-Ottoman officers needed employment (before disgruntlement might translate into opposition to the new regime), a belief that a central military could act as a unifying force for the new state, and an understanding of the need for a strong armed forces to deal with internal security problems.

Second, the armed forces became critical to the security of the regime due to the army's role in holding off or defeating various insurgencies by the Kurds in the north and the tribes (though the Kurdish rebellions were never fully subdued until the 1970s), as well as increasing demands for autonomy by the Assyrian minority. (A small ethnic minority practicing Christianity, the Assyrians did not engage in widespread open revolt. But they were not viewed as welcome in an increasingly Arab-nationalist Iraq.) This growing importance led the army to demand a greater say in decision making, and it was difficult for the government to refuse. It was not until after World War II and direct British intervention in the country that the army was, more or less, removed from politics. The army returned to political prominence in the 1958 revolution, after which it remained an important contender in the political process. When Saddam Hussein exerted complete control in 1979, the military ceased again to be a main force on its own in policymaking.

Military interference in politics became direct on October 29, 1936, when the first military coup, under General Bakr Sidqi, took place. His government was overthrown less than a year later, on August 11, 1937, in another military coup. As in Syria, the Iraqi army was divided into various factions, each with its own ideology and ties to specific civilian politicians and groups. Some were more interested in economic and social reform while others wanted to maintain the status quo; still others were concerned about the necessity of autocratic government to impose reforms, which would of course undermine the old notables and the monarchy; finally there were differences between those groups that preferred an Iraqi nationalism that was not tied to the rest of the Arab world, and a pan-Arab nationalism—a belief that Iraq was only one part of the larger Arab nation and so could only be considered in this framework (though the differences between these factions were far narrower than was the case in Syria).

The peak of army influence came in the late 1930s and early 1940s under the Golden Square—a group of four high-ranking army officers with pan-Arab leanings led by Salah al-Din al-Sabbagh. It then became impossible to separate the military from the political process. The army avoided direct rule, instead installing civilian leaders affiliated with the specific faction in power at the time or with shared ideas about governance and the British. But no civilian politician was able to remove the army from politics or prevent it from intervening when it considered its interests to be threatened or believed that politicians were doing a poor job of running the country; five more army coups followed after the 1937 coup.

The Golden Square was responsible for the Rashid Ali movement, which removed the monarchy for the first time. This coup and its aftermath had a profound influence on the military in later years, playing some part in the desire for a return to military rule in 1958. On April 1, 1941, the Golden Square overthrew the monarchy (at that time led by a regent in the name of the young Hashemite king) and placed Rashid Ali al-Gaylani in power as prime minister. In addition, the coup swept from power the old establishment politicians, most of whom supported the status quo and many of whom accepted close ties with Britain.

Sympathetic to the German cause during the war, Rashid Ali began negotiations with the Axis powers. Alarmed, the British invaded Iraq and by the end of May drove Rashid Ali and the Golden Square from power. It was their intervention (the British remained in the country until 1945) that pushed the army out of the direct role it had played in politics. Pro-British politicians were re-entrenched in the government and parliament, and it seemed for a time that their position was not easily assailable. The return of the old regime also brought into government far more Kurds and Shi'ites than usual, which caused some resentment among the Sunnis (who formed the majority of the plotters of 1958 and after).

In this context Iraq after the war seemed to stabilize. The British-supported regime had weathered the storms of the war and military involvement, and by the 1950s some economic growth was being registered. However, the army was out but not down, and the 1952 Free Officers coup in Egypt served as an inspiring example to them of what the military could do. The Rashid Ali affair of 1941 also served to motivate them, both in returning the army to politics and expelling the old notables and the British from power.

Like the other Arab states, Iraq was in the throes of societal and ideational change. In addition, growing nationalism (which had begun to spread widely in the 1930s, in part in opposition to British influence), widespread poverty, and the rise of new middle and working classes interested in breaking into the traditional power structures facilitated both the willingness of the army to overthrow the regime, tied as it was to foreign powers, and the willingness of the population to welcome a new one. Finally, developments in Mandatory Palestine, followed by the Israeli victory in the 1947–1949 war, intensified the military's anger at being directed by what it perceived as incompetent civilians and fomented a pan-Arab nationalism that could not exist at the same time as a pro-British orientation. This hardened attitudes among other groups against both the establishment and the British, and facilitated a willingness to overthrow the old regime by violence.

From Revolution to Saddam Hussein

In domestic terms, Iraq was more or less stable in the period between 1941 and 1958, and indeed was in the process of real economic and educational expansion. Still, the regime, controlled as it was by old-time politicians who were engaged in increasing suppression of any opposition to the government, resisted opening up the system to the new movements and parties that were forming in Iraq, particularly among the Left (Communists, socialists, and the recently established Baath Party).

Perhaps more importantly, regional developments had a profound impact on Iraqis, particularly the pan-Arab nationalists. The war in Palestine/Israel in 1947–1949, the Baghdad Pact of 1955, the Suez crisis in 1956, and finally the formation of the United Arab Republic in February 1958 all had repercussions among the pan-Arabists in Iraq as well as those who were frustrated with the government's focus on foreign rather than domestic affairs. These events underlined their resentment at British influence and the support of the old Iraqi regime for a strong British connection at the expense of strengthening ties with the Arab states in the region.

Underlying all of these conditions was dissatisfaction in the military, which had been greatly displeased with the use of British force to overthrow the 1941 Rashid Ali regime. When civil conflict broke out in Lebanon in May 1958, Jordan's King Hussein asked for Iraqi soldiers to protect the Jordanian monarchy. Instead of crossing into Jordan as ordered, the military instead moved into Baghdad to overthrow the Iraqi regime in the most bloody coup in all of the Arab world until that time.

On July 14, 1958, Brigadier Abdul Karim Qasim and Colonel Abdul Salam Arif led the Free Officers in the coup. The Free Officers, formed in 1957 and modeled on the Egyptian Free Officers, were determined to remove all traces of the old establishment and British influence. The royal family was killed, along with several old-time politicians, including the most prominent among them, Nuri al-Said. This marked the end of the old regime (the monarchy and the notables) and the beginning of a new one. A republic replaced the monarchy, and there was never a return to the previous system.

The revolution ushered in an era of coups and coup attempts that differed significantly from the changes that had marked the old regime. Under the monarchy, there had been fifty-nine governments in thirty-seven years, between independence and revolution. But these had simply been a reshuffling of the same politicians rather than wholesale changes in government. After 1958, coups brought different groups to power, some with radically different ideologies and policy ideas.

Problems began almost immediately under the new regime. The Iraqi Free Officers did not have a strong ideological position or carefully crafted policy agenda, and they were especially divided on foreign policy. Qasim preferred a more independent Iraq and a slower approach to Arab unity, while Arif favored a more aggressive pan-Arab policy, which included drawing closer to Nasser and Egypt more quickly. The Baath supported Arif's stance. The issue came to a head at the beginning of November 1958, and Arif attempted another coup. He was arrested and jailed. As different factions struggled for control, Qasim eliminated them each in turn, becoming more authoritarian, and in this way ended up alienating all his original bases of support; coupled with a new Kurdish uprising in 1961, he was soon viewed as a liability for Iraq.

On February 8, 1963, the Baath led their first coup with the help of sympathetic army officers. Yet the new government that took power was itself soon divided into two groups: one wanted to impose more radical social change in Iraq and to distance Iraq from Egypt; the other preferred a more moderate domestic policy and a closer relationship with Egypt. The struggle between the two factions undermined the party. It was also a weak government. The party itself had a small membership, was inexperienced, and had not made major inroads in the military—a critical necessity in the era of military coups. Finally, the party was damaged from without: after the failure of the United Arab Republic in 1961 and the failure of further unity talks between Egypt, Syria, and Iraq, Egyptian president Nasser verbally assaulted the Baath in both Syria and Iraq, challenging its legitimacy. Arif, released from prison and made nominal president, led a group of non-Baathist officers and overthrew the Baathist regime later that year, on November 18.

Arif's rule concentrated on moving closer to Egypt and engaging in the nationalization policies that marked Nasser's Egypt and Baathist Syria. His government lasted until April 13, 1966, when he died in a helicopter crash. His younger brother, Abdul Rahman Arif, took power with the support of the military and continued to bring the state into direct control of the economy. His rule lasted less than two years, and, like all regimes since 1958, was based on personal rule with no support from allies who could defend the ruler himself. The younger Arif was never successful in balancing the various groups that, for their part, still wanted to return to power, especially the Baath. The lack of a supporting institutional structure, in political terms, coupled with Arab defeat in the 1967 war against Israel (in which Iraq had backed Egypt and Syria), discredited the Iraqi regime (as it had the Syrian and Egyptian regimes). On July 17, 1968, a group of Baathist and independent officers took power in another coup. On July 30, the Baath ousted its erstwhile allies and took power solely for itself in its second and final coup, and it remained in power until the U.S. invasion of 2003.

Iraq Under Saddam Hussein

It is often thought that Saddam's rule began in 1979, the year he took complete power for himself and became the sole leader in Iraq. But he was a major force in the Baathist regime that came to power in 1968, and he became second in command of the regime during the 1970s, under the original coup leader, General Ahmad Hassan al-Bakr. During that time he was responsible for many of the regime's policies.

The Baathists initiated a period of relative stability in Iraq after quickly removing the independent officers from the regime. Though it was far less of a mass party than its counterpart in Syria (membership numbered only in the tens of thousands, and frequent purges reduced these even more), the Baath created strong political institutions to support its rule. This was a new development in post-1958 Iraq. Previously, none of the regimes were able to build a strong institutional base and were only governed by individuals or factions.

The Iraqi Baath was stronger in 1968 than it had been in 1963, and more tightly organized. Its structure was similar to the Syrian Baath. At the lowest, neighborhood level was the Cell (sometimes referred to as the Circle), containing only three to seven members. Two to seven Cells made up a party Division, which operated in larger urban areas, offices, factories, and so on. Party Divisions also existed in the civil service and the military as parallel units designed to maintain conformity and loyalty to the regime. Two to five Divisions formed a party Section, which worked in even larger urban areas. Next was the Branch, existing at the provincial level (though Baghdad had more than one Branch). The Branches came together in a party Congress, which then elected the Regional Command—as in Syria, the highest body in the party.

The provisional constitution, promulgated on July 16, 1970, set out the principles of the Iraqi state, which were also the principles of the Baath—Arab socialism and pan-Arabism. Islam was also made the state religion. The Revolutionary Command Council (RCC) was made the highest decision-making body in the state, with both executive and legislative powers, and by the end of 1977 its members also had to be members of the Regional Command. The president was given wide powers, including chairmanship of the RCC. The top leaders in government were thus also top leaders in the party: Bakr was secretary-general of the party, president and prime minister of the republic, and commander of the armed forces. (Saddam followed his example and held these same positions after 1979.)

The RCC had greater powers than the country's parliament, the National Assembly. The Assembly did not meet until 1980, but even then its members were vetted and the electoral campaign controlled by the RCC. Its main purpose was to ratify or reject legislation passed on to it from the RCC. In addition, it had powers of oversight of the government, but none of these were ever exercised independently. Finally, the constitution guaranteed citizens a number of rights, such as freedom of religion, speech, assembly, even to form political parties. But these rights were severely curtailed in practice, and allowed only where they suited the regime's purpose.

In addition, the Baath under Saddam used the influx of oil wealth after 1973 to embark on a major program of development, expanding the bureaucratization and power of the state. Saddam used both carrots and sticks with the Kurds. In the early 1970s he offered them significant autonomy and several political and cultural rights within the Iraqi state. He also continued the military campaign against them and forcibly moved many Kurds out of the north, replacing them with Arabs brought to live in Kurdish or mixed Kurdish-Arab areas, in order to weaken Kurdish unity.

Finally, the regime strengthened itself internally in two ways. First, it expanded its paramilitary and intelligence capabilities. This gave it the capacity to watch for dissent and to move quickly to intimidate or coerce critics into silence. Second, many of the top leaders were also tied to one another by tribal links. Tikritis dominated the government. These were Sunni Arabs from an area northwest of Baghdad who were related through tribal, clan, and familial connections. Both Bakr and Saddam were Tikritis, and in fact were relatives.

Saddam played the key role in developing the party and the regime's capacities after 1968. Even before the 1968 coup he had been heavily involved in organizing the clandestine activities of the party, including its military units. He had participated in a Baath attempt to assassinate Qasim in October 1959. This prepared him well for the consolidation of power both under Bakr and, when he retired Bakr and took complete power for himself, after 1979. Between 1968 and the mid-1970s he was the strongman of the party and the regime, overseeing the purges (including murders) of enemies and would-be plotters within the party, government, and society. Saddam also played an important role in the development and modernization of Iraq in the 1970s. He saw through the nationalization of the country's oil industry in 1972. Bakr was older and carried more prestige, and Saddam was content to be his deputy for some time. But Saddam was an active worker, and while he strengthened the regime he also consolidated his own power by removing those he did not trust and filling positions with loyalists.

The party still had its own internal divisions. It was separated into two groups—a military and a civilian wing. Similar to the divisions in Syria, the military element was less radical in both domestic and foreign policy, while the civilians were more ideological and therefore more committed to radical change in both areas. The military wing, led by Bakr, was dominant in the beginning. The civilian group, weaker at first but increasingly stronger in the 1970s, was led by Saddam Hussein. He asserted the civilian wing's dominance at the expense of the military wing, and his own personal power at the expense of Bakr, who was already beginning to withdraw from active politics due to illness.

On July 16, 1979, Saddam seized total power, making Bakr resign for "health reasons." On July 22 he convened a meeting of party leaders in which he read out the names of sixty-eight people who were labeled as disloyal, removed from the room, and tried as traitors. Many of them were later executed. Saddam had the meeting videotaped and then sent the tape around to various individuals in the country to let them know that he had taken power and would tolerate no dissent.

Saddam purged the top positions in the party, state, government, and military and refilled them with tribal kin loyal to him or with individuals dependent on him for their own positions. A paranoid and violent man, he continued to purge the government and party on a regular basis. He expanded the domestic intelligence and security organizations, and used money from oil exports to build a stronger, more centralized (and bureaucratic) state. He also greatly expanded literacy programs and education, and under him Iraq's public health system became one of the best in the region. He enlarged the role of women in society and in work, and undermined the influence of Islam, particularly in Iraq's legal system.

Like his Syrian counterpart Hafez al-Assad, Saddam had learned that factionalism in politics contributes to instability. Under Saddam's guidance, therefore, the regime did not even pretend to create a loyal opposition party. There was no room for one, because it was feared this would lead to the instability and coups that marked Iraqi politics between 1958 and 1968. In 1974 the Progressive National Front was set up as an alternative party to the Baath, but as in Syria, the Baath was dominant within the Front and its non-Baath members were carefully vetted.

Saddam also built up a cult of personality unlike any other Iraqi leader before him. Pictures and likenesses of him adorned walls (inside and outside of buildings), statues, government offices, stores, and schools. In order to project an image as father to all the Iraqi people, there were pictures of Saddam dressed in a variety of outfits, each calculated to appeal to a particular segment of Iraq's fractured population: modern leader (in suits), military commander (in uniform), Kurdish sympathizer (in traditional Kurdish clothing), and devout Muslim (in a traditional robe). One quip that made the rounds in Iraq was that the country's population was actually 28 million—14 million people and 14 million images of Saddam.

Saddam had a tendency to micromanage his regime. He rejected advice contrary to his own preferences, which made it impossible for him to have proper counsel from his coterie of supporters. Instead, they were essentially all yes-men who told Saddam what he wanted to hear. In this way, it has been argued, Saddam made monumental miscalculations about American intentions and Iraqi capabilities in 1990 and 2003. He had created a climate of fear that made his advisors afraid to tell him the truth about domestic and regional conditions, as well his own megalomania.

Saddam's Wars

Saddam Hussein engaged in what, at least in hindsight, has been classified as reckless foreign policy. His two major foreign policy adventures were the invasion of Iran in 1980 and the invasion of Kuwait in 1990. Together, they created the conditions that would, in 2003, lead to his overthrow by a U.S.-led coalition. These decisions are critical because, compared to the leaders of the other two major radical-nationalist states, Syria and Egypt, the Iraqi leader did not moderate his foreign policy. His continued aggressiveness undermined the regime's legitimacy and capabilities (though not in domestic security) and created the conditions for its eventual overthrow in 2003.

Saddam invaded Iran on September 22, 1980. The reasons were varied and complex. First, underlying the contemporary tensions, Iraq and Iran had a long history of conflict and competition in the region as previous Arab and Persian kingdoms and empires. Second, their geopolitical struggle resulted in Iran supporting Kurdish rebellions in Iraq throughout the 1960s and beginning of the 1970s. In addition, in 1975 Iraq and Iran had concluded the Algiers Accord. This pact set the boundary between Iraq and Iran at the thalweg line of the Shatt al-Arab waterway—the critical river that gave Iraq an important outlet to the Persian Gulf (the thalweg line was the middle of the waterway). Previous arrangements had the border closer to the Iranian side. Now that the border was moved to the middle it represented a greater threat to Iraqi interests.

Third, even before the onset of the Iranian Revolution in 1979, Iranian clerics, including Ayatollah Khomeini, had been encouraging Shi'ite agitation in the south of Iraq against the Sunni-dominated central government. This was a direct threat to the Baathists and, especially, Saddam's new regime. When Khomeini came to power in 1979, he posed both an ideological and a political challenge to Saddam: a powerful Shi'ite neighbor that was already trying to undermine the Baath's legitimacy could now act as a lightning rod for the disaffected Shi'ites in the south of Iraq and mobilize them against the Iraqi regime. Saddam calculated that since Iran was in the middle of the revolution, its decision making would be hampered by internal problems and it would not put up an effective resistance. Regime security—fear that the power, wealth, and lives of the Iraqi leaders, especially Saddam, were under threat—drove Baghdad to launch the invasion.

The war lasted until August 20, 1988, with over a million casualties. At first Iraq did well, capturing a significant portion of Iranian territory (about 10,000 square miles). But Saddam misperceived the extent to which an Iraqi invasion would unify Iran. Indeed, most segments of Iranian society banded together in the face of this external threat and put up a very strong resistance. Loyalty to its government galvanized the Iranian population. The Iranian army was also in better shape than Baghdad had believed.

By 1982, Iran had succeeded in pushing Iraq back to its own territory, and after that, much of the war was fought in Iraq. The conflict became a war of attrition punctured by brutal acts of violence, such as the "war of the cities," in which both sides rained missiles down on each other's major cities. Iran engaged in "human wave" attacks, in which Iranian youth ran en masse across minefields and charged the Iraqi positions. Finally, Saddam used poison gas against both Iranian soldiers and his own Kurdish population in the north when he feared the latter was rising up against him by joining with Iranian forces that had captured parts of Kurdish northern Iraq.

A UN-sponsored cease-fire finally came into effect in August 1988. Iraq did not achieve any of its war aims (Saddam agreed to restore the Iraq-Iran border at the thalweg line in the Shatt al-Arab) and ended up devastating its own economy. By the time of the cease-fire, Iraq's oil industry had been severely damaged. This was disastrous for the Iraqi economy; in 1979, oil exports represented 90 percent of Iraq's revenue. Production was limited as early as 1983, when Iraqi oil fields in the south were put out of order by Iran and the shipping lanes in the Gulf were under threat as both countries attacked ships trading with the other. Iraq had incurred massive war debt to finance its campaign, especially after the damage to its oil industry—over $80 billion, much of it held by Saudi Arabia and Kuwait. The debt also meant that Iraq could not return to its pre-invasion program of expanding its infrastructure because much of its revenue had to go to servicing the debt.

One important outcome of the war for Iraq was that the regime became determined to protect itself. Some estimates point out that, based on oil revenue, Iraq could have recovered economically in a reasonable period of time. Instead, though, the regime decided to spend much of its income on a vast expansion of the military, which now numbered over a million. Iraq thus devoted a significant portion of its energy to developing its own domestic arms production, including weapons of mass destruction (WMD—chemical, biological, and nuclear weapons). In 1988 and 1989, it spent $10 billion on the military. The need for revenue was part of the motivation for Iraq's invasion of Kuwait in 1990, just two years after the end of the war with Iran.

Yet Saddam's reasons for invading Kuwait were also varied. He was angry at what he perceived to be the lack of gratitude from Kuwait, Saudi Arabia, and the other small Gulf monarchies for Iraq's long war with Iran, which Saddam argued was a continuation of centuries-old conflict between the Arabs and the Persians. He also was angry that Kuwait refused to forgive Iraq war debts. Finally, he believed at that time that his regime was again threatened. He alleged that Israel was preparing for another attack on Iraq like the one in 1981, when it destroyed Iraq's nuclear reactor at Osirek. He also believed that the United States was actively trying to encircle Iraq with enemies in preparation for the overthrow of his regime, and that Kuwait and the UAE were involved in the global conspiracy against him.

Saddam also believed that internal conspiracies were afoot, supported by these foreign powers; hundreds of officers were arrested and either executed or purged from the military. In this same vein, Baghdad accused Kuwait of "slant drilling" into the Iraqi section of the shared Rumaila oil field, thus depriving Iraq of its own revenues. Iraq also had long-standing claims on Kuwait, having argued since at least the 1960s that Kuwait was historically part of Iraq and therefore should be reincorporated into the Iraqi state. Iraq accused Kuwait and the United Arab Emirates of producing more oil than was allotted to them through OPEC, which reduced the market price of oil and, again, deprived Iraq of needed revenue.

Saddam believed that by invading Kuwait he would solve most of these problems: he would be able to strengthen Iraqi oil revenues and thus the economy, remove a key conspiring enemy (Kuwait itself), unite the Iraqi people around his foreign objectives, and demonstrate to the United States and others that Iraq was still very strong. To this end, on August 2, 1990, he invaded Kuwait and occupied the country.

The story of the invasion and its aftermath is well documented elsewhere. The United States immediately began to build up its troops in the region (Operation Desert Shield) while putting together an international coalition of states to participate in the coming conflict or support the American efforts. Economic sanctions were imposed. Even the Soviet Union did not support its ally in the event, instead supporting American action. When Saddam did not meet the U.S. deadline for withdrawing, the coalition attacked on January 16, 1991, (Operation Desert Storm) and easily defeated the Iraqi forces. On February 27, U.S. president George H.W. Bush declared Kuwait liberated.

The 2003 American Invasion

But the coalition forces did not attack Iraq itself, except for strategic targets, and left the regime in power. Partly on the encouragement of the United States (particularly President Bush) and partly due to years of marginalization and suffering under the Baathist regime, the Kurds in the north and Shi'ites in the south rose up against the regime. Both at first scored some successes, but the regime quickly regrouped. The Shi'ite revolt in the south did not have an organized leadership, and by the end of March the Iraqi army—still very strong—crushed the rebellion and restored central government control, executing hundreds of Shi'ites in the process.

In the north the Kurds were much better organized and set up local administrations immediately after seizing towns and cities. But the Kurds still could not stand up to the Iraqi military once it turned its attention to them after defeating the Shi'ites. Iraqi advances induced a panicked flight among the Kurdish population, much of which fled to Turkey and Iran (about 2 million people). Hundreds of thousands set up camps in the mountains in northern Iraq, and thousands died under the harsh conditions. Turkey refused to let the Kurds in, out of fear they would destabilize Turkey, and the images of so many Kurds trapped in the mountains galvanized international public opinion and leaders.

Led by the United States, no-fly zones were established in the Kurdish north and Shi'ite south. Here, the Iraqi army was forbidden to enter and American, British, and French forces protected the areas from the central government. In the north especially, the Kurds used this cover to set up their own autonomous political and administrative structures, building a separate yet viable society and economy.

With Baghdad's control thus reduced to the center of the country, the United States again led the effort to impose a United Nations weapons inspection system (the United Nations Special Commission on Iraq, UNSCOM) on Iraq to destroy its chemical, biological, and nuclear programs and its ballistic missiles. For the next twelve years the UN and United States struggled with Iraq to follow the weapons inspections to the end while Saddam worked hard to avoid complying as much as possible with the inspectors. The Iraqi people (with the partial exception of the Kurds) suffered as economic sanctions remained in place (except for food and medical supplies) while the regime remained in power and, indeed, was able to continue rewarding its loyal elites with wealth and resources.

Then came September 11. The terrorist attacks on the United States led to a very different psychological framework among American leaders. Greater awareness of the will of their enemies to attack and kill many innocent people engendered fear in the George W. Bush administration and a determination to prevent any further attacks on the country. In addition to possessing a preexisting desire to overthrow the Saddam Hussein regime, the Bush administration claimed that Iraq posed a serious threat to the United States by virtue of its WMD programs, its links to terrorist organizations, and Saddam's dangerous foreign policies. (The administration also argued that it wanted to liberate the Iraqi people from the tyrannical regime of Saddam.) The WMD and the terrorist links were later found to be negligible, but in the event, after a prolonged and ultimately unsuccessful attempt to have the United Nations legitimize and support an invasion, Washington led a coalition of dozens of other countries to attack Iraq on March 20, 2003, in Operation Iraqi Freedom. (Many other countries disagreed with the invasion and did not support it.)

Once again, the Iraqi military collapsed in the face of overwhelming firepower. On April 9, 2003, coalition forces took Baghdad. On May 1, President Bush announced the end of major combat in Iraq (although this would prove excessively premature), and on December 14, U.S. forces captured Saddam Hussein in a hideout. The old regime was now, without question, gone.

Governance in the New Iraq

The story of governance in Iraq since 2003 is one centered on two intertwined themes: American involvement in governing, and societal divisions and subsequent violence between insurgents and sectarian groups that have hampered effective administration. These factors underlay an evolving process of governance as the Americans and the Iraqis sought to establish credible, legitimate, and permanent political decision-making structures. The story can be better told through a chronological discussion of events after the overthrow of the old regime.

Washington wanted to impose a democratic political structure on Iraq as part of its broader Middle East policy. It believed that it could do so easily, and that Iraqis would be eager to provide legitimacy to such a structure. But the United States underestimated the extent of ethnic and sectarian divisions in the country, the desire of some Shi'ite groups to assert their dominance over the entire country, and the will and capabilities of an insurgency composed of numerous elements, including supporters of the erstwhile regime and al-Qaeda terrorists.

The United States was determined to hand over governing power to Iraqis as soon as was possible; indeed, Washington believed Iraq would be secure and stable enough that U.S. staff could govern Iraq for a short interim, help establish a constitution and political structure, and then withdraw. This was overly optimistic. At the beginning of 2011 the Iraqi political system was still wracked by mistrust, ethnic and sectarian divisions, and a violent uprising, though levels of violence were declining relative to the immediate years after the invasion.

On April 21, 2003, the United States established the Coalition Provisional Authority (CPA) in Baghdad. This was designed to be a transitional government. The country's political structure had been swept aside, there was no time to organize a proper government of Iraqis, and an American hand at the helm was perceived to be necessary to guide Iraq through the beginning of the process in the face of continuing military activities and domestic and external threats. Moreover, the Iraqi people had no democratic political culture, and it was deemed necessary to educate Iraqis on how a democratic system worked, what their responsibilities were, and what their options were.

At the same time, the CPA sought to break down the Baathist structure of the Saddam era and rebuild the country almost from scratch. To this end, it disbanded the Iraqi military, engaged in a program of "de-Baathification," and in July established the Iraqi Governing Council (IGC). The IGC was made up of twenty-five members appointed by the CPA, representing the various sectarian elements within Iraqi society. Though the CPA had ultimate authority, it was anxious to prove to Iraqi citizens that it was not just the United States that was ruling the country, but Iraqis themselves. The council therefore was to advise the CPA on governing Iraq. It also had the power to appoint interim ministers and, most important, to draft the Transitional Administrative Law (TAL), the provisional constitution that would govern Iraq and its election to a fully staffed and more permanent government (though with American input and advice).

The CPA was designed to govern Iraq for a limited time. But Iraqis quickly grew uncomfortable with the idea of the Americans directly controlling their affairs, and an insurgency was just beginning that called into question the Americans' ability to impose security on the country. In addition, ethnic and sectarian divisions were clearly emerging by then, between Kurds and Arabs and between Sunnis and Shi'ites, both at the political level and in the street, where different factions with their own militias were beginning to fight each other as well as the American-led forces. Finally, the increase in American casualties and a growing awareness among observers in the United States that it was more difficult to govern Iraq than Washington had originally thought put pressure on the administration to transfer authority to the Iraqis more quickly than originally intended.

On March 8, 2003, the IGC signed into effect the TAL, which was to govern Iraq as the provisional constitution until the writing and adoption of a permanent constitution. The CPA and the IGC then together nominated the Iraqi Interim Government (IIG). It was headed by a former member of the IGC, Prime Minister Ayad Allawi, and was designed to be the government of Iraq, operating under the TAL. The IIG became the Iraqi government on June 28, 2004, when the CPA dissolved itself. Crucially, the IIG was recognized by both the United Nations and the Arab League as the rightful, sovereign government of Iraq. This gave it much-needed legitimacy, particularly as the United States still maintained tens of thousands of troops in the country, was responsible for Iraq's internal and external security, and continued to advise the government.

In April, extremist Shi'ite groups, most particularly the Mahdi militia, headed by radical Shi'ite cleric Muqtada al-Sadr, began to openly defy U.S. authority, prompting a failed attempt by the United States to arrest him. The Americans were reluctant to openly challenge Sadr and use the necessary force to bring him in, fearing a negative reaction among the Iraqi population, especially the Shi'ites. This later proved, many observers agree, to be a major strategic mistake, as Sadr was able to continue defying U.S. and Iraqi government authority and, once he won a seat in the December 2005 elections for parliament, promote his radical agenda. His policies, and those of his allies and supporters, helped alienate the Sunnis of Iraq, without whom the government could never claim complete legitimacy and authority.

Once it took power in June 2004, the IIG's main purpose was to guide the country to elections that were to be held on January 30, 2005, for a new government that would write a permanent constitution. The IIG was, like the IGC, plagued with domestic problems, particularly growing rifts between Sunnis and Shi'ites, Kurdish demands for significant autonomy in the north, an insurgency that was growing more violent, and the continued presence of U.S. troops. Iraqis themselves tended to mind the troops less, but did not appreciate American involvement in Iraqi political decision making.

The elections were held as scheduled on January 30, 2005. For the first time since 1958, Iraqis were genuinely free to choose their representatives in a parliament that was not just a rubber stamp for the regime. Over 100 lists competed. Legislators were chosen for the 275-seat Majlis al-Watani (National Assembly), which was the structure that was created in the 1970 provisional constitution under the Baath regime. The United Iraqi Alliance won 48 percent of the vote, giving it 140 seats, while a Kurdish party came in second with 26 percent of the vote. The Alliance is composed of over twenty parties and movements, but is primarily Shi'ite. It contains the two most influential Shi'ite parties in Iraq, the Islamic al-Dawa Party (a conservative, some would argue militant, party dedicated to an Islamist state) and the Supreme Council for the Islamic Revolution in Iraq (now called the Supreme Islamic Iraqi Council, considered to be more moderate than al-Dawa but also devoted to fostering an Islamist state in Iraq).

Talks began almost immediately between the Alliance and other Iraqi parties to form a coalition government. The elections and the new government that was formed in April were, however, undermined by the fact that Sunnis largely boycotted the election. Though Sunnis make up about 35 percent of the population, their largest party in the new Assembly won less than 2 percent of the vote. This undermined the legitimacy of the elections and the new government because it indicated Sunni disatisfaction with the new political structures and, more importantly, the advent of Shi'ite power. Sunnis had long been the dominant group in Iraqi society, and there was disgruntlement and resentment at the new assertion of Shi'ite demographic weight. There was also widespread fear that the Shi'ites might take their revenge against the Sunnis for the violence of the Saddam Hussein regime.

But the new government was formed, and the IIG was dissolved in May. The new government, now called the Iraqi Transitional Government (ITG), began to work on a permanent constitution for the country. The process was stipulated in the TAL: the deadline for the formulation of the new constitution was set at August 15, 2005, and for the submission of the document to a national referendum for October 15, 2005.

However, societal divisions soon imposed themselves on the constitutional negotiations. First, there were disagreements over the role of Islam in the country's political and social structure. Some of the more powerful Shi'ite parties wanted a greater, if not all-encompassing, role for Islam. More secular parties opposed this effort. Second, the Shi'ites and, especially, the Kurds wanted a weaker form of federalism than the Sunnis did. The Sunnis feared that they would be left with a rump, a landlocked state in central Iraq with no open waterway and little or no access to oil (which is concentrated in the Kurdish north and Shi'ite south). Third, there were disagreements over the division of economic wealth, the specific powers to be held by the government, and how hard de-Baathification should be pursued. But there was a strong desire for consensus, to prove the legitimacy of the government and convince Sunnis that the country would not be run by Shi'ites indifferent to their needs, and consequently to undermine the legitimacy of the Sunni-led insurgency. Parliament was convened to extend the deadline for the constitution.

On August 23, just before midnight, the constitution was submitted to the Assembly for a vote, though the vote itself was delayed for three more days to give the parties more time to negotiate Sunni support. With no agreement yet between Sunnis, and Kurds and Shi'ites, the deadline was extended again on August 26 for one more day. Still negotiations continued, but the Sunnis did not in the end agree to support the constitution. The constitutional committee, dominated by Kurds and Shi'ites, then submitted the document to the parliament (which they also dominated) on August 29 for a vote. The constitution could then be submitted to the population at large.

The referendum on the constitution took place on October 15, 2005. Ten days later the results were announced: at a 63 percent turnout, support for the constitution was set at 79 percent. In the three Sunni Arab majority provinces, the results were overwhelmingly against the constitution; in al-Anbar province, 97 percent of those who went to the polls voted "no." However, despite this opposition, the constitution was approved. The TAL had stipulated that it could be rejected only if in three provinces two-thirds of the electorate rejected the constitution. In the third majority Sunni Arab province, however, only about 50 percent, not two-thirds, voted "no." The constitution was accepted.

The success of the referendum paved the way for elections on December 15, 2005, of a permanent Iraqi government. Representatives were elected to a 275-seat Council of Representatives (Majlis an-Nuwwab), which now replaced the old National Assembly. Turnout was estimated to be around 70 percent. Again, the Shi'ite and Kurdish parties dominated. The United Iraqi Alliance won just over 40 percent of the vote (128 seats), and the Democratic Patriotic Alliance of Kurdistan received 22 percent of the vote (53 seats). The Iraqi Accord Front, a mainly Sunni Arab party, came in third at 15 percent of the vote (44 seats). (In the January 2005 elections the largest Sunni party had received only five mandates in the Assembly.) In April and May 2006, the new government of Iraq was established through bargaining between various parties in the Council, giving a role to all three communal groups (the Kurds, the Sunnis, and the Shi'ites). This led to the creation of the first genuinely democratic government in Iraqi history.

The executive is now structured like any executive in any democracy: there is a prime minister at its head (with a more ceremonial president and two vice presidents), a bicameral legislature (the Council of Representatives—now expanded to 325 seats—and a higher body, the Federation Council—Majlis al-Ittihad—which is designed to represent Iraqis on a more regional level, but has yet to be installed or its power delineated), and an independent judiciary. In short, Iraq's political structure is now democratic; this represents a major shift from all previous regimes and, in this context, represents a major new form of government in the Arab world.

The Future of Governance in Iraq

Many questions remain regarding the future stability of the Iraqi political system. The democratic structure that has been built is somewhat fragile. The government faces a lingering insurgency that, despite an intensive American effort, shows no sign of ending. Tensions between Sunnis and Shi'ites have broken out into open violence between the two communities, such that some observers refer to a civil war in Iraq. Iran has been jockeying for influence in the country, particularly through the Shi'ites. Sunnis are still resentful, wary, and reluctant to grant full legitimacy to the new government.

Divisions among the politicians, partly related to the existence of armed militias associated with various political parties, have not been easily bridged. The death toll of Iraqi civilians (and American soldiers) under the conditions of sectarian violence and brutality and the uprising remains high, though the number of deaths began declining per month. Into 2011, though, violence began to spike again, and crime was increasing considerably. Economic growth has not been substantial enough, and the central government has had problems delivering the services it is responsible for, such as basic plumbing, health care, and security. Many Iraqis have given their loyalty not to Baghdad but to various tribal groups and chiefs, religious sects or leaders, and ethnic communities. There is, in short, widespread mistrust, suspicion, resentment, and wariness about the new government and system.

Political instability continues as well. Due to contradictory stipulations in the constitution, there was some uncertainty when elections would take place in 2010. The Supreme Court considered the issue, and in May 2009, ruled that elections would be held at the end of January 2010. However, the elections were postponed over internal disputes and politicking, as parties were unable to agree on basic electoral rules. A political crisis ensued at the end of 2009/beginning of 2010, when political and judicial officials banned hundreds of candidates from running based on ties to the now-disbanded Baath Party. The decision raised fears about political disenfranchisement of many Iraqis, particularly Sunnis, as well as a renewal of violence after months of decline—both of which threatened to undermine the legitimacy and stability of the governing system. Elections did take place in March 2010, with the results in many ways similar to previous elections: The Iraqi National Movement under former prime minister Ayad Allawi and composed of Shi'ite and Sunni parties won ninety-one seats; the State of Law Coalition under former prime minister Nouri al-Maliki, composed of Shi'ite parties received eighty-nine mandates; the National Iraqi Alliance, a largely Islamist Shi'ite group, took seventy seats; and the Kurdistan List received forty-three. As before, disputes among the parties prevented a government from being formed until the end of 2010: not until December 22 did al-Maliki receive parliamentary approval to form a government.

Finally, determined to meet his campaign pledge to withdraw from Iraq, President Barack Obama oversaw the removal of many combat troops from Iraq by August 19, 2010, and committed to the withdrawal of all additional American soldiers by December 2011 (though some troops and military advisors are expected to remain). This has prompted many to wonder whether the Iraqi military, police, and security forces will be equipped to deal with the insurgency and other challenges by then on their own.

The U.S. invasion in March 2003, and the imposition of democratic order in the aftermath of the overthrow of Saddam Hussein's regime, is really only the latest episode in a long history of revolution, coups, rebellions, and violence that has characterized modern Iraqi politics. The American intention is to make this new order last. Therefore, what the United States decides to do in the near future, what Iran decides to do, and how Iraqis decide to handle themselves and the development of their political system will have an impact on the future of the new Iraq.

References and Further Reading

Bengio, Ofra. *Saddam's Word: Political Discourse in Iraq.* Oxford: Oxford University Press, 1998.

Diamond, Larry. *Squandered Victory: The American Occupation and the Bungled Effort to Bring Democracy to Iraq.* New York: Henry Holt, 2005.

Hiro, Dilip. *The Longest War: The Iran-Iraq Military Conflict.* London: Grafton, 1989.

Marr, Phebe. *The Modern History of Iraq.* 2nd ed. Boulder, CO: Westview Press, 2003.

Postscript

This study has covered the general period up to 2010. However, as mentioned throughout, sudden new developments took place at the end of 2010 and beginning of 2011 that require some clarification and discussion. Referred to variously as the demonstrations in the Arab world, the "Arab spring," or the Arab uprising, these have been a series of protests and civil disobedience campaigns by populations in many Arab states against their regimes. Together they have contributed to what Marc Lynch has called "structural" changes in the Arab populations that, whatever the final outcome, have changed the pattern of state-society interactions in the Arab world forever.

Though there were specific immediate causes for the onset of the revolutions in Tunisia and Egypt, the popular protests were not unexpected. Certainly few anticipated the timing and the extent, but the conditions in the Arab countries described above—stagnating economies, very young populations, repressive and tired regimes and their lack of legitimacy among the populace—were widely considered to be fertile conditions for change. The regimes did, as could have been predicted, respond violently to the protests, but what was perhaps most surprising was the relatively low levels of violence. Compared to past reactions by the regimes, security forces did not engage in as widespread violence as in the past. Equally important, the leaders of the regimes seemed surprisingly weak, as they gave in to the protests very quickly. Some simply fled the country, while others promised (and to one degree or another began to enact) changes to open up the political and economic systems to greater participation.

The demonstrations began in Tunisia. The proximate cause was the self-immolation of Mohamed Bouazizi. Bouazizi sold vegetables, but apparently did not have an official license to do so. When on December 17, 2010, the police confiscated his cart, slapped him, and refused to hear his complaint, he set himself on fire (he died in a hospital a few weeks later). Small protests began against the heavy-handed reaction of the regime, and two more Tunisians killed themselves in protest. The demonstrations swelled and expanded to other cities, and focused on the lack of economic opportunities available to the people. They also took aim at the president of Tunisia himself, Zine el Abidine Ben Ali. As the regime responded with increasingly harsh tactics, including beatings, shootings, and curfews, other groups joined the protests. On January 14, Ben Ali abruptly fled the country, and although efforts were made after that to retain some structure of the old regime in place, it was clear that deeper changes would be forthcoming.

Much is made of the role of social and electronic media (such as al-Jazeera, Twitter, and Facebook) in implementing and spreading the revolutions. Certainly, the greater awareness of what was happening around the Arab world contributed to an inspiration and call to action not seen since the days of Nasser and his radio addresses. After Tunisia, unrest spread to other Arab states, including Algeria, Libya, Jordan, Yemen, Saudi Arabia, Egypt, Syria, and Bahrain. In these Arab states, varying levels of violence have been used by the regimes against the demonstrators, combined with vague promises of political and economic reform. Such reforms reached their peak in Egypt, where President Hosni Mubarak also eventually fled, and in Yemen, where President Ali Abdullah Saleh announced he would step down from government in 2013.

In some places the protests have become part of broader regional and global dynamics. In Bahrain, the regime has successfully altered the narrative of the protesters from one of a struggle for human rights and civil liberty to one of a larger fight between Shias and Sunnis over the future of the region. This has helped bring the Saudis into the country, to provide protection for the Sunni al-Khalifa regime. And in Libya, a vicious civil war was waged by dissidents and rebels who, believing momentum was on their side, initiated an armed insurrection against Libyan leader Muammar Qaddafi. Qaddafi's reactions were among the most violent, and until his death in October 2011, he publicly promised to mete out severe punishment to those struggling against him. These hints of brutality combined with Libya's geostrategic position brought the United States and NATO into the country to enforce United Nations Security Council–approved no-fly zones over parts of the country, in order to protect the rebels and give them room to advance against Qaddafi.

In none of these countries are the outcomes certain, and at best we can only make informed guesses about the future. In Egypt, for example, the military retains a powerful position in the post-Mubarak era, and it is leading the shift away from the old regime. In such cases it is unlikely the military will give up its share of power easily. In other states, entrenched minorities, tribes, sectarian groups, and economic elites all benefit from maintenance of the old regimes, and they, too, are not likely to give up so quickly.

Another prominent consideration is the role of Islamist groups. As mentioned previously, these groups—wanting to impose strict Muslim law and norms on society—posed the greatest threat to the regimes because they are the best organized and most widely supported, and because of their direct appeal to the cultural and spiritual norms and personal preferences of many of the region's inhabitants. The weakening and disappearance of the very regimes that had suppressed them have provided room for their public activities, including political participation.

Again Egypt provides a clue to these developments. There the Muslim Brotherhood was banned under Mubarak, its leaders alternately arrested or kept out of politics. But with no other organization capable of competing with it in terms of its mobilization, familiarity, and attraction (with a partial exception of the regime's National Democratic Party) it is poised to do best in any elections that occur in the immediate future. Despite the Brotherhood's efforts to reassure Egyptians and outsiders to the contrary, this raises for many the specter of an Islamist state similar to the Iranian model, with its consequent repression of human rights and its antipathy to Western interests and values. Even more, concerns have begun to be voiced that extremist Islamist groups could easily take advantage of the chaos and new public space in the Arab world to advance their own violent jihadist agenda. Discussion of al-Qaeda's appearance in Libya is pointed out as an example.

To repeat: the politics and state-society interactions in the Arab world seem to have changed forever. The relatively mild reactions of the Arab regimes to the protests and threats to their position, in comparison to past responses, indicate that even the regimes are aware of the new era. Moreover, the populations have shown themselves willing to chance violence and even death in order to promote a new relationship between the state and the populace. Aware of their growing power, demonstrators—particularly among the youth—seem set on changing the structure of the Arab world.

In the past analysts often lamented that the waves of democracy that swept the world after the Cold War were blocked in the Middle East by the barriers of regime fears. These dams now appear to have been broken, and while they may be repaired to some extent, it is doubtful they can ever be as fully functioning again as they once were.

Further Reading

Lynch, Marc, Blake Hounshell, and Susan Glasser, eds. *Revolution in the Arab World: Tunisia, Egypt, and the Unmaking of an Era*. Foreign Policy Magazine: Digital edition, 2011.

Part II

Middle East Economics

Patrick Clawson

Economics in the Middle East

An Introduction

In many ways, the Middle East seems to fit poorly with the rest of the world. At a time when armed conflict in Europe has become unthinkable and the Cold War is a distant memory, the Middle East is torn by instability and war, from global terrorism to the violence in Iraq to the Palestinian-Israeli conflict. While much of the world celebrates tolerance and diversity, many in the Middle East wish the state to impose rigid adherence to a strict social code and deny full rights to religious minorities. Many in the region admire suicide bombers, prepared to kill innocent civilians and themselves in the name of their cause. How to integrate the Middle East more fully into the world community is arguably the great challenge of our times. As long as the heartland of Islam remains so troubled, there is a threat of instability spreading to other Muslim communities, ranging from Western Europe south to tropical Africa and east to China.

In addition to its social and political problems, much of the Middle East has not done well economically, though some countries—especially Israel and the oil-rich monarchies of the Persian Gulf—have been exceptions. That mixed record comes despite many advantages that should have helped the region prosper, such as its proximity to massive European markets and its ample oil wealth. What went wrong in some Middle Eastern countries, and why have other Middle Eastern economies done better?

The region's principal economic problem has been lagging globalization. The World Bank's 2003 *Trade, Investment, and Development in the Middle East and North Africa* shows that in 1950, Middle Eastern economies had seven times the world average export performance, with exports at 45 percent of gross domestic product (GDP) when the world average was 6 percent. Fifty years later, the Middle East had slipped and the rest of the world had caught up, so that both the Middle East and world average export share of GDP were about 17 percent.

Fundamental Differences

Any understanding of how Middle Eastern economies have performed must start with appreciating the extraordinary diversity among the region's twenty countries—Israel, Iran, and the eighteen main Arab League members, excluding the small, peripheral Arab League states of Comoros, Djibouti, Mauritania, and Somalia (note that this volume excludes Turkey, which has many unique characteristics that separate it from the core Middle East countries).

Consider the stereotype of the region as one rich in oil and poor in water. To be sure, oil is produced in fifteen of the twenty countries—all except Morocco and the Levant states of Israel, Lebanon, Jordan, and the Palestinian territories. But there is a world of difference between the annual output of 500 barrels per person in Qatar or 320 barrels in Kuwait and the 7 barrels in Yemen, 4 in Sudan, or 3 in Egypt.

Water availability differs nearly as much as oil. Iraq has more renewable water per person than does Great Britain, while Iran and Sudan have more than Germany. The water in Iraq, Iran, and

---

The emphasis in this analysis is on long-term trends which will almost certainly persist for years to come. That said, the Middle East is a constantly changing region. This analysis reflects developments as of 2009.

Sudan is not equally distributed across the country; each has vast desert areas. The Gulf monarchies and Libya have deserts but not the offsetting rivers. They have the lowest renewable water per person of any countries in the world; Kuwait's renewable water per person is less than 1/400th that of its neighbor Iraq.

Like oil and water resources, income in the Middle East varies vastly. The gap between the average income in the poorest state (Yemen) and the richest (Israel and the small Gulf monarchies, especially Kuwait and Qatar) is more than 25:1. That is a much greater divide than among the states of Africa, Europe, North America, or South America.

Even greater than the gap in resources and income are the cultural differences. Israel, for example, is in many ways more a part of Europe than of the Middle East when it comes to its political, economic, and social culture, yet its main political ally is the United States. Much analysis of the Middle East simply leaves Israel out, and it is generally not included in World Bank data on the averages for the "Middle East and North Africa" (MENA) region.

While the post-1979 emphasis of the Iranian Revolution on the Islamic element in politics may make Iran seem similar to the eighteen Arab countries, Iranian society is vastly different from the societies of the Arab countries. At every level, from language to social behavior and family life, the way that Iranians conduct their lives differs sharply from Arab sensibilities. The civilizational divide between Iran and its Arab neighbors has been deep and profound for 2,500 years, centuries before Islam came on the scene.

For that matter, even among Arab League members, differences are large enough to make dubious the concept of an "Arab world" or "Arab street." The North African states known as the Maghreb—Morocco, Algeria, and Tunisia, sometimes including Libya—are much more oriented toward Europe than toward the Arab east. Egypt has a long and proud history of separate nationalism; the attachment of the Nile Valley's children to its land is not easily broken. Sudan is in many ways a part of sub-Saharan Africa rather than the Arab world. The six Gulf monarchies in the Gulf Cooperation Council (GCC)—Saudi Arabia, Kuwait, Bahrain, Qatar, Oman, United Arab Emirates (UAE), and Oman—are in many ways a world apart. Until only a few decades ago, they were profoundly poor and deeply isolated from the rest of the world. It is hard to appreciate how recent have been the changes for these oil-rich states. In 1966, Abu Dhabi—the richest part of the UAE—had exactly 6 primary schools with 587 students, students who in 2010 would be aged 50 to 56.

Among the factors affecting their economic performance, perhaps the most important differences among Middle Eastern countries has been political evolution. For decades, the region has been the most war-torn part of the world. Lebanon is struggling to recover the income level it had before the civil war started in 1975. Only with the post-2005 oil boom did Algeria exceed its 1959 pre-independence income level. Iraq remains below its 1982 peak at the start of what was twenty-seven years of near-continuous war. Palestinian incomes in 2009 were well below the level of 1993, when Israel and the Palestine Liberation Organization signed Oslo "Declaration of Principles" for peace.

Less dramatic than war but almost as debilitating has been the slow corrosion of the economy from deadening hand of state control. Many Arab states imitated the "Arab socialism" model heralded by Egyptian president Gamal Abdel Nasser in 1960, which after a few years led to sharply lower economic growth. By contrast, the region's success stories have taken place in countries that embraced entrepreneurialism and globalism, such as the United Arab Emirates and Qatar.

Given the profound differences among Middle Eastern countries and the extraordinary importance of politics in explaining economic outcome, country-by-country stories should be emphasized. Less important are regional averages and the evolution of such economic indicators as productivity growth and the efficiency of capital investment. The account that follows is unabashedly political economy rather than quantitative analysis. Furthermore, the country accounts themselves emphasize historical evolution, because the political constraints to improving policy in the future can only be understood by analyzing how the present set of policies evolved.

Historical Context and Present Challenges

To an economist comparing the Middle East with other developing regions, the Middle East's economic performance has been moderate—not the levels of growth of East Asia, but also not the stagnation of much of sub-Saharan Africa. But that is not how the peoples of the region judge the situation. The first *Arab Human Development Report* in 2002, written by leading Arab thinkers, had harsh criticism of the region's performance, especially its failure to turn higher income into broader development, leading to deficits in freedom, women's empowerment, and human capabilities/knowledge.

The Arab peoples have a general self-conception that the Middle East should have great and powerful societies. The Iranian self-conception is even higher, namely, that Iran still is a great and powerful society, undervalued by the rest of the world. After all, the Middle East was once a world power center. A mere 300 years ago, the Ottoman Empire, which at the time included the Arab Middle East all the way to North Africa, stood at the gates of Vienna; it was defeated only by combined armies of Europe. Only 200 years ago, with Napoleon's invasion of Egypt, did the Arab world perceive its backwardness relative to Europe. At about the same time, Iran began to lose half of its territory in a series of wars against Russian and British Indian forces.

More recently, consider how the Mediterranean looked on the eve of World War II. With fascist rule in Spain and Italy, its European shores were arguably less democratic than the imperfect parliamentary democracies in Egypt and Iraq. Alexandria and Cairo were arguably more liberal socially, freer intellectually, and generally more cosmopolitan than southern Europe. Islam had less of an oppressive role in Egypt than did the Catholic Church in Italy and Spain or the Orthodox churches in southeast Europe. In *Egypt at Mid-Century*, Charles Issawi provides a description of the relative income of various Mediterranean economies in 1950: Egypt's income per person was 80 percent that of Greece and 45 percent that of Italy. And French Algeria was much richer than Egypt. The best estimate is that on the eve of World War II, the gap in income between the Mediterranean's northern and southern shores—between southern Europe and North Africa and the Levant—was no more than the 2:1 gap existing then between the northern and southern parts of the United States. By contrast, World Bank data show that in 2009, Egypt's income was a mere 12 percent that of Greece and 7 percent that of Italy.

Years of Development

Indeed, as recently as the mid-1980s, the Middle East looked like an economic success story. In the period 1960–1985, its growth was well above the world average, at 3.7 percent per person per year in real terms. The Middle East grew vigorously both when the rest of the world did in the 1960s and when the rest of the world economy was in the doldrums in the 1970s (the exception was Israel, where there was an economic crisis).

Middle East governments misused the 1960–1985 boom years, laying the foundations for later problems. The public sector's weight in the economy expanded massively; private investment was only a modest share of national income while massive sums were poured into public investments. Much of that public investment went either into overbuilt infrastructure well in excess of needs or into inward-oriented industries that were uncompetitive and intensive users of expensive imported inputs and nonrenewable natural resources, as well as being highly polluting. At least as damaging was the steering of the benefits of the sustained economic growth to key constituencies, especially civil servants and workers in state-owned enterprises. This was at the root of the "authoritarian bargain" in which the public acquiesced to autocrats controlling politics in return for jobs and generous public services for the privileged middle classes. Furthermore, the "redistributive state" entrenched and empowered bureaucrats who extended and deepened their control over the economy.

Economic Stagnation

From 1985 to 2000, most of the Middle East economies outside Israel fell badly behind the rest of the world, growing at a slower rate than even sub-

Saharan Africa. The region did not fall backward in an absolute sense; it just stopped moving forward. For the Middle East and North Africa overall (excluding Israel), the International Monetary Fund calculated that 2002 per capita income was no higher than it had been at its peak in 1977, twenty-five years earlier. The region largely missed the global 1990s boom; only Israel grew rapidly in that decade, although some of the modestly reforming non-oil economies, especially Tunisia and Egypt, grew at respectable rates. The inward-oriented, uncompetitive Middle East industries were not able to take advantage of the explosion in world trade in manufactured goods; in 2003, the entire Arab Middle East exported fewer manufactured goods than did the Philippines. The World Bank estimates that exports other than oil are one-third of what they could be, given the characteristics of the Middle East.

Meanwhile, for all the talk of economic reform, bureaucracies proved highly resistant to change. In its *Trade, Investment, and Development in the Middle East and North Africa* report, the World Bank summarized the problem as a "lack of commitment by the leadership in governments of the region to new policy directions." Furthermore, the report noted that much of civil society—including public-sector employees, unions, media opinion leaders, and private enterprises—"remains deeply wedded to the security and benefits of the old order." The problems were further exacerbated by a lack of commitment to economic reform.

Decrease in Economic Gaps

After 2000, the gap in economic performance between the Middle East and the rest of the world largely disappeared, partly because of solid growth in much of the Middle East and partly because of poor growth in the industrial countries. In 2000–2007, the oil-producing countries of the Middle East benefited from rising oil prices. Oil prices stabilized in 2008–2009 at a level much higher than the average of preceding decades (even when the prices of earlier years are adjusted for inflation). Sharply higher export earnings provided governments with ample revenue. On the whole, the money from the post-2000 oil boom has been better used than was the revenue of the 1973–1985 oil boom. A notable exception was the city-state of Dubai in the United Arab Emirates, where the government encouraged frenzied real estate speculation financed by heavy borrowing. The 2008 world financial crisis hit Dubai hard, but had less of an impact on most Middle Eastern economies than its effect on the industrial countries.

The post-2000 experience suggests that at least in some parts of the Middle East, the approach to economic development is undergoing a profound shift. For many decades, the most striking similarity across Middle Eastern economies has been that political agendas trump economic considerations. That has been true whether the political agenda was Zionism, Palestinian nationalism, Arab unity, or Islamic revolution. In contrast with the region's fascination with politics, Arabs in particular have been much less interested in economic development. In *The Arab Economies in a Changing World*, Howard Pack and Marcus Noland document the relative absence of Arab voices in contemporary debates about development strategy and how little Arabs discuss the development experiences of other countries and regions, such as East Asia's success. China came through its Cultural Revolution determined to put economic development above ideological purity; in the words of Chinese Communist Party leader Deng Xiaoping, "To get rich is glorious." Many in the Middle East would disagree with that ordering of priorities.

And even those Middle Easterners who care about economics frequently have had a zero-sum mentality. In the Middle East, mutual benefit is not necessarily seen as a good thing. Locals may view political adversaries as an enemy whom they do not want strengthened—an attitude often evident in Israeli-Palestinian dealings on economic matters. Or they may fear that if the foreigner benefits in a deal, that means they are being cheated and exploited—a belief heard often in Arab and Iranian objections to dealings with international oil companies and other foreign investors. Such an atmosphere—where politics matters more than prosperity, where mutual benefit is regarded with suspicion—is far removed from the "rational economic man" assumed in economic theory. These Middle Eastern attitudes do much to explain why so many in the region are ambivalent, if not hostile, to globalization in all its aspects. Integrating the

Middle East more fully with the rest of the world will be a long-term struggle.

References and Further Reading

Abed, George T., and Hamid R. Davoodi. "Challenges of Growth and Globalization in the Middle East and North Africa." Available at www.imf.org/external/pubs/ft/med/2003/eng/abed.htm.

Alnsarawi, Abbas. *Arab Nationalism, Oil, and the Political Economy of Dependency.* Westport, CT: Greenwood, 1991.

Glain, Stephen. *Mullahs, Merchants, and Militants: The Economic Collapse of the Arab World.* New York: Thomas Dunne Books/St. Martin's, 2004.

Henry, Clement, and Robert Springborg. *Globalization and the Politics of Development in the Middle East.* Cambridge, UK: Cambridge University Press, 2001.

Iqbal, Farrukh. *Sustaining Gains in Poverty Reduction and Human Development in the Middle East and North Africa.* Washington, DC: World Bank, 2006.

Owen, Roger, and Şevket Pamuk. *A History of Middle East Economies in the Twentieth Century.* Cambridge, MA: Harvard University Press, 1999.

Pack, Howard, and Marcus Noland. *The Arab Economies in a Changing World.* Washington, DC: Institute for International Economics, 2007.

Richards, Alan, and John Waterbury. *A Political Economy of the Middle East: State, Class, and Economic Development.* Boulder, CO: Westview Press, 1990.

Rivlin, Paul. *Arab Economies in the Twenty-First Century,* Cambridge, UK: Cambridge University Press, 2009.

Shafik, Nemat, ed. *Economic Challenges Facing Middle Eastern and North African Economies: Alternative Futures.* New York: St. Martin's Press, 1998.

———. *Prospects for Middle Eastern and North African Economies: From Boom to Bust and Back?* New York: St. Martin's Press, 1998.

World Bank. *Trade, Investment, and Development in the Middle East and North Africa: Engaging with the World.* Washington, DC: World Bank, 2003.

Yousef, Tarik. "Development, Growth, and Policy Reform in the Middle East and North Africa Since 1950." *Journal of Economic Perspectives* 18:3 (Summer 2004): 91–116.

Section 1. Common Issues

Oil

Oil is of vast importance in the Middle East, and its impact on the region has been magnified by the volatile character of global oil prices. Many commentators emphasize political factors or fundamental resource shortages to explain the periodic dramatic price increases, although in fact the industry's history is as full of dramatic price declines. The classic economic explanation for the industry's unstable character is in P.H. Frankel's 1946 *Essentials of Petroleum.* He argued that the oil industry lacks the usual self-adjusting mechanism in which price increases quickly lead to more supply and less demand; instead, supply and demand adjust very slowly to price changes because of the uncertain results of exploration, the high overhead costs at all stages of the industry, and the unresponsiveness of demand in the short run to price increases. Frankel's thesis has only been strengthened by the growth since 1946 of oil nationalism, that is, political movements demanding greater control over the industry by the producing-country governments. The initial impact of that nationalism was to depress oil prices: uncertain how long their concessions would last, oil companies had an incentive to raise output. After nationalization, the bias has been toward higher prices. Having taken over from the oil companies, governments could more effectively act as a cartel to restrict output, thereby putting a floor under prices. Meanwhile, their exclusion of potential investors impeded the expansion of output in the most promising areas, thereby limiting the usual process that puts a ceiling on prices.

The Middle East's oil resources are broad and deep. Of the twenty countries in the Middle East and North Africa, fifteen produce oil; the exceptions are Morocco and the four Levant countries of Israel, Lebanon, Jordan, and the Palestinian territories. The region has two-thirds of the world's oil reserves. In 2008, it produced 31 million barrels a day (b/d) of oil—38 percent of the world total—while consuming only 8 million b/d of oil. Its 23 million b/d of oil exports were half of the world's oil exports. The Middle East and North Africa's role in natural gas is not quite as dominant. It has 45 percent of the world's gas reserves, but in 2008 its production was only 18 percent of the world's total. Furthermore, three-fourths of that production was consumed at home, much of it in energy-intensive industries, with the result that Middle Eastern gas is a small part of energy consumption in Europe, Asia, and the Americas.

The West's Involvement

From the discovery of oil in the Middle East just before World War I until the early 1970s, the terms on which oil was produced in the Middle East were largely dictated by the West. In the early decades, Western governments such as that of Great Britain were the principal actors, whereas the international oil companies (IOCs) became the main players in the 1950s and 1960s.

1911–1953

Oil was first discovered in Egypt in 1911 and Iran in 1913. This was a time of colonialist European empires that locked up access to raw materials, constructing elaborate mechanisms to keep trade within the empire; only the United States was somewhat interested in an "open door" policy, as Washington's phrase went, and that by no means precluded direct political pressure on behalf of U.S. corporations. Middle Eastern oil was firmly kept within this system in which politics rather than economics determined development, and where local officials had a limited say.

The most obvious case of European government control over Middle Eastern oil was in Iran. In conjunction with his decision to convert the Royal Navy from coal to oil, Winston Churchill, as First Lord of the Admiralty just before World War I, managed to persuade the British government to purchase 51 percent of the new Anglo-Persian Oil Company, which went on to become British Petroleum decades later. Since it reaped dividends and taxes on Anglo-Persian's profits, the British government had every incentive to keep profits high by reducing as much as possible the payments to the Iranian government, while on the other hand it also had every incentive to see Iran become one of the world's major oil producers, which it quickly did. For decades, Iranian leaders were unhappy about the unfavorable terms of the concession agreement.

After World War II, nationalist tensions within Iran about oil propelled to prominence the populist politician Mohammed Mossadegh. He successfully opposed an oil concession for the USSR in northern Iran, agreed on in 1946 as part of the package deal to end Soviet occupation of northwest Iran (the Soviets had invaded Iran during World War II). After he became Iran's prime minister in 1951, Mossadegh nationalized the Anglo-Iranian Oil Company, as it was then called. Even though the Labor government in Britain had been actively nationalizing many basic industries in the UK, it was outraged at Mossadegh's action. Britain successfully organized an international boycott of Iranian oil, blocked efforts by the Truman administration to work out a compromise with World Bank financing, and persuaded the new Eisenhower administration in 1953 to help organize Mossadegh's overthrow. In the aftermath, Anglo-Iranian had to yield to a consortium with 40 percent ownership by American oil companies, 6 percent by the French national oil firm, and 14 percent by its half-British rival Royal Dutch Shell.

Contentious as the disputes were between the Iranian government and the Western powers about oil, it was in this setting that the oil industry took root. By contrast, in Iraq, byzantine politicking among outside powers and stubborn stances by local politicians slowed oil development for decades. From 1900 on, Britain, Germany, and France used every tool at their disposal to secure oil concessions from the Ottoman authorities, which in 1913 were consolidated into the Turkey Petroleum Company. After World War I, the company's fate was subject to the same sort of political jockeying, with the intriguing twist that 5 percent of the renamed Iraq Petroleum Company ended up in the hands of C.S. Gulbenkian, the promoter who successfully arranged the final allocation among U.S., British, and French firms. The complexity of the deal can be illustrated by the provision that for twenty-five years, 10 percent of all royalties due to the Iraqi government were owed to the Turkish government.

Today, the Gulf monarchies from Kuwait in the west through Saudi Arabia to Oman in the east are the center of Middle Eastern oil riches. By contrast, for decades after the demand for oil took off after World War I with the rapid growth of the motorcar industry, geologists nearly unanimously deemed Gulf Arab monarchies so unpromising that there was little reason to look for oil in their territories. But the persistent efforts of the New Zealander Major Frank Holmes persuaded several American oil firms to back exploration in various places. The British, who dominated the Gulf, were intensely annoyed, but had to let in the Americans under pressure from Washington. Saudi Arabia, where British influence was smallest, was pleased to be able to use the U.S. presence to counteract London's preeminent regional role. Oil was found first in Bahrain in 1932, followed by Kuwait and Saudi Arabia in 1938. However, production prior to World War II was small. Even after the war, the importance of the Gulf Arab monarchies was not appreciated. In the late 1940s, the general figure for Saudi oil reserves was 5–7 billion barrels, a gross underestimate: by 2006, Saudi Arabia had produced more than 120 billion barrels and still had 264 billion barrels in proven reserves, as well as potentially another 300–500 billion barrels of oil yet to be solidly confirmed. Oil production in the Arab Gulf monarchies did not really take off until Iran's exports ceased during the 1951–1953 nationalization crisis.

1953–1970

The 1950s and 1960s were a period of extraordinary expansion for the oil industry, and Middle Eastern oil led the way. In 1946, global oil output was 8 million b/d, of which only 0.7 million b/d came from the Middle East. At that time, the United States dominated the world oil business, providing 5 million b/d. From 1946 to 1972, global output increased more than sixfold, with over half of that increased output from the Middle East. In 1972, global oil production was 54 million b/d, of which 24 million b/d were from the Middle East, while U.S. output was only 11 million b/d. It is no exaggeration to say that the discovery of giant oil fields in the Middle East fueled the postwar economic boom. Furthermore, the Middle East had come to dominate the industry, replacing the preeminence of the United States.

A leading reason for the post–World War II economic boom was a breakdown of the prewar system of imperial preferences. Oil was a prime case in point; the oil business increasingly became a seamlessly integrated entity across the free world, leaving out only the Eastern bloc. As part of this process, the leadership of the industry in many ways passed from governments to IOCs, especially the "Seven Sisters"—Standard Oil of New Jersey (later Exxon), Socony Mobil, Standard of California (later Chevron), Gulf, Texaco, British Petroleum, and Royal Dutch Shell—but also the Compagnie Française des Pétroles (CFP). That said, the oil business was hardly a free market activity: regulations, close political connections, and oligopolistic practices preserved special privileges for the large firms. High on the list of what kept control of the industry in these firms' hands were their monopoly concessions in Middle Eastern oil-producing states. While Western governments fiercely defended those concessions, they were also seen at the time as being advantageous for Middle Eastern rulers. There were few cases of closer collaboration between a producing country government and the IOCs than in Saudi Arabia, where the Arabian-American Oil Company (Aramco) was a joint venture between Standard Oil of California and Texaco.

The large and highly profitable IOCs were the subject of much resentment, and many theories pervaded about their political power. However powerful, the oil companies did not always get their way. Inspired by Venezuela's action—which it actively publicized throughout the Middle East—the region's oil producers were able in the early 1950s to get more favorable terms, under which oil profits were split fifty-fifty between the government and the IOCs. The U.S. government strongly supported these revised terms because Washington wanted to prop up the conservative Middle Eastern oil-rich states as part of the global struggle against the USSR and leftist forces. A decade later, in the early 1960s, came another dispute about how to react to a glut of oil, a recurrent problem from the 1920s through 1960s. Faced with Soviet exports at half their prices, the IOCs unilaterally cut prices. Furious, Gulf producers joined with Venezuela to form the Organization of Petroleum Exporting Countries (OPEC) to increase their bargaining leverage with the IOCs. They were soon joined by Algeria, where oil was found in 1956, and Libya, where oil was discovered in 1959.

By 1970, the power of the IOCs was being hollowed out by forces few fully appreciated at the time. Within a few short years, the governments of the oil-producing countries in the Middle East had assumed control over the oil industry, setting prices and appropriating nearly all of the profits from oil production. The governments' domination has continued ever since. They have had a checkered record at ending the cyclical character of the oil business, as prices have periodically soared and crashed.

The 1971–1985 Boom

Oil use rocketed after 1965; global demand grew from 32 million b/d that year to 54 million b/d a mere seven years later in 1972. Middle Eastern and North African producers supplied two-thirds of that extra demand, as they increased their output from 10 million b/d in 1965 to 24 million in 1972. With oil demand growing so quickly and with no place other than the Middle East to get that additional oil, Middle Eastern oil producers were in position to change the rules of the game in their favor, and that is exactly what they did. The first to act was Libya, which had attracted the smaller oil firms known as the "independents" as well as the larger IOCs. The independents were less able to resist Libya's pressure for unilateral revisions in the terms of the concessions and its demands for higher prices for its much-desired high-quality oil. Seeing Libya's success in 1970, the other producers wanted similar terms. The February 1971 Tehran Agreement between OPEC and the IOCs marked the end of the IOC era and the start of the OPEC era. In the next few years, the IOCs had to cede control and ownership of the oil reserves to the local governments, with varying degrees of compensation being paid (very little in the more radical states such as Iraq, generous amounts in the more conservative states such as Saudi Arabia).

The implications of the transformation in the oil industry were not understood by Western leaders until the 1973 October War between Israel and Egypt and Syria. Furious at U.S. support for Israel, first Saudi Arabia and then the other Arab oil producers (with Iraq as the exception) embargoed oil shipments to the United States, as well as to Israel-friendly Portugal and the Netherlands. The 5 million b/d reduction in Arab oil output caused what can only be described as panic in the West, as governments suddenly realized their economic and strategic vulnerability to Arab oil pressure. The price of Arabian Light oil on the spot market, which had been $1.90 a barrel in 1972, reached $10.41 in 1974. The burden of higher payments for oil added to the pressures on the world economy, which was already slipping into recession at the same time that inflation was soaring. Western economies went through several years of "stagflation"—slow economic growth accompanied by roaring inflation—in part due to the difficulties of adjusting to the oil price increases, made worse by the poorly formulated policies of Western governments.

While the Arab oil embargo ended within a few months, Middle East oil producers now knew they were in the driver's seat and took advantage of the situation. For the rest of the 1970s, OPEC was split about how much to push up prices. While the shah of Iran was a close political ally of the United States, on oil prices, he opposed U.S. wishes by being the price "hawk." He wanted to maximize how much Iran could earn from its fast-diminishing oil reserves. U.S. preferences were reflected by the price "doves" led by the Saudi kings, who at the time were somewhat reserved in their attitude to the United States because of U.S. support for Israel. They wanted to ensure that consumers did not switch from oil to other energy sources, since Saudi Arabia's vast reserves guaranteed the kingdom would be a major oil producer for at least a century. As Iranian and Saudi policies illustrate, governments adopted oil price policies which fit their economic interests, rather than using oil prices to advance political relations with foreign powers. In practice, the Saudis prevailed; the spot price for Arabian Light rose only modestly at a time of raging inflation, to $13.03 in 1978. But then came the 1979 Iranian Revolution, when Iran's oil output was disrupted by strikes before being cut 3 million b/d by the new revolutionary government. Panic broke out anew, and Arabian Light soared to $29.75 in 1980 and $35.69 in 1981. Oil prices then drifted slowly lower, to $27.53 a barrel in 1985.

The 1986–1999 Crash

The boom carried the seed of its own destruction. High oil prices reversed decades of rapid demand growth; from the peak of 64 million b/d in 1979, demand fell to 59 million b/d in 1985. Plus, the high prices stimulated production in high-cost areas. Under the twin impact of these two forces, Middle Eastern and Northern African oil output fell from the peak of 28 million b/d in 1979 to a mere 15 million b/d in 1985.

Saudi Arabia absorbed the lion's share of the reduction in a bid to keep prices firm. Worried at how much this policy was cutting their income, the Saudis ramped up production in 1986, which caused prices to crash. The spot price for Dubai oil (the equivalent of Arabian Light) fell to $13.10 per barrel in 1986. Once they had demonstrated their power to control prices, the Saudis were able to play the lead in getting OPEC members to agree to quotas. As economic theory would predict, cheating on the quotas was rampant, but OPEC members were able to maintain greater solidarity when prices softened and a crash loomed. That said, the real power in setting prices was not so much OPEC as the Saudis, who maintained sufficient excess production capacity that they could always threaten to flood the market if other producers did not agree to more or less respect quotas.

The Saudi strategy was evidently to maintain oil's reputation as a reliable energy source, so that consuming countries did not find alternatives to Middle Eastern oil. The strength of the Saudi strategy became apparent in 1990, when the loss of both Iraqi and Kuwaiti production was offset by bringing on stream excess production capacity to such an extent that during that crisis, Middle Eastern oil production remained steady. Nevertheless, consumers remained leery of oil prices. Throughout the 1980s, energy conservation and shifts to energy sources other than oil kept oil demand stagnant. On the other hand, the United States abandoned its "Project Independence," designed to end reliance on imported oil, shutting the door of a multi-billion-dollar synthetic fuel plant.

Over time, world oil demand recovered but at a very slow pace. Only in 1993 did world demand recover to the level it had reached in 1979. Further limiting the demand for Middle East oil was output growth in high-cost areas outside the region. Only in 1999 did Middle Eastern output reach its 1979 peak of 28 million b/d. Two decades of no output growth were a dramatic contrast to the years of breakneck growth pre-1973: from 1965 to 1972 alone, Middle Eastern oil output shot up from 10 million b/d to 24 million b/d. Corresponding to the stagnant demand for Middle Eastern oil was a stagnant price. From 1986 to 1999, the spot price for Dubai crude rose only gently, from $13.10 per barrel to $17.25 per barrel, with one spike (to $20.45 in 1990) and one plunge (to $12.21 in 1998).

With oil income low, Middle Eastern oil producers reconsidered whether to involve IOCs, which could finance the many billions of dollars of investment needed to replace aging infrastructure. However, the national oil companies resisted, arguing that they had the necessary technical capacity and were better placed to serve the national interest. In the end, the only substantial IOC investments were in Algeria and in Iran's offshore waters.

The Second Boom Since 2000

Over the course of the 1990s, the supply/demand balance in the oil industry changed slowly, in a smaller-scale version of the changes in the 1960s. In both cases, the main driver was a buoyant world economy, which drove up oil demand. Added to that, neither the IOCs nor the producing countries made much investment. The situation was ripe for a price increase, which Saudi Arabia and Iran engineered in a 1999 agreement about how to reduce OPEC quotas. The spot price of Dubai crude went from $17.25 a barrel in 1999 to $26.20 in 2000, and it remained about that level through 2004 despite a softening in world economic growth. When after 2005 world growth took off again, so did the price of oil, which shot up to $49.35 in 2005 and then to $68.19 in 2007. The year 2008 was particularly turbulent; oil prices rose in early 2008 to $150 a barrel, before sinking to $35 after the world financial crisis began later in the year. The 2008 annual average price was $94.34; the 2009 price was about two-thirds that level. To keep the price that high, OPEC producers have to hold their output to about 5 million b/d below their production capacity.

Predicting the future course of Middle East oil income is an inexact art. Over the last forty years, the record of the best oil forecasters has been at best spotty; they have been way off as much as, if not more than, they have been in the ballpark. The oil forecasters make very different predictions about all three of the major factors determining how much Middle East countries earn from oil exports: how much oil the world demands, how much of that oil comes from the Middle East, and what is the price of oil.

In coming years, oil demand will almost certainly grow at a slower pace than the rate of world economic growth. This drop in the "energy intensity"—the amount of energy needed to produce a dollar of output—reflects two factors: first, the declining weight of energy-intensive heavy industry compared to energy-light high technology and services, and second, explicit government policies to reduce oil demand as a means to curb global warming. Forecasts of how much oil demand will grow in coming decades vary enormously because of different assumptions about these two factors as well as about how fast the world economy will grow. The U.S. Department of Energy forecast that 2030 world oil output will be 25 percent higher than in 2010. The International Energy Agency estimates the growth will be 1 percent a year, or 105 million barrels a day by 2030 compared to 85 million barrels a day in 2008. The largest IOC, Shell, forecasts the growth will be 8 percent under one scenario or 2 percent under another.

Any prediction about how much of the world oil supply in 2030 will come from the Middle East depends on assumptions about politics as much as economics, or for that matter geology. Middle Eastern countries are implementing their announced plans for large increases in their oil output capacity. Iraq alone expects to increase its capacity by 5 million b/d, and though that may take longer than Iraq hopes, it certainly can be done years before 2030. The Middle East will almost certainly have the capacity in 2030 to produce 10 million b/d more than it produced in 2009. But how much of that capacity will be used is not clear. Middle Eastern producers have long had a policy of restraining their output if necessary to keep prices high. The level of Middle Eastern oil output therefore depends very much on how much is produced in the rest of the world. Oil production in the rest of the world depends primarily on what policies governments outside the Middle East will adopt. Recently, the U.S. government has been encouraging the production of biofuel oil while simultaneously tightening environmental restrictions on conventional oil production—two policies with contradictory impact on how much oil is produced in the United States. In many other oil-producing countries, nationalist sentiment has led governments to insist that the local state-owned oil company have a larger share in oil output. Almost everywhere, that has slowed investment and therefore reduced the growth in oil output capacity. The most likely scenario for the next twenty years is that political issues like nationalism and environmental concerns will become even tighter constraints on oil production outside the Middle East. If so, the Middle East will increase its share of world oil output.

Middle Eastern oil income depends both on the level of output and the price. Despite periodic predictions that oil prices are inevitably headed upward, in fact oil prices have fluctuated both down and up. By picking a starting year when prices were low—say, 1998—one can claim that prices are trending upward. By picking a starting year when prices were high—say, 1980—one can claim that prices are flat or even trending downward. How prices will go in the future is entirely unclear. If we assume low world economic growth, greater energy efficiency, increasing concern about global warming, and robust investment to increase oil output capacity, demand might fall and supply rise, with the result that prices drop. But the opposite assumptions are equally plausible. The safest forecast is that oil prices will continue to behave in unexpected ways.

Oil as a Mixed Blessing?

The Middle East illustrates both the advantages and the problems that come from ample oil and gas resources. Without oil, the Persian Gulf states would be dirt poor instead of upper-middle-income or rich. But it could be argued, although the evidence is mixed, that oil income has fueled devastating wars, undermined economic development, and entrenched autocratic rulers.

Funding War

The Middle East has been a zone of violence primarily because of the many deep political differences in the region. That said, oil income has provided the wherewithal to make wars particularly deadly and to sustain conflicts longer than they might have lasted otherwise. The most obvious case has been the Iraq wars, namely, its 1980–1988 war with Iran, its 1990 invasion of Kuwait and 1991–2003 resistance to UN inspections, and the insurgency since 2003. In particular, the Iraq-Iran war eventually exhausted both sides; indeed, the letter from Iranian supreme leader Ayatollah Ruhollah Khomeini explaining his decision to end the war explicitly argued that Iran could not afford the economic burden. Besides the Iraq wars, other conflicts in the region arguably fueled by oil income include the various civil wars in Sudan, Libya's prolonged interventions in Chad, and the Algerian civil war.

The most famous conflict in the region has been the Arab-Israeli conflict. For all the emotional intensity of that dispute, it has been argued that the conflict waxed hot when Arab states found outside funding for the fighting, including cash grants from the oil-producing countries. Egypt in particular has been explicit over the years that maintaining the conflict with Israel placed an unacceptably heavy burden on the country, necessitating a peace even though the Palestinian issue had not been settled.

On balance, then, it would appear that oil income has contributed to the Middle East's sad record of continuing wars.

Undermining Economic Development

The Middle East's oil-producing countries have had generally poor economic policies. Across the globe, there is much evidence that natural resource booms undermine economic growth. The boom feeds state revenues, leading governments to increase public spending so much they may go deeply into debt. As the economy overheats, costs rise to the extent that normal economic activity becomes uncompetitive: nonresource exports fall and imports soar, in a process known as "Dutch disease" (for the classic analysis of what happened in the 1960s when the Netherlands enjoyed high income from its natural gas exports). The economy is wracked by inflation, government deficits, and balance-of-payments problems. This pattern has hardly been unique to the Middle East; it has also afflicted petro-states such as Nigeria and Venezuela—indeed, OPEC founder Juan Pablo Pérez Alfonzo described oil as "the devil's excrement." For that matter, sixteenth-century Spain earned an emperor's ransom from Latin America's gold and silver mines, and the result was that Spain soon became one of Europe's poorer countries, a process described and decried in Adam Smith's *Wealth of Nations*.

This ample precedent certainly gives reason to suspect that oil has something to do with the generally poor economic performance of the Middle Eastern oil producers. On the other hand, an argument can be made that their weak growth record was not due to the oil income but instead to the pernicious influence of unsound economic theories promoting industrialization and state control over the economy. After all, the track record of the Middle Eastern countries with little oil income, such as Egypt and Syria in the 1960s and 1970s, was on the whole worse than that of the oil producers.

While the evidence is only suggestive rather than conclusive about oil income's negative impact on government policy, one way in which oil income has clearly undermined economic development is by fostering a profoundly pernicious "petro-culture."

Entrenched Autocratic Rulers

Scholars of the Middle East often argue that oil income impedes democratic reform. The argument is hard to evaluate, because the entire Middle East has so few countries that have experienced democratic reforms: the oil-poor states have been as autocratic as the oil-rich. Indeed, the modest steps toward democracy in some Gulf oil monarchies—most notably Kuwait—are arguably the furthest that any Arab state has gone toward political reform. And the smaller Gulf oil producers on balance have at least as good a record of allowing free debate and personal freedoms as do other Arab states, though Saudi Arabia and Iran are among the most repressive states in the region.

However, studies that compare countries across the globe have permitted fuller evaluation of the thesis that oil impedes democracy, and the results are convincing. Three separate effects, each of which empirical study has found to be statistically significant, are at work:

- Governments use oil revenue to buy off the populace, which has accepted a social bargain in which the ruling elites deliver prosperity and in return are allowed to control the state. Oil revenue allows greater spending on patronage as well as lower taxation—or what Lisa Anderson has referred to as "no representation without taxation." A particularly pernicious problem is that the middle classes in Middle East oil-rich states largely work for the state. Because they are dependent on state largesse, they are less likely to form independent civil society groups pressing for political rights.
- Oil income gives governments the resources with which to expand internal security apparatuses.
- Oil income, unlike other forms of economic activity, does not require a large skilled labor force for its creation, with the result that oil development is not as much associated with rising education levels and with modern work habits of independent action and thought—which are principal ways in which modernization contributes to democracy.

References and Further Reading

Adelman, M.A. *The World Petroleum Market.* Baltimore, MD: Johns Hopkins University Press for Resources for the Future, 1972.

Amuzegar, Jahangir. *Managing the Oil Wealth: OPEC's Windfalls and Pitfalls.* London: I.B. Tauris, 2001.

Anderson, Lisa. "The State in the Middle East and North Africa." *Comparative Politics* 20:1 (1987): 1–18.

Askari, Hossein. *Middle East Oil Exporters: What Happened to Economic Development?* Cheltenham, UK: Edward Elgar, 2006.

Bamberg, James. *British Petroleum and Global Oil, 1950–1975: The Challenge of Nationalism.* Cambridge, UK: Cambridge University Press, 2000.

Blair, John. *The Control of Oil.* New York: Pantheon Books, 1976.

BP Statistical Review of World Energy. Available at www.bp.com/statisticalreview.

Crystal, Jill. *Oil and Politics in the Gulf.* Cambridge: Cambridge University Press, 1990.

Dunning, Thad. *Crude Democracy: Natural Resource Wealth and Political Regimes.* Cambridge, UK: Cambridge University Press, 2008.

Ford, Alan. *The Anglo-Iranian Oil Dispute of 1951–52.* Berkeley: University of California Press, 1954.

Frankel, P.H. *Essentials of Petroleum: A Key to Oil Economics.* London: Chapman and Hall, 1946.

Gause, Gregory, III. *Oil Monarchies.* New York: Council on Foreign Relations Press, 1994.

International Energy Agency. *Middle East Oil and Gas.* Paris: OECD, 1995.

———. *World Energy Outlook.* Available at www.worldenergyoutlook.org.

Karl, Terry Lynn. *The Paradox of Plenty: Oil Booms and Petro-States.* Berkeley: University of California Press, 1997.

Keating, Aileen. *Mirage: Power, Politics, and the Hidden History of Arabian Oil.* Amherst, NY: Prometheus Books, 2005.

Marcel, Valérie. *Oil Titans: National Oil Companies in the Middle East.* London: Chatham House (The Royal Institute of International Affairs), 2006.

Mikesell, Raymond, and Hollis Chenery. *Arabian Oil: America's Stake in the Middle East.* Chapel Hill: University of North Carolina Press, 1949.

Morse, Edward, and Amy Myers Jaffe. "OPEC in Confrontation with Globalization." In *Energy and Security: Toward a New Foreign Policy Strategy*, ed. Jan Kalicki and David Goldwyn, 65–96. Baltimore, MD: Johns Hopkins University Press, 2005.

Noreng, Oystein. *Crude Power: Politics and the Oil Market.* London: I.B. Tauris, 2006.

———. "The Predicament of the Gulf Rentier State." In *Oil in the Gulf: Obstacles to Democracy and Development*, ed. David Heradstveit and Helge Hveem, 9–40. Aldershot, UK: Ashgate, 2004.

O'Connor, Harvey. *World Crisis in Oil.* New York: Monthly Review Press, 1962.

Penrose, Edith. *The Growth of Firms, Middle East Oil, and Other Essays.* London: Frank Cass, 1971.

Ross, Michael. "Does Oil Hinder Democracy?" *World Politics* 53 (April 2001): 325–361.

Shell. *Shell Energy Scenarios to 2050.* Available at www.shell.com/scenarios. Accessed 2008.

U.S. Energy Information Administration. www.eia.doe.gov.

Yergin, Daniel. *The Prize: The Epic Quest for Oil, Money, and Power.* New York: Simon & Schuster, 1991.

Water

The Middle East is an arid region in which access to adequate water supplies has often been a highly charged issue. Furthermore, some of the region's largest rivers flow across hostile boundaries. Nevertheless, cooperation about water has been and continues to be more common than disputes. The region has learned how to manage water, both from an economic and a technical point of view. In addition to the long-standing efforts to increase water supply, many Middle East governments are now also reducing demand. Since approximately two-thirds of the region's water use is for agriculture, demand management is largely a matter of changing the mix of crops grown and the farming techniques used. The continuing problems in household water supply in several countries are mostly due to inefficient management of a public service, not of physical water availability.

Not all of the Middle East is particularly short of water. Counting only renewable water (without desalinated water), Iraq has more than 3,000 cubic meters per person per year, while Iran and Sudan have about 2,000, which is well above the 1,700 cubic meters level that many researchers call water stress. To be sure, there remain important problems of getting the water where and when it is needed in those arid countries. Two other Middle Eastern countries—Syria and Lebanon—are a bit above the 1,000 cubic meters level that marks water scarcity, and two others—Morocco and Egypt—are close to that level. Desalination provides much of the water in seven Middle East countries, namely, Libya and the six Gulf monarchies. That leaves six countries that face absolute scarcity of less than 500 cubic meters of water per person per year: Tunisia, Algeria, Israel, Yemen, the Palestinian territories, and Jordan, in descending order of water per person.

The problem of water shortage is primarily an issue of how much agriculture can be carried out. Even Jordan, the country facing the most difficult situation, has 165 cubic meters of water per person per year, compared to the usual norm of 40 cubic meters needed annually for household consumption. On average, the Middle East consumes about 800 cubic meters of water per person per year, or about the same amount as Europe.

Security, Law, Engineering, Economics, and Environment

Water problems are viewed in distinctly different ways by various actors, which can result in deep disagreement about what is at stake, as well as how to address the difficulties. The most common perspective—among politicians, journalists, and much of the general public—has been to see water supply as a profoundly important issue, central to the very existence of society and the environment. By contrast, economists and many engineers have argued that water is simply one of many resources, albeit one that requires careful government policies to manage, though economists and engineers have often deeply disagreed about how to manage water. Indeed, there are five main approaches to Middle East water problems, as laid out by Mostafa Dolatyar and Tim Gray in *Water Politics in the Middle East:* they are security, law, engineering, economics, and environment.

Security

The dominant view of water among politicians, people at large, and writers on the issue has been that water is vital to national security and survival. It is often claimed that water disputes are a major potential cause of conflict in the Middle East. In fact, however, the only conflict in which water played an important role was the 1967 Arab-Israeli war, and even there, the dispute about Arab efforts to divert Jordan River waters (after Israel built its National Water Carrier, taking some Jordan water south along the Mediterranean coast) was not at the center of the war. For all the political problems among them, governments have been much more prone to cooperate in practice than to fight. The de facto cooperation among Turkey, Syria, and Iraq—three states that have generally been at odds in recent decades—and even among Syria, Jordan, Israel, and the Palestinian territories, is described below. Meanwhile, Middle Eastern politicians have increasingly realized that an important part of the answer to water supply problems is to manage resources more efficiently and to adopt more appropriate policies, in particular, reducing subsidies that encourage wasteful consumption. Given that all aspects of water supply and treatment generally take only between 1 and 3 percent of national income, economists do not view water as some particularly precious commodity. They argue that if a country needs more water, it can be readily produced at only a fraction of the amount being spent on national defense.

Law

Muslim water law, like that in much of the world, is based on the principle of prior appropriation: he who is using water is entitled to that water. That principle conflicts with the principle of territorial sovereignty: he who controls a territory can use the water found on it. Acting on the second principle, some Middle Eastern property owners pump more water from deep wells on their property, causing their neighbors' wells to go dry, even though that contravenes traditional water law. This is also an issue between Israelis and Palestinians, who generally disagree about which principles should govern water allocation. The more common international political problem in the region is about transborder rivers: does the upstream country have the right to increase its use of river waters if that interferes with the quantity and quality of water that the downstream country has counted on? This question has arisen particularly in the Jordan, Euphrates, Tigris, and Nile river basins. While there are more than 100 treaties around the world restricting the freedom of action of upstream countries, each of those treaties is specific to a particular case; no general rule has won broad acceptance. Not surprisingly, given the difficult political relations between many Middle Eastern states that share rivers, the "region has a striking absence of inclusive and comprehensive international water agreements on its most significant trans-boundary water courses," according to the World Bank's *Making the Most of Scarcity.*

Engineering

Confronted with water shortage, Middle Eastern governments have often responded by investing in large projects to tap new supply sources. One of the most spectacular was the Aswan High Dam built in the 1960s by Egypt's Gamal Abdel Nasser on the Nile, but there have also been other grand projects, not all of them dams, as described below. Many of these have been quite inefficiently used. For instance, Iran has 85 dams and plans to build 171 more, even though only 13 percent of the land that could be irrigated by the existing dams is in fact being served. In recent years, more attention has been paid to increasing the efficiency of water use, which was often low. Saudi irrigation systems have overall water efficiency rates of 45 percent compared to the 75 percent standard practice for the types of systems they use. In most Arab cities, less than 70 percent of the water that leaves purification facilities arrives at consumers' homes due to leaky pipes. In the West Bank, less than 40 percent of the water put into the system can be counted as arriving at people's homes; because so much water leaks out of the pipes, consumers in many parts of the West Bank have water service for only a few hours a day.

Economics

Economists view water scarcity as a matter of price: highly subsidized water—actually, often free water—encourages excessive consumption and discourages investment to take advantage of potential supply sources. Middle Eastern politicians long resisted the economic approach to water almost as bitterly as did their counterparts in the western United States, but both have given way since the late 1990s. The big gains to be made are in agriculture, which uses most of the water consumed in every Middle Eastern country, even in the Gulf oil states, where most water is desalinated. Indeed, agriculture uses 75 percent of the water consumed in Jordan and 95 percent in Yemen, two countries where water consumption exceeds the long-term sustainable supply. Saving agricultural water is often a matter of changing water allocations to encourage farmers to grow different crops. The World Bank estimates that in the Middle East, growing wheat brings 8 cents per cubic meter of water used; growing vegetables brings 50 cents per cubic meter. But many governments continue to chase the chimera of food self-sufficiency by encouraging the growing of cereals. Protection of cereals and legumes in Tunisia costs four times gross domestic product (GDP) per capita for each job created, according to the World Bank. A better approach is to import water-intensive commodities such as wheat and cotton, rather than producing them locally. By using international trade to provide "virtual water" in this way, Jordan saves 5.0 billion cubic meters of water a year, compared to 1.1 billion cubic meters from all other sources.

Environment

Middle Eastern governments have historically not given much weight to environmental concerns. Water management policies that emphasize agricultural and urban needs have put at risk the region's rich biodiversity. One such risk is the threat to wild varieties of cereals that might one day be invaluable for protecting against future diseases: for example, thirty-two of the world's fifty-six species of large seeded grasses, including wheat and barley, are indigenous to the region. Perhaps 40 percent of Iran's forest land has been lost since the mid-twentieth century. Forests and grasslands in many countries have been converted into crop land. Modern technology, like pump-driven wells, permit overexploitation of groundwater resources that were managed in a sustainable manner by traditional technologies, such as Iran's *qanat*s—gravity-flow tunnels that brought water from mountain slopes onto the surrounding plains. Middle Easterners are beginning to be more concerned about these "light green" issues, that is, caring for the environment because it is in humankind's interest to do so. So far, however, the region has seen little expression of the "deep green" perspective, which holds that the environment has an intrinsic value regardless of its utility to human beings.

The Water-Poor But Oil-Rich States

Three specific water systems in the Middle East have generated great interest: the desalinated water plants of the bone-dry, oil-rich states; the two great river basins of the Nile and the Tigris/Euphrates; and the hotly contested Jordan River basin.

The bone-dry, oil-rich states use a great deal of water—more per person than in southern Europe. They have two basic strategies for supplementing their renewable water: desalination and "water mining." The Middle East has 70 percent of the world's desalination capacity, producing more than 2.8 billion cubic meters a year. Most of that is in the Gulf. Saudi Arabia alone produces more than 1.0 billion cubic meters a year. Kuwait, Qatar, and the United Arab Emirates are almost entirely dependent on desalinated water. Bahrain and Oman each have as much renewable water per person as Jordan, but they use desalinated water to supplement those supplies. Outside the Gulf, Libya uses desalinated water in coastal cities, and Algeria has plans to do the same, building plants to desalinate 0.7 billion cubic meters a year. In addition, as of 2009, Israel produces about 0.4 billion cubic meters of desalinated water a year; it is planning to increase that to 0.7 billion. There are also small plants serving isolated areas in Egypt, Jordan, and Tunisia.

Important as desalination plants are, they produce much less water than a little-noted practice central to Saudi and Libyan water supply. Both countries withdraw much water from ancient aquifers deep below the desert sands in a process best known as "water mining." Saudi Arabia uses as much as 17 billion cubic meters a year of aquifer water. Libya uses as much as 3 billion, though that will rise to over 4 billion with the completion of the ongoing Great Man-Made River project, a water transport system conveying water hundreds of miles to the north from the aquifers in the south. These aquifers are not being recharged; once the water is used up, it is gone. Essentially, all this water is used for agriculture, producing crops that would be cheaper to import. In other words, Saudi Arabia and Libya subsidize their farmers in addition to using up nonreplaceable ancient water reserves, all for the purpose of growing food crops at home rather than relying on international trade to provide food at much less cost.

Great Rivers: Nile and Tigris/Euphrates

Nile water flowing into Egypt from nine upstream countries provides more than 90 percent of Egypt's water. Water flowing from Turkey in the Tigris and Euphrates provides much of the water for northern Syria, and in turn those waters, plus additional Tigris waters from Iran and northern Iraq, provide more than 50 percent of Iraq's water. Both river systems get most of their water from upstream states. While these great rivers are life-givers to the desert lands along their lower course, they would not provide a steady, reliable water supply even if there were no problems in the upstream countries. The water flow in both river systems varies strongly over the course of the year, and the average flow in some years is three times that in others. From 1871 to 1965, the discharge of the Nile at Aswan varied from 1.0 billion cubic meters in April 1900 to 28.9 billion in August 1874; the flow in the March–June low period was typically well under 10 percent that in the August–October peak, which confined farmers to planting one crop a year, even though Egypt's weather could readily accommodate two crops. Annual average flows varied from 137 billion cubic meters in 1879 to 46 billion in 1913. Data for the Tigris at Mosul, Iraq, from 1919 to 1952 and the Euphrates at Birecik, Turkey, and Hit, Iraq, from 1937 to 1964 show slightly less variability during the year but slightly more variability across years. The peak months for the Tigris/Euphrates are April–May and the low months are July–November, which is detrimental to farmers who want the rivers' waters during the peak summer growing season.

The combination of foreign origin, high variability, and central importance makes those who depend upon these two river systems nervous. This, along with the emotional importance attached to water supply, creates a situation ripe for conflict among the countries that share a river. Many books describe the potential for water wars in the Middle East. But in fact there has been much more cooperation than there has been conflict. In the Nile Valley, Egypt reached an agreement with Sudan about the sharing of the river waters in 1959 before beginning to plan the Aswan High Dam. The eight sub-Saharan African Nile Basin countries were not party to that agreement, however. In the 1990s, Egypt launched the large New Valley Project to use Nile water to put desert land into cultivation, while Ethiopia began a program to build mini-dams in the Blue Nile Basin to permit more irrigation there. It will be difficult to accommodate both these schemes if the region experiences another period of low rainfall similar to that of 1979–1987. In recent years, all ten countries in the basin launched a Nile Basin Initiative, with a permanent staff and technical advisory committees to resolve potential problems and plan cooperative efforts.

The disputes about the Euphrates were a good example of bitter rhetoric but mutually advantageous cooperation. After Turkey began construction in the early 1980s on a series of dams along the Euphrates, Turkey, Syria, and Iraq exchanged much venom before the 1987 agreement to maintain the flow at the Turkish-Syrian border at a minimum of 500 cubic meters per second. Turkey installed eight electricity generators at the Ataturk Dam, each of which requires 225 cubic meters per second to work at full capacity, meaning that Turkey would have to let 1,800 cubic meters per second flow to get the maximum benefit from the electricity, but it bitterly refused the Syrian-Iraqi demand that it guarantee 700 cubic meters per second in each month. Meanwhile, Syrian and Iraqi complaints about the 500 cubic meters Turkey guaranteed ignored the fact that, according to the 1937–1964 data, the Euphrates' natural flow during the peak growing months of August–November had been below 400 cubic meters per second, meaning that Turkey's offer was better for Syrian and Iraqi farmers than the pre–Ataturk Dam situation.

The rise of activist governments after 1960 brought several decades of grand water projects in both the Nile and Tigris/Euphrates basins. Dams were designed to generate electricity and to trap floodwaters that could then be used to expand the irrigated area (and in Egypt, provide water for a second annual crop). Egyptian president Nasser's break with the West in 1955–1956 was in no small part occasioned by the World Bank and U.S. decision not to fund the Aswan High Dam project about which he cared so deeply. Egypt then turned to the USSR for assistance to build that dam, which was much more massive than the two dams the British built across the Nile in the early twentieth century—one at Aswan, upstream from the High Dam, and one for the Gezira irrigation project in Sudan. Also with Soviet assistance, in the early 1970s, Syria built the al-Thawra, or Tabqa, Dam, creating Lake Asad along the Euphrates. In the early 1970s, Turkey built the Kaban Dam along the Euphrates, followed up in the 1980s and 1990s with the South-East Anatolia Project to build six dams along the Tigris and seven along the Euphrates, including the giant Ataturk Dam.

The track record of the great dams and irrigation schemes has been mixed. The worst has been the Syrian al-Thawra Dam. Not only has its fill been limited by poor construction quality, but the soil in the surrounding area contains so much gypsum that it cannot be cultivated. Iraq's water projects have been characterized by inadequate drainage of the water applied; evaporation of the excess water has left behind salts that have ruined large areas of previously productive land. Compounding the damage was the draining of southern Iraqi marshlands in the early 1990s following rebellions there against the Saddam Hussein government; more than 200,000 people were displaced. By contrast, the Egyptian Aswan High Dam has turned out much better than the World Bank anticipated in the 1950s. The High Dam was built large enough to smooth out water from low-flow years, as occurred in 1979–1987, as well as to protect from floods, such as in 1964, 1975, and 1988. One great worry was that the Egyptian government would skimp on the drainage of the irrigation water, which is not as dramatic as the construction of the dam but is every bit as essential for successful agriculture. To its credit, the Egyptian government created an efficient agency that invested more than $1 billion on innovative subsurface drains, which have worked well. Overall, the High Dam is estimated to have generated a net positive benefit to Egypt equal to at least 2 percent of national income.

Jordan River Basin

The most contentious water issues in the Middle East have been between Israel and its neighbors in Syria, Jordan, and the Palestinian territories (Lebanon has been peripherally involved). Water scarcity is only part of the problem. After all, the Gulf states are much drier. Supplying water to the 4 million residents of the Saudi capital Riyadh is at least as hard as any problem in the Jordan Basin, Riyadh being 240 miles (386 km) from the sea and 2,000 feet (610 m) above sea level.

The amounts of water in dispute are less than a half-billion cubic meters a year, even if each party insisted on the most maximalist interpretation of what it is entitled to. The experience of the Gulf states—which desalinate four times that much water—suggest that desalinating the amount in dispute would cost less than $0.5 billion a year, even with all the required infrastructure; this is compared to the more than $4 billion a year the Jordan River states receive in foreign aid, and the $10 billion a year they spend on defense. Indeed, for all the heated talk in the region about water, relatively little money is spent on it. Jordan devotes 2.3 percent of its GDP to water, more than any other state in the region.

In short, the root of the problem between Israel and its neighbors has not been technical or economic, but instead the attitude Miriam Lowi captured in her book *Water and Power*, namely, "neither side has been willing to engage in any activity that could help the adversary become stronger."

Compounding the problem have been deeply held attitudes on each side. On the Israeli side, the historic Zionist dream of reclaiming the land gave farming a powerful patriotic mystique. From Independence in 1948 to 1957, Israel massively expanded its use of water for agriculture from 0.2 billion cubic meters a year to 1.0 billion before running into supply problems. In the early 1960s, it built the National Water Carrier to bring 0.4 billion cubic meters a year of Jordan River waters from north of the Sea of Galilee to the country's south; farmers absorbed essentially all the increased supply. But that was about as far as the country's water could be stretched. Since the 1980s, Israeli agriculture has been forced by government pressure to reduce water use and to make more use of brackish and recycled urban water. Much complicated political maneuvering was involved. For instance, cities prefer to discharge lightly treated wastewater into the sea rather than to treat the water up to the standard required for reusing in irrigation. Still, Israeli agriculture seems en route to using as little as 0.5 billion cubic meters a year of fresh, high-quality water.

On the Palestinian side, many are convinced that the basic water problem is that Israel takes too much water, and that without the water stolen from the Palestinians, Israel could not absorb Jewish immigrants or build settlements in the territories it occupies. The corresponding Israeli myth is that an independent Palestine could bring Israel to its knees by cutting off the 0.4–0.5 billion cubic meters a year Israel gets from West Bank aquifers. The facts are much more mundane. Israel could survive without the West Bank water, either by reducing agriculture or desalinating water; the annual cost would be about the same as one or two fighter planes. Palestinian water problems are caused less by Israel than by subsidized prices, which encourage excessive consumption (especially in agriculture), insufficient treatment facilities to provide farmers with recycled water, and leaky municipal pipes that lose half the water put into the system.

Water has also been a central issue in Israel's relations with Jordan and Syria. In the 1950s, the United States sponsored a study by Eric Johnston that proposed how to develop and divide the Jordan River's waters among the three countries (with a tiny share for Lebanon); the study was rejected. In the mid-1960s, the Arab League proposed a plan grandly described as diverting the Jordan's headwaters away from Israel, although in fact it would have diverted a mere 0.2 billion cubic meters a year. Israel attacked several construction projects in 1965–1967. Writers about water issues describe this dispute as central in the build-up to the 1967 Six-Day War; historians of that war generally disagree. Similarly, it is not clear what role Syria's claim to a Sea of Galilee coast played in torpedoing the Israeli-Syrian peace negotiations in 2000: Syria certainly made the claim and Israel certainly resisted, but it is by no means obvious there would have been a treaty had the issue been settled. Nor is it clear how much the ability of Israel and Jordan to compromise about some long, contentious water issues was important to reaching their 1994 peace treaty.

The Middle East continues to inspire grand water project ideas. A "Red-Dead" canal has been proposed to provide water for Jordan's population centers and to stop the drying up of the Dead Sea, which no longer receives sufficient water from the Jordan River. The canal might almost pay for itself. From an economic point of view, a better way to solve Jordan's urban water problems would be to curtail agricultural water use, now 0.8 billion cubic meters a year compared to 0.2 billion in the 1960s; Jordan's total urban use, for households and industry combined, is less than 0.3 billion cubic meters. But rather than tackling farmers' privileges—such as paying only 30 percent of the cost of the water they receive—Jordan, like Israel, has thrown itself into recycling urban water for irrigation, making more use of brackish water, and increasing the efficiency of urban water use. It also has built several dams to catch floodwaters, mostly along the Yarmouk River, a tributary of the Jordan.

In closing, the importance of water to conflict in the Middle East is easy to exaggerate. Water is in fact rather cheap, despite the arid character of much of the region. Even those countries with massively subsidized consumption supplied by desalination plants spend only a small percentage of their GDP on water in all its aspects. The region's water scarcity has generated more heated rhetoric than real economic pain.

References and Further Reading

Albert, Jeff, Magnus Bernhardsson, and Roger Kenna. *Transformation of Middle Eastern Natural Environments: Legacies and Lessons.* Yale School of Forestry and Environmental Studies Bulletin No. 103. New Haven, CT: Yale University, 1998.

Allen, J.A., ed. *Water, Peace and the Middle East: Negotiating Resources in the Jordan Basin.* London: Tauris Academic Studies, 1996.

Clawson, Marion, Hans Landsberg, and Lyle Alexander. *The Agricultural Potential of the Middle East.* New York: American Elsevier, 1971.

Dolatyar, Mostafa, and Tim Gray. *Water Politics in the Middle East: A Context for Conflict or Co-operation?* New York: St. Martin's, 2000.

Haddadin, Munther, ed. *Water Resources in Jordan.* Washington, DC: Resources for the Future, 2006.

Hillel, Daniel. *Rivers of Eden: The Struggle for Water and the Quest for Peace in the Middle East.* New York: Oxford University Press, 1994.

Lowi, Miriam. *Water and Power: The Politics of a Scarce Resource in the Jordan River Basin.* Cambridge, UK: Cambridge University Press, 1993.

Medzini, Arnon. *The River Jordan: Frontiers and Water.* London: University of London School of Oriental and African Studies Water Research Group, 2001.

Sherman, Martin. *The Politics of Water in the Middle East: An Israeli Perspective on the Hydro-Political Aspects of the Conflict.* New York: St. Martin's, 1999.

World Bank. *Making the Most of Scarcity: Accountability for Better Water Management Results in the Middle East and North Africa.* Washington, DC: World Bank, 2007.

World Resources 2002–2004: Decisions for the Earth: Balance, Voice, and Power. World Resources Institute, United Nations Development Programme, United Nations Environmental Programme, and World Bank. July 2003, pp. 274–277. www.wri.org/publication/world-resources-2002-2004-decisions-earth-balance-voice-and-power.

Demography

In the Middle East as in much of the rest of the world, the demographic story of the mid-twentieth century was rapid population growth, which placed a heavy burden on economies. That is coming to an end, in no small part because of social changes, especially the modest progress toward empowering women. The Middle East is now making a "demographic transition" that offers the prospect of twin "demographic dividends" if governments can create the right environment. First, there is the opportunity that comes from much of the population being of working age, with a low burden of caring for the young and the elderly; then, in coming decades, there is the opportunity of increased capital from the savings of middle-aged workers preparing for retirement. But these opportunities could turn into dangers if insufficient jobs are created for the youth flooding into the labor markets and if not enough is saved for what will within a few decades be a rapidly growing elderly population. Central to both challenges will be how women's social role evolves, especially women's employment opportunities outside the home.

Slowing Population Growth

The Middle East experienced explosive population growth from 1950 to 2000. The region's population grew from 92 million to 349 million—a 3.8-fold increase, or 2.7 percent a year. All of the countries in the region had much the same experience: Israel grew at 3.2 percent a year, Iran at just over 2.7 percent, and the Arab countries at just under 2.7 percent on average. For most countries, the reason was a sharp decline in death rates: infant and maternal care improved, the physician/population ratio rose briskly, and so did the hospital beds/population ratio. For Israel, Libya, and the Gulf monarchies, immigration was another important factor. Indeed, the large number of resident noncitizens in Libya and the Gulf monarchies complicates interpretation of population figures in various ways. For one thing, trying to minimize the importance of foreign residents leads some governments to exaggerate the number of citizens; the most careful study of Saudi Arabia's 1970 citizen population suggests it was only 60 percent of the figure reported in the usual international statistics (which are those used here), and there is every reason to believe that discrepancy remains.

Policymakers and the general public are only slowly realizing that the Middle East's long population boom is coming to an end. The Middle East is experiencing the same "demographic transition" to slow growth that hit Europe and North America in about 1900 and Asia and Latin America in the late twentieth century. In some countries, the change has been particularly dramatic. In Iran, the number of births peaked in 1986–1987 at 2.2 million, then dropped by half in less than twenty years; since 2004–2005, births each year have averaged 1.1 million. In other countries, the demographic transition has not yet started. In particular, in Yemen and the occupied Palestinian territories, the United Nations projects that population growth rates in 2000–2050 will be about the same as they were in 1950–2000. For the Middle East as a whole, the annual population growth rate from 2000 to 2050 will be 1.3 percent, or less than half of the 1950–2000 level. From 2000 to 2050, the region's population will not quite double, compared to the almost fourfold increase from 1950 to 2000. And the growth rate is continuing to drop; in 2020–2050 it will be 0.6 percent a year.

The immediate reason for the slower population growth is a drop in the number of children born to the average woman over her life span, which is called the "total fertility rate" (TFR). The

World Bank reports that for its Middle East and North Africa region (which excludes Sudan and Israel), the average TFR fell from 6.2 in 1980 to 2.8 in 2007. The World Bank reports that TFRs are falling across the Middle East. For instance, in Egypt, the TFR dropped from 7.1 in 1960 to 3.2 in 2003. Iran's 2007 TFR of 2.0 is at the "replacement level," the rate needed to sustain a steady population.

When demographers explain why the TFR declined in Europe or developing Asia or Latin America, they make reference to a host of factors absent in the contemporary Middle East, such as the declining influence of conservative religious views or industrial take-off. The breadth and depth of the demographic revolution in the Middle East have therefore been a surprise to demographers and seem to have been the product of three factors. First, and least important, was increased availability of contraception, which appears to have primarily speeded along a process that was occurring anyway. Contraception prevalence rose sharply in much of the region in the 1980s and 1990s. In Egypt, with ample funding from U.S. aid and an effective government effort, the rate of contraception usage rose from 30 percent of married women in 1984 to 57 percent in 2000. Over the same period in Algeria, the rate went from 7 percent to 64 percent. The second factor contributing to the falling TFR was urbanization. Whereas child labor on the farm is an economic boon, parents working in the fields can readily watch the children, and housing is not a particular burden, all this is reversed in urban settings: children often cannot help in urban jobs, they often require day care, and larger apartments are a real economic burden. The third factor in the demographic revolution, which statistical analysis shows to have been the most important, was empowerment of women, especially rising female education rates. For instance, a study of Oman in 1995 found that illiterate women's TFR was 8.6, but women with secondary education had a TFR of 3.8.

While TFRs have become much lower, the number of women of childbearing age remains high, and so the population growth rate is falling more slowly than the TFR. And even as the population growth rate falls, the absolute number of people being added to the population stays high. The United Nations forecasts that from 2000 to 2050, the population of Middle Eastern countries will increase by 329 million (from 349 million to 678 million), which is actually more than the increase in population of 258 million from 1950 to 2000. But by 2050, the absolute size of the annual increase in the population will have slowed to a crawl.

When the population was growing quickly, the number of children was skyrocketing, but there were few elderly, that is, people over the age of sixty. From 1950 to 2000, the number of children under age fifteen in the Middle East grew by 92 million. About one-third of the Middle East's population increase was children under fifteen, while only one-twentieth was elderly over age sixty. As population growth slows, the composition of the population changes to fewer children and more elderly. From 2000 to 2050, the proportions in the population growth will reverse: one-third will be elderly and one-twentieth will be children. Indeed, after 2020, the number of children in the Middle East will fall slowly, with considerable social implications; for instance, schools will need fewer teachers. This reduction in school-age population is already very noticeable in some countries; for instance, in Iran, the number of children under fifteen in 1990 was 25.3 million, while in 2010 it will be only 18.7 million. In contrast to what is happening to the number of children, from 2000 to 2050, the number of elderly over age sixty in the Middle East will skyrocket by 107 million, rising sixfold from 21 million to 127 million. Because of the rapid growth in the number of elderly and the modest growth in the number of children, by 2050, the number of Middle Easterners over sixty will almost equal the number under fifteen (127 million compared to 143 million). Indeed, in 2050, the population over sixty will be larger than that under fifteen in twelve of the region's twenty countries—45 percent greater in Iran.

In short, the Middle East is leaving behind the population explosion and entering a new demographic era in which youth are a smaller share of the population and the elderly a much larger share.

Youth Unemployment and Preparing for Retirement

The current demographic transition taking place in the Middle East presents an opportunity as well as a challenge. The opportunity comes in the form of several decades in which the economy will face a relatively light burden in caring for children and the elderly. To capture the combined cost of caring for the young and the old, demographers calculate the dependency ratio, that is, the ratio of those under fifteen or over sixty to those ages fifteen to sixty. During the height of the Middle East's population explosion from 1960 to 1980, the dependency ratio was about 1.0, that is, one dependent per working-age person. As the births drop off but the numbers of elderly are still small, the ratio is falling; it was 0.75 in 2000 and will bottom out at 0.58 in 2030. Then, as the numbers of elderly start to increase, the dependency ratio will rise again, reaching 0.66 in 2050 (forecasting out much further than that becomes quite speculative). But especially in the period 2010–2040, when the dependency ratio ranges from 0.58 to 0.63, the Middle East will have a light burden in caring for the young and old. This could be a golden period for economic growth—what demographers refer to as the "demographic dividend."

However, the Middle East can only take advantage of this opportunity if it can create enough jobs for the young people born during the years of rapid population growth. That did not happen in the 1990s. A destructive cycle set in, whereby young people were prepared to remain unemployed for years in hopes of securing a public-sector job at higher wages and more security than available in private firms. In response to students' dreams of obtaining public-sector jobs, the education system became oriented toward preparing bureaucrats rather than providing the skills needed by the private sector—the result being that private employers often offered graduates lower wages than the graduates felt they deserved.

The situation improved markedly after 2000. Vigorous private-sector growth created enough jobs so that, despite the rapidly growing labor force, unemployment across the World Bank's Middle East and North Africa region dropped from 14 percent in 2000 to 11 percent in 2005, though these numbers should be viewed with caution, because unemployment data are unreliable in many Middle Eastern countries (for one thing, the issue of unemployment is so politically sensitive that governments may not want unemployment measured accurately). However, that number is kept low by the many people, especially women, who do not look for work. In 2005, across the region, one in two people aged fifteen to sixty-four did not have a job.

Sustaining vigorous job growth will be a great challenge. The oil-rich countries may be able to expand government employment enough to absorb many of those joining the labor force, but other Middle Eastern states will not have the resources necessary to do so. Private-sector job growth will require substantial amounts of capital. In *The Arab Economies in a Changing World*, Howard Pack and Marcus Noland show that under favorable assumptions—including a modest number of jobs required and efficient use of capital—Middle Eastern countries would still need to have investment equal to 28 percent of national income. That is about 10 percentage points more than Middle Eastern countries invested in 2000. To attract that kind of capital would require changes in policies to make the business environment more attractive and to encourage foreign investment (or at least to persuade locals to invest at home rather than placing their funds abroad). On the bright side, if Middle Eastern countries were able to make that kind of investment, then the additional capital along with the extra labor would be sufficient to produce a real gross domestic product growth rate of 5.4–5.7 percent a year.

Another approach to providing youth with jobs would be to displace foreign labor in the nine countries in the region in which the number of foreign workers exceeds the number of unemployed. The countries concerned are not only Libya and the six oil-rich Gulf monarchies, but also Jordan and Israel, which have become dependent on foreign labor to perform low-wage jobs that nationals refuse to do at the wages offered. The governments in each of these nine countries have periodically campaigned to replace foreign workers with locals, but these efforts have been ineffectual. A particularly striking example occurred in mid-1990s Israel, which had substantial unemployment among the recently arrived immigrants from the former Soviet Union. The country's booming economy created demand for unskilled workers. Israel responded by permitting employers to hire tens and tens of thousands of foreign workers from Asia, Africa, and Eastern Europe, while unemployment was high among Israelis. Encouraging locals to do manual labor or service jobs is hard; such work is often seen as undesirable. Plus, private firms in many Arab countries have a long history of resisting employment of locals, who are seen as much more trouble than they are worth. In short, the solution that would seem obvious to outsiders—solve the unemployment problem by displacing foreign workers—would not be easy to implement.

Yet another solution to the Middle East's employment challenge is emigration. Many countries in the region have had substantial emigration for decades; France has several million residents of North African descent. However, the prospects for continuing emigration are limited. The oil-rich states are more likely to turn to cheaper labor from South and East Asia. And while Europe faces a labor shortage tied to its aging population, the skills and education of young Middle Easterners do not match up well with Europe's labor requirements. The World Bank estimates that about 1.3 million young Middle Eastern workers will emigrate in the decade 2010–2020, which would be a somewhat slower pace than the emigration in the prior decade.

Unemployment is more than an economic problem for Middle Eastern countries; it also has a social and political dimension. Research on what determines happiness suggests that employment is an extremely important factor, independent of income. While extended family networks allow young people to disguise their unemployment for years by living with their parents and pretending that they are gainfully occupied at something that in fact does not take up much of their time, the reality of their limited prospects weighs heavily on young Middle Easterners. Iran has seen a wave of unemployed youth turning to antisocial behavior, especially drug addiction and prostitution. Political extremists from Algeria to Palestine and Iraq have been able to recruit readily among young people who face a bleak future.

The labor market in the Middle East will likely undergo a dramatic change by midcentury when the working-age population will largely stop growing. In six of the region's twenty countries, the population aged fifteen to sixty will likely shrink between 2040 and 2050; in Iran, it is projected to shrink 9 percent in that decade. By then, the working-age population will likely only be increasing in the countries in which the demographic transition started late: Sudan, Iraq, and especially the Palestinian territories and Yemen. At just the same time that the working-age population is no longer growing much, the numbers of elderly will likely start to soar.

The steady working-age population combined with the increasing numbers of elderly will likely combine to produce a sharp decrease in the ratio of working-age people per elderly, which is the key determinant of how much of a burden society faces for financing retirement. For the Middle East as a whole, the ratio of working-age population to the elderly has been around 9:1 since 1950, reaching a peak of 9.6:1 in 2000. But the ratio will likely start to decline precipitously after 2010, and is estimated to plunge to 3.2:1 in 2050. Iran will likely face the most acute problem, going from 9.2 people of working age for each person over age sixty in 2000 to only 2.2 in 2050. (Israel will likely have only 2.3, but it has long had proportionately more elderly—the ratio was 4.4:1 in 2000—so it is well on the path to adjusting by encouraging later retirement and more savings.) Note that these figures all relate to population of working age, not to actual workers. In particular, if current patterns persist, in which only 30 percent of women work outside the home, and factoring in the usual nonworking people aged fifteen to sixty (e.g., students, unemployed, and disabled), then the number of active workers may be only half the number of people aged fifteen to sixty. That would mean that for each person over sixty, the Middle East on average would have 1.6 active workers—and Iran would have 1.1. That will be an unsustainable burden for the region's pay-as-you-go retirement systems, which rely on the contributions of those now working to fund the payments made to the retired.

The challenge of paying for retirement could be an opportunity—what is referred to as a second "demographic dividend" when the middle-aged save for their retirement—because those savings could fund investment that raises national income. That, however, would require policies that encourage financial savings, such as reliable banks (as distinct from government-owned bureaucratic dinosaurs that treat customers badly), attractive interest rates, well-regulated insurance firms, and bond markets. On the whole, Middle Eastern financial systems leave much to be desired. For example, while in many ways a developed economy, Israel has a weak financial system in which a handful of institutions dominate the banks, stock markets, and insurance firms. Several Gulf monarchies have vigorous stock markets, but they have been subject to speculative waves, with strong public pressure to rescue local investors when bubbles burst. The $90 billion public bailout of Kuwaiti investors after the 1982 stock market crash created the impression that stock markets are as much an instrument for distribution of government largesse as a place in which capital is raised for productive purposes. Given the history of the region's financial systems, it will be a challenge to persuade locals to hand over the savings with which they expect to fund their retirement. While any estimate is uncertain, it seems plausible that Middle Easterners have put several hundred billion dollars in international financial markets rather than home markets—and that is on top of the well over a trillion dollars that Gulf governments have invested in those markets, mostly from secretive "future generation" funds designed to supplement income if oil receipts fall.

Women's Economic Role

In recent decades, Middle Eastern women have made great progress at gaining more equal access to education, but that has not yet translated into more access to employment outside the home. What happens to women's employment status will do much to influence how the region develops.

Throughout the region (with the exception of the poorest countries, Yemen and Sudan), girls as well as boys have nearly universal access to primary education. By 2000, female primary school enrollment was 90 percent of the school-age children in the World Bank's Middle East and North Africa region (which excludes Sudan and Israel). Access to secondary education in the region has sharply increased in recent decades for both boys and girls: enrollment rates in 1980 were 52 percent of boys and 32 percent of girls, whereas in 2000, the rates were 77 percent of boys and 73 percent of girls. In the oil-rich states—including those with strict Islamic rule, such as Saudi Arabia and Iran—women now make up half or more of the undergraduate university students. Indeed, the increasing dominance in universities by women is becoming a matter of social concern; it appears that young men have better work opportunities and so do not stay in school as long. Kuwait University has introduced a formal affirmative action program to attract more male students.

Women's increased skills, combined with the urbanization that the Middle East has been experiencing, would be expected to lead to more women working outside the home. However, to date, women's labor force participation has lagged behind trends in much of the rest of the world. In East Asia and sub-Saharan Africa, women's labor force participation has for decades been at 60 percent or more. By contrast, the proportion of working-age women in the labor force grew modestly in the World Bank's Middle East and North Africa region from 22 percent in 1960 to 32 percent in 2006. One way to read these data is that the Middle East is going down the same route as Latin America, where women's labor force participation has been slowly rising for decades, from 26 percent in 1970 to 55 percent in 2006.

So far, Middle Eastern women's employment has been much higher in the public sector and in agriculture than in private, urban firms. Part of the problem is that women face legal barriers and restrictions in many countries. Yet the single most important factor explaining the low level of women's employment in the region is cultural attitudes, such as the code of modesty restricting interactions between men and women, the centrality of the family rather than the individual, and the common assumption that the man is the family's sole breadwinner. While some have argued that privatization and other economic reform programs have also hurt women's efforts to find work, there is scant evidence to back this up.

Another problem women face is discrimination in pay. The World Bank calculates that in its Middle East and North Africa region, the average women's wage would go up 32 percent if discrimination were eliminated (women make on average 73 percent of what men make, but part of the difference is due to lower education and experience).

If women increasingly seek to join the labor force in the next few decades, it will add to the pressures of creating sufficient jobs for the "youth bulge." For instance, a 10 percentage point increase over the next decade in the women's labor force participation rate—which would still leave Middle Eastern women well below the average in other developing countries—would almost double the number of job seekers being added to the labor force. To create anywhere near the number of jobs needed to employ all these workers would require far-reaching reforms across the region: attracting foreign financing, reducing the bureaucratic burden on entrepreneurs, and, in many countries, displacing foreign workers. On the other hand, if the women graduating in increasing numbers from the region's universities are left with poor or no employment opportunities, it will be a great waste of a valuable resource, as well as potentially a source of serious social if not political tension.

While employing women could be a serious challenge in the next few decades, women's employment could become a savior by midcentury as the number of youth falls off at the same time that the elderly population begins to soar. Having a pool of women to add to the work force could do much to meet the challenge of funding retirement for the rapidly increasing elderly population. In other words, the economic pressures for bringing women in the labor force will grow as the population ages.

References and Further Reading

Clarke, J.I., and W.B. Fisher, eds. *Populations of the Middle East and North Africa: A Geographical Approach.* London: University of London Press, 1972.

Fargues, Philippe. "Demographic Explosion or Social Upheaval?" In *Democracy Without Democrats? The Renewal of Politics in the Muslim World*, ed. Ghassan Salamé, 156–182. London: I.B. Tauris, 1994.

Handoussa, Heba, and Zafiris Tzannatos, eds. *Employment Creation and Social Protection in the Middle East and North Africa.* Cairo: American University in Cairo Press, 2002.

Lee, Ronald, and Andrew Mason. "What Is the Demographic Dividend?" *Finance and Development* 43:3 (September 2006): 16–17.

Moghadam, Valentine. *Women, Work, and Economic Reform in the Middle East and North Africa.* Boulder, CO: Lynne Rienner, 1998.

Robinson, Warren, and Fatma El-Zanaty. *The Demographic Revolution in Modern Egypt.* Lanham, MD: Lexington Books, 2006.

Salehi-Isfahani, Djavad. *Labor and Human Capital in the Middle East: Studies of Markets and Household Behavior.* Reading, UK: Ithaca Press, 2001.

Sirageldin, Ismail, ed. *Human Capital: Population Economics in the Middle East.* New York: Macmillan, 2003.

United Nations, Department of Economic and Social Affairs. Population Division. www.un.org/esa/population/unpop.htm.

United Nations Development Programme (UNDP), Arab Fund for Economic and Social Development, and Arab Gulf Programme for United Nations Development Organizations. *Arab Human Development Report 2005: Towards the Rise of Women in the Arab World.* New York: UNDP, 2006.

United Nations Economic and Social Commission for Western Asia. www.escwa.org.lb.

U.S. Census Bureau, International Data Base. www.census.gov/ipc/www/idbsprd.html.

Winckler, Onn. *Arab Political Demography: Volume One, Population Growth and Natalist Policies.* Brighton, UK: Sussex Academic Press, 2005.

World Bank. *Gender and Development in the Middle East and North Africa: Women in the Public Sphere.* Washington DC: World Bank, 2004.

———. *Shaping the Future: A Long-Term Perspective of People and Job Mobility for the Middle East and North Africa.* Washington, DC: World Bank, 2009.

———. *The Status and Progress of Women in the Middle East and North Africa.* Washington DC: World Bank, 2009.

Governance

The Middle East has been plagued by governments that try to do too much and do it poorly. Among the region's great problems in the economic arena has been the heavy hand of the state, intervening in areas where the market would do better. On the other hand, governments do not deliver effective basic services and rule of law.

In the 1980s, the term "poor governance" was often used as a euphemism for corruption. Since then, research on the role of political institutions and arrangements in economic development has advanced considerably. Researchers have found that the two major categories of governance that matter for economic development are accountability and inclusiveness—that is, nondiscrimination in access to services, and equality before the law. By contrast, freedom and democracy, which many thought to be important for development, have less impact on economic growth.

In 2003, the World Bank study *Better Governance for Development in the Middle East and North Africa* found that the Middle East and North Africa region, compared to other regions of the world, "ranks at the bottom on the index of overall governance quality." While the World Bank has not updated that comparison, it has documented the considerable progress many Middle Eastern countries made from 2003 until 2008 toward improving the overall business environment.

The Middle East Freedom and Democracy Deficit

The problem of bad governance is often reduced to the absence of democracy or, more generally, of political freedom. Perhaps counterintuitively, democracy and freedom are not in fact the most important governance issues for economic development.

The most obvious characteristic of Middle Eastern political systems is the "freedom deficit," in the words of the first *Arab Human Development Report* in 2002. That report, prepared by leading Arab intellectuals for the United Nations Development Programme (UNDP) and the Arab Fund for Economic and Social Development, bluntly identified the lack of freedom as the first of three key deficits plaguing the region; the others were the women's empowerment deficit and the human capabilities/knowledge deficit. The report pointed out that on the "freedom scores" prepared annually by the UNDP as a component of its "human development index," the Arab world's score was less than half that of any other part of the world and less than one-fifth that of North America. An equally bleak picture emerges from the detailed Freedom House annual reports, *Freedom in the World*. In 2009, the Middle East had exactly one of the world's eighty-nine "free" countries, Israel. By contrast, the Middle East's twenty countries included thirteen of the world's forty-three "not free" countries. Looked at another way, whereas 46 percent of the world's peoples lived in free countries, only 2 percent of Middle Easterners lived in free lands. While 36 percent of the global population lived in not free states, 80 percent of Middle Easterners were in not free lands. However, the Middle East's record was improving slightly; over the preceding few years, some countries had graduated from "not free" to "partly free."

The Freedom House index is based on a checklist of ten political rights and fifteen civil liberties, such as the right to organize political parties, realistic possibility for the opposition to gain power, a political process free of domination by the military or other unelected group (e.g., religious hierarchies), freedom from pervasive corruption, full political rights for minority groups, freedom of the press, freedom of assembly, free trade unions, independence of the judiciary, an open government operating with full transparency, rule of law, equal treatment for the various segments of the population, the right to own property, and personal social freedoms. As these criteria illustrate, the concept "freedom" is much broader than the question of whether a country has elections. Many Middle Eastern states have elections, but subject to significant limitations, such as pre-vetting of candidates for acceptability to the authorities (e.g., Iran), regime scrutiny of ballots as they are cast by the voter (e.g., Syria), or severely limited powers of the elected officials (e.g., the advisory character of the partially elected, partially appointed Bahraini Majlis). The only one of the twenty Middle Eastern states that Freedom House rated in 2009 as an electoral democracy is Israel. By contrast, it rates 118 of the 174 states outside the Middle East as electoral democracies. Thus, 5 percent of Middle Eastern states are electoral democracies, whereas in contrast, 68 percent of non–Middle Eastern states are electoral democracies.

Scholars have vigorously debated the reasons for the "Middle East democracy exception." The most common factor cited is that many Middle Eastern countries are "rentier states," to use Vladimir Lenin's evocative expression: the government gets its revenue without having to tax the people, either from oil income or foreign aid (much of it from oil-rich Middle Eastern states). Lisa Anderson coined the phrase "no representation without taxation," arguing that "the taxed devise ways to be represented." This thesis is hard to evaluate by looking at the Middle East's experience, since both rentier and nonrentier states in the Middle East are generally undemocratic; however, statistical studies of the global experience offer support for the theory.

Other explanations for the absence of democracy in the Middle East outside Israel include cultural and ideological factors. The particular cultural factors cited by authors to make this case have varied over time; the current favorite seems to be "neopatriarchy," that is, traditional patterns of gender relations and authority within the family. A particularly sensitive issue has been whether and to what extent Islam explains the Middle East's poor record at freedom and democracy. The historical record offers little reason to think that is the case. When Europe was deep in the Dark Ages, Muslim societies were much more tolerant, offering greater freedoms for intellectuals and minorities. Nor do the Muslim sacred books and the teachings of the major Muslim religious leaders show attitudes to freedom and democracy that contrast to those of Christianity or Judaism. Indeed, the fairest interpretation of the texts and conventions of all three monotheistic traditions is that they are not particularly enthusiastic nor particularly hostile to political freedom. Yet empirical studies of what holds back democracy have found that the proportion of Muslims in the population is a statistically significant factor. Of course, it is only one of several such factors, none of which by itself explains in full the absence of democracy in any society. The loudest and most extreme opposition to political freedoms in the contemporary world comes from the radical Islamist fringe, whose views resonate with some Middle Eastern youth.

However, the poor Middle Eastern record on freedom and democracy is not necessarily a major factor in the region's weak record at economic development. The link between economic growth and freedom, much less democracy, seems weak. As Nobel Prize–winning economist Amartya Sen put it in *Development as Freedom*, a book dedicated to arguing the merits of freedom, "the hypothesis that there is no relation between them in either direction is hard to reject."

While political and civil rights might not affect economic growth as such, they do seem connected to some other aspects of economic well-being. In particular, in freer societies, popular pressure forces governments to be more responsive to natural disasters, such as famines and earthquakes. The weight of scholarly consensus is that democratic societies are less likely to engage in war. Finally, the case can be made that freer societies are more stable politically, less prone to be torn apart by ethnic and religious tensions. However, the evidence on this point is not completely firm. Consider the contrast between Lebanon, with its relatively free politics and its raging religious tensions, including a fifteen-year civil war, and Syria, with its strict authoritarian politics, which has kept a cap on ethnoreligious tensions in a deeply divided society (the Syrian government is controlled by a minority group, the Alawites, who are despised by many in the majority Sunni Arab community). In sum, the argument for freedom and democracy should not rest on the economic advantages, which do not seem major; instead, the case for political openness should be made on noneconomic grounds.

Accountability

While the economic impact of freedom and democracy is open to debate, that is not the case for two major elements of good governance, accountability and inclusiveness.

Government accountability means that those acting in the name of the people are answerable to the people for their failures and credited for their successes. It has three main components. First is explaining and disclosing actions to the people, which is known as "transparency." Equally important is being held responsible by citizens for actions, through elections or other processes that allow citizens to choose among alternatives—what is known as "contestability." Third is being subject to checks by other government agencies, such as when parliament must approve executive proposals, audit agencies investigate ministries, or courts rule on the legality of executive actions. All three of these components are sorely lacking in many nondemocratic Middle Eastern countries. The World Bank places public accountability in the Middle East as well below the average among developing countries.

The lack of transparency in the Middle East takes many forms. Freedom of the press to report on government actions is limited in all the nondemocratic countries; in most countries, the media rarely report on government shortcomings and carefully avoid any criticism, even implicitly, of the ruler. But the problem of nontransparent government is even more basic than the lack of a free press: there is simply little information made available to citizens about the government's policies and rules. No nondemocratic Middle Eastern country guarantees citizens the right to government information. In some countries, not even the government budget is published except in the briefest of summaries. Indeed, citizens may not have access to information about the laws and regulations by which they are supposed to abide. The World Bank's explanation about Egypt in its 2003 *Better Governance* report is all too typical of the region: "In Egypt, the ambiguity and lack of knowledge about relevant laws are exacerbated by the new laws issued frequently by the legislature, the binding presidential decrees issued by the executive branch, and other binding decrees issued by relevant departments. There are also inconsistencies between some of these laws and the way they are enforced. Moreover, the new laws are often published only after a considerable time lag, or they are not published at all."

The poor regional record regarding transparency is duplicated with regard to contestability. Only two of the countries in the region have ever replaced a sitting leader through elections: Israel and Iraq (Iran's peculiarities are discussed below). Only a handful of parliaments in the region have any real power. Few countries have elections for local office, and even rarer are the cases where elected local leaders have any substantial authority. The region is poor at even more limited sorts of contestability, namely, within government bureaucracies: appointment to and advancement within the civil service are often determined on the basis of personal connections rather than merit. In the nondemocratic Middle East, at every level of government from the simplest clerk to the head of state, poor performance is rarely punished and good work is rarely rewarded. In that environment, it is hardly surprising that governments work badly at providing needed public services.

Internal checks and balances are as poor in most nondemocratic Middle Eastern governments as transparency and contestability. The excessive concentration of power in the hands of the executive is obvious in the seven monarchies, but it is also characteristic of republics such as Syria, Egypt, Algeria, and Tunisia. National leaders have, in effect, the power to do as they wish, irrespective of law. What is particularly striking to Americans is that Middle Eastern constitutions are more advisory than binding; indeed, the norm for such documents is to make rights subject to conditions that can be changed at will. Article 38 of the Syrian constitution states, "The state guarantees the freedom of the press, of printing, and publication in accordance with law." More direct is Article 13 of Libya's 1969 constitution: "Freedom of opinion is guaranteed within the limits of public interest and the principles of the Revolution."

The norm for the nondemocratic Middle East is uncontested elections and an unchecked executive. For the first twenty-five years after the 1979 revolution, the Islamic Republic of Iran was the exception to this rule with its vigorously fought elections for parliament and the presidency. The Iranian parliament played an active role checking the executive; it rejected a larger proportion of ministers nominated by the president than any other parliament in the world, and each year it significantly altered the government budget proposed by the executive. As a further check, the Council of Guardians must approve the constitutionality and compatibility with Islam of each parliamentary action, and the separate Expediency Council is empowered to override both the parliament and the Council of Guardians in order to resolve differences between them. The contested elections and checks and balances provided a way to correct the system's course in response to public complaints.

However, the Islamic Republic's structure has one great flaw that severely undercuts the significance of the elections and the checks and balances—namely, the unlimited power of the Supreme Leader. As justified by the theory of "rule of the jurisprudent" (*velayat-e faghih*), the Supreme Leader has the absolute authority to overrule any decision by any government body. He further directly controls the key institutions; for instance, he is the military's commander in chief, and he appoints the director of the state television and radio. In other words, he is the true executive, while Iran's president is not particularly powerful. While the Supreme Leader is elected by an Assembly of Experts, those elections, like the ones for parliament and presidency, are controlled by a body he appoints, which carefully vets who can run. Since 2000, the power of Supreme Leader Ali Khamenei has steadily grown, and he has shown less and less tolerance for dissent. In 2009, protests over widespread accusations of fraud in the presidential elections drew 3 million Tehranis onto the capital's streets. When Khamenei dismissed the significance of the objections, he became the object of the protestors' wrath. A harsh crackdown against dissent included mass arrests and show trials of journalists, opposition politicians, and academics; allegations of prison rape and torture further inflamed public opinion. Iran's system thus increasingly looks like that of the other nondemocratic Middle Eastern countries, in which elections are shams and the power of the leader is unchecked.

Inclusiveness

Inclusiveness means that all citizens have equal rights before the law and equal opportunities to exercise those rights. If some class of citizens is systematically excluded or treated unfairly, then the country's economy is deprived of the full contribution they could make.

The most glaring problem of inclusiveness in the Middle East is the status of women. The region's economies do not effectively use the skills of women. The World Bank reports that in 2006 in its Middle East and North Africa region, only 32 percent of working-age women were in the labor force. Part of the problem is government policies; conservative countries such as Saudi Arabia place great barriers against the employment of women working alongside men. But the principal explanation is social attitudes, which limit women's public role. Those attitudes are evolving, as seen in the region's dramatic progress in women's education. In 2006, on average, nine Middle Eastern girls were enrolled in primary and secondary schools for every boy. In the oil-rich countries, women predominate in the universities, making up more than 60 percent of the undergraduates in such countries as Iran and Saudi Arabia. One reason for this is that women have such poor access to the job market that many stay in school instead.

The Middle East has a poor track record at making full use of the economic potential of people irrespective of ethnic and religious background. Minorities frequently face discrimination in the provision of public services and barriers to full economic participation. Examples of large minorities long facing discrimination include Algeria's Berbers, Egypt's Copts, Sudan's Southerners, Syria's Kurds, Saudi Arabia's Shia, Israel's Arabs, and Iran's Kurds. The ruling minority Alawites in Syria and Sunnis in Bahrain have used their hold on power to grant themselves considerable economic advantages. On a similar note, generous government programs aid the nationals of Kuwait, Qatar, and the United Arab Emirates but exclude the noncitizens who make up the vast bulk of those countries' residents.

The Middle East also suffers from the same problems as other parts of the world in ensuring equitable treatment of the poor and those who live in the countryside and in disadvantaged regions. In Egypt, infant mortality is more than twice as high in the historically disadvantaged southern governorates as in the metropolitan governorates, and schools enroll more than 80 percent of those in the top income bracket (the highest 20 percent of income earners) but less than 50 percent of those in the bottom income bracket.

A pervasive problem throughout the region is clientelism—government decisions made on the basis of personal connections, be it membership in the ruling political party or nepotism in favoring family or clan members. Clientelism divides the population into two categories: the included and the excluded. The two have unequal access to the government—the former are favored for services like university enrollment, for government jobs, and for administrative decisions like permission to start a business or build a house. The excluded have to devote considerable time, and often money, to secure from the government that which should be available to all citizens.

While the accuracy of corruption indices is not entirely clear, measures such as that from Transparency International regularly show the Middle East as suffering from a serious corruption problem. As Sen argues in *Development as Freedom*, "the temptation to be corrupt is strongest when the officers have a lot of power but are themselves relatively poor." That obviously applies to highly regulated Middle Eastern economies such as Egypt. But it also fits the case of the oil-rich Gulf states, where government officials make decisions about the allocation of vast sums; their incomes may be substantial by the scale of what public servants in similar posts earn in Western developed countries, but those incomes are still small in comparison to the amounts in play.

Improved Business Environment

For decades, nearly every Middle Eastern country suffered from burdensome regulation and inadequate rules enforcement. A 2003 World Bank study of the Middle East and North Africa region found that registering a new business on average took sixty days and cost 62 percent of per capita income, compared to 11 percent in developed Western countries. The study also found that dispute resolution was cumbersome and protracted: the average time to complete a commercial court case was more than two years in Jordan and Lebanon, while the average time in Egypt exceeded six years.

Shortly after the turn of the millennium, the situation began to change. Israel and several of the oil-rich Gulf monarchies began to introduce reforms that eased the cost of business. They went on to deepen and extend those reforms, while their example influenced some of their neighbors. In its 2010 annual report *Doing Business*, the World Bank reported that seventeen of the nineteen countries in its Middle East and North Africa region had made reforms in the areas it monitors, which include the ease of starting a business, registering property, getting credit, employing workers, enforcing a contract, paying taxes, and closing a business. In the World Bank's 2010 rankings of the ease of doing business in 183 countries, 4 of the Gulf monarchies—Saudi Arabia, Bahrain, United Arab Emirates, and Qatar—plus Israel scored above the average for EU members.

While the regulatory environment has improved, many Middle Eastern countries still suffer from government-caused problems that drive up the costs of doing business. One of the most obvious indicators of poor governance is inadequate basic infrastructure, a common problem in the region. A World Bank study concluded that Yemen averages seventy-five days a year without electrical power, while Algeria averages sixteen outages a year, 70 percent of them lasting up to five days. Businesses are forced to rely on high-cost generators or to make do without electricity for days at a time.

In conclusion, despite some progress at improving the business environment, the Middle East is plagued by exclusive, unaccountable, undemocratic, and unfree governments. The region's bad governance has been a factor holding back Middle Eastern economic development. In addition, the governance shortcomings have had many other ill effects, such as wars and the loss of basic political freedoms.

References and Further Reading

Anderson, Lisa. "The State in the Middle East and North Africa." *Comparative Politics* 20:1 (1987): 1–18.

Freedom House. *Freedom in the World 2009*. New York: Freedom House, 2009.

Pack, Howard, and Marcus Noland. *The Arab Economies in a Changing World*. Washington, DC: Institute for International Economics, 2007.

Salamé, Ghassan, ed. *Democracy Without Democrats? The Renewal of Politics in the Muslim World.* London: I.B. Tauris, 1994.

Sen, Amartya. *Development as Freedom.* New York: Anchor Books, 1999.

UNDP and Arab Fund for Economic and Social Development. *Arab Human Development Report 2002: Creating Opportunities for Future Generations.* New York: UNDP, 2002.

UNDP, Arab Fund for Economic and Social Development, and Arab Gulf Programme for United Nations Development Organizations. *Arab Human Development Report 2004: Towards Freedom in the Arab World.* New York: UNDP, 2005.

World Bank. *Better Governance for Development in the Middle East and North Africa: Enhancing Inclusiveness and Accountability.* Washington, DC: World Bank, 2003.

———. *Doing Business 2010: Reforming Through Difficult Times.* Available at www.doingbusiness.org.

———. *Gender and Development in the Middle East and North Africa.* Washington, DC: World Bank, 2004.

———. *The Road Not Traveled: Education Reform in the Middle East and Africa.* Washington, DC: World Bank, 2008.

SECTION 2. SOCIETIES

Gulf Monarchies

One Western stereotype of Arabs is as oil-rich sheikhs. Aside from Libyans, the only Arabs who come even close to that Western image are those residing in the six Gulf monarchies that belong to the Gulf Cooperation Council (GCC): Bahrain, Kuwait, Oman, Qatar, Saudi Arabia, and the United Arab Emirates (UAE). The nationals of the Gulf monarchies account for fewer than 8 percent of Arabs; even including the many foreigners living in those countries, their total population is only 12 percent of the total for all Arab countries. Yet their oil income gives them great weight in the economy of the region; the gross domestic product (GDP) of the GCC states is as large as that of all the other Arab states combined. Three of the Gulf monarchies—Kuwait, Qatar, and the United Arab Emirates—are profoundly rich, with average income levels equal to or higher than those in advanced industrial countries such as the United States. The other three—Bahrain, Oman, and Saudi Arabia—have more modest per capita incomes, on the order of such southern European countries as Greece or Portugal and also of Israel.

Management of oil income has converted the Gulf monarchies from poor societies into countries with high standards of living that are well integrated into the world economy. However, in the Gulf monarchies, as in other oil-producing countries, high oil revenue undercuts the rest of the economy. Reforms that address serious socioeconomic problems are repeatedly postponed in the hope, often realized, that oil income will eventually rise sharply, providing the resources to allow the regimes to avoid economic reforms. In particular, the Gulf monarchies have become dependent on foreign labor, first out of necessity because of the lack of local skills, then out of choice, as the habit of hard work faded. For decades, analysts have warned that oil income will be insufficient to provide the rapidly rising populations with the same generous social programs and government employment. But time and again, buoyant world demand for oil and gas has offset growing social pressures.

Background, Pre-Oil to 1972

Before oil, the Gulf monarchies were poor and weak. Kuwait, Bahrain, Oman, Qatar, and the Trucial Coast—which became the United Arab Emirates upon independence in 1971—were all British colonies. All but Oman had to rely on pearl diving for export revenue, and the market for natural pearls crashed in the 1930s. The economies of Saudi Arabia and Oman depended mostly on livestock and agriculture, which the Saudis supplemented with revenue from pilgrims making the hajj to Mecca. There were basically no public services like schools or hospitals, much less utilities like water or electricity. The monarchs were not particularly strong, being dependent on the powerful merchants who paid the taxes that sustained them. In the 1930s the Saudi *majlis*—the council composed of merchants and tribal leaders—regularly dictated to the Saudi kings as to what they could and could not spend money on, while the merchants in the 1938 Kuwait majlis came close to deposing the emir. In other words, rather than being a tradition deeply rooted in history and custom, the current pattern of extraordinarily powerful rulers who dispense patronage to subjects with little if any voice in public affairs arose only with the oil income.

Oil income has smoothed over many of the region's deep historical divisions, but these same divisions were the basic organizing principle for pre-oil life. While today the Gulf monarchies seem to be a nearly uniform bloc, in fact, long-standing enmities among countries undercut many seemingly obvious economic cooperation efforts. The region was often on the brink of war over boundary disputes, most notably between Saudi Arabia and Abu Dhabi and between the historical enemies Bahrain and Qatar. Though theoretically resolved, these disputes make themselves felt from time to time, such as a 2006 dustup between Saudi Arabia and the UAE about their border. And then there is the historical uniqueness of Oman, which had been a major naval power (it chased the Portuguese out of the Gulf in the seventeenth century) and had its own empire, which was split in 1856 with one wing of the ruling family controlling the African coast from Mogadishu to the island of Zanzibar where it was based. Then a bitter civil war was fought off and on for decades until the 1960s between the sultan and the imamate, the religious leadership of the main Muslim group among Omanis, the Ibadis. From 1963 to 1975, Dhofar, Oman's southern region, was the scene of a bitter war pitting a local communist movement against British special forces and later thousands of Iranian troops.

Within countries, there were deep social divisions. The seven emirates of the UAE have often not gotten along well; Dubai has a long tradition of regarding itself as more sophisticated than Abu Dhabi, and some of the smaller five northern emirates were historically much more prominent than they are today (even at independence in 1971, they had 40 percent of the country's population; in 2010, they had less than 10 percent). Bahrain's majority Shia population continues to regard the ruling Sunni al-Khalifa family as foreigners, even though they took power more than two centuries ago. Perhaps a quarter of Kuwait's citizens are Shia, as are a large portion of the Saudis living in the area along the Gulf (Shia make up at least 10 percent of Saudi citizens overall). Saudi Arabia has deep regional and tribal divisions. The more cosmopolitan residents of the Red Sea coast (known as the Hejaz), which was ruled for most of a millennium by the Hashemite family now on the Jordanian throne, long felt they had little in common with the royal family from the central Nejd region around Riyadh. To this day, Hijazis feel profoundly different from Nejdis, including more sophisticated and liberal. In short, the GCC states are complex, heterogeneous societies. Economic development has often shaken up the sociopolitical balance within states. For instance, with increasing oil income, power in Saudi Arabia dramatically shifted from Hejazis to the Nejdis, symbolized by the move of the capital from the Hejazi city of Jeddah to the Nejdi city of Riyadh.

The historical divisions with and among Gulf societies are very much alive for this generation, which is still in many ways the product of the pre-oil era. While oil production began in Bahrain, Kuwait, and Qatar in the 1930s, society changed only slowly at first. Oil income was minor until well into the 1950s: the volumes produced were small, and the institutional arrangements in colonial times gave nearly all the income to the foreign oil firms. Kuwait was the pioneer, developing social services and infrastructure soon after independence in 1961. While Saudi Arabia's oil income was rising rapidly by then, its government was paralyzed until 1964 by a dispute within the royal family. During that dispute, a group known as the Young Princes, unhappy at the limited development to that date, pushed hard for more rapid economic, social, and political modernization. They were pushed aside, and Saudi Arabia continued to evolve slowly, admittedly fitting the general temperament of Saudi society, with the high priority it places on tradition and social consensus. Public opinion surveys in the 1980s confirm the continuing Saudi caution about change, with 95 percent of respondents agreeing with the statement, "Social change should not be instituted at the expense of traditional values."

It is hard for Westerners to appreciate how poor Gulf societies were only a few short decades ago. Consider that in 1971–1972, at a time when Saudi Arabia had at least 3 million citizens, only 3,279 Saudis graduated from secondary schools—graduates who in 2010 would be 57 years old, at the height of their careers in business or politics.

Late development was all the more true in the UAE and Oman, where oil production only began in the late 1950s and 1960s, respectively. In 1962, Abu Dhabi ruler Sheikh Shakhbut turned down the British development plan because it was too ambitious, containing such elements as a hospital, water supply, and electricity system for Abu Dhabi island, plus a bridge to connect it to the mainland. In 1966, Abu Dhabi had exactly 6 primary schools with 587 students—students who in 2010 would be aged 50 to 56. And yet Abu Dhabi's school system was more advanced than that of Oman: when Qaboos became Oman's sultan in 1970 by overthrowing his father Said, the capital Muscat had no central electricity and the city gates were still locked at night. Sultan Said had established a few schools and hospitals, but so few that Sultan Qaboos sent 700 Omanis to elementary school in the UAE. This is well within the memory of many among the contemporary Omani elite.

Oil Boom, 1973–1985

The extraordinary increase in income for oil-producing countries during the 1970s had a great impact on the Gulf monarchies. Their oil revenue rose about fivefold between 1972 and 1974—all the more impressive given that in 1972, the revenue was already 60–80 percent of GDP (except in Kuwait, where in 1972 oil revenue was a mere 53 percent of GDP). With this flood of money, the Gulf monarchies built an amazing amount of infrastructure: roads, airports, ports, water systems, government buildings, schools, hospitals, housing, and more. The process was often inefficient, with much money wasted in the rush to build quickly, but on the whole, these countries had more money than time, and so they were quite prepared to pay a higher price in order to get quicker development. Perhaps nowhere was the price higher and were the results poorer than in arms purchases. But even in the military sphere, the image of oil sheikhs foolishly wasting their money is grossly overstated. Saudi Arabia, for instance, in the boom years spent less than 10 percent of its GDP on defense, and rather than buying a lot of arms, it mostly built defense infrastructure such as air bases, which turned out to be quite important for accommodating U.S. forces during the 1990–1991 crisis with Iraq.

While the Gulf states shared the common experience of rapidly rising income, how they used that money differed considerably. The oil boom accentuated the preexisting differences in the development strategies. Already by the late 1960s, the various Gulf monarchies had chosen different paths for how to develop in the face of ample cash but limited human capital and small local markets. The different monarchies followed four general development strategies: industrial, gas, financial, and trading. By the 1960s, Abu Dhabi, Qatar, and Bahrain were all interested in industrial development; they were soon joined by Saudi Arabia. Industrialization was at first thought of as primarily producing for the local market, in line with the economic development theory popular in the 1960s known as import substitution industrialization, but then later shifted to energy-intense products for world markets in line with the economic development theory of the 1980s known as export-led industrialization. Gas was the route chosen by Qatar, with its limited oil but massive natural gas reserves, which it has developed for use both in industry and as liquefied natural gas for export. Investing wealth abroad has been a major activity for Kuwait, which early on established a formal reserve fund to be invested abroad to generate earnings for future generations; the domestic economy was dominated by commerce and services for the local population. Being a trading center has been Dubai's ambition for decades, at least since Sheikh Rashid came to power in 1958. Dubai developed as a regional trade entrepôt, with extensive port and airport facilities and a welcoming attitude toward foreign investors.

The rapid rise in income of the early 1970s was quickly equaled by a rise in spending. After all, the Gulf states (other than Kuwait and to a lesser extent Bahrain) were at such a low level of development in 1972 that their needs were enormous. By 1977–1978, the Gulf states were running up against financial constraints. Saudi Arabia's government budget fell into deficit. The financial problems were exacerbated in the late 1970s by softness in world oil markets as demand shrank in response to the 1973 price increase. The Gulf monarchies' finances were saved by the 1979–1980 dramatic oil price increases associated with the Iranian Revolution. Once again, these states were awash in cash, and grand development plans were reinvigorated. Times were good in the early 1980s. Governments had resources to waste; for instance, Kuwait bailed out its half-million citizens' $90 billion loss when a speculative stock market bubble burst.

The Slow Years, 1986–2004

The oil boom came to an end with the spectacular 1985 oil price crash, followed by twenty years of mostly modest prices and little demand growth. Gulf monarchies were forced to implement cutbacks; in Saudi Arabia, those came only after a 1985–1986 run-up in unpaid bills to contractors. The squeeze on local businesses was all the worse because local banks no longer had ample deposits they were looking to lend; indeed, the Saudi banking system was increasingly financing the government deficit, while trying to clean up balance sheets weakened by defaulting local borrowers. Meanwhile, governments were facing bills coming due to sustain development projects launched during the boom days. Saudi Arabia, for instance, had promoted agricultural development with generous subsidies, which resulted in a twentyfold increase in land under cultivation, mostly with highly subsidized water; wheat output rose so much that the kingdom became the world's sixth-largest wheat exporter (the subsidized purchase price was finally cut in 1988; output then stabilized).

Especially for Kuwait and Saudi Arabia, the economic problems were massively compounded by the 1990–1991 Iraqi invasion of Kuwait. While neither government has ever provided a clear accounting of the crisis's costs nor of their financial situation on its eve, it appears that Kuwait exhausted nearly all its reserve fund of about $100 billion, and that the Saudi government spent nearly as much, including contributions-in-kind for the U.S. forces based in the kingdom during the crisis and $20 billion in grants to states for their participation in the anti-Iraq alliance. Riyadh ran up a large debt, and while most of that was owed internally, the Saudi government did borrow some on international markets in 1991–1992 and insisted on loans for major purchases, for instance of arms. To be sure, all that government spending resulted in something of an economic boom, though in Kuwait that was of little comfort, since the impressive postliberation reconstruction spending was only rebuilding what had been there before. In contrast to the economic problems the war caused in the northern Gulf, the UAE earned much more from the temporarily higher price and demand for oil associated with the Kuwait crisis than it spent in support of the allied war effort.

After the brief war uptick in oil prices, world oil markets stagnated until the late 1990s. As their oil income slowly rose in 1999–2004, the Gulf monarchies used the money cautiously while continuing, or even accelerating, their economic reform efforts. Saudi Arabia paid down much of its debt to the local banking system, which had peaked at close to 100 percent of GDP in 1999, with the result that banks could vigorously lend to private business. Particularly striking was that military budgets and arms purchases fell significantly despite the higher oil income. It would appear that Gulf states' high levels of military spending in the 1980s and 1990s were based on the perception of real threat from Iraq and Iran, and as that threat faded, so too did their spending. Furthermore, they spent more wisely on their military, acquiring weapons well designed for their needs.

While the Gulf states implemented economic reforms in 1999–2004, it is by no means clear that the pace of reform matched the scale of problems facing these societies. In particular, unemployment is a massive social challenge. The rapid population growth since 1970 has created a rapidly growing labor force. At the same time, public expectations have been shaped by decades of easy-to-get, well-paid government jobs. Locals hold few private-sector jobs, which are mostly filled by foreigners who work harder and for considerably lower wages than locals would accept. While the data about employment in the Gulf monarchies are unreliable, from the most careful accounts available, it would appear that about three-fourths of those employed in the Gulf monarchies are foreigners. According to the 1995 UAE census, of the 114,000 employed nationals, 102,000 worked for the public sector and 12,000 for the private-sector; that made nationals 27 percent of public-sector employment but only 1.3 percent of private-sector employment.

The heavy reliance on foreign labor creates two profound socioeconomic problems. The first is unemployment, a subject so sensitive that there are no reliable figures. For instance, serious estimates for unemployment among Saudi males in 2002 ranged from 10 percent to 30 percent. And the problem is getting worse because the rapid population growth rate of the past decades is translating into a rapidly growing pool of young people joining the labor market, many of them university graduates. In 2000–2010, the UAE national labor force grew at 10 percent per year. To be sure, the extended family network cushions the social impact of unemployment, which generally takes the form of young men having to stay in their parents' home for years until they finally land a government job. But those idle young men are both an economic waste and a potential political problem. Another problem, set to mushroom in the next decade, is unemployment among women, who by 2010 made up a majority of university students in every Gulf country but whose participation in the labor force has been at only about 10 percent of the working-age population. Since 2000, that participation rate has risen in Kuwait, but many of the women seeking jobs have not found them, so female unemployment has been increasing.

The second problem caused by heavy reliance on foreign labor is the social tension created by the predominance of foreigners in the local population. The situation is most extreme in the UAE, where the tone of public life is set by foreigners. Furthermore, the overwhelmingly male foreign labor force means that 67 percent of the UAE population is male. The young adult population has an even higher proportion of males, creating a socially explosive situation in a society with conservative sexual mores. The heavy dependence on foreigners also creates security concerns of many sorts, from conflicts among foreigners of different nationalities (e.g., Pakistani and Indian) to infiltration by foreign subversives (e.g., radical Islamists). In Bahrain, the Shia majority of the local population is deeply embittered by what it perceives as a concerted government campaign to give citizenship to Sunni foreigners in a bid to change the country's religious mix.

Gulf monarchies have had limited success at addressing the problem of heavy reliance on foreign labor. Programs requiring private firms to hire locals have had mixed results at best. Many private firms treat such programs as in effect a tax, with the hired locals not being expected to be seriously competitive with their foreign co-workers. Some small reforms have been instituted to make education more responsive to labor-market needs. But the expectations of locals about how much effort they should put forth at work and how much income they should expect have changed incrementally, at most. On the whole, the response of Gulf societies to the employment problem has been to continue with the old model—foreign labor for private-sector work, nationals working for the government—and hope for the best. After all, it would only take modest adjustment in the proportion of new jobs going to nationals rather than foreigners to absorb the growth in the national labor force. Consider that between 1999 and 2004, employment in the UAE rose by 929,000 while the national labor force rose by 96,000. Had the share of nationals among those being hired been only 11 percent, national unemployment would have been eliminated; instead, it reportedly more than doubled to a total of 29,000 (other reputable estimates of Emirati unemployment in 2006–2008 range from 17,000 to 35,000).

The Second Boom After 2004

After several years of steady increases in prices and demand, the world oil market took off in 2005, creating a second oil boom for the Gulf. The income windfall was stunning, and this time the governments did not rush to spend it all. The big exception was in Dubai, where the local government teamed with the private sector in a speculative boom that crashed in 2009.

In the early years of the second boom (from 2004 to 2006), Gulf governments reacted cautiously. Saudi Arabia used most of the windfall to turn a 2002 budget deficit into a $60 billion surplus in 2006. Spending initiatives were modest: a 15 percent government salary increase (the first in almost twenty years), an $8 billion program for basic infrastructure, a $19 billion purchase of seventy-two Eurofighter Typhoon jets to replace an aging force. By the end of 2006, the Saudi government had slashed the national debt to less than half its 2002 level of $250 billion. In both Kuwait and the UAE, governments constrained spending such that by 2006, budget surpluses were over 25 percent of GDP.

While governments were relatively restrained in the face of the new money flood, the private sector was not. In 2003–2006, private-sector enthusiasm in much of the Gulf caused some unsustainable bubbles, especially in the stock markets. The capitalization of the GCC stock markets went from $129 billion in early 2002 to $499 billion at the end of 2004. After the capitalization rose further in 2005, in 2006 came the crash that badly hit many small investors who entered the market late. The Saudi market started 2006 at a $645 billion valuation before losing 52 percent of its value during the year. In 2006, the Abu Dhabi market dropped 43 percent, Dubai 44 percent, and Qatar 47 percent (the Kuwaiti stock market index is calculated in a unique way that makes it a poor indicator of what is happening to the value of stocks). Investors demanded a public bailout in the face of the 2006 drop, but governments refused. After all, despite the 2006 crash, the markets were up 55 to 91 percent over the three-year period of 2004–2006.

Oil markets grew even hotter in 2007–2008. GCC GDPs grew by 42 percent, from $732 billion in 2006 to $1,073 billion in 2008. While each country took a slightly different path, in each one, oil and gas exports rose by at least that much, and government revenue rose correspondingly. Faced with such large increases in revenue, it would have been politically impossible and economically unnecessary for governments to completely constrain spending. In the context of the oil income flooding it, Saudi Arabia was relatively restrained when it raised spending 15 percent per year in 2007–2008. Kuwait boosted its spending 27 percent per year in 2007–2008, while the UAE opened the floodgates with a 38 percent increase per year. The increase in UAE government spending was more than matched by the private sector. Investors in Dubai led the way, encouraged by the Dubai government, which was a partner in many of the biggest projects. The eye-catching activities in Dubai included construction of the world's tallest building, an artificial island in the shape of palm tree, with over 4,000 luxury villas, and a 100-meter-high indoor ski slope.

It was poor timing, in that many of the Dubai projects had just opened or were under construction when the global financial crisis hit in late 2008. Real estate prices in both Dubai and Abu Dhabi fell 60 percent from July to October 2008 as the foreign investors who had been driving the market disappeared. Making the problem worse was that Dubai's development depended to a large extent upon borrowed funds, which dried up after the global financial crisis hit. The Dubai government had to swallow its pride and turn to the Abu Dhabi government for a $19 billion line of credit, something the Dubai authorities were loath to do as they had long derided their neighbor for not being as successful in business as they were. The Dubai government minimized the debt problems of the various firms in which the authorities are partners, a debt which informed observers estimated at between $60 billion and $90 billion when the crisis broke in 2009. The Dubai authorities took a tough position in their negotiations with creditors, insisting on write-downs and longer repayment periods. It appears that restructuring has resolved the debt crisis, though it is unclear how much the losses creditors had to accept will hurt Dubai's reputation as a good place to do business. The impact on Dubai of the debt crisis will be felt for years; with less credit available, construction of housing, offices, hotels, and shops will all be at a much slower pace than in the pre-2008 boom.

While the UAE was hit worst, none of the Gulf monarchies escaped the effects of the 2008–2009 global financial crisis. The GDP of the GCC countries as a group fell from $1,073 billion in 2008 to $887 billion in 2009, a 17 percent drop—but that left GDP in 2009 21 percent higher than in 2006. Lower oil earnings hit government revenue hard, at a time when many governments were gearing up for development projects planned during the earlier boom. While Saudi Arabia increased its spending in 2009 by a relatively modest 9 percent, the drop in revenue meant that spending equaled revenue, whereas in 2008, revenue had been twice as much as spending. The real pain from the global financial crisis was felt not by government budgets, which were cushioned by large reserves built up during the boom, but in stock markets and real estate. From January 2008 to March 2009, the average drop for the six GCC stock markets was 63 percent; while they recovered 40 percent on average by September 2009, that still left them 48 percent below the January 2008 level. While real estate conditions varied from market to market, prices fell throughout the GCC. As of mid-2009, residential real estate prices were 20 percent off their peak in the Saudi capital Riyadh and 15 percent off in the Saudi commercial capital Jeddah. The real estate crashes had less implication for the banking system than similar crashes would have in the West, because most homes are purchased with cash. (This is the reason only half of Saudis live in homes they own, as young people must stay with their parents for years until they save up enough to pay cash for a house.) In contrast to the home mortgage lending system common in the United States, bank lending in the GCC is usually based on family reputation. In a worrying development for banks, two prominent Saudi business families that had borrowed $20 billion from banks got into a very public bankruptcy dispute in 2009, dragged through the courts in New York and London.

The prospects for 2010 and the subsequent few years are for a recovery in oil markets, with prices firm and the volume demanded higher. With higher earnings and continued restrained spending policies, the Gulf monarchies should return to substantial budget surpluses and modest GDP growth, according to International Monetary Fund (IMF) forecasts. So long as those conditions prevail—relatively firm oil markets and relatively modest government spending—the Gulf monarchies will be on a sustainable macroeconomic path. Another reason the Gulf monarchies have good prospects is that they are good places to do business—that is, each of the governments has continued to implement business-friendly reforms. All the Gulf monarchies rank in the top third of countries in the World Bank's 2009 *Doing Business* index; by contrast, four European Union members, including Italy, rank below any of the Gulf monarchies.

Until the 2009 crash, the route forward for the Gulf monarchies seemed to lie along the path chosen by Dubai, which prospered by embracing globalization and entrepreneurship, as well as being socially open. The 2009 crash substantially changed that picture, with many in the Gulf concluding that Dubai's success was artificial and that Western-style economies are vulnerable to periodic crises. It is not at all clear to what extent the various Gulf monarchies will fall back on the old ways of depending on oil and gas, and to what extent they will concentrate on plans for a post-oil future. Voices of doom have long predicted that by relying on oil and gas while delaying reforms, the region will be overwhelmed by the obvious socioeconomic and political problems. That has repeatedly proven wrong. But the path forward is not as clear.

Yemen

Sharing the Arabian Peninsula with the oil-rich monarchies is the populous and poor country of Yemen. Yemen has remained weak and backward, showing what could have happened to the Gulf monarchies had they not found oil.

Until reunification in 1990, Yemen was split into two countries: the more populous and always independent North Yemen and the ex-British colony South Yemen—more formally, the communist-run People's Democratic Republic of Yemen. North Yemen's modern history begins with the overthrow of the monarchy in 1962; the new republic abolished slavery and began modernization under Egyptian tutelage, with many of the same Nasserist state-led policies as Egypt. A nasty civil war followed, as the Saudis backed the royalists and Egypt sent 50,000 troops to support the republicans. With the withdrawal of the Egyptian forces in the aftermath of the 1967 Six-Day War, North Yemen's civil war ended with a conservative republic, which was then replaced in 1978 by the more left-leaning government of Ali Abdullah Saleh, who rules to this day. Both North and South Yemen depended upon foreign aid—Saudi and Soviet respectively—and most especially on remittances from workers in Saudi Arabia. In the 1970s, one-fifth of the North's labor force and one-third of the South's were employed abroad, and for both countries, remittances made up the vast majority of foreign exchange earnings, reaching 40 percent of the South's GDP.

After the newly reunified Yemen supported the 1990 Iraqi invasion of Kuwait, Saudi Arabia expelled Yemeni workers and cut off aid. Fortunately for Yemen, oil production soon began, though at the modest level of 450,000 barrels per day. The country's fortunes were now tied to its oil income, which made up three-fourths of government revenue. However, with revenues from oil income the government lost interest in economic reform, which it had been previously pursuing.

Yemen remains desperately poor, with a per capita income below $1,000 at purchasing power parity. The 2009 UN Development Programme's Human Development Report ranks Yemen 138 out of 179 countries, by far the lowest human development index of any Arab country. Most of the population is rural; agriculture remains largely traditional, with modernization largely confined to the growing of qat, a moderate narcotic universally chewed in Yemen, usually daily. Yemen's long-term prospects are not good, clouded by declining oil production and continued delays in undertaking needed reforms. Indeed, the World Bank and IMF projections are for a bleak future of rising debt and stagnant income, unless the government substantially changes policies.

References and Further Reading

Abdulsadiq, Ahmed Ali. "Problems of Development Planning in the People's Democratic Republic of Yemen." In *Economy, Society, and Culture in Contemporary Yemen*, ed. B.R. Pridham, 12–21. London: Croom Helm, 1985.

Allen, Calvin, Jr., and W. Lynn Rigsbee II. *Oman Under Qaboos: From Coup to Constitution, 1970–1996.* London: Frank Cass, 2000.

Askari, Hossein. *Middle East Oil Exporters: What Happened to Economic Development?* Cheltenham, UK: Edward Elgar, 2006.

Birks, J.S., and C.A. Sinclair. *Arab Manpower: The Crisis of Development.* London: Croom Helm, 1980.

Boucek, Christopher. *Yemen: Avoiding a Downward Spiral.* Carnegie Papers 102 (September 2009). Available at www.carnegieendowment.org/files/yemen_downward_spiral.pdf.

Bradley, John. *Saudi Arabia Exposed: Inside a Kingdom in Crisis.* New York: Palgrave Macmillan, 2005.

Chaudry, Kiren Aziz. *The Price of Wealth: Economies and Institutions in the Middle East.* Ithaca, NY: Cornell University Press, 1997.

Cordesman, Anthony. *The Gulf and the West: Strategic Relations and Military Realities.* Boulder, CO: Westview Press, 1988.

———. *Saudi Arabia Enters the Twenty-First Century: The Political, Foreign Policy, Economic, and Energy Dimensions.* Westport, CT: Praeger, 2003.

Cordesman, Anthony, and Nawaf Obaid. *National Security in Saudi Arabia: Threats, Responses, and Challenges.* Westport, CT: Praeger Security International, 2005.

Crystal, Jill. *Oil and Politics in the Gulf: Rulers and Merchants in Kuwait and Qatar.* Cambridge, UK: Cambridge University Press, 1990.

Davidson, Christopher. *Abu Dhabi: Oil and Beyond.* New York: Columbia University Press, 2009.

———. *Dubai: The Vulnerability of Success.* New York: Columbia University Press, 2008.

———. *The United Arab Emirates: A Study in Survival.* Boulder, CO: Lynne Rienner, 2005.

El Mallakh, Ragaei. *The Economic Development of the Yemen Arab Republic.* London: Croom Helm, 1986.

El-Wady Ramahi, Seif A. *Economic and Political Evolution in the Arabian Gulf States.* New York: Carlton Press, 1973.

———. *Saudi Arabia: The Rush to Development.* Baltimore, MD: Johns Hopkins University Press, 1982.

Erbas, S. Nuri. "Labor Market Issues." In *United Arab Emirates: Selected Issues and Statistical Appendix.* IMF Country Report 05/268 (August 2005): 27–41.

Gause, F. Gregory III. *Oil Monarchies: Domestic and Security Challenges in the Arab Gulf States.* New York: Council on Foreign Relations Press, 1994.

Govil, Rajan. "Kuwait and Other GCC Stock Markets." In *Kuwait: Selected Issues and Statistical Appendix.* IMF Country Report No. 05/234 (July 2005).

Heard-Bey, Frauke. *From Trucial States to United Arab Emirates.* London: Longman, 1996.

International Bank for Reconstruction and Development (World Bank). *The Economic Development of Kuwait.* Baltimore, MD: Johns Hopkins University Press, 1965.

International Monetary Fund. *Kuwait: 2006 Article IV Consultation—Staff Report.* IMF Country Report No. 06/132. April 7, 2006. Available at www.imf.org/external/pubs/ft/scr/2006/cr06132.pdf.

———. *Public Information Notice.* No. 09/109 (August 18, 2009). Available at www.imf.org/external/np/sec/pn/2009/pn09109.htm.

———. *Regional Economic Outlook: Middle East and Central Asia* (October 2009). Available at www.imf.org/external/pubs/ft/reo/2009/MCD/eng/mreo1009.pdf.

———. *Republic of Yemen: 2004 Article IV Consultation—Staff Report.* IMF Country Report No. 05/111. March 23, 2005. Available at www.imf.org/external/pubs/ft/scr/2005/cr05111.pdf.

———. *Republic of Yemen: 2008 Article IV Consultation.* IMF Country Report No. 09/100. March 24, 2009. Available at www.imf.org/external/pubs/ft/scr/2009/cr09100.pdf.

———. *United Arab Emirates: 2006 Article IV Consultation—Staff Report.* IMF Country Report No. 06/257. July 14, 2006. Available at www.imf.org/external/pubs/ft/scr/2006/cr06257.pdf.

Kapiszewski, Anrezej. *Native Arab Population and Foreign Workers in the Gulf States.* Krakow, Poland: Universitas, 1999.

Knauerhase, Ramon. *The Saudi Arabian Economy.* New York: Praeger, 1975.

Knights, Michael. *Troubled Waters: Future U.S. Security Assistance in the Persian Gulf.* Washington, DC: Washington Institute for Near East Policy, 2006.

Malik, Monica, and Tim Niblock. "Saudi Arabia's Economy: The Challenge of Reform." In *Saudi Arabia in the Balance: Political Economy, Society, and Foreign Affairs*, ed. Paul Aarts and Gerd Nonneman, 85–100. London: Hurst and Company, 2005.

MEED. "2006 Gulf Economic Review." *MEED: Middle East Economic Digest*, January 28, 2006, pp. 1–72.

Naumkin, V.V. "Evaluation of Socio-economic Development in the People's Democratic Republic of Yemen." In *Economy, Society, and Culture in Contemporary Yemen*, ed. B.R. Pridham, 1–11. London: Croom Helm, 1985.

Niblock, Tim, with Monica Malik. *The Political Economy of Saudi Arabia.* London: Routledge, 2007.

Peterson, J.E. *Yemen: The Search for a Modern State.* London: Croom Helm, 1982.

Roberts, Gwilym, and David Fowler. *Built by Oil.* Reading, UK: Ithaca Press, 1995.

Skeet, Ian. *Muscat and Oman: The End of an Era.* London: Faber and Faber, 1974.

"Special Report on Saudi Arabia." *Financial Times*, September 23, 2009.

Stookey, Robert. *South Yemen: A Marxist Republic in Arabia.* Boulder, CO: Westview Press, 1982.

Townsend, John. *Oman: The Making of a Modern State.* New York: St. Martin's Press, 1977.

Vassiliev, Alexei. *The History of Saudi Arabia.* London: Saqi Books, 1998.

Wilson, Peter, and Douglas Graham. *Saudi Arabia: The Coming Storm.* Armonk, NY: M.E. Sharpe, 1994.

World Bank. *Country Assistance Strategy for the Republic of Yemen,* Report No. 36014, May 17, 2006. Available at http://info.worldbank.org/etools/wti/docs/wti2008/brief208.pdf.

———. *Yemen: Development Policy Review.* Washington DC: World Bank, 2008.

Iraq

While Iraq is a country with ample oil, water, and fertile land, it has also had the worst governance in the region. The most obvious sign is the never-ending series of wars: civil war with Kurds 1961–1975; war with Iran 1980–1988; invasion of Kuwait and sanctions 1990–2002; and the 2003 U.S.-led invasion and insurgency-cum-civil-war. In addition, for decades, Iraq has been plagued even during peacetime by administrative inefficiency, overambitious plans, and political disputes that stand in the way of development projects—and these same factors continue to hold back growth post–Saddam Hussein. The story of Iraq is a lesson in how little can be accomplished in the face of ineffective governance.

Pre–Saddam Hussein, 1958–1978

Although Iraqi oil production had begun on a small scale before World War II, Iraq only began to earn substantial income from oil in the early 1950s, as production rose quickly, reaching 700,000 barrels a day by 1955. Encouraged by the World Bank, Iraq set up a Development Board in 1950, which received all of the oil income. Under the pro-British monarchy that ruled Iraq until 1958, the board opposed industrial development as inappropriate for a country lacking in skilled workers and so well endowed with rich agricultural land. It refused to touch the landholding pattern, in which the landlord received between one-half and five-sevenths of the crop, and it spent little on social programs such as education in a country where 90 percent of the people were illiterate in 1950. In addition, in the six years after it started fully functioning in 1951–1952, the board only spent 70 percent of the funds available to it. Private efforts, not the board's actions, explain the considerable agricultural growth Iraq experienced during this period; 70 percent of the people earned their living from agriculture.

The July 1958 revolution, which brought to power Abdul Karim Qasim, rejected the Development Board approach, which the new authorities (inspired by "Arab socialism" of the Nasserist sort) saw as consolidating feudalism, failing to develop public-sector leadership, neglecting industrialization, and deepening dependence on oil and foreign oil companies. In its five years in office, the Qasim government stepped up development spending, which still remained less than half of budgeted amounts. Consistent with the government's philosophy, public-sector industry received generous funding, with little results. To some extent, this pattern continued under the three leftist governments that followed each other in quick succession in 1963–1968, although the political instability impeded decision making and delayed many investment projects.

The main impact of the Qasim government and its successors on development was the 1958 Agrarian Reform Law, which disrupted the existing system (land tenure, financing inputs, marketing, and so on) but did not establish a clear alternative. Agricultural output fell precipitously after the reform, though some of the drop was due to other factors such as drought. By 1961, Iraq, which had exported grain not just for centuries but millennia, was importing rice and wheat to cover 40 percent of consumption. However, even the scholarly account most sympathetic to the reform—namely, Kamil Mahdi's *State and Agriculture in Iraq*—concludes that the insufficient reforms were unable to solve the land, irrigation, and drainage problems.

The case of land reform is an important example of a problem that continues to plague Iraq to this day, post-Saddam: the heavy-handed imposition of ideological models untempered by knowledge of the local scene and implemented woodenly by an ineffective bureaucracy.

After the radical Arab socialist Baath Party seized power in a 1968 coup, beginning its thirty-five-year rule, agriculture suffered from the second main problem that plagues Iraq's economy to this day: the lack of attention to the productive economy by governments overly reliant on oil income. This was the period when oil income shot upward, thanks to the oil boom of the 1970s. During this time, many schools, roads, power plants, factories, and other development projects were built. However, continuing the pattern prevailing since the monarchy, development spending rose much less than did oil revenue. The government's priority was extending state control, more than increasing output or social welfare. In the first Baath decade from 1968 to 1977—the period before Saddam Hussein assumed control—more than half of all the jobs created were in the government. The government's share in total employment rose from 12 percent in 1968 to 21 percent in 1977, and these data may understate the case since they evidently exclude the rapidly expanding military. The share in gross domestic product (GDP) of what official statistics call "the socialist sector"—that is, government-owned enterprises—rose from 31 percent in 1968 to 80 percent in 1977 as the government took over such sectors as foreign trade. Farmers were hard hit by the post-1970 state takeover of marketing, which eventually extended even to fruits and vegetables. Agriculture did not keep pace, with its share in GDP dropping from 17 percent to 7 percent and its share in employment falling from about half to roughly a third. Government policy was designed to satisfy urban consumers, not farmers; crop prices were set well below world market levels. Not surprisingly, production suffered; the value of agricultural output in 1975 was exactly the same as in 1957, the last year before the land reform. Industrial output expanded, but since the state development funds were poured disproportionately into capital-intensive heavy industries, especially military-related industries, which functioned poorly, the increase in industrial output and employment was low considering the money spent.

The Saddam Era, 1979–2003

When in 1979 Saddam stepped up from his number two slot to become president, Iraq was well positioned for unparalleled prosperity: oil prices were high and about to go higher. However, Saddam plunged the country into a series of wars that reversed decades of economic gains; at its low point in 1996, Iraq was no better off economically than it had been when the monarchy was overthrown in 1958. In addition, many hundreds of thousands of Iraqis lost their lives during the years of war and political repression, such as the 1987–1988 Anfal scorched-earth campaign against the Kurds.

One feature of the Saddam years was obsessive secrecy. As a result, economic data became unreliable and largely unavailable. In moments of great need, the government would sometimes release data supporting its claims about the country's dire situation; their accuracy is unknown. On other occasions, Iraq would release a considerable amount of seemingly accurate information, such as its report to the UN on its foreign debt after the 1991 Kuwait war.

As Saddam's rule began, Iraq was enjoying the five most prosperous years it would ever know—1978–1982. Saddam's grand ambitions led him to pursue a guns-and-butter model, involving costly policies both abroad and at home. Miscalculating that he could make quick and easy gains, Saddam invaded Iran in September 1980 while at the same time spending billions on prestige projects, such as the $7 billion reportedly spent in anticipation of a major political event (the summit of the nonaligned movement, to which most developing countries belong) that was to have been held in Baghdad in 1982 but was canceled due to the war. Iraqi investment spending rose some fivefold from 1976 to 1982. Nonmilitary imports at least quadrupled from 1978 to 1982, to over $15 billion a year. Employment grew briskly, not least because the military expanded by 350,000, absorbing much of the labor force growth.

These actions and events strained government finances. The war was costing more than $10 billion a year, according to some estimates, much of it spent on imported arms. (Interestingly, the Iraqi government's claim after the fact that during the eight-year war it spent $102 billion for foreign arms is about twice the estimate of most Western observers.) For once, Iraq had broken the long-standing pattern of being unable to spend its oil income. In fact, oil income fell to about $10 billion a year because after the September 1980 Iraqi invasion, Iran responded by sinking ships in the narrow Shatt al-Arab waterway through which Iraq exported nearly all its oil, and Syria, in solidarity with Iran, closed the pipeline across its territory, which was Iraq's other export route. Iraq was reduced to trucking oil through Jordan and speeding construction of a pipeline through Turkey. The shortfall brought on by decreased oil income and the guns-and-butter spending was financed at first by drawing down the country's reserves, which may have been $40 billion when the war started, and appealing for aid from the Gulf monarchies, who contributed billions.

However, reality caught up; after all, with oil output down, in 1981–1983 real GDP per capita had fallen in half from its 1979 peak of $3,000 (at 2007 prices) back to the level before the 1973 oil price boom. Iraq had to turn to borrowing from suppliers and friendly governments—Western, Soviet, Third World, and Gulf Arab. In 1991, Iraq acknowledged its wartime borrowing had been $42 billion, excluding unpaid interest and most Soviet and Gulf Arab debt, which those creditors claimed was $8 billion and $40 billion respectively. By 1983, Iraq had run out of resources and willing lenders, and battlefield reverses required adding another 350,000 soldiers who had to be equipped. The 1983 cutbacks were dramatic; civilian imports may have been cut by as much as 80 percent from the prior year's levels; development spending was slashed similarly, while salaries were frozen and many benefits dropped. But all of this was not enough since oil prices fell sharply in 1985, reducing both Iraqi income and Arab aid at just the time Iraq stepped up its military efforts. In 1987, the Iraqi government pared its expenses further by carrying out a vigorous privatization campaign, much more extensive than any other such reform in the Middle East. The government also removed most price controls and freed up most foreign trade, with the result that businessmen were blamed for the high inflation that resulted from the sinking value of the Iraqi dinar on the parallel markets. But the private-sector response was anemic, in no small part because it was apparent to all that the government was acting out of desperation and not out of any conviction that the private sector should be allowed to prosper. This led to the entirely accurate suspicion that at the first opportunity, the government would reassert control.

Iraq expected prosperity following the end of the war with Iran in August 1988. But just the $5 billion a year debt service and the constrained civilian imports absorbed the country's oil export revenue of no more than $12 billion a year. Saddam's son-in-law Hussein Kamil, in charge of a super-ministry of industry and ministry industrialization, pushed ahead with ambitious projects the country could not afford, while talk circulated about major arms deals. Iraq could have had a bright future had it scaled back its ambitions and awaited the extra income from expanded oil output, income that would have been generated from investment in new fields by international oil companies for which Iraq sensibly announced detailed plans in 1990. However, when world oil prices fell from a temporary peak of $20/barrel in January 1990 to $14 in June, closer to the level of the previous three years, Saddam was not alone in attributing the inability to sustain the increase to Kuwaiti production in excess of its OPEC quota.

The August 1990 Iraqi invasion of Kuwait and the subsequent noncooperation with UN-ordered arms inspections amounted to economic disaster. Despite the difficulties of the 1980s, Iraq's social indicators in 1989 were still roughly on a par with those of Turkey or Iran. That changed sharply for the worse in the 1990s. Under the impact of sanctions, GDP per capita bottomed out in 1993 at below the 1950 level, less than one-eighth the 1979 peak. Still, Saddam smuggled oil in violation of the UN sanctions, taking advantage of the unwillingness of the United States to stop the smuggling to Jordan and Turkey; by contrast, U.S. forces devoted considerable effort to eliminate smuggling at sea, where the political complications were fewer. The money from oil smuggling financed a minimal diet for Iraqis through a rationing program that was surprisingly well administered in the Arab areas of Iraq; the Kurds, who had de facto autonomy after their postwar rebellion, got little. Saddam cynically used the suffering of ordinary Iraqis in his campaign to have the UN sanctions ended. The Health Ministry regularly issued inflated estimates of premature deaths due to the sanctions; already by April 1993, its count was the uncharacteristically precise 264,738.

Under pressure from church and other humanitarian groups, the United States agreed to loosen the restrictions on Iraq, allowing it to accept the UN's long-standing offer to participate in an Oil-for-Food program. The program, implemented in 1997, freed Iraq to export oil sufficient to finance humanitarian goods, but Saddam soon corrupted it to divert the funds to purposes he thought more important—the source of a scandal when the Iraqi records were opened after Saddam fell. The UN further loosened the rules to allow Iraq to import essentially anything other than arms or dual-use goods. Saddam still objected to, among other things, the 30 percent of the oil export proceeds channeled to pay compensation for the Kuwait war damages.

Nevertheless, the economy took off. Imports rose from perhaps $2 billion a year to $10 billion a year. Real GDP doubled from 1997 to 2001, although that still left real income per person below the 1972 level. The increased income barely dented the great drop in living standards Iraq had suffered since 1989. Education spending was down from $620 per pupil in 1989 to $47 in 2002, with a quarter of school-age children not attending classes. Health funds were cut 90 percent from the 1989 levels. Even though malnutrition stabilized after the start of the Oil-for-Food program, one-third of the children in the south and center remained malnourished. Agricultural output dropped 15 percent from 1989 to 2002. Installed electrical capacity fell from 9,295 megawatts in 1990 to 4,500 before Saddam's fall. Iraqis' expectations about electricity supply are in no small way shaped by the memory of how reliable and ample the supply had been before the invasion of Kuwait.

Prospects Post-Saddam, 2004–2010

The Iraqi people's standards for where their economy should be are shaped not so much by where the country was when Saddam fell, but by the memory of the 1988–1990 interwar interlude or of the peak of prosperity in 1982. Measured by that metric, post-Saddam Iraq falls way, way short. To be sure, GDP per person rose by 2009 to at least 30 percent above the prewar level, but many social indicators have improved little. While it is early to be sure, there are preliminary indications that this may change with the waning of the 2005–2008 violence, which prevented normal functioning of schools, hospitals, commerce—indeed, any aspect of public life.

The principal reasons for the slow pace of development post-Saddam are the same factors identified decades earlier: political instability, overly ambitious plans, and administrative inefficiency. Of these, instability was the most debilitating. The deteriorating security situation prevented foreign firms from becoming involved either as contractors or investors. Many Iraqi businessmen found themselves targets of one violent group or another, be it common criminals or insurgents—two groups which are not always that distinct, as many criminals claim to have adopted a political program, and many insurgent groups recruit from the criminal classes. But overly ambitious plans were also a serious problem, especially during 2003–2004, when Iraq was run by the Coalition Provisional Authority (CPA), the UN-sanctioned U.S.-led occupation. Worse were ideologically motivated policies proposed by some CPA officials with a background in U.S. political battles but little experience in developing countries, who wanted to replicate in Iraq the initiatives on which they had worked in America, despite the vast differences between the economic and political circumstances of the two countries. A few CPA policies worked very well, particularly the abolition of all tariffs and restrictions on foreign trade, which enabled Iraqis to enjoy easy access to many imported goods formerly in short supply or simply unavailable, such as automobiles and mobile phones. But many of the policies could only be described as out of touch with the realities of developing economies and Iraq's political culture. Meanwhile, the CPA made little if any progress at changing some of the most debilitating Saddam-era policies, especially the subsidies to be discussed below.

As for the third traditional constraint—administrative effectiveness—most civil servants stopped showing up for work after the looting of government offices upon Saddam's downfall, and the problem of rebuilding the ministries was compounded by the purging of many senior staff under the CPA's order barring Baath Party full members from government posts. But the new administration was able to carry out the operation of exchanging the Saddam-era currency for new bills, and it was able to pay the vastly increased salaries on time (mid-level civil servants saw their monthly wages increase from $10 a month under Saddam to $200 a month by the end of 2003). When Iraqi politicians took over the government in 2004, many key ministries became highly politicized, with personnel and policy decisions being based on partisan advantage rather than national interest.

As is often the case in Iraq, the constraint on development has not been money. Many otherwise informed observers in the United States assume that Iraq's stalled development must mean that cash is short; after all, the needs are great, so if they are not being met, surely the reason is inadequate funds. That mistaken view about how developing economies work is evidently what underlay the overly enthusiastic $21 billion U.S. Iraq Relief and Reconstruction Fund, supplemented by 2007 with $11 billion in other U.S. funding for relief. While much of this money went for training and equipping the Iraqi army and police, many low-priority items were also included, such as redoing Iraq's postal code system, as were many projects such as hospitals, for which Iraq lacked the resources to sustain once completed. Much of the money was spent with little supervision, with the inevitable result being considerable corruption and waste, and large sums had to be diverted to provide security for project personnel. In a similar vein, by 2007, little of the $13 billion pledged for Iraq at an October 2003 aid conference by international agencies and governments other than the United States had been used.

In post-Saddam Iraq, as is often the case in weak and fragile societies, the fundamental constraint on development has not been money but the limited ability to make and carry out decisions—what economists call absorptive capacity. The UN/World Bank "Joint Iraq Needs Assessment" had been widely misunderstood when it stated that Iraq's "reconstruction needs" were a staggering $55 billion for 2004–2007; as the assessment explained, Iraq's limited absorptive capacity suggested that even if all these funds were available, Iraq would only be able to spend $22 billion over the period. In fact, Iraq managed to spend $26 billion, which still looks rather more modest compared to the $101 billion in oil export earnings during those four years. In its 2006 report *Rebuilding Iraq*, the World Bank does not once mention a need for more resources. By contrast, it writes, "managing public investment is critical."

The major reason to worry about Iraq's financial situation at the time of Saddam's fall was the foreign debt. Iraq had a crushing foreign debt burden from Saddam's 1980s borrowing binge and the $52 billion Kuwait war damages awarded by the UN Compensation Commission before closing off claims in 2005. That said, the debt problem was not as bad as many foreign observers anticipated prewar. For instance, in *A Wiser Peace: An Action Strategy for a Post-Conflict Iraq* (2003), Frederick Barton and Bathsheba Crocker note that "Iraq's financial burden is estimated at $383 billion," including items such as $172 billion in claims before the UN Compensation Commission; in the end, only $9 billion of those claims were upheld by the commission. In any case, a phased debt reduction was agreed to by the major creditors which by 2009 reduced the debt to $33 billion, well in line with what Iraq can service, even including the burden of paying 5 percent of oil exports to settle the Compensation Commission awards.

Post-Saddam, Iraq largely paid for its own economic recovery while the United States largely paid for the war. In 2004–2008, the Iraqi government paid for 80 percent of public investment; foreign aid covered the other 20 percent. By contrast, in 2004–2008, the Iraqi government security expenditures were $18 billion while the U.S. government apparently spent $500 billion on its own forces (there is considerable dispute about how to separate out the cost of operations in Iraq from the cost of normal U.S. military operations). In 2009–2010, Iraqi security spending increased sharply to $20 billion, while U.S. spending began to shrink, but U.S. spending is still several times that of Iraqi.

In 2004–2008, despite the bad security situation, Iraq had substantial economic growth. GDP rose from $26 billion in 2004 to $91 billion in 2008. Most of this growth was because of the oil price boom; Iraq's oil exports rose from $17 billion in 2004 to $61 billion in 2008. In addition, Iraq took impressive steps to open up to market-oriented growth and to free up more resources for investment.

The biggest policy change in post-Saddam Iraq was the reduction of subsidies. In 2005, subsidies from the government were estimated at 53 to 67 percent of GDP, with the main ones being on fuels, food, and inputs used by farmers. Besides wasting resources, these huge subsidies encouraged serious economic distortions, such as the rampant smuggling of fuel to neighboring countries where prices are higher—a significant source of revenue for the insurgency. In 2006–2008, the government phased out most of the subsidies on fuels, and in 2009, it began a planned program to restrict the food subsidies. The International Monetary Fund's forecast for 2010 is that subsidies will be 12 percent of GDP.

The Iraqi economy hit a rough spot in 2009. Because of lower prices, oil exports fell $25 billion in 2009. That slashed budget revenue just as the government was gaining the capacity to spend more, especially on security and development projects. The budget went from surplus to a $17 billion deficit. However, Iraq had substantial financial reserves on which to draw, including $47 billion in foreign exchange reserves, and the government has been cautious, cutting spending despite those substantial reserves. While finances were tight, the improved security situation meant the government could deliver more services. For instance, in mid-2009, electricity production finally exceeded the 6,000 megawatt target that had been established in August 2003—about three times the postwar low during some conflict-ridden months of 2006–2007—though increased demand in the interim meant that periodic blackouts continue.

The medium-term prospects for government revenue are excellent. The year 2009 saw the signing of major contracts with international oil companies, which offer the prospect of substantially increasing Iraq's oil production. Oil production had only slowly increased from 2.0 million b/d in 2004 to 2.5 million b/d in 2009. With the new projects under way, production could double within five years, though it is unlikely to reach the government target of tripling within that time. Even at the more likely slower pace of increase, Iraq's oil revenue will increase by many billions of dollars a year even if prices decline from their 2009 levels.

The prospects for Iraq's economy depend not primarily on the financial resources it will have available but on the country's political stability. The degree of stability will determine the extent to which a safe and secure environment can be created. And stability is the prerequisite for building the political consensus needed if the government is to function more effectively, making the complicated decisions needed about economic reform and about development projects. The most likely prospect is that for the foreseeable future, Iraq will remain a weak society in which stability is fragile. That would seriously constrain economic development.

References and Further Reading

Alnasrawi, Abbas. *The Economy of Iraq: Oil, Wars, Destruction of Development and Prospects, 1950–2010.* Westport CT: Greenwood Press, 1994.

Barton, Fredrick, and Bathsheba Crocker. *A Wiser Peace: An Action Strategy for a Post-Conflict Iraq.* 2003. Available at http://csis.org/files/media/csis/pubs/wiserpeace.pdf.

Batatu, Hanna. *The Old Social Classes and the Revolutionary Movement in Iraq.* Princeton, NJ: Princeton University Press, 1978.

Chandrasekaran, Rajiv. *Imperial Life in the Emerald City: Inside Iraq's Green Zone.* New York: Alfred A. Knopf, 2006.

Chaudry, Kiren Aziz. "On the Way to Market: Economic Liberalization and Iraq's Invasion of Kuwait." *Middle East Report* 170 (May–June 1991): 14–23.

Clawson, Patrick. *How Has Saddam Hussein Survived? Economic Sanctions 1990–93.* McNair Paper No. 22, Institute for National Strategic Studies of the National Defense University, 1993.

Crocker, Bathsheba. "Reconstructing Iraq's Economy." *Washington Quarterly* 27:4 (Autumn 2004): 73–93.

Dreze, Jean, and Haris Gadar. *Hunger and Poverty in Iraq, 1991.* Monograph No. 32, Development Economics Research Programme of the London School of Economics, 1991.

Foote, Christopher, Keith Crane, William Block, and Simon Gray. "Economic Policy and Prospects in Iraq." *Journal of Economic Perspectives* 18:3 (Summer 2004): 50.

Henderson, Simon. *Instant Empire: Saddam Hussein's Ambitions for Iraq.* San Francisco: Mercury House, 1991.

Independent Inquiry Committee into the United Nations Oil-for-Food Programme. www.iic-offp.org/documents.htm.

International Monetary Fund. *Iraq: Second Review Under the Stand-By Arrangement.* December 2008. IMF

Country Report No. 08/383, September 15, 2008. Available at www.imf.org/external/pubs/ft/scr/2008/cr08303.pdf.
———. *Iraq: 2005 Article IV Consultation—Staff Report.* IMF Country Report No. 05/294, August 16, 2005. Available at www.imf.org/external/pubs/ft/scr/2005/cr05294.pdf.
———. *Regional Economic Outlook: Middle East and Central Asia*, October 2009.
Jalal, Ferhang. *The Role of the Government in the Industrialization of Iraq, 1950–1965.* London: Frank Cass, 1972.
Mahdi, Kamil. *State and Agriculture in Iraq: Modern Development, Stagnation, and the Impact of Oil.* Reading, UK: Ithaca Press, 2000.
Marr, Phoebe. *The Modern History of Iraq.* 2nd ed. Boulder CO: Westview Press, 2004.
Office of the Iraq Programme Oil-for-Food. www.un.org/Depts/oip.
Penrose, Edith, and E.F. Penrose. *Iraq: International Relations and National Development.* London: Croom Helm, 1978.
Republic of Iraq, The Coalition Provisional Authority. 2004 Budget. Available at www.cpa-iraq.org/budget/budget2004.html.
Simmons, John. "Agricultural Development in Iraq: Planning and Management Failure." *Middle East Journal* 19:2 (Spring 1965): 129–140.
Special Inspector General for Iraq Reconstruction's (SIGIR). Quarterly Reports to Congress. Available at www.sigir.mil/publications/quarterlyreports/index.html.
UN Compensation Commission. www.uncc.ch.
World Bank. *Interim Strategy Note for the Republic of Iraq for the Period Mid FY09–FY11.* Report No. 47304-IQ, February 19, 2009.
———. *Rebuilding Iraq: Economic Reform and Transition.* Report No. 35141-IQ, February 2006.

Arab Levant

The four Arab Levant economies—Lebanon, the Palestinian territories, Jordan, and Syria—share several important characteristics. First, they have strong endowments of human capital but no great oil wealth. Though Syria produces some oil, oil has played less of a role in the Levant than almost anywhere in the Muslim Middle East. Besides Jordan, Lebanon, and the Palestinian territories, the only other Muslim Middle East state not producing oil is Morocco (leaving aside such peripheral Arab League members as Somalia or the Comoros). All the Arab Levant states have been affected by spillover from the oil booms of their neighbors, however, thanks to aid flows, trade opportunities, and work for emigrants.

Second, all of the Arab Levant economies have been profoundly shaped by geopolitics, namely, wars, and principally the Arab-Israeli conflict but also domestic sectarian infighting. Economic performance in the Palestinian areas and Lebanon has been largely determined by geopolitics: in the Palestinian territories by the conflict with Israel, and in Lebanon by the civil war. Unlike the latter two, Syria and Jordan have avoided protracted warfare, but they have been buffeted by the wars around them as well as by the ethnic tensions within their own countries—in Syria, between the politically dominant Alawites and the rest of the population; in Jordan, between the politically dominant Transjordanians (from east of the Jordan) and the ethnic Palestinians.

While their circumstances have important commonalities, the Levant countries have followed quite different economic policies, and that has led to divergent economic performance. Syria's persistent state control has damaged its economy, whereas Jordan's more open policies have brought better results despite its limited resources.

Lebanon

Before its civil war began in 1975, Lebanon had a strong economy that was thriving. When the war ended in 1990, the economy had shrunk to one-third its prewar level and the state had been weakened. Heavy borrowing financed the start of recovery, but by the late 1990s the debt burden had slowed the economy. The corruption and inefficiency of the civil war years were only reinforced by the dead end of the Syrian occupation from 1990 to 2005. The departure of Syrian troops left Lebanon vulnerable to continuing serious ethnoreligious cleavages, which are a greater threat to economic prosperity than the many continuing shortcomings in governance.

Most Advanced Arab Economy Before 1975

In the 1950s and 1960s, not only was Lebanon's income level well above that of any other Arab country except oil-rich Kuwait, but its literacy rate—at about 60 percent by the early 1960s—was a multiple of that of most Arab states. As late as 1970, Lebanon's student enrollment rate was twice that of any other Arab country. In the 1950s and 1960s, its macroeconomic policy was by far the best in the Middle East: inflation averaged less than 3 percent, government budget deficits were small, and the exchange rate was stable. Thanks to the sound economic environment and the strong human capital base, Lebanon's economy grew briskly at an average annual pace of 7 percent from 1950 to 1975 (a bit faster in the 1950s, a bit slower from 1960). Lebanon was by far the Arab leader in finance and many other services. In addition, its industries were rapidly growing; merchandise exports were 19 percent of gross domestic product (GDP).

Despite a strong economy, prewar Lebanon had many serious social problems in which economics played a role. For instance, the poor were disproportionately Shia Muslims and the rich disproportionately Christians, which exacerbated religious tensions.

Civil War, 1975–1990

Lebanon fell into a complicated, multisided civil war in 1975 because of the country's deep political and social fissures. Once the civil war began, greed became one of its key sustaining factors. Over the fifteen years of the war from 1975 to 1990, foreign financial assistance may have been $30 billion, added to which the militias may have earned another $15 billion from contraband, drug trafficking, and outright thievery. That averages out to $3 billion a year, in a country with a GDP at war's end of under $6 billion.

The war caused grievous losses. In a country of 3 million people, 150,000 were killed, perhaps another 600,000 emigrated, and 750,000 were internally displaced. By the time of the Israeli invasion in 1982, GDP had fallen to 40 percent of its prewar level. After a considerable recovery to 1987, GDP collapsed again, ending up in 1990 at one-third the prewar level. Unemployment soared, especially among the unskilled. Had prewar growth (at about 6 percent a year) been sustained, the 1990 economy would have been eight times larger than it actually was. And in the absence of a civil war, the growth in 1975–1990 could have been even higher than the prewar pattern, because prewar Lebanon offered many of the services—tourism, banking, health care, and the like—for which demand was soaring in the Gulf Arab states after the 1973 oil price increases.

Shaky Recovery Since 1990

The 1989 Taif Accord among the main contending parties and the 1990 ouster of a hard-line Christian government ended the civil war with what was in effect a Syrian occupation. The divided lines of authority established by the Taif Accord meant that Lebanese politicians often called upon Syria to be the ultimate decision maker.

The postwar Lebanese government implemented an ambitious public investment program, but growth fell short of the objective: 1995 GDP was only 60 percent of the prewar level, rather than the planned 100 percent. The problem was that private-sector response was limited by lingering political uncertainty and the fact that other regional centers such as Dubai had emerged during the war years to provide the services Lebanon used to offer to oil-rich Arab states. The situation was made worse by questionable macroeconomic policy, namely, continuing massive government deficits that undermined faith in the currency (the U.S. dollar continued to be widely used in place of the Lebanese pound). The budget deficit and the currency weakness were sustainable only with high interest rates, which attracted foreign funds to finance the government and to cover the balance-of-payments deficit, but those high interest rates discouraged investment, holding back economic growth.

The problems only became more acute as time progressed. Administrative reform was never seriously attempted. Corruption grew steadily, with the Syrian occupying forces often implicated but by no means the main actors. The combination of poor administration and corrupt practices resulted in unreliable and costly electricity, overly expensive communications, inefficient ports and border crossings, and burdensome delays in business licensing. The balance of payments deteriorated, with merchandise exports a mere 6 percent of GDP and Lebanon running a deficit on services, whereas prewar services like tourism and finance had been a major source of income. Government borrowing continued at high levels; the modest adjustment measures adopted in 2002 only served to stabilize the debt at 165–170 percent of GDP, which is still by far the world's highest and is simply unsustainable. From 1997 to 2005, average annual GDP growth slowed to about 2 percent.

The departure of Syrian troops in 2005 created a brief wave of optimism that the fundamental structural economic problems would be addressed, even if politics remained frozen by ethno-religious splits. However, once again, geopolitics trumped economics, the continuing lesson of the Levant. Failure to resolve the independent armed status of Hezbollah led to a destructive Israeli bombing campaign in summer 2006, which not only ruined much of the rebuilt infrastructure but, at least as destructive, dented confidence in Lebanon's stability. Fortunately, the violence ended quickly so that Lebanon was able to benefit from providing services such as tourism to the booming oil-rich Arab states. Lebanon also benefited from the cautious banking policies imposed by its regulators, which left Lebanese banks largely unaffected by the 2008–2009 global financial crisis. GDP growth averaged 8 percent in 2007–2008, slowing to half that rate in 2009–2010 under the impact of the global financial crisis.

Over the longer term, Lebanon's economic prospects look good if it can make planned progress at slowly reducing its debt-to-GDP ratio. However, all of that is dependent on the political situation. The lesson of the Lebanese economic experience has been that political stability is the absolute prerequisite to sustained economic growth.

The Palestinian Territories

From 1921 to 1948, Mandatory Palestine included what in 1948 became Israel as well as what became the Gaza Strip and the West Bank, which together form the Palestinian territories. During the mandatory period, the economies of the Jewish and Arab communities were quite closely integrated; despite Zionist efforts to create a separate Jewish economy, it is hard to speak for that period of separate Palestinian and Israeli economies. From 1949 until the 1967 Six-Day War, Gaza was administered by Egypt and the West Bank was part of Jordan, with no economic interaction with Israel. Neither area was thriving economically. Egypt placed many restrictions on the movement of people and goods into and out of Gaza, which in any case was a long way from Egypt's economic heartland in the Nile Valley. Jordan concentrated its development efforts on the East Bank, whose weight in the national economy rose steadily relative to that of the West Bank. Under Israeli occupation since 1967, the Palestinian territories have had a mixed growth record: rapid at first, but then slower than in the Arab countries to which Palestinians compare themselves. The 1993 Oslo Peace Accords between Israel and the Palestinian Liberation Organization (PLO) created much hope for better times economically as well as politically, but over time political stalemate has brought increased economic hardship.

Integration with the Israeli Economy, 1967–1986

As a result of the 1967 war, about 170,000 people fled the West Bank, leaving it with 600,000 residents outside of east Jerusalem, of whom 106,000 were refugees from the 1948 war. The Gaza Strip had 356,000 residents at the time of the war, including 205,000 refugees; from September 1967 to March 1968, Israel and Jordan permitted Gazans to move to Jordan, and about 35,000–40,000 people did so. A further 65,000 people lived in East Jerusalem, which had been until 1967 an integral part of the West Bank but which Israel annexed, with the result that its residents became more integrated with Israel than did residents of the rest of the West Bank. The economic impact at first was rather limited, except in East Jerusalem, where incomes rose sharply as thousands found jobs in the western part of the city. The West Bank's trade with Jordan continued uninterrupted; already by autumn 1967, hundreds of trucks carrying goods crossed daily on a gravel bed across the shallow river. Given that Israel did not check the papers of those crossing in 1967–1970, tens of thousands from throughout the Arab world were able to cross into Israel, mostly for tourism.

As Israel recovered from recession and its demand for labor grew, it eagerly sought Palestinian workers. The number of West Bank and Gaza residents officially working in Israel shot up to 68,000 by 1974. With many more working unofficially, more than 30 percent of all employed Gazans and West Bankers were working in Israel in the mid-1970s, attracted by the higher wages (though competition forced wage levels in the Palestinian territories to rise quickly). Annual per capita income rose briskly, from below $1,200 in 1968 to about $2,500 in 1975 (at 2007 prices). A similar improvement was recorded in social indicators, such as infant mortality and caloric consumption.

While the first decade of the occupation was a period of rapid economic growth, the second decade was a time of slower economic progress, largely because of Israel's mounting economic problems, which culminated in a 1985 economic crisis. Annual per capita income in 1987 was less than $3,500 at 2007 prices. This was particularly disappointing to Palestinians because much of the Arab world was undergoing an economic boom. Jordan, home to a large Palestinian community and therefore a natural point of comparison for many in the West Bank, had a difficult decade up to 1975, but in the next ten years, per capita income doubled (though still remaining 30 percent below West Bank/Gaza income). In other words, Palestinians saw their economy doing not particularly well because it was tied to a stagnant Israeli economy, while those to whom they compared themselves in the Arab world were enjoying rapid growth as a by-product of the 1970s oil price increases.

Separation from Israel and Stagnanation Since 1987

In 1987, Palestinians began a violent uprising known as the *intifada*. It was as much a rebellion of the poor as a nationalist uprising. The results, however, belied the goal: per capita income dropped 35 percent from 1987 to 1990. Repeated general strikes and transport blockages meant that hours worked in Israel by Palestinians dropped 19 percent during that time. Even more devastatingly, the Palestinian strikes during the intifada began a process of separating the Palestinian and Israeli economies, a rift that would only deepen during the 1991 Gulf War by the U.S.-led coalition against Iraq, during which Israel closed off the West Bank and Gaza for weeks. Such blockades would become a customary feature of Israeli action after Palestinian terrorist attacks in the 1990s.

Declining opportunities in Israel and difficult access to broader international markets dashed hopes for a new Middle East cooperation following the 1993 Declaration of Principles, known as the Oslo Peace Accords, between Israel and the PLO, headed by Yasser Arafat. Instead, because Israel insisted that security concerns required that it retain total control over the external borders of the West Bank and Gaza, including those with Jordan and Egypt, the closures prevented nearly all exit of goods and people from Gaza; the West Bank was somewhat less affected only because geographic proximity allowed informal crossings, usually on foot. Intense international effort went into finding ways to address Israeli security concerns without closures, and many practical suggestions were made, only to crash on the shoals of political ill will and intransigence on both sides.

The closures continued, evolving into a lasting separation of the two economies. The 1996 closures, after a wave of terror attacks, cost the Gaza/West Bank economies $962 million, equal to a significant percentage of national income. While the situation improved in 1997–1999, the outbreak of violence in September 2000 led to long-lasting closures that only worsened when, in 2002, the Israeli Defense Forces reentered Palestinian cities. In the years 2000–2002, per capita Palestinian income declined 35 percent before leveling off in 2003–2005. The construction of physical barriers—in most places fences, in some sensitive areas a wall—between Israeli-controlled areas and Gaza and the rest of the West Bank made for more definitive separation between the Israeli and Gaza/West Bank economies. In 2005, Israel withdrew from Gaza and imposed tighter restrictions on the flow of goods and people into and out of the territory. The European Union and the United States tried to facilitate movement of goods and people from and to Gaza via Egypt, and avoiding Israel, but that plan had largely failed by 2006 due to Palestinian violence and Israeli objections about the movement of terrorists and arms.

The worsening economic situation deepened Palestinian dependence on international aid. The high political profile of the Palestinian-Israeli conflict had long meant that both sides received aid at levels well above most developing areas. After the 1993 Declaration of Principles, billions in aid flowed into the West Bank and Gaza; in the next decade, the Palestinian territories received more than ten times as much aid per capita as that which went to sub-Saharan Africa, which is much poorer. The aid brought few benefits due to inappropriate projects (almost always at donor insistence), immense Palestinian corruption, and renewed political tensions, which led Israel to either block aid-financed goods or to destroy aid-built projects, such as the Gaza airport. Generating the aid levels on which the Palestinian economy had come to depend became more and more difficult as donors became disillusioned. Periodic outbreaks of violence have produced renewed high donation levels: grants remained at about $1.7 billion to $1.9 billion a year through 2009.

The already dim prospects for the Palestinian economy grew even less bright after the 2006 election victory of the Hamas movement, a victory that owed much to reaction against the corruption by the then-ruling Fatah Party. In 2007, Hamas seized complete power in Gaza, while Fatah reasserted control in the West Bank, handing the Palestinian Authority ministries over to technocrats. With the 2007 political split, the economic situation in Gaza and the West Bank began to diverge significantly, which was only intensified by a brief December 2008–January 2009 war between Israel and Hamas in Gaza. From mid-2006 to mid-2009, average wages (adjusted for inflation) fell 30 percent in Gaza while remaining constant in the West Bank. In 2009, unemployment was 37 percent in Gaza and 18 percent in the West Bank. Furthermore, the International Monetary Fund (IMF) forecasts for 2010–2012 growth prospects suggest the differences will grow, with real per capita income remaining constant in Gaza while growing 4 percent a year in the West Bank (the World Bank is more pessimistic).

The reasons for the divergence between Gaza and the West Bank are twofold. First is the tough treatment of Hamas by the outside world. Both the United States and the European Union classify Hamas as a terrorist organization and therefore have cut off aid to Hamas-controlled institutions, directing their aid to Gaza through international and nongovernmental organizations. After the brief 2008–2009 war, the donors did not increase aid to Gaza despite the considerable destruction. Since Hamas came to power, Israel stepped up its closures such that by 2008, it was in effect allowing only humanitarian movements into and out of Gaza. The Hamas government was unable to keep open the crossings from Gaza to Egypt, and was reduced to encouraging smuggling via tunnels. By contrast, donors maintained the level of aid to the West Bank Palestinian Authority despite their disillusionment with past results. Israel lessened the burden of the security checkpoints throughout the West Bank, especially by reducing waiting times at such places.

The second reason for the divergence in economic performance was that the Palestinian Authority in the West Bank began to match the improvement in government services that Hamas had been making in the areas it controlled. The post-2007 technocratic Palestinian Authority reformed social assistance programs, public pensions, civil service employment practices, utility subsidies, and police practices, among other areas. As a result, the gap between the public services Hamas delivered and those provided by the Palestinian Authority shrank noticeably.

Since 1987, the Palestinian economic situation has generally gotten worse as the Palestinian link to Israel's economy has been reduced with nothing put in its place. Since 2008, the Palestinian Authority in the West Bank has taken initial steps to strengthen state institutions and develop economic infrastructure independent of Israel. It remains to be seen how far that will go, and what will be the future of the Gaza Strip.

Jordan

Jordan has had impressive results for an economy with so many strikes against it: a poor natural resource endowment, repeated refugee inflows, and regional instability threatening domestic tranquility. However, Jordanians remain scarred by the collapse of the hothouse economy of the late 1970s, when the economy was artificially overheated by generous aid from oil-rich Arab states as well as ample remittances from Jordanians working in the Gulf. Only in 2010 did Jordan regain the prosperity it had in 1982. However, if one takes as a starting point 1970, when Jordan suffered a short civil war, then Jordan has experienced significant growth, especially considering the external shocks.

Jordan was completely transformed by the 1948 war with Israel, after which its population more than tripled, primarily from the refugee flow from Israel and Jordan's takeover of the West Bank (more populous than Transjordan, also known as the East Bank). In the years that followed, government policy systematically promoted economic development in the East Bank, the poorer part of the kingdom, which embittered many ethnic Palestinians. The West Bank was lost in the 1967 Six-Day War, and the new flow of Palestinian refugees to the East Bank resulted in ethnic Palestinians being a majority there. There followed the greatest crisis Jordan has ever experienced as the PLO set up what amounted to a competing government. In the short but bloody 1970 civil war, the monarchy and its East Bank allies reasserted control.

Ever since then, the de facto social contract in Jordan has been that East Bankers dominate the government while allowing ethnic Palestinians to dominate the private sector outside of agriculture.

The government's work force is 75 percent East Bankers. By contrast, 63 percent of the employees in the 500 top companies work in firms controlled by ethnic Palestinians. The market value of firms controlled by ethnic Palestinians is 83 percent of the capitalization of the stock exchange. By some estimates, ethnic Palestinians control 90 percent of small and intermediate commerce as well as owning much of the urban real estate. Within this context, changing the relative economic power of the state and private sectors has profound sociopolitical implications.

The recovery from the 1970 war started slowly, held back by Jordan's ostracism by other Arab states. But after King Hussein's 1974 recognition of the PLO as the sole representative of the Palestinian people, Jordan received substantial Arab aid, which swelled due to the oil boom. Official data appear to leave out much of the aid, such as much military assistance; nevertheless, they show aid flows averaging about 20 percent of GDP during the boom decade of 1973–1982. Added to that, during this period, the perhaps 300,000 Jordanians working in the Gulf sent home remittances averaging as much as 30 percent of GDP. The money flood financed substantial state spending, including infrastructure and industrial investment. By 1982, per capita income had approximately doubled from the 1971 level. Jordan seemed on the road to become a solidly middle-income country.

However, Jordan had not created an economic system that could be sustained in the absence of the foreign financing. When that dried up as the Gulf's oil income shrank precipitously in the mid-1980s, Jordan was left in the lurch. Its economic fall was made much, much harder by the vain effort into the late 1980s to sustain spending despite the drop in financing. Foreign debt mushroomed to more than twice GDP, and the government had to borrow on harsh terms from international banks rather than receiving concessionary government loans on terms so soft as to be almost grants. Signs of trouble mounted in 1988 with several financial scare-cum-scandals. After years of denying any structural problem, the Jordanian government finally had to face the truth in 1989, when it was unable to service its debt.

When this crisis came, Jordan had to agree to an IMF program cutting subsidies on a wide range of consumer staples, provoking rioting in the southern cities at the heart of the East Bank community, the regime's main political base. The economic situation worsened with the 1990 Kuwait crisis. Jordan's pro-Iraqi stance led to a near complete cutoff in aid, both Arab and Western (although Japan stepped in at the most difficult moment in 1991, its aid quickly returned to low levels). Jordan also had to absorb around 300,000 Jordanian nationals exiting the Gulf states for Jordan, nearly all of them ethnic Palestinians (as a result of Arafat's warm endorsement of Saddam's invasion of Kuwait, Kuwait and other Gulf states pushed Palestinians to leave). The bottom was reached in 1991, when per capita income dropped back to where it had been two decades earlier, right after the 1970 civil war with the PLO.

Recovery was slow. The Gulf returnees brought with them perhaps $2 billion, but much of the money went into real estate or other unproductive purposes; the effect was a temporary boom, which quickly dissipated. Hopes were high that the 1994 peace treaty with Israel would bring substantial Western aid on the model of what Egypt got after the 1978 Camp David accords, but aid flows were modest: Jordan was still paying the price for its stance during the Kuwait crisis. Jordan had asked primarily for debt relief, of which it got more than a billion dollars, but that had little public visibility, so the popular perception was that Jordan got little for peace. Public skepticism about the peace dividend hardened after the government was forced to acknowledge in 1998 that official economic data had overstated the growth rate for 1996–1997 by eight percentage points. Meanwhile, Jordan was burdened by the continuing sanctions on Iraq, especially since the United States insisted until well into the 1990s on inspecting every ship going into Jordan's Aqaba port on the suspicion that Jordan was complicit in smuggling to Iraq; the inspections slowed deliveries and raised shipping costs. The main bright spot was Iraq's provision of low-cost oil, which turned Iraq into Jordan's largest donor through the 1990s. Overall, during the 1990s, income per capita was stagnant.

King Abdullah II, who came to the throne in 1999 with the death of his father King Hussein (ruled 1951–1999), has gone considerably farther with economic reform. As a result, GDP growth picked up from 3.5 percent a year in 1996–2000 to 6 percent a year in 2001–2010. Jordan benefited from Hussein's initiatives in negotiating a free trade agreement with the United States and establishing qualifying industrial zones (QIZs) that allowed quota-free access to the U.S. market for products such as textiles, usually subject to strict limits for goods made jointly in Jordan and Israel. Largely due to the QIZs, Jordan's exports to the United States rose from under $30 million a year in 1995 to over a billion dollars a year by 2005. In 2005, 54,000 people were employed in the QIZs.

At least as important, Abdullah launched in 2002 a "Jordan First" campaign and a companion "Socio-Economic Transformation Plan," which was extended by the ten-year "National Agenda" prepared in 2005 by a broad-based commission. These various initiatives were designed to more fully integrate the ethnic Palestinians into Jordanian society and thereby reduce the political tensions associated with economic reforms that benefit the Palestinian-dominated private sector over the East Bank–dominated state sector. Under King Abdullah, the main areas of growth of the Jordanian economy have been manufacturing exports to world markets and services provided to the booming Gulf oil states, which are areas of the economy traditionally dominated by ethnic Palestinians.

The country continues to be buffeted by regional tensions. The 2003 overthrow of Iraqi dictator Saddam Hussein by the U.S.-led invasion meant that Jordan lost access to cheap Iraqi oil; compounded by the oil price increases, Jordan's oil import bill rose fourfold from 2003 to 2008, increasing to 16 percent of GDP. Plus, as violence in Iraq mounted, Jordan sustained a large influx of refugees—by some estimates, over 800,000 by 2007, meaning 12 percent of Jordan's population. To be sure, some of those immigrants brought cash, which they invested in Jordan, but more of them arrived looking for jobs and with few resources.

The Iraqi refugees are not the only foreigners employed in Jordan. Indeed, Jordan employs a large number of foreigners even while it suffers from a serious unemployment problem. Numbers in each category are disputed, but there is little doubt that the number of foreigners working in Jordan exceeds the number of unemployed Jordanians. Throughout the decade 2000–2009, the unemployment rate appears to have been about 13 percent. Even though many jobs were created in 2000–2005, the World Bank estimates that half of them went to foreigners. Part of the problem is that 60 percent of the new jobs are in the capital of Amman, while many of the unemployed live in other cities. Another issue is that employers prefer foreigners, who are perceived to be more productive and have better work habits. Furthermore, many Jordanians are falsely optimistic about their chances of finding high-paying work, and so they refuse to consider jobs paying less. Solving these problems will be a great challenge.

On balance, Jordan will be challenged to meet its objective of doubling per capita income from 2005 to 2015, but that may be possible if Abdullah persists with reforms and the world economy recovers steadily from the 2008–2009 crisis. The general lesson of the post-1970 period is that Jordan has managed to survive serious external political shocks that have repeatedly dealt heavy blows to its economy. During those times, such as 2000–2009, when the government implemented some economic reforms, the growth record has been good; during other times, such as the 1980s, when the government ignored possible reforms, serious imbalances built up and eventually resulted in economic crisis.

Syria

In 2010, Syria's per capita income was among the lowest in the Arab world, better only than those of Yemen and Sudan. Syria's growth record since the late 1950s has been poor. In *Syria: Development and Monetary Policy*, author Edmund Asfour estimates that Syrian per capita income in the late 1950s was $120–180, which translates in 2007 dollars to about $1,800, depending how one adjusts for inflation. By contrast, the World Bank lists Syrian national income per person for 2007 as $1,760 while IMF reports imply the per capita income was $1,950 (note that for international comparisons, per capita income is often calculated on a "purchasing power parity basis," adjusting for lower prices in countries like Syria; were that basis used, the per capita income both in 2007and in the late 1950s would be higher). Only with the boom after 2004 did Syrian per capita income exceed the late-1950s level.

Syria's reduced situation is a historical reversal. A detailed 1955 World Bank report on Syria concluded, "One of the most noteworthy features of the Syrian economy has been its rapid growth over the last two decades." Until the 1970s, Syria was rather well off by Arab standards. When the short-lived union of Egypt and Syria known as the United Arab Republic broke up in 1961, one of the reasons was Syrian complaints that the Egyptians had descended upon their rich country like locusts; now Syria's income is notably lower than that of Egypt, and not because Egypt has had stellar growth rates.

The reason for the decline of Syrian fortunes is due to restrictions in the private sector. The same 1955 World Bank report explained why Syria had done well up to that point: "A characteristic feature of Syria's rapid economic development is that it has been almost wholly due to private enterprise." The Baathist Party, which has ruled Syria since coming to power in a 1963 coup, sharply limited the private sector, starting with a 1964–1965 wave of nationalizations and vigorous implementation of the languishing 1958 land reform, accelerating after the hard-line leftist wing of the Baath took power in a 1966 coup. The economic results of the Baathist takeover can best be described as revolutionary: the economic system was substantially remodeled and a new elite took power. The defining characteristic of the economy became bureaucratic control; for instance, the agricultural cooperatives control finance, provision of inputs, and most marketing. After Hafez al-Assad took power gradually in 1969–1970, there was a limited economic opening, with some additional reforms in 1973–1974. But the main feature of the 1970s was an extraordinary burst of state-led investment in industry, much of it ill conceived. While all that investment created a temporary economic boom, Syria ran up an unsustainable foreign debt, and the new industries proved inefficient and uncompetitive. Despite the massive sums spent on the new industries, Syria's economy remained largely agrarian.

As the 1980s opened, Syria entered into a deep economic crisis, made worse by Assad's overly ambitious bid to achieve strategic military parity with Israel, though nearly all of that arms buildup was financed by oil-rich Arab states and the Soviet Union. Industrial investment more or less stopped for the entire decade. Faced with an acute foreign exchange shortage, each industrial unit could only import inputs if it itself generated the funds from exports or sales for hard currency on the local market. After a decade of rapidly expanding public-sector payrolls, public employment was frozen after 1985 (except for education and health). The military went into a nosedive made all the steeper by the collapse of the Soviet Union; Russia refused to even sell Syria spare parts for hard cash unless Syria serviced its huge debt, which Syria was unwilling and unable to do.

While the Syrian economy was already slowly righting itself by the late 1980s, the country got a tremendous boost from the large cash foreign aid contributions from oil-rich Arab states in 1991, when Syria surprisingly joined the American-led coalition to liberate Kuwait. In addition, by the late 1980s, Syria's modest oil output rose sharply as a result of the ideologically painful decision to allow a greatly expanded role for Western oil companies. Because of these windfalls, Syria never implemented the economic reforms urged on it by Western donors, led by the World Bank and the IMF. Instead, it maintained its system of tight control over the economy by the government, with power increasingly centralized in the hands of the presidency. When in the late 1990s the country was once again on the brink of a serious economic crisis, Assad's response was to patch up the long-chilly relations with Iraqi dictator Saddam Hussein. By allowing Iraq to ship its oil to Syria in violation of UN sanctions (it was used to replace Syrian oil in the domestic refineries, permitting Syria to sell more of its own oil abroad), Syria may have been able to increase its exports by one-third.

When Hafez al-Assad died in June 2000, Syria's economy was still in poor shape for such a potentially rich country. The Ministry of Planning reported that 40 percent of public-sector workers made less than $44 per month, while another 50 percent made $60 to $100 a month, while the country's revenues from oil exports were equal to $75 per month for every person in the labor force. The widespread expectation was that Assad's successor and son, Bashar al-Assad, would devote himself to reviving the economy by opening it up. Not only was Bashar al-Assad trained in the West (as an ophthalmologist), but as chairman of the Syrian Computer Society he had been instrumental in allowing access to the Internet—not an easy step for a regime that keeps tight control over all aspects of society. In a February 2001 interview, the younger Assad said his "general vision" for Syria could be summed up in a single proposition: "to see Syria more prosperous." But reforms were slow in coming and modest in scope. For instance, the 2003 banking reforms, described as radical by Syrian officials, were modeled on the 1950s Lebanese regulations.

The Syrian economy grew briskly from 2004 to 2008 at an average rate of 5 percent a year (adjusted for inflation), led by non-oil exports and tourism. Partly that growth was due to the growing impact of the continuing reforms. An additional factor was the spillover from the Gulf oil boom, especially tourism and investment by individuals from the oil-rich Gulf states. These factors offset the declining oil output. In 2007, Syria became a net oil importer, because it has refused to offer sufficiently attractive terms to foreign investors and because the United States imposed sanctions in 2007, reinforcing the impression that Syria is a risky place to do business. The IMF forecasts that Syrian oil imports will grow steadily to $4 billion a year in 2013.

Only by sustaining the 2004–2008 growth can Syria hope to create enough jobs to absorb the 200,000 youth joining the labor force each year (that is an estimate; official data are conflicting and not necessarily accurate). In 2005–2006, the unemployment situation was aggravated by the return from Lebanon of at least a hundred thousand unskilled Syrians and the influx of several hundred thousand Iraqi refugees.

While it is difficult to separate out the various influences that have blocked reform in Syria, one important factor has been the sectarian element. The Syrian government has for decades been dominated by the Alawite community, who make up about one-eighth of the country's population; Alawites, a religious community on the fringes of Islam with some highly heterodox practices, were long marginalized in Syrian society before rising to political power thanks to a strong presence in the military. By contrast, Alawites have historically not been important in the private economy. The rise of state-run industries has disproportionately benefited Alawites. They have also been able to take advantage of the state's tight control over private business; for instance, having an Alawite business partner could not hurt in relations with the state. Any real opening of the economy would reduce the economic advantages of this group.

To summarize the experience of the Levant, economic performance has heavily depended on geopolitics, especially the Arab-Israeli dispute and domestic sectarianism. Many Levant Arabs put more importance on their political agenda than on their prosperity. Where governments have been prepared to put economics first, the result has been faster growth. For instance, Jordan has opened up its economy to some extent, even though the gains have accrued disproportionately to ethnic Palestinian Jordanians, with the result that Jordan has on average had better economic growth than its neighbors, despite its poor resource endowment and the difficult external shocks to its economy. Elsewhere, limited reforms in Syria under Bashar al-Assad have been a factor in Syria's higher growth rates after 2004. Unfortunately for the people of the Levant, the area has often been buffeted by political turmoil, and the economy has suffered as a result.

References and Further Reading

Abed, George, ed. *The Palestinian Economy: Studies in Development Under Prolonged Occupation.* London: Routledge, 1988.

Arnon, Arie, A. Spivak, and J. Weinblatt. *The Palestinian Economy: Between Imposed Integration and Voluntary Separation.* Leiden, Netherlands: E.J. Brill, 1997.

Asfour, Edmund. *Syria: Development and Monetary Policy.* Cambridge, MA: Harvard University Press, 1967.

Berthélemy, Jean-Claude, Sebastien Dessus, and Charbel Nahas. "Exploring Lebanon's Growth Prospects." *World Bank Policy Research Working Paper* 4332, August 2007.

Brynen, Rex. *A Very Political Economy: Peacebuilding and Foreign Aid in the West Bank and Gaza.* Washington, DC: USIP Press Books, 2000.

Carroll, Katherine Blue. *Business as Usual? Economic Reform in Jordan.* Lanham, MD: Lexington Books, 2003.

Clawson, Patrick. *Unaffordable Ambitions: Syria's Military Build-up and Economic Crisis.* Washington, DC: Washington Institute for Near East Policy, 1989.

Clawson, Patrick, and Zoe Danon Gedal. *Dollars and Diplomacy: The Impact of U.S. Economic Initiatives on*

Arab-Israeli Negotiations. Washington, DC: Washington Institute for Near East Policy, 1999.

Clawson, Patrick, and Howard Rosen. *The Economic Consequences of Peace for Israel, the Palestinians, and Jordan.* Washington, DC: Washington Institute for Near East Policy, 1991.

Diwan, Ishac, and Radwan Shaban, eds. *Development Under Adversity: The Palestinian Economy in Transition.* Washington, DC: Palestine Economic Policy Research Institute, 1999.

El-Hafez, Ramzi. "The Business Environment: Barriers to Remove, Opportunities to Develop." In *Options for Lebanon*, ed. Nawaf Salam, 135–172. London: Centre for Lebanese Studies/I.B Tauris, 2004.

Farsakh, Leila. *Palestinian Labour Migration to Israel: Labour, Land, and Occupation.* London: Routledge, 2005.

Fishelson, Gideon. *Economic Cooperation in the Middle East.* Boulder, CO: Westview Press, 1989.

Gaspard, Toufic. "Towards a Viable Economy." In *Options for Lebanon*, ed. Nawaf Salam, 117–134. London: Centre for Lebanese Studies/I.B. Tauris, 2004.

Gharaibeh, Fawzi. *The Economies of the West Bank and Gaza Strip.* Boulder, CO: Westview Press, 1985.

Greenwood, Scott. "Jordan's 'New Bargain': The Political Economy of Regime Security." *Middle East Journal* 57:1 (Spring 2003): 248–268.

Hinnebusch, Raymond. *Authoritarian Power and State Formation in Ba'thist Syria: Army, Power, and Peasant.* Boulder, CO: Westview Press, 1990.

———. *Peasant and Bureaucracy in Ba'thist Syria: The Political Economy of Rural Development.* Boulder, CO: Westview Press, 1989.

International Bank for Reconstruction and Development (World Bank). *The Economic Development of Syria.* Baltimore, MD: Johns Hopkins University Press, 1955.

International Monetary Fund. *Lebanon: 2009 Article IV Consultation.* IMF Country Report No. 09/131, April 23, 2009. Available at www.imf.org/external/pubs/ft/scr/2009/cr09131.pdf.

———. "Macroeconomic and Fiscal Framework for the West Bank and Gaza: Fourth Review of Progress." Washington, DC: International Monetary Fund. September 22, 2009. Available at www.imf.org/external/np/wbg/2009/pdf/022509.pdf.

———. *Syrian Arab Republic: 2006 Article IV Consultation—Staff Report.* IMF Country Report No. 06/294, August 9, 2006. Available at www.imf.org/external/pubs/ft/scr/2006/cr06294.pdf.

———. *Syrian Arab Republic: 2008 Article IV Consultation—Staff Report.* IMF Country Report No. 09/55, February 13, 2009. Available at www.imf.org/external/pubs/cat/longres.aspx?sk=22702.0.

———. *West Bank and Gaza: Economic Performance and Reform Under Conflict Conditions.* Washington, DC: International Monetary Fund, 2003.

Kanovsky, Eliyahu. *Economic Impact of the Six-Day War: Israel, The Occupied Territories, Egypt, Jordan.* New York: Praeger, 1970.

Knowles, Warwick. *Jordan Since 1989: A Study in Political Economy.* London: I.B. Tauris, 2005.

Leverett, Flynt. *Inheriting Syria: Bashar's Trial by Fire.* Washington, DC: Brookings Institution Press, 2005.

Makdisi, Samir. *The Lessons of Lebanon: The Economics of War and Development.* London: I.B. Tauris, 2004.

Mattar, Mohammad. "On Corruption." In *Options for Lebanon*, ed. Nawaf Salam, 173–208. London: Centre for Lebanese Studies/I.B. Tauris, 2004.

Nizameddin, Talal. "The Political Economy of Lebanon Under Rafiq Hariri." *Middle East Journal* 60:1 (Winter 2006): 95–114.

Perthes, Volker. *The Political Economy of Syria.* London: I.B. Tauris, 1995.

Reiter, Yithzak. "Economic and Political Power in Jordan: The Palestinian Transjordanian Rift." *Middle East Journal* 58:1 (Winter 2004): 72–92.

Van Arkadie, Brian. *Benefits and Burdens: A Report on the West Bank and Gaza Strip Since 1967.* New York: Carnegie Endowment for International Peace, 1977.

World Bank. *Country Assistance Strategy for the Hashemite Kingdom of Jordan.* Report No. 35665, April 6, 2006. Available at http://web.worldbank.org/WBSITE/EXTERNAL/COUNTRIES/MENAEXT/JORDANEXTN/0,,contentMDK:20148051~pagePK:141137~piPK:141127~theSitePK:315130,00.html.

———. *Country Assistance Strategy for the Republic of Lebanon.* Report No. 34463-LB, November 2005.

———. *The Economic Development of Syria.* Baltimore, MD: Johns Hopkins University Press, 1955.

———. *Four Years—Intifada, Closures, and Palestinian Economic Crisis: An Assessment.* Washington, DC: World Bank, 2004.

———. *A Palestinian State in Two Years: Institutions for Economic Revival.* Washington, DC: World Bank, 2009.

———. *Resolving Jordan's Labor Market Paradox of Concurrent Economic Growth and High Unemployment.* Washington DC: World Bank, 2008.

———. *Stagnation or Revival? Israeli Disengagement and the Palestinian Economic Prospects.* Washington, DC: World Bank, 2004.

Zisser, Eyal. *Commanding Syria: Bashar Al-Asad and the First Years in Power.* London: I.B. Tauris, 2007.

Nile Valley

Reliance on the Nile River's waters has shaped the economy and history of Egypt and Sudan, making them quite distinctive within the broader Arab community. For many periods in its long history, Egypt was the preeminent regional power, and a prosperous one as well. While the Industrial Revolution left Egypt far behind northern Europe economically and in political power, Egypt was at mid-twentieth century still within striking distance of southern European standards. In 1950, Egypt's income per person was 80 percent that of Greece and 45 percent that of Italy, and Alexandria was arguably as rich as Athens or Naples. However, the Arab socialism instituted by President Gamal Abdel Nasser slowed growth and entrenched Egypt's bureaucracies, which have resisted change ever since 1974, when President Anwar Sadat launched the country on the path toward a market economy. Reforms have been fitful, as has been growth. In 2005, Egypt's income was a mere 11 percent that of Greece and 6 percent that of Italy, a drop since 1950 by a factor of seven in relative income. Sudan, long Egypt's poorer cousin, has since 1999 seen its fortunes improve thanks to oil, though that could change if Southern Sudan becomes independent as seems likely.

Egypt's Classical Agrarian Market Economy Until 1956

To understand the economic problems of Egypt in the mid- to late twentieth century, it is instructive to look at how well the Egyptian economy performed in the preceding 150 years. In 1800, Egypt's population was 2.5 million, only 40 percent of what it had been in Roman and early Arab days, and its economy can best be described as feudal: small cities, and peasants who had no property rights and were tied to the soil. Shaken by the French invasion (1798–1801), the old regime was overthrown by Muhammad Ali (ruled 1805–1849), who launched the country on a dramatic and rapid path of modernization. Within the space of a few decades, private property in land became the norm, agricultural production was oriented toward world markets, and extensive infrastructure was built (irrigation works to water the new crops; railways, roads, and ports to carry the harvest to markets in Europe). As a result, agricultural output soared. With cotton as the main crop, the American Civil War gave Egypt years of extraordinary prosperity. Also important were sugar and wheat, though the latter's share fell under pressure from New World and Australian producers. Egypt's economy was intensely integrated into the world economy, attracting massive foreign investment. The heavy debts for constructing infrastructure, most especially the Suez Canal, led to a debt crisis and Anglo-French intervention in 1882. In effect, Egypt became a British colony, though retaining its ruling kings, who were nominally subject to the Ottomans until 1914. Sustained growth continued under British rule, as the role of cotton in the economy deepened. Contemporary observers during the nineteenth century thought that one of Egypt's major economic problems was a labor shortage in the face of the booming economy, even though its population rose fivefold from 1800 to 1917 (to 12.7 million).

After World War I and nominal independence in 1922 (the British retained considerable control), nationalist sentiment led private Egyptian businessmen to found a local bank—Bank Misr, Misr being the name of Egypt in Arabic—as well as local industries, which grew considerably during World War II and the prosperous years following. Egypt was certainly not a rich country under the monarchy, but neither was it a particularly poor country by the standards of the day. From 1800 to 1950, Egypt had kept pace with the explosive growth in Europe under the Industrial Revolution; its population and income per person rose at rates roughly comparable to Europe's.

The monarchy was overthrown by the Free Officers' military coup in 1952; by 1954, Nasser had emerged as the new leader. At first, the Free Officers did not have a clearly articulated economic philosophy, though they were profoundly hostile to the old oligarchy—that is, the closely interlinked group of large landowners and industrial/financial capitalists. In its early years, the new government made few changes to the free market economic orientation, in which the state's role was largely limited to providing infrastructure. Indeed, the Free Officers reduced taxes on business and wooed foreign investors, though they did retain state ownership of the industrial properties confiscated from the monarchy. The one substantial change was land reform. Individuals were not allowed to own more than 200 *feddans* (a feddan is 1.04 acre or 0.47 hectare); almost 15 percent of agricultural land was redistributed in the 1950s from the large landholders to those owning less than 5 feddans. The aim of the reform was to break the power of the oligarchs and to consolidate political support from the smallholders.

Egypt's Arab Socialism, 1956–1973

The Free Officers' hostility to the old oligarchy pushed them toward Arab socialism, with the shift away from a free market economy accelerating greatly in 1956. The precipitating episode was the failure of negotiations with the United States, Great Britain, and the World Bank for the financing of the Aswan High Dam on the Nile. Combined with a 1995 Egyptian decision to purchase Czech arms and Nasser's demand that Britain give up its military bases near the Suez Canal, the West's concern was that Egypt was falling under Soviet influence; this translated into detailed conditions, both economic and political, accompanying the offer to finance the dam. Nasser found these conditions humiliating. Thinking Nasser had no alternative way to finance the dam, and wishing to teach him a lesson, the U.S. and British governments withdrew their financing offer in July 1956. Nasser responded by nationalizing the Suez Canal in order to use the revenue from its tolls to finance the dam. The entire Arab world was electrified, bursting with pride at Nasser's action—a feeling that only intensified after the failure of the October 1956 Anglo-French invasion designed to reverse the nationalization (the simultaneous Israeli invasion of Sinai was, by contrast, successful).

The Suez invasion led Egypt to seize the considerable British and French assets within its borders, greatly expanding the state's role in the economy. The next stage of the revolution was the nationalization of Egyptian-owned assets. In 1960, the two large Egyptian banks that dominated the financial sector were nationalized. In 1961 came what the regime called the "Socialist Revolution," starting with state control over trade in the all-important cotton crop and extending to the state takeover of hundreds of firms. In late 1961, after Syria seceded from the brief United Arab Republic union of Syria and Egypt, the property of hundreds of wealthy Egyptians was sequestrated—effectively, confiscated. Practically all exports and imports were taken over by government ministries or state-owned firms. The reduction of the private sector to a minor role was then enshrined as the centerpiece of the government's 1962 statement of its plans for the future, called the National Charter.

While economists are often thought of as partisans of free markets, in the early 1960s, Nasser's policy of state control was seen by the best economic minds as a reasonable choice for a developing economy. A 1967 study sponsored by Yale University's Economic Growth Center concluded, "Perhaps the most important result of the nationalizations has been to give manufacturing establishments more possibilities of borrowing from commercial and Central banks, thereby raising the rate of investment in industry." This attitude persisted. A 1976 study by Oxford University economists argued, "The difficulties experienced by Egyptian industries after 1964 cannot be attributed, on the evidence available, to the extension of public ownership." Tellingly, the U.S. government continued a large aid program, providing Egypt with the wheat it could no longer afford because foreign exchange was being wasted on inappropriate investments and overly ambitious initiatives. While the size of the U.S. aid program fluctuated, the storms in the Egyptian-U.S. relationship were over geopolitics; the United States simply did not raise objections to Nasser's economic politics.

In the 1960s, right after the nationalizations, Egypt's economic performance continued much as before. But in retrospect, that continued growth was because Egypt benefited from an extraordinarily favorable world economic environment, in which markets for its products were growing briskly. That favorable environment masked the growing problems caused by the nationalizations. While in the 1960s Egypt was pouring resources into industry, all that investment had remarkably little positive effect. Consider the automobile industry. Three factories were built whose full-scale production would have required foreign inputs equal to one-fifth of the total value Egypt could afford for imports of all goods; peak production was less than 10,000 vehicles a year. In fact, post-nationalization, despite the priority accorded to industry and the gross overstaffing of state firms, manufacturing's share in new jobs created was actually less than it had been before (16 percent for 1960–1970 versus 18 percent for 1937–1960).

Parallel to the nationalizations was the so-called land reform of 1961, which quickly became the assertion of state control over agriculture. The state pressed farmers into state-run cooperatives, which made the most important decisions, such as which crops to plant; the result was that prices had little impact on farmer actions. In any case, the government set prices for inputs and crops, both of which it alone marketed, at levels completely disconnected from world market prices. By the late 1960s, the Egyptian state had greater control over the economy than did states in parts of Eastern Europe, such as Poland, where agriculture was largely private. The result was that agricultural output rose modestly despite the improvement in irrigation made possible by the High Dam. As a result, many farmers deserted the countryside for the cities, given that labor was in short supply on the farms.

The Egyptian government issued only one Five-Year Plan, covering 1960/61–1964/65. In other words, economic policy was entirely disconnected from the plan. That was rather typical of Egypt's planning experience. Preparing that plan took five years of work by the National Planning Committee set up in 1956. The committee gathered input from world-class economists, but then the plan was largely a collection of projects proposed by overly enthusiastic ministries, with the financial needs "planned" by making wildly enthusiastic assumptions. The policies actually adopted by the government, such as the nationalizations and state control over agriculture, were not what the plan envisaged. Even as economic performance fell increasingly short of hopes, the government continued to adopt expensive policies. The most disastrous was the 1964 institution of the right of high school and college graduates to a guaranteed government job after a waiting period. As government employment shot up, the wage bill ate up funds that could otherwise have gone for investment.

Meanwhile, the inward-looking policies that ignored exports in favor of import substitution caused exports to shrink from 21 percent in 1950 to 12 percent in 1970. The government was running large deficits, and the country was running out of foreign exchange. Egypt had come to depend on the Soviet Union, which had become the largest aid donor as U.S. aid ended. Although politically very sympathetic to the Nasser government, the USSR in 1965–1967 pushed Egypt to adopt retrenchment policies in the style of the International Monetary Fund (IMF) and curtailed its aid. From 1970 on, new Soviet aid was less than the debt repayments Egypt had to make to the Soviets.

Nasser had grand ambitions for Egypt—as a leader of the global Non-Aligned Movement, a group of countries not formally allied with either side in the Cold War, along with Nehru in India and Tito in Yugoslavia; as the prophet of Arab socialist unity (witness the 50,000 Egyptian troops dispatched to fight in the Yemeni civil war); and as the leader in the Arab cause against Israel. After the catastrophic defeat in the 1967 Six-Day War, in which Egypt lost 80 percent of all its weaponry, Nasser decided to prioritize the confrontation with Israel. The resources required for that effort meant he had to abandon pursuit of many of his other objectives. Egypt had to sacrifice its best minds to the military, as conscription was extended to cover high school and university graduates. The government had to raise substantial sums for war costs; given its limited ability to collect taxes, it had to resort to inflationary borrowing, which at the peak covered 53 percent of all spending. Plus, Egypt turned to oil-rich Arab states and the Soviet Union to finance a vast flow of weapons from the

Soviet Union, which shipped $2.3 billion in arms from 1967 to 1973 and provided 15,000 advisors at the peak.

Whereas in many countries such national mobilization for war strengthens the state's hand in the economy, in Egypt the paradoxical effect was exactly the opposite. Both Nasser's government and, after his 1970 death, that of his successor Anwar Sadat realized that the sacrifices Egyptians were making for the war effort were straining the limits of social acceptance and threatening political stability. As a result, they pulled back from plans for new socialist measures and curtailed Egypt's broader international agenda, for instance, recalling the troops from Yemen. Nevertheless, by the time of the 1973 war with Israel, the Egyptian economy was in desperate straits: as Sadat warned, "Our economy has fallen below zero."

Though a massive conflict, the 1973 war itself had relatively limited economic impact. The cost of the war was largely covered by substantial cash aid from the oil-rich Arab states. Unlike their pattern in the preceding six years when they pledged aid they did not deliver in full, the oil-rich Arabs, with their coffers swelled by the 1973 oil price increases, came through with billions in cash, though the exact amounts remain shrouded in secrecy. The arms lost in the war were replaced by the Soviet Union at low cost. While the war did not add as much as might have been expected to Egypt's economic travails, neither did it reduce the crushing prewar problems, nor was it clear how long Arab and Soviet generosity would persist.

Egypt's Modest and Slow Reform, 1974 Onward

Faced with a desperate economic situation and a continuing high military burden, in 1974 Sadat launched an economic opening toward more of a role for market forces and for foreign trade and investment, which he called the open-door strategy, or *infitah*. Despite the grand pronouncements made by the government, the infitah brought little change. Throughout the 1970s and 1980s, the modest initiatives announced were further watered down by the opposition of key cabinet ministers and their bureaucracies. When small reforms were proposed, such as selling the state-owned hotels, which had 3.5 employees per room, protests ensued (the purchaser wanted 1.4 employees per room). In 1990, the public sector was about as dominant as it had been in the 1960s, accounting for 65 percent of value added, 70 percent of investment, 80 percent of foreign trade, and 90 percent of banking. Of the 15 million people working in Egypt in 1992, 5 million worked for the public sector, 6 million in agriculture, and 3.5 million in the informal sector, with only a half million in private firms with ten or more employees. Weighed down by the bloated public labor force and by subsidies, which averaged 18 percent of gross domestic product (GDP), the government budget deficit averaged 16 percent of GDP.

One of the major impacts of the infitah was to facilitate the inflow of Arab funds. On that score, it worked: 1974–1981 was a period of very rapid growth in Egypt, driven by the windfalls from the oil boom and peace with Israel. While neither Egypt nor the donor Arab states have published clear or consistent data, a careful study showed that Arab aid from 1973 to 1978 probably averaged $2.5 billion a year, including $700 million in military aid, before being cut off in 1979 in retaliation for Egypt's peace with Israel. The drop-off in aid was counterbalanced by an increase in the remittances from Egyptians working in oil-rich Arab lands. While data are estimates since much money came through unofficial channels, remittances seem to have risen from $1 billion a year in the late 1970s to at least $3 billion a year in the 1980s.

Israel and Egypt signed a peace treaty in 1980. Peace resulted in several substantial economic windfalls. First, Israeli withdrawal brought the return of the Sinai oil fields. With the oil price increase, oil income by 1981 was $3 billion, equivalent to 13 percent of GDP. That alone was more than the Arab aid lost because of the treaty with Israel. A second benefit of peace was the reopening of the Suez Canal, revenues from which quickly rose to $909 million in 1981–1982. Third, defense spending dropped to 9 percent of GDP in 1978 from 16 percent in 1970; had the military burden continued at the early level, this would have been $2 billion a year higher. Fourth, U.S. aid restarted, averaging about $2.5 billion a year from 1976. Most of the $1 billion in civilian aid was general support to the government, while much of the rest was for infrastructure.

After 1981, President Hosni Mubarak continued the economic policy of his assassinated predecessor Sadat, that is, the policy of high spending and resistance to reform, despite the end of the oil windfall. Prices were determined more by government orders than market forces, inefficient government-owned firms were sheltered from competition, and the government bureaucracy was swollen and incompetent. With Arab aid cut off after the peace with Israel and remittances falling as job opportunities in oil-rich states shrank, Egypt had to rely on borrowing to fill the growing gap in its foreign accounts. At first that worked; economic growth remained robust in 1982–1987. However, by 1987, total foreign debt was $40 billion, or 180 percent of GDP; arrears alone were over $4 billion. Despite the dire situation, Mubarak stalled for another four years, trading on Egypt's strategic worth to the United States and Gulf oil countries to generate just enough aid and debt relief. Serious reform only came in 1991.

Egypt concluded an economic reform program with the IMF in May 1991 and with the World Bank in November 1991. The budget deficit went from 15 percent of GDP in 1991 to 6 percent in 1992; further tightening brought it under 1 percent by 1995. This was mostly due to cutting expenditures, such as subsidies and government investment, but 4 percentage points of the change came from the cancellation of $23 billion in debt in the wake of Egypt's participation in the U.S.-led coalition to liberate Kuwait. Employment at public enterprises was cut by nearly 500,000 to fewer than 600,000. The immediate impact of the changes was painful, but Egypt persisted with reforms. From 1995 to 2000, the economy grew at a respectable 5.3 percent a year. Perhaps more important, job growth was higher after the reform program than before, despite the public-sector layoffs: from 1992 to 2000, employment rose 460,000 a year, compared to 250,000 a year from 1976 to 1992. For one thing, tourism increased sharply, with foreign tourism receipts up from $1.1 billion in 1990 to $4.3 billion in 2000. The stock market boomed as the value of listed stocks (the market capitalization) went from 5 percent of GDP in 1994 to 20 percent in 2000.

Mubarak's interest in economic reform has waxed and waned. For several years after 2000, the reform momentum stalled. Subsidies crept back up, going from 3 percent of GDP in 1998–1999 to 10 percent in 2005–2006; the budget deficit climbed back to 9 percent of GDP. Then in July 2004, Mubarak appointed a new cabinet filled with reformers who took action on some long-stalled issues, such as privatizations. Trade reform moved ahead, with a tariff reform and an agreement with Israel and the United States creating qualifying industrial zones (QIZs) in Egypt, which are eligible to export textiles and other goods free of restrictions to the United States. The results were impressive, with GDP going from $107 billion in 2005–2006 to $163 billion in 2007–2008, driven by 70 percent increases over the two years in tourism and exports other than oil and gas. The world financial crisis of late 2008 hit Egypt's economic prospects, but the economy continued to grow in 2009. If current policies remain in place, Egypt is likely to sustain growth of around 5 percent a year from 2010 onward.

Egypt's prospects depend on how much the government does about the deep structural problems, largely rooted in the continuing impact of Nasser's Arab socialism fifty years after the 1956 wave of nationalizations set the country on the wrong path. The dead hand of bureaucracy raises costs; for instance, the state-owned monopoly ports charge fees triple those of Egypt's competitors, raising the cost of imports by over 10 percent. Government services are needlessly inefficient; for instance, because the tax authorities audit every single taxpayer, audits may take place many long years after the return is filed, which leaves taxpayers not knowing how much they will have to pay—a system that only encourages rampant underpayment. Only by tackling the long list of problems identified by the World Bank and Egyptian economists can Egypt expect to achieve the growth necessary to absorb the growing labor force.

Sudan: Transformed by Oil

Before the end of the Anglo-Egyptian Condominium, which ruled Sudan from 1898 to 1956, the Sudanese debated whether to unify with Egypt or seek independence before deciding on the latter course. While Sudan retains deep cultural and political links with Egypt, economic links are few. Sudan's economy is better studied in the context of sub-Saharan Africa. Civil wars along ethnic and religious lines have been the overwhelming determinant of economic development for decades. A particularly disturbing dynamic has been periodic famines, the product as much of political maneuverings as of natural conditions. The 2003–2007 genocide in Darfur followed almost to the letter the same patterns seen in the two famines of the 1980s.

Two similarities with broader Middle East economic developments bear mentioning. First, Sudan experimented with Egyptian-style "Arab socialism," including extensive nationalizations and interventionist policies. However, political instability prevented Sudan from imitating Nasser's excesses until 1969, and the most detrimental policies were soon reversed after a failed communist-led coup attempt in 1971. But Sudan spent much of the 1970s trying to carry out an overambitious, state-centric, poorly conceived development program, which left the country so deeply in debt that it has still been unable to dig itself out.

The second similarity with other Arab economies came with the start of oil production in 1999. Output rose briskly until reaching a plateau of 650,000 barrels a day in 2006. At the high 2008 prices, oil exports reached $12 billion, or about $325 per person—no small sum for a country where GDP per capita had been $500 only five years earlier, in 2003. With the high oil income of 2008, Sudan's per capita income was $1,400, which was two-thirds that of Egypt, probably a historical high for that ratio. The challenge for Sudan will be to avoid the "oil curse," whereby the high oil income has undercut the rest of the economy while the oil revenues have been largely wasted.

The lower oil prices in 2009 as compared to 2008 have posed a serious problem for Sudan, with government oil revenue falling from 14 percent of GDP to 8 percent. Nevertheless, the outlook is for sustained, if modest, growth. The IMF forecasts that real GDP growth in 2009 and 2010 will be 4.5 percent a year. The prospects for realizing that growth will depend in part on resolving the post-2003 conflict in Darfur. Not only has that conflict kept military spending from falling as much as it might have with the end of the war in the south, but more importantly, it has led to a variety of international sanctions and boycott campaigns by human rights organizations, all of which has hurt Sudan's image as a country with which to do business.

One hopeful sign for the economy is that military spending decreased in the aftermath of the 2005 Comprehensive Peace Agreement, which ended the twenty-year civil war between the central government in Khartoum, dominated by Arabs, and forces in the south, with its African, non-Arab population. That agreement called for sharing oil revenues with the south, and Khartoum decided to apply this to the other states; the IMF reports that such transfers in 2008 were 67 percent of oil revenue. On a more troubling note for Sudan's economic prospects, the Comprehensive Peace Agreement provides for a 2011 referendum in the south on secession. If, as seems likely, Southern Sudan opts for independence, the newly independent country will have at least 80 percent of Sudan's oil production. All of that oil is exported via a pipeline running through northern Sudan. The best that the Khartoum government can hope for is revenue from the pipeline and a few oil fields in areas contested between the north and south, meaning that even in the best case, Khartoum's oil revenue will drop sharply. Alternatively, Khartoum and independent Southern Sudan may deadlock over the pipeline fees or even descend into war, in which case the economic situation in both parts of Sudan could become quite dire.

Southern Sudan is culturally, linguistically, and historically more a part of sub-Saharan Africa than the Middle East. An independent Southern Sudan will not be a part of the Middle East in any meaningful sense.

References and Further Reading

Abdel-Fadil, Mahmoud. *Development, Income Distribution and Social Change in Rural Egypt (1952–1970): A Study in the Political Economy of Agrarian Transition.* Cambridge, UK: Cambridge University Press, 1975.

Adams, Richard, Jr. *Development and Social Change in Rural Egypt.* Syracuse, NY: Syracuse University Press, 1986.

Amin, Galal. *Egypt's Economic Predicament: A Study in the Interaction of External Pressure, Politcal Folly, and Social Tensions in Egypt, 1960–1990.* Leiden, Netherlands: E.J. Brill, 1995.

Bach, Quintin. *Soviet Economic Assistance to the Less Developed Countries: A Quantitative Analysis.* Oxford, UK: Clarendon Press, 1987.

Barnett, Michael N. *Confronting the Costs of War: Military Power, State, and Society in Egypt and Israel.* Princeton, NJ: Princeton University Press, 1993.

Benin, Joel, and Zachary Lockman. *Workers on the Nile: Nationalism, Communism, Islam, and the Egyptian Working Class, 1882–1954.* Princeton, NJ: Princeton University Press, 1987.

Brown, Richard. *Public Debt and Private Wealth: Debt, Capital Flight and the IMF in Sudan.* London: Macmillan, 1992.

Burns, William. *Economic Aid and American Policy Towards Egypt, 1955–1981.* Albany: State University of New York Press, 1985.

Davis, Eric. *Challenging Colonialism: Bank Misr and Egyptian Industrialization, 1920–1941.* Princeton, NJ: Princeton University Press, 1983.

Feiler, Gil. *Economic Relations Between Egypt and the Gulf Oil States, 1967–2000: Petro-wealth and Patterns of Influence.* Brighton: Sussex Academic Press, 2003.

Financial Times. *Special supplement on Egypt*, December 7, 2005.

Goldberg, Ellis. *Tinker, Tailor, and Textile Worker: Class and Politics in Egypt, 1930–1952.* Berkeley: University of California Press, 1986.

Hansen, Bent. *The Political Economy of Poverty, Equity, and Growth: Egypt and Turkey.* Oxford: Oxford University Press for the World Bank, 1991.

Hansen, Bent, and Karim Nashashibi. *Foreign Trade Regimes and Economic Development: Egypt.* New York: Columbia University Press for the National Bureau of Economic Research, 1975.

Harik, Iliya. *Economic Policy Reform in Egypt.* Gainesville: University Press of Florida, 1997.

Ikram, Khalid. *The Egyptian Economy, 1952–2000: Performance, Policies, and Issues.* London: Routledge/Taylor and Francis, 2006.

———. *Egypt: Economic Management in a Period of Transition.* Baltimore, MD: Johns Hopkins University Press for the World Bank, 1980.

International Monetary Fund. *Arab Republic of Egypt: 2008 Article IV Consultation—Staff Report.* Country Report No. 09/25, January 2009.

———. *Sudan: 2006 Article IV Consultation—Staff Report.* Washington, DC: International Monetary Fund. Country Report No. 06/182. May 24, 2006. Available at www.imf.org/external/pubs/ft/scr/2006/cr06182.pdf.

International Monetary Fund. *Arab Republic of Egypt: 2006 Article IV Consultation—Staff Report.* Washington, DC: International Monetary Fund. Country Report No. 06/253, July 11, 2006. Available at www.imf.org/external/pubs/ft/scr/2006/cr06253.pdf.

———. *Sudan: Staff-Monitored Program for 2009–10.* Country Report No. 09/218, July 2009.

Issawi, Charles. *Egypt at Mid-Century.* London: Oxford University Press, 1954.

———, ed. *The Economic History of the Middle East 1800–1914: A Book of Readings.* Chicago: University of Chicago Press, 1966.

Keen, David. *The Benefits of Famine: A Political Economy of Famine and Relief in Southwestern Sudan, 1983–1989.* Princeton, NJ: Princeton University Press, 1994.

Landes, David. *Bankers and Pashas: International Finance and Economic Imperialism in Egypt.* London: Heinemann, 1958.

Mabro, Robert, and Samir Radwan. *The Industrialization of Egypt 1939–1973: Policy and Performance.* Oxford: Oxford University Press, 1976.

Mead, Donald. *Growth and Structural Change in the Egyptian Economy.* Homewood, IL: Richard D. Irwin, 1967.

Niblock, Tim. *Class and Power in Sudan: The Dynamics of Sudanese Politics, 1898–1985.* Albany: State University of New York Press, 1987.

O'Brien, Patrick. *The Revolution in Egypt's Economic System: From Private Enterprise to Socialism, 1952–1965.* London: Oxford University Press, 1966.

Owen, Roger. *The Middle East in the World Economy, 1800–1914.* London: Methuen, 1981.

Posusney, Marsha. *Labor and the State in Egypt: Workers, Unions, and Economic Restructuring.* New York: Columbia University Press, 1997.

Rivlin, Helen. *The Agricultural Policy of Muhammad 'Ali in Egypt.* Cambridge, MA: Harvard University Press, 1961.

Sidahmed, Abdel Salam, and Alsir Sidahmed. *Sudan.* London: RoutledgeCurzon/Taylor and Francis, 2005.

Tignor, Robert. *State, Private Enterprise, and Economic Change in Egypt, 1918–1952.* Princeton, NJ: Princeton University Press, 1984.

Toth, James. *Rural Labor Movements in Egypt and Their Impact on the State, 1961–1992*, 133–163. Gainesville: University Press of Florida, 1999.

Vitalis, Robert. *When Capitalists Collide: Business Conflict and the End of Empire in Egypt.* Berkeley: University of California Press, 1995.

Waterbury, John. *The Egypt of Nasser and Sadat: The Political Economy of Two Regimes.* Princeton, NJ: Princeton University Press, 1983.

Weinbaum, Marvin. *Egypt and the Politics of U.S. Economic Aid.* Boulder, CO: Westview Press, 1986.

World Bank. *Country Assistance Strategy for the Arab Republic of Egypt for the Period FY06–FY09.* Report No. 32190-EG.

———. *Sudan: Stabilization and Reconstruction. Country Economic Memorandum.* Report No. 24620-SU, 2003.

Maghreb

Algeria, Libya, Tunisia, and Morocco—what is known in Arabic as the Maghreb—have been largely oriented toward Europe economically, politically, and culturally. In fact, the four fall into two very different pairs, each of which has followed broadly similar economic paths, though of course with unique features in each country.

Algeria and Libya were the quintessential practitioners of revolutionary state-dominated economics, with Libya being the more extreme. The results were nothing short of disastrous, with both economies in serious difficulty by the early 1990s. Since then, both countries have engaged in modest economic reforms, creating more space for the private sector in what are still strongly state-dominated economies. The one area where each has made the most change is in opening up to foreign investment in the oil and gas industry; the ensuing production increases, combined with higher oil prices, led to sharply higher income in 2004–2007.

Tunisia and Morocco have been an anomaly in the Middle East in that their economic performance has not been as buffeted by revolutionary winds or war as in other countries in the region. In fact, their experience has been much more like that of developing countries in Latin America, Asia, and southeastern Europe than like the politics-tossed Middle East. Each has followed the trends for economic development: at first, import-substituting industrialization led by the state, then export-oriented, private-sector-driven growth. Tunisia has been much more consistent and successful; Morocco has experienced many more problems, political as well as economic.

Algeria and Libya: The Failure of Revolutionary Economics

Algeria and Libya followed much the same path of Third World socialism as did Gamal Abdel Nasser's Egypt. However, unlike Egypt, they had ample oil income and governments that remained committed to this policy path for decades. As a result they ran their economies into the ground by the mid-1990s. Recovery was slow; strong growth only came with the oil boom after 2004.

Pre-Socialism

In many ways, the economic situation under the old regime—pre-1961 French colonialism in Algeria, pre-1970 monarchy in Libya—was better than what followed in both Algeria and Libya. Though they claimed that their anti-Western, anticapitalist policies would improve people's well-being, the policies did not yield such results.

During the 1950s, even though the pro-independence war was getting under way, the Algerian economy grew briskly. Per capita income, adjusted for inflation, rose 6.3 percent a year from 1951 to 1959, achieving a level of income higher than Algeria would have anytime in the next forty-five years (only with the oil boom since 2005 has Algeria reached and then exceeded its colonial per capita income).

Libya's oil wealth is due in no small part to excellent economic policy. At independence in 1951, Libya was a desperately poor country not thought to have particularly promising geology for oil. But the 1955 Petroleum Law was skillfully designed to attract the smaller, independent oil companies who were locked out of opportunities elsewhere. They rushed to invest, and by the early 1960s, Libya was a major oil producer. Throughout the next decade, Libya had by far the most sophisticated oil policies in the world, through which the state steadily increased its per barrel income while structuring incentives in such a way that output rose as well. The monarchy was ill equipped to deal with the rush of oil money, which raised per capita income from $35 in 1951 to $2,000 in 1969 (in current dollars)—a higher income level than Libya had at the end of the twentieth century. The government had been almost nonexistent pre-oil;

indeed, only in 1963 were the independent-minded provinces welded into a unitary state.

Initial State Capitalism

Algeria at independence and Libya after the overthrow of the monarchy each fundamentally changed economic direction, toward state capitalism. The governments in both countries were inspired by revolutionary socialist movements, and in particular by Nasser's example in Egypt.

Newly independent Algeria in 1961 faced the legacy of a bitter war of independence; it claimed that 1 million (10 percent of the population) were killed during the war and another 3 million were regrouped into strategic hamlets, though French figures suggest the numbers were perhaps one-fifth that level. Furthermore, several hundred thousand people went to France after independence, leaving behind much property but taking with them a substantial proportion of the country's savings and abandoning many medium- and small-sized businesses. The country was faced with problems due to the emigration and extensive nationalizations of foreign-owned property (including all foreign-owned agricultural estates). President Ahmed Ben Bella spoke much about workers' self-management but that quickly became an empty facade covering the usual bureaucratic state control. His revolutionary government soon extended its reach far into the economy; in March 1963, it even nationalized hotels, restaurants, and movie theaters, but it continued to allow large foreign firms to operate.

The 1969 overthrow of the Libyan monarchy was widely expected, but the surprise was that the coup was carried out by extremely junior and radical officers. Their initial economic policy was a close imitation of what Nasser had done in Egypt: state-led industrialization and agrarian reform. Yet those policies were singularly inappropriate for a country with as few trained workers as Libya. This resulted in ill-designed and expensive programs to bring water to land previously used as pastures, leading to a sharp drop in agricultural output, still the income source for most Libyans. Meanwhile, the new regime's inexperience working with, and hostility toward, foreign firms brought a rapid reversal to the oil industry. Output fell from 3.3 million barrels per day in 1970 to 1.5 million in 1975.

After Problems, Intensified Radicalism

Faced with initial difficulties in their radical policies, both the Algerian and Libyan governments responded by turning sharply leftward. In each case, the oil boom of the 1970s provided the resources to sustain state socialism, which was increasingly hollowing out the productive economy.

In Algeria, a 1965 coup put power into the hands of the military. The new government, headed by Houari Boumédiènne, was firmly committed to industrialization. Oil production had begun in 1958, ramping up quickly to 560,000 barrels a day by 1964. Oil income, which had been 10 percent of the 1964 budget, rose sharply. The resources were poured into investments in heavy industry. The Ministry of Finance and the State Secretariat for Planning stated that the country could not afford the industrialization drive and that agriculture was being neglected, but their advice was ignored after the 1973 oil price rise brought dramatically more money to the state coffers. Government spending accelerated the shift in Algerian society away from the countryside and agriculture; the 1977 census found that agricultural employment was only 1.0 million out of a population of 17 million, down from 1.3 million out of a population of 12 million in the 1966 census.

Libya's crisis came in 1975 because of a sharp drop in government revenue, the product of a ban on oil exports to the United States, which had previously been an important market for Libya's low-polluting crude. Modest reform was proposed by Planning Minister Umar al-Muhayshi, who had been the architect of the state-capitalist industrialization plans, but he had to flee after his plans for a coup failed. De facto head of state Muammar al-Qaddafi relented on the oil export ban (oil output bounced back to 2 million barrels a day), but he insisted on a dramatic shift toward more extreme state control, especially over commerce. At first Qaddafi concentrated on creating political structures, which he described in the first volume of his *Green Book* as direct popular rule. The replacement of traditional government institutions, such as ministries, by revolutionary bodies devastated economic policymaking. Economic policy got worse in 1978 when Qaddafi issued the second volume of the *Green Book* with the grand subtitle "The Solution to Economic Problems."

He propounded his "Third Universal Theory" (neither capitalist nor socialist), which proclaimed wages and private property to be contrary to God's natural law. Aside from being unsound from an economic point of view, Qaddafi's theories were also heresy in the eyes of many Muslim clerics, especially when he claimed the right to innovate from what the Quran dictated. The merchants and small businessmen who had hitherto been the backbone of support for the revolution were now described by Qaddafi as parasites. The state took over all commerce and abolished all private professional practice, for instance, by lawyers and doctors.

The economy did not function for long under Qaddafi's central lack of planning, in which the state controlled everything but neglected organization and bureaucratic development, hollowing out the economy. His erratic politics hit the oil industry hard; production fell from 3 million barrels at the fall of the monarchy and 2 million barrels in 1975 to an average of 1.1 million barrels a day in 1982–1989. On top of this, Qaddafi wasted much on foreign policy adventures, for instance, spending $12 billion importing arms from 1979 to 1983. His radical foreign policy seriously compounded Libya's economic problems. After the 1986 raid in response to Libya's role in the bombing of a Berlin discotheque, which killed U.S. soldiers, the United States imposed comprehensive economic sanctions on Libya. In 1992, in response to Libya's role in the 1988 bombing of Pan Am 103 over Lockerbie, Scotland, the United Nations Security Council imposed limited economic sanctions, particularly targeting the oil industry and foreign travel.

Initial Reforms

With oil income declining, both Algeria and Libya were forced to make modest adjustments in their economic policies—more willingly and earlier in Algeria, more reluctantly and under greater external pressure in Libya. But the initial reforms were much too timid to have the necessary impact.

Algeria's state-led, heavy-industry-centered approach to development began to change slowly after Chadli Bendjedid became president in 1979 on the death of Boumédiènne. The government tried to strengthen the management of state-owned industries, which were running massive losses. However, the entrenched bureaucracies and the continuing hold of socialist thinking meant the process went slowly at best. The billions of dollars sunk into restructuring the state enterprises were a heavy burden on government finances, which slipped deeply into the red after oil prices collapsed in the mid-1980s. With the state unable to afford social services (such as public housing), people had come to rely upon or to expand public-sector employment, pauperizing large segments of society. The extensive October 1988 riots shook the regime. But rather than abandoning the path of economic reform, it decided to add political reform to the mix, permitting elections. However, the only well-organized forces other than the government were the Islamist opposition, and that is to whom the voters turned out of disgust at the ruling party's poor record over the decades. With the Islamists poised to take power after the first round of the December 1991 national elections, the army forced Bendjedid out and the second round of the elections was canceled. The Islamists launched a bloody and disorganized civil war in which perhaps 50,000 people were killed before it petered out a decade later. The increasing violence, including vicious attacks on any foreigners in the cities, added to the economic woes, though the all-important oil and gas industry centered deep in the desert remained largely immune.

By contrast to Algeria's early recognition of the need for reform, Qaddafi was extremely reluctant to abandon his revolutionary policies. He tried to muddle through with limited economic reforms, namely, the 1987 permission for self-management enterprises and the 1990 permission for private firms. But he continued to spend vast sums on grandiose projects. For instance, he spent billions of dollars on his Great Man-Made River project to transport water hundreds of miles from ancient underground aquifers in the deep desert to farms near the coast; the value of the additional farm output in no way covers the cost of the water.

Crisis and Intensified Reforms

In both Algeria and Libya, economic problems only grew despite the modest reforms. Both governments were eventually forced to adopt much more extensive reform programs—and, in Libya's case, to abandon adventurist foreign policy approach.

After 1988, Algeria lived from year to year on short-term loans so massive that paying back the interest and principal took three-fourths of their exports each year. By 1994, creditors were no longer willing to extend new loans to replace those being repaid. Algeria had no alternative but to reschedule the debts, and the creditors insisted it agree to a program with the International Monetary Fund (IMF). The next decade saw an inconsistent reform record: successful and sustained at the macroeconomic level on such matters as the government budget, unimpressive and patchy at the microeconomic level. Anecdotal evidence suggests that the failure to create employment opportunities for the flood of young people entering the job market complicated the war effort, as disaffected youth facing a bleak life were attracted to Islamist extremism.

In the end, the Qaddafi government abandoned its previous active role of supporting revolutionary and terrorist movements in no small part because of the sanctions. Libya is one of the rare cases in which economic sanctions were instrumental in forcing a government to reconsider its basic foreign policy orientation. The 1999 decision to allow the extradition of the Libyans accused of the Lockerbie bombing led the UN to suspend its sanctions, which were fully lifted in 2003, followed a year later by the end of U.S. sanctions after Qaddafi gave up his missile and weapons of mass destruction programs.

The end of sanctions was accompanied by an intense debate in Libya about economic reform. The task was daunting. When sanctions ended in 2003, three-fourths of employment was still in the public sector. Private business was subject to complex regulations and onerous labor rules, plus businessmen had to worry about whether the government would once again shift direction, given the legacy of policy reversals.

Higher Oil Income

One area where both Algeria and Libya made real reforms was in offering more attractive terms to foreign investors in the hydrocarbon industry, that is, oil and gas. It takes years after a policy change to negotiate agreements and then for the foreign firms to drill the wells and build the pipes to carry the oil and gas, so the effects are felt only after a long lag.

In Algeria's case, the increased production was perfectly timed to catch the dramatic increase in oil and gas prices after 2004. Oil production, which had been stuck at 1.3 million barrels a day from 1988 to 1995, rose to 2.0 million in 2005; gas production, which had plateaued at 5.2 billion cubic feet a day from 1991 to 1994, rose to 8.5 billion in 2005. Combining higher volumes and higher prices, Algeria's oil and gas exports tripled from 2002 to 2006, reaching $55 billion. However, the reassertion after 2005 of nationalist objections to international oil and gas companies led to stagnation or modest decline of Algeria's output of oil and gas in 2006–2009. With output flat, the rise in oil and gas exports to a $77 billion peak in 2008 was due solely to price increases. The prospects are that the production projected for 2014 will likely not exceed the 2005 level.

The Qaddafi government also had good timing. By 2006, oil production had increased to 1.8 million barrels a day—which was 50 percent above the 2002 level, but still only 55 percent of the 1979 level. Production stayed at about that level in 2007–2009. As of late 2009, investment projects under way raised output projections to 2.5 million barrels a day by 2014, finally (almost) restoring production to the 1979 level. Higher output combined with much higher prices raised Libya's oil and gas income sharply from $10 billion in 2002 to $60 billion in 2008. Over the same period, gross national product (GDP) tripled from $30 billion to $90 billion. At that higher level, GDP per capita was $14,500 a year, which is at the high end of the range for developing countries but still below the level in such newly industrialized countries as South Korea and way below the level in the Gulf monarchies. Given the additional oil and gas output likely by 2014, the prospect is that Libya will likely have substantial growth, but it will not be as rich a country as the Gulf monarchies.

The Impact of Reforms

Both Algeria and Libya used their higher oil income to resolve macroeconomic problems, such as Algeria's heavy foreign debt. But the impact on reforms differed sharply in the two cases. In

Algeria, the higher oil and gas revenue after 2001 was used to pay off the foreign debt, which had disappeared by 2006, and then to sharply increase government spending. The 2008 supplementary budget included substantial increases in government salaries and in subsidies, which do little to contribute to growth. On a more positive note for growth prospects, government investment went from 8 percent of GDP in 2001–2004 to 12 percent in 2005–2006 and 15 percent in 2007–2008. Meanwhile, reforms stalled. The slow pace of reforms has meant that the atmosphere for private business remains poor; in 2009, the World Bank ranked Algeria as having one of the worst climates for doing business in the Middle East. Despite wage rates only 15 percent above those in China, profitability is held down by cumbersome bureaucratic procedures. Labor productivity has been slipping; relative to Algeria's trading partners, productivity was 95 percent in 2003 but only 63 percent in 2008.

With oil and gas prices high and reforms stalled, the Algerian economy has become more dependent than ever on oil and gas income. Exports other than oil and gas are trivial, as is foreign investment in fields other than oil and gas. That leaves Algeria highly exposed if oil and gas prices were to fall sharply. For 2001–2008, when oil and gas prices were high, the dependence on oil and gas looked good. Increasing oil and gas prices fueled higher government spending, which in turn created jobs. Unemployment fell from 26 percent in 2001 to 11 percent in 2007. Youth unemployment remained stubbornly high at about 20 percent in 2007. The most likely prospect is that unemployment will shrink further after 2010, but that is primarily because the number of those entering the job market each year will fall quickly after 2010.

In Libya, the Qaddafi government made some modest reforms but the pace was slow and erratic. For instance, Libya applied in 2004 to join the World Trade Organization (WTO) and made some 2005 reforms to what had been one of the most restrictive foreign trade systems in the world, but as of late 2009 Libya had not done much to move its WTO application along or to follow up on the earlier trade reforms. Similarly, in 2006, the Libyan government announced that state-owned firms would as of 2009 face competition from the private sector, but it is not at all clear if that is happening in practice. It appears that change, if it does come, will come only slowly.

Tunisia and Morocco

The economies of Tunisia and Morocco have been strongly oriented toward Europe, which has been the main market for their goods, the main source for foreign investment funds, and the main place to which emigrants have gone for work. The rough analogy would be the relationship between the United States and Mexico and Central America. Indeed, the economies of Tunisia and Morocco have developed more along the lines of Latin American or Asian economies than most of the Middle East. Whereas most Middle East economies have been shaped by political turmoil or by the vagaries of the world oil markets, Tunisia and Morocco have experienced the usual developing country problems of finding industries in which they can be competitive on world markets. Both countries also avoided the worst of the Third World socialism that ravaged their neighbors.

Morocco has generally been one to two decades behind Tunisia from an economic point of view. That has its roots in the events of 1956, when both countries became independent. Several hundred thousand Europeans and Jews emigrated from the new Moroccan state—possibly as many as left Algeria after its bloody independence war. The first fifteen years saw the Moroccan state playing a minimal economic role as the monarchy under Hassan II (ruled 1961–1999) concentrated on asserting its power vis-à-vis parliament and the military (1971–1972 saw two coup attempts) and integrating the former Spanish protectorate with the larger ex-French territory, which did not go easily. During this time, the economy slipped. One important indicator was the gap in per capita income between Morocco and Spain, then still under Franco and not well integrated with Europe; from 1960 and the mid-1970s, the gap went from 3:1 to 5:1.

Import-Substitution Industrialization Led by the State

The first development approach adopted both in Tunisia and Morocco was for the state to sponsor industries whose product would substitute for what had previously been imported. Import-substitution industrialization was the approach advocated by many Western economists before the 1980s. In many ways, this was a lighter version of Third World socialism, with a much larger role for the private sector and a concern about comparative advantage rather than a single-minded pursuit of heavy industry.

After Tunisia's independence in 1956, President Habib Bourguiba's priority was top-down political directives reflecting his secularist and pro-Western orientation. With the economy stagnating, in 1961 Bourguiba appointed Ahmed Ben Salah as minister of planning and national economy, who acted from this position as the main influence on economic policy until 1969. His focus was on promoting industry and agricultural cooperatives. Both this economic policy and Bourguiba's foreign policy orientation fit well with what the United States was advocating at the time; hence from 1962 to 1970, U.S. aid was enough to cover most public investment.

In 1973, Morocco announced several policies to Moroccanize the economy and implement import-substitution industrialization policies. At first there was much enthusiasm that the state could afford extensive investment based on the 1973 tripling in the price of phosphate, a fertilizer of which Morocco has long been a principal source. But the high phosphate prices only lasted two years. In addition, the country became bogged down in a war to hold on to the former Spanish Western Sahara, which it annexed in 1975, against separatists strongly supported by Algeria; in 1977, the war absorbed more than 30 percent of the government budget. Export implemented several changes mid-1970s through 1983. The government persisted with heavy state investments, relying increasingly on foreign borrowing to cover the costs. The economy grew rather quickly; indeed, the gap in per capita income between Morocco and Spain narrowed from 5:1 to 4:1. Dissatisfaction with austerity measures and the poor economic situation led to a 1978–1979 strike wave and 1981 riots.

Modest Reform, Modest Results

Both Tunisia and Morocco eventually announced a reorientation in economic policy toward more reliance on the private sector and greater focus on exports and foreign investment. However, the actual changes were less modest than the announcements, as both governments persisted with extensive investments and tight regulation. The results were as modest as the reforms.

In 1969, Bourguiba dismissed Ben Salah; the next year, he put economic policy in the hands of former Central Bank governor Hédi Nouira whom he appointed prime minister. Nouira announced a pro-market strategy of economic liberalism, which he called *al-infitah.* In practice, the new policies opened up space mostly for family-run small private businesses. Tunisia's textile industry took off: textiles went from 2 percent of Tunisia's exports in 1971 to 30 percent in 1986, mostly sold in the European market. The economy became much more open to foreign trade; exports went from 12 percent of GDP in 1969 to 40 percent in the early 1980s. At the same time, the state continued to make about half of all industrial investment in 1970–1976 and an even larger share in the next decade, as the state dominated heavy industry such as fertilizer (made from Tunisia's low-grade, often unprofitable phosphate), as well as controlling transport and utilities. For all its announced intentions to emphasize the private sector, the state was not able to resist the bureaucratic pressure from state enterprises when income from the modest oil production rose with oil prices. Tunisia's oil production, which averaged 100,000 barrels a day during the 1970s and 1980s, was enough to raise oil's share in GDP to 11 percent in 1981, the peak price year. The oil revenue allowed the government to afford transfers to cover the growing deficits of the state firms as well as their investments.

Morocco's inability to service its debt forced it to turn to the IMF in 1983. The sharp subsidy reductions resulted in riots in which 400 were killed, but the government persisted. To promote exports, the currency was devalued repeatedly, the tax system was thoroughly revised, and trade was liberalized. Morocco experienced respectable growth at 2.2 percent per capita on average (after inflation) from 1982 to 1991, but then the economy flattened out with per capita income barely rising through the rest of the 1990s. One reason may have been that the reform momentum flagged badly after the initial burst. Furthermore, Morocco's economy remains subject to the vagaries of the weather; agricultural output varies tremendously from year to year depending upon rainfall.

Greater Reform, Greater Results

Tunisia (since 1986) and Morocco (since the mid-1990s) have had quite favorable economic circumstances: political stability, proximity to major European markets, and generally solid economic policies. Tunisia has had good but unspectacular growth. At least until 2000, Morocco's economy barely grew, though more recently it may have finally begun to see consistent if modest growth. The reasons for the modest results from such encouraging inputs are not clear. The sad reality is that while economists have a good understanding of why economies crash and burn, they simply do not have a good handle on what explains economic growth under more normal circumstances.

Tunisia faced a serious economic crisis in 1986, as low oil prices plummeted. The government was forced to adopt an austerity budget and enter into programs with the IMF and World Bank, which deregulated prices and lifted import restrictions. The situation was complicated by the incapacity of the aging Bourguiba, who was eased out in 1987 by his protégé Zine el Abidine Ben Ali. The new president went on to implement a continuing series of reforms that year by year reduced the state's role in the economy: privatization, deregulation of prices, ending credit controls, reducing tariffs, and ending quantitative restrictions on imports, among other measures. The year 2006 saw the sale of much of Tunisie Télécom for $2.3 billion, equal to 7.5 percent of GDP. He also persevered at reorienting the economy to be more open to world trade by simplifying procedures for foreign investment, realigning the tax system to encourage exports, and making the exchange rate more competitive. Ben Ali made slow progress at curtailing reliance on foreign borrowing, bringing it down by 2010 to 50 percent of GDP, which is a sustainable level. As sound policies have been sustained longer and longer, the economy has responded more and more. Real per capita GDP rose on average 3 percent a year in the first decade under Ben Ali (1987–1996), rising to 4 percent a year on average from 1997 to 2005, and then 5 percent a year in 2006–2010. Growth has been led by increasing exports, as well as being helped by investments in oil and gas, which made Tunisia a small net energy exporter.

Yet for all its progress, unemployment remains high at 14 percent in 2010; Tunisia continues to face a challenge creating enough jobs for all the young people entering the labor force. And Tunisia is not satisfied with its current income level, which at purchasing power parity (that is, adjusting for differences across countries in prices) is similar to that of Turkey. By 2020, it wants to catch up with Mexico or Poland, which would require Tunisia to have growth rates 2 percent or 4 percent a year higher than in those respective countries. That may be overly ambitious. But already Tunisia has left the rest of the Middle East far behind, other than Israel and the richest oil producers.

Morocco considerably intensified its economic reform program after the mid-1990s. For the rest of that decade, it tried to boost growth rates with vigorous government spending financed by an equally vigorous privatization program, and then after 2000, it emphasized structural reforms such as making education fit better the needs of the labor market and refocusing agriculture on higher-value, less water-using crops. The results were hard to read because agriculture—which has for thirty-five years retained its share at about one-fifth of the economy—is highly volatile depending on the rains. For instance, GDP growth in 2005 and 2007 was only 3 percent a year due to low rainfall, while GDP growth in 2006 and 2008 was 8 percent a year due to ample rainfall. Overall, growth improved steadily if slowly after the mid-1990s. Whereas in the late 1990s per capita income stagnated, it then grew 3 percent a year after the turn of the millennium. Exports and tourism did particularly well during the boom before the world financial crisis of 2008, rising from $17 billion in 2005 to $27 billion in 2008.

Despite the more modest results than could have been hoped for from the substantial reforms in Tunisia and Morocco, the two countries are solidly on a path to steadily increasing income. By contrast, Algeria and Libya are still grappling with how to achieve sustainable growth and overcome the legacy of decades of failed socialist policies. Both Algeria and Libya remain highly dependent on the ups and downs of the world oil market, which has proven a fatal trap for so many oil producers around the world.

References and Further Reading

Aghrout, Ahmed. *Algeria in Transition: Reforms and Development Prospects.* London: RoutledgeCurzon/Taylor and Francis, 2004.

Anderson, Lisa. *The State and Social Transformation in Tunisia and Libya, 1830–1980.* Princeton, NJ: Princeton University Press, 1986.

Bearman, Jonathan. *Qadhafi's Libya.* London: Zed Books, 1986.

Bennoune, Mahfound. *The Making of Contemporary Algeria, 1830–1987: Colonial Upheavals and Post-Independence Development.* Cambridge, UK: Cambridge University Press, 1988.

International Monetary Fund. *Algeria: 2004 Article IV Consultation—Staff Report.* IMF Country Report No. 05/50, February 2005.

———. *Algeria: 2005 Article IV Consultation—Staff Report.* IMF Country Report No. 06/93, March 2006.

———. *Algeria: 2008 Article IV Consultation—Staff Report.* IMF Country Report No. 09/108, April 2009.

———. *Morocco: 2006 Article IV Consultation—Staff Report.* IMF Country Report No. 06/413, November 2006.

———. *Morocco: 2009 Article IV Consultation—Staff Report.* IMF Country Report No. 08/304, September 2008.

———. *Socialist People's Libyan Arab Jahariya: 2004 Article IV Consultation.* Country Report No. 05/83, March 2005.

———. *Socialist People's Libyan Arab Jahariya: 2004 Article IV Consultation.* Country Report No. 06/136, April 2006.

———. *Tunisia: 2006 Article IV Consultation—Staff Report.* IMF Country Report No. 06/207, June 2006.

Murphy, Emma. *Economic and Political Change in Tunisia: From Bourgiba to Ben Ali.* London: Macmillan, 1999.

O'Sullivan, Meghan L. *Shrewd Sanctions: Statecraft and State Sponsors of Terrorism.* Washington, DC: Brookings Institution Press, 2003.

Sensenbrenner, Gabriel. "Algeria's Business Climate: Tax Reforms for Faster Job Creation." In *Algeria: Selected Issues*, 23–45. IMF Country Report No. 06/101, March 2006.

Stewart, Charles. *The Economy of Morocco, 1912–1962.* Cambridge, MA: Harvard University Center for Middle Eastern Studies, 1964.

Vandewalle, Dirk. *A History of Modern Libya.* Cambridge, UK: Cambridge University Press, 2006.

White, Gregory. *A Comparative Political Economy of Tunisia and Morocco: On the Outside of Europe Looking In.* Albany: State University of New York Press, 2001.

World Bank. *Kingdom of Morocco Country Economic Memorandum: Fostering Higher Growth and Productive Diversification and Competitiveness.* World Bank Report No. 32948-MOR.

———. *Republic of Tunisia Development Policy Review: Making Deeper Trade Integration Work for Growth and Jobs.* Report No. 29847-TN, October 2004.

Zartman, I. William, ed. *Tunisia: The Political Economy of Reform.* Boulder, CO: Lynne Rienner, 1991.

Iran

Iran had spectacular economic growth while its oil income was modest; indeed, the oil revenue fueled that growth. Because its oil income was limited, the shah was forced to undertake far-reaching structural reforms in the early 1960s—reforms that then resulted in rapid growth.

But after the 1973 oil price rises, Iran became overly reliant on oil while the rest of its economy suffered. Through the many political changes Iran has experienced since 1973—Islamic revolution, an eight-year war with Iraq, reform/hard-line confrontation—one constant has been erratic and inappropriate economic policies that have frittered away the country's impressive economic potential. When the shah tried to force-step growth at an unachievable pace after 1973, the economy stalled and social problems mounted, setting the scene for the Islamic Revolution in 1979. Once in power, the revolutionary authorities implemented Third World socialism, with the result that the economy headed downhill—a situation made only worse by the long war with Iraq. Postwar, sporadic economic reforms resulted in modest growth, barely sufficient to absorb the many young people entering the labor force.

Imperial Rule to 1973: Rapid Growth

During the early decades of the twentieth century, Reza Shah Pahlavi modernized Iran by creating a modern education system, establishing a National Bank, building hundreds of modern factories, and establishing a modern legal framework. His signature project was the Trans-Iranian Railway, running from the Persian Gulf to the Soviet border, which took 32 percent of all government expenditure at the peak of construction in 1937. He paid for this ambitious modernization program through onerous taxation, avoiding foreign loans. While oil production began in 1906, revenues to Iran from the rapidly growing oil business remained less than 10 percent of government income, despite pressure by Reza Shah on the Anglo-Iranian Oil Company (the precursor of British Petroleum), majority owned by the British government, which earned vastly more from its operation than did the Iranian government.

Reza Shah was forced to abdicate by the British and Soviet governments, who invaded Iran in 1941, suspecting the shah of being pro-German. Momentum for modernization was lost under the weak parliamentary governments that largely eclipsed Reza Shah's son, Mohammed Reza Pahlavi (ruled 1941–1979). Society was polarized, with a large communist party (called Tudeh, or Masses) and an active extremist Islamist movement. Hostility to the Anglo-Iranian Oil Company extended across the political spectrum; in 1951, the *majlis* (parliament) insisted on nationalizing it. To implement the nationalization, the shah appointed as prime minister Mohammed Mossadegh, an effective nationalist. Faced with bitter British opposition to the nationalization, including an effective British blockade of all international sales of Iranian oil, Mossadegh refused to compromise, even though the economy stagnated as a result. In 1953, Mossadegh was overthrown, largely because he lost support at home but in part due to Central Intelligence Agency assistance to his opponents.

From 1953, Mohammed Reza Pahlavi ruled actively and his priority was economic development. In the first decade, his record was mixed. But the economy shot forward after substantial reforms in the early 1960s, especially a far-reaching land reform, a currency devaluation that made Iranian products more price-competitive, and changes to the banking system to encourage lending to entrepreneurs. For the next decade, rapid economic growth only partly based on oil was the foundation for the shah's spectacular drive to transform Iran and to assert its national power on the regional stage.

The Oil Foundation

Throughout the two decades between Mussadiq's fall and the 1973 oil shock, oil exports accounted for more than 80 percent of Iranian foreign exchange income. Broadly speaking, without oil, the Iranian government would have been half the size it actually was. Iran used its oil income effectively in the period through 1972, funding generally reasonable development projects and social infrastructure spending. The proof is Iran's exemplary record of economic growth: in the decade 1963–1972, non-oil gross domestic product (GDP) rose on average 8.7 percent per year.

The shah pushed to expand Iran's oil output way past the prenationalization peak of 0.6 million barrels per day. The expansion in Iranian output was driven by the shah, not by the companies in the consortium of international oil companies running the concession area from which nearly all of Iran's oil was produced. In his single-minded pursuit of raising Iran's oil output—and therefore his revenue—the shah used every method at his disposal, from playing off consortium members against each other to appealing to the U.S. and British governments to press the companies if they wanted his continued strategic cooperation. As he got more control, the shah expanded Iranian oil output at breakneck pace. At the 1959 founding of the Organization of Petroleum Exporting Countries (OPEC), Iran was the group's smallest producer, behind Venezuela, Saudi Arabia, Kuwait, and Iraq, OPEC's other founding members. Iran's output was 4.6 percent of world production. By 1966, Iran's output was second only to that of Saudi Arabia, the longtime OPEC lead producer. In that year, Iran's production continued to rise, peaking at 6.1 million barrels a day in 1974, by which time it had more than doubled its share of world oil output to 10.3 percent. The headlong expansion of output was not good for the country's oil fields. Too much production can cause field pressure to decline, making it hard to extract oil. There are various ways to maintain the pressure in the oil field, such as injecting natural gas, with which Iran is amply endowed, but Iran did little in this regard. In the 1970s, economists projected that Iran was going to have difficulty sustaining large-scale oil exports past the 1980s, as production fell and the expected industrialization and associated prosperity caused consumption to rise.

While the shah was a close political ally of the United States and other Western powers, he was no friend of the international oil companies. He spent twenty-five years pushing the companies as hard as he could to get more for Iran. The concession he negotiated with a consortium of international oil companies after Mussadiq's overthrow was much more favorable to Iran than the prenationalization agreement; the consortium had to divide the profits 50–50 with the Iranian government. By 1960, revenue was more than eight times the 1950 level, only partly because of a 50 percent increase in output. In the 1960s and 1970s, Iran's rapidly growing oil industry enabled the shah to play a central role in shaping the world oil industry, which was part of his ambitions for Iran to be important on the global stage. Iran worked at eroding the Western oil companies' power, both on its own and through OPEC, which it was urging to be more active. Iran continuously pushed for better terms from the oil companies. The National Iranian Oil Company (NIOC) was founded in 1955 as the Iranian government's vehicle for encouraging more competition to the international consortium running the concession area. It sought out smaller oil companies willing to accept a 25–75 profit split in favor of Iran for developing fields outside the concession area. These agreements strengthened Iran's hand in bargaining with the consortium. Under constant pressure from NIOC, the consortium agreed to increase Iran's share of net profits to more than 60 percent in 1970. The shah kept pushing for more revenue. This laid the basis for the historic February 1971 "Tehran Agreement" between the major Middle Eastern OPEC producers and the international oil companies, in which the countries forced the majors to agree to higher prices and better terms. By 1973 the Iranian government, not the oil companies, was in control, setting prices, owning the oil fields, and determining production levels.

Rapid Industrialization

Within a few years after Mossadiq's fall, government policies such as ample credit and a competitive exchange rate facilitated rapid industrialization. In the late 1950s and early 1960s, industrial output grew as much as 20 percent a year. For instance, the production of cotton textiles increased 665 percent in seven years. The government invested heavily in the infrastructure to back up this industrial growth, building roads and utilities for the rapidly expanding cities. The breakneck pace of industrial and infrastructure growth continued from 1963 to 1973, the years covered by the 1963–1968 Third Plan and the 1968–1973 Fourth Plan. Manufacturing employment more than doubled from 1956 to 1972; indeed, one-third of all jobs created in Iran during that time were in manufacturing. Manufacturing output rose by 11.3 percent a year over the decade 1963–1972. To give some examples of what that meant: the annual output of motor vehicles went from a few hundred to 71,000, and that of radios and televisions from zero to 406,000.

The normally cautious World Bank summarized the changes in Iran as of 1971: "However impressive the rise in the macroeconomic aggregates, they do not even begin to show the truly radical transformation of the Iranian economy. In less than 15 years, modern roads and air services have reduced distances many fold. In provincial centers, sleepy repositories of a crumbling past, new industries have sprung up, urban facilities are being built up to truly European levels. . . . In the new factories and on the construction sites, a nation of farmers and nomads has learnt the technical skills of the modern age. . . . Iran has built itself the bases of a large, complex, modern economy."

A more quantitative analysis comes from the International Monetary Fund (IMF), which in a 2004 report concluded, "During 1960–76, Iran enjoyed one of the fastest growth rates in the world: the economy grew at an average rate of 9.8 percent in real terms, and real per capita income grew by 7 percent on average."

The rapid growth of the decade 1964–1973 rested in no small part on the entrepreneurial skills of Iranians, which government policy empowered. A good example of the new industrialists was Ahmad Khayami: when his dried-fruit exporting business was bankrupted by the economic disruption of World War II, he started a car wash business, from which he moved to being the local agent for Mercedes-Benz, then into car repair, and then to assembling cars. Once he began making Peykan cars, which still dominate the Iranian car business, he handed over the Iran National firm to his brother and started Kouroush Stores, the first large-scale retailers in Iran.

Despite the rapidly rising incomes, the shah got little credit from the people for the country's economic success. Part of the problem was that not everyone in society benefited equally from the prosperity. While the spending power of even poor Iranians increased, so too did the gap between rich and poor. There was also huge geographic disparity; in 1971, average household expenditures in Tehran were more than two-and-a-half times those in the impoverished southeastern province of Kerman.

But the bigger political problem for the shah was that economic modernization was not well accepted by Iranian intellectuals. The dominant intellectual trend was Third Worldism, which is a mixture of socialism and anti-imperialism that blames the West, especially America and the local elites who work with it, for the shortcomings in developing countries. In Iran, Third Worldism went beyond the usual neo-Marxism to take on a strong nativist element. One of the most influential books of the period was a 1962 volume by an important modern Iranian author, Jalal al-Ahmad, with the title in Persian *Gharbzadegi,* a made-up word usually translated as "Westoxication" or "Occidentosis." Al-Ahmad's theme was that Iranians are abandoning their traditions to ape the West, at the cost of losing their culture and history. *Gharbzaedgi* combined a criticism of Western culture with a neo-Marxist perspective on economics that rejected capitalism and blamed imperialism as the main source of Iran's problems.

Land Reform

At first, agriculture, which remained the main source of income for most Iranians, did not share in the boom. While the data are poor, it appears that output of the staple food crops rose less than 2 percent a year from 1953 through 1962. This agricultural stagnation was the background for the shah's surprising 1962 decree of Iran's first real land reform. The shah combined the land reform and other modernizing measures such as women's suffrage into what he called "the White Revolution" (as distinct from Marxist red revolutions). The economic effects of this program were much less than its political impact.

Clerics led a fierce opposition to the White Revolution. They linked the White Revolution to the shah's pro-American policies, such as an agreement about stationing U.S. forces in Iran, and opposed them both. Incendiary speeches by an ambitious cleric named Ruhollah Khomeini led to his arrest in June 1963. Rioting broke out in several cities, and Khomeini was sent into exile.

Even though it took years to really get going, the land reform resulted in striking change in the countryside. Before land reform, only 10 to 12 percent of the land was in the hands of small proprietors; the rest belonged to the crown, large landlords (of whom there were perhaps 100,000), and religious endowments. The land reform's first phase, begun in 1962, was in theory rather bold, but in practice there were many ways landlords could retain their land, so less than 10 percent of Iran's rural population became landowners in this first phase. The second and third phases of the land reform reached more farmers. By the 1970s, about half of cultivated land belonged to small farmers, but these figures are by no means precise.

However, landownership is not necessarily the most important issue for Iran's rural population. The heart of the Iranian agricultural dilemma is water, not land. The basic problem for Iranian farmers has been how to improve access to water and share risk in the event of drought. Water was so important that in the customary formula for sharing the crop, one-fifth of the crop went to he who owned the water. The other four shares were for the land, the seed (effectively also the credit), the oxen, and the labor. The landowner provided the first three; a village rich man typically provided the oxen; and the farmer got only the one-fifth share for labor. The traditional system for water delivery was through water channels (*qanats*), underground aqueducts that carried water, sometimes for miles, from mountains onto alluvial plains.

In some parts of Iran, land was owned and rented for cash in a system similar to that in the West. In most of Iran, however, access to land was more complicated than in the Western-style ownership system. The landowner shared control over the land with a large minority of the rural population, perhaps 40 percent, who held traditional land-use rights. Those farmers were organized into multifamily teams that worked the land together. The farmers' rights to the land were not tied to a particular plot of land. Each year, the village headman redistributed the land in order to rotate access to the portions of land with better access to water. Another large minority of the rural population, perhaps another 40 percent, had no land-use rights and were seasonal laborers.

Into this complex system came a land reform that was largely if not entirely designed around landownership, on the implicit assumption that all of Iran had tenant farmers paying cash rent to absentee landlords for access to fixed land plots, without paying attention to water. The effect of this reform was to disrupt the traditional water-use system, because it was hard to sustain qanats under a system of pure individual private ownership, especially when some owners bought pumps, which lowered the water level to the point that the flow of water in the qanat was reduced.

The land reform distributed land only to those with land-use rights. The impact of the land reform on each individual depended on whether he was allocated land with good water rights or with mediocre ones. Those with no land-use rights—typically the poorest farmers—lost all access to land and were forced to seek wage employment, either on farms or more typically in cities. All in all, there is no clear evidence on how the ordinary Iranian farmer was affected by the land reform.

Despite these disruptive institutional changes, agricultural output grew 4 percent a year between 1963 and 1972. To be sure, that was only slightly faster than population growth. And because Iranians were becoming richer, they were eating more food, so Iran was importing more and more food.

The land reform and the rapid industrialization capped the transformation of Iran from a rural to an urban society. By the 1976 census, only a bare majority of Iranians remained in rural areas. The 1976 census recorded fewer people working in agriculture than had the 1956 census: in 1976, only one-third of Iranians worked in agriculture, compared to 56 percent in 1956. In the decade before the 1976 census, more than two million people moved from the countryside to the cities. Even more spectacular was the decline of nomadism. Nomads had been a significant force during the nineteenth century—certainly more than 10 percent of the population, perhaps twice that. The nomads were pressed to settle in villages and cities, in the process shattering tribal identity. Their numbers fell to less than 1 percent of the national population.

Boom, Revolution, War, and Recovery, 1974–1996

The 1979 Iranian Islamic Revolution was not about economics, but the economic situation played no small role in undermining the shah. The key problem was that the oil price revolution of 1973 led the shah to predict an unrealizable rapid transformation of Iran into an advanced industrial country, whereas what actually happened was that much of the oil wealth was wasted due to economic mismanagement. Perhaps some rejected the rapid social change on the grounds that it was un-Islamic, as is often alleged by those who think the revolution was due to too-rapid modernization, but certainly many others rebelled because they could see little good coming from all the money being spent.

Once the revolutionaries came to power, the economic situation deteriorated sharply under the dual battering from ill-thought-out quasi-socialist policies and the war with Iraq. Every time it looked like the revolutionaries would be forced to compromise their hard-line stances, oil income came to their rescue. By the time the war ended in 1988, average incomes had dropped by more than half. The grand hopes for postwar recovery at first looked like they would be fulfilled with a rush of investment. But soon the entrenched revolutionaries who benefited from the complex government regulations reasserted their power, and the government fell back into its old ways of muddling through on the strength of oil income. In short, the decades from 1974 to 1996 were a lost economic opportunity in which Iran's progress was held back by oil wealth, which permitted avoiding difficult decisions.

Unmet Expectations and the Revolution

Paradoxically, the flood of oil income after 1973 led to slower growth: too much was attempted, and the resulting logjams stopped progress. In contrast to its impressive record at managing growth in 1963–1973, the imperial government badly mismanaged the economy after the 1973 oil price increases. Government revenue from oil rose from $5 billion in 1973 to $19 billion the next year. With this flood of money, the Fifth Plan covering the five years 1973–1978 was revised in August 1974 to raise spending from $44 billion to $123 billion. In effect, the shah decided to press ahead full steam on every front, ignoring the serious constraints to implementing so many projects and so many policy changes simultaneously. The dramatically higher spending on everything from the military, infrastructure investments, and government salaries to social welfare programs increased demand for goods and services to a level the domestic economy could not supply. Nor could Iran's transport system handle the ensuing demand for imports; in 1975, ships had to wait 160 to 250 days to enter Iran's principal port, Khorramshahr, at the tip of the Persian Gulf. Iran had to pay more than $1 billion in demurrage charges. The result was a sharp increase in inflation to an average of 15 percent per year in 1973–1978 from less than 4 percent in the preceding five years.

The Fifth Plan was quickly abandoned in practice; every government agency assumed it had priority. The scramble for scarce skilled manpower and inputs became extraordinarily wasteful. Despite contracts signed and money spent, planned programs were unable to proceed in an orderly manner due to the supply constraints. During the entire 1973–1978 oil boom period under the shah, despite billions of dollars spent, not one new petrochemical plant, steel mill, or nuclear power plant was completed, and many industrial projects contracted for prior to 1973 remained unfinished. Meanwhile, the demand for labor on government projects pushed wages up to a level at which private industry had serious problems competing with imports.

The changes Iran was undergoing in 1973–1978 caused much social disruption and undercut the impact of higher income. Even among the relatively affluent Tehran middle class, the raging inflation hit hard, with consumer prices doubling between 1973 and 1978. Planned improvements in social services were only erratically met; for instance, while more than a million housing units were planned, only 124,000 were built. Added to which, the government tried to blame economic problems on price-gouging merchants, and student squads hauled merchants accused of violating price controls before special courts. Meanwhile, the shah alienated industrialists and benefited few workers when he ordered that 49 percent of shares in major companies be distributed to workers to offset the impact of inflation. And the modern professional and industrial classes were unhappy at the high salaries paid to the 60,000 foreign workers, whose very presence insulted the proud Iranian nationalists. Also fueling the economic discontent was the devastating impact of the overheated economy on the mainstays of traditional Iranian life. The carpet industry, which employed 300,000 people scattered in villages across Iran, could not compete with the salaries available in towns.

Some of the worst policies after 1973 were in the countryside. What little development funds the government allocated to rural areas were often diverted into mechanized agriculture corporations, which operated at massive losses and did not increase the well-being of the farmers. The main impact of the oil boom on agriculture lay in the devastating impact on farmers of the pro–urban development policies. The government used oil revenue to subsidize imports of grain, meat, and milk products, which served to reduce the prices received by farmers. Meanwhile, the government imposed price controls on key crops, many of which had to be sold through government-run marketing monopolies. And the cost of inputs soared while labor was attracted away by the better opportunities in the cities. The result was stagnant production. By the time of the Islamic Revolution, agriculture provided only 15 percent of non-oil output and just 9 percent of overall output.

By late 1976, the economy was in a bad state, with national income growing only slowly while shortages of electricity, water, cement, and some foodstuffs constrained output and fed popular discontent. The shah reversed course, acknowledging he had wrongly pushed too fast. He appointed a new prime minister who suspended many development projects and introduced an IMF-style stabilization program in March 1978. The overheated economy began to cool and inflation abated. But the price of curtailed government spending was fewer new jobs and falling real incomes, while the supply constraints meant that shortages persisted. The economic constraints played no small part in feeding the political discontent that exploded in Iran's streets in 1978.

The general mood of the time was one of unmet expectations. The shah had promised the Iranian people European-style income, and he could not deliver. In one 1974 interview, the shah promised, "In 25 years Iran will be one of the world's five flourishing and prosperous nations . . . I think that in 10 years' time our country will be as you [Britain] are now." The shah's forecast, which reinforced proud Iranians' self-conception of their country's natural greatness, only exacerbated the gap between what they expected and what they had. Adding to their frustration was the shah's profligate lifestyle and all-pervasive influence. Few sectors of the economy were untouched by the activities of the Pahlavi Foundation, which managed much of the shah's wealth.

The Revolutionary War Economy

While disappointment about the economy contributed to the shah's unpopularity, the revolution was about politics, not economics. The economy was not a priority for the new revolutionary leader, Ayatollah Ruhollah Khomeini. His comment about economic concerns was, "I do not accept that any prudent individual can believe that the purpose of all these sacrifices was to have less expensive melons." Some of his followers—bazaar merchants and traditionalist clerics—opposed almost any state intervention as incompatible with traditional Islamic jurisprudence. Others of his followers were Western-oriented technocrats who wanted state sponsorship of rapid development. Neither of these two groups prevailed. Within two years after the revolution, the levers of power were firmly controlled by a Third Worldist group wanting comprehensive state control in the name of social justice. Faced immediately after the 1979 revolution with chaos in the factories and a banking system close to collapse, the new government nationalized much of the economy. At the same time, extensive assets of the former shah and his supporters were confiscated and transferred to new revolutionary foundations (*bonyads*), which were controlled by revolutionary ideologues. Only smaller industries remained in private hands.

Over time, the state's control over the economy grew even further. After war with Iraq started in 1980, the state controlled prices, parceled out foreign exchange only to the politically favored, effectively banned foreign investment, and strictly regulated all economic activity through an unwieldy permit system. Rationing was introduced for staples, with ration coupons distributed at mosques. Since the prices of rationed goods were well below market prices, the producers of such goods, primarily farmers, had little incentive to increase output and felt cheated because their income suffered. The manufacturing sector suffered from a stranglehold of price controls and severe shortages of tightly rationed foreign inputs; profits depended on manipulating the complicated regulations. In this atmosphere of legal confusion and bureaucratic restriction, the companies that did best were those owned by the state or by the various *bonyads*.

The official exchange rate was not adjusted even though prices soared; as a result, the price of the dollar on the black market became more than ten times its official rate, and anyone who could get permission to buy dollars at the official rate (in order to import goods) was then able to sell the dollars (or, more often, the goods imported with those dollars) at a huge markup. The foreign exchange situation was made worse by bouts of high government spending which exhausted the available foreign exchange, followed by periods of excessive restrictions, including periodic bans on "luxury" imports that largely served to enrich those who were able to use connections to get permission to import such items.

The economy performed badly under the impact of these poorly designed policies. Adjusted for inflation, national income fell more than 20 percent between 1977 and 1989, while the population rose at a brisk clip, with the result that per capita income fell by nearly half, at a time when the economy was benefiting from considerable investment and the labor force was increasingly better educated. By the IMF's calculation, these factors should have led to economic growth of 7.2 percent a year, whereas the economy actually shrank 2.4 percent a year. The government's surveys on household budgets confirm the dramatic decline in living standards; adjusted for inflation, the average urban household's income fell in 1989 to less than half its 1978 level. The modern middle classes, such as professionals, were particularly hard-hit, while those with good political connections did well.

Having criticized the shah for excessive dependence on oil exports, the revolutionaries did worse: oil's share in government revenue and exports rose, as non-oil revenues and exports fell. Oil exports, which were badly hurt in 1980–1982 by the continuing impact of the revolution and then the start of the war, recovered in 1982–1983 to 1.7 million barrels a day and then stayed more or less at that level throughout the 1980s.

Blocked Postwar Recovery

The economy did well after the war ended in 1988 and Ali Akbar Hashemi Rafsanjani took over as president in 1989, at about the same time that Khomeini died. Rafsanjani, the first Iranian revolutionary leader to put a priority on economic development, forced through the majlis the Islamic Republic's first Five-Year Plan, which sought to downsize the state control from the wartime era. Under the limited reforms he introduced, the economy recovered, with GDP rising 8 percent per annum in real terms during 1989–1993. Iran increased its oil production from 2.6 million barrels per day in 1989 to 3.9 million in 1993. But even the extra oil income was not enough for the government's ambitious plans. Determined to show that the privation of the war years was over, the Rafsanjani government ran up a $28 billion foreign debt, much of it short-term borrowing. This money, raised mostly in Europe, financed a wave of imports, which more than doubled to $24 billion a year.

Personal income rose 20 percent in the first three years after the 1988 ceasefire ending the war with Iraq. But that did not impress Iranians, who had been told for years that once the war ended, times would be even better than they had been under the shah. That did not happen: the 1992 income was still only 62 percent of the prerevolution level. On the other hand, the revolutionary government had been able to dramatically improve the basic social indicators. Infant mortality was cut in half; consumption of staples like meat, sugar, and rice increased significantly; and ownership of consumer items like telephones and washing machines rose dramatically.

After 1993, Rafsanjani ran into strong resistance to further reform from entrenched revolutionary interests determined to protect their sinecures. Rafsanjani was unwilling to risk a confrontation. The very limited character of reforms can be seen by the experience with privatization, gasoline, and foreign exchange. Privatization, in many cases, consisted of selling shares in the state-owned firms on the stock market where nearly all were bought by the state-owned banks. Gasoline prices remained highly subsidized; Oil Minister Gholam-Reza Aqazadeh warned that fuel subsidies cost $6 billion in 1994. Foreign exchange remained subject to complicated rules that only encouraged corruption. Inaction on such issues undercut Rafsanjani's standing as a reformer, especially when his family members enriched themselves and openly engaged in influence peddling. Indeed, at around this time, the term *aqa-zadeh*—son of an important person—entered Iranian parlance to describe the family members of high-ranking figures in the Islamic Republic who cashed in on their positions. When Rafsanjani's presidential term ended in 1997, the economy remained weighed down by corrupt revolutionaries and powerful foundations that could use their political connections to stifle any competition, for example, the Imam Reza Foundation that owned 90 percent of the arable land in Khorasan, and the Foundation for the Oppressed and Self-Sacrificers (Bonyad-e Mostazafan va Janbazan) that controlled $12 billion in assets with 400,000 workers.

In 1993–1999, the economy was hit hard by a weakening of the oil market. As the price of oil fell in 1993, Iran was no longer able to service the substantial foreign debt it had run up to pay for the postwar boom. The Rafsanjani government had little choice but to use Iran's oil income to repay its foreign debt. To generate $5 billion for foreign debt payments, imports were cut almost in half in 1995. Reducing imports that much required reversing the postwar market reforms and returning to the unpopular government-controlled allocation of foreign exchange. The debt crisis, which lasted from 1993 to 1997, brought an end to the postwar boom. The popular mood was sour, and the blame was put firmly on hard-line policies, especially isolation from the United States, which complicated Iran's efforts to reschedule its existing debt and to arrange new loans. The Iranian debt crisis of the 1990s is a classic example of oil's double curse: not only is high oil income often wasted, but the temptation is great to borrow against the inflated views of the country's prospects, such that when prices crash—as they inevitably do—the economy is hit both by the lower oil income and the foreign debt burden.

The Rafsanjani government had hoped to offset the worst effects of the foreign debt crisis by opening the country up to foreign direct investment in oil and gas production—a remarkably bold initiative given the historical sensitivity in Iran about oil nationalization. But, again, the reality fell far short for two main reasons. First was the sharp deterioration in U.S.-Iranian relations, which led President Bill Clinton in March 1995 to forbid U.S. firms from making oil investments, torpedoing the deal that Iran had negotiated with the U.S. oil firm Conoco. Clinton reinforced that policy two months later with a general U.S. ban on investment in and trade with Iran. The U.S. Congress enacted a 1996 law designed to press European and Japanese firms to eschew investment in the Iranian oil industry.

The second reason for little foreign investment in Iran's oil and gas fields was that Iran did not offer attractive business terms. Rather than allowing a straightforward foreign investment, it insisted on complicated "buy back" arrangements in which the foreign oil company puts in money up front and then receives oil in payment. Further complicating foreign investment was Iranian nationalistic pride, exaggerated expectations about Iran's importance to oil firms, and a suspicion that oil firms were cheating Iran by not offering good enough terms. As on previous occasions, Iran had assumed that its oil wealth would in the end prove its trump card, which once again it did not.

Reform and Counter-Reformation, 1997–2009

The deep discontent that led to the surprising 1997 election of reformist president Mohammed Khatami was fueled at least as much by social restrictions as by economic despair. Furthermore, Khatami had no clear economic ideas, unlike his well-formed and articulately stated views on political and social reform. His long-awaited August 1998 Economic Rehabilitation Plan was blunt in description of the problems but modest in its proposals, as was the Third Five-Year Plan (2000–2005). The different political factions all agreed that the economy was in bad shape and that drastic steps were needed. Indeed, this was a favorite theme of Supreme Leader Ali Khamenei (Ayatollah Khomeini's successor), who argued the government's priority should be fixing the economy rather than political reform. But no one was willing to tackle the entrenched interests, be it the subsidies for consumer goods that drained the public coffers or the rampant corruption that enriched the politically well-connected but scared away foreign investors. As an example of the distortions, extraordinarily cheap domestic energy prices, especially for gasoline, meant that Iran, with 1 percent of the world's population, consumed 9 percent of the world's energy production.

Failure to make much headway on reform meant that the economy remained lackluster during the 2000–2005 Third Plan period, despite the dramatic increase in oil income from rising oil prices. To be sure, consumption grew handily (6.6 percent per year) and unemployment fell some, but that was not an impressive result when the price of oil was three times the plan's forecast of $12.50 per barrel. Indeed, the Third Plan years were characterized by increasing reliance on oil, which provided 64 percent of the government's income, not counting the massive implicit subsidies from cheap energy. The growing disillusionment with Khatami was fed by the obvious diversion of the new oil wealth into the pockets of a few—and the reformers were as implicated in corruption as were the hard-liners.

President Mahmoud Ahmadinejad, who assumed office in 2005, was committed to reviving the spirit of the early revolutionary years, which was a period when economic policy was particularly poorly managed. During his election campaign, Ahmadinejad promised to bring the country's oil wealth to the people's tables (literally, to their *sofreh*, which is the cloth spread on the floor under serving dishes in traditional Iranian homes, where meals are eaten while seated on the floor). He also adopted a variety of other populist stances, such as expressing doubts about whether foreign investment benefited Iran. Once in office, Ahmadinejad put many of his populist policies in place. He fired two Central Bank governors who refused to cut interest rates as he directed. He ordered the state-owned banks to direct much of their lending to causes he favored irrespective of the ability of the borrower to repay; banks in 2009 were estimated to hold $38 billion in nonperforming loans. He rejected advice from professional economists, disbanding the long-important agency historically known as the Plan and Budget Organization (the name was later changed to Management and Planning Organization).

Ahmadinejad deepened the confrontation with the international community over Iran's nuclear and missile programs, which led by late 2009 to four UN Security Council resolutions imposing sanctions. Those sanctions were primarily aimed at Iran's nuclear and missile programs as well as "dual use" items, that is, those with both military and civilian uses. However, the UN sanctions, combined with the worsening Iranian human rights record after the contested 2009 presidential elections, have created in some business circles the impression that Iran is a problematic country. For instance, Siemens and Nokia received considerable negative publicity for the role that technology they had sold Iran played in censoring the flow of news about the 2009 protests. An active U.S. government campaign to warn banks about the risks to their reputations from doing business in Iran led most European banks to curtail or cease their activities in Iran.

To his credit, Ahmadinejad implemented some policy reforms that his predecessors had long discussed but never acted on, despite urging from the IMF and World Bank. The most important reform was to reduce oil subsidies, which the IMF estimated if unchanged would have cost Iran $32 billion—equivalent to 11 percent of GDP—in

2007. In that year, Iran introduced a two-tier gasoline pricing system, with a ration available at the subsidized price of $.05 a liter and then unlimited amounts available at a much higher price ($0.40 a liter as of late 2009). As of late 2009, Ahmadinejad is pressing the parliament to accept similar reforms to phase out the other subsidies, replacing them with cash payments to needy families. His government also introduced a value-added tax, a reform long urged by the IMF.

The reform Ahmadinejad emphasized the most was a privatization program, which had such complicated and conflicting provisions that it ended up doing little to reduce the state's influence in the economy. Instead, it reinforced a trend toward increasing economic influence for the Islamic Revolutionary Guard Corps (IRGC). Using their political connections (for instance, to have competitors excluded on dubious national security grounds), firms linked to the IRGC have purchased some of Iran's largest firms. They have also secured multibillion-dollar contracts from the government and state companies for work, such as construction projects, which they are manifestly unable to do; they typically subcontract the jobs to firms they had pushed aside during the bidding, with the IRGC-linked companies pocketing a large commission. This sort of corruption has become more rampant as the IRGC's role in Iran's political life has grown after the contested 2009 presidential elections, which led to widespread protests.

In 2005–2009, economic reforms had only a modest effect on the economy compared to the massive increase in oil revenue due to the high oil prices. During Ahmadinejad's first term (2005–2009), Iran's oil exports were three times what they had been during the eight years under his predecessor, Khatami. The $37 billion increase in oil exports from 2005 to 2008 translated into $35 billion in additional government revenue. During that period, the government raised spending by $15 billion on grants and benefits, mostly to the politically well-connected, and $11 billion on "other" unidentified items, which is a category used in the past for national security spending such as the nuclear program or financial assistance to groups such as Lebanon's Hizballah. It is not apparent if either the grants or the "other" spending contributed much to economic growth.

The high oil income should have made possible an extraordinary boom in 2005–2009, such as that enjoyed by Iran's southern neighbors in the oil-rich Arab monarchies of the Gulf. Instead, Iran's economy grew modestly in 2005–2009 under Ahmadinejad, averaging about 5.5 percent a year. That growth has not been rapid enough to create sufficient jobs for the approximately 800,000 people joining the labor market each year. One result is the annual emigration of somewhere around 100,000 educated men and women, a brain drain Iran can ill afford.

Iran faces some serious potential vulnerabilities. The IMF estimated that Iran would have run a budget deficit in 2010 if oil prices were below $90 a barrel, even without new populist initiatives, increased political turmoil that affects business, or additional UN sanctions. But the priority for the Ahmadinejad government continues to be its populist policies and its support for the IRGC. Nothing could better capture the oil curse that has afflicted Iran for decades. So long as difficult decisions are postponed on expectation that oil income will save the day, Iran's economy will not realize its great potential.

References and Further Reading

Afshar, Haleh, ed. *Iran: A Revolution in Turmoil.* Albany: State University of New York Press, 1985.

Al-Ahmad, Jalal. *Occidentosis: A Plague from the West*, trans. R. Campbell. Berkeley, CA: Mizan Press, 1984.

Alikhani, Hossein. *Sanctioning Iran: Anatomy of a Failed Policy.* London: I.B. Tauris, 2000.

Alizadeh, Parvin, ed. *The Economy of Iran: Dilemmas of an Islamic State.* London: I.B. Tauris, 2000.

Amid, Javad, and Amjad Hadjikhani. *Trade, Industrialization, and the Firm in Iran: The Impact of Government Policy on Business.* London: I.B. Tauris, 2005.

Amuzegar, Jahangir. *The Dynamics of the Iranian Revolution: The Pahlavis' Triumph and Tragedy.* Albany: State University of New York Press, 1981.

———. *Iran: An Economic Profile.* Washington, DC: Middle East Institute, 1977.

———. *Iran's Economy Under the Islamic Republic.* London: I.B. Tauris, 1993.

———. "Iran's Third Development Plan: An Appraisal." *Middle East Policy* 12:3 (Fall 2005): 46–63.

———. "Iran's 20-Year Economic Perspective: Promises and Pitfalls." *Middle East Policy* 16:3 (Fall 2009): 41–57.

———. "Islamic Social Justice, Iranian Style." *Middle East Policy* 14:3 (Fall 2007): 60–78.

Ansari, Ali. *Modern Iran Since 1921: The Pahlavis and After.* London: Longman, 2003.

Bakhash, Shaul. *The Reign of the Ayatollah: Iran and the Islamic Revolution.* New York: Basic Books, 1984.

Beck, Lois. *The Qashqa'i of Iran.* New Haven, CT: Yale University Press, 1986.

Bharier, Julian. *Economic Development in Iran 1900–1970.* London: Oxford University Press, 1971.

Buchta, Wilfried. *Who Rules Iran? The Structure of Power in the Islamic Republic.* Washington, DC: Washington Institute for Near East Policy and the Konrad Adenauer Stiftung, 2000.

Clawson, Patrick, and Michael Rubin. *Eternal Iran: Continuity and Chaos.* New York: Palgrave, 2005.

Esfahani, Hadi Salehi, and Farzad Taheripour. "Hidden Public Expenditures and the Economy in Iran." *International Journal of Middle East Studies* 34:4 (November 2002): 691–718.

Gheissari, Ali, ed. *Contemporary Iran: Economy, Society, and Politics.* Oxford: Oxford University Press, 2009.

Goodell, Grace. *The Elementary Structures of Political Life: Rural Development in Pahlavi Iran.* New York: Oxford University Press, 1986.

Graham, Robert. *Iran: The Illusion of Power.* Rev. ed. New York: St. Martin's Press, 1980.

International Monetary Fund. *Islamic Republic of Iran: Selected Issues.* IMF Country Report 04/308, September 2004.

———. *Islamic Republic of Iran: Staff Report for the 2005 Article IV Consultation.* IMF Country Report No. 06/154, February 2006.

Kanovsky, Eliyahu. *Iran's Economic Morass: Mismanagement and Decline Under the Islamic Republic.* Washington, DC: Washington Institute for Near East Policy, 1997.

Katousian, Homa, and Hossein Shahidi, eds. *Iran in the 21st Century: Politics, Economics, and Conflict.* London: Routledge, 2008.

Kazemi, Farhad. *Poverty and Revolution in Iran: The Migrant Poor, Urban Marginality, and Politics.* New York: New York University Press, 1980.

McLachlan, Keith. "Economic Development 1921–79." In *The Cambridge History of Iran. Volume 7: From Nadir Shah to the Islamic Republic*, ed. Peter Avery, Gavin Hambly, and Charles Melville. Cambridge, UK: Cambridge University Press, 1991.

———. *The Neglected Garden: The Politics and Ecology of Agriculture in Iran.* London: I.B. Tauris, 1988.

Najmabadi, Afsaneh. *Land Reform and Social Change in Iran.* Salt Lake City: University of Utah Press, 1987.

World Bank. *Iran—Medium Term Framework for Transition: Converting Oil Wealth to Development.* Washington, DC: World Bank, 2003.

Israel

While the differences with its Muslim-majority neighbors are many, Israel's economy has suffered from much the same pattern of up-and-down growth. In its case, however, the ups have gone farther and the downs have been less significant. Years of rapid growth pre-1973 gave way to a war economy suffering from increasingly poor management until the country reached the brink of hyperinflation in the mid-1980s. In 1985 a sharp change in direction stabilized the situation, setting the stage for the rapid growth in the 1990s, fed by Russian immigration and an effective move into high technology. In the new millennium, as the high-tech boom collapsed and conflict with the Palestinians escalated, the economy stumbled, though it ultimately recovered with renewed reforms and de facto separation from the Palestinians.

The record of Israel's economic performance can be read as demonstrating the economic impact of the Arab-Israeli conflict, but it can also be interpreted as evidence that domestic economic policy matters more than international politics. Indeed, it is striking that outside observers attribute much influence over the Israeli economy to the Arab-Israeli conflict, whereas professional economists utilizing statistical tools place much stress on the impact of Israeli economic policies.

Stellar Record, 1948–1972

Israel underwent dramatic transformation in the first twenty-five years after its establishment in 1948. Driven by immigration, the population rose almost fourfold, from 870,000 in 1948 to 3.3 million in 1973, which translates into an increase of about 5.5 percent per year. In spite of the burden of absorbing so many immigrants, income per person doubled and national income rose at least sevenfold—an average growth rate of about 9 percent per year.

Upon independence in 1948, the new country faced a mixed situation. On the plus side were experienced administrators, a substantial industrial sector, and decent infrastructure; on the minus side were damage from the independence war, a trade boycott by all its neighbors, and the departure of many Palestinian Arabs, who through their dominance in agriculture had previously supplied most of the country's food. The overwhelming factor, however, was immigration: the country's population doubled in four years. Few of those arriving spoke the national language (Hebrew); many of the 40 percent arriving from Asia and Africa were illiterate. Most immigrants had job skills of limited use in their new land, which needed agricultural laborers more than merchants. Expanding employment was further limited by severe capital shortage, as well as the rigid labor policies of the extraordinarily powerful Histadrut national labor federation. Domestic agricultural and industrial production could not supply demand, requiring a level of imports the country could ill afford. In Israel's early years, transfers—that is, grants, private and public—covered much of the cost of imports.

The economic situation eased by the mid-1950s and remained solid through 1965. Unemployment, which had been in the double digits, declined to 4 percent by the late 1950s and stayed there through 1965. The import gap shrank relative to gross domestic product (GDP), and after 1953, 75 percent of the gap was covered by transfers, including German reparations of $850 million from 1953 to 1964 (in addition to a larger amount of German restitution payments to individuals). Despite a sharp recession in 1965–1966 and the shock of the 1967 Six-Day War, the economy resumed its solid growth by 1968. To be sure, the seeds of future problems were starting to grow. After the 1967 war, Israeli military spending rose sharply, reaching an average of 22 percent of GNP in 1968–1972 compared with 10 percent in 1962–1966.

War Economy and Crisis, 1973–1985

The defense burden on Israel's economy was magnified after the 1973 war. Defense spending rose to an extraordinary 28 percent of gross national product (GNP) on average in 1974–1980, as Israel was caught in an arms race with Arab states well financed by oil income and having access to the most modern Soviet arms on very favorable terms. In 1974–1980, Israel spent an average of $1.9 billion on defense imports per year—12 percent of its GNP—while receiving only $0.6 billion a year in U.S. military aid grants. That may overstate the defense burden, since in 1974–1980 Israel also received an average of $0.4 billion a year in U.S. economic grants. It also borrowed from the U.S. government an average of $1.2 billion a year, $0.9 billion of which was for arms purchases; however, all the U.S. loans were at market interest rates. Besides the pressure this placed on the balance of payments, the expenditure was a burden on the budget, which had to bear the cost of local expenditures for the military, such as wages and Israel's own arms output, which averaged an additional 16 percent of GNP in 1974–1980. The strain of defense spending only increased after 1982, when Israel invaded Lebanon and found itself caught in an unexpected and harsh occupation of the southern part of that country. In addition, Israel was determined to develop its own arms to the maximum extent possible, including building an advanced fighter plane, the Lavi. The heavy defense budget would have posed a challenge for the best-managed economy; it was all the worse for an economy hobbled by ineffective government policies.

While Israel certainly faced a difficult international security situation, domestic policy played no small role in the economic deterioration post-1973. Indeed, many Israeli economists present strong reasons to identify bad policies as the key culprit in the mounting economic problems. In particular, public-sector labor militancy in an economy stretched taut by military mobilization led to unsustainable public spending fed by wage increases, a generous welfare state, high defense budgets, and wage-price controls. Service on the national debt rose from 4 percent of GNP in 1973 to 7 percent in 1982. At the same time, other transfer payments—such as pensions, child allowances, and subsidies to firms—rose from 15 percent of GNP to 20 percent.

When the Labor Party, which had ruled Israel from 1948, gave way to the conservative Likud Party in 1977, the same set of disastrous economic policies remained. Indeed, as part of its campaign to undermine the Histadrut labor federation, which had long been central to Labor's political power, the Likud championed the welfare state and extensive government protection for inefficient enterprises. The bitter political conflict between the two parties, which centered mostly on their stance on the Arab-Israeli conflict (this being the period of Israel's peace treaty with Egypt), led each to play up unwise populist economic policies, such as undercutting tax enforcement at the same time as increasing education, health, and other social spending. Yawning budget deficits fed inflation, to which the response was a mix of price controls and indexation to protect wages. Expansionary monetary policy combined with a balance-of-payments crisis only added fuel to the inflationary fires.

By 1985, Israel was headed for economic disaster. Inflation, which escalated to 200 percent in 1983 and reached almost 450 percent in 1984, continued to rise in 1985. A series of stabilization packages from 1983 through early 1985 accomplished little. Wage/price freezes had a small impact in the face of the almost universal price indexing. The national unity government formed after the stalemate in the 1984 elections was at a loss about how to proceed. The stage was set for the dramatic summer 1985 stabilization program designed by Israel's leading academic economists. A "Law of No Printing" was adopted which prohibited the Bank of Israel from lending money to the government. Budget cuts and tax increases slashed the budget deficit from 12 percent of GNP to under 2 percent. Meanwhile, monetary policy was so tight that real interest rates on lines of credit peaked at over 160 percent, and the Israeli shekel was devalued by 42 percent in one month. At the urging of U.S. secretary of state George Shultz, a distinguished economist, the United States supported the stabilization program with an emergency aid package of $1.5 billion spread over two years.

Reform and Boom, 1986–2000

While the 1985 stabilization program rescued Israel from hyperinflation, the consensus throughout the late 1980s was that the prospects for the economy were gloomy. The pessimism was unwarranted. From 1984 to 1999, employment rose 50 percent, GNP nearly doubled, and exports rose almost fourfold.

The gains from the 1985 reforms were slow to make themselves felt. They were in part offset by the 1987 outbreak of the first intifada—extensive Palestinian violent resistance to Israeli occupation. The violence affected the Israeli economy in three main areas. First, the civilian labor supply shrank due both to the large numbers of reservists mobilized to combat chaos in the Palestinian territories and, more importantly, to the shortfall of workers from the West Bank and Gaza, who served in low-paying jobs in the labor-intensive agricultural sector and who constituted 40 percent of the work force in Israeli construction. Second, a component of Israel's economic success had rested on the high numbers of tourists entering the country each year, a trend that slowed significantly during the first years of the intifada as a result of increasing unease about traveling to a war zone. In 1988, for example, foreign tourism decreased by 15 percent, representing a loss of $120 million. Finally, exports to the West Bank and Gaza fell drastically, with the sale of industrial goods to the territories declining from $850 million in 1987 to $250 million in 1988, under the combined impact of a Palestinian boycott of Israeli goods and Israeli security measures, which greatly impeded the movement of goods into the Palestinian territories. All in all, Israeli economy and finance ministers placed the annual loss from the violence at somewhere between $900 million and $2 billion. Nevertheless, thanks to the positive impact of the economic reforms begun in 1985, the GDP continued to grow at about the same rate as the population.

The economic situation improved sharply from 1990. The good times were fed by three unexpected factors: immigration from the former Soviet Union, a high-tech boom facilitated by government policies, and advances in the peace process.

Soviet Immigration

From 1990 through 1997, about 700,000 immigrants arrived in Israel from the former Soviet Union, boosting the population more than 15 percent above its previous level of 4.5 million. In 1990 alone, 190,000 immigrants arrived. The immigrants were a highly skilled group; in just the first four years, 57,000 described themselves as engineers compared to 30,000 engineers in Israel in 1989, while 12,000 described themselves as medical doctors compared to 16,000 in Israel in 1989. The immigration energized the Israeli public, excited at the renewal of the Zionist dream of ingathering the exiles, but it also created deep anxiety about how Israel could afford their absorption. In the event, this turned out to be much less of a problem than anticipated during the highly contentious 1991–1992 dispute with the Bush administration about $10 billion in U.S. government loan guarantees for immigrant absorption that Israel thought had been promised when it stayed out of the 1991 Iraq war despite the Scud missiles falling on Israel. However, the George H.W. Bush administration was unwilling to provide the loan so long as right-wing Israeli prime minister Yitzhak Shamir was unforthcoming in the peace talks launched at the November 1991 Madrid peace conference. The dispute became moot after Shamir was defeated in 1992 elections; the Bush administration liked the new government led by Yitzhak Rabin, which was committed to peace talks.

Economic Reform

The economic reforms begun during the 1985 crisis accelerated in subsequent years. Mostly, that was a product of strong domestic support for reform in the face of determined resistance from some quarters. A lesser contributor was U.S. insistence, using its aid as leverage. The U.S. role was particularly large in the 1986–1987 decision to halt a multibillion-dollar program to produce the Lavi advanced fighter plane. The end of the Lavi program was a major reason for employment in the defense sector dropping from 70,400 in 1985–1986 to 49,400 in 1991. The extensive layoffs in this highly sensitive sector sent a strong signal that the days of government protection for inefficient firms were at an end.

The Lavi cancellation was only one of many structural reforms to challenge the privileged position of powerful political groups. Foreign trade was liberalized, through elimination of export subsidies and discriminatory taxes and compulsory licensing of imports. Labor regulations were changed to reduce the burden on business of social security contributions, unemployment compensation, cost-of-living adjustments, and the minimum wage. The financial system was reformed to reduce many detailed regulations, though the banking system remained highly concentrated with little competition.

One of the most important reforms was shrinking the size of the government. Driven by a reduction in transfer payments by 12 percent of GDP along with a reduction of the same size in defense spending, total government spending fell from 75 percent of GDP in 1980–1984 to 54 percent in 1994–1998, still much higher than in the United States and Japan, but not that far off from the levels in Western Europe. With spending lower, Israel was able to reduce its dependence on foreign aid, which over the period remained roughly level in dollar terms but fell as a percentage of GDP by 7 percent. Nevertheless, generous U.S. aid was a factor in Israel's boom. From 1987 through 1998, U.S. aid was maintained at $3 billion a year: $1.8 billion in military aid and $1.2 billion in economic aid (excluding loan guarantees). Israel's rising income made it seem an unlikely candidate for so much economic aid. However, Israel's friends pointed out that only thanks to a generous debt rescheduling had the economic aid been sufficient to cover Israel's debt service on past U.S. loans, about 90 percent of which were for military purchases. These loans were made at a time when Israel was on the front lines of the Cold War, confronting advanced Soviet weaponry provided to Arab states at cut-rate prices by the USSR. As the debt service phased out in the decade after 1997, so did the economic aid, though half the reduction was added to military aid.

The phasing out of U.S. economic aid was symbolic of Israel's emergence as a developed economy with a vibrant private sector. Despite the sharp reduction in government protection for sectors with strong political backing, manufacturing output rose 74 percent in real terms from 1985 to 1998. The growth leader was electronics—that is, high-tech computer and communications equipment—which went from 13 percent of manufacturing output to 22 percent in that period. Israel developed a world-class high-tech sector, which attracted substantial foreign investment that further fueled the growth of the industry. While traditionally most foreign capital flows to Israel were arguably politically motivated—such as the Israeli government bonds bought mostly by those politically sympathetic to Israel—Israel in the 1990s began to attract significant amounts of direct foreign investment; by some estimates, as much as $20 billion from 1995 to 2001. Multinational companies such as Intel, Motorola, Cisco Systems, and IBM built major production and research and development facilities there. At the same time, Israeli firms were able to raise funding on international markets. At the market peak, the value of Israeli companies traded on U.S. stock markets reached $33 billion; Israel had more companies listed on Nasdaq than any other foreign country except Canada.

Peace Process

In contrast to the considerable economic impact of the Soviet immigrants and economic reform, the peace process had a more muted effect on Israel's economy, despite the grand hopes in the early 1990s. Its impact can be divided into two parts: a small direct impact and a larger indirect impact. When the peace process began with the 1991 Madrid conference, great hopes were placed in the potential for direct economic cooperation; Shimon Peres's *New Middle East* (1993) captured the optimism about the opportunities peace would bring for economic prosperity throughout the region. However, the direct impact was limited by the insistence of most Arab states that substantial improvement in economic relations with Israel should await final peace settlements, which undermined the optimism about joint projects that prevailed at a 1994 Casablanca economic summit attended by many prominent Israeli and Western businessmen, as well as quite a few Arab investors. Israel and three Arab neighbors (Egypt, Jordan, and the Palestinian Authority) proposed at a 1995 Amman economic summit a Middle East Economic Development Bank; while a charter was negotiated with participation by many industrial and Middle East countries, the bank never came into existence, as the peace process faltered in subsequent years.

As for trade, the Arab economic boycott was not formally abandoned by most Arab states, though the economic impact of that ban on direct Arab-Israeli trade was limited. The greater indirect impact of the peace process on Israel's economy, compared to its limited direct effect, is well illustrated by the Arab boycott. The Arab boycott of Western companies active in Israel—known as the secondary boycott—effectively ended after 1991. That gave Israel greater access to products such as high-tech goods from some firms, notably Japanese and South Korean, which had previously stayed out of the Israeli market (meanwhile, Arab countries continued the primary boycott, that is, their refusal to trade with Israel).

A second indirect effect of the peace process was to make Israel appear a safer place and therefore one international investors were more willing to consider. To what extent the 1990s foreign investment boom should be ascribed to this factor is unclear, since economic reforms were also making Israel a more attractive place to invest. The third and most important aspect of the indirect economic impact of the peace process was lower defense spending, though arguably this was due primarily to the end of the Soviet Union, which had provided Arab states with advanced weaponry at low or no cost. In any case, Israeli defense spending fell from 21 percent of GDP in 1980–1984 to 9 percent in 1997–1998.

A Twentieth-Century Developed Economy

In the twenty-first century, Israel's economic situation is quite like that of the advanced industrial states and quite different from that of the developing world. Thus, in its economy much as in its cultural outlook, Israel resembles Europe more than it does the rest of the Middle East.

Recovery from Twin Blows, 2000–2010

As the new millennium dawned in 2000, Israel's economic outlook looked excellent. That year, GDP rose 8 percent to $113 billion, or more than $17,000 per person, equal to about one-half the U.S. level. The contrast could not have been greater with the Arab world, which was suffering from low oil prices and stalled economic reforms. Israel appeared to have left the Middle East behind, to have become part of Europe, despite the geography of its location. Self-confidence was high.

But that changed sharply in the first years of the new millennium, which were tough for the Israeli economy. The country went through its worst-ever recession, with GDP shrinking in 2001 and 2002. Anemic growth in 2003 was not enough to restore output to its 2000 level. The budget deficit ballooned from under 1 percent of GDP in 2000 to 5.6 percent in 2003. Unemployment, already at a disappointing 8.7 percent in 2000, shot up to 10.8 percent in 2003.

What happened in 2000 was that Israel's economy was hit by two serious blows. In a familiar pattern, the economy was hurt both by fallout from the Arab-Israeli conflict and by more normal economic problems unrelated to that conflict. Once again, many observers emphasized the economic impact of the former, while many economists thought the latter was more important from the economic point of view. The novelty was that the normal economic problem for once was not rooted in bad government policies. Instead, market forces—the globalization on which Israel had placed such high hopes—disappointed. The bursting of the global high-technology bubble seriously affected the industry in which Israel had become a significant world player. Employment in high-tech areas fell from 66,000 in 2000 to 53,000 on average in 2001–2003. Israeli economists estimated that the high-tech downturn was responsible for about two-thirds of the decline in GDP.

The other one-third of the GDP decline came from the September 2000 outbreak of violent conflict with Palestinians, known as the second intifada (the first intifada was the Palestinian popular uprising against Israeli occupation in the late 1980s). Continuing and dramatic suicide bombings caused a 50 percent drop in tourism income, which had accounted for 3 percent of GDP in 2000; indeed, Israelis' wariness about congregating in public seriously affected restaurants, entertainment centers, and even shops. Lack of access to Palestinian labor imposed serious adjustment costs on agriculture and construction, which had returned to using Palestinian workers during the relative calm of the late 1990s. The Bank of Israel estimated the cost of the violence in 2001 to be $2.6 billion.

The combination of the high-tech bubble bursting and the onset of violence with Palestinians seriously eroded business confidence; instead of the significant foreign investment of the boom years, foreign capital flowed out of Israel. To add insult to injury, many Arab economies were booming as oil prices firmed; now it was Israel's turn to look like the vulnerable party, stumbling as the region boomed. Meanwhile, many around the world were blaming Israel for the catastrophe that had befallen the Palestinian economy, rejecting Israel's argument that by tolerating or encouraging terror attacks on Israelis, the Palestinians had brought upon themselves the border closures and Israeli attacks that devastated their economy. The mood in Israel was sour, with the economy suffering, international opinion hostile, and the number of terror attacks increasing.

Starting in 2003, Israel's economy began a recovery made all the more surprising by its cause, namely, structural economic reforms long bitterly resisted by the beneficiaries in government-protected industries. While Israel had tackled several times the macroeconomic imbalances in the government budget and balance of payments, most notably in 1985, it had made but slow progress in dismantling the extensive net of regulations that created privileged pockets throughout the economy. For decades politicians had preferred to patch together coalition governments by buying off one small constituency after another; the parties supported by the ultra-religious in particular benefited from this practice. This pattern was broken by Benjamin Netanyahu, a politician whose previous career had been plagued by accusations that he lacked the courage to put into effect the fine words he proclaimed. While serving as finance minister in 2003–2005, Netanyahu implemented bold reforms. He took on powerful bastions of government-protected privilege, such as the port workers whose restrictive work rules had driven costs sky high. He pushed through extensive privatizations, such as the national airline El Al and part of the Bezeq telephone service. He began tackling the greatest bastion of protected privilege, namely, the banking industry, by privatizing the number three bank, Israel Discount Bank.

The impact of the economic reforms was considerable. In 2004–2008, GDP after inflation rose by 5 percent a year on average. Per capita GDP reached $28,000 in 2008, 60 percent of the U.S. level. By 2006, exports of goods and services had more than doubled from their 2002 trough to $85 billion, enough to cover more civilian imports, with the defense imports largely being covered by U.S. aid. Israel had reduced its public debt to a sustainable level; three-fourths of the small foreign debt was either guaranteed by the U.S. government or in the form of bonds held mostly by Israel's political friends.

Most Israelis worry much less about debt and deficits than they do about social inequality and poverty. Economic reforms were widely blamed for worsening social problems, whereas the evidence suggests that the opposite was the case. Unemployment was 11 percent when the Netanyahu reforms began in 2003; in 2008, unemployment was 6 percent. Israel faces a problem about welfare programs and pensions. Israelis generally support generous state welfare programs and pensions on the north European model, but the country is nowhere near rich enough to afford benefits on the north European scale. Despite the pressure for more generous social programs and higher pensions, Israel managed in 2007 to balance the government budget.

The Israeli economy was hit by several shocks in 2006–2009. The higher price of oil raised Israel's oil import bill by $6 billion from 2003 to 2008, which is equivalent to 3 percent of Israel's GDP. Israel fought two short wars, one in 2006 with the Lebanese Hezbollah movement and one in 2008–2009 with Hamas, the militant Islamist organization controlling the Gaza Strip. The 2008–2009 global financial crisis reduced demand for Israel's products, though Israel's banks were largely spared because their conservative practices left them unexposed to losses on the complex financial products that collapsed in value during the crisis. Israel slipped into a shallow recession in early 2009; as of late 2009, Israel seemed likely to have only very modest economic growth in 2010. On balance, Israel's economy was hurt less by the

2008–2009 global financial crisis than were most advanced economies.

For decades, Israel was a prosperous developing country on a quasi-socialist path. That, however, is the past. Israel's self-conception is increasingly that it is an advanced industrial economy, similar to those in the European Union (EU) and North America. That is largely accurate. Not only is Israel's per capita income at about the EU average, but the structure of Israel's economy is rather like that of the industrial countries: a rapidly growing high-tech service sector, a diverse industrial base, and a small but highly productive agricultural sector. As a mature industrial economy, Israel is likely in the coming decade to have solid but unspectacular growth.

A Final Word on Peace and Prosperity

The centrality of the Israeli-Palestinian conflict to the political scene can lead to an exaggerated view about its economic impact on Israel. The impact on Israel's military budget of peace with Palestinians would not necessarily be particularly large at first. Israel's military costs are driven in large part by the threat from hostile states such as Iran as well as by the potential that a hostile government could come to power in one of its Arab neighbors, such as Egypt. That is the threat which forces Israel to buy expensive advanced weapons like antimissile systems and fighter planes. To be sure, the hostilities with the Palestinians have been expensive, but since Israel is likely to keep its guard up for years after any permanent agreement with Palestinians, it is by no means clear that the counterterror costs would decline much for years even if there were a peace agreement.

The economic benefits of peace for each side would be much greater if the peace resulted in open borders for the flow of goods and people, including workers. Such a "peace of cooperation" looks increasingly less likely than a "peace of separation" in which the two sides have little to do with each other. Such separation has become the norm, beginning with the prolonged closure during the 1991 Iraq war. Political troubles have periodically blocked Palestinian laborers' access to Israel, with the result that Israeli employers were less and less interested in relying on Palestinian workers. The road closures and declining Palestinian incomes made Israeli businessmen less and less interested in the Palestinian markets. However, even in the unlikely event that peace results in a return to the close economic interaction that characterized 1967–1986, when Israelis would regularly visit West Bank and Gaza shops and restaurants, the impact on the Israeli economy would be quite limited. The Palestinian economy is tiny relative to that of Israeli, with the GNP never at the peak reaching 4 percent of Israel's. Starting with the 1991 closures, Israel replaced Palestinian workers with foreign laborers, primarily from Asia and Eastern Europe.

A particularly emotional question for both sides has been the conflict over water. As discussed in the chapter on resources, while water issues inflame emotions, they do not involve large financial sums for an advanced economy such as Israel. Even if Israel were to end all use of water from sources connected to the West Bank, the replacement cost could be less than 1 or 2 percent of GDP.

If Israel and all its Arab neighbors were to reach a peace agreement, Israel's economy would certainly benefit. Businessmen would be more receptive to investing in and trading with an Israel that was seen as peaceful and accepted by its neighbors. Absent any new threats, Israel would be able to reduce its defense budget and to release young people from the obligation of compulsory military service. It is possible Israel would also profit from direct economic interaction with its neighbors, although the record to date with Jordan and Egypt suggests that such interaction would be limited. Trade between Israel and those two countries is small, except in the context of the qualifying industrial zones (QIZs), which provide privileged access to the U.S. market for goods made jointly in Israel and QIZs located in Jordan or Egypt. However, the long-standing animosity may make the post-peace Israeli-Arab economic relationship rather like that between Greeks and Turks: correct but limited.

Arabs and Israelis are more likely to accept the difficult compromises required for peace if they could expect a real improvement in their lives after the peace agreement. In addition, cooperative projects that bring benefits to both sides could reinforce a peace deal. These are arguments for generous international support to meet the transition costs associated with a peace agreement, such as population shifts (settling refugees, moving settlers), and to ensure a post-peace economic boom. However, Israel's considerable prosperity makes it unlikely that any donor other than the United States would consider providing such assistance in the event of a peace treaty.

References and Further Reading

Ben-Bassat, Avi, ed. *The Israeli Economy, 1985–1998: From Government Intervention to Market Economics.* Cambridge, MA: MIT Press, 2002.

Ben-Porath, Yoram, ed. *The Israeli Economy: Maturing Through Crises.* Cambridge, MA: Harvard University Press, 1986.

Clawson, Patrick, and Zoe Danon Gadal. *Dollars and Diplomacy: The Impact of U.S. Economic Initiatives on Arab-Israeli Negotiations.* Washington, DC: Washington Institute for Near East Policy, 1999.

Feiler, Gil. *From Boycott to Economic Cooperation: The Political Economy of the Arab Boycott.* London: Frank Cass, 1998.

Fischer, Stanley, Dani Rodrik, and Elias Tuma, eds. *The Economics of Middle East Peace.* Cambridge, MA: MIT Press, 1993.

Halevi, Nadav, and Ruth Klinov-Malul. *The Economic Development of Israel.* New York: Fredrick A. Praeger in cooperation with the Bank of Israel, 1968.

International Monetary Fund. *Staff Report for the 2005 Article IV Consultation.* February 2006.

———. *Staff Report for the 2008 Article IV Consultation.* February 2009, Country Report 090/57.

Kanovsky, Eliyahu. *The Economic Impact of the Six-Day War: Israel, the Occupied Territories, Egypt, Jordan.* New York: Praeger, 1970.

Lewin-Epstein, Noah, and Moshe Semyonov. *The Arab Minority In Israel's Economy.* Boulder, CO: Westview Press, 1993.

Michaely, Michael. *Foreign Trade Regimes and Economic Development: Israel.* New York: Columbia University Press for the National Bureau of Economic Research, 1975.

Myre, Greg. "High-Tech Industry in Israel Goes from Bust to Boom." *New York Times,* December 26, 2005, C3.

Pack, Howard. *Structural Change and Economic Policy in Israel.* New Haven, CT: Yale University Press, 1971.

Peres, Shimon. *The New Middle East.* New York: Henry Holt, 1993.

Razin, Assaf, and Efraim Sadka. *The Economy of Modern Israel: Malaise and Promise.* Chicago: University of Chicago Press, 1993.

Rivlin, Paul. *The Israeli Economy.* Boulder, CO: Westview Press, 1992.

Rose, Tom. "Bibi Does Economics." *The Weekly Standard,* March 10, 2003, 19–20.

Shalev, Aryeh. *The Intifada: Causes and Effects.* Tel Aviv, Israel: Jaffee Center for Strategic Studies and Boulder, CO: Westview Press, 1991.

Shaley, Michael. "The Contradictions of Economic Reform in Israel." *Middle East Report* 207 (Summer 1998): 30–33, 41.

———. *Labour and the Political Economy in Israel.* Oxford: Oxford University Press, 1992.

Sharaby, Linda. "Israel's Economic Growth: Success Without Security." *Middle East Review of International Affairs* 6:3 (September 2002). Available at www.gloria-center.org/meria/2002/09/sharaby.html.

Zakheim, Dov. *Flight of the Lavi: Inside a U.S.-Israel Crisis.* Washington, DC: Brassey's, 1996.

Conclusion

Great Opportunities, Unimpressive Results, Modest Prospects

How one evaluates the Middle East's growth record depends in no small part on what time period one considers and what expectations one has. Over the last few decades, the region's performance has been middling in comparison to other developing regions. But the longer the time frame adopted, the more consideration given to the region's inherent advantages, and the more that the point of comparison is the absolute gap with the industrial West rather than the growth rate relative to other developing countries, the more disappointing the Middle East's performance has been. The region was well placed for rapid growth in the last fifty years, being close—physically, historically, and often culturally—to the booming European market, having many countries well endowed in natural resources or human capital (though seldom in both), and in many cases having powerful friends prepared to extend significant assistance. But despite these advantages, only Israel and the Gulf oil monarchies have since the mid-twentieth century narrowed the gap between themselves and the advanced industrial economies, while almost all other Middle Eastern countries have fallen further and further behind the West. And fifty years is a short period of time for the history-conscious people of the Middle East, whose point of reference for how their societies should be fairing is often the days of glory in centuries past, when the Middle East was more advanced and more powerful than Europe.

Those who have done best in the Middle East over the last fifty years have been Israel and the Gulf oil monarchies. Israel has transformed itself from a poor country into an advanced industrial economy much like those in the middle of the European pack. The Gulf oil kingdoms have gone from being some of the most backward and isolated countries on earth—well behind sub-Saharan African countries such as Ghana, Kenya, or Ivory Coast—to being both well-to-do and modern. It is striking that these high performers have been the countries excoriated by the regions' radicals—leftists in the past, Islamists now—for their close relations with the United States. And the other Middle Eastern countries which have done relatively better than most, such as Tunisia and Jordan, have also been more friendly to the United States than most. By contrast, the region's worst economic performers have been Iraq and Algeria, both with per capita incomes barely above the levels of forty years ago—and both are countries that for most of the last few decades had radical governments sharply hostile to the United States.

It would be quite wrong to say that the reason for Israeli or Gulf monarchical prosperity has been good relations with the United States or that the cause for Iraqi and Algerian stagnation has been bad relations with the United States. Instead, both the economic performance and the state of relations with the United States have flowed from the same cause: the absolute priority placed on radical political ideology at the expense of all else. Placing priority on politics has been a major problem for economic development across the region, whether that ideology was Zionism, Palestinian nationalism, Arab unity, Islamic revolution, or anything else. Most obviously, those ideologies have been at the root of the region's many wars, some of which have devastated economies—witness the state of the Iraqi economy after more than twenty-five years of war. In addition, ideology has often impeded sensible economic policymaking; leaders have been unwilling to challenge long-held shibboleths, afraid that the short-term political risks would outweigh the long-term economic advantage. The priority on politics over economics has become a self-reinforcing cycle in which poor economic performance creates discontent off of which radical ideologues can feed. Prosperity could facilitate the solution of the region's political problems: people who are more satisfied are more likely to consider difficult political compromises.

For decades, the region's various political ideologies converged on much the same economic approach, which can best be described as Third-World socialism. The most charismatic articulator of this approach was Egyptian president Gamal Abdul Nasser, whose eloquent rhetoric about Arab socialism captured the imagination of a whole generation of Arabs and Iranians in the early 1960s. Ironically, many of the elements of "Nasserism" were similar to the economic policies long applied by the Labor socialists in Israel, both of which were openly inspired by Marxism. The Third-World socialist economic policies were much like the left wing of European social democracy: the leading role of state-owned firms in all aspects of the economy, be it finance, industry, services, or even agriculture; strict government regulation of private enterprise; large government bureaucracies that provided employment for the politically well connected; redistributive policies that heavily taxed the wealthy and provided extensive subsidies. The Middle East's experience with these policies has not been that different from Europe's: at first, good growth and improved well-being, but increasing problems as bureaucracy become entrenched, until the spreading of inflexible regulation impedes growth and drags down efficiency. Unfortunately for the Middle East outside Israel, the problems of Third-World socialism were masked for a decade by the post-1973 oil boom. While politically influential Egypt spoke loudly about opening the economy as early as the mid-1970s, in practice, little happened until the late 1980s. And in Egypt as throughout most of the region, Third-World socialism still retains significant support among intellectuals, despite its dismal track record.

Since the 1979 Islamic Revolution in Iran, the ideology sweeping the Middle East has been political Islam. Despite the political Islamists' slogan "Islam is the solution," they have in fact had few economic ideas except the old socialist ways. When the Islamist revolutionaries came to power in Iran in 1979, they proceeded to implement much the same economic program that Nasser had developed in the early 1960s with much the same result: modest results at first, followed by steadily worse problems. The Iranian revolutionaries made few attempts to introduce clearly Islamic elements in their economic policy. For instance, faced with the problem of how to ban the charging of interest as required by most interpretations of Islamic law, they decided on blatant hypocrisy, simply renaming "interest" as "profit-sharing" while in fact doing nothing to change the underlying economic reality. The twenty-first century political Islamists barely refer to economic issues and rarely argue that Islam will solve the region's economic problems. Perhaps they agree with the comment often attributed to Ayatollah Ruhollah Khomeini, "Economics is for donkeys" (though it is not clear if he ever said those words).

While neither Third-World socialism nor Islam has been the answer to the region's economic problems, what has worked at delivering prosperity in the Middle East has been globalization and economic reform. While outside observers have often dismissed the Gulf kingdoms' prosperity as artificial and temporary because it was dependent on oil exports, in fact their export-based approach has done better than the region's inward-looking economies. Algeria and Iran have wasted vast sums—as did Iraq when it had the money—on the vain pursuit of import-substituting industrialization, only to end up with uncompetitive factories that are able to survive only if competing imports are blocked and inputs subsidized. Iran's automotive industry produces a million vehicles a year, but the cost of imported inputs exceeds what Iran would pay for importing those vehicles; that is, the net value added by Iran's automotive industry is negative. To be sure, world markets are uncertain, but they have proved a better engine for growth than trying to make do on one's own. Consider how Israel's economy bounced back by 2005 after suffering from the 2000 collapse of the high-tech industry in which it had so concentrated.

If one important part of the answer has been globalization, another has been economic reform. The Middle East has been bedeviled by well-entrenched elites that resist needed change. Economic policies and institutions need to evolve to fit changing times; no solution is perfect for all time. Resistance in the Middle East to pro-growth reforms is deep, in no small part because the bureaucracies which employ most of the region's middle class are suspicious that easing their control over the economy will undercut their political and economic power. Perhaps as damaging has been the bureaucrats' refusal to keep up with the times. For instance, the region's educational systems are largely geared to producing bureaucrats rather than entrepreneurs or technicians, which may have been appropriate when government bureaucracies were expanding rapidly, but that was decades ago. The poor quality of governance in the region is more than a matter of the Middle East's often noted "democracy gap." The governance problem stems also from unaccountable, nontransparent bureaucracies which discriminate on political or ethno-religious grounds in access to services and administration of the law. It does not seem accidental that the region's most democratic country, Israel, has also been its most consistent reformer—or that the most consistent reformer has had the best economic results in the region, especially once it finally conceded in 1985 to make changes to long-established institutions and policies.

The single most important reform needed in most countries of the region is greater openness to the world economy by reducing administrative barriers to trade and investment. In *Reducing Vulnerability and Increasing Opportunity*, the World Bank provides an excellent checklist of the other top reform agenda items:

- Sounder macroeconomic management, especially countercyclical rather than procyclical fiscal policy, that is, saving the windfalls when oil prices are high to use when prices drop;
- Better governance, with more transparency, respect for law and liberties, and more efficient bureaucracies;
- Reformed labor markets, including trade union rights and bans on ethno-religious discrimination;
- Smaller price distortions, especially lower tariffs, more realistic exchange rates, and smaller subsidies for water, gasoline, and food;
- Strengthened regulatory institutions, especially enforcing property rights and competition;
- More efficient education and health expenditures targeted on the poor, while providing a framework to encourage private providers; and
- Mitigation of and relief for the risks faced by the most vulnerable, with government social expenditures focused where they can be most efficient rather than tackling too many problems at once.

The prospects for the Middle Eastern economies depend on the ability to surmount the great barriers of the past, namely, the priority of political ideology over prosperity, the suspicions about the outside world, and the resistance to change. Many countries will be hard-pressed to create enough meaningful jobs to take advantage of the number of young people joining the labor market from 2010 to 2020, nor will they prepare adequately for the rapid growth in elderly populations thereafter. The "demographic transition" the Middle East is undergoing could be the basis for rapid economic growth, but most countries seem likely to miss the opportunity. The second oil boom, which began in 2000, has provided many countries a substantial windfall. The challenge is to retain the sense of urgency about reforms, because windfalls do not make a sustainable basis for continued growth.

References and Further Reading

Abed, George T., and Hamid R. Davoodi. "Challenges of Growth and Globalization in the Middle East and North Africa." Available at www.imf.org/external/pubs/ft/med/2003/eng/abed.htm.

Alnsarawi, Abbas. *Arab Nationalism, Oil, and the Political Economy of Dependency.* Westport, CT: Greenwood, 1991.

Glain, Stephen. *Mullahs, Merchants, and Militants: The Economic Collapse of the Arab World.* New York: Thomas Dunne Books/St. Martin's, 2004.

Henry, Clement, and Robert Springborg. *Globalization and the Politics of Development in the Middle East.* Cambridge, UK: Cambridge University Press, 2001.

Iqbal, Farrukh. *Sustaining Gains in Poverty Reduction and Human Development in the Middle East and North Africa.* Washington, DC: World Bank, 2006.

Owen, Roger, and Şevet Pamuk. *A History of Middle East Economies in the Twentieth Century.* Cambridge, MA: Harvard University Press, 1999.

Pack, Howard, and Marcus Noland. *The Arab Economies*

in a Changing World. Washington, DC: Institute for International Economics, 2007.

Richards, Alan, and John Waterbury. *A Political Economy of the Middle East: State, Class, and Economic Development.* Boulder, CO: Westview Press, 1990.

Rivlin, Paul. *Arab Economies in the Twenty-First Century.* Cambridge, UK: Cambridge University Press, 2009.

Shafik, Nemat. *Prospects for Middle Eastern and North African Economies: From Boom to Bust and Back?* New York: St. Martin's Press, 1998.

———, ed. *Economic Challenges Facing Middle Eastern and North African Economies: Alternative Futures.* New York: St. Martin's Press, 1998.

World Bank. *Reducing Vulnerability and Increasing Opportunity: Social Protection in the Middle East and North Africa.* Washington, DC: World Bank, 2002.

———. *Trade, Investment, and Development in the Middle East and North Africa: Engaging with the World.* Washington, DC: World Bank, 2003.

Yousef, Tarik. "Development, Growth, and Policy Reform in the Middle East and North Africa Since 1950." *Journal of Economic Perspectives* 18:3 (Summer 2004): 91–116.

PART III
MIDDLE EAST MEDIA

The Middle East Media

An Introduction

Haim Koren

The Middle East is known as a region where media freedom is limited. Nevertheless, the media are of the greatest importance in promoting support for the existing governments, oppositions, and ideologies.

The Worldwide Press Freedom Index, published by the nongovernmental organization Reporters Without Borders (RSF) and which evaluates freedom of the press in different countries, ranks Middle Eastern states poorly. Saudi Arabia and Iran were 161st and 162nd respectively, out of 168 countries, while the top-ranking Middle Eastern state was Israel, in 50th place. Aside from Israel, there is no country in the region that has an independent media not under state control.

Freedom House, a Washington, D.C.–based nongovernmental organization that has published a ranking of global media since 1980, has ranked the majority of media in the Middle East and North Africa as "Not Free" every year. Freedom House reported in 2006 that the Middle East and North Africa have the lowest ranking of all parts of the world, with 84 percent of the countries receiving a "Not Free" rating. The trend can be seen in the fact that 1980 was the region's best year, when just 57.9 percent of print media and 84.2 percent of broadcast media were "Not Free." During these twenty-six years, only Israel has earned a "Free" ranking (this does not include the Palestinian-ruled West Bank and Gaza).

The state has tried to control the media throughout the Middle East. According to Middle East media expert Abdelwahab El-Affendi, a complete state monopoly over print media, radio, and television exists in Egypt, Iran, Iraq, Libya, Saudi Arabia, and Syria. In these countries, the state seeks to suppress any criticism of its policies or leaders, using direct control, financial power, and intimidation, while employing the media as a propaganda instrument. El-Affendi concludes that this has brought about "a blanket dark age extending from Indonesia to the Atlantic."

Among the public in the Arabic-speaking states and Iran, there is indeed a predominant belief that the purpose of the media is to either reinforce the existing system, which is the government's point of view, or to overthrow it, which is the radical Islamist and in some places radical Arab nationalist conception. Liberal forces are a distinct minority: they see the media as a nonpartisan and independent force that can expose corruption or other problems regardless of who is being criticized.

Ideas taken for granted in the West, like freedom of the press or the public's "right to know," are largely absent. The Middle Eastern media have echoed, rather than challenged, the government viewpoint in each country. Journalists—especially in radio and television—are often state employees, either directly or indirectly, whose loyalty lies with the state rather than the search for truth. Without a strong enough independent economic basis—including a weak advertising base—or a framework of legal protection, the print media were always vulnerable to pressure or prosecution.

This is only somewhat less true for the "new media"—that is, the Europe-based Arabic press, satellite television, and the Internet, which have assumed a growing importance in the region. Even here, a key factor allowing for limited apparent freedom is the propensity of wealthy Saudis, usually with links to the royal family, to invest in the media. The editorial content is then dependent on the wishes of this or that prince, who might or might not allow a measure of flexibility for the editors.

Two additional factors are the ability of countries to bar newspapers from entry, giving them economic leverage, and the tendency among Islamic clergy and Islamist groups to launch campaigns against any article that displeases them. Attempts to control the Internet and satellite television are tougher, yet have also been seen to some extent.

Origins of the Arab Media

The Arab media include media of all Arabic-speaking countries, including the Levant, the Gulf, and North Africa. The Arabic-language press was the first stage of the modern Arab media. It has accompanied political and historical developments in the Middle East since the second half of the nineteenth century. As the Ottoman Empire declined, Arab nationalism sprouted, and with it a debate on the role of Islam in politics and culture.

From its very beginning, the Arab press was strongly influenced by writers, poets, and intellectuals. It did not just convey news but served as a platform for essays on society, culture, religion, and politics. To this day, newspaper editors as well as radio, television, and electronic media officials form a large portion of each nation's intellectuals, often playing roles that in Western countries might be filled by academics and book publishers. Given relatively low levels of literacy and formal education, especially at the outset, the print media addressed a small elite that could appreciate highly cultured writers of classical Arabic (*fusha*). This literary Arabic prevailed in journalism of that period, which had little impact on the masses, who spoke the vernacular language (*amiyyah*).

The early media were often tied either to ideological movements or to the existing regime. Yaacov (James) Sanu, an Egyptian Jew (1839–1912) and pioneer of the Arabic press, published a satirical paper called *Abu Nazarah.* His friendship with the country's ruler, Khedive Ismail, did not spare him royal wrath after he expressed scathing criticism of the ruler, and he was forced to leave for Paris with his friend and collaborator Abdullah Nadim. They continued to circulate their paper to an avid Middle Eastern readership. They aimed not to entertain but to promote cultural and social reform.

Similarly, Jamal al-din al-Afghani and Muhammad Abduh, two of the most important forerunners of modern political Islamic thought, published in Paris a paper called *al-Urwa al-Wuthqa*, which lamented the weakness of Islam and offered a platform for Muslim thinkers and writers, mostly liberals, who sought to return Islam to its former glory. The paper became the focal point for a group of Arab political-literary intellectuals that came together in 1918 at the American University in Beirut as a society of teachers and students from Arab countries. This society saw pan-Islamism as the answer to the downfall of the Ottoman Empire and wished to bring back Islam's hegemony. Another Muslim scholar who put his thoughts in writing was Rashid Rida, a student of Abduh and founder of *al-Manar*, a weekly and then monthly journal.

The periodicals *Filastin* and *al-Carmel*, published in Jaffa and Haifa respectively, represented the nationalist view, followed by *al-Hayat* and *al-Nahar* of Beirut. *Al-Urwa al-Wuthqa* and *al-Manar* represented the pan-Islamic view. Beirut was indeed the center of Arab media in the 1920s, although newspapers appeared also in Damascus, Jerusalem, Baghdad, Amman, Cairo, Mecca, and Sana'a.

In the late 1930s, the cultural, political, and media center of the Arab world moved to Cairo, flourishing under British rule. The weekly *Ruz al Yusuf*, established in the 1920s, was joined by other dailies that displayed various approaches to local politics, including *al-Wafd* and later *al-Ahram*, which became the flagship of the Egyptian press.

Structural Changes

By the early 1950s the colonial powers were in retreat and the Arabic-speaking states managed their own affairs, some as conservative monarchies (Saudi Arabia and Jordan) and others as secular revolutionary republics run by military juntas (Egypt and Syria).

Substantial changes occurred in the Arab media. A Middle Arabic dialect (*wusta*) was eventually used by the media to make newspapers more accessible to every Arab through the use of a common language. This language filled the space between high literary Arabic and the local dialects.

Aside from technology itself, the key historical event of the time was the July 1952 Free Officers revolution in Egypt, which produced a charismatic leader, Gamal Abdel Nasser, who used the media very effectively. Nasser championed pan-Arabism against a local, state-based nationalism. More conservative Arab leaders saw Nasser as a threat to both themselves and the independence of their states. The struggle of *qawmiyyah* ("local" nationalism) against *wataniyyah* (nationalism for a united Arab world) was reflected in the tension between the other Arab countries' media and an Egyptian media committed to its leader's pan-Arab vision.

Nasser was able to build on Cairo's centrality in the Arab world and soon saw the advantage of using the radio to spread his message. He already understood that usage of the new medium would be much more effective than relying on written journalism only. The portable transistor radio became a potent weapon in the hands of the new junta, so much so that the Free Officers revolution was called "the transistor revolution." Nasser's rhetoric ranged from classical Arabic to popular slang, creating a magic appeal to his audience. And by appealing directly in his own voice, he overcame the problem of illiteracy and popularized the Middle Arabic dialect that was to be used widely by the media.

The transistor radio functioned as the "clan's campfire" for the Arab masses, and Nasser's message was easily understood by the peasant in the field. Nasser declaimed from the balcony on Tahrir Square in Cairo to the people below, and his voice was carried everywhere by radio, reaching each and every home effectively, gaining him immense popularity. His messages sometimes contradicted those of other Arab leaders, who were being circumvented and unable to censor him. This way, Nasser brought *qawmiyyah* nationalism into homes in the Middle East and beyond, and also to his listeners' hearts. He also patronized the Thursday concerts of the popular singer Umm Kulthum, and so enlisted the national-cultural message for political ends. His speeches were valued not only for their message but for his mastery of Arabic style.

The 1967 Arab defeat in Israel challenged Nasser's predominance. And his death in 1970 carried him away before he was able to use television, which was only beginning to reach the Arabic-speaking world. His old rivals had also been learning how to use the media to their own benefit, countering what had previously been a largely one-sided media battle. But Nasser's control of the media laid the groundwork for much of the state of Arab media from the 1960s onward.

As of the mid-1970s, oil magnates of the Gulf states used their earnings from rising oil incomes to take over leadership of Arab media, buying newspapers and radio stations where possible in order to promote their ideologies and gain regional significance. Their new understanding of the importance of information and control over it moved the media's center of gravity from Cairo to the Gulf (especially Saudi Arabia and Kuwait). They hired the best Arabic journalists (Lebanese, Palestinian, Egyptian, and others), published newspapers on high-quality paper, and cultivated a professional style. The Saudi *Ukaz* was modeled on the British *Financial Times*; *al-Ray al-Aam* in Kuwait maintained high standards of content and production.

If the 1950s were the age of the transistor, the 1970s became the age of the recorded media. Ayatollah Ruhollah Khomeini of Iran cleverly used taped sermons from France to spread his message in Teheran in order to prepare the ground for the 1979 Islamic Revolution in Iran. Although Khomeini's efforts were known as "narrowcasting," the use of tapes quickly spread to "broadcasting" since the messages on the tapes, initially intended for a limited target audience, were passed on to other opponents of the shah.

The next stage of media development was the advent of the fax machine in the late 1980s and early 1990s. As Arab newspapers migrated to Europe (*al-Sharq al-Awsat, al-Quds al-Arabi, al-Hayat*, and *al-Wasat* to London; *al-Watan al-Arabi* to Paris), the necessity for fax editions emerged. This meant that Arab decision makers in the Middle East found on their desks every morning Arab newspapers sent from Europe and setting the Arab agenda. For the first time, it was possible to reach readers despite geographic distance and without fear of the censorship that was such an important tool of Arab dictators. Local government media officials with a *wataniyyah* agenda found themselves at odds with the international *qawmiyyah*-oriented media. Professional rivalries between writers added to the tension, when the more talented ones were recruited to work for the international Arab media.

The introduction of satellite television and the Internet in the 1990s brought about two further important developments. All Arabs were now an accessible audience for ideological debate, including those living in closed, nondemocratic countries where censorship still existed. The "man in the street" was suddenly exposed to critical and often subversive ideas—to the extent that international Arab media were willing to provide them.

An interesting example of a career in the new international Arabic media is that of Faysal Qasem, a Syrian Druze. He worked for the BBC while studying for his doctorate in Manchester, gaining much experience. When al-Jazeera TV was established in 1996, Qasem was taken on and became one of its main figures. As producer and presenter of its flagship show, "al-Ittijah al-Muakis" ("The Opposite Direction"), he claimed, "In the BBC I did not enjoy even 20% of the freedom of expression that I have in al-Jazeera." But at a media experts' meeting, Qasem admitted that he did not always enjoy backing or have a free hand at al-Jazeera either, and was often directed as to topics and participants. His statements reveal the tension between the wealthy TV station owners and the journalists who work for them.

Media ownership is of prime importance. MBC TV, headquartered in London, is controlled by a Saudi prince who is close to the Saudi king; al-Mustaqbal TV was owned by the late Lebanese prime minister Rafik Hariri; al-Jazeera belongs to the government of Qatar; ANN belongs to the uncle of Syrian president Bashar al-Assad (though he opposes the regime); *al-Quds al-Arabi* stockholders are Iraqi and Palestinian; and most of the Arab satellite TVs are still operating from Europe.

However, it seems the hopes that "soft news" and advertising might percolate to the Arab viewer and thus "soften" and modify "hard news" and messages have been dashed. Despite a higher level of debate and exposure to controversial topics, the Arab audience does not respond to Western values and rejects messages that conflict with its own culture. Muhammad bin Salman has scornfully called al-Jazeera "a new form of pornography," arguing that its Arab speakers were encouraged to trash Arab values, principles, and beliefs. They challenge the creation of the Quran and raise questions as to the relevance of Islamic shariah law.

Yet in its coverage of conflict with the West and Israel, al-Jazeera has in fact tended to go beyond the balanced reporting of MBC and Orbit. The intifada and the terrorist events of September 11, 2001, were treated by al-Jazeera in a distinctly Arab, anti-Western mode, so much so that the station has been accused by Arab journalists of acting as a spokesman for al-Qaeda.

Functions of the Media

As in other countries around the world, media in the Middle East convey news and information, interpret and explain events, provide information about society in order to reinforce social and cultural norms, entertain, and offer information on commercial products and services. The way in which these functions are performed in the Middle East, however, is distinct from the way in which they are done elsewhere.

In terms of news and commentary, the editorial stance of the media in the Arabic-speaking world and Iran tends to be fairly obvious. The media do not serve as forums for the exchange of different views, and opinions expressed tend to be limited to those of a small elite. Nor is there much room for criticism of the government. In the same vein, Middle Eastern media do not perform the "watchdog function"—that is, to expose the mistakes and corruption on the part of governments and other institutions—of their Western counterparts.

William Rugh, a leading Western expert on the Arab media, writes that it is the editor who exerts the greatest control by selecting news pieces and placing them in such a way as to shape opinions. Editors do this, Rugh continues, "by omitting parts of the story, by emphasizing other parts by putting them in the lead paragraph or headline, by juxtaposing elements of the story to create a certain impression, by printing as unattributed fact information from only one source on a controversial issue, by uncritically publishing information from a doubtful source, or by outright fabricating."

Unconscious cultural bias might be one reason for this, while conscious political bias is another. Political bias might lead to editorial choices that reflect the government's policies and preferences, sometimes in direct response to the regime's orders. Rugh asserts that if one sets aside distortions based on cultural biases, instances in which political bias leads to untruthful distortion of the news are rare. Political news stories, he continues, are an exception to this rule, and if the reader has access to several sources he can detect the bias. In Arabic-speaking countries and Iran, however, such access is often limited.

In these countries, journalism is not held in high regard as a profession. Many avoid the profession, wary of the associated political and financial risks. In the Arabic-speaking world, journalists are sometimes viewed as little more than political hacks or mouthpieces. Not all observers of the Arab press agree with this assessment, however.

The reinforcement of cultural norms through media is accomplished in several ways. One is through the inclusion of literature, sometimes by noted local literary figures, in the newspapers. Poetry and plays are written for radio and television, furthermore. Language serves a similar function, and the use of specific Arabic words and phrases can have a greater impact than the facts they describe.

Broadcast media provide more entertainment than their print counterparts. This is because broadcast media are more accessible to the masses, whereas publications are intended for a more elite audience. Arab newspapers have a far more limited readership in proportion to the population than do Western counterparts, partly due to relatively low literacy rates, unavailability of newspapers in the provinces, and people being unable to afford newspapers. The Arabic press does not carry much advertising because commerce has not been a major priority, and radio and television carried little if any advertising because they were all run by the state, though this has to some extent changed with the rise of Arabic satellite channels such as al-Jazeera.

Media Systems and the Press

Newspapers are the backbone of Middle Eastern media and have existed in the Middle East for some two centuries. Napoleon Bonaparte introduced periodicals to Egypt during the French occupation of 1798–1801. *Journal al-Iraq* is believed to be the first Arab newspaper; it was published in Arabic and Turkish in Baghdad in 1816. Cairo had two Arabic newspapers in the 1820s; Iran (which is considered a Middle Eastern country, but one based on its own language and heritage—Persian and not Arabic) had its first in 1835, Algeria in 1847. The first newspaper in Beirut was published in 1858, and by 1900 forty newspapers and other periodicals had been published. Tunis saw its first in 1861, Damascus in 1865, Libya in 1866, Yemen (Sana'a) in 1879, Casablanca and Khartoum in 1889, and Mecca in 1908.

The relatively open atmosphere for publications changed with the 1952 coup that brought Nasser to power in Egypt. The proponents of the Arab nationalist ideology saw the media as a powerful tool for mobilizing support for the government, inspired by both fascist and communist models, including the Soviet Union and Nazi Germany. State control of the media became a top priority, followed by the media's use in backing the leaders' policy at home and abroad. More traditional Arab regimes, such as Saudi Arabia, noted this offensive and tried to follow suit, though more slowly and with less success.

Beirut became the locus of the Arabic press—especially those newspapers that were more independent or secretly subsidized—due to less government intervention, greater journalistic freedom, better technical facilities, and low costs for publishers. Yet with growing instability in Lebanon given the general anarchy followed by the civil war, beginning in the 1970s journalists headed in two directions: toward the Gulf, where the oil boom brought high salaries, and to London.

The open political and social atmosphere in Europe theoretically offered the Arabic media greater freedom, but they still needed access to the Gulf. The greater costs of working and publishing in Europe, furthermore, led to continuing or even greater dependence on outside financial support, which usually meant Saudi Arabia, Iraq, or the smaller Gulf Arab states. According to El-Affendi, the Gulf states maintain a blacklist of critical Arab journalists.

El-Affendi also refers to a phenomenon called the "blackmail rag." These are irregularly published low-cost papers that provide favorable publicity about Arab leaders who pay them and report on the scandals and secrets of those who do not. The willingness of some regimes to resort to violence against their critics also discourages critical reporting. After Saddam Hussein's downfall in 2003, writers joked about "Saddam's widows and orphans," meaning the journalists and newspapers that lost their subsidies from Baghdad.

The Arabic press has been essentially an elite institution because of its limited circulation. Lebanon was an exception to this general rule because the literacy rate there (more than 85 percent by 1980) was higher than in the rest of the region. Kuwait and the United Arab Emirates may also have been ahead, Rugh suggests, because of their literate expatriate populations. Moreover, the Arabic press was intended for an elite audience, and some dailies had very low circulation figures. In Egypt in the 1950s, for example, the highest-circulation daily sold 7,000 copies, though most dailies did not exceed circulation rates of 2,000. Small populations in some countries meant that a domestic newspaper could not be sustained: Qatar did not get one until 1975; Bahrain not until 1976. The authoritarian nature of the Arabic-language media means that only a select few people—national leaders and trusted supporters—know the truth.

In his 1979 book *The Arab Press*, Rugh introduces a categorization that remains useful today. He explains that the press falls into three subcategories—mobilization press, loyalist press, and diverse press. In 2004, Rugh introduced a new category—transitional print media. Rugh's categories will serve as the framework for the discussions on media that follow, and two non-Arab states, Israel and Iran, will be assessed in addition.

Mobilization Press

A mobilization press—found in Algeria, Egypt, Iraq until 2003, Libya, Syria, South Yemen, and Sudan—does not criticize government policies, particularly foreign policy. Domestic policy is generally out of bounds, too, although newspapers can carry items criticizing shortcomings at the local level, such as power outages or a lack of potable water. Likewise, lower-level officials can be criticized but national leaders are left alone, even if scurrilous information about them is public knowledge. They can engage in what Rugh calls a limited level of "constructive criticism."

There can be several newspapers in countries with a mobilization press, but they offer no diversity because their editorial stances and news stories operate from the same pro-government base. The press is expected to mobilize the people in pursuit of the cultural, economic, political, and social goals espoused by the leadership.

Countries with a mobilization press share several characteristics. First, power is in the hands of a small group that does not face an organized opposition and does not permit its domestic authority to be challenged. Second, the ruling group views itself as a revolutionary vanguard that is fighting for domestic social change, stressing a nationalist line as a defender of the country against foreign enemies. Third, passive acceptance of the ruling elite is not enough; popular support is pursued. Fourth, the ruling group has just one political party behind it, and the political system does not allow for multiple parties.

Algeria, Egypt, Libya, and Sudan all had a mobilization press and one ruling party that owned the major newspapers. In the Egyptian case, Law Number 156 of May 1960 decreed that a newspaper could not be published without permission from the National Union (later the Arab Socialist Union) Party. Under this law, ownership of four private publishing houses was transferred to the National Union, which already owned one. The National Union was tasked with appointing directors of the newspapers. The situation changed slightly in 1975 with the creation of a Higher Press Council that received 40 percent ownership of the press and the power to issue press licenses. The change was superficial, however, because government and party officials had leading roles in the council.

The Algerian government in 1963 put all but one of the country's newspapers under President Ahmad Ben Bella's National Liberation Front (FLN). The one exception already supported the government, and that newspaper was eventually merged with an FLN mouthpiece. State domination of the Algerian media continued until 1989. During this time, the regime censored private publications and established more than ten publications to reflect its own views. In 1973, the government banned private newspapers completely. Strict press controls continued, regardless of who was in power (Ben Bella, overthrown in a 1965 coup, was succeeded by Houari Boumedienne, who died in 1978 and was followed by Chadli Bendjedid).

In Sudan, President Jafar Numeiry's Sudanese Socialist Union Party owned the press jointly with the government. An August 1970 press law gave ownership to a public corporation. About one year later, all publishing houses that produced newspapers and magazines were made party property. A 1973 law enunciated this arrangement: "The Minister [of Culture and Information] shall be responsible for the daily direct control of newspapers in order to ensure harmony with the general information line commitment to the political plan of the Sudanese Socialist Union."

There were multiple parties in Iraq, South Yemen, and Syria, but the ruling party effectively controlled the press nevertheless.

Personnel practices are one of the means by which the ruling party controls the press in these countries. Newspapers are run by people associated with the ruling party. This applies to editors, and, in what approaches self-censorship, journalists intuit how they are expected to report. Failing this, they can be dismissed, suspended, or even arrested. In Egypt in 1973, for example, the professional licenses of some one hundred reporters were suspended for six months. Journalists whose work is deemed supportive of the government are rewarded with improved access. Direct censorship is possible, too, but the close relationship between the press and the government makes this unnecessary. If they do not receive direct guidance, editors and journalists can determine the desired nature of their work by following the statements of top officials.

Loyalist Press

The loyalist press shares some of the traits of the mobilization press, but differs in important ways. The commonalities include a tendency not to attack national policies, to avoid criticism of regime leaders, and a lack of diversity in portrayal of significant issues. The loyalist press will, however, report critically on government services that do not fulfill public needs, and it will publish reports that expose the corruptness of government officials. The loyalist press tends to be more passive than the mobilization press. It avoids hot topics and uses more subdued language. Investigative reporting is infrequent.

Bahrain, Jordan, Qatar, Saudi Arabia, Tunisia, and the United Arab Emirates (UAE) all have what can be categorized as a loyalist press. The newspapers are mostly in private hands but are loyal to and supportive of the government. The rare exceptions to this rule are in Tunisia, where two dailies belong to the Destorian Socialist Party, and the UAE, where a pre-independence daily remained in government hands until its 1976 transfer to a semi-independent publisher. From 1971 to 1974, *al-Ray* was run by the Jordanian government before private owners took over.

There are several reasons for the emergence of a privately owned, loyalist press. One is that the government usually has legal powers it can use to influence the press. For example, the Emirate of Transjordan, an entity established by the United Kingdom in May 1923, created a press law in March 1927. The wording of the law was vague because the sole local publication, the weekly *al-Sharq al-Arabi*, printed state announcements and laws, and therefore required little regulation. More strict laws passed in 1939 and 1945 gave the government censorship powers and control over the media, reflecting concern about German and Ottoman influence. The 1948 press law was even stricter due to Jordanian government concern over the influx of Palestinian refugees.

Two laws passed in 1953 affected the Jordanian press. One made joining the Communist Party or possessing Communist literature illegal. The Law of Publications (modified in 1955 and 1973) authorized the Jordanian government to distribute and withdraw newspaper licenses and licenses for printing presses. The laws also specified what was prohibited in the press.

In 1967, after the press criticized the military's inadequate response to Israeli raids, Jordan's prime minister declared the press had not met its responsibilities and he withdrew all publishing licenses. Under a press law passed that year, partial ownership of newspapers by the government was made mandatory—the government had to provide at least 25 percent of a newspaper's capital. The government then licensed four dailies and dictated that they should merge into two papers—*al-Dustour* and *al-Difa'a*. The Jordanian government again closed two dailies in the summer of 1970, after they published a communiqué from Palestinian militants who had taken over parts of the country. A pro-Palestinian daily emerged in their place, so the government reinstated their licenses. After the government crushed the Palestinians in September 1970 and their publication disappeared, the government revoked the license of one of the offending dailies again.

Censorship of the Jordanian press continued in the 1980s. The government dissolved the boards of directors of three dailies in 1988, and forced private individuals to sell their ownership shares to the government, which subsequently appointed many top newspapers' managers. The editor in chief of the *Star*, Osama El-Sherif, described this as "the black days of the Jordanian press," adding that the government even forced owners to sell the newspapers and let them be taken over by state-appointed personnel.

Governments also derive influence from their funding of the press. This is done through the purchase of advertising and subscriptions, and by distributing subsidies. The press contributes to its own vulnerability by failing to report independently and failing to establish financial independence. It thus approaches its responsibilities from a position of weakness. In the cases of Bahrain, Qatar, and the UAE, which gained independence in 1971, this can be attributed to the lack of time for a domestic journalism to develop. The media in these countries were staffed by expatriates. Political upheavals in other countries contributed to the relocation of journalists.

The political environment in these countries (Bahrain, Jordan, Qatar, Saudi Arabia, Tunis, and the UAE) contributed to the emergence of a loyalist press. Most lacked independent legislatures, and there was no institutionalized political opposition. Elites supported reform, but they backed the authoritarian governments and the general status quo. The media's general sensitivity to the political and social climate ruled out the need for much government censorship or even guidance. The regimes made their views known through official policy statements and through state broadcast media, and the press acted accordingly. Reports from the official news agencies fulfilled a similar role.

Diverse Press

There were just a few cases of a diverse press in the Arabic-speaking world in 1979. In these cases, privately owned newspapers had distinct and different political views and content, and they published news and opinion that did not necessarily support the regime. This arrangement provided readers with choices. Lebanon is the best example of this, and Kuwait and Morocco were somewhat similar.

Lebanon had fifty licensed newspapers and forty-five political weeklies, though their quality and regularity of publication varied greatly. Many of the publications depended on financial contributions for survival, but there was enough variety in points of view that readers had a choice. This level of variety existed even after the civil war began in 1975, and Rugh writes that the public continued to believe (in several cases on a solid basis, in some of them not) that *al-Nida*, *al-Sharq*, *al-Safir*, and *al-Kifah* were subsidized by Russia, Syria, Libya, and Iraq. Similar suspicions related to *al-Hayat* (Saudi Arabia), *al-Muharri* (Palestinians), and other publications.

The Lebanese press, furthermore, took its role of government oversight seriously. Its exposure of election rigging and corruption in the late 1940s led to the imposition of restrictive press regulations and the suspension of newspapers. A president resigned in the early 1950s due to press activities. First, a newspaper editorialized that President Bishara al-Khuri was installed by foreigners, and the government reacted by suspending the newspaper and jailing its editor. Other newspapers republished the editorial, and they too were closed. Thirteen were eventually suspended, leading to a sympathy strike by the national press.

Lebanon's next government lifted the suspensions and passed new laws, and the press became more influential as political figures recognized its potential. Nevertheless, the government did suspend some opposition papers and censor others during the 1958 civil war, and it also banned imports of foreign publications. A 1962 press law forbade publication of news that undermines national security or insults a foreign leader. A 1974 press law loosened the restrictions somewhat by making civil courts responsible for press cases. Nevertheless, some media figures were fined or even jailed, and sometimes the government asked newspapers not to publish news that threatened national security. In such cases, the newspapers published blank spaces on their pages to signify the missing story.

As a result of the civil war that began in 1975, the Lebanese government decided that censorship was needed. The subsequent Interior Ministry guidelines were marginally less vague than those in the 1962 press law, so although the press was more cautious, it continued to criticize the government.

A diverse press could be found in Kuwait and Morocco, too, although their situations differed from the Lebanese one. Kuwait had seven dailies with a total circulation in excess of 100,000 (out of a population of less than one million and a literacy rate below 60 percent) by 1979. On top of this, there were sixteen weeklies. The Morocco of 1979 had ten "important" dailies (five in French, five in Arabic), with a circulation that surpassed 240,000, and there were dozens of other publications. The press in both Kuwait and Morocco was in private hands, and newspapers expressed views that differed from those of the government. The publications spoke for parties that were not in power, and they questioned the status quo.

In Morocco in the 1970s, two dailies—*Le Matin* and *Maroc Soir*—defended government policies and the status quo. They were published by King Hassan II's cousin, former government minister Moulay Ahmed Alaoui. *Al-Maghrib* and *al-Mithaq al-Watani* also supported the government, but they favored Alaoui's rival, Prime Minister Ahmed Osman. Contributing to the diversity of views in Morocco was the publication of two low-circulation dailies associated with a Marxist party.

In the Kuwaiti and Moroccan cases, newspapers were owned by individuals who recognized the publications as a way to make their voices heard and thereby benefit politically and professionally. Moreover, both countries had political systems in which competition could take place, while the governments also wanted to cultivate a democratic image on the international level.

Transitional Print Media

Rugh introduced a new category—transitional print media—in his 2004 book, *Arab Mass Media.* Falling into this new category was the press from Algeria, Egypt, Jordan, and Tunisia, where authoritarianism had eased its degree of control without giving up its ultimate authority. The change was also due to recognition of the need for a broader media institution if development was going to take place, as well as the obvious discrediting of the state-controlled media.

Newspapers in these countries are owned by a number of actors, including the government, political parties, and private individuals. The party papers serve as mouthpieces, though they can sometimes criticize specific government policies. A 1990 press law in Algeria, for example, allows parties and individuals to own publications. The government owned four newspapers, and two independent dailies were close to the government. Three independent dailies favored Islamist parties (which were banned from newspaper ownership), and one independent French-language daily opposed the Islamists.

The government, individuals, and parties own newspapers in Tunisia. Two dailies are connected with the ruling Democratic Constitutional Rally Party—the party provides funds, and members are on the editorial staff and the boards of directors. Two other newspapers also were run by the regime, and there are four independent dailies. Furthermore, there are at last five independent weeklies. Jordanian law also allows private newspaper ownership, although the owners must be Jordanian. The government is a shareholder in two major dailies, while individuals and parties own many weeklies.

In transitional print media countries, the government wields control over the media through licensing, suspensions and closures, and the fining or arrest of journalists and other staff. There are various legal prohibitions on reporting. Libeling government officials—a category broad enough to be invoked against unwelcome stories or statements—is banned, as is insulting the head of state. Criticism of the military or revealing national security information is banned, too. In Jordan, for example, news about the royal family cannot be published without its approval. A 1998 Jordanian law allows the imposition of fines, closure of newspapers, and withdrawal of licenses, and there is a special court for press cases.

The government in countries with a transitional press can use economic pressure to control what is published. This includes purchasing advertising, controlling access to printing facilities, distributing newsprint, and providing subsides. In 1993 the Tunisian government withdrew its advertising from a magazine in response to the publication of a negative article about the country, and in 1999 the Jordanian government stopped all its advertisements in *al-Arab al-Yawm* after it published articles critical of the prime minister. In Algeria, the government controls newsprint imports through a state-owned firm, owns five printing companies, and bans private printing presses.

Yet Rugh goes on to say that there is diversity and criticism of the government in countries with a transitional print media. In countries with a diverse system, the pro-government print media generally has much larger circulation and can therefore influence the public debate more effectively. Algeria's pro-government dailies defend it consistently, whereas independent ones can be critical. In Algeria, however, independent newspapers have much higher circulation figures. *Al-Ra'y*, the Jordanian daily with the closest ties to the government, defends it against foreign criticism and has a generally optimistic tone.

The so-called "transition" in the Jordanian media began in the late 1980s and coincided with parliamentary elections. The government repealed several aspects of martial law after it took office in December 1989, and it took steps that effectively ended state control over newspapers. The parliament legalized political parties in September 1992, and publications associated with the parties, which expressed opposition to the government, emerged soon thereafter. The new press law of 1993 relaxed the situation even more, although the government retained the right to issue and revoke press licenses, and restrictions on permissible subjects remained in force. On the other hand, government ownership in the press did not decrease.

Clearly, this is not a smooth evolution. A temporary 1997 press law strengthened capital requirements, according to Middle East media expert Abeer Najjar, and this led to the closure of thirteen publications. The law further restricted subjects on which the press could report. Reporters would no longer be imprisoned, but fines for press offenses were increased. In early 1998, Jordan's high court determined that the temporary press law was unconstitutional, and the country no longer requires such measures.

The new Jordanian monarch who came to power in 1999, King Abdullah II, advocated greater press freedom and encouraged the prime minister to take steps to increase privatization. Press restrictions were reinvigorated in August 2001, however, with the arrest of some editors and newspaper closures, and these have continued due to regional tensions.

The Algerian "transition" began in 1989, when the country adopted a new constitution that called for a multiparty parliamentary system. A 1990 Information Law permitted political parties and other nongovernmental institutions to own newspapers, and the government actually provided funds to unofficial publications. Algerian print media flourished from 1989 to 1991, Rugh notes, with the number of newspapers and magazines increasing from 13 to 160. Ownership was spread between the government, political parties, private individuals, and associations.

This pattern was reversed in early 1992, when the military intervened after the Islamic Salvation Front (FIS) won the first round of national elections. The military canceled the second round of elections, and clashes between security forces and Islamists ensued. A committee replaced the president, and new laws restricted press freedom. The government could suspend a publication for up to six months without a court hearing, and reports on security-related topics required governmental approval. The government later established committees at printing presses to review publications for security-related material.

Journalists were targeted by the Islamists and scores lost their lives. As the security situation improved around 1996, restrictions on the media were eased. The press had greater latitude in reporting on security subjects, and a variety of opinions—including the Islamists'—appeared in independent publications.

Broadcast Media

Radio broadcasting got off to a much later start in the Arab world. Only after 1945 did it begin to become more available, or in some cases exist at all. Radio reached a higher proportion of the population than did newspapers. Low-cost receivers were available and people often listened in groups, especially at cafés. As for television, it was not until the late 1950s that transmitters were set up in Baghdad and Beirut, and few people watched regularly until much later due to the cost of the sets and the weakness of the transmissions. Countries in North Africa made do with French TV, while broadcasts by ARAMCO, the Saudi state-owned oil company, were viewed in Saudi Arabia, as were broadcasts of the U.S. military in Libya. Television's popularity grew quickly in the 1970s, particularly in the wealthier Arab states, where locals could afford to purchase sets.

Arabic broadcast media were, for the most part, owned by the state, due to cost, the perceived propaganda value (and to stop control by oppositionists), and the European model (as in either Britain or the Communist states). By the 1990s, however, cheaper technology, the development of the advertising potential, and the use of satellites brought privately owned channels into the field. In the UAE, advertising was an important source of television revenue; in contrast, Algeria, Libya, and Oman did not allow advertising on radio or television.

The Arab countries that had a mobilization press—Algeria, Egypt, Iraq (until 2003), Libya, Syria, South Yemen, and Sudan—had broadcast media organized along these lines. Bahrain, Jordan, Kuwait, Morocco, North Yemen, Oman, Qatar, Saudi Arabia, Tunisia, and the United Arab Emirates have all taken a looser approach, and their governments have not invested as heavily in the broadcast media. The broadcast media there are loyal, meaning they do not cause trouble for the government and the authorities consequently leave them alone. The Lebanese broadcast media do not fit into either of these groups because of their relative diversity.

When Sudan gained independence from the United Kingdom in 1956, control of broadcast media was quickly transferred from a semi-autonomous committee to the government. State radio went from low-power transmissions eight hours a day to a national network that transmitted seventeen hours a day. Similar development of broadcast media took place in Algeria, Libya, and South Yemen in the 1960s.

Among Arabic-speaking countries, Iraq was the first to establish a noncolonialist (British) locally controlled television station, in 1956. This station had only enough power to reach the city of Baghdad. But following the 1958 coup, which brought to power an Arab nationalist regime, the government increased the station's power and built new transmitters throughout the country. The content of the programs was made more political. Egypt and Syria built up their television capabilities in the 1960s. The newly independent Algerian government began rebuilding its television system in 1962 and changing the content of the programs. The Sudanese government worked to improve television capabilities intermittently in the 1960s, and by the mid-1970s television was reaching a much greater audience. The revolutionaries who took power in Libya in the late 1960s also saw television as an important means of extending their influence over the population.

In terms of content, the mobilization broadcast media mainly relayed news about the regime's accomplishments. Politically, they broadcast information of an anti-Western, leftist, and Third World nature (which was represented mainly by the nonaligned states). State broadcast media frequently hosted pro-Palestinian programming that focused on important issues similar to those common on the Voice of Palestine radio. Rugh notes that while these states were broadcasting anti-U.S. material, they also were broadcasting American TV series and movies. But these were apolitical programs; the regimes still tried to block the entry of foreign ideas, such as those on the BBC and Voice of America, with jamming.

Countries that do not use broadcasting to mobilize support are more traditional and maintain their political base through traditional appeals. Jordan, for example, took over British transmitters in 1948 but did little until it faced hostile Egyptian broadcasts. It subsequently expanded the facilities in Amman in 1956. The first Saudi Arabian radio station opened in 1948, but it was only audible in

Jidda and Mecca. Riyadh did not get a radio station until 1963. At the same time, Saudi shortwave transmissions were reaching Muslim audiences in Pakistan and Indonesia.

Kuwaiti radio broadcasting commenced in 1952 and expanded after the country gained independence in 1961. Qatar and Abu Dhabi, which later became part of the UAE, opened radio stations in the late 1960s. The UAE itself took over British facilities in 1971 after gaining independence. Although Morocco gained its independence in 1956, it did not take over all broadcasting facilities until 1959. Tunisia put radio broadcasting under government control shortly after independence in 1956, but it was not until 1964 that a member of the ruling party was appointed director of the radio service.

The countries in this category (which preferred to concentrate on the radio medium mobilization) showed even less interest in television. Morocco and Tunisia gained independence in 1956, but they did not set up television stations until 1962 and 1966, respectively. During the intervening years, people in these countries could watch television programs from across the Mediterranean in Europe and also from Algeria. Jordan was motivated to commence television broadcasts in 1968, according to Rugh, because citizens had more than 10,000 TVs with which they were watching programs from other countries.

The Lebanese broadcasting situation differed from that of other countries. The government—first through the Interior Ministry and then through the Information Ministry—took over Lebanese Radio when the French withdrew in 1946. The government did little to increase broadcasting power until the early 1960s, but a 1974 survey found that roughly 25 percent of the population did not listen to state radio even once a week.

The Lebanese government issued television licenses, but stations were privately owned and depended on advertising income. The government's licensing power allowed it to dictate editorial policy to these networks, although it rarely did so unless there was a political crisis. The Compagnie Libanaise de Television (CLT) began work in June 1959, and by the 1970s it had four channels. French involvement with CLT was so extensive, Rugh writes, that the French government was involved with the licensing negotiations. Another firm, Tele-Orient, began broadcasting in 1962, and by the 1970s it had two channels. Tele-Orient has a major British shareholder and depended more on British and U.S. support.

The government's agreement with CLT dictated that programming would not impinge on public security or morality, would not threaten religious groups, and would not back politicians or political parties. CLT, furthermore, agreed to broadcast information provided by the Information Ministry. When CLT renewed its license in 1974, the Lebanese government required a government censor to be on site and also required the station to provide a nightly block of one hour for a government program.

Lebanese political factions' involvement with broadcasting was triggered by the civil war that began in 1975. Several clandestine radio stations began operating in an effort to overcome limited newspaper circulation. The situation became more complicated in March 1976. The group that had seized power from President Suleiman Franjieh controlled several AM and FM radio transmitters, and it also dictated CLT newscasts because it controlled the area where the company was located. President Franjieh's supporters controlled the area north of Beirut where the main AM and shortwave transmitters were located, and they controlled the area where the Tele-Orient facilities were located. Installation of a new president in late 1976 led to improvements in the security environment and restoration of control of the main transmission facilities.

The state of the broadcast media, however, remained in flux. During the next ten years, political factions established seven unauthorized radio stations. These included the Phalange's Voice of Lebanon and the leftist, Nasserite Murabitun's Voice of Arab Lebanon. The Christian Lebanese Forces had Radio Free Lebanon, Christian forces in southern Lebanon had the Voice of Hope, and in 1978 President Franjieh split from the Lebanese Front and established the Voice of United Lebanon. The Islamic Charitable Society established Voice of the Nation in 1984, and Walid Jumblatt, leader of the Druze minority and the Progressive Socialist Party, created the Voice of the Mountain.

In 1978, furthermore, CLT and Tele-Orient decided to merge. The outcome of their agreement with the government was Tele-Liban. Under this arrangement, the government owned half the shares, and the other two entities owned a quarter of the shares each. Division of Beirut into Christian and Muslim halves in 1984 resulted in the relocation of station personnel on the basis of religious identity. This affected the tone of the broadcasts noticeably, because, according to Rugh, Muslims from West Beirut wrote the Channel 7 newscast and the Christians from Hazmiyyah wrote the Channel 5 newscast.

Similar situations exist to the present, with the Lebanese media reflecting the complex communal and political differences of that small country. Following the Syrian withdrawal in 2005, the press in particular blossomed, but followed generally partisan lines. There are news media backed by Syria, Hezbollah, and the anti-Syrian ruling parties. This is, then, a highly politicized pluralism. A roughly similar system developed in Iraq after U.S.-led foreign coalition forces overthrew Saddam Hussein in 2003. Various Sunni Muslim and Shia groupings predominate. In both Lebanon and Iraq, the government itself has only limited control over the media, especially the print media.

Iran is a unique situation. Following very tight controls until the 1990s, which continue absolutely regarding television and radio, there was an opening up toward print media. On one hand, there is a fair amount of freedom, but this is circumscribed by constant closing of newspapers, withdrawal of licenses, and judicial prosecutions. In Iran, then, there is a fair amount of freedom of the press, but for any given newspaper it does not last very long.

Another special case is Israel, which basically follows Western patterns. Israel did not get television until the 1960s and for many years had only one channel, modeled on the BBC and supported by television user fees. Radio was also conducted along British-style lines. In the 1990s, however, television went from only a single channel to a half dozen (or scores if widely available cable is included), while many local and private radio stations were licensed.

By the 1950s, Hebrew-language newspapers were largely in private hands and independent. By far the largest has been *Yediot Aharnot*, read by well over half of the market, followed by *Ma'ariv*, taken by roughly one-third. Somewhat over 10 percent read the English-language *Jerusalem Post* with a similar percentage who read *Ha'aretz*, which generally takes both a leftist and free-enterprise line, and has been more influential due to its elite audience. There are a range of newspapers for the Jewish religious and Arabic-language sectors as well.

Satellite TV, Interactive TV, and Social Media

In the early 1990s, advanced technology led to the creation of Arab satellite television, which continues to operate mainly from Europe. This development sparked an intense debate regarding the role of Arab satellite TV in bringing greater openness to Arab societies and regimes. The globalization of the Arab media (print, broadcast, and televised), which has become known as the "Arab international media," raised expectations of transferring values of pluralism, liberalization, and moving toward a form of democracy in Arab societies.

Even al Jazeera TV, which operates from its center in the capital of Qatar, Doha, has clearly been challenging the Arab social-religious-political agenda. Al-Jazeera earned the image of a provocative medium, one that did not necessarily maintain journalistic ethics and was used for nonjournalistic agendas. Nevertheless, satellite TV became the most popular medium, and al-Jazeera and others succeeded in bringing many taboo issues out in the open for discussion and debate. Interactive television channels such as Orbit—which operated from Rome in the 1990s—held live interviews with Arab leaders—even presidents—and accepted call-ins from Arab viewers worldwide. This enabled the Arab public in some Middle Eastern states (Egypt, Lebanon) to speak out and be heard in a way that they had never experienced before.

These developments along with other technologies have shown that with the globalization process, the people can bring change. The use of Internet chat and blogs (although censored and limited) in the early 2000s opened the way for what became known during the first half of 2011 as the "Arab Spring." In addition, the development of social media outlets such as Facebook and some movements and personalities who dared to favor human rights publicly (the Egyptian Kifaya movement and Professor Saad Eddin Ibrahim, for example) opened new horizons for the Arab public.

As happened elsewhere in the world, the Middle Eastern media scene was very much affected by the advent of the Internet and of satellite television channels. On one hand, this greatly opened up the choices available while also often circumventing the government controls that had hitherto been so effective. On the other hand, however, the new Arabic-language media fell largely into two categories—the entertainment-oriented and the ideological, with the latter meaning either radical Arab nationalist or Islamist.

While such Arabic-language media were often less beholden to an individual government, the amount of liberal-style, democratic-oriented media in the Western style remained limited. There was no democratic revolution in Middle Eastern media, and its function remains largely similar to that filled in the past. This means that in many ways the bulk of the media remains more of an obstacle to reliable information and fair reporting than a vehicle for delivering such things.

The beginning of the twenty-first century is marked by the feeling—common to Middle Eastern regimes, media, and public opinion alike—of rejection by the West in political and social terms, accompanied by a rejection of Western values. Middle Eastern regimes have learned to live with criticism in the media, and their interpretations of it are colored by their own cultural viewpoints.

Middle Eastern journalists are aware of "red lines that may not be crossed" in their criticism of their leaders, and exercise self-censorship, so that public anger is directed outward, and the West is invariably blamed. But the question of assimilating modernity into the Middle Eastern media remains open, because the process is still under way.

References and Further Reading

Ajami, Fouad. "The Arab Inheritance." *Foreign Affairs* 76:5 (September/October 1997): 133–148.

Alterman, Jon B. *New Media, New Politics: From Satellite Television to the Internet in the Arab World.* Washington Institute Policy Papers no. 48 (1998), pp. 15–44.

Amin, Hussein. "Freedom As a Value in Arab Media: Perceptions and Attitudes Among Journalists." *Political Communication* 19:2 (2002): 125–35.

Ayalon, Ami. *The Press in the Arab Middle East: A History.* New York: Oxford University Press, 1995.

Bin Salman, Muhammad. "Arab and Another Kind of Pornography." *Al-Jazeera* [Riyadh-based Saudi daily], February 13, 1998.

Boyd, Douglas. "Satellite Broadcasting in the Middle East and North Africa: Regulations, Access and Impact." *Transnational Broadcasting Studies (TBS)*, no. 2 (Spring 1999), www.tbsjournal.com/Archives/Spring99/Documents/article19.html.

Cohen, Jonathan, and Haim Koren. "Nothing New Under the Sun: How the Media Revolution Failed to Transform Politics in the Middle East." *Review of Communication.* Washington, DC: National Communication Association, October 2003, pp. 415–419.

al-Din al-Miladi, Nur. "Are We Witnessing an Arab Public Sphere in the Making?" Conference on Broadcasting in the Arab World: Challenges and Prospects. London: Westminster University, June 10, 2003.

Eickelman, Dale F. "The Coming Transformation in the Muslim World." *Current History* 9:633 (January 2000): 16–20.

Gershoni, Israel. "Egyptian Liberalism in an Age of 'Crisis of Orientation': Al Risala's Reaction to Fascism and Nazism, 1933–1939." *International Journal of Middle East Studies* 31 (1999): 551–576.

Gilboa, Eytan. "The Evolution of Israeli Media." *Middle East Review of International Affairs (MERIA)* 12:3 (September 2008), www.gloria-center.org/meria/2008/09/gilboa.html.

Hofheinz, Albrecht."The Internet in the Arab World: Playground for Political Liberalization." *Internationale Politik and Gesselshcaft* (*IPG*) 3 (2005): 78–86, www.fes.de/IPG/arc_05_set/set_03_05d.htm.

Hourani, Albert. *Arabic Thought in the Liberal Age, 1798–1939.* Cambridge, UK: Cambridge University Press, 1993.

Khalidi, Rashid. *Palestinian Identity: The Construction of Modern Consciousness.* New York: Columbia University Press, 1997.

Khalil, Joe F. "Inside Arab Reality Television: Development, Definitions and Demystification." *Transnational Broadcasting Studies (TBS)* 15 (2005), www.tbsjournal.com/Archives/Fall05/Khalil.html.

Koren, Haim. "The Arab Citizens of the State of Israel: The Arab Media Perspective." *Israel Affairs* 9:1–2 (Autumn/Winter 2003): 212–26.

———. "The Development of the Arab Media: Cultural and Ideological Aspects and Their Relation to Politics and Regimes in the Middle East." *Diplomatic Notes*, no. 2, *Policy Monographs on International Relations, Security and International Law* (December 2007), www.mfa.gov.il/NR/rdonlyres/E417FE65-4DF9-4F89-B569-244E74B9139F/0/DiplomaticNotes2.pdf.

McLuhan, Marshall. *Understanding Media: Extensions of Man*. New York: McGraw-Hill, 1964.

Miles, Hugh. *Al-Jazeera: The Inside Story of the Arab News Channel That Is Challenging the West*. New York: Grove Press, 2005.

Moreh, Shmuel. "Ya'qub Sanu: His Religious Identity and Work in the Theatre and Journalism According to Family Archives." In *The Jews of Egypt*, ed. Shimon Shamir, 111–129. Boulder, CO: Westview Press, 1987.

Najjar, Orayb. "Freedom of the Press in Jordanian Press Law 1927–1998." In *Mass Media, Politics, and Society in the Middle East*, ed. Kai Hafez, 77–107. Cresskill, N.J.: Hampton Press, 2001.

———. "The Middle East and North Africa." In *Global Journalism: Topical Issues and Media Systems*, 5th ed., ed. Arnold de Beer, 253–92. New York: Pearson Ally and Bacon, 2008.

Qassem, Faysal. Interview in *al-Sharq al-Awsat*, TV supplement, March 16, 1998, p. 7.

———. "The Opposite Direction: The Making of a New Era." Conference on Broadcasting in the Arab World: Challenges and Prospects. London: Westminster University, June 10, 2003.

Rugh, William A. *Arab Mass Media: Newspapers, Radio, and Television in Arab Politics*. Westport, CT: Praeger, 2004.

———. *The Arab Press: News Media and Political Process in the Arab World*. Syracuse, NY: Syracuse University Press, 1979.

Sakr, Naomi. *Satellite Realms: Transnational Television, Globalization and the Middle East*. London: I.B. Tauris, 2001.

The Syrian Media

Kathleen Ridolfo

The Syrian constitution supports free speech and freedom of the press, of printing, and publication "in accordance with the law." However, the government does not do so in practice. A 1963 emergency law authorizes the Syrian government to monitor all publications and communications, and to arrest those who commit crimes that threaten the safety and security of the state. It is illegal to criticize the president, his family, the military, and the Baath Party. Under the 1963 emergency law, the government has the power to determine "at will" what constitutes illegal reporting. For example, "false reporting," which opposes the goals of the revolution, is prohibited, according to author William Rugh. The government can also override the constitution under the emergency law if it deems action by the press a threat to the country's sovereignty or to Baathist ideology. Moreover, Rugh notes, Syrian journalists are in effect employees of the Baath Party and therefore must promote and support Baathist ideology.

As in other Arab states, the first newspapers began operating in Syria in the late nineteenth century. What was perhaps the first Syrian newspaper, the government-run *Suriya*, began printing in 1865. Privately owned newspapers were also published during this period. Ottoman control over the media prevented the development of a vibrant press until the Young Turk Revolution of 1908, in which a group of Turkish nationalist officers and students seized power. They were intent on modernization and knew that a strong press was a key element in any such program. Consequently, they encouraged literacy, the import of printing presses, and the spread of newspapers over the next ten years. Syria passed from Ottoman control to a French mandate after World War I. Under the French, the press continued to grow, but articles critical of the mandate government were subject to censorship.

Syria gained independence just after World War II. In the independence period, which lasted until 1946, Syria experienced decades of political turmoil, which influenced the development of its media system. The media eventually came under the control of the government in the 1960s, which used them as tools to maintain state control. Journalists who went too far in their criticism of government policy were imprisoned.

From 1946 to 1958, Syria passed through what Rugh characterizes as the factional press stage, marked by a high degree of partisan political activity, a rapid turnover in governments, and heated competition for power and control. Virtually every newspaper was run by a politically oriented editor tied to a party, interest group, powerful family, or politician. Due to the influence of these actors on the press, there were no truly independent newspapers. By contrast, the government remained weak, and therefore could not exert pressure on the press or control its activities.

The situation changed with the establishment of the United Arab Republic (UAR) in 1958. The short-lived republic, which merged the Syrian state with Egypt under Gamal Abdel Nasser, banned all private newspapers and political parties. The government established its own media machine, which it tightly controlled. Following the 1961 coup in Syria, which marked the collapse of the UAR, the new regimes prevented the development of a free and independent press. The Baath Party came to power in 1963 and has controlled the state ever since. The Correctional Movement within the Baath, under Hafez al-Assad, came to power in 1970. The Assad family has controlled Syria ever since.

The Assad regime's control over every aspect of political life ensured no real criticism would be made in the press. Following his ascension to the presidency in 1970, Assad maintained power through corrupt elections. The government slightly relaxed its censorship of the media from 1996 to 1999. For example, regional issues, including the peace process between Israel and Syria, were covered factually, whereas had such issues been covered in the press before, the facts would have been presented in a light that was favorable to the regime. The government also repealed its ban on the import of Jordanian newspapers in 1999.

In what was to be his last term in office, Assad was elected to his fifth seven-year term in 1999, with 99.9 percent of the vote. Upon his death in June 2000, his son Bashar took power after he was unanimously nominated by the Baath Party to succeed his father.

More than a decade into the new millennium, ownership of the press is not all formally in the hands of the government, but no free press exists since there are very tight controls. The largest daily in circulation is the government-owned *al-Baath.* The second largest is *al-Thawra*, published by the Ministry of Information, which also publishes the popular daily *al-Tishreen.* The government also publishes the English-language *Syria Times.* The ministry controls the Syrian National News Agency (SANA), which reports in both English and Arabic.

In 2001, the government granted permission for a pro-Baath faction of the Communist Party to publish its newspaper *Sawt al-Sha'b* following a forty-three-year ban on the daily. Two new privately owned weekly newspapers, the satirical *al-Domari* and the Nasserist *al-Wahdawi*, were also allowed to publish, but the government set limits on content. Some 150 magazines were also in publication.

Another private political newspaper, *al-Watan*, began operating in November 2006 with a very small print run. *Al-Watan*, while privately owned, maintains an editorial line basically indistinguishable from the government owned press, and some observers consider that it is intended to enable the regime to depict itself as reformist, rather than constituting a real step toward greater media freedom.

The Baathist Media Machine

Under Hafez al-Assad, a member of Syria's minority Alawi sect, Alawis maintained power and relative popularity through a vast propaganda effort, the main goal of which was to secure favorable public opinion for the regime through the mass media. Manipulation of newspapers, radio, and television was only part of the propaganda effort, which also included the organization of mass rallies, oversight of school curricula, the publication of books praising Assad, and other efforts promoting the personality cult around the leader.

According to Mordechai Kedar, the Syrian press under Assad served a dual function: first, to bring the reader information and articles on a wide variety of subjects, and second, to act as a conduit for the words and messages of the regime. The dual role did not allocate space to contradictory opinions. Assad, viewed by many as a dictator exerting complete control over the population yet rattled by insecurities, used the press as a tool for creating legitimacy for himself as president and for the systems he operated to implement his rule. Accordingly, the press functioned to propagate the regime's message and provide legitimacy for Assad, while at the same time blocking messages that threatened the regime's legitimacy. As is the case with other Arab leaders, Assad was acutely aware that large segments of the population did not view his regime as legitimate.

Syrian media were long managed by Information Minister Ahmad Iskandar Ahmad, who served the president from 1974 until 1983. According to Patrick Seale, Ahmad streamlined Syria's media by welding into a team the heads of state-run television, radio, and print media; the state news agency SANA; advertising; and press distribution—all to the greater glory of Assad.

In a 1985 interview, the editor of the daily *al-Thawra* contended that the goals of the Baath Party's mass media machine were, on the one hand, to educate and turn the individual into "the new man," an Arab nationalist and patriot who supports the party's goals, and on the other, "to direct the consciousness and the culture of the masses," in order to "fuse" and "mold" the sectors of the population into a consolidated whole.

The Media Under Bashar al-Assad

On the day Bashar al-Assad came to power in 2000, he called for a new transparency and openness, indicating that earlier restrictions on the press and other areas of civic activity would be relaxed. Bashar instructed the media to end the practice of blanketing the pages of their publications with praise for the president. The move prompted Information Minister Adnan Omran to announce that the press could talk about anything without a problem.

The experiment was not to last, yet for a brief period publishers tested the limits of the regime. For example, *al-Domari*, the first privately owned newspaper to begin operating in four decades, began publicly criticizing state ministers, and *al-Thawra* featured articles by former political prisoners and intellectuals previously barred from publication. As Rugh notes, a fine line existed in the press, where local press reports and editorials were allowed to criticize government services, but senior regime leaders were off limits. By autumn 2001, new restrictions on the media were in place. The government issued a press law that imposed additional restrictions on journalists. Along with the restrictions came the stillbirth of political reforms, including a much-anticipated opening for political opposition.

Syria's 2001 press laws, while allowing for a free and independent press, also cite grounds for libel. The prime minister has the right to shut down newspapers and arrest journalists who harm the national interest. Information that could harm national security, the unity of society, military security, the economy or monetary system, or Syria's relations with its neighbors is banned from publication. Under the law, violators can be imprisoned for up to three years and fined up to 1 million Syrian pounds (about $20,000).

Communications minister Amr Salim issued an order in July 2007 requiring Web site administrators to identify individuals posting material to their sites by name and e-mail address.

Sanctioned Criticism Acts as Safety Valve

Though the Syrian government severely restricts criticism of the state, it does allow for some criticism in the government-owned press. For example, in April 2007, the Middle East Media Research Institute (MEMRI) reported that dozens of articles had been published in the state-run press in the weeks leading up to parliamentary elections that criticized candidates, "describing them as freely scattering promises, but not doing anything once elected apart from actions that serve their personal interest."

One such critique, which appeared in *al-Tishreen* on April 30, 2007, asserted that many Syrians had no desire to participate as candidates or as voters in the elections since they believed the parliament and regional councils did not fulfill their function as outlined in the constitution, thus making them nominal rather than active institutions. The schizophrenic nature of the regime means, however, that what is permissible changes on a near daily basis, making it difficult for writers who wish to work in the media.

Moreover, the government uses the media when necessary to launch attacks at rival Arab states and the West. Syrian government dailies routinely published articles attacking Detlev Mehlis, the first commissioner of the UN team investigating the assassination of former Lebanese prime minister Rafik Hariri, killed in a 2005 truck bombing in Beirut, which many claim was carried out by Syrian intelligence. Syrian state media attempted to smear Mehlis's credibility, claiming he had been paid off by Lebanese leaders and that he led a life of luxury, sailing on Lebanese yachts, drinking wine, and losing his objectivity.

Other articles, particularly since the 2003 start of the U.S.-led war in Iraq, have accused neighboring Arab states of aiding a so-called U.S. imperialist agenda across the Arab world. A July 2007 article in *al-Tishreen* noted: "The joint plan by Washington and Tel Aviv is being implemented by others who are supposed to be loyal to the [Arab] nation and motherland. The United States has managed to set up a natural experiment and a model for dividing society throughout the entire region."

Similarly, an article published in *al-Thawra* just days later, read: "Our nation at the moment is experiencing disintegration and a rift of unprecedented proportions, and is in need of resistance, values and culture. . . . We have no choice but to return to the culture of resistance, now that Iraq has been turned into a kind of American state, and Lebanon into a backyard of the White House, and in view of what is being planned for Syria, Sudan, and all Arab countries as part of the American-Zionist plan."

Like many other Arab states, the Syrian regime employs one media message for the outside world and another for its domestic audience. When Bashar al-Assad gave an interview to the *New York Times* in November 2003, the translation that appeared in Syrian newspapers was heavily edited. In an article posted on the Web site of the Syrian Communist Party, journalist Subhi Hadidi noted that the Syrian version in Arabic was over 2,000 words shorter than the Arabic translation of the interview published in the London-based daily *al-Sharq al-Awsat.* "The part that was omitted included questions and answers regarding [Syria's] domestic situation, Iraq, Hizballah, normalization with the Hebrew State [Israel], and U.S.-Syrian security cooperation," wrote Hadidi.

Radio

Radio broadcasting was launched in Syria in 1946, the year the state-run Syrian Broadcasting Organization was founded. Unlike other Arab states, Syria invested little effort and few resources in the broadcasting system. Thus, it lagged behind neighboring countries such as Lebanon and Israel until the early 1960s.

In 1950, Syria had four medium-wave transmitters operating from its two main cities, Damascus and Aleppo. State-run radio was on the air for nine hours a day, with foreign-language broadcasts running one hour a day, presenting programs in English, French, and Turkish, among others. Syria also began broadcasting in Hebrew in the 1950s.

Douglas Boyd writes that the brief 1958–1961 union between Egypt and Syria known as the United Arab Republic had a strong influence on broadcasting because it brought many Egyptians to Damascus. Egypt, which had a strong broadcasting system, also provided training to Syrians in broadcast technology and the art of propaganda. A radio-broadcasting complex was built in Damascus, and transmitters were set up throughout the country to serve both domestic and neighboring populations. Although the Syrian system failed to rival that of its neighbor in scale, by 1965, the country boasted sixteen transmitters.

Shortwave transmitters were not well maintained and were eventually deactivated in 1978, when the country launched a new system that included five 250-kilowatt transmitters. Boyd notes that Syria also acquired a Czech-made 1,500-kilowatt Tesla medium-wave facility that boasted a switchable omnidirectional and directional transmission. The antenna was aimed at Iraq and the Gulf States in 1979. The transmitter was prohibitively expensive, requiring sixteen tons of oil per day to operate. The acquisition of this new powerful transmitter allowed Syria to broadcast news, dramas, and other programs that defended the regime's Baathist policies and its occupation of Lebanon.

Syrian citizens have also turned to Western radio stations. Popular among them have been BBC's Arabic service, Radio Monte Carlo, and to a lesser extent the Voice of America. Another radio station that has succeeded in attracting an audience is the Arabic service of the Israeli radio, though more for its daily broadcast of Umm Kulthum songs than its news.

Television

Television came to Syria under the UAR, and the first broadcasts began on July 2, 1960—the same day Egypt started broadcasting. Broadcasts were beamed from a main transmitter in Damascus, with smaller stations operating out of Aleppo and Homs. In the 1970s, a nationwide network linked regional stations by microwave to the main station in Damascus.

Boyd writes that due to poor economic development and the 1967 and 1973 wars with Israel, there was little growth in the field of television between 1960 and 1975. Frequent regime change was also to blame for the poor media development. Moreover, following the Arab League's decision to boycott the Radio Corporation of America (RCA) in the late 1960s, which was responsible for the construction of the television system in Syria, spare parts became difficult to obtain. Eventually, Syria purchased Polish cameras to replace outdated and broken RCA equipment. The regime overhauled the system in 1975, bringing SECAM color, and new transmitters were installed to broaden domestic and international reach.

The regime's decision to upgrade the television system in the mid-1970s was influenced by the increasing availability of foreign broadcasts in Syria from neighboring Israel, Iraq, and Jordan, all of which had relay stations close to their borders with Syria.

Syrian programming has always been domestically produced, and few programs are brought in from foreign states. Films and documentaries from non-Arab states—particularly from Soviet satellite countries—are shown, but few Western programs are regularly broadcast. Syria has had more success in the export of its dramas to regional states, as the programs are considered top-notch across the Arab world. With the rise of satellite television, they have become more accessible across the region. Special programming during the holy month of Ramadan draws thousands of viewers from across the region. In 2007, Syrian dramas were hailed regionwide for addressing taboo subjects rarely addressed so openly in Arab society, such as prostitution, terrorism, and AIDS. The dramas, while filmed in Syria, were broadcast mainly on regional satellite channels rather than on state-owned channels, most likely because the government would not approve such content for broadcast.

The Syrian government finances television through a combination of government funding and advertising. According to Boyd, 30 percent of advertising revenue is retained by Syrian television, with the remaining 70 percent going to the Ministry of Finance.

Syria's first privately owned television channel opened, and closed, in 2006. Sham TV began running trial transmissions in May 2005 from Dubai's Media City. Just days before it was to go on the air with live transmission, the channel's manager was summoned to the Information Ministry and told of the decision to withdraw the channel's license. According to media reports, no explanation was given. Sham TV was, in effect, stillborn. Some observers speculated that the channel was viewed by the regime as a threat to state-run television, though that was probably not the main reason for its ban.

The Syrian government opened the Damascus Media City in March 2006. Located at the Damascus International Fairgrounds, the 65,000-square-metere media zone was billed by Deputy Information Minister Taleb Qadi Amin as part of the government's desire "to develop media performance and to use true information in the service of the country and citizens."

Internet

The Internet began officially operating in Syria in 1998, but few Syrians had access to it due to registration requirements and fees. Until 2005, the only two service providers were government owned. Two privately owned providers opened that year. By 2000, there were an estimated 30,000 Internet users in Syria. Since that time, the number of Syrians going online has increased dramatically, even though access has remained difficult and expensive for a large percentage of the population. The Web site www.openarab.net reported in 2006 that the per-hour cost of accessing the Internet in Internet cafés was between 50 and 100 liras (US$1–2). The gross domestic product per capita in 2009 was estimated at $2,474.

By the end of 2004, there were some 800,000 Internet users, according to openarab.net. According to the 2008 edition of the CIA *World Factbook*, that number had grown to 1.5 million by 2006. There were 119 Internet hosts by 2007, in a country with a population of 19.3 million, skewed to a younger age range. The Amman-based consulting firm Arab Advisors Group estimated that the number of Internet users would surpass 1.7 million by 2009. In fact, by June 2010, there were 3.9 million Internet users in Syria.

Though usage has proliferated, the government still controls access through a variety of mechanisms. For example, openarab.net reported in 2006 that Syrian intelligence paid millions of dollars in 2005 to purchase modern censorship equipment from Germany and the Netherlands in order to restrict access to the most popular Web sites.

The Internet in Syria was developed so that all access must go through a proxy. Critics contend that the regime operates from the position that all content is forbidden unless it can be proved useful or of no harm to state interests. Moreover, Syrians were banned from accessing any service excluding browsing web pages using http protocol, according to openarab.net.

The Syrian government blocks all types of Web sites, but especially opposition sites and those critical of government policy, as well as Islamist sites. The sites of pan-Arab dailies, which are often critical of the Assad regime, are also banned, including *al-Sharq al-Awsat* and *al-Quds al-Arabi.*

The elaph.com news Web site, which is funded by the Saudi government, is also blocked, and the government has also blocked access at times to Yahoo!, Hotmail, Google's blogging engine www.blogspot.com, and Maktoob, as well as some access to YouTube and the social networking site Facebook. Facebook was officially unbanned in February 2011 in the face of protests. Young Syrians had in any case long accessed both Facebook and YouTube using proxy international servers. Pro-Kurdish Web sites and sites registered with Israel's country suffix .il, as well as sites for international human rights organizations, are also banned.

Openarab.net reports that the state-owned Public Telecommunications Foundation signed a contract with an Italian company to launch satellite Internet service and construct a series of Internet cafés in Syria. However, the agreement stipulated that the service would be a reception only, meaning that any subscriber wishing to send anything via the Internet would have to go through the servers of the Public Telecommunications Foundation, which are heavily monitored by the state. According to media reports, it is possible to get around Syrian restrictions by requesting use of a "Lebanese server" at Internet cafés. The connection then runs through a long-distance phone call to a Lebanese Internet service provider (ISP) not subject to Syria's controls. However, the practice, while reportedly widespread, is considered illegal. In November 2005, media watchdog Reporters Without Borders named Syria as one of fifteen enemies of the Internet around the world.

Communications and Technology Minister Amr Salim told *al-Hayat* in July 2007 that Syria obtained a license to import technological equipment from the U.S. telecommunications sector after a several-month delay due to sanctions under the Syria Accountability Act. The equipment purchase came amid demands for high-speed wireless ADSL, he said.

Salim confirmed in the interview that his ministry began experimental implementation of a wireless Internet project, which would be available through the two cellular telephone companies later in the year. The companies allowed the ministry to use their infrastructure to secure wireless Internet, he said, adding, "the service will be offered by the private-sector Internet Service Providers [ISP] in order to strengthen competition over the prices and sectors." He said the agreement would lead to reduced prices for users, and that wireless Internet would first be available in Damascus and Aleppo, offered free of charge for three months to new subscribers. A recent survey by the Syrian Telecommunications Establishment determined the number of Internet subscribers had reached 5.5 million, he added.

Bloggers have become a frequent target of security services. The Syrian authorities began detaining online commentators as early as 2002, with some serving sentences of three years or more on charges of violating the press law. In 2005, there were only five Syrian bloggers online, according to a 2006 report by openarab.net. Within a year, that number had increased to thiry-five.

By October 2007, Syria had been holding two men in detention for nearly five months for expressing their views online, Human Rights Watch reported. The authorities refused to tell the men's families where they were being detained. One month earlier, the Supreme State Security Court had sentenced a third man to two years in prison for posting online comments critical of Saudi Arabia, which the Syrian government said adversely affected its relations with the state, the watchdog said. "The fact that Syria arrests people solely because they criticize the state speaks volumes about the government's utter disregard for the most basic human rights," said Sara Lea Whitson, Middle East director at Human Rights Watch.

Bloggers have recounted to several international media watchdogs that Syrian intelligence often places plainclothes agents in Internet cafés to spy on users' activities. One Syrian who posted comments on an opposition Web site based outside Syria was arrested and detained for a month along with a relative after the owner of an Internet café filmed him posting the comments.

Minister Salim issued a decree in July 2007 requiring all Web site owners to display "the name and e-mail of the writer of any article or comment [appearing on their site] . . . clearly and in detail, under threat of warning the owner of the website, then restricting access to the website temporarily and in case the violation is repeated, permanently banning the website," according to Human Rights Watch.

The brief opening experienced by Syrian media in 2001 became known as the "Damascus Spring." Though it was not to last, it provided a window for Syrian journalists to test the limits of the regime. There was some increase in flexibility over what existed under Hafez al-Assad, but only to a very limited extent.

2011 Uprising

The role of social media in facilitating the widespread protests of 2011 was enormous. Activists communicated with each other and organized demonstrations using Twitter and Facebook, and they broadcast messages to the world via YouTube. However, at the time of writing, the regime is bloodily suppressing protests, and the print media remain the outlets for regime propaganda. The Assad regime is doing its best to close down media coverage in Syria. It has banned foreign journalists from entering the country. Even the satellite phones that provided contact between journalists in Lebanon and activists in Syria were reportedly shut down by the regime. Bashar al-Assad appears determined to freeze development in his country. For as long as he succeeds, the severe restrictions on media activity in the country are likely to continue.

References and Further Reading

"Attacks on the Press in 2007: Worldwide Survey by the Committee to Protect Journalists." Committee to Protect Journalists. Available at http://cpj.org/2008/02/attacks-on-the-press-2007.php.

Boyd, Douglas A. *Broadcasting in the Arab World: A Survey of Electronic Media in the Middle East.* 3rd ed. Ames: Iowa State University Press, 1999.

Campagna, Joel. "Syria Briefing Sept. 2001: Stop Signs." The Committee to Protect Journalists. Available at www.cpj.org/Briefings/2001/Syria_sept01/Syria_sept01.html.

CIA World Factbook. "Syria." Available at www.cia.gov/library/publications/the-world-factbook/geos/sy.html#Intro.

"Criticism of the Upcoming Parliamentary Elections in the Official Syrian Press and Among the Syrian Opposition." MEMRI, Inquiry and Analysis Series—no. 345. April 20, 2007.

Halpern, Orly. "Syria Opens 'Free Media City.'" *Jerusalem Post*, March 14, 2006.

Hammond, Andrew. "The State of Syria's Media: 'Damascus Spring' or Indian Summer?" January 3, 2002. Available at www.worldpress.org/Mideast/886.cfm.

"Harsh Criticism of Arab Countries in Syrian Press." MEMRI, Special Dispatch Series—no. 1666. July 25, 2007.

Human Rights Watch. "Syria." In *False Freedom: Online Censorship in the Middle East and North Africa.* Available at www.hrw.org/reports/2005/mena1105/6.htm#_Toc119125736.

"In the Syrian Media: Personal Attacks on Head of International U.N. Committee Investigating Al-Hariri Assassination." MEMRI, Special Dispatch Series—no. 1001. October 11, 2005.

Kedar, Mordechai. *Asad in Search of Legitimacy: Message and Rhetoric in the Syrian Press Under Hafiz and Bashir.* Brighton, UK: Sussex Academic Press, 2005.

Kraidy, Marwan M. "Syria: Media Reform and Its Limitations." *Arab Reform Bulletin* 4:4, Carnegie Endowment for International Peace, May 2006.

Rugh, William A. *Arab Mass Media: Newspapers, Radio, and Television in Arab Politics.* Westport, CT: Praeger, 2004.

The Egyptian Media

Barry Rubin

From the 1950s onward, the Egyptian media was predominant in the Arabic-speaking world. This was partly because Egypt's size and political influence (especially in the 1950s and 1960s) was so powerful, as was its centrality in terms of cultural significance. The Egyptian media had lively newspapers, with *al-Ahram* considered the best newspaper in the Arab world. There was censorship, but they had a lot of latitude.

Over time, this role steadily declined for a number of reasons: the death of President Gamal Abdel Nasser in 1973; the isolation of Egypt by other Arab states from the late 1970s and into the 1980s after its peace agreement with Israel; the development of media in other countries; the growth of an Arabic press located in Europe; a turning inward by the Egyptians themselves; and finally, the creation of new media, especially satellite television networks, in other countries.

Still, Egypt remains extremely important in the world of Arabic media. It is also an excellent case study for the extent and limitation of media freedom along with the methods of government control and ideological orientation.

The Egyptian Press

Newspaper publishing in Egypt can be traced to the era of Napoleon's presence (1798–1801), which opened Egypt to Western influence and started its people thinking about many new ideas and inventions. The early newspapers were put out by the French and later by the Egyptian government. While the Ottoman Empire returned in 1805, a native-born dynasty soon rose to power, founded by Muhammad Ali, which was very interested in modernization. After the British seized control in 1882, they continued this development, as did the opposition Egyptian nationalist movement and the monarchy, which achieved a modicum of independence in the 1920s. Private newspapers emerged in the 1860s and 1870s, while those associated with political parties began in the 1880s. In some instances, newspapers were established, attracting similarly inclined writers, and they would eventually establish a party. These were mainly elite publications, and furthermore, the government restricted the commentary and reporting in them.

One newspaper in particular, *al-Ahram*, came to have a significant reach in the Arabic-speaking world and was particularly influential among politically active Egyptians. The newspaper was created in the late 1870s by two Lebanese journalists, the brothers Salim and Bisharah Taqla, who had fled censorship at home, where the Ottoman Empire still ruled. They ran it as a family firm, and Bisharah's son, Gabriel, took over in 1908.

Gabriel Taqla introduced several innovations, including a network of foreign reporters in major international capitals, as well as a wire service. Until then, Egyptian newspapers depended on foreign news agencies to provide them with information. Taqla also built a modern printing plant and had the newspaper publish photographs. While Egyptian newspapers were generally identified with political parties, the Taqla family's wealth allowed *al-Ahram* to avoid being connected with any single faction. The paper, therefore, was openly critical of political parties and prominent individuals. It did not criticize the royal family, however.

Egyptian Nationalism

Being under British rule inspired nationalist sentiments among Egyptians. The British allowed the monarch, Faruk I, to remain in place, while keeping effective power in their own hands. When in 1919 the British exiled the leader of the nationalist Wafd Party, the resulting revolutionary turmoil led to the declaration of Egyptian independence in February 1922. Effective British control stayed in place, however, and a 1936 treaty between Egypt and the United Kingdom permitted British troops to stay in Egypt to protect the Suez Canal for the next twenty years. Still, the 1920s and 1930s were something of a golden age in the development of a liberal Egyptian intellectual elite determined to reform the country into a more European-style state and society.

The 1952 Revolution

Resentment over colonial rule and anger with King Faruk's ruling style led to a coup in July 1952. The Free Officers Movement, from which Nasser emerged as leader, overthrew the monarch. General Mohammad Naguib became president as figurehead for this group of more junior officers in September 1952.

The Arab nationalists believed Egypt should become the Arab world's leader, and guide it toward unity within and opposition to Western influence. This meant that the new regime had a tremendous interest in propaganda and ideological matters as well as in influencing other Arab countries. Following the Soviet and fascist models to some extent, the Egyptian government believed that it should have a monopoly on conveying information and that news should conform to its political line.

Soon thereafter, the Dar al-Tahrir publishing house was established to convey the new leadership's views to the public. *Al-Tahrir*, a bimonthly magazine, first appeared in September 1952. It was leftist, anti-imperialist, and revolutionary, and it backed the ruling Revolutionary Command Council. *Al-Gomhuria*, a daily newspaper with a similar stance, started in December 1952.

In addition to putting out its own publications, the Revolutionary Command Council acted against the private newspapers. General Naguib announced in January 1953 the creation of a party called the National Liberation Rally. He banned all other parties and their associated publications on the grounds that they undermined the national interest.

The Media Under Nasser

Nasser briefly revoked some aspects of censorship after he became president in February 1954. But since criticism of his government was intense, censorship was reinstated within a month. The regime was particularly concerned since the popularity of several private newspapers—*al-Ahram*, *Akhbar al-Yawm*, and *al-Misri*—surpassed that of the government's own *al-Gomhuria*.

For example, *al-Misri*, which reflected the views of the banned Wafd Party, had a circulation surpassing 120,000. It criticized Nasser in 1954, calling for a real parliamentary system and urging the military to return to the barracks. The Revolutionary Command Council (RCC), the body which formally controlled Egypt after the 1952 revolution, revoked its license in April 1954. Private publishing was not eliminated, but pressure from the military government brought about a significant level of self-censorship by the media and effectively halted serious criticism of the government. The government's power to issue press licenses, as well as other forms of legal authority, was used against critical journalists and publications.

This control of the media continued with a May 1960 regulation (Law Number 156) stating that a newspaper must be authorized by the country's sole political party, the Arab Socialist Union (previously the National Union). Law Number 156 transferred ownership of several private publishing houses (Dar al-Ahram, Dar Akhbar al-Yawm, Dar al-Hillal, and Dar Rose al-Yusif) to the sole political party. The law also required that the party appoint newspapers' directing boards, effectively giving the government control over all aspects of the press. But because the state itself did not take direct control of the newspapers, the regime asserted that this was not nationalization. Egyptian law referred to organization of the press rather than nationalization, for example, and the Arab Socialist Union technically was not part of the state.

The Media Under Sadat

Anwar Sadat succeeded Nasser in 1970 upon Nasser's death, and this development heralded changes in handling of the press. Sadat ended press censorship in 1973, but in the same year more than

100 journalists had their licenses suspended. Press censorship was abolished formally in 1974. Sadat favored democracy as a concept, but he also feared that opponents would exploit the situation. In addition to its other responsibilities, the Supreme Press Council that was created in 1975 was tasked with creating a code of conduct for journalists.

Sadat decreed in 1976 that the Arab Socialist Union would have three distinct platforms—leftist, centrist, and rightist—that would compete against each other in the upcoming parliamentary elections. The three entities officially became political parties, and 1977's Law Number 4 permitted members of parliament to create new parties. Sadat abolished the ASU in June 1977. Law Number 148 of 1980 dealt with powers of the press and gave the upper house of parliament (the Shura Council) ownership of the five major publishing houses. The council appointed the chairman and majority of each house's managing board. As the debate on the press law was taking place in the parliament in 1977, Sadat pointed out that from his perspective the public must control the press in a democracy. The new parties published weeklies, but by September 1978 they had mostly faded away.

It became obvious that while Sadat wanted party activity, he only wanted a circumscribed public debate. Looking ahead to the June 1979 parliamentary election, in late 1978 Sadat created the National Democratic Party. The party's weekly—*Mayo*—benefited from good financing, access to news and information from the government, and exclusive interviews with Sadat himself. The opposition created the Socialist Labor Party meanwhile, and this produced the *al-Shaab* newspaper. The National Progressive Unionist Grouping's *al-Ahali* weekly appeared shortly before the election. The latter two criticized the government's polices, such as the 1979 peace treaty with Israel, and had some legal problems, but they continued to publish.

Consequently, at first the press enjoyed greater freedom during the presidency of Sadat, and some of the journalists who were imprisoned or exiled under Nasser were rehabilitated. Press restrictions were eased even more in 1974, and the media discussed topics that were previously off-limits, including Nasserism, the need for political parties, student politics, and press freedom. Two Islamist monthlies—*al-Dawa* and *al-Itisam*—that were closed under Nasser were reinstated. However, the Marxist monthly *al-Taliah* was replaced by a science magazine after it attributed January 1977 disturbances over price increases to mass disgruntlement, and the editor of *Rose al-Yusif*, Muhammad al-Tabi, was replaced for similar reporting about the disturbances.

A 1977 parties' law permitted the publication of weekly newspapers by political parties. The *Garidit Masr* of Sadat's party began in June 1977, *al-Ahrar* of the rightist Liberal Party began in November 1977, and *al-Ahali* of the leftist Progressive Party began in February 1978. These publications ran into financial problems and found it difficult to compete with the major publishers. Moreover, the prosecutor seized copies of *al-Ahali* in May 1978 on the grounds that they contained antidemocratic content. Also in May 1978, the Sadat regime secured approval in a referendum of a law that banned political activities by Marxists and others. By September 1978 all the party weeklies had ceased activities, although the Islamist ones, *al-Dawa* and *al-Itisam*, continued.

Several factors contributed to the relative diversity of the Egyptian press during this period. Journalism is a respected and even prestigious profession with a long tradition, and a number of journalists working in Egypt have the best reputations in the Arab world. Moreover, a diversity of views can be found on a publication's staff. Journalists who support government policies get improved access and are favored by the leadership, but even those who fall out of favor are rarely imprisoned or prevented from earning a living. In 1973, many journalists were suspended but continued to draw their salaries, and eventually they were reinstated. Sadat said later that he only wanted the journalists to behave responsibly and stand by Egypt.

By the end of the 1970s the situation was changing. The Supreme Press Council was established in 1975 and authorized to issue licenses to publications and journalists. This council influences the distribution of newsprint and advertising, which in turn gives it power over publications. The upper house of parliament was established in 1980 and given ownership of the press. The council and the upper house are effectively controlled by the ruling party, which gives the president the power to select editors in chief.

In September 1981 Sadat had had enough of critical debate and reinstated government control of the press. Several newspapers were closed and others were suspended, journalists were arrested, and there was a crackdown on the opposition. *Mayo*, the ruling National Democratic Party's newspaper, continued its activities, as did the Liberal Party's *al-Ahrar.* Emergency laws passed after the October 1981 assassination of Sadat were renewed for two years in May 2006.

The Media Under Mubarak

Sadat was assassinated in October 1981 and succeeded by Hosni Mubarak, who stayed in office well over a quarter of a century. Mubarak's attitude toward the press was similar to Sadat's, and the conflict with Islamist elements contributed to the regime's repressiveness. Initially, Mubarak lifted some of Sadat's press restrictions and had oppositionists and journalists freed. *Al-Ahali* and *al-Shaab* resumed publication by spring 1982, and a dormant opposition party called the New Wafd resumed activities in autumn 1983. Within six months the new party's weekly—*al-Wafd*—was selling in excess of 500,000 copies. Restrictions on Muslim and Coptic Christian publications were lifted in 1984. During this decade, press criticism of government policies was allowed to appear in print, and even the older, mainstream dailies occasionally published articles that made the government look bad.

By the middle of the 1990s the press appeared to be flourishing. At least five of the party papers' circulations exceeded 100,000, and the three national dailies had circulations ranging from 400,000 to one million. According to William Rugh in *Arab Mass Media*, 263 newspapers had licenses.

Simultaneously, the regime used its counterterrorism campaign to justify media restrictions. Antiterrorist Law 97 of 1992 outlines vaguely defined deeds—such as "spreading panic"—as grounds for actions against a publication. The government passed Press and Publications Law Number 93 in 1995, making penalties more severe and placing the burden of proof on the press in libel cases. The law was so restrictive that it elicited widespread objections from the press syndicate, journalists, and even government-appointed editors. The head of the press syndicate met with Mubarak in June 1996, and negotiations between the government and the press resulted in passage of Press and Publications Law Number 96 in 1996.

In July 2005, the Egyptian media underwent another shake-up, when the Higher Press Council appointed new chairmen of three major state-owned publishing houses and replaced editors in chief of the main newspapers. The *al-Ahram*, *Akhbar al-Youm*, and *al-Tahrir* publishing houses got new and younger leaders, and *al-Ahram*, *al-Akhhar*, and *al-Gomhuria* got new editors. The official reason for the replacements was that the editors had passed retirement age. There was speculation, however, that the appointments reflected an official effort to reform the media as a counter to the emergence of independent Arabic-language dailies such as *al-Masry al-Youm* and *Nehidat Misr.*

Pressures to improve the media, which meant giving it at least a greater appearance of freedom to increase its popularity, came about due to three factors. First, the popularity of Arabic satellite news channels gave a growing number of people an alternative source of information quite independent of government control and often including criticisms, though frequently from a more radical rather than more moderate direction.

Second, international pressure for democratization came from the United States and Europe. Egypt could, however, defuse this development or even at times turn the situation to its own advantage by showing reform from above. For example, the government created its own journal on democracy, whose potential impact on Egypt was diminished and its public relations value maximized by its being published only in English. The journal was also apparently forbidden from writing about Egypt itself.

Third, the radical challenge stemming from political Islamism also forced the regime to defend itself and its policies against a potentially popular internal foe for the first time since the 1950s. Thus, the success of Muslim Brotherhood candidates in the November–December 2005 parliamentary elections resulted in critical commentary from the state-owned *al-Ahram.* Specifically, the National Democratic Party (NDP) was condemned for failing to deal with the difficulties encountered by average citizens, and there were demands for a new party as an alternative to the NDP and the Muslim Brotherhood.

Levels of Control

The Egyptian press initially fell into the mobilization category, in which the purpose of the press was to mobilize support for the regime and its policies. By the 1990s, however, it fell into the transitional print media category. During the mobilization phase, the Egyptian press avoided editorials that attacked the regime's foreign policy. Moreover, editorials did not criticize government policies at all, and any political discussion that did occur did so within the context of state policy. Individual officials could be criticized, but changes in the leadership were not recommended.

The newspapers did not function directly as government mouthpieces, however, so it was not mandatory—in comparison to the media in Syria or under Saddam Hussein in Iraq, for example—for them to publish an entire presidential speech. Even when state censors were assigned to newspapers during crisis periods, there was a level of discussion between them and the editors over what would be published.

Editors always had the freedom to engage in indirect criticism. They would publish poetry or short stories, for example, that might serve this purpose. Rugh writes, "There is evidence of vitality and professionalism in Egyptian journalism, though it is often restrained by the political system for the sake of current efforts by the leadership at unity in order to deal with overriding problems such as the Arab-Israeli conflict or economic development."

The publications generally cover identical news stories, but their styles vary. *Al-Ahram*, which is read by state officials, academics, and businesspeople, tends to be conservative, whereas the higher-circulation *al-Akhbar*, which has a livelier and more sensationalist style, is read by students, bureaucrats, and more of a mass audience. *Al-Gomhuria* tends to focus on Arab socialist issues and leftist causes, and therefore has a following among leftist intellectuals and workers. Leftists were active in print media during Nasser's presidency (1953–1970), and Marxists had a monthly journal call *al-Taliah*. The weekly *Rose al-Yusif* engaged in what Rugh terms "irresponsible yellow journalism that carried the government's anti-imperialism and other policies to excess."

The state also controls access to foreign print media. The Interior Ministry can claim protection of public order when banning a foreign publication, and the Defense Ministry can ban reporting on security issues. Furthermore, print media from abroad must be approved by the Information Ministry's Censorship Department. For example, *al-Hayat*, a London-based newspaper, was seized in 1992 because of the way it reported on the government's handling the aftermath of an earthquake, and it was seized again in 1993 when it published an interview with Sheikh Omar Abdel Rahman. *Al-Hayat* was seized yet again for its 1998 interview with an Islamist figure, Rugh writes in 2004. Some newspapers that are not allowed to publish in Egypt have moved their offices to Cyprus and send copies to Egypt.

Egyptian journalists can be fined or imprisoned for insulting the country's president or a foreign president, state officials, the military, or the legislature. Emergency and counterterrorism laws permit additional press restrictions if vaguely worded rules are broken. A publication can be banned for printing news about a national security case, and prepublication censorship is permitted.

Political parties continue to have the legal right to publish newspapers, and five out of sixteen parties had publications in 2003. These included the daily *al-Wafd* of the Wafd Party, as well as several weeklies (such as *al-Ahali* of the leftist Tagammu party and *Mayo* of the NDP). The Labor Party's *al-Shaab* was a platform for Islamist views until its suspension in 2003.

Radio

Any discussion of media in Egypt, or in the Arabic-speaking world generally, should stress that radio, during the second half of the twentieth century, as well as television, especially in the twenty-first century, had far larger audiences, proportionally, than print media. For example, a survey conducted in 2003 by InterMedia, a U.S. company, found that newspapers were far less important than television as a source of news for Egyptians.

The efforts of a private business brought radio broadcasts to Egypt in the 1920s. The Egyptian monarchy took over in 1947, but the semi-autonomous governing board exercised control loosely.

When the revolutionary leadership took over in 1952, serious efforts to ramp up broadcasting ability got under way so Egyptians would be more effectively informed about government policy. A new Ministry of National Guidance was created and given responsibility for radio, and the new radio service—Voice of the Arabs (Sawt al-Arab)—was created in July 1953. Aside from Egypt itself, this radio was to have relatively more political influence in the Arabic-speaking world, at least during the early Nasser era, than virtually any equivalent situation elsewhere in the world.

The new leadership had recognized that a powerful medium-wave signal would make reception possible without special equipment. Signal strength was increased and programming improved with large financial investments. Transmitter power grew twenty-eight times stronger in just ten years. Specific cultural programming was designed for intellectuals, and political indoctrination programs were prepared for the lower classes. There was a European program in six languages, Sudan Corner, a Palestine program, and even a Hebrew one. The licensing fee for radio receivers was eliminated to improve access. Domestic broadcasting went from 18 hours a day in 1952 to 72 per day in 1960 to more than 120 hours per day in the 1970s. By the late 1970s, some 85 percent of the urban adult population said it listened to state radio.

Gamal Abdel Nasser contributed to the service's popularity through his use of the Arabic language, writes Douglas Boyd. Nasser combined colloquial Egyptian Arabic with classical Arabic. Colloquial Egyptian Arabic was understood throughout the region because Egyptian films were so popular, and classical Arabic appealed to a more literate audience. The nature of the Arabic language also contributed to the broadcasts' ability to influence listeners. According to Boyd, the language's combination of "vagueness, rich grammar and repetitive style facilitate[s] exaggeration and the painting of vivid mental pictures."

Voice of the Arabs focused its attention on developments in North Africa during its first three years. Its programs supported the Neo-Destour Party of Habib Bourguiba in Tunisia and the anti-French revolutionaries in Algeria. The Algerians maintained an office in Cairo, and they were allowed to use the Egyptian radio service.

Other Arab states were not ignored, however, and specific times of day were allocated to programs for Lebanon, Syria, the Persian Gulf states, and the southern portion of the Arabian Peninsula. Programming essentially blended news and commentary, with the addition of press reviews, speeches, interviews with Arab politicians, radio dramas, and music.

Voice of the Arabs became more open in advocating Nasser's pan-Arab and anti-Western ideology from 1955 onward. Jordan's pro-British monarchy was one target, particularly because its army (known as the Arab Legion) was headed by an Englishman, General John Bagot Glubb (better known as Glubb Pasha). Glubb's March 1956 dismissal may have been more closely linked with his disagreements with King Hussein, but his being a target of hostile Egyptian broadcasts is also widely believed to have been a factor.

The significance of the Voice of the Arabs was demonstrated during the Suez Crisis, triggered by Nasser's nationalization of the Suez Canal Company in July 1956. During raids that preceded the October 1956 invasion by Britain, France, and Israel, British aircraft bombed transmitters near Cairo. The raid had little impact, and the conflict ended with a U.S.-backed UN resolution demanding a withdrawal by the invaders. British and French forces had withdrawn by December 1956, and the Israelis left some three months later. The outcome of the Suez Crisis contributed to Nasser's prestige, and it also persuaded the Egyptians to have more radio transmitters and to spread out their sites.

Similar to its actions regarding Jordan, Egypt waged what Boyd refers to as a "propaganda war" against Iraq's pro-Western prime minister Nuri al-Said until that country's 1958 revolution overthrew him. Nasser's actions were triggered by Iraq's joining the Western-supported Baghdad Pact (which included Iran, Pakistan, Turkey, and Britain) in 1955. The Voice of the Arabs called for the killing of the Iraqi royal family and Prime Minister Said by 1957. Said and King Faisal II were both killed in the July 1958 coup, and the chief announcer of Voice of the Arabs, Ahmad Said, was sent a portion of the premier's finger as a sign of appreciation, according to Boyd.

The Voice of the Arabs then turned its attention to Lebanon, where U.S. forces landed in 1958 to help end a civil war, and Jordan, which saw the simultaneous arrival of British forces. Also in 1958, Nasser brought state radio under the control of the presidential office. Despite these developments, the impact of Voice of the Arabs actually declined from the late 1950s. Boyd suggests that Middle Eastern radio audiences had become more sophisticated and, therefore, were less open to the exaggerations and falsehoods of the Egyptian broadcasts.

Moreover, other Arab countries improved their radio and television capabilities. When Egypt began criticizing the Saudi rulers, connecting them with the United States and accusing them of squandering the country's oil wealth, the Saudis reacted by establishing their own radio service. This service emphasized the rulers' religious credentials, and it noted that Egyptian troops were fighting other Arabs in Yemen. Saudi Arabia also established a television service and set up a facility to jam television broadcasts from Egypt.

Voice of the Arabs' inaccurate reporting on the June 1967 Six-Day War led to an overall loss of its influence. The station kept claiming that Egypt was about to defeat Israel, and other Arab stations repeated these claims. The reality, of course, was quite the opposite. Alarmed by Egyptian expulsion of UN observers from the Sinai Peninsula and other military activities, Israel launched a preemptive strike against Egypt. Jordan then attacked Israel in a conflict that eventually involved Algeria, Iraq, Kuwait, Saudi Arabia, and Syria. By the time the conflict was over, Israel had occupied the Sinai Peninsula and Gaza Strip, as well as the West Bank and the Golan Heights.

Television

Egyptian television got off to a later start than radio, going on the air in 1960. In the ensuing years, twenty-nine transmitters were built, and the purchase of communal receivers in poorer areas was subsidized. Eleven television studios were built in Cairo, and thousands of staff members were hired. State-run television is controlled by the Information Ministry through the Egyptian Radio and Television Union (ERTU), per a 1970 decree.

Egypt's Channel 1 television went on the air in July 1960 with three hours a day of programming, and Channel 2 followed the next year with mostly foreign programs. Channel 3 appeared in October 1962 with cultural programming for the Cairo area, and it stayed on the air until 1976. It returned in 1985. The introduction of regional channels began in 1988. As of 2005 there were eight domestic channels.

A survey conducted in 2003 by InterMedia, a U.S. company, found that television was the most important source of news for Egyptians. Roughly three-quarters of the respondents cited Channel 1 as their most important source, followed by Channel 1 and al-Jazeera. The programming depicted President Mubarak as a defender of Arab causes and interests and a promoter of democratic reform, while simultaneously rejecting U.S. pressure to reform. Thus, phrases such as "civil society" occurred frequently, while President George Bush's comments on democracy in the region were rejected as "foreign-imposed reform." Programming rejected Islamist extremism, and the weekly Friday Prayer sermons broadcast by Channel 1 featured apolitical topics.

The significance of television was demonstrated in the run-up to the September 2005 presidential elections, particularly in President Mubarak's campaign. Rather than televising official appearances, which is what was done in the past, he gave a lengthy exclusive interview to al-Arabiya satellite television. The terminology used in his speeches and statements, and his speaking directly to the camera at other times, also reflected appreciation of this medium.

Television coverage was important for the Egyptian opposition, too. Opposition parties staged frequent street demonstrations, and they had women and minorities participate in their events to increase their telegeneity. State media to some extent covered opposition activities, particularly those of Ayman Nur of the al-Ghad Party and Numan Jumah of the al-Wafd Party. Moreover, interviews with opposition candidates appeared in the state-owned press. Although Mubarak won the election, Nur got 12 percent of the vote and Jumah earned roughly 5 percent. Of course, both the relative proportions of coverage and the manner of conduct of the election were designed to ensure the incumbent's reelection.

Satellite Television

Arab League members established the Arab Satellite Communications Organization in 1976. The

Arabsat satellite system was put into orbit roughly one decade later. Egypt was not a participant, however. It was kicked out of the Arab Satellite Communications Organization (and the Arab League) due to its signing the Camp David Accords with Israel in 1978 and then a peace treaty with Israel in 1979.

Egypt was readmitted to the Arab League in 1990, and in December of that year the Egyptian Space Channel (ESC) began using Arabsat. Cairo paid $2 million annually for this privilege, and the initial object was to provide Egyptian soldiers based in Saudi Arabia with news from home. ESC programs were identical to Egyptian state television's terrestrial ones.

Naomi Sakr writes in *Satellite Realms: Transnational Television, Globalization and the Middle East* that ESC became popular with Saudis who were dissatisfied with their own national offerings. Algerian and Moroccan viewers also welcomed the more entertaining mix of music and drama offered by ESC and made available to them by local distributors.

The dependence on Arabsat did not sit will with the Egyptians, who resented their earlier exclusion from its activities. Nilesat-1 was launched in April 1998, therefore, and for symbolic reasons began operating on May 21, the country's official Media Day. The Egyptian Radio and Television Union (ERTU) held 40 percent shares in Nilesat and was the biggest producer of television programs in the region. It saw the satellite as a means of distributing Egyptian programs and making use of its vast television and film archives. Interestingly, other Arabic language television networks leased frequencies on Nilesat so they could have access to the Egyptian market of roughly 80 million people.

The country's media strategy at the time also entailed creation of a gigantic Egyptian Media Production City. This would have more than ten production studios, as well as sets, hotels, and theme parks, and it would cost in excess of $1 billion. ERTU also created two international satellite channels that could be viewed in Asia, Australia, Europe, Latin America, and the United States.

The emergence of Egyptian satellite television and its aggressive media strategy coincided with the proliferation of other Arabic-language satellite channels. Recognizing the popularity of the innovative programs on these channels, ERTU decided to act aggressively in order to counter them. This required imitating the popular talk-show format, and ERTU even tried to hire popular presenters away from other networks. The Egyptian shows were more subdued than their competitors, but they did address previously taboo topics such as female genital mutilation, unemployment, and sex discrimination. Observers of Egyptian media note that the programs can be edited because they are prerecorded rather than live, and self-censorship also takes place.

There were efforts in the 1990s to establish private television channels, but they were blocked by the government. El Mehwar, the first Egyptian private space channel, was launched on Egypt's new Nilesat 102 in late 2000. A wide variety of other such stations followed.

On balance, then, by the time of the fall of President Hosni Mubarak, the Egyptian government still had a great deal of control over the media, and the ability to shape, through various carrots and sticks, even the private channels. But there was more diversity of both media type and information than at any time since the current regime was established in the 1950s.

The role of the media, and in particular online and social media, in the Egyptian revolution of 2011 was very significant. Facebook groups were instrumental in mobilizing the large demonstrations that challenged Mubarak and led to the situation in which he was eventually forced to resign by other elements in the regime. Following Mubarak's resignation, changes began to be introduced in state-run media. On March 30, 2011, official changes were announced. Seventeen new people were appointed to chief editor and chairman of the board positions in seven state-run newspapers. Most importantly, the editor at the flagship *al-Ahram* newspaper was replaced. Most of the people fired were Mubarak associates. But the people who replaced them also had long careers in state-run media. This "purge" suggested that while the new government wanted to cut ties with the former regime, this did not in itself mean that the strong government role in media in Egypt would end as a result of Mubarak's fall. Rather, there is a sense of flux in Egypt at the moment, and it is not clear whether a new regime may seek to reimpose its heavy hand on the media, or whether the new greater independence will prove long-lasting.

References and Further Reading

Abu-Lughod, Lila. *Dramas of Nationhood: The Politics of Television in Egypt.* Chicago: University of Chicago Press, 2004.

Armbrust, Walter. *Mass Culture and Modernism in Egypt.* Cambridge, UK: Cambridge University Press, 1996.

Boyd, Douglas A. "Development of Egypt's Radio: 'Voice of the Arabs' Under Nasser." *Journalism Quarterly* 4 (1975).

Dajani, Karen Finlon. "Egypt's Role as a Major Media Producer, Supplier and Distributor to the Arab World: An Historical-Descriptive Study." Doctoral dissertation, Temple University. Ann Arbor, MI: University Microfilms International, 1980.

Haroutunian, Mourad R. *Media, Politics, and Religion in Egypt: An Analysis of the Impact of the Relationship Between Government and Religion on Egyptian Media Content, 1950–1995.* Cairo: Author, 2000.

Kays, Doreen. *Frogs and Scorpions: Egypt, Sadat, and the Media.* London: F. Muller, 1984.

Rachty, Gehan Ahmed. *Mass Media and the Process of Modernization in Egypt After the 1952 Revolution.* Ann Arbor, MI: University Microfilms International, 1972.

Rugh, William A. *Arab Mass Media: Newspapers, Radio, and Television in Arab Politics.* Westport, CT: Praeger, 2004.

———. *The Arab Press: News Media and Political Process in the Arab World.* Syracuse, NY: Syracuse University Press, 1987.

Sakr, Naomi. *Satellite Realms: Transnational Television, Globalization and the Middle East.* London: I.B. Tauris, 2002.

Iraq
From Captive to Relatively Free Media

Kathleen Ridolfo

Between 1967 and 2003, Iraqi media operated in what author William Rugh describes as the mobilization stage; private newspaper ownership was banned and all politically important newspapers were controlled by an agent of the ruling regime. During this stage, the key duty of the press was to mobilize support for the regime.

The overthrow of Saddam Hussein and the institution of greater freedom under a new elected Iraqi government created an entirely different situation for the media in Iraq. The country already had a relatively rich history in terms of media development, though it had been greatly constricted under the dictatorships that had ruled between 1958 and 2003.

Law No. 155, issued in 1967, six months after the six-day Arab-Israeli war, stated that it was necessary for the state to control the press so as to ensure the press was "guided on sound national lines to meet the responsibilities of the battle," and to "prevent infiltration of the press" and "preserve the state."

The Baath Party seized power in a 1968 military coup, and subsequent laws solidified state control over the media. The 1968 Press Act banned articles addressing twelve specific subjects, including those considered detrimental to the president, the Revolutionary Command Council (RCC), and the Baath Party.

The Penal Code of 1969 stated that any person who publicly insults the National Assembly, the government, the courts, the armed forces, or any official or semi-official departments or agencies, was subject to detention, a fine, and up to seven years in prison. Any person who insults another can be jailed up to one year and fined by the court. "If such an insult is published in a newspaper or publication or medium it is considered an aggravating circumstance." Moreover, under paragraph 438, which concerns the disclosure of confidential information, any person who publishes a picture, remark, or information regarding the private or family life of another, even if this information is true, is subject to fine and imprisonment for up to one year.

In 1986, the RCC issued Decree No. 840, which called for the death penalty for insulting the president, Baath Party, RCC, or high-level government officials. In 2001, the RCC amended the decree so that anyone found criticizing Saddam Hussein would have their tongue cut out.

Following the 1991 Gulf War, Iraq's Kurdish region fell under international protection. As a result, a relatively thriving media environment emerged, with numerous newspapers, terrestrial and satellite television channels, and a dozen radio stations. While journalists had far greater freedom in terms of what they could report, they operated under the watchful eye of the region's two leading parties, the Patriotic Union of Kurdistan and the Kurdistan Democratic Party. Moreover, the majority of media outlets operating in Kurdistan were tied to one of the two parties. After 2003, the Kurdistan regional government would exert tighter controls on the press, detaining and prosecuting journalists deemed to have damaged the Kurdistan Regional Government or its leaders in the press.

The Iraqi Press

Baghdad would be at the forefront of modern Arabic-language publishing. Indeed, Iraq was one of the first countries in the Middle East where newspapers were published, beginning in the mid-nineteenth century. By the early 1900s, when the country was under Ottoman rule, the print media were flourishing. Following the fall of the Ottomans, during the British Mandate era (1920–1932), writers and editors had a great deal of freedom to publish with little censorship, though direct criticism of the government was not permitted.

The end of the British Mandate brought with it a very diverse press. Since most newspapers represented specific factions and parties, however, they were rarely independent. The government took little interest in controlling the press in the early days of the Iraqi state, thus there was greater freedom of the press at that time than in later years.

The years 1932 to 1963 were a period of vibrant, open political discussion, in which parties and individuals, competing for power in a relatively unstable political environment, sought support from newspapers in promoting their interests. There was rapid turnover in newspapers, but diversity remained, particularly in the years following World War II. Government intervention in the press was rare, and when it did occur, it was usually to target a specific publication for a perceived transgression, rather than targeting the press as a whole. Yet the limited government intervention in the press during this period was a product of the political instability plaguing Iraq. Since no one group or party monopolized power, neither did anyone consolidate total control over the newspapers.

The British installed a monarchy under the rule of King Faisal in 1921. Over the next eighteen years, Iraq saw three monarchs. The 1930s were plagued by political turmoil, tribal uprisings, and media wars. Yet the Iraqi press had the most freedom under the monarchy. By the time the monarchy was overthrown in 1958, the country had seen ten general elections and more than fifty cabinets. In the decade following 1958 there were four changes in regime and many coup attempts, such as the 1963 coup that overthrew General Abdul Karim Qasim and brought the Baath Party briefly to power.

In the early months following the 1958 revolution, which brought to power a dictatorship based on a nationalist Communist coalition, there was a thriving media environment. At least fifteen dailies were being published, each catering to its own political or social constituency, including Communists, Baathists, Arab nationalists, Islamists, and the Kurdish nationalist movement. But as the regime suppressed the Communists, it also closed down those parts of the media it did not directly control. Finally, only those newspapers fully supporting the regime were allowed to operate.

The state further institutionalized control over the press during the regime of Abdul Salam Arif, who seized power in a 1963 military coup and then was succeeded by his brother, Abdul Rahman Arif, until that regime was overthrown in 1968. At the beginning of the Arif era, there were twenty newspapers publishing in the Iraqi capital. Abdul Salam Arif outlawed opposition political parties and their newspapers. In 1964, the Arif government enacted Press Law No. 53, which enabled the government to censor newspapers critical of the regime. Newspapers accused of jeopardizing the state's security would have their licenses revoked.

In 1968, the Baath Party seized power. It had a coherent ideology of comprehensive statist control in which the media functioned to further the survival and policies of the government. As in Communist states, the party and government would directly and fully supervise the press to ensure 100 percent support, while those who deviated from the political line faced execution or imprisonment.

Once the Baath Party became entrenched in office, and especially with the ascension of Saddam Hussein to total power, the methods used to control the media became more violent. According to Reporters Without Borders, judicial harassment, arrests, threats, prolonged detentions, and incidents of torture and executions increased dramatically. The International Alliance for Justice has estimated the Hussein regime killed more than 500 writers, journalists, poets, and artists between 1968 and 2002. An estimated fifty journalists fled Iraq in 2001 alone.

Under Saddam, the Iraqi government and the Baath Party owned and controlled all print and broadcast media in Iraq. Satellite television was publicly banned and only senior officials had access to it. Journalists were required to join the Baath Party if they expected to work.

Uday Hussein (Saddam Hussein's eldest son from his first wife) took control of the journalists' union in 1992, turning it into an instrument for monitoring members and controlling the media. In addition to his role as head of the union, Uday also built a media empire that included *Babil* newspaper, an FM radio station, and al-Shabab (The Youth) television channel. Uday Hussein used his position as head of the union for reprisal against his rivals and to suppress journalists. In March 2002, for example, he expelled thirty journalists from the union, effectively ending their careers, because he disliked them personally.

Foreign journalists also worked in tightly controlled conditions. All media outlets were housed within the Information Ministry complex, and journalists were not allowed to travel without a ministry-appointed chaperone, who doubled as a censor. Travel outside the capital was rare and required government permission.

The Coalition Provisional Authority (CPA), the governing body established by coalition forces following the downfall of the Saddam Hussein regime in 2003, issued Order Number 14 in June 2003, which addressed "Prohibited Media Activity." The order prohibited the media from broadcasting or publishing material that incited racial, ethnic, or religious violence, violence against coalition forces, or civil disorder. Media advocating a return of the Baath Party to power or media purporting to represent the Baath was also banned. Any media organization found in violation of the order would be subject to arrest and closure, and a fine of up to $1,000. Order Number 14 was used to close the *Al Hawza* newspaper operated by Shia cleric Muqtada al-Sadr, in March 2004, on the grounds that it incited Iraqis to violence.

The CPA issued Order Number 65 establishing the Iraqi Media and Communications Commission (IMCC) in March 2004, creating the country's first modern telecommunications policy. The IMCC's main function is to manage the communications and licensing process in Iraq for telecommunications, broadcasting, and information services. The IMCC can enforce its rules and procedures through warnings, financial penalties, suspending licenses, and by forcibly closing and seizing the equipment of media outlets that violate the law. Order Number 66, issued in conjunction with Order Number 65, established the Iraqi Media Network (IMN), Iraq's public service broadcaster.

The CPA issued Order Number 100 in June 2004 on the day the CPA transferred authority to the Iraqi Interim Government, which gave the prime minister the authority to enforce Order Number 14 and impose sanctions on the media. Previously, only the IMCC had the authority to regulate the media. The change in essence gave the premier the power to crush media critical of his performance.

Radio

In Iraq, as in Egypt and Syria, the electronic media operated under strict government control; radio and television were used to reach and mobilize the largely illiterate masses. The first radio station in Iraq, the Republic of Iraq Radio, was government owned and began broadcasting in the mid-1930s. Broadcasting was overseen by a government committee that included a representative from the Ministry of Education. Insufficient government funding in the 1930s was supplemented by a one-half Iraqi dinar tax on the sale of radio receivers, which supported the salaries of seven full-time employees.

King Ghazi also began intermittent broadcasts from his own station based inside the palace, where he acted as the sole broadcaster. Ghazi was known for his pro-Nazi broadcasts, including German-supplied news bulletins. The broadcasts ended with Ghazi's death in 1939.

Until 1939, government radio was on the air five hours per day. In 1939, the programming began to include fifteen-minute news bulletins in Kurdish. British assistance widened the transmission reach over the next decade, but broadcasts did not by any means blanket the country (they did not reach the far northern or southern parts, for example).

As Douglas Boyd writes in *Broadcasting in the Arab World: A Survey of the Electronic Media in the Middle East*, by 1945, Iraq's Arabic programming was on the air from 4:25 P.M. to 10:05 P.M. daily and included news, music, poetry, and drama. Kurdish broadcasting was on the air from 3:25 P.M. to 4:25 P.M. daily. The government did not appear to target other minorities in its broadcasting.

In the mid-1950s, the government began to realize the importance of a country-wide broadcast infrastructure. Prompted by regional political developments, Iraq sought U.S. assistance to set up shortwave and medium-wave transmitters to counter Egyptian broadcasts into Iraq that were aimed at destabilizing the regime of Prime Minister Nuri al-Said.

Egyptian president Gamal Abdel Nasser, angry that Iraq had joined the U.S.-sponsored Baghdad Pact (in which Iran, Pakistan, Turkey, and the United Kingdom also participated), sought to incite Iraqis against the Western-backed government and prevent other Arab states from joining the new alliance. Egypt's Voice of the Arabs radio launched a vicious campaign against Said, joined by an Egyptian-based clandestine channel identified as Radio Free Iraq. The anti-Said broadcasts prompted Baghdad to seek U.S. help in countering the media attack. According to Boyd, the bureaucratic inefficiency of the U.S. State Department prevented the delivery of the transmitters. The Egyptian broadcasts helped inspire the 1958 coup that ousted the royal family and installed the government of Abdul Karim Qasim.

The 1958 post-revolution government saw radio as a key vehicle for propaganda aimed at both an internal and external audience. Radio broadcasts were expanded to fifteen hours per day, and the programming reflected a revolutionary and anti-Western agenda. The regime used the radio to fight propaganda battles with both Egypt and Syria. Qasim sought help from the USSR in boosting Iraq's transmission power, and within three years, Iraq's transmission power equaled that of Egypt. Broadcasts glorified Qasim, and substantial airtime was devoted to the Iraqi leader and his policies. The only songs broadcast on radio and television were those praising him. Subsequent leaders followed suit, including the Baathist regime that came to power in 1968.

Transmission continued to improve, as did Iraq's focus on regional broadcasting. By 1970, Iraq was broadcasting 189 hours each week in Arabic, 70 hours in Kurdish, 28 each in Turkmen and Persian, and 7 hours each in Urdu, Turkish, English, German, French, Hebrew, and Russian.

By 1980, Iraqi state radio was broadcasting twenty-two hours per day, with programming targeting both a national and regional audience. The Iraqi regime promoted an anti-Egypt tone, intent on seeking Arab leadership in place of Egypt, which had been blacklisted by Arab states for signing the Camp David peace treaty with Israel. According to Boyd, one of the more popular programs was broadcast over the short- and medium-wave Voice of the Masses service, called the Arabist Voice of Egypt, which aired at the peak evening broadcast time, focused on Islam, peasant life, and music. The entire theme of the service was anti-Sadat, and listeners said the programs were appealing in part because the announcers were Egyptian. Egypt jammed the transmissions in response.

Under the Baathist regime, Iraq continued to improve its broadcast capabilities. A French-built short- and medium-wave transmission facility was erected in Balad in the 1980s, located some 70 kilometers north of Baghdad. The complex cost $180 million to build and was reputed to house the largest shortwave transmitter facility in the world. The facility was destroyed in 1991 during Operation Desert Storm, the U.S.-led response to Saddam Hussein's 1990 invasion of Kuwait. The 1991 war destroyed virtually all of the country's broadcast capability, including a 2-megawatt medium-wave facility in Maysan Governorate, in southeast Iraq.

Some effort was made to rebuild Iraq's broadcast capabilities following the Gulf War. Those efforts were largely blocked by international sanctions, which prevented the transfer of equipment such as transmitters to Iraq. Nevertheless, Iraqis under sanctions had access to international radio broadcasts from outlets such as the British Broadcasting Corporation (BBC), Radio Monte Carlo, and U.S.-funded broadcasters Radio Free Europe/Radio Liberty's (RFE/RL's) Radio Free Iraq, Voice of America, and, after March 2002, the U.S.-produced channel Radio Sawa.

According to U.S. government estimates, in 1998 there were nineteen AM stations in Iraq (five of which were inactive), fifty-one FM stations, and four shortwave stations. However, it is important to note that many Iraqi stations operated only intermittently or had ceased broadcasting altogether after the 1991 Gulf War. In mid-October 2002, there were reports of Iraqi plans to maintain state radio broadcasts in the event of war by using mobile transmitters. In fact, Iraq Radio did function throughout Operation Iraqi Freedom, which began in March 2003, but according to reports from inside Iraq, its signal was weak and sporadic.

Prior to the downfall of the Hussein regime, there were five major Arabic-language dailies in Iraq and nine major weeklies, all of which operated under state control and several of which were run directly by Uday Hussein, who was killed in a gun battle with U.S. troops in July 2003. Economic sanctions against Iraq resulted in newsprint shortages, leading to print-run limitations since 1993. Hussein's regime maintained a total monopoly on printing facilities and distribution.

Television

Iraq was the first Arab state to have broadcast television, with the national station launched in 1956, four years before its appearance in Egypt and nine years before Saudi Arabia. The first station to open in Baghdad was a modest facility of 500 watts, which aired a program mostly seen only in that city. With the downfall of the monarchy two years later, the station's power was increased substantially. As with radio, Abdul Karim Qasim sensed the importance of television as a medium for social and political change.

In 1959, a new 2-kilowatt transmitter began operating, and in 1961 there were 50,000 sets. Qasim decided to use television and radio to promote his political agenda. He broadcast the trials of former regime officials, known as the Mahdawi trials, after the head of the Special Supreme Military Court, Fadhil Abbas al-Mahdawi, Qasim's cousin. The televised proceedings were marked by showmanship and performances that resembled a work of theater more than a court trial. Qasim's regime was overthrown by a 1963 coup. He was killed in the fighting, and, perhaps ironically, images of his dead body were broadcast on television to prove the old ruler was dead and the new regime in control.

From 1965, television broadcasting and transmission expanded rapidly. Government-owed local television channels opened in Basra, Mosul, and Kirkuk. The government began broadcasting in Kurdish in 1974. By the mid-1970s there were 350,000 sets in Iraq. In 1981, the Iraqi government built a modern television broadcast facility in Baghdad.

Under Saddam Hussein's regime, television remained an important means for maintaining regime control and promoting Baathist, anti-Western doctrine. Managed by the Ministry of Information, television was used by Saddam to promote his self-designed image as a leader for all seasons, often dressed in military uniform, but sometimes in a suit, presiding over his cabinet through countless meetings, visiting the poor, meeting with hospital patients, and inspecting his army.

During the 1980–1988 Iran-Iraq war, the regime used footage from the battlefield, often graphic in nature, to rally the Iraqi people around the Hussein regime at the time of an immense threat. A similar approach was adopted during Iraq's 1990 invasion of Kuwait and the ensuing 1991 Gulf War. Boyd writes that virtually every minute of airtime during that period was devoted to the invasion of Kuwait. The aim was twofold: the government wanted to keep morale high at home, while using television and radio broadcasts to back up its territorial claim to Kuwait as the nineteenth Iraqi governorate.

In the months following the war, television broadcasts dedicated substantial time to Hussein's supposed attempts at reconciliation with the Shia population after a Shia rebellion that had been brutally crushed by his forces in the south.

While the state controlled all domestic television, satellite television was banned, largely preventing Iraqis from seeing news of the outside world. Though they had access to a handful of radio broadcast channels from abroad, only high-level regime officials had access to satellite television. Recognizing the importance of satellite television as a means to promote the regime and its regional and international agenda, the government started its own satellite television channel geared for a regional and Western audience in 1998. That same year, coalition air strikes temporarily disabled satellite and terrestrial television and radio operating from the Iraqi capital.

As with other media, Iraqi television broadcasting was transformed following the 2003 invasion by U.S.-led coalition forces. State-run television was taken off the air seven days into the war and was soon replaced by coalition-run media. Satellite dishes flooded the market, providing Iraqis with a plethora of never-before-seen choices, including access to English-language news broadcasts like CNN and BBC. Satellite television penetration became one of the highest in the world in the two years that followed the invasion, and Iraq went from having three prewar national TV stations and fourteen officially sanctioned Arab channels (available only to a select group of high-level regime members) to access to over 300 satellite channels virtually overnight.

Today, there are more than thirty terrestrial and satellite channels operating in Iraq, but few independent channels exist. Every major political party operating in Iraq owns at least one television channel, the content of which reflects the party's position and goals. The result is that in terms of independent, unbiased content, few choices are available.

Internet

The Internet came to Iraq in 1999 and was accessible only through government servers at some thirty Internet cafés across the country. Access to sites such as Hotmail was forbidden. The controls over access and the high costs of usage at a time when the population was suffering under international sanctions made it virtually impossible for the average citizen to go online. At the onset of Operation Iraqi Freedom, there were an estimated fifty to seventy Internet centers in Iraq, located in places such as luxury hotels, universities, state ministries, and research and industrial facilities. According to U.S. prewar estimates, the number of Internet users in Iraq in 2001 was just 12,500 in a country with a population of more than 24 million.

Today the Internet is accessible through hundreds of Internet cafés across the country. It is also widely available on university campuses and at homes through private subscriptions at a variety of rates. However, home subscriptions remain prohibitively expensive for the average Iraqi family. Younger Iraqis tend to use the Internet far more frequently and in a more varied way than their elders, who use it rarely, if at all.

There do not appear to be any government controls or regulations on Internet access in Iraq. Web sites and online e-mail services are widely used, including Yahoo!, Hotmail, and Google.

The Post-2003 Media Environment

A vibrant media environment erupted virtually overnight following the downfall of the Saddam Hussein regime. On March 24, 2003, four days after coalition forces launched Operation Iraqi Freedom, the United States initiated a campaign to end the regime's state-run media system. Official Iraqi television channels 1 and 2 were taken off the air. Likewise, Iraq Satellite Television was knocked off the air by mid-April. That pro-regime channel broadcast to the wider Arab world and had been for foreign consumption only.

By fall 2003, there were some 100 newspapers operating in Iraq. In less than one year, the number would double, though printing was sporadic. Numerous newspapers that claimed to be dailies would publish only a few days each week, probably due to funding shortages and weak institutional capacity. The BBC estimated in 2007 that there were about fifty newspapers publishing on a regular basis throughout the country. About a dozen of those are published in the capital. The majority of publications in print are affiliated with political parties, but a few independent newspapers do exist.

The availability of online media is extensive, from newspaper Web sites to sites that act as clearinghouses for several media outlets. Blogging by Iraqis living inside Iraq continues to grow, and several such blogs serve as a source of information for their readers and, at times, for media outlets hindered by the security situation.

The sectarian tensions that erupted in Iraq after 2003 have been reflected in the tone of broadcasting, with some media being pro-Sunni and some pro-Shia. Arab Sunni-Shia tensions, reflected in broadcast content, appear to have peaked in 2006 following the February 16 bombing of the al-Askari Shrine in Samarra.

Moreover, sectarian violence has affected the ability of all media outlets to operate effectively on the ground in Iraq. Between March 2003 and October 2007, some 233 media professionals were killed in Iraq—the majority were Iraqi nationals—targeted by sectarian militias, some operating under the guise of legitimate security forces, or killed accidentally by U.S. military forces. The targeting of media professionals—unprecedented in the history of violent conflicts—has changed the way media outlets cover news and events. Media managers, whether they work for print, radio, or television broadcast, have said they measure the value of sending journalists into the field against possible dangers. The costs of providing security details to staff journalists have also severely impacted costs for fledgling media outlets, forcing smaller outfits to close, reduce broadcast hours, or purchase reports from larger outfits more capable of carrying the costs of security.

Even Western-based news outlets have seen their reporting affected. Major outlets like CNN rarely send their Western journalists into the field, instead relying on Iraqi journalists to provide them with content and footage of an event. Western print outlets also frequently use stringers or local correspondents to relay a story to a Western journalist, who then writes it up for publication.

The Coalition Provisional Authority (CPA), Iraq's transitional government, established the Iraqi Media Network (IMN) in April 2003 to replace the former Interior Ministry–managed state television network. The goal was to model the IMN on public broadcaster agencies like the BBC or PBS. The U.S. government awarded the contract to set up a twenty-four-hour satellite news channel, al-Iraqiya television, two terrestrial channels, two FM radio stations, a national newspaper called *al-Sabah*, and a satellite television sports channel to California-based Science Applications International Corporation (SAIC). According to media reports, the contract was severely mismanaged and was eventually re-awarded to another company, U.S.-based Harris Communications. Established under CPA Order Number 66, the IMN was required to air programs in the major Iraqi languages of Arabic, Kurdish, Assyrian, and Turkmen.

State-run al-Iraqiya was met with skepticism by Iraqi nationals, who regarded the channel as pro-United States. With time, viewership increased. According to a February 2004 survey by Oxford Research International, 50 percent of Iraqis polled expressed confidence in the channel. However, though state-run, the channel is not without problems.

The IMN is managed by a director-general and a nine-member board of governors. At times, the board has been unable to act due to vacant seats. Senior IMN representatives said the board's paralysis enabled political officials to exert influence over al-Iraqiya and prevented adequate management oversight. Today, the channel is pro-Shia, reflecting the views and goals of the Shia political parties that have dominated the post-Hussein governments.

Prior to the transfer of authority from the CPA to the new Iraqi government in June 2004, action was taken against broadcasters who promoted sectarian tension or incitement to violence. Pan-Arab television channels al-Jazeera and al-Arabiya were banned for two weeks in September 2003 from covering official government events and from reporting in the field after the Iraqi Governing Council said the news channels gave too much airtime to the ousted Hussein regime and promoted the fledgling insurgency. Al-Jazeera was banned altogether from broadcasting from Iraq in 2004 because of its frequent airing of insurgent footage. The Iraqi government later shut down pan-Arab broadcaster al-Arabiya television for thirty days in 2006 for inciting sectarianism and promoting violence.

In March 2004, the CPA issued Order Number 65, establishing the Iraqi Media and Communications Commission (IMCC). Under the order, the IMCC was granted the exclusive authority to license and regulate telecommunications, broadcasting, and information services in Iraq. The IMCC would act as an independent body, with limited oversight by the Iraqi parliament. Its funding comes from licensing fees.

The IMCC is headed by a CEO; a nine-member board of commissioners provides strategic guidance, including writing the IMCC's rules of conduct, codes, and regulations. In order for rules to be approved, six board members must vote favorably. As of January 2006, three of the board members had resigned citing dissatisfaction over the management of the IMCC. New board members must be appointed by the prime minister and approved by a parliamentary majority.

In July 2005, the IMCC issued the Interim Broadcasting Program Code of Practice, which sets minimal content restrictions for broadcasters. Incitement to violence, publicizing terrorist messages, encouraging public disorder, and knowingly airing false content are prohibited. The board also monitored coverage of Iraq's January and December 2005 national elections, issuing a media code of conduct during elections that required broadcasters to provide candidates with equal time, show balance in their coverage of contenders, and promote electoral education for voters. The code also called for a media blackout for the two days preceding the opening of the polls. The IMCC also took control of licensing, but according to authors Monroe Price, Douglas Griffin, and Ibrahim al-Marashi, a number of broadcasters remain unlicensed and are in essence broadcasting illegally. In addition, though required to obtain a broadcasting license from the IMCC, most Kurdish media outlets do not hold such a license, though they do hold licenses with the central government.

Although the IMCC has made some progress in setting a regulatory framework on par with international standards, much work needs to be done in terms of staff regulation, training, and increased staff capacity. As long as security remains a factor and the government remains weak in enforcing existing laws, little progress can be expected.

References and Further Reading

Boyd, Douglas A. *Broadcasting in the Arab World: A Survey of the Electronic Media in the Middle East.* 3rd ed. Ames: Iowa State University Press, 1999.

Coalition Provisional Authority. Official Documents. Available at www.iraqcoalition.org/regulations/.

Price, Monroe E., Douglas Griffin, and Ibrahim al-Marashi. "Policy Recommendations Concerning Broadcasting in Iraq: Communications and Media Commission of Iraq." Stanhope Centre for Communications Policy Research, 2007. Available at www.cardozoaelj.net/issues/07/Stanhope.pdf.

Reporters Without Borders. "The Iraqi Media: 25 Years of Relentless Repression." Available at www.rsf.org.

Ridolfo, Kathleen. "RFE/RL Iraq Report." April 2, 2004. Available at www.rferl.org.

Rugh, William A. *Arab Mass Media: Newspapers, Radio, and Television in Arab Politics.* Westport, CT: Praeger, 2004.

Iraqi Politics and Control of the Media

Ibrahim al-Marashi

A recurring theme in debates on Iraq involves the conflict between the Sunni and Shia Muslim sects. The media affiliated with the major Sunni and Shia Islamist parties play a crucial role in these developments, which in turn shape the post-Saddam media. The pluralism of a private media sector in post-Baathist Iraq has been a positive development, yet has also allowed for the emergence of local media along religious sectarian lines, reinforcing the country's sectarian divisions.

Differences between Shia and Sunni Arabs have been ever present in Iraq but were rarely articulated in official, public debate, or used by politicians or religious and community leaders as a basis to criticize the others. Even in Baathist Iraq, while members of every community may have suffered discrimination, the media rarely employed the terms "Shia" and "Sunni" in a negative manner, as it would harm national unity. Following the 2003 Iraq war, the emerging media mentioned such sectarian terms for Iraq's people, but in the context of calling for national unity. However, the debates prior to the adoption of the Iraqi Constitution in October 2005 and the December 2005 election of a permanent Iraqi Assembly marked an emerging trend in Iraq's politics: a divisive sectarian discourse that has proliferated into the media.

Following the February 2006 bombing of the revered Shia al-Askari Shrine in the city of Samarra, a spiral of violence consumed the center of Iraq, including Baghdad, where sectarian killings between Arab Sunni and Arab Shia groups became daily phenomena. These tensions manifest themselves in the political sphere, as certain Arab Shia Islamist parties have advocated the creation of a federal entity in the predominantly Shia south as a means of separating themselves from the violence-ridden center dominated by Arab Sunni Islamist parties.

In postwar Iraq, private Iraqi media have emerged, with ownership in the hands of competing Islamist political factions, reflecting the country's conflicting sectarian agendas. This Islamist media have taken on a public advocacy role as well, pressing policymakers to address deficiencies and shortcomings in providing security and infrastructure needs by highlighting these problems and giving Iraqi citizens a platform to express their views. However, these sectarian channels conduct public advocacy primarily on behalf of their communities.

A professional and independent media that can allow views expressed by all of Iraq's sectarian communities is an important step toward establishing a viable democracy. Nevertheless, in a country relatively new to independent media, freedom of expression can be abused. Iraq's Islamist-owned sectarian media are laying the psychological groundwork for bitter divisiveness and conflict, with one channel already making direct exhortations for violence against other Iraqi communities. Media divided along religious and sectarian lines have the potential to further the gap between Iraq's communities and weaken any kind of national belonging. Most Islamist factions have at times used their media to stress unity among Iraq's communities, but they nevertheless have the potential to instigate conflict with these means if it suits their interests.

According to surveys, more than 90 percent of Iraqis receive most of their information, whether it is news or entertainment, from satellite TV stations. According to a report by International Media Support, many people believe the satellite channels provide all the news and that buying newspapers is therefore unnecessary. By using satellite broadcasts, Iraqi Islamists send their messages not only to local Iraqi audiences but also to the Arab world and the large Iraqi diaspora, which provides financial support for many of Iraq's political parties. Religious-sectarian factions among the Sunni, Shia, and Christians all have their own means of communicating to their ethno-sectarian constituencies in Iraq and abroad in the Iraqi diaspora.

Media Owned by Political Islamists

Islamist parties among Iraq's sectarian groups have formed media empires and are a pervasive element in Iraq's Fourth Estate.

Arab Shia Media

All the Shia political parties operate their own radio stations, newspapers, and satellite channels. The strongest Shia parties are political Islamist groups that seek a greater role for Islam in the state and public life, though they may differ on how large a role Islam should play in Iraq. The four prominent Shia Islamist political factions include the Supreme Council for the Islamic Revolution in Iraq (SCIRI), the al-Dawa Party, the Sadr Trend of Muqtada al-Sadr, and the Iraqi Hezbollah.

Each of these factions owns various newspapers, radio stations, and terrestrial TV channels, such as SCIRI's Ghadir TV, the Dawa Party's al-Masar TV, the Sadr Trend's al-Salam TV, and Ayatollah Sayyid Hadi al-Mudarissi's short-lived Ahl al-Bayt TV. SCIRI owns and finances the al-Furat satellite channel, based in Baghdad. Al-Furat, which began broadcasting in November 2004, is run by Ammar Abd al-Aziz, the son of the party's leader.

The dominant themes on al-Furat are the "progress" SCIRI is making as the largest constituent party in the Iraqi government in terms of "reconstruction" and providing "security." Therefore, the channel's content supports the government, as well as the possibility of a federal Iraq. It marks victimization in terms of attacks by Sunni Arab militants referred to as *takfiri*. *Takfiri* is a euphemistic term that literally means "those who condemn others as 'unbelievers,'" and usually refers to Sunni members of al-Qaeda in Iraq, or in general foreign volunteers from the Arab world who came to Iraq to combat the U.S. and Iraqi security forces. Nevertheless, Iraqi Sunni argue the term is used as a justification for operations against their community for allegedly giving tacit or overt support to their co-religionists fighting in Iraq.

Since al-Furat is owned by SCIRI, a Shia political Islamist group, much of its programming is religious, but the channel does not focus on issues of ethnicity and avoids direct references to the Shia as a distinct religious group. Rather, it emphasizes Iraqi unity based on an inclusive Iraqi Muslim identity. In other words, the channel tries to gloss over the ethnic differences between Arabs and Kurds, and stresses the unity of Islam in Iraq, both Shia and Sunni. The news program rarely refers to Iraq as part of the "Arab world" as do other Arab Sunni or independent Iraqi satellite channels.

Religious programs include "The Talk of Friday," which broadcasts interviews of religious figures, and "The Most Virtuous People on Earth," a cartoon show with Islamist themes. The station has coverage of Friday sermons, primarily from Shia mosques. The channel also prominently features the activities of the leader of SCIRI, Abd al-Aziz al-Hakim. During the run-up to the December 15, 2005, elections for the permanent National Assembly, al-Furat featured campaign ads only for the Shia coalition, the United Iraqi Alliance, and not for other parties. As part of its religious programming, female presenters on this channel don the Islamic headscarf.

Given that SCIRI is dominant in the government, this channel tends to frame violence in Iraq with a pro-government stance, similar to the al-Iraqiya channel. Since members of SCIRI have a prominent role in the armed forces, the channel prominently features the role of the security forces and their efforts to "eliminate terrorism" in Iraq by reporting on their activities in the first few minutes of the news programming as well as providing extended coverage of security operations. When some of these security forces were implicated in a scandal involving a secret underground prison maintained by the Interior Ministry (headed by a SCIRI member), these incidents were played down on the al-Furat channel.

The channel has also featured speakers who have criticized other Arab states for failing to condemn the violence committed by "terrorists" in Iraq. Promotional ads (public service spots paid for by the government) on the channel also serve to condemn the violence. One ad features what appears to be a handwritten note by a child in Arabic, with a stick figure of a child looking at another stick figure of what appears to be an angry insurgent. The text of the note reads: "I wish I could stop you. If I were bigger and stronger, I would not let you destroy my country. I would hand you over to the police because you are bad, and Iraq needs everything you have stolen from it."

Intersectarian violence against Iraqi Shia Muslims is prevalent in al-Furat's coverage, although the station does not advocate revenge but rather patience and obedience to those Shia leaders who have called for restraint. The channel frames a federated Iraq (one of the primary political platforms of SCIRI) as a positive development and calls on all Iraqi communities to unite.

Public advocacy programs include a live call-in program "al-Furat and the People" and "al-Furat Reports," an investigative show that deals with domestic issues affecting the lives of everyday Iraqis. "Deported in the Homeland" profiles internally displaced families who have relocated due to sectarian violence. It can be gleaned from the last names of those interviewed, and the phrases used, that most of the victims on this show are Shia. While the channel has a distinct Shia leaning, songs in between programs support peace and unity among Iraq's various ethnic and sectarian communities.

Al-Furat's programming is mostly religious. It does not feature popular entertainment shows such as Arabic-dubbed Latin American soap operas, Hollywood films, or music videos from Arabic pop stars.

Arab Sunni Media

The Arab Sunni Islamist factions developed political associations later than their Shia and Kurdish counterparts in Iraq's postwar dynamics. While Sunni Arabs provided most of the Baath Party leadership, Kurds and Shia made up some of its party cadres. Iraqi Sunni Arabs, however, were also involved in forming exile organizations, such as the Islamist Iraqi Islamic Party, and many of them returned to Iraq to represent their constituencies in postwar Iraq. Other prominent Sunni groups include the General Dialogue Conference, the Association of Muslim Scholars (technically not a political party), and the Unified National Movement.

These parties coalesced into the al-Tawafuq Front. The satellite channels that represent the front's political agenda are the Rafidayn Channel and the Baghdad Satellite Channel. The latter began to transmit in August 2005 and will be the focus here. The channel primarily depends on advertising from the Arab Sunni community, but also receives advertising revenues from the Sunni political parties in Iraq.

A dominant theme on this channel is "resistance" to the U.S. military forces, referred to as "occupation forces." This view of violence in Iraq mirrors that of al-Tawafuq. Unlike al-Iraqiya or al-Furat, this station refers to insurgents as "armed men" rather than "terrorists." It views a future federated Iraq as a "foreign scheme" to divide the nation, reflecting Arab Sunni fears of Kurdish and Shia entities in the north and south of Iraq, respectively, that would leave them in a landlocked rump state. Another prominent theme is that of the Arab Sunni as the victims at the hands of "militias" that are linked to the government or have "infiltrated" the security forces.

Given the Baghdad Satellite Channel's sympathies to the al-Tawafuq Front, it featured campaign advertisements for the front exclusively during the Iraqi elections in December 2005, and carried live press conferences of the front. Such sympathies manifest themselves in a news program that features the headlines from various Iraqi newspapers with Sunni Arab Islamist tendencies. Islamist themes are also evidenced by anchorwomen who don the headscarf, similar to the SCIRI's al-Furat channel. Religious programming includes "Explaining the Holy Quran," where Arab Sunni clerics offer religious interpretations of the sacred text; "In the Shadow of the Shariah," discussing topics on Islamic law; and "Fatwas on the Air," which examines various religious rulings. Political programs feature a mix of guests, including government officials, but mostly Arab Sunni politicians.

The channel also has programs for Iraqis to express themselves, and many vent their frustrations over unemployment and the lack of basic utilities. "Baghdad Daily" features on-the-street interviews to give the "common man's" view of current events in Iraq, particularly related to the security situation and the reconstruction efforts. "Your Place Is Empty" focuses on the plight of Iraqi prisoners, a good number of whom happen to be Arab Sunni, showing the circumstances of the prisoners' arrests through interviews with their families. While most prisoners who appear on this show are Sunni Arabs, there are no accurate figures on Iraq's prison population, so it is difficult to ascertain whether the program accurately represents the prison population.

Although the Baghdad Satellite Channel's shows are mostly religious in nature, some deal with culture, the arts, and sports. The channel imports other programs that deal with Islam, but does not feature popular entertainment shows such as soap operas or films, either imported from the region or internationally.

Media Owned by Entities Calling for Sectarian Violence

Though the Iraqi media described in the preceding sections belong to sectarian factions and at times expose sectarian tensions and give the impression that their communities are under attack, they usually call for restraint and national unity, and do not specifically exhort viewers to engage in violence. However, at least one channel has emerged that not only calls upon Iraqis to take part in violence, but also serves as a means for insurgent groups to publicize their attacks. The al-Zawra channel is not owned by an Islamist group but airs videos by an Islamist insurgent faction, the Islamic Army in Iraq. Additionally, it plays a prominent role in inciting religious tensions between Shia and Sunni.

The Case of al-Zawra

The al-Zawra satellite channel is owned by the family of Mish'an al-Juburi. It first emerged as an entertainment channel and later served as a mouthpiece for Mish'an's December 2005 parliamentary bid. With Mish'an's expulsion from the Iraqi National Assembly, the channel eventually evolved into a platform for insurgents.

Mish'an comes from the northern Iraqi city of Mosul, from the Juburi tribe. He was a member of the Baath Party and became the leader of the post-2003 Arab Front for Reconciliation and Liberation and a parliamentarian in the postwar National Assembly. He later fled Iraq on charges of embezzlement. His son Yazin al-Juburi is the managing director of the station and was the target of an assassination attempt.

The channel's slogans include "al-Zawra, The Voice of the Excluded and Marginalized," and "al-Zawra Favors the Nation, the Nation as a Whole." The station does not have a fixed schedule, but rather regularly airs videos produced by the insurgents, with footage of attacks against multinational forces. For a period following a government crackdown, old footage was looped continuously, twenty-four hours a day.

When former Iraqi president Saddam Hussein's death sentence was announced on November 5, 2006, al-Zawra featured videos and songs supportive of the outlawed Baath Party, as well as exhortations for Iraqis to join groups fighting the U.S. "occupation forces" and the Iraqi government and its "sectarian gangs." The Iraqi government ordered the station closed down on charges of "inciting violence." The closure order came from the Iraqi Interior Ministry, which also ordered the closure of the less well-known Salah al-Din satellite channel. The closure was justified by the ministry, not under regulation of the Communications and Media Commission (CMC) but under the Anti-Terrorism Law, a distinction that Juburi made clear in a January 2007 interview with the Arab *al-Sharq al-Awsat* newspaper: "The decision to close the station was issued by the Interior Ministry and not by a relevant body, like the Iraqi Communication and Media Commission, which is responsible for granting transmission and frequencies licenses." Al-Sharqiya, an independent channel with Arab Sunni sympathies that will be discussed later, carried footage of Iraqi security forces allegedly raiding the offices of the two channels.

However, the station has been able to circumvent the closure through its use of transnational satellites. It is unclear where its operations are now centered: Mish'an claims that the station still has many centers in Iraq, protected by Iraqi "resistance groups." Other conflicting reports claim that the channel is based in Irbil, in the north of Iraq, or in Syria. Both the Kurdish Regional Government and the Syrian government deny such claims.

As al-Zawra has shifted transmission tactics, its content has become increasingly incendiary. After the government closed its office, the channel's content focused on footage of insurgent attacks against U.S. and Iraqi forces. The channel produces its own announcements that directly incite violence by calling on Iraqis to join the "jihad" against "U.S. and Iranian occupation." Its attacks on Iran reflect a pro-Iraqi Arab Sunni sentiment that alleges Iran is aiding its co-religionists in Iraq. Announcements on the channel denounce the "crimes of Muqtada and of the gangs of Aziz al-Hakim," a reference to Muqtada al-Sadr, leader of the primarily Shia Sadr Trend, and Abd al-Aziz al-Hakim, leader of the SCIRI group. The station calls upon the "free youth of Iraq" to join the groups that are "defending" the nation to keep "Baghdad free from the Safawis," referring to the Safavid Empire of Iran (c. 1502–1736), but meant as a derogatory characterization of Iraq's Shia. The channel also features footage of what it alleges are "Sunni civilians" being attacked by Shia militias. Iraqis now speak of such ideas as a "Misha'an" rhetoric.

Al-Zawra's news anchors—a man and a woman wearing the veil—are dressed in military uniforms and regularly read statements delivered by Iraq's insurgent groups. Most of their news footage is provided directly by groups such as the Islamic Army in Iraq, an Islamist organization primarily comprised of Iraqis. It also carries relatively sophisticated documentaries produced by the insurgent groups, which feature English subtitles and are directed to Western viewers. One documentary claims that an armed group "wiped out" an entire American unit; the same documentary claims that 15,000 Americans have been killed by improvised explosive devices. The station also carries video footage of attacks carried out by Nizar al-Juburi, who achieved notoriety in Iraq as the "Baghdad Sniper." Foreign reporting of this channel has claimed that al-Zawra is an "al-Qaeda channel." However, though the channel often features grisly footage of insurgent activity, it has never aired videos produced by the al-Qaeda in Iraq organization, and its owner has declared that he refuses to do so.

There are no statistics on the number of viewers of this channel, but there are scattered reports about viewer reactions in Iraq and the Arab world. In Iraq, parliamentary critics of the station have been vocal about the station's content, and its owners have received death threats. At the same time, one correspondent in Iraq quoted one of the channel's young fans as saying, "I watch this channel every night. I don't like encouraging violence, but it is something unusual in the argument against the Americans. I am hooked." Another report stated how a Saudi cleric has issued fatwas, or religious declarations, encouraging Saudis to watch "the channel of the *mujahideen* [religiously inspired fighters]," stating, "it teaches the art of jihad, a matter the youth of our Umma [religious community] desperately need."

In terms of the effectiveness of Iraqi government actions, as quoted in the same report, Mish'an al-Juburi claims that the al-Zawra channel still broadcasts "from underground areas controlled by the Iraqi resistance, especially in northern Baghdad all the way to Mosul and al-Ramadi, using mobile transmission equipment out of fear of the U.S. forces shelling them." He also claims that the station's "six correspondents remain on the run, roaming the Iraqi countryside in a satellite truck, from which they beam their programming to an Egyptian satellite distributor called Nilesat, which then retransmits the channel across the Middle East." Journalist Lawrence Pintak interviewed Mish'an and described how his channel continued to operate: His teams in Iraq have sporadically managed to feed video to Cairo through satellite news gathering, or SNG, which apparently refers to the same kind of portable satellite dishes used by television news teams to transmit their material from the field. He says the material is recorded on a "server" in Cairo, then forwarded to Nilesat. "And it keeps transmitting even if we are not transmitting from Iraq," he adds. Much of the footage is shot on inexpensive video cameras and cell phones.

In February 2007, al-Zawra also began transmission on the Saudi-based regional satellite system Arabsat, on the BADR-4 satellite. This means that audiences in Iraq as well as the greater Arab world can watch it. Misha'an al-Juburi has also sought to broadcast the channel via European carriers such as Eutelsat in France.

The Iraqi and U.S. governments tried to have the Egyptian satellite provider, Nilesat, shut down the channel's satellite transmission over its transponders. More than a month after the closure of its terrestrial operations and offices in Iraq, in late December 2006, al-Zawra began to broadcast what it claimed was new footage of "Iraqi resistance" activities over its satellite channel. In January 2007, according to the *New York Times*, al-Zawra was broadcasting continuous footage of old jihadist videos, a trend that continued until the end of February. This suggests that Nilesat, bowing to pressure, had stopped transmitting new al-Zawra broadcasts sent from undisclosed locations in Iraq.

Al-Juburi has claimed that the Egyptian government caved in under U.S. pressure and prevented Nilesat from broadcasting any new material. The Egyptian culture minister challenged this claim, however. The chief engineer of Nilesat said that it was al-Zawra that asked the satellite carrier to continue transmitting old material. In regard to the issue of diplomatic pressure, the chairman of Nilesat denied ever receiving an Egyptian government request or an American or Iraqi government request to cut the channel's transmission.

Egypt's information minister stated that Iraqis had threatened the Egyptian diplomatic mission in Baghdad if Nilesat continued carrying al-Zawra. Some Egyptian sources claimed that these threats came from Muqtada al-Sadr's militia, the Mahdi Army, and led to the decision to stop broadcasting new material. This does not explain why Nilesat continues to loop al-Zawra's jihadist footage, which the Iraqi government and Sadr's militia would likely find offensive.

The case of al-Zawra, an entertainment channel that evolved to an insurgency channel, represents a worst-case scenario for the Iraqi media, demonstrating the ineffectiveness of punitive measures, such as the closure of its Baghdad office, in the face of new transnational transmission technologies. It is plausible that a channel owned by other Islamist sectarian factions, or even an independent channel, could undergo a similar transformation. Punitive legislation and action against media that incite violence is only a partial solution. Even the speaker of Iraq's parliament declared that the al-Zawra channel incident demonstrated the dangers of shutting down a channel and called for media responsibility.

The Future of Iraq's Media

Well before the 2003 Iraq war, the Iraqis were viewed by foreign media through a "tri-ethnic prism" focusing on divisions between Shia, Sunni, and Kurds, while ignoring Turkmens, Assyrian and Chaldean Christians, Yazidis and Sabaens, as well as the country's more traditional fault lines, such as class, rural-urban, religious-secular, and tribal divisions within the three communities. Iraqis' placement into three "ethnic" categories has led to erroneous notions such as characterizing Iraq's Shia as an "ethnic" group or neglecting the fact that the majority of Kurds are also Sunnis.

Nevertheless, an examination of the media sphere in Iraq suggests that such categorizations have become reality. Indeed, Iraq's media are increasingly divided along sectarian lines, with independent organizations competing for audiences that have grown weary of sectarian media. Author Paul Cochrane refers to this situation as the "Lebanonization" of the Iraqi media: "With Iraq's TV menu growing increasingly sectarian, it is possible to draw a parallel with Lebanon's highly sectarianized hodgepodge of channels—linked directly or loosely with political parties—which regularly report sect-specific news."

The Iraqi media are pluralistic, but also fragmented. This plurality can be positive. If the Iraqi media served as the outlet for all of Iraq's communities, that would be beneficial for Iraq's painful transition to democracy. However, there are negative aspects of pluralism when it emerges as a result of chaos. Media pluralism in Iraq allows for sectarian political groups to consolidate powerful media empires—including print, radio, and TV—and broadcast in Iraq and internationally. While there is freedom of the press, the freedom of journalists to cover a story or obtain access to information is severely restricted. Certain political parties are content when their media express their political platform, but will violently target journalists and media professionals who report on news in a way that displeases them. Pluralism, without regulation, can also lead to the rise of media that can be abused as a means of encouraging violence.

Four phases are necessary for the emergence of a conflict media: (1) a strong ideology, (2) sectarian control over mass media, (3) psychological preparation to hate, and (4) a call to violence. I would argue that Iraq's sectarian media have entered phase three. Following the bombing of the Shia al-Askari Shrine in Samarra in February 2006, the various sectarian and ethnic media outlets escalated tensions but eventually called for restraint among Iraq's communities.

A content analysis of the various sectarian channels did not find that coverage directly demonized the other communities. However, each sectarian group uses its media to show that its members are the victims in Iraq's ongoing violence. While they do not explicitly exhort violence against other communities, as would happen in phase four, their continued portrayal of victimization serves as a means of encouraging Shia and Sunni to "defend" themselves in the ensuing sectarian violence. After the 2006 shrine bombing, for example, the Arab Sunni–oriented Baghdad Satellite Channel focused its coverage on the Arab Sunni killed in retaliation, while the Arab Shia–oriented al-Furat focused on the actual damage to their sacred structure. According to journalist Nir Rosen, "al-Furat was even more aggressive, encouraging Shia to 'stand up for their rights.' On a Shia radio station's talk show, one caller announced that those responsible for the attack were Abu Bakr, Omar, and Othman, the three first caliphs whom Sunni venerate and whom Shia reject as usurpers of the position that rightfully belonged to Imam Ali, the prophet Muhammad's cousin and son-in-law."

When a particular channel reports a violent incident in Iraq, as, for example, an Arab Shia militia killing an Arab Sunni family in their home, or when another channel reports on Arab Shia killed in a marketplace by Arab Sunni suicide bombers, neither party directly calls for revenge against the other. In these cases, the channels may not even invoke the terms "Shia" or "Sunni." Usually viewers can identity the victims by the location of the attack, or the perpetrators by the method of attack. If, for example, Baghdad Satellite Channel states that the Abu Hanifa Mosque was attacked by mortar rounds, an Arab Sunni viewer will most likely infer that the rounds were launched by the Shia Mahdi Army from the adjacent neighborhoods. The respective audience members that feel victimized may take matters into their own hands in "self-defense," which in most cases manifests itself in revenge attacks. Even if the "victimized" parties fail to act, the worsening security situation may generate support for the respective militias, and not the state, to provide protection.

Ahmed Rikabi, an Iraqi journalist with extensive experience in postwar media, reflected on the bias and sense of victimization in Shia and Sunni reporting. Speaking on the CNN program "International Correspondents" (October 13, 2006), he said in reference to Iraqi media:

> The sectarian tension is so strong in Iraq today. And I think this guy whose name is Omar . . . this is a Sunni guy, when he goes and tries to cover an incident in a Shi'ite area, he feels like one of the victims. He doesn't go and feel like a neutral person covering this. And so is the case for the Shi'ite Ali, who goes to that Sunni area . . . trying to cover [a story]. You also feel the fear. He feels that those people standing there, they might kill him as well. So that probably also affects him somehow. . . . Whether he is very objective or whether he is very normal or neutral or unbiased . . . he can't help it that he's got a certain name. And that name might get him killed. And that will influence his way of thinking or approaching the subject.

A month later, also on CNN, Rikabi stated explicitly that the media in Iraq have emerged as tools of conflict: "We are witnessing a civil war. And this civil war is conducted by different religious groups and different political groups. And of course, the media is an extension of this sectarian violence we are witnessing today."

If Iraqi sectarian media have reached phase three, they are laying the psychological groundwork for hating the other. To reach stage four, these factions would need to make direct exhortations to violence. If the security situation were to worsen, the other political factions would have the option of using their media as mouthpieces to exacerbate the conflict by whipping up ethnic and sectarian feelings, or even directing the conflict. So far, these other factions have used their media to stress unity among Iraq's communities, but they nevertheless have the potential to instigate conflict with these means if it suits their interests.

According to the author's fieldwork on the media in Iraq, a common perception held among the Iraqi public, and even journalists themselves, is that different factions have used the newspapers, radio, and TV as "tools of war." As the Iraqi political parties rarely communicate directly with each other, they have expressed their grievances through the media, with some media discreetly encouraging violence against the incumbent government. While observers of the situation in Iraq argue whether a "civil war" has emerged in Iraq, a "civil war of words" has certainly emerged in the Iraqi media, according to some Iraqi journalists.

One of these, Muhammad Sahi, wrote a critical essay in *al-Zawra*, a weekly published by the Iraqi Journalists Association (unrelated to the al-Zawra satellite channel), published March 27, 2006. His article serves as a lament for the state of the Iraqi media. Sahi writes: "They [the media] not only increased sectarianism and deepened ethnicity in society, but also are responsible for the fading of the concept of nationalism and patriotism and their actual dimensions." He cites a list of the vast array of media aligned to political factions, which, he argues, are "mere fronts, whose main goal is to promote the ideologies and ideas of their affiliated political parties and forces," and "have confused the Iraqi citizens and created a psychological barrier, in one way or another, between them."

According to Sahi, the pluralism in the Iraqi media—which often results in conflicting news reports about the same event on different satellite channels, depending on affiliation—has divided, confused, and enraged the Iraqi viewer. Sahi admits that some channels are trying to avoid promoting sectarianism, but they do cover statements made by Iraqi politicians divided by "sectarian inclinations that escalate sectarian tension and crisis." In a final assessment of the Iraqi media, Sahi writes that "the Iraqi street and viewers are being divided with regard to their favored channels and news coverage based on their political loyalties and inclinations." He believes it is inevitable that viewers will "adopt the political discourse of their favored television channels and . . . act in accordance with the statements made by political leaders."

The Media and Iraq's Future

Iraq's pattern of media development is a matter of concern for the country's long-term stability. Sectarian divisions have proliferated in the electronic and print spheres as well, and have the potential to exacerbate tensions. This potential was demonstrated in light of events that occurred in predominantly Shia Sadr City in late November 2006, when multiple car bombs caused the highest number of casualties in a single incident. The Iraqi government accused various networks, both foreign Arab and Iraqi, of inflaming the conflict through their coverage, and threatened to prosecute these channels, and Iraqi president Jalal Talabani blamed the media for inciting the violence.

The fact that government officials have been so vehement in their criticism of various television channels and newspapers is an indirect acknowledgement of the power of the media. Their criticisms also reveal the challenge of dealing with the violence in Iraq that plays out not only on the streets, but also in the media sphere. The government sought to make an example of the al-Zawra station in November by closing down its office. However, satellite television and the Internet have proven that punitive measures are ineffective in dealing with media that can be transmitted transnationally.

Events in Iraq could stabilize, and as a result the Iraqi media might play a constructive role. Nevertheless, in the long term, various sectarian media outlets in Iraq still could prove problematic in another fashion. Rather than a media sphere, Iraq has sectarian media "spherecules" that have the potential to further the gap between Iraq's communities, developing identities along sectarian lines and weakening any kind of national belonging. The media "spherecules" owned by Islamist groups have the potential to increase sectarian nationalism in the guise of political Islam in Iraq.

Appendix: Sample of Sectarian Media in Iraq

Arab Shia Media:

SCIRI
al-Adala (Justice) daily paper
al-Wahdah (Unity) weekly paper
al-Ghadir radio station
al-Furat (The Euphrates) satellite channel

The Da'wa Party:

al-Da'wa (The Call) daily paper
al-Bayan (Announcement) weekly paper
al-Masar radio station
al-Masar TV channel

Sadr Trend:

Ishraqat al-Sadr weekly daily paper
al-Hawza al-Natiqa (The Active Hawza) weekly paper
al-Salam radio station
al-Salam TV station

Iraqi Hezbollah:

al-Bayyinah (Evidence) paper

Arab Sunni Media:

Iraqi Islamic Party: Dar al-Salam (The House of Peace) radio station; *Dar al-Salam* (The House of Peace) daily paper
General Dialogue Conference: al-Itisam (The Guardian) daily newspaper
The Unified National Movement: al-Sa'ah (The Hour) biweekly newspaper
The Association of Muslim Scholars: al-Basa'ir (Insights) daily newspaper

References and Further Reading

Alexis, Monique, and Ines Mpambara. "IMS Assessment Mission: The Rwanda Media Experience from the Genocide." International Media Support Report, 2003.

Choi, Jingbong. "The Framing of the 'Axis of the Evil.'" In *The Global Media Go to War: Role of News and Entertainment Media During the 2003 Iraq War*, ed. Ralph Berenger. Spokane, WA: Marquette Books, 2004.

Cochrane, Paul. "The 'Lebanonization' of the Iraqi Media: An Overview of Iraq's Television Landscape." *Transnational Broadcasting Studies* (June–December 2006).

International Media Support. "Media Development in Post-war Iraq Report." London, April 2003.

IREX. "Media Sustainability Index—Iraq." IREX Europe, 2006.

Karlowicz, Izabella. "The Difficult Birth of the Fourth Estate: Media Development and Democracy Assistance in Post-Conflict Balkans." In *Reinventing Media: Media Policy Reform in East-Central Europe*, ed. Miklos Sukosd and Peter Bajomi-Lazar. Budapest, Hungary: Central European University Center for Policy Studies, 2003.

Mroue, Bassem. "Sectarian TV Main Source of News in Iraq." Associated Press, July 7, 2006.

Noor Al-Deen, Hana. "Changes and Challenges of the Iraqi Media." *Global Media Journal* 4:6 (Spring 2005).

al-Qazwini, Iqbal Hassoon. "On the Role of Media in the Current Transition Phase in Iraq." *Transnational Broadcasting Studies* (Fall 2004).

Rosen, Nir. "Anatomy of a Civil War: Iraq's Descent into Chaos." *Boston Review* (November/December 2006).

The Iranian Media Under President Muhammad Khatami

Barry Rubin

Control of the press has been a central battle in the factional political struggle within Iran. Newspapers supporting President Muhammad Khatami, who held that office from 1997 to 2005 leading a reformist faction, were closed or harassed, as are those whose criticisms of government policy or the regime's ideology go too far in the eyes of the powerful conservative faction. This discussion takes a detailed look at the period between 1998 and 2001, one of relative media freedom in Iran.

Despite Khatami's election, or perhaps because of it, Iranian hard-liners increasingly targeted the press through arrests, persecution, and harassment as part of their struggle to retain power. Khatami was unwilling or unable to respond. As a result, the Committee to Protect Journalists (CPJ) placed Iran's Supreme Leader Ayatollah Ali Khamenei at the top of its annual "Enemies of the Press" list in May 2001; he was the runner-up the previous year.

Iranian publisher Shahla Lahiji was awarded the 2001 PEN/Barbara Goldsmith Freedom to Write Award as she faced a three-and-a-half year prison sentence for acting against national security and another six months for describing the dangers faced by Iranian writers. Iranian editor Mashallah Shamsolvaezin was already in jail when he received the International Press Freedom Award from the New York–based Committee to Protect Journalists. There were at least twenty Iranian journalists in prison and about fifty Iranian publications closed by the government in the second half of 2000 and the first half of 2001. Afterward, the situation became even worse, especially after Khatami left office.

When Khatami was first elected in May 1997, one might have expected a real increase in press freedom. Khatami appointed the moderate Ataollah Mohajerani as Islamic Culture and Guidance Minister. In the first year of Khatami's presidency, 226 publications received licenses. But at the same time, newspapers were closed for violating vague and unevenly enforced regulations, and despite the existence of the Press Law, Iranians who work in the fields of journalism and publishing frequently complain about vague rules. Following the Islamic Revolution of 1979, journalists were on occasion tried, incarcerated, and sometimes prevented from practicing their profession. There were also cases in which journalists were murdered or were made to disappear.

In an interview with RFE/RL's Persian Service, Ali Nazari, managing editor of *Arzesh* magazine, said: "Every time the press in Iran is warned by officials, we are told that we have crossed a red line, although no one has bothered to tell us where that red line is."

Under the guise of clarifying these limits, a revision of the Press Law was proposed in October–November 1998. In *Asr-e Ma* on November 18, 1999, the Majlis Research Center said this would eliminate "ambiguous points and defects in the press law," though later that month the Islamic Republic News Agency (IRNA) reported that not all officials agreed that this was needed.

There was general unhappiness with the proposed amendment, particularly among journalists. A letter from the Press Association, cited by *Jomhuri-ye Islami* in June 1999, said, "Tabling bills which are restrictive and which undermine freedom would not only not make the press [corps] law-abiding, but would place them under [a] monopoly by a few people and drive society toward samizdats and other methods." *Neshat* reporter Minoo Badii was quoted by Islamic Republic of Iran Broadcasting (IRIB) in July 1999 as saying: "To attain a civil society and achieve political development we need to have numerous newspapers and publications, [but] if you look at the proposal to amend the press law you will see that it would restrict this trend." Even Khatami was critical, saying that all press cases should go before a jury and not a special court, IRNA reported that June.

A hint of parliament's view came when 228 parliamentarians signed a letter, cited by *RFE/RL Iran Report* of June 1999, declaring their concern about "The cultural inroad of the enemy in the form of a plot for transformation and overthrow of the system" and would "foil such a conspiracy." Parliament approved the law on July 7.

The law says that a complaint against a publication can be filed without any statute of limitations. It calls for a reporter to be held responsible for individual writings while general responsibility lies with the publication's director or chief editor. Press accreditation was made more restrictive. The bill stipulates that a cleric and the head of the Islamic Propagation Organization shall serve on the Press Supervisory Board, and that Revolutionary Courts are qualified to hear press offenses, whereas Article 168 of the constitution only permits press courts to do so.

Just before the vote, Deputy Minister of Intelligence and Security Said Emami wrote in *Salam* that since journalists' activities "cause security problems for the Islamic Republic of Iran," every writer who endangers security must be confronted "individually, using the law, in order to ban them from writing or publishing." The goal should be, he concluded, that pro-government forces "can be strengthened and hostile elements driven away." In January 1999, Emami was arrested for his part in the 1998 murders of writers and dissident political figures. It would seem that he was implementing part of the plan proposed in his letter. Emami died the following June, allegedly committing suicide while in custody.

Shortly before its final session, the fifth parliament strengthened the Press Law and defined the "red line" more clearly. The new law was used to close some thirteen publications in one week in April 2000 and at least forty-four publications by April 2001. When the new, predominantly reformist, sixth parliament tried to change the press law in August 2000, Supreme Leader Khamenei blocked the debate.

Nevertheless, publications and journalists took on more and more controversial subjects during that time, despite numerous press closures. These two developments led to the creation of what Iranian hard-liners term "serial newspapers" and what Iranian reformists would term "serial plaintiffs."

High Expectations

When President Khatami was elected on May 23, 1997, there were expectations of increased press freedom for several reasons. Khatami had been forced out of office in 1992 after almost ten years as minister of Islamic culture and guidance due to accusations that he was too lax with the media. Mohajerani, Khatami's choice for minister of Islamic culture and guidance, was considered by some observers as too moderate to win parliamentary approval, according to a *New York Times* article of August 15, 1997. Later that month, Reuters reported that one parliamentarian criticized Mohajerani for being too "culturally tolerant and politically weak vis-à-vis the West." Another asked Mohajerani if he would kill novelist Salman Rushdie if he met him. A third member of parliament is reported to have said, "[a] ll the shrewd and cunning foreign media are supporting Mohajerani's nomination. Let us all disappoint them." Mohajerani made no attempt to hide his views, delaring, "I disagree with almost all of the present practices in the culture ministry. We have to protect artists and provide an atmosphere for creativity, tranquility, and freedom." He added, "Everybody who has accepted the Islamic Republic and its constitution must be subject to tolerance. . . . I condemn the burning of bookshops, the beating of university lecturers and attacks on magazine offices."

During his presidential campaign, Khatami promised increased openness, civil society, and governmental accountability and transparency. On the day his victory was announced in May 1997, Khatami's spokesman, Ahmad Burqani, was quoted by the *New York Times* as saying that "of course Mr. Khatami will not continue the present restrictions on the press and media. He will have an open policy toward them." In his first extended remarks after winning the election, Khatami said it was time to ensure more democracy in Iran, and that the Islamic Republic was stable enough to give its citizens full constitutional rights, including free thought, life, employment, assembly, and association. "We hope to gradually witness a more legal society," he said, "with more clearly defined rights and duties for citizens and the government." Khatami also called for the creation of an independent press in his first address after taking office.

Some Expectations Met

The first year of the Khatami presidency saw the emergence of a reinvigorated press. Notable was the publication of the daily *Jameah*, which was the first to report on the Islamic Revolution Guards Corps (IRGC) commander's closed-door speech in which he threatened to "cut the necks and tongues" of political opponents. In July 1998, the *New York Times* reported that the daily had also run interviews with Abbas Amir Entezam, who had served fifteen years in prison on charges of being an American spy, in which he described torture in the prison system and the need to separate religion from politics. Publications like this questioned the status quo and also served as vehicles for reform-oriented political figures to express their views.

Simultaneously, one saw trends emerging that would gain momentum later. Student leader Heshmatollah Tabarzadi was beaten up and his newspaper closed in late 1997 after he commented that the supreme leader should be elected directly by the people for a limited term, rather than by the Assembly of Experts, a directly elected eighty-six-member clerical body. *Jameah* had its license suspended in June 1998, although it resumed publication the next month with the same staff under the name *Tus*. According to a July 1998 article in the *New York Times*, editor Mashallah Shamsolvaezin explained, "We are a test case of how much openness the government can tolerate." The answer came in August, when the judiciary ordered the closure of *Tus* for "publishing lies and disrupting public order," and members of the hard-line Ansar-e Hezbollah vigilante group beat up Shamsolvaezin, according to Agence France-Presse. The daily was permanently closed in September for questioning Tehran's tough policy toward the Taliban in Afghanistan, a rather unwise move at a time when the regime to the east had just murdered a group of Iranian officials.

Just as press closures and violence against journalists took on a pattern, so did the continued publication of a banned newspaper under a new name and the use of an unused press license. *Jameah* became *Tus*, and after that license was revoked, the newspaper came out as *Neshat*. After its closure, *Neshat* took over the dormant license of *Akhbar* and resumed publication as *Akhbar-e Eqtesad*, employing *Neshat* staff. Other *Neshat* personnel were employed by *Asr-e Azadegan*, which after its closure was succeeded by *Gunagun* weekly. Until its closure, this weekly employed staff from *Tus*, *Neshat*, *Asr-e Azadegan*, and other reformist publications. Other *Jameah* alumni created *Aftab-e Imrooz*. Hard-line political commentators, such as Seyyed Jalal Fayyazi, Amir Mohebbian, and Mohammad Imani, complained about the "serial newspapers" in issues of *Qods*, *Yalisarat al-Hussein*, and *Fayzieh*, *Kayhan*, respectively.

Factional issues played a big part in press closures. The hard-line judiciary closes reformist publications, while hard-line ones that commit similar violations are rarely punished. Furthermore, many reformist publications, plus a few hard-line ones, have been closed through the enforcement of vaguely worded rules and regulations. After a brief respite following Khatami's 1997 inauguration, there was a clampdown against the more vocal press.

Continued Repression

Other publications encountered legal problems for exposing corruption of local officials. For example, the director of provincial newspaper *Kosar Kavir Kerman* claimed his offices were set on fire after publishing articles about the improper use of nationalized property in Kerman province, as reported by *Kar va Kargar* on January 31, 1999. The publisher of Sanandaj's Kurdish-language *Sirwan* weekly was summoned "for publishing falsehoods and slander against an adviser of the head of the judiciary," although more likely the real issue was an article on financial mismanagement in the Kurdistan province governorate, according to *Hamshahri*, a major national daily newspaper, on April 14 of that year. The situation in Gilan province seemed especially bad. Ali Sebati, director of *Payam-e Shomal*, was arrested by the local Ministry of Intelligence and Security, or MOIS, *Khordad* reported in February. In all, seven journalists were imprisoned there, according to an April edition of *Neshat.*

Neshat further reported that the *Sobh* newspaper was warned in April about a critical article on government managers. Nasser Safarian, the movie critic from *Salam*, a moderate, pro-Khatami newspaper, was held for two days and questioned for signing a letter demanding answers about the murders of dissidents. In a not-so-subtle hint, he was released on the road to the Behesht-e Zahra cemetery.

Conservative figures have blamed the press for the country's problems. Iranian Revolutionary Guards Corps general Yahya Rahim Safavi opined, "The influence of the anti-revolutionary elements in the country's press should be stopped." On April 19, 1999, the state-linked daily newspapers *Jomhouri-e Islami* and *Kayhan* quoted a letter from four senior ayatollahs to Khatami, asking him to confront the press's "violation of religious principles, efforts to undermine Islamic belief, and distortion of ethics."

Islamic Republic of Iran Broadcasting (IRIB)

Because newspapers and print media have a limited circulation outside Iran's main cities, radio and television play a powerful role in opinion making. The Islamic Republic of Iran Broadcasting, however, is subject to frequent criticism for its biased coverage of domestic political issues. For example, its coverage of the 1997 presidential election heavily favored conservative candidate Hojatoleslam Ali-Akbar Nateq-Nuri. On the other hand, IRIB's coverage of his chief rival, Khatami, was less frequent and much less favorable. In January 1999, a daily from Rasht, *Khabar va Nazar*, claimed that IRIB directed "propaganda attacks" against Khatami since "they called him a 'liberal' and even hinted he was against the *velayat-e faghih*," referring to the concept of a ruling clerical spiritual guide for the country promulgated by Ayatollah Ruhollah Khomeini.

Serious unhappiness with IRIB and its director, Ali Larijani, resumed in January 1999. At that time, a guest on the "Cheraq" program claimed Khatami's allies were behind the murders of intellectuals, dissidents, and journalists the previous autumn. Eighty-eight members of parliament sent a letter to Supreme Leader Ayatollah Ali Khamenei requesting reforms in the IRIB. In the letter they complained that state broadcasting was not impartial, and "instead of safeguarding national interests, it was evidently backing a certain faction." *Zan*, a newspaper focusing on women's rights, quoted the parliamentarians as writing that such behavior would "encourage tension, discredit the important media to the people, and ultimately deal fatal blows to our holy Islamic system."

In March 1999, IRIB was criticized for its coverage of Khatami's trip to Italy. Although the president's speech at the European International University in Florence was broadcast live, the applause after the speech was not broadcast in its entirety. This, and the fact that the speech was not rebroadcast nor was it mentioned in news reports the next day, showed that IRIB has an anti-Khatami bias, claimed the newspaper *Iran.*

Islamic Culture and Guidance Minister Mohajerani

While the Islamic Culture and Guidance Ministry issues press licenses, the courts are authorized to close publications. Leading liberal daily *Neshat* was closed in September 1999 because of articles critical of aspects of the regime. On the same day that *Neshat* was closed, Chief Judge Ayatollah Mahmud Hashemi-Shahrudi met with Islamic Culture and Guidance minister Ataollah Mohajerani. In September, IRNA reported that Judge Hashemi-Shahrudi said the ministry should "render useless any grounds for attacks against the principles and basic tenets of the system." He told Mohajerani that if his ministry did its job, the judiciary's intervention would be unnecessary.

In April 1999, thirty parliamentarians submitted a motion for Mohajerani's removal. The motion stated that Mohajerani had not restrained the press sufficiently and had questioned the judiciary's performance in shutting down newspapers. He had advocated separation of religion and politics, as well as the establishment of relations with the United States. Mohajerani was also guilty of founding the writers' association. "The ministry failed to support intellectual and cultural movies and instead films were produced with the aim of making profits," read one critique, which would have preferred films glorifying the Sacred Defense (Iran-Iraq war). Finally, Mohajerani was accused of misappropriating funds.

Waging a successful defense on April 31 and May 1, Mohajerani survived narrowly, by a vote of 135 to 121, with 7 abstentions. This was seen as a victory for the reformers. Even after the closure of *Neshat*, Mohajerani did not abandon his principles. His ministry rejected the closure by the court and permitted *Neshat* to reopen under the name *Akhbar-e Eqtesad.*

The April 1999 motion to remove Mohajerani brought renewed criticism of the IRIB. Abbas Abdi, editor of the pro-reform newspaper *Khordad*, said that if the parliament wanted to fire Mohajerani for what is in newspapers, it should instead target the IRIB, which, after all, is the institution producing broadcasts whose "unethical programs" far exceed that found in all the newspapers combined.

Criticism of the Moderate Press by Hard-liners

Events in the first two years of the Khatami presidency pale in comparison to what happened in 2000 and 2001, when about fifty publications were closed in a fifteen-month period. This trend started in March–April 2000, when Supreme Leader Khamenei delivered several sermons and speeches criticizing the reformist press specifically.

In one sermon, Khamenei complained about unnamed promoters of "Americanized reforms" and seemed to indicate they were acceptable targets of violence. In another, he claimed that the West first attacked Iran via its radio stations, but now was building a "stronghold" in Iran through the press, creating anxiety, discord, and pessimism. On April 20, 2000, Khamenei spoke on the Voice of the Islamic Republic of Iran, saying, "It seems as if ten or fifteen newspapers are being directed from the same center to publish articles with similar headlines. They make mountains out of molehills . . . kill the hope among the youth . . . weaken the people's trust . . . offend and insult." The supreme leader added that Khatami was unhappy with the press as well. "We are trying to stop the enemy from realizing his propaganda conspiracy."

Such statements inspired the following statement from the IRGC on the Vision of the Republic of Iran on April 16, 2000: "If necessary, our enemies, be they small or large, will feel the reverberating impact of the hammer of the Islamic revolution on their skulls and the impact will be so strong that they will never be able to engage in hatching plots or committing crimes." Then in just one day, April 23, 2000, twelve publications were closed. It was quite clear that the closures related to the publications' criticism of the hard-liners and support for reformist causes.

After the initial closures, an unnamed judiciary official explained that a committee formed to investigate the press had concluded that, "despite frequent warnings given to them, they continued with their anti-Islamic and anti-revolutionary activities," and "the tone of material in those papers had brought smiles to the faces of the enemies of the Islamic Republic and hurt the feelings of devout Muslims at home and even the leader of the Islamic revolution." In April 2000, according to the *Tehran Times*, the same official warned, "We are also trying to detect the foreign links of some of these newspapers."

Supreme Leader Khamenei continued his criticism of the media during a July 26 speech broadcast on the Voice of the Islamic Republic of Iran, stating, "The journalists stop the officials from carrying out their duties and this is an act of treason. Talking about matters that are desirable by the CIA and Mossad, or writing about issues in order to please them [CIA and Mossad], or taking stances for their benefit, do not serve the people's interests."

On August 6, Khamenei warned that "should the enemies of Islam, the revolution and the Islamic system take over or infiltrate the press, a great danger would threaten the security, unity and the faith of the people and, therefore, I cannot allow myself and other officials to keep quiet in respect of this crucial issue." Khamenei went on to say that "the current [press] law, to a degree, has been able to prevent the appearance of this great calamity, and [therefore], its interpretation [amendment] and similar actions that have been anticipated by the parliamentary committee are not legitimate and not in the interest of the country and the system."

This outraged reformist deputies. Scuffles broke out in the chamber, and there was a walkout. Speaker of Parliament Hojatoleslam Mehdi Mahdavi-Karroubi reacted by reminding the protestors that the supreme leader's action was legally permissible. As he later told state radio, "The constitution emphasizes the Absolute Rule of the Jurisconsult [*velayat-e motlaq*] and this is how it is. And, you voted for it."

Radio Free Europe/Radio Liberty's Persian Service asked reformist journalist Masud Behnud why the press law had been made so strict in the first place. In the August 2000 issue of the *RFE/RL Iran Report*, Behnud explained that after the hard-liners lost the elections, the loss was attributed solely to the press, which demonstrated its role as a decisive factor in elections. Thus, according to Benhud, the hard-liners made a small number of major changes to the press law.

In addition to the aforementioned government shutdown of more than fifty daily newspapers, weeklies, and monthlies, numerous provincial and student publications were closed. And these figures do not include publications whose licenses were revoked by the Press Supervisory Board.

Closures in the Provinces

Press closures and persecution of journalists were most noticeable in Tehran, but also happened in the provinces, as noted above. Editors from Rasht, Shiraz, and Tabriz described some of the problems they faced in a roundtable organized by RFE/RL's Persian Service in September 2000. The most pernicious problem is self-censorship. After seeing what happened in Tehran and noting how long their colleagues were unemployed, provincial journalists became very cautious. The provincial publications have other problems, including lack of money and modern printing facilities. This means they have low circulation and limited reach.

Provincial journalists face legal problems, too. For example, it was reported in September 2000 that Davud Bayat, managing editor of Zanjan's *Farda-ye Roshan* weekly, was charged with printing defamatory articles, publishing falsehoods to divert public opinion, and vilifying institutions, according to a complaint from the Justice Department and public prosecutor. The court ordered the weekly's closure in August 2001. Meanwhile, also in September 2000, Mohammad Reza Nabaie, managing editor of the weekly *Andalib*, was summoned to court following a complaint from a former parliamentarian, Hassan Zamani, who claimed that an article in the publication insulted the people of his district, distorted his words, and contained lies.

Serial Plaintiffs

Four institutions that regularly go after journalists and publications are what could be called "serial plaintiffs." They are the IRGC, MOIS, the counterintelligence unit of the Law Enforcement Forces, and the IRIB. They and other, similar bodies file most of the complaints that lead to press trials in which the courts revoke press licenses and send people to prison.

When the *Ava* weekly from Najafabad, Isfahan province, was suspended in April 2000, it faced complaints from the MOIS, the Press Supervisory Board, the Ministry of Islamic Culture and Guidance, the Special Court for the Clergy in Qom, the Islamic Revolution Guard Corps in Qom, and the city of Najafabad. *Ava* editor Mustafa Izadi was sentenced in early July. Attorney Muhammad Aghassi said that Izadi's chief problem was the perception that he was a supporter of a dissident faction, according to the July 2000 *RFE/RL Iran Report*.

In June 2000, *Hayat-e No* reported that the managing director of Tabriz's *Ahrar* weekly faced complaints from counterintelligence chief Brigadier General Muhammad Reza Naqdi, the IRGC, and the East Azerbaijan Basij of the Dispossessed (a pro-regime militia). *Bayan* managing editor Hojatoleslam Ali Akbar Mohtashemi-Pur was summoned by the Special Court for the Clergy to face complaints from a counterintelligence unit, the IRIB, the Tehran municipality, and hard-line cleric Hojatoleslam Ruhollah Husseinian, stated *Iran* in June.

As a result of all these developments, Reporters Without Borders referred to Iran in an April 2001 press release as the biggest jail for journalists in the world. And often people disappear in a prison system that is run by a myriad of unaccountable security agencies. Other journalists have been murdered (for example, Majid Sharif, Mohammad Mokhtari, and Mohammad Jafar Puyandeh) or disappeared (for example, Piruz Davani).

As president, Khatami was unable to defend reformist newspapers and journalists, even when they were his strong supporters. The courts closed the reformist *Hambastegi* daily on August 8, 2001, the very day Khatami took his oath of office. And once Khatami was out of office and the regime prevented reformist candidates from running for election at all, the pressure rose even more.

To get around press limitations, Iranians resort to foreign media via shortwave radio or the Internet. State radio and television already had a powerful role in opinion making because newspapers and print media have a limited circulation outside the main cities. The closure of so many publications only increased this advantage. But the IRIB was also widely criticized for being one-sided in its news reporting. *Iran Daily* cited shopkeepers as saying that the demand for shortwave receivers in Iran increased after press closures in May 2000.

Internet

Another alternative media is the Internet. Many Iranian newspapers, such as *Hamshahri*, *Jomhouri-e Islami*, and even *Khabar-i Jonub* from Shiraz, are available on the Internet. So too are weeklies like *Donyaye Varzesh*. But the government also has means of retaliating even here. Reporters Without Borders identified Iran as one of the leading "Enemies of the Internet" for controlling or blocking access. An operator of an Internet café reportedly told a visitor to Tehran that a condition for getting a license to operate an ISP was a promise to the MOIS to provide a listing of all Web sites used by any given member at any given time, according to the *Tehran Times* on July 18, 1999.

This is not to say that the Iranian media, if left alone by the state, would be perfectly objective and unbiased. Many publications serve as party organs and voice the viewpoints of political factions and pressure groups. As Professor Sadiq Zibakalam wrote in *Jameh-ye Salem* in August 1997, even the more independent newspapers, like *Salam* and *Hamshahri*, reflect some of the more populist and reactionary views in foreign policy. Zibakalam gave as an example the lack of nuance and general double standards in response to international human rights reports about Iran. The authors of such reports are criticized as "agents of Zionism" and the reports denounced as attacks against Iran's prestige.

Still, the Iranian press has been a lively forum for discussion of many issues, including a willingness to dare question government policies. In October 1999, *Der Spiegel* reported that a Tehran public prosecutor asked *Asr-e Azadegan* editor Mashallah Shamsolvaezin how long the game of cat-and-mouse between government and journalists would continue. Shamsolvaezin says, "I told him that I would continue until the cat realized that the mouse had a right to live."

References and Further Reading

Fayyazi, Seyyed Jalal. "Elections: Free or Secular." *Qods*, December 14, 1999.

Imani, Mohammad. "May God Save Us from Dishonest Friends." *Kayhan*, February 15, 2001.

"Iran's Moderate President Faces Dissent over Cabinet Choices." *New York Times*, August 15, 1997.

Kinzer, Stephen. "Moderate Leader Is Elected in Iran by a Wide Margin." *New York Times*, May 25, 1997.

"Mohajerani's Period of Ministership: Cultural Triteness, or Cultural Corruption?" *Fayzieh*, January 3, 2001.

Mohebbian, Amir. "The Executives of the System Must Be Brought Under the Sword of Criticism." *Yalisarat al-Hussein*, December 6, 2000.

Samii, A.A. "The Contemporary Iranian News Media." *MERIA* 3:4 (December 1999).

———. "Sisyphus' Newsstand: The Iranian Press Under Khatami." *Middle East Review of International Affairs (MERIA)* 5:3 (September 2001).

Sciolino, Elaine. "Iran's Alternative Voices Now Demand to Be Heard." *New York Times*, July 19, 1998.

The Israeli Media

Eytan Gilboa

Despite its small population and territory, absorption of 2 million immigrants, and the constant burden of national security, Israel has been able to support, develop, and maintain a flourishing, diversified, and free media. Israelis are probably the largest consumers of news in the world. Israeli society is very dynamic and closely monitors significant events and developments in the Arab-Israeli conflict. The society is also very active and outspoken, and this is both reflected and nourished by the mass media. The print media have always been independent and respected, and in general has been able to adjust to social, economic, and technological challenges and innovations.

Today, the Israeli media includes four general daily newspapers, three daily financial newspapers, hundreds of local papers and magazines, three national television channels, popular cable and satellite services, two public radio networks, fourteen regional radio stations, and thousands of Web sites and portals. This diversified media world, especially in broadcasting and new media, has emerged only since the late 1980s, due to technological, economic, and political changes. Until the early 1990s, there was only one public television channel and two public radio networks. The political establishment resisted efforts to open up the electronic media market because it exercised some political control and influence over the institutions regulating and operating television and radio broadcasts. The revolution in communications technologies, the ability to broadcast—often live—from almost every place in the world to almost any other place, and the Internet created global news networks, consumers, and economic interests. Accompanied by unprecedented prosperity in the Israeli economy, the communications revolution brought enormous pressure on the government to expand the electronic media through privately owned commercial networks.

Since the late 1980s, Israeli media has undergone a complete transformation. Most of the political and ideological party newspapers have disappeared, and the single public television channel has lost substantial numbers of viewers to new commercial television channels and to cable and satellite services. New media have stormed the country, and the proportion of households connected to the Internet is one of the highest in the world.

The Israeli Press

The media in Israel predated the official establishment of the state in 1948. Hebrew newspapers were an integral part of the Jewish revival in the land of Israel, beginning in the middle of the nineteenth century. The first Hebrew newspapers were established in Jerusalem in 1863. *Ha'aretz* (The Land), one of Israel's leading existing dailies, was founded in 1918, and the most popular daily today, *Yediot Aharonot* (Latest News), was established in 1939.

Despite the existence of military censorship, freedom of speech and freedom of the press are strongly protected and widely practiced in Israel. Table 1 lists major Israeli newspapers currently published in four languages: Hebrew, English, Russian, and Arabic. Four major independent daily Hebrew newspapers appear in Israel today. There are three additional financial dailies. Although through the years many newspapers have closed, especially party dailies, a new daily, *Israel Hayom* (Israel Today), started in 2007, and a new financial newspaper, *Calcalist* (Economist), began publication in 2008. *Ha'aretz* is an elite newspaper, while *Yediot Aharonot* (hereafter referred to as *Yediot*), *Ma'ariv* (Evening), and *Israel Hayom* are popular tabloids, except that unlike other such papers around the world, they devote substantial space to news and commentary. *Israel Hayom* is circulated for free in

Table 1

Daily Newspapers

Newspaper	Language	Owner	Year Founded
Independent Newspapers			
Ha'aretz	Hebrew	Schocken	1918
Yediot Aharonot	Hebrew	Moses, Fishman	1939
Ma'ariv	Hebrew	Nimrodi	1948
Israel Hayom	Hebrew	Adelson	2007
Financial Newspapers			
Globes	Hebrew	Fishman	1983
TheMarker[1]	Hebrew	Schoken	2008
Calcalist	Hebrew	Moses	2008
Party Newspapers			
Hatzofe[2]	Hebrew	National Religious Party	1938
Hamodia	Hebrew	Agudat Israel	1949
Yated Ne'eman	Hebrew	Degel Hatorah	1985
al'Ittihad	Arabic	Hadash[3]	1948
Other Languages			
Jerusalem Post	English	Mirkay Tikshoret & Canwest Global Communications	1932
Ha'aretz /International Herald Tribune	English	Schocken & *New York Times*	1997
Vesti	Russian	Moses	1992
al'Sinarah (Weekly)	Arabic	Mashur	1983

[1]In 2005, *TheMarker* became the financial section of *Ha'aretz*, but since January 2008 it is also separately sold.
[2]Merged with Makor Rishon on April 25, 2007, and is no longer affiliated with the National Religious Party.
[3]Arab-Jewish Communist-Socialist Party.

central locations across the country, and to a list of subscribers. *Ha'aretz* was a morning newspaper while *Yediot* and *Ma'ariv* were evening papers, but today they all are published and distributed in the early morning hours. Politically, *Ha'aretz* is liberal-Left while the other three are mainstream.

All the daily newspapers are owned by families who also own commercial conglomerates. The Moses family owns *Yediot* and a financial newspaper, *Calcalist* (a Hebrew wordplay on the name Economist), local newspapers, newspapers in Russian and Arabic, and a publishing house. It is also a partner in a music firm. The Nimrodi family owns *Ma'ariv*, local newspapers, magazines, a record company, a publishing house, an advertising company, and firms in the areas of insurance, real estate, and health. The Schocken family owns *Ha'aretz*, *TheMarker*, local newspapers, and a publishing house. Sheldon Adelson, an American Jewish tycoon, owns *Israel Hayom*. Eliezer Fishman owns *Globes* and is a minor partner in the ownership of *Yediot*. The literature on newspaper ownership is filled with claims about the control and influence of owners on news and content of their respective newspapers. Experts who are not necessarily neo-Marxists also claim that by owning a newspaper, the rich acquire too much influence on politicians and government officials. At least in Israel, no evidence has been produced to verify such claims.

Of the many party newspapers published in the pre-independence period and subsequent years, only four survive. All of the Hebrew-language party papers are affiliated with Orthodox religious parties: *Hazofe* (the Observer) was affiliated with Mafdal, the National Religious Party, but in 2007 merged with *Makor Rishon* (The First Source), a right-wing weekly news magazine. *Yated Ne'eman* (Loyal Stake) is affiliated with the Haredi Degel Hatorah Party, and *Hamodia* (The Announcer) is aligned with Agudat Israel, an ultra-Orthodox party. *Hamodia* also publishes an English-language version for readers in the United States and the United Kingdom, and *Yated Ne'eman* publishes a weekly U.S. edition in English. The religious papers have been able to survive because their readers are captive and faithful. The same idea applies to the fourth surviving party paper, the Israeli Arab *al-Ittihad* (The Union), which has always been identified with the Israeli Communist Party under all its various names over the years (Maki, Rakah, and Hadash).

The English-language *Jerusalem Post* was established in 1932 under the name the *Palestine Post* and for six decades faced no competition. In 1997, *Ha'aretz* started an English-language version, which is distributed together with a short version of the *International Herald Tribune*. English-language newspapers primarily serve immigrants from English-speaking countries, foreign reporters, diplomats, and foreign businessmen. Foreign reporters use the English version of *Ha'aretz* extensively as a source of information about Israel. As liberal-left newspaper, however, *Ha'aretz* represents only a fraction of the Israeli polity and society, and those depending on it receive a slanted view of Israel and the Arab-Israeli conflict. In 1992, following massive Russian immigration to Israel, *Yediot* started *Vesti* (News), a major newspaper in Russian. The Israeli Arab minority has several weekly papers including *al-Sinarah* (Lighthouse) and *Kul al-Arab* (All the Arabs).

Yediot and *Ma'ariv* have been engaged in a fierce competition ever since a group of prominent journalists left *Yediot* and in 1948 established *Ma'ariv*. In the 1950s and the 1960s, *Ma'ariv* was the most popular daily in Israel, but in the 1980s *Yediot* became the dominant paper. *Ha'aretz* lagged far behind. *Yediot* became known as the "state's newspaper," while *Ma'ariv* presented itself as "a newspaper for everybody." *Ha'aretz* did exactly the opposite by appealing mostly to political, social, economic, and intellectual leaders via the slogan "a newspaper for thinking people."

In recent years, the veteran general newspapers have all experienced declining exposure. From 2001 to 2010, exposure to *Yediot* and *Ma'ariv* declined by about 14 percent while exposure to *Ha'aretz* declined by about 3 percent. Data published in July 2010 reveal a revolution in exposure: *Israel Hayom* became the most read newspaper in Israel with 35.2 percent, *Yediot* fell to second place with 34.9 percent, *Ma'ariv* occupies third place with 12.5 percent, and *Ha'aretz* is last with 6.4 percent.

Hundreds of local newspapers, mostly weeklies, are published in every city. Many also serve a group of adjacent towns. Most are operated by chains created by the owners of *Yediot, Ma'ariv*, and *Ha'aretz*. The rest are independent and privately owned. They appear mostly on Friday and are added without cost to papers delivered to regular subscribers of the national newspapers. They are also available for purchase at local outlets. More than half of the local newspapers in Israel operate in the central sector of the country, while the rest are almost equally divided between the north and the south. Many local newspapers contain mostly advertising, with little news content and are delivered free to all households. A typical local paper includes reports on city or town matters and sections on movies, music, theater, exhibitions, education, sports, leisure, public safety, gossip, and so on. City government issues, sports, and gossip are the most popular. Newspapers from the big chains also include syndicated columns, particularly on sports, arts, and leisure. Hundreds of magazines, mostly weeklies and monthlies, are also published in Israel. They cover a variety of general and specific topics, including women, youth, children, traveling, cars, entertainment, education, business, and health.

Radio

Radio service in Hebrew started in 1936 with the establishment of the country's leading radio network, Kol Israel (Voice of Israel), which started as the Voice of Jerusalem. Today it operates seven channels: A for culture and education; B for news;

C for popular Israeli music; D for the Arabic network; classical music; 88 for FM-quality music; and Reka, broadcast in foreign languages for new immigrants. Galei Zahal (IDF Radio, owned and operated by the Israeli Defense Forces) was established in 1950 and operates two channels. The main network broadcasts primarily news, talk shows, and music, and the second (Galgalatz) focuses on traffic and music. The junior staff consists mostly of young soldiers, both women and men, who perform their compulsory military service at the station. The station is very popular among young people primarily because of the informal presentation style and modern music. For many years the station has served as the main training school for broadcast journalists; today, former professionals of the station occupy many leading positions in the Israeli media.

The communication revolution in broadcasting also facilitated the establishment of commercial regional radio stations. The first stations began broadcasting in September 2005. Today there are twelve regional stations spread all over the country and two stations designated for specific audiences, one in Arabic for Israeli Arabs and the other for Orthodox Jews. Five stations are located at the center of Israel, three in the south and four in the north. All the regional stations are operated by private franchises and financed by advertising revenues.

Ownership, funding, financing, and regulation patterns for the three types of radio networks are similar to the pattern of television ownership. Liberal democracies use three models to develop and regulate broadcast media: public networks, commercial networks, and a mixed model of both public and commercial networks. Israel began with the first model. Until 1989, all the television and the radio networks were public. Since then, the government has adopted the mixed model. It kept the public channels but awarded broadcasting licenses to private television and radio companies. This way, the government has maintained some influence on the media.

The Voice of Israel is funded by the television and radio fee and by advertising. It is supervised by a BBC-type public body, the Israel Broadcasting Authority (IBA). IBA's chair, board of directors, and general director are selected and appointed by the government through a minister responsible for the organization. The IDF Radio is owned and funded by the Ministry of Defense and sponsors. The station's nonmilitary programs are also regulated and supervised by IBA. The commercial regional and designated stations are funded by advertising and are regulated by the Second Authority for Television and Radio (SATR). The chair and members of this authority are selected and approved by the Ministry for Communication. The cable and satellite services are regulated by another body—the Council for Cable and Satellite Broadcasting.

In recent years, Galei Zahal has become the most popular radio station in Israel, with Kol Israel closely behind. The commercial stations collectively occupy third place, maintaining a steady audience share of about 34 percent.

Television

Israel began television broadcasts only in the late 1960s. The view of Israeli founder David Ben-Gurion, the first prime minister, was that television would corrupt culture and arts, and that watching television would reduce reading of books and attendance at cultural events such as theater, concerts, and exhibitions. Also, the Israeli economy was weak and the people consumed only basic commodities. The market could not sufficiently support commercial television networks, and the government did not want to spend tax money on television. This attitude changed in 1965, when the government authorized privately funded educational television broadcasts for the first time. Israel is probably the only country in the world where an educational channel existed before the launching of a general television channel.

Another significant change occurred after the 1967 Six-Day War between Israel and the armies of Egypt, Jordan, and Syria, in which Israel won despite the fact that the Arab media had been reporting an Arab victory. During the war, Arab television networks enjoyed a monopoly over pictures from the battlefields. They mainly broadcast propaganda and the coverage was highly distorted and misleading. Consequently, the Israeli government decided to establish a public television station, Israel Television, which began broadcasting in 1968. Israel Television and Educational Television shared the same channel; the former broadcasted in the evenings and the latter in the mornings. In 1994, Israel Television also established Channel 33, a second public channel.

Israel's first commercial channel, Channel 2, began broadcasting in November 1993. A second commercial channel, Channel 10, began broadcasting in January 2002. With the introduction of commercial television channels, Israel Television became Channel 1. Only channels 1 and 2 are terrestrial, while the others are available only through cable or satellite services. Multichannel cable television started in 1989, and DBS (direct broadcasting satellite) began in 2000. Both are operated by private commercial companies, "HOT" and "Yes" respectively. Various government ministries and regulatory bodies supervise and regulate television broadcasts in Israel. Channels 1 and 33 are funded mostly via annual fees paid by every household and by sponsorships. They operate via IBA. Educational Television is funded by the Ministry of Education and sponsors.

The two commercial channels, 2 and 10, are financed via advertising revenues and are regulated by SATR. Today, two private communication firms, Keshet and Reshet, jointly operate Channel 2, dividing and rotating broadcasting days between them. Together with SATR they operate one news department. In 2010 the news budget of Channel 2 was about $27 million. Channel 10 is operated by one company. Educational Television operates its own cable channel, 23, but also has slots on channels 1 and 2. The network broadcasts about 215 hours weekly, and about 40 percent of the programs are produced in-house, while the rest is imported. Broadcasts include news and cultural programs, documentaries, and shows geared for children and adolescents.

In 2008 there were about 1.69 million family households in Israel. Most households, both Jewish and non-Jewish, own television sets. The percentage for Jews (91 percent) is slightly less than the percentage for the total population (92 percent), mainly because ultra-Orthodox Jewish leaders don't allow the owning of television sets or the watching of television. Among non-Jews, many Bedouins also do not own television sets.

In August 2003, the founding cable companies merged into one company (HOT) in order to better compete in the fixed telephone and Internet market and with the Yes/digital broadcasting satellite services. The cable and DBS channels are obligated to carry a basic package including the major public and commercial stations, but they also offer a large variety of local and foreign channels in many general and specific areas and in many languages. In 2010, about 75 percent of all households (1.2 million) subscribed to the cable services, while about 28 percent (500,000) subscribed to the Yes-DBS service. Cable operators introduced digital transmission technology in 2001. As of 2010, about 82 percent of all multichannel subscribers received digital service, including interactivity options. This is one of the highest digital ratios in the world. The cable and satellite services are regulated by another body—the Council for Cable and Satellite Broadcasting.

Figure 1 depicts the distribution of top-rated television programs by genre. Most viewers surveyed preferred to watch news, reality, and comedy. While news programs are particularly popular among Israelis, because of security, political, and economic tensions, including periodic war and violence, they frequently escape to the world of reality TV and comedy. Except for news, the distribution of the highest-rated programs in Israel is similar to the distribution of top television programs in the United States and many other developed countries. For several years, a popular satire show, *A Wonderful State*, has topped the list with an average rating of 30 percent. The show presents a mockery of current events, politicians, and celebrities via a humoristic simulated news program. The top comedy programs primarily include original series, while the reality programs include original and adapted foreign formats such as *Survivor* or *American Idol*, and foreign programs such as *Seinfeld*. The most popular sports telecasts include broadcasts of basketball games in the Euroleague. Israel's Maccabi Tel Aviv has won several European championships. A very popular quiz show has been a local adaptation of *One Against 100*.

Channel 2 overwhelmingly dominates Israeli television. On average, it has consistently captured the top 10 slots on the weekly rating list. Channel 10, with a highly popular reality show and improved news programs, has begun to chal-

Figure 1 **Distribution of Top-Rated Television Shows by Genre, January 2008**

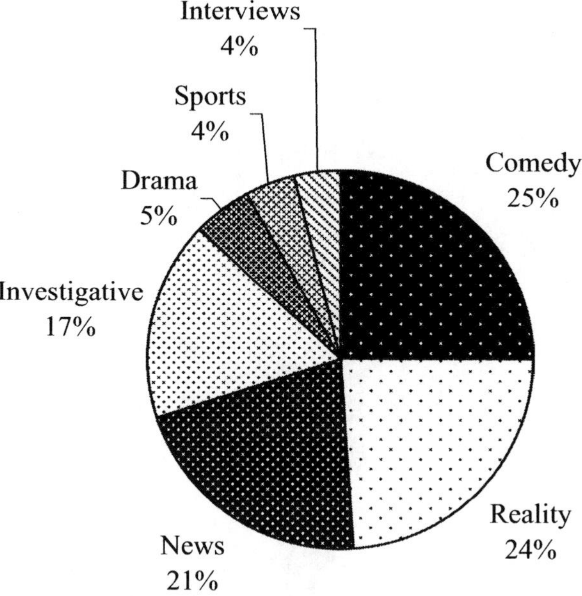

Programs aired between January 6 and 12, 2008.

Source: The Israel Audience Research Board, Tele-Gal, TNS.

lenge Channel 2. Since April 2007, the monthly average rating of Channel 1's top programs have rarely made the monthly list of the top twenty-five programs. News programs on Israeli television channels are highly prestigious and garner high ratings.

Internet

Israel is a world leader in Internet technologies and applications, and Israeli companies operating in the field have achieved enormous success. Israel's international high-tech reputation is also recognized on the home market, and influences local interest and use. Since 2003, Internet penetration in Israel has grown rapidly. In 2010, five major and about seventy-five smaller Internet service providers served more than 4.6 million users over age thirteen, including 58 percent of households and 77 percent of businesses. Cellular phone companies introduced wireless Internet in 2001. Israel's national phone company, Bezeq, began asymmetric digital subscriber line (ADSL) services in 2000, and the cable companies started to provide broadband cable modem access in 2002. There has been a considerable and steady increase in overall Israeli household connections to the Internet. It has risen from about 5 percent in 1997 to 82.5 percent in 2010.

A survey by Dun and Bradstreet revealed that in 2006 the broadband penetration rate for Israel's Jewish households was 69 percent and that figure placed Israel in eighth place in the world. In 2008, Israel's penetration rate reached 77 percent, which placed it seventh in the world. Israel's connection rate is lower than the rates of South Korea, Hong Kong, the Netherlands, and Denmark, but is higher than those of the United Kingdom and the United States. Surveys also found that on average, Israeli Web surfers spend 37.4 hours online per month. Worldwide, only Canadian surfers spend more time on the Internet (39.6 hours per month). Demographic data on surfing in Israel revealed interesting results. Ninety-nine percent of young Israelis, between ages thirteen and seventeen, surf the Web. In the eighteen-to-twenty age category the penetration rate is 79 percent, and among people over fifty the rate is 45 percent. Jewish males (69 percent) surf more than women (63 percent), and secular Jews (80 percent) surf more than both traditional Jews (62 percent) and Orthodox Jews (50 percent).

Table 2 shows that Israeli surfers use the Internet primarily to seek information (35 percent) and to send and receive e-mail (35 percent). When adding "first activity" and "second activity," searching for information becomes the dominant activity (66 percent). Only 16 percent look first for news, probably because television and radio extensively cover all events, including breaking events, in real time. Still, 28 percent defined searching for news as their first or second activity on the Internet. A total of 14 percent and 11 percent respectively use the Internet primarily for shopping and chatting. Very few surfers use the Internet first for other functions. Surprisingly perhaps, reading blogs in Israel is not yet a major activity for Israeli local surfers.

The October 2006 survey displayed in Table 2 was conducted among adults by the Netvision Institute for Internet Studies and indicated that television was the main source of news for Israe-

Table 2

Most Popular Activities on the Internet in Israel

Activity	First Activity (%)	Second Activity (%)	Total (%)
Searching for information	35	31	66
Using e-mail	35	23	58
News	16	12	28
Consumer sites (shopping, banking, etc.)	4	10	14
Chats/discussion groups/Instant messaging	3	8	11
Software and games	3	3	6
Downloading music/media files	3	1	4
Listening to radio, watching TV shows	0.5	1	1.5
Reading blogs		0.5	0.5
Other/no opinion		10	10

Source: Netvision Institute for Internet Studies, Tel Aviv University, October 2006; adults above 18 surveyed.

lis by far, while Internet occupied second place. Thirty-five percent said that television was their primary source of news, 26 percent used primarily the Internet, 23 percent used newspapers, and only 14 percent said that radio was their primary news source. When responses to using the Internet as "an additional source" were added to responses on using this medium as a "primary source," the gap between television and the other media widened. A total of 73 percent said they used television as a primary or secondary source of news, while 51 percent named the Internet as their primary or secondary source.

All the major daily newspapers produce online editions. Several have established separate editorial, marketing, and advertising departments for these editions. The online edition of *Ha'aretz* is both in Hebrew and English (Haaretz.com), *Israel Hayom* (www.israelhayom.co.il/site/today.php?id=549) and *Globes* are almost identical to their printed editions, but *Yediot*'s Ynet (www.ynet.co.il) and *Ma'ariv*'s NRG (www.nrg.co.il) are different and include many reports, interviews, and columns written especially for them. Ynet also publishes an English version (www.ynetnews.com). The *Jerusalem Post* (www.jpost.com) also maintains an online edition.

Most radio stations broadcast live on the Internet, while the television networks broadcast only selected programs. Israel Broadcasting Authority (IBA) has one site in Hebrew and English for both radio and television programs (www.iba.org.il/). The news company of Channel 2 has a Web site (www.reshet.tv/newsite), while Channel 10 collaborates with Nana-a news portal (http://10tv.nana10.co.il/).

Several independent portals include Walla (www.walla.co.il), Tapuz (www.tapuz.co.il), and Arutz Sheva (www.israelnn.com)—which broadcasts in Hebrew, English, and Russian. *TheMarker* (www.themarker.com) is a major online source for economic and financial news, and One (www.one.co.il) is a major sports portal. A December 2010 survey of exposure to sites shows a phenomenal rate for Google—91 percent—while Facebook occupied second place with 67.5 percent, and Walla placed third with 65.9 percent. YouTube's exposure was 63.7 percent, while Ynet dropped to 58.5 percent.

Most of the traditional and new media in Israel depend on advertising revenues. Economic prosperity increases advertising budgets, while recession reduces them. The more advertising outlets a society develops, the stiffer the competition and the scarcer the allocations of funds for each medium. Overall advertising expenditures in Israel have not dramatically changed in the last ten years. Total expenditures in 2005 were smaller than the sum spent in 1995. In 2007, the total increased by 8.3 percent, reaching $898 million. Despite the global economic and financial crisis, in 2008 the total expenditure for advertising rose to $921 million.

Changes in the distribution of expenditures among the different media are very interesting. The print media still receive the largest portion of revenues, but since 1990 the total sum has decreased by almost 50 percent. Television went in the other direction, from a meager 4.2 percent in 1990 to 39 percent in 2008. Expenditures for television advertising went up because of the introduction of commercial channels. Advertising on the Internet has grown rapidly, from a mere 1.2 percent in 2002 to 12 percent in 2008. Despite the proliferation of commercial regional radio stations, the volume of radio advertising remains relatively unchanged throughout the period. In 2008, television led advertising expenditure with 39 percent, followed by the print media (38 percent), the Internet (12 percent), billboards (5 percent), radio (5 percent), and cinema (1 percent). The share of the print media in advertising will continue to decline, while that of the Internet will grow exponentially at the expense of the other media.

The Evolution of Israeli Media

Since the 1990s, the major revolutions and transformations in Israeli media have occurred in the electronic and new media. Until then, Israel had only one public television channel and two public radio stations, which operated under some government control. Today, the media world is much more independent, rich, and vibrant. New commercial television and radio channels and cable and DBS services vigorously compete for audiences and revenue. Occasionally, the competition leads to the broadcast of trash programs in an attempt to appeal to the broadest possible audience, but this is a worldwide television problem, not just an Israeli one. New media have been rapidly developing, and Israel is ranked at the top of advanced societies with very high levels of Internet penetration and utilization.

Like media in the Western and developed world, the mainstream media in Israel do not sufficiently cover the periphery and the concerns of ethnic, national, and religious minorities, but the availability of several channels and new media have reduced this problem. Military censorship still exists. Since Israel is engaged in a protracted and sometimes violent conflict with several of its neighbors, emergency periods may be justified. Moreover, the enemies of the Israeli state are autocratic and severely restrict freedom of the press. By denying access to reporters or limiting them to certain areas or topics, they exercise censorship at the source. In the new media world, however, censorship has become much less effective and is easily circumvented. Today, Israeli newspapers can publish any information published abroad, even if it wasn't cleared by the censorship body. Local reporters can leak information to colleagues abroad, and after its publication in a foreign outlet they publish the same information in their own medium. In the future, Israel is likely to abolish this instrument of information control.

In many ways, the media in Israel operate like the media in the Western and developed world. They fully exploit the advantages of the information age, but at the same time they suffer from weaknesses and pressure created by fierce competition and scarce resources. One major challenge is public broadcasting. After many years of monopoly, IBA and Channel 1 have failed to properly adjust to the newly diversified media world and have suffered from very low ratings, financial crises, inflated work force, failures to recruit young talent, and ineffective management. Politicians and experts alike have recommended closing IBA, but every society needs public communication, especially Israel. There are too many separate regulation bodies for the commercial channels, cable and DBS services, and the new media, and these bodies are controlled extensively by politics and bureaucracy. Major reform is required.

At this writing, the dynamic Israeli economy is able the support independent newspapers, commercial television and radio networks, and new media channels. Yet the media need to take into consideration recessions and other potentially damaging events and processes, such as wars. Trends show a continuing decline in revenues for the print media and substantial increases for the new media. Newspapers are coping with this challenge by starting and developing online editions, but this may not be sufficient if they continue to cut back on talented editors and reporters. In sum, the Israeli media are among the most advanced and free in the world, and have a very good chance to further develop and serve Israeli society.

References and Further Reading

Avraham, Eli. *Behind Media Marginality: Coverage of Social Groups and Places in the Israeli Press.* Lanham, MD: Lexington Books, 2003.

Caspi, Dan. "On Media and Politics: Between Enlightened Authority and Social Responsibility." *Israel Affairs* 11:1 (January 2005): 23–38.

Caspi, Dan, Hanna Adoni, and Akiba A. Cohen. "The Red, the White and the Blue: The Russian Media in Israel." *Gazette* 64:6 (2002): 537–556.

Caspi, Dan, and Yehiel Limor. *The In/Outsiders: The Media in Israel.* Cresskill, NJ: Hampton Press, 1999.

Doron, Gideon. "The Politics of Mass Communication in Israel." *Annals of the American Academy of Political and Social* Science 555 (January 1998): 163–179.

Gilboa, Eytan. "The Evolution of Israeli Media." *Middle East Review of International Affairs,* 12:3 (September 2008): 88–101.

———. "The Media in the 2003 Israeli Elections." *Israel Affairs* 10 (Summer 2004): 217–241.

Katz, Elihu. "Television Comes to the People of the Book." In *The Use and Abuse of Social Science,* ed. I. Horowitz, 249–271. New Brunswick, NJ: Transaction, 1971.

Katz, Yaron. "The 'Other Media': Alternative Communications in Israel." *International Journal of Cultural Studies* 10:3 (2007): 383–400.

Koren, Haim. "The Arab Citizens of the State of Israel: The Arab Media Perspective." *Israel Affairs* 9:1, 2 (Autumn/Winter 2003): 212–226.

Lehman-Wilzig, Sam, and Amit Schejter. "Israel." In *Mass Media in the Middle East,* ed. Y. Kamalipour and H. Mowlana. Westport, CT: Greenwood Press, 1994.

Levi-Faur, David. "The Dynamics of the Liberalization of the Israeli Telecommunications: Policy Emulation and Policy Innovations Outside the Joint-Decision Trap." In *European Telecommunications Liberalization,* ed. E. Kjell and M. Sajovaag. London: Routledge, 1999.

Liebes, Tamar. "Performing a Dream and Its Dissolution: A Social History of Broadcasting in Israel." In *De-Westernizing Media Studies,* ed. J. Curran and M.J. Park, 305–324. London: Routledge, 2000.

Limor, Yehiel. "Israel and the New Media." In *New Media and the New Middle East,* ed. P. Seib, 157–169. New York: Palgrave, 2007.

Limor, Yehiel, and Hillel Nossek. "The Military and the Media in the Twenty-First Century: Towards a New Model of Relations." *Israel Affairs* 12:3 (July 2006): 484–510.

Nossek, Hillel, and Hanna Adoni. "The Social Implications of Cable Television: Restructuring Connections with Self and Social Groups." *International Journal of Public Opinion Research* 8:1 (1996): 51–69.

The Second Authority for Television and Radio (SATR). www.rashut2.org.il/english_index.asp.

Tal, Rami. "The Israeli Press." *Ariel: The Israel Review of Arts and Letters,* no. 99–100 (July 1995).

Weimann, Gabriel. "Cable Comes to the Holy Land: The Impact of Cable TV on Israeli Viewers." *Journal of Broadcasting & Electronic Media* 40:2 (Spring 1996): 243–257.

———. "The Israeli Media: Future Challenges." *Middle East Institute Viewpoints: Israel: Growing Pains at 60,* May 12, 2008, pp. 16–18.

———. "Zapping in the Holy Land: Coping with Multi-Channel TV in Israel." *Journal of Communication* 45:1 (Winter 1995): 96–102.

The Palestinian Media and Anti-Americanism

Hillel Frisch

Palestinian radio and television are controlled by the Palestinian Authority. There are also half a dozen small, nominally independent newspapers, but all of which are very much influenced by the regime. *Al-Hayat al-Jadida* is the most "official" newspaper of the three Palestinian dailies, which also include *al-Quds* and *al-Ayyam*. After the 2006 elections to the Palestinian Legislative Council and Hamas's resounding victory, two new outlets sponsored by Hamas, al-Aqsa television and *Felesteen*, have prominently waged a battle of the minds between the Palestinian Authority controlled by Mahmud Abbas and the Hamas government that has controlled Gaza since 2007.

The example of Palestinian media is not an atypical case of the way such institutions are structured in the Arabic-speaking world. There is a strong element of government control, coupled with some at least nominally separate publications. Overall, coverage is directed by ideology and goal-oriented politics. These factors replace the professional ethos associated with an accurate and independent media that focuses on reporting news and issues on their own merits.

An interesting and useful example of this phenomenon is how the Palestinian media report on the United States. Built into this situation is at least an apparent contradiction. On the one hand, U.S. policies since the early 1990s have been quite helpful to the Palestinian Authority. At the same time, though, America is defined as an enemy by the movement's doctrine.

Hajj Amin al-Husayni (the Grand Mufti of Jerusalem from 1921 to 1948), arguably the most popular Arab Palestinian leader of all time, had much to say on pan-Arabism, pan-Islamism, and local nationalism in his writings. By contrast, he said virtually nothing on democracy and liberalism, allying with Nazi Germany. Yasser Arafat, founder of resurgent Palestinian nationalism and chairman of the Palestine Liberation Organization (PLO), also never indicated any views that drew him to the American vision of civilization. Since the mid-1980s, the main new development in Palestinian political thought has been the rise of a radical Islamist movement. The proportion favoring liberal standpoints has remained minute, according to surveys conducted by Palestinian research centers.

It is difficult for Palestinians to acknowledge that the United States has often followed policies in their favor, including devoting great effort over decades to peace plans and processes aimed at achieving a diplomatic settlement—one that, at least since the late 1980s, might have resulted in the establishment of an independent Palestinian state.

Divergence over interests and ideology between Palestinians and the United States, of course, extends far beyond the Palestinian-Israeli arena. Both Palestinian officials and the media take a radical pan-Arab stance on almost all issues related to the Arab world. The basic view that Western imperialists are bent today, as in the past, on dividing and subordinating the Arab world, and that the United States leads this campaign, is as prevalent in Fatah as it is in the more radical factions. These ideas enter the Palestinian media through two channels: as a natural result of the views of those who manage and work in the media, and as a result of political directives and adherence to the political line of groups or movements that these individuals follow or belong to.

Consequently, virtually everything the United States does in the Middle East is regarded as negative. This does not merely mean that the Palestinian media conclude that American actions are hostile, but that they neither report nor consider such a bias in the course of their stories.

Assessing Palestinian Anti-Americanism

It is not surprising under these ideological and political conditions to find numerous and rabid displays of anti-Americanism in the Palestinian media to translate and disseminate. For example, the opinion that U.S. involvement in Palestinian politics reflects a historic and bitter clash of civilizations can be found in a sermon broadcast on the Palestinian Authority's (PA) television station on September 5, 2003, by Palestinian Authority religious leader Ibrahim Madiras:

> If we go back 1,400 years in time, we find that history is repeating itself. . . . The Prophet Muhammad . . . was besieged by two powers, Persia in the east and Rome in the west. These represent the Soviet Union and America of today. . . . Persia fell first in the East, just as Russia fell first in the East, and America will fall . . . just as Rome fell in the West. . . . The Prophet succeeded, through Muslim unity and arousing faith, in overcoming the America of then, just as we will defeat America, as long as it supports our enemy, as long as it adheres to its positions against our people, our issue and our holy places, and against our people and its leadership, as long as it adheres to these wicked positions.

Official Palestinian sentiment in the context of postwar Iraq is equally clear. In a piece entitled "Shaa'hid and the Shahid" (The Witness and the Martyr—a play on words), one writer in the Palestinian daily *al-Ayyam* condemned Iraq's Shia religious leaders for cooperating with the United States when they should join the ranks of the martyrs killing American soldiers to fight against Iraq's occupation.

Palestinian anti-Americanism is also reflected in political cartoons. Particularly striking are a series using the image of the World Trade Center to portray Iraqis and Palestinians as the victims of U.S. policies and actions. A cartoon depicting the two smoldering towers of "Iraq" and "Palestine," for example, appearing in late 2003, was so well received after it was printed in *al-Quds* that it was reprinted two days later in *al-Hayat al-Jadida*, the semi-official daily. Other popular cartoons were copied from other Arab dailies. For instance, in one, a fearful Uncle Sam runs away in terror being chased by the date "September 11." In another, the U.S. response to September 11 is said to be immoral and imperialistic: the Twin Towers are depicted over a mass of dead bodies, victims of American "imperialism." Another variation shows the towers as forming a hammer that attacks the Muslim-Arab world in a cartoon marking the second anniversary of the attack, with the text reading: "September 11—the day of the greatest conspiracy against the Arabs and Muslims."

Depictions of the United States in Palestinian Media

The appearance of specific items may indicate a certain intent, but not the overall impact of these articles, news items, and cartoons. The effect of an anti-American article once a week is different from the appearance of such an article on a daily basis, and different weights must be given according to where such a piece appears in a newspaper. A content analysis of the media over time is helpful in this regard. The following is an analysis of *al-Hayat al-Jadida* appearing in the first seven days of February 2003.

A quantitative account, illustrated in Table 3, clearly demonstrates a strong anti-American bias. Over three-quarters of the forty-nine news items and articles regarding U.S. policy and actions printed in *al-Hayat al-Jadida* during that week were critical of the United States. Only 10 percent either objectively represented the U.S. administration's perspective on Iraqi affairs—the issue most of these news items addressed during that week—or related positively to American considerations or actions.

Generally speaking, the articles from foreign sources, most of which were translations of articles from the United States and Western press, were mild in tone and substance. (In distinguishing between the "foreign" and "Arab" press, I follow the common Middle Eastern practice of identifying "foreigner" [*ajnabi*] versus either Muslim or Arab. This model is used even on the sports pages to describe the origins of players on teams.) In contrast, the Arab and Palestinian articles and news items tended toward a more hostile perspective. Most neutral were short news items, usually reported by foreign news wire services. Considerations of space (measured by square inch) or placement in the newspaper (headline, front versus back page, etc.) did not have any impact on the general findings.

Table 3

Articles on the United States by Author's Origin and Content

	Foreign	Arab	Palestinian	Israeli	Total
Pro	5				5
Anti	21	6	10		37
Neutral	4	2		1	7

Nor is anti-American sentiment, prevalent as it may be, the major theme of the Palestinian media. The reason is simple: enmity or even hatred of Israel is by far its all-consuming focus. Of the approximately 150 articles and news items that appear daily in *al-Hayat al-Jadida* (minus culture, sports, and business items) over one-third are devoted to hatred of Israel. By contrast, there were a total of only forty-nine news items and articles relating to the United States during one week—equaling one day's coverage of Israel.

The difference is also qualitative. Almost all the coverage on Israel is vociferously critical. By contrast, coverage on the United States is more variegated despite its being overwhelmingly negative. The contrast is highlighted best in comparing the two headlines that appeared on February 1, the first issue analyzed. The headline regarding Israel read: "The Leadership Emphasizes Its Adherence to the Choice of Peace Despite Israeli Arrogance [*ghatrasa*] and Barbarism." The headline concerning U.S. policy, while critical, was more veiled: "President [Arafat] Criticizes the Silence of the International Community Regarding the Israeli Government's Infringement of the Accords." In the body of the news item it becomes clear that what was meant was an alleged U.S. criticism of Israel: "He [President Arafat] asked, 'How could . . . Israel be allowed to violate agreements signed at the White House?'"

Even when the headlines about Iraq, printed later in the week, clearly expressed opposition to moves by the United States, they were still mild in comparison to coverage of Israel. On February 5, a main headline read: "The War Plan: The Occupation of Iraq and Its Division into Three States." The title suggesting that the United States was eager to divide Iraq into three *duwaylat* (the pejorative term for a balkanized state in pan-Arab rhetoric) fits well into the prism of a long-term attempt on the part of the "West" to divide and rule the Arab world through which so many American moves in the Middle East are construed. The main headline appearing on February 6 read: "Most of the States in the Security Council Are Not Convinced by 'Proof' of Powell Against Iraq." Quotation marks in Arabic are used as a means of casting doubt on the word within them. In this case, doubt was being expressed regarding the quality of the evidence Powell presented.

Anti-Americanism is also less blatant than anti-Israelism because the top Palestinian leadership and the personalities involved in international negotiations such as Mahmud Abbas, Abu Ala'a, Sa'ib Ariqat, Nabil Abu Rudayna, and Yasir Abd al-Rabbu refrained as a general rule from disparaging or condemning the United States. For the media, this effectively means that the considerable criticism of the United States does not often appear as a leading headline or on the front page.

Use of the Foreign Press

Al-Hayat al-Jadida relies mainly on foreign and Arab sources in its coverage of non-Palestinian affairs. The overriding issue during the week surveyed was Iraq, particularly U.S. preparations for war and Secretary of State Colin Powell's attempt to curry support for such a policy within the United Nations. One could safely assume that had a time period in which the United States was involved in mediation between Israel and the Palestinians been chosen, more Palestinian commentators would have written on the United States as well.

Most of the articles on the subject were taken from the foreign press. As a general rule, they reflected a list of distinguished analysts writing in equally prominent newspapers. Four articles, one each by Jon Alterman, head of the Middle East program at the Center for Strategic and International Studies in Washington, D.C., David Francis of the *Christian Science Monitor*, Nicholas Kristof culled from the *International Herald Tribune*, and Patrick Seale "The American Empire on the Eve of a Strike," appeared on the same page in the February 1 edition. All were critical of U.S. policies in Iraq. On February 2, it was the turn of Paul Kennedy, a well-known professor of history from Yale University, to argue on the basis of historical precedent against U.S. involvement in Iraq.

Three other articles, which appeared in the middle section of the newspaper—two by Americans, one by a Spanish analyst—concurred. Geoffrey Kemp, another prominent American policy analyst, took a mildly anti–U.S. administration approach the following day. On February 4, six translated articles authored by Americans and European analysts and thinkers were published. The piece by Michael Walzer, a well-known political philosopher, could be considered mild, even bordering on neutral. Walzer, though opposed to direct U.S. intervention, called upon the international community to acknowledge the threat Iraq posed and called for a strong international authority to impose all sanctions short of war, including military means, against Saddam. James Zogby, the veteran Arab lobbyist in Washington, authored one of the more militant articles.

The two pro-administration news items aired in the newspaper were both connected to senior administrative officials. On February 6, a half-page interview with Condoleezza Rice was culled from the Egyptian *al-Ahram*. A lengthy article written by Colin Powell stating the administration's position appeared the next day.

All in all, the newspaper's choice of articles from the international press, though biased against the U.S. administration, was probably little different from the fare presented in the average European newspaper. However skewed, it was nevertheless impressive in quality and even slightly variegated. At least two of the other types of coverage under review, articles authored by Arabs and the news items, presented a less benevolent perspective regarding the United States and its interests in the area.

Arab and Palestinian News Sources

The only Palestinian commentators who wrote on U.S. policy in Iraq dealt with it solely through the prism of Palestinian interests. Nabil Amer, the former minister of parliamentary affairs and confidant of Yasser Arafat, argued that a U.S. war in Iraq was likely to increase the Palestinian predicament as a national movement contending with an established state in turn supported by a superpower. Amer was one of the most outspoken advocates of reform and moderation in Fatah. He argued that only reform and real institution building will address this increasing imbalance—an obvious jab at his former mentor, Arafat. He warned that the Israelis were likely to try to use the time they gained by the U.S. focus on Iraq to create facts on the ground inimical to Palestinian interests. Amer argued that only putting an end to the armed conflict against Israel would serve Palestinian interests during this difficult experience. Hasan al-Kashif presented a similar argument.

These almost neutral perceptions contrasted sharply with a long, bitterly critical article written by Mohamed Hassanein Heikal, a prominent journalist and confidant of former Egyptian leader Gamal Abdel Nasser, which appeared in the newspaper on February 1. Identifying the United States's wars as imperial and wasteful, Heikal claims that the Arabs could react to such imperialism and hegemony in three ways, all with dubious effectiveness. The first would be to extend the arm of friendship, a strategy that has become impossible since 1948. Equally implausible would be reacting through outright confrontation. The third would be to slowly slide into a confrontation, and the fourth, most plausible, would be to sweat it out.

Even the latter alternative would be difficult to achieve, argues Heikal, since the United States is so intermeshed in the affairs of the Arab world. In short, the Arabs were in a difficult predicament. Heikal's analysis of the United States is unflattering, to say the least. The country, he claims, runs its affairs like a business, bereft of soul and dignity and driven exclusively by the calculation of costs and benefits as the treatment of the late shah of Iran after his fall, in which he was denied asylum in the United States. Heikal also claims that the United States drains the Third World of its finest brains without investing a cent and exploits its immigrants to death as slaves. Politically, the United States does not recognize borders and is forever engaged in war.

On the following day, an article by former Egyptian field marshal Halim Abd-al Halim Abu-

Ghazaleh asserted that the U.S. goal was not the mere removal of Saddam but to create a state that will be under its own control. In another article titled "The State of the Union . . . or the State of Iraq," Ahmed Umrabi questioned who the real aggressor was: "You would think that Saddam had encircled the United States by land, air and sea! Is Iraq really threatening?" Obviously, he concluded, hidden agendas such as Iraqi oil, Israel, and the resolve to maintain the present state of Arab weakness were the determining factors behind the U.S. drive against Iraq and Saddam Hussein.

On a slightly different issue, a professor from Qatar in an article published on February 3 reacted to Colin Powell's statement on American plans of democratization in the region by asking how the United States was only willing to spend $29 million to democratize the Arab world compared to the billions it expended on Israel. Powell's initiative, he maintained, also placed the Arab intellectual in a catch-22 situation: he ought to support democratization, yet how can he support it when it is seen as a directive from outside, especially as part of a larger American imperial plan in the region to force the Arabs to abandon the rights of the Palestinian people? He continued by pointing out what happened to the Palestinian leadership that had placed its trust in the Americans. Only deep reform of individual Arab regimes and Arab collective action could counter imperialism in general and U.S. imperialism in particular.

There were also Arab analysts who wrote milder articles. A Saudi Arabian political scientist could not understand how Uncle Sam could stop the *zakat* (charity) from flowing to groups accused of terrorism and also claimed the United States had accused Islam of terrorism. Khairi Mansur, in his "America . . . and the Forty Noble Souls," praises the forty Nobel Prize winners who had decided "to stand up against the madness in the White House since 9-11." They are warning "of the follies of going into war without assessing its ramifications. Why should the United States citizen think that the generals are any smarter in strategy than these men of such intellectual stature?" Buhan Salih, joint prime minister in the regional Kurdish government in Iraq, wrote the only article in support of war authored by a resident in the area. He, however, is not Arab.

The Officially Orchestrated Anti-American Campaign

One can safely assume that only a small, though perhaps influential, elite read the long articles by Western, Arab, or local Palestinian commentators that account for most of the news items surveyed. This is perhaps why it is so important to take into account the nature of the short news items, particularly those focusing on Palestinian involvement in developments related to Iraq. These suggest not only the prevalence of anti-Americanism in Palestinian political circles, but its propagation by the official leadership. In fact, it was the Palestinian Authority and the PLO who, in organizing "the street" or "the masses," caused anti-Americanism to take on a rabidly radical coloration.

On February 4, secondary students organized what was described as a "massive" procession in northern Gaza in solidarity with the Iraqi people. An accompanying photograph showed demonstrators with posters of Saddam Hussein. A similar news item covered a demonstration in Qalqilya organized by the Popular Committee of Support for Iraq. In the context of Palestinian media behavior, the very fact that the newspaper covered these events reflected official approval. After the capture of Saddam Hussein, for example, *al-Hayat al-Jadida* did not cover many larger demonstrations that occurred in Gaza.

On February 5, the same day in which the article about a purported U.S. plan to divide Iraq in three appeared, a lengthy news item reported that Interior Minister Hani al-Hasan warned that preparations must be made to confront the difficulties that Palestinians will face "in the wake of the aggression on Iraq." He was addressing the graduation ceremony of a military training program in Ramallah. The affair was organized by the Commission of Political and National Guidance for the PA's security forces.

On the same day, the National Center for Research and Documentation, an official PA body, organized, in conjunction with a private research group, a roundtable to discuss events in Iraq. The newspaper reported that "political speakers and jurists emphasized that Iraq and Palestine face the same enemy and that their resolve and steadfastness in the face of aggression is the common denominator in bringing about the defeat of the enemies of the Arab nation, renewing their call to strengthening the spirit of steadfastness and resistance and [the obligation] of the Arab masses in bearing their historical responsibility in blocking the aggression on sisterly Iraq."

On the following day, it was the turn of the National and Islamic Forces, the loose coalition between Fatah, Hamas, and the Islamic Jihad, which called for a procession in Ramallah in support of Iraq and against the aggression. They condemned the vicious campaign of preparations for war. During the procession, Sakhar Habash, a veteran member of the Fatah Central Committee and the keynote speaker, described the U.S. president as "no more than an oil merchant and a trader in the blood of peoples." "The Iraqis were able to win through steadfastness twelve years ago and they will do so now," he promised.

In Qalqilya at a conference held under the slogan "In steadfastness and resistance we will defeat the plot of American and Zionist aggression against Palestine and Iraq," the governor of the province, Mustafa al-Maliki, condemned the planned American attack on Iraq and the double standard concerning weapons of mass destruction and Israel. He produced a long list of America's "true" motives behind its Iraq policy. They included: stealing Iraqi oil, protecting Israel, dividing Iraq into three confessional and weak states as a preparatory move toward doing much the same in other Arab states (also known as the Sykes-Picot paradigm), drawing away scientists and controlling the world, and, finally, dealing with the Palestinian problem according to Zionist desires. The mayor of the town spoke as well. Needless to say, both officials would have never attended without Arafat's approval, as they were beholden to him for their positions.

By 2008, it was clear that the change at the helm of the PA after Arafat's death and the seemingly overwhelming Hamas challenge to President Mahmud Abbas's rule, first by defeating his party in the 2006 legislative elections and then by defeating his forces and militia to take over Gaza in July 2007, have gone a long way in taming anti-Americanism in the nationalist camp.

In *al-Ayyam*, most probably the leading PA newspaper in the post-Arafat era, a discourse over interests has clearly eased out expressions of visceral emotion against the United States. In an op-ed piece by Talal Ukal summarizing President George W. Bush's visit to Israel and the PA as "A Payoff Yielding Less Than Zero," Bush is portrayed as a leader eager to expand his commitments to Israel at the Palestinians' expense. Ukal expresses himself, however, in moderate prose, little different from the style found in a sampling of articles from the *Washington Post* on the Democratic candidates in their race for the party nomination. In any event, any slack in anti-Americanism in the PA newspapers is more than made up for by *Felesteen*, the new semi-official daily published in Hamas-controlled Gaza and banned in the areas under Abbas's control.

Assessment

Palestinian media are clearly anti-American as reflected in the analysis of *al-Hayat al-Jadida*, the unofficial organ of the Palestinian Authority. At the same time, a variety of viewpoints are presented, many from foreign sources, although they are hardly balanced. However, the small airing of opinions expressing a deviation from the common anti-American content of most articles appears in the most "elitist" type of journalistic writing—the long, analytical articles that are probably the least read. Even so, the overall message of the newspaper remains anti-American. Suffice it to note that throughout its coverage, the term used to describe the approaching U.S. campaign against Iraq was *'udwan* (the "American aggression").

Palestinian anti-Americanism was far more prominent in official Palestinian Authority institutions, especially those with a mass base or deep reach into Palestinian society such as Fatah or the security forces, as demonstrated in the analysis of the actual content of the news items in *al-Hayat al-Jadida* regarding the positions taken by these institutions. Not only do these organs reflect anti-Americanism, they propagate it. That these institutions are related to the PA, which enjoys direct and indirect U.S. aid—and, in the case of the Palestinian security forces, have even been the beneficiaries of

U.S. professional training—had little bearing on their actions or positions.

Over time, there has also been some change, however. The PA media, from the vantage point of 2008, seem to have lowered the polemical flames, although the Hamas-supported media are more than willing to fuel them.

References and Further Reading

Abu Amr, Ziyad. *Usul al-Harakat al-Siyasiya Fi Quta Ghazza 1948–1967* [The Origins of the Political Movements in the Gaza Strip 1948–1967]. Acre, Israel: Dar al-Aswar, 1947.

Frisch, Hillel. "Territorializing a Universal Religion: The Evolution of Nationalist Symbols in Palestinian Fundamentalism." *Canadian Review of Studies in Nationalism* 21:1–2 (1994): 45–50.

Marcus, Itamar. "PA Uses Twin Tower Image to Mock USA." *Palestinian Media Watch Bulletin*, September 16, 2003.

———. "Palestinian Authority Hatred of USA Continues." *Palestinian Media Watch Bulletin*, September 11, 2003.

———. "Palestinian Incitement to Kill and Hate Americans." *Palestinian Media Watch Bulletin*, November 5, 2003.

The Virtual Frontiers of the Iranian Blogistan

Liora Hendelman-Ba'avur

The promotion of information technology (IT) and its integration into local public sectors became one of Iran's most important national goals in the postwar era, especially from the 1990s onward. Iranian printed and broadcast media have been strongly regulated by the state since the establishment of the Islamic Republic in 1979. Yet the expansion of telecommunication networks and proliferation of Internet infrastructure and online culture over the past two decades also entailed the emergence of an alternative media channel that contests once-impregnable state monopolies over access to information. The emergence of Blogistan, the Iranian cybersphere of online self-publishing journals, has posed various challenges to the Islamic Republic of Iran from the early 2000s. A decade after the formation of the first blog service providers, blogs continue to rank high on the list of the top ten most popular Web sites for browsing.

The Iranian authorities confront new challenges with the emergence of the Iranian Blogistan. Yet the bulk of Internet challenges the Islamic Republic is facing—cyber-crimes; sedition; disinformation and imbalanced reporting; harassment; defamatory, hateful, obscene, and immoral content; and others—is not unique to the Iranian case and could apply to other countries as well. In setting up an advanced telecommunications infrastructure, each state chooses its own strategy for managing new information and communication technologies. Yet the loss of a stranglehold on the flow of information reaching its populace and the advent of a hard-to-regulate public sphere, such as Blogistan, pose additional challenges for regimes in China, Egypt, North Korea, Saudi Arabia, Syria, Tunisia, and Iran. The ways in which these countries chose to regulate the domestic use of the Internet have positioned them on the Reporters Sans Frontières (Reporters Without Borders) list of the top "Internet Enemies" and on the Committee to Protect Journalists' (CPJ) list of "10 Worst Countries to Be a Blogger."

Frontier of Blogistan

The term "blog" (short for "Weblog") was scarcely familiar prior to 1999. Since then, however, blogs have become the building blocks of one of the most vibrant "virtual communities" online. Early attempts to define blogs elaborate on their rapid growth and evolution in terms of volume and Web application frameworks. In her seminal work *We Are Iran: The Persian Blogs* (2005), Nasrin Alavi characterizes the blog as a type of diary or journal that appears on the Internet. Author Alireza Doostdar defines a blog as a Web site consisting of regularly updated writings arranged in reverse chronological order and which is posted online, usually by a single author. A more detailed definition is offered by Erin Simmons, who defines blogs as hyperlink-driven sites containing a mixture of hyperlinks, commentary, personal thoughts, and essays. Positioning blogs in the context of online interactivity, Dan Gilmore further identifies a chain of online communications (e-mail lists, forums, chatrooms, news groups, etc.) and categorizes blogs as somewhere in between the Web and e-mails. He emphasizes that blogs also link to other Web sites and blog postings, and many bloggers allow readers to comment on their original posts, thereby encouraging discussions.

Earlier stages in the formation of the Iranian Blogistan are attributed to the spontaneous and private initiative of three Iranian students—Salman Jariri, Hossein Derakhshan, and Nima Afshar Naderi—who separately launched the first three Iranian blogs in late 2001. Two years later, in 2003, Iranian Blogistan was the fastest growing cybersphere in the Middle East, and it became a prominent feature in defining the new global phenomenon of online communities. By 2006, Iran ranked ninth in the world for the number of blogs, and Persian was reportedly among the top ten languages in terms of posting volume.

The exact number of blogs is hard to ascertain, whereas the 2008 report of the Berkman Center for Internet and Society at Harvard University estimated there to be about 60,000 routinely updated Persian blogs. According to the evaluation of Hamid Ziaee-Parvar, editor of the science and technology desk at the Iranian daily *Hamshahri*, there are probably 700,000. The disparity of figures partly stems from the fact that blogs are abandoned at the same rate at which they are created. The ultrarapid growth of this virtual global village—known variously as the blogosphere, blogtopia, blogomania, blogalization, weblogistan, and blogistan—makes the process of tracking blogs, especially those that are active (or frequently updated), a highly challenging endeavor.

Additionally, blogs tend to share a basic layout format—a template, a headline, an archive arranged in reverse chronological order, blogrolls, and so forth—yet the dynamic evolution of this medium has presented new methodological difficulties for research and typology. Following the growing popularity of online personal journals, consumer-generated advertising on blogs (for which bloggers are paid for sponsored content according to page viewers) became another dominant feature in the blogosphere, thus offering a new ad platform for marketing and some supplementary income for bloggers. The implementation of advanced blogging tools, which improve managing, presentation, and navigation features, has also initiated the emergence of different types of blogs (photo, video, life blogs, etc.). In turn, online communication patterns are also being altered. As the blogosphere continues to flourish and evolve, the definition of what exactly constitutes a blog has also become more complicated. Many personal Web sites have adopted blog applications or are produced with blogging software, thus it is difficult to differentiate them from genuine blogs.

Exploring the relationship between technology and online behavior, Quentin Jones suggests that the community's cyberspace is a socially produced "virtual settlement." Drawing on archaeological methodology and practices, Jones identifies four preliminary characteristics of the virtual settlement: interactivity, a variety of communicators, sustained membership, and a virtual common public space. He further stipulates that a virtual settlement is "symbolically delineated by topic of interest within which a significant proportion of interrelated computer-mediated communications occur." Referring specifically to the blogosphere, Steve Fox defines it as "the new imagined community," inspired by Benedict Anderson's well-known book, which focuses on the creation and sustainability of the modern nation. Identifying the cybersphere as a metropolis, Michael Hauben observes the developing sense of responsibility shared by what he has termed "netizens," citizens of the Internet, or those who play an active role in contributing to the development of the Internet.

Accordingly, Iranian Blogistan can be defined along two contour dimensions. According to the first dimension, Blogistan is composed of various virtual settlements in the cyberspace, which are delineated by technical boundaries set by international and Persian blog service providers (BSPs). The second dimension involves Iranian personal blogs written in the form of diaries by netizens or bloggers (the term used to describe the authors of blogs) who share a sense of community and belong to one or more of the following groups. The first group in current Blogistan includes personal blogs written in Persian by bloggers who are permanent residents of the Islamic Republic of Iran. The second group consists of personal blogs published by Iranians residing outside the Islamic Republic, the bulk of whom live in North America and Western Europe. A third group contains personal blogs published by Iranians in languages other than Persian (mainly English, French, Urdu, and Arabic), in another language in addition to Persian, or in many different languages. A fourth group comprises blogs published in Persian by Kurdish, Afghani, and Tajik bloggers. A fifth group includes multilingual blogs by scholars, specialists, analysts, journalists, and readers of different ethnic identities who are interested professionally or otherwise in different issues pertaining to Iran and who dedicate their blogs to the subject. A sixth group consists of no-individual blogs, such group blogs, news blogs, and corporate blogs.

There are numerous variations of these virtual Blogistan settlements. Some include writers both inside and outside of Iran. For example, groups three, four, and five might include both residents and nonresidents of the Islamic Republic. Blogs also cover a wide array of topics and interests. Additional subcategories in current Blogistan might include different types of blogs.

The variety of groups constituting Blogistan serves as an indication of its extensive social boundaries. Since 2001, Blogistan has developed at a formidable pace and attained widespread popularity. Four out of the top ten most popular Web sites in Iran are blog providers. Although its origins may be found in Western countries and technologies, it is the joining of bloggers from Iran that has given Blogistan its edge.

The Rise of Blogistan—A Brief Background

Blogistan surfaced in the Islamic Republic against the backdrop of tangible transformations during Mohammad Khatami's presidency (1997–2005). This period witnessed growing investments in the local telecommunications infrastructure, which was promoted by the government and increased availability of relatively low-cost computers from East Asia. This was followed by a proliferation of Internet service providers (ISPs), the rapid expansion of the Internet, and improved access technologies, especially in the major urban centers. Exponentially, growth was indicated by domestic usage and public access points, such as in universities, research centers, libraries, and Internet cafés. In one decade, Internet usage in Iran reportedly increased from 250,000 users in December 2000 to 33.2 million in June 2010. Accordingly, Iranians represent approximately 31 percent of all Internet users of the entire Middle East region, including Egypt and Turkey (roughly about 107 million as of 2010).

Further technological advancements during the late 1990s and early 2000s were central to the rise of Blogistan. Most notably in this respect were the international incorporation of the Unicode system—a multilingual text character encoding system that supports Persian texts—and the launching of the first provider of free Web pages and publishing tools in Persian. PersianBlog commenced operation by hosting Persian blog tools in June 2002. It was followed by other blog services such as BlogFa, Mihanblog, Blogsky, Parsiblog, Aftablog, and Iranblog. The Persian blog hosts, similar to the international prototypes (published in English), offered free service accompanied by easy-to-use software. Henceforth, Internet accessibility and basic computer skills were all that were required for rapid self-publishing in Persian on the World Wide Web.

News of Blogistan swiftly spread throughout the Islamic Republic by old and new forms of mass media. Rumors, instructions, and invitations to join the blogosphere passed by word of mouth, e-mail, newsgroups, and even graffiti posting URLs (Uniform Resource Locators) on street walls, postboxes, and bus seats.

In addition to the implications of a decade of war with Iraq, a troubled economy, and massive waves of immigration to and from Iran, the late 1990s were also marked by the Second of Khordad reform movement (referring to the local date of Khatami's election in 1997) and an atmosphere seemingly hospitable to change. Relating to this period, Azadeh Moaveni, *Time* magazine's Tehran correspondent, observed in her memoir how "young people were busy launching blogs . . . intellectuals were writing innovative, sparkling satire, graphic designers were creating websites for the west. Their interest was turning intensely outward, to the world of ideas outside." Ongoing factional political disputes regarding the extent of the state's control over mainstream media became more overt among senior officials of the Islamic Republic. Promises of greater freedom of the press also appeared in Khatami's preliminary election manifesto, but eventually amounted to recurrent crackdowns on local newspapers, especially during his second term in office. From April 2000 to April 2001 the authorities closed down more than 57 newspapers and publications (most of which were pro-reform), leaving approximately 1,500 press industry workers, including journalists, unemployed. Under such circumstances, Iranian writers and journalists diverted their activity from printed to electronic media and joined other netizens in Blogistan.

The sense of revitalization encouraged both individuals and social groups to retest the limits of the state's forbearance. With 40 percent of Iran's population (in 2007, estimated at around 68.5 million) between the ages of fifteen and thirty-rive—the most active age group of net users and bloggers—the country's unique demography has contributed to the high receptiveness of the new cybersphere activity. The option to choose what personal details to reveal online, as well as the ability to publish anonymously under pseudonyms, aliases, and even invented identities, granted rights such as freedom of expression and freedom of information, which had previously been restricted.

Young and ordinary citizens from across the country have articulated their sense of self, grievances, spontaneous thoughts, casual ideas, and intuitive emotions in public. Referring to the active and open debates that transpired in Blogistan, Minister of Culture and Islamic Guidance Hossein Saffar-Harandi stated that such conditions allowed everyone to "comment on current affairs as if he or she were president." As bloggers were drawn to Blogistan for various reasons (curiosity, experimentation, influence of others, entertainment, etc.), the blog was initially based on the guiding principal of traditional personal journals, that is, self-documentation. For instance, in his blog's introduction a twenty-seven-year-old blogger writes: "I am just an ordinary simple Iranian boy who wants to share his thoughts, beliefs, favorite [issues], country, society." In a different blog, a thirty-one-year-old oil industrial worker shares his daily life and his hobby of photography. A Tehran-based English teacher posts on her experiences as a young single woman and human rights activist in her blog; in yet another blog, a professor of social science shares his thoughts on Islam and Iran.

Iranian blogs have sprouted up around myriad domains such as music, sports, health and hygiene, lifestyle, caricatures, jokes, and current affairs. Exact figures relating to Blogistan are hard to obtain, since the number of blogs constantly changes. Audience demographics recorded by the Web information company Alexa reveal that over 93 percent of the site's visitors are based in Iran. They further indicate that relative to the general Internet population, the dominant age group of BlogFa users is eighteen- to twenty-four-year olds, the majority of whom are males, usually browsing the Net from home.

Similar indicators were listed in AftaBlog, ParsiBlog, and IranBlog in the summer of 2010. Based on their total listing of over 400,000 registered Iranian blogs, the following figures reflect on some of the major tendencies of the communities of Blogistan. In BlogFa (Figure 2), a quarter of the registered blogs were initially listed under the category of "personal" journals, 24 percent were dedicated to issues pertaining to the Internet, computers, and technology, and 17 percent to subjects relating to literature and art. AftaBlog (Figure 3), formed in 2006, offers about seventy themes for blogs' layout and 200 MB of space for photos. Its listing indicates hosting about 38,000 registered blogs of which 22 percent are under the category of "entertainment" and 18 percent relate to "computer" issues. ParsiBlog (Figure 4), established in 2003, owes over 96 percent of its traffic to Iranian residents, and compared with global figures, people without a college education are overrepresented among its guests. Similar to the trends on BlogFa and AftaBlog, the category of "computers" (22 percent) is at the top of the list of bloggers' choice among ParsiBlog's 22,000 blogs. Social issues (12 percent) are the second most popular subject upon registration to ParsiBlog, followed by religious themes (9 percent). IranBlog (Figure 5), initiated in 2002, presents a listing of over 110,000 blogs. Unlike the subject inclination in the previously mentioned blog hosts, 85 percent of the blogs on IranBlog were registered under the unbinding category "general."

The distribution of blogs by subject is based on the initial categorization of each blog, and as such it may change over time and depending on circumstances. Despite the risks involved, highly opinionated and frequently well-informed Iran-based bloggers also comment on domestic and international politics. Debates on political affairs are especially high during times of national crisis. Events such as the December 2003 earthquake in Bam, 2006 concerns over Iran's nuclear capabilities, and the local and national elections (in 2004 and 2008 for the Majlis, in 2005 for the presidency, and in 2006 for municipalities and the Assembly of Experts) affected seasonal currents in Blogistan. Ad hoc blogs proliferated during the postelection mayhem in June 2009 as well. As international media correspondents were requested by the authorities to leave Iran, the Internet became the

Figure 2 **Distribution of Blogs in Blogfa by Subject** (August 2010)

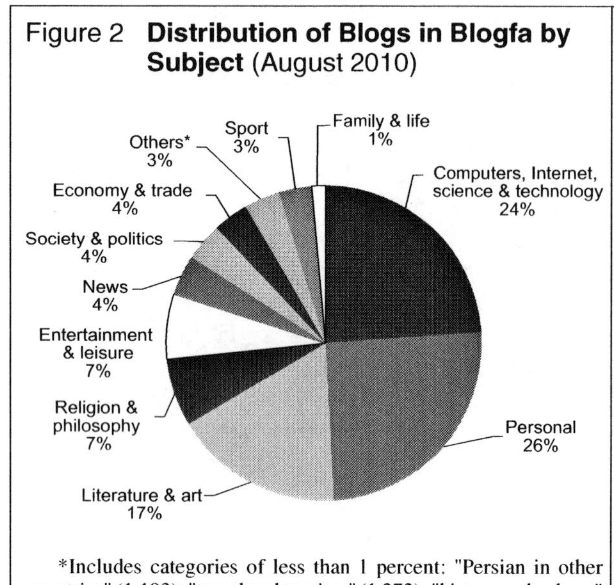

*Includes categories of less than 1 percent: "Persian in other countries" (1,193); "travel and tourism" (1,272); "history and culture" (2,396); and "photoblog" (3,023).

Figure 3 **Distribution of Blogs in AftaBlog by Subject** (August 2010)

News 6%
Politics 4%
Society 8%
Religion 8%
Entertainment 22%
Family 5%
Reference 11%
World 7%
Computers 18%
Art 11%

Figure 4 **Distribution of Blogs in ParsiBlog by Subject** (August 2010)

Geographical regions 2%
Leisure (fun) 6%
Marketing & trade 5%
Chidren and teenagers 3%
Computer 22%
Art 7%
Home 3%
News 6%
Ethics & spirituality 6%
Islamic Revolution 4%
Iran's history 3%
Sports 6%
Society 12%
Religion 9%
Science 6%

Figure 5 **Distribution of Blogs in IranBlog by Subject** (August 2010)

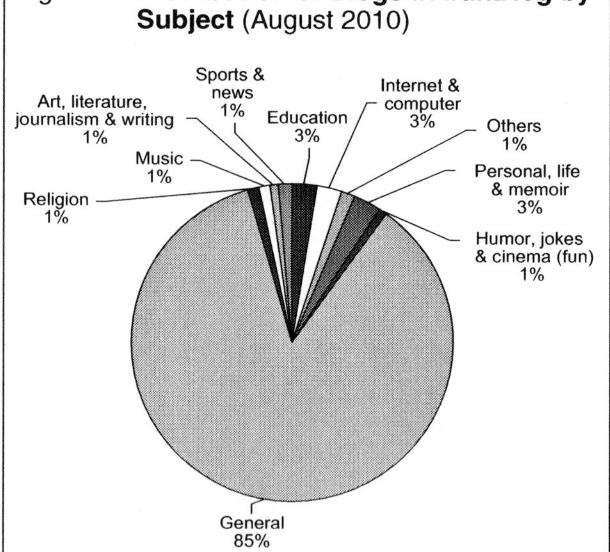

sole channel through which news and audio files of the 2009 demonstrations and "the green wave" protest spread worldwide.

Hence, other than being a public route for individuals' self-expression according to changing circumstances, blog connectivity has enabled interactions and collective networking among like-minded savvy Net users as well as the discussion of topics of mutual interest worldwide. Sharing ideas and opinions, technological knowledge, and audiovisual files have also become a central feature of Blogistan. Another form of online collaboration is group blogs, maintained by several authors. For instance, students at the Sharif University of Technology tend to use blogs for conversations, community forums, and discussion groups. Another interesting example is the unofficial Iranian cultural documentation of visual street arts in blogs, where young artists document and display graffiti, urban signs, and stickers in support of underground artists living in Iran.

A focal feature of collective networking in Iranian Blogistan is promoting online petitions for the release of political prisoners—the most well-known cases are the intellectuals Akbar Ganji and Ramin Jahanbegloo—and endorsing campaigns in support of human rights and freedom of speech in Iran (see, for instance, freeganji.blogspot.com and releaseraminjahanbegloo.blogspot.com). Commemorating specific occasions, especially the official Students' Day on December 7 (the 16 of Azar) and July 8 (the 18 of Tir) in memory of the 1999 student riots, serves as yet another focus to promote campaigns for the release of social activists and detained students.

This discussion of the circumstances that cultivated Blogistan and its considerable growth in the Islamic Republic highlights some of the major challenges Blogistan has posed to the Islamic Republic in recent years. By facilitating worldwide interactions and national collaborations, Blogistan has been compromising many of Iran's social and political restrictions.

The Challenges of Blogistan

Emerging as an integral part of the international blogosphere, Blogistan developed within a global space that did not abide by any standards of ethics or practices. Since the Islamic Republic has promoted public Internet use, in particular from the mid-1990s, Blogistan was initially allowed to develop without legal restrictions or any serious filtering and blocking measures by the authorities. In 1994, Iranian academic institutes joined the global network, and in 1998, the Iranian National Academic Network (INAN) was established, linking 230 scientific centers. That same year, eleven universities across the country initiated Information and Communication Technology (ICT) departments. As such, blogs embody potential hazards to expression and behavioral taboos that have prevailed in the country ever since the establishment of the Islamic Republic.

By cutting across age, class, ethnic, and geopolitical boundaries, the Internet in general and blog connectivity in particular have been loosening some of the state's fundamental perceptions concerning social order and its sex-segregation policies. Free and anonymous expression mediated by computers and practiced in the privacy of one's home (or an isolated computer station) has also enabled the dismantling of social and physical restraints. The unedited and informal nature of blogs has turned them into a source of empowerment for Iranian youth and especially for Iranian women. Blogistan enables them to access critical information (such as on health and law), form online communities, gain social support, and experience mixed-gender interactions. Since the early 1980s, the Islamic Republic has displayed sheer consistency in enforcing sex-segregation measures. The most conspicuous forms are the compulsory *chador* (veil) for women and routine moral patrols clamping down on parks, restaurants, and other public places where young couples tend to group. Indeed, moral concerns over indecent and subversive Internet content are not exclusive to the Islamic Republic, yet they have been a central concern for states such as Iran and Saudi Arabia, which restrict interaction between men and women who are not related.

Beyond redefining personal connectivity in the Islamic Republic, Blogistan has also been an outlet through which unmonitored content makes its way into the country. The free flow of information, along with foreign cultural invasion—mainly from the United States—has slowly diminished the cultural isolation imposed on the local population by the state. All the more so, this flow of information stands in contradiction to the Islamic Republic's doctrine. On the one hand, it has contested the propagation of proper Islamic and revolutionary values. On the other hand, it has challenged the campaign against the Anglo-American cultural onslaught, or "Westoxication" (*gharbzadegi*). Thus, while satellite television dishes are confiscated and American movies are banned, Iranian-based bloggers are discussing Harry Potter, Nicole Kidman, and Beyoncé. The legislature considered ending the 1995 ban on satellite dishes and receivers in 2001 and again in 2002, but seasonal crackdowns in which rooftops are searched for dishes are still occasionally launched. According to an estimate released in November 2009 by the deputy director of Islamic Republic of Iran Broadcasting (IRIB), about

40 percent of the population had satellite access. The breach opened by Blogistan also managed to bypass the state's traditional controls over the mainstream media (MSM) and its monopoly (with the exception of retail Internet service provision) over the telecommunications market until 2006.

Another challenge posed by Blogistan for the Islamic Republic has been the free flow of information coming out of the country. Soon after they began to multiply in 2002, Iranian personal blogs managed to attract the attention of the international MSM, and a new kind of grassroots reporting and participatory journalism was born. Blogs published by Iranian resident citizens and firsthand observers commenting on the happenings in Iran were gaining recognition, especially by the Western media, as supplementary or alternative sources to the Islamic Republic's official news outlets. A notable case in point was the coverage of the June 2003 demonstration and the launch of a solidarity campaign by bloggers worldwide in support of Iranian students.

Blogs proved highly beneficial, especially in covering news on domestic policies that the authorities had deliberately withheld from the national and international public or that had been disregarded as not newsworthy. Iranian-Kurdish bloggers, for instance, were able to expose details of the July 2005 clashes between the local Kurdish population and the Iranian security forces in the town of Mahabad, when no other news coverage was available.

Another notable blog captured on camera the violent suppression of the June 12, 2006, women activists' protest in Tehran's Haft Tir Square. Female demonstrators and male supporters protested against civic and labor discrimination, such as the minimum legal age at which a person may be charged and tried as an adult (currently nine for girls and fifteen for boys), the value of a woman's testimony in court (which currently carries only half the weight of a man's), and equal parental rights in child custody. The peaceful demonstration turned violent when security forces began to spray-paint (a tactic used in order to be able to identify the women protestors, who are all veiled) and arrest demonstrators. Several hours after the incident, photographs of the clash between the protestors and armed policewomen were circulated through Blogistan. One of the photos, taken by Mansour Nasiri, even won the Kaveh Golestan photojournalism award later that year, but the Ministry of Culture banned its public display. The protest impregnated the widely advertised campaign of "change for equality," which aimed to collect one million signatures in support of a petition addressed to the Iranian Parliament asking for the revision and reform of current laws that discriminate against women.

In June 2008, a group of students from Zanjan University exposed a sex scandal on their campus through the use of Blogistan and YouTube. The blog Zanjan1387 published a petition demanding the resignation of a professor from the Persian Language and Literature Department who was allegedly sexually harassing a female student. An audio file of the professor, caught on camera in his office while in the company of a young unveiled female student, was also posted on YouTube and attracted over 67,000 views during the first week (the original blog, Zanjan1387.BlogFa.com, is no longer available online).

The extensive coverage of the phenomenon of blogs in the international media has raised Blogistan's status and played a role in the international agenda of Western mainstream media. Yet international attention has also put Iranian-based bloggers in a tight spot. On the one hand, blogs have gained recognition as an important forum for debate and a valuable source of information. On the other hand, they have become targets of government efforts to limit freedom of expression and information.

Confronted with these challenges, the Islamic Republic began to apply multiple measures, passing new laws and implementing existing ones, and activating comprehensive Internet filtering and control-monitoring over Blogistan, especially since 2003. At first, the authorities vehemently denied claims of any filtering activities, and even today Iranian officials rarely address the actual extent of state censorship over Internet use and blogs in particular. Yet online, the filtering of Blogistan is highly transparent, and Internet users are notified (occasionally both in Persian and English) if a blog is blocked.

Campaigning Against Blogistan

The April 2003 arrest of blogger, former journalist, and film critic Sina Motallabi signaled that Blogistan had aroused the attention of the authorities in Iran. Charged with threatening national security, Motallabi was released the following month after posting a very high bail. His arrest dissuaded other bloggers, and they removed past postings and adopted self-censorship for fear of similar acts of reprisal by the authorities. Such concerns were soon realized, as Motallabi's case was the first in a series of crackdowns on bloggers and other Internet dissidents.

In February 2004, a proposed legislative article "on punishment of crimes linked to the Internet" was first introduced as a supplement to the country's press law. The new article specified a prison sentence of one to three years for publishing information considered a threat to national security, and five to fifteen years for disclosing sensitive information to foreign states or organizations. The article also specified about twenty forms of online violation, such as offenses against Islamic and revolutionary values, Iran's leadership, top clerics, and Khomeini's teachings. In the spirit of the law, the head of the judiciary, Ayatollah Mahmoud Hashemi Shahroudi, announced that anybody disseminating information whose purpose was to "disturb" the public mind via computer systems would have to deal with the consequences. Later that year, the judiciary also set up a special division to investigate and prosecute Internet dissidents. Further instructions were passed to all ISPs and Internet content providers (ICPs) in the country ordering them to close every proxy server port used to bypass filtration.

Under this new legislative framework, more than twenty bloggers and Internet journalists, mostly in their early twenties, were detained between August and November 2004. Among them was Mojtaba Samienejad, a twenty-seven-year-old student who was sentenced to two years' imprisonment for "insulting the Supreme Guide" and ten more months for inciting "immorality." With the election of the new Majlis that year, 2004 witnessed perhaps the most disturbing clampdown on bloggers and Internet dissidents. The wave of arrests included Mahboubeh Abbas-Gholizadeh, the editor of the women's rights journal *Farzaneh*, and Fereshteh Ghazi of the daily *Etemad*. The two women were accused (among others things) of endorsing democracy online and "immoral behavior." After being held in custody for a couple of months, they were released on high bail, and together with fellow blog-journalists Hanif Mazroi, Massoud Ghoreishi, and Arash Naderpour filed a formal complaint for being mistreated, tortured, and violently interrogated during their detention. Following the appeal, the head of judiciary, Shahroudi, ordered the formation of an internal investigation committee to probe the bloggers' claims, and in December 2004 the group appeared before a special presidential committee. During the course of the procedures, some of the bloggers reported attempts to obstruct the investigation by the underlings of Judge Saeed Mortazavi, Tehran's general prosecutor. By the time the special committee completed the investigation and finished its report, a new government had come into office under Mahmoud Ahmadinejad.

Despite such attempts to receive justice by local bloggers and human rights activists, as well as harsh criticism by the international media, the Islamic Republic continues to employ stern measures in persecuting bloggers. In March 2009, Blogistan commemorated the death of twenty-nine-year-old Omid Reza Mir-Sayafi, the author of the cultural news blog Rooz Negar, who died in Evin prison while serving a sentence for allegedly insulting Iran's religious authorities.

Further state sanctions in the form of technical filtering and blocking were also implemented in the Iranian cybersphere. Iranian blogs such as Faryad-e Beseda, published by Najmeh Omidparvar, were "disabled due to terms of service violation." The blocking of Omidparvar's blog followed her arrest in March 2005. Based on evidence found on her confiscated computer and CD ROMs, the Revolutionary Court in the city of Rafsanjan found her guilty of acting against the regime by showing disrespect to former president Khatami on her blog. Omidparvar, pregnant at the time, was released after twenty-four days, but her husband and co-blogger, Mohammad Reza Nasab Abdolahi, was sentenced to six months' imprisonment and a heavy fine for insulting the state's leaders, writing antigovernmental propaganda, and working with foreign media.

The responsibility for filtering indecent Web sites and blogs from outside the country, as well as regulating domestic Internet activity, was assigned to Iranian ISPs, which filter Internet content by using various commercial filterware products of their choice. According to Nart Villeneuve, director of technical research at the University of Toronto's Citizen Lab, the implementation of different filtering software has resulted in a lack of standardization with regard to the content blocked in Iran. Thus, Web sites and blogs that are blocked on one Iranian ISP could be accessible on another. Western filtering technology originally intended to enable parental control and deny access to pornographic sites is now used to block secret lists of immoral and politically offensive sites in countries such as Iran, Saudi Arabia, Sudan, Tunisia, the United Arab Emirates, and Yemen, writes Villeneuve, although every country outlines its own filtering. Iranian Internet service providers must be approved by both the Data Communication Company and the Ministry of Culture and Islamic Guidance. Failure to comply with the state's filtering strategy is punished by heavy penalties and the revocation of licenses.

Yet this filtering policy has not always produced the intended results. First, this is due to the advancing nature of online communication technology. Iranian-based Net users are offered technical assistance (or counterfiltering technology) from outside the country in the form of anonymous blogging software and online gateways for censored sites. Second, using filterware (or content filtering) sometimes hinders the state's online projects as well, as it can also filter out useful content along with undesirable content. For instance, in October 2006, a special seminar was held, titled "Women and the Internet in the Third Millennium." The seminar was sponsored by the Women's Affairs Department of the Islamic Revolutionary Guards Corp and received online coverage. For the potential target audience in Iran, the official announcement of this seminar was filtered because of an illicit word. Since online searches for the word "women" may generate "immoral" results (e.g., pornography), many of the women's organizations and social NGOs in Iran are filtered as well. Nonetheless, these technical glitches have not prevented the authorities from continuing to tighten their control and filtering policies over the Internet and Blogistan. Also in October 2006, the government instructed all asymmetric digital subscriber line (ADSL) providers to limit private users and Internet cafés to a maximum connection speed of 128 kbps, thus making the transmission and downloading of large files—especially images and videos—very difficult.

Members of the religious establishment have also expressed their discomfort with the entire phenomenon of the Internet and its devastating effects. In a lecture delivered to deputies of the Political Department of the Islamic Guard Corps on February 15, 2006, the Grand Ayatollah Nasir Makarem-Shirazi (b. 1924) stated that satellites and the Internet were destructive to the morality and belief tenets of the young generation in Iran and that some of the publications were destructive tools in the hands of the enemy. The specific nature of Makarem-Shirazi's important message did not prevent it from being posted on his personal Web site, however.

Nonetheless, so far the most acute criticism of the Internet by Iranian senior officials followed the "green wave" protests against the reelection of Ahmadinejad in June 2009. Since the oppression of the movement, members of the ruling elite frequently denounce the role of the Internet in advancing the postelection frenzy as part of what they considered to be "a soft war" waged by the West against Iran's Islamic Revolution. Accordingly, local Majlis members like Gholam Ali Haddad Adel, former spokesman of the parliament, suggest the Islamic Republic should equip itself by similar means for the purpose of self-defense.

Co-opting the Medium for the Message

The Internet as a new digital medium already played a key role in Iran's May 1997 presidential election, when leading candidates Mohammad Khatami and Speaker of Parliament Ali Akbar Nategh Nuri formed official Web sites publishing their political platforms. In 2003, Mohammad Ali Abtahi, vice president during Khatami's second presidential term, was the first acting cabinet member in the Islamic Republic to launch a personal blog. Regardless of Abtahi's failed attempts to convince the former president to publish his own blog, by the 2005 presidential elections blogs were incorporated into the local political campaigns. Ali Akbar Hashemi Rafsanjani's fans, for instance, endorsed his presidential candidacy through several semi-official blogs, and Mostafa Moeen, professor of pediatrics and former minister, met regularly with bloggers and began publishing his own journal online.

Over the course of two years, from 2003 to 2005, most of the country's prominent grand ayatollahs assimilated the new digital technology into their routine public activity. By publishing their biographical notes, speeches, written works, official visits, and photo galleries, they established what became known unofficially as the "Webatollah." Senior clerics thus initiated their personal multilingual official Web sites, managed by a board of advisors, office staff, translators, and theology students.

Additional special projects were also launched by other leading clerics. Grand Ayatollah Yousef Saane'i (b. 1927) hosted a special chat room during the month of Ramadan. Internet users were encouraged to ask him questions about human rights, religion, and women's rights during fixed hours of the day. By supplying immediate and direct answers online to questions ranging from a request for permission to use contraceptives, to inquiring whether or not looking at a non-Muslim woman's body parts is lawful, and even asking for guidance in voting in presidential elections, Saane'i and other Iranian senior ayatollahs have been making themselves available and transparent to the public.

Many of Iran's leading clerics are highly active on the World Wide Web, and their propensity toward modern technology is by no means new. Modern technology played a key role in mobilizing the popular movement of the 1979 revolution against Mohammad Reza Shah. Khomeini's oppositional messages and teachings made their way from his exile in France to the people of Iran via cassette tapes and fax machines, by now old-fashioned communication technologies. The current online presence of the ruling elite also bears the mark of the e-government (or e-state) project under the framework of the TAKFA national reform program. The general program, approved by the Iranian cabinet in 2002, was designated to advance all governmental branch services to the public via electronic channels. Further shifts to improve the government's interactions with the business sector and public organizations were initiated through e-commerce, e-banking, and e-education. An initial budget of 100 million dollars was approved by the Majlis for the program.

Various forms of information and communication networks, promoted in Iran ever since the establishment of the Islamic Republic, have also proved instrumental to the propagation and dissemination of the Shia doctrine in other Islamic countries. The Internet's potential to reach millions around the world was soon found to be more compelling and effective than radio and television. Addressing this issue, Ali Akbar Javanfekr, Ahmadinejad's presidential press advisor and director of the Islamic Republic News Agency (IRNA), announced that government agencies were starting Web sites because of the shortcomings of the traditional news outlets. Aalulbayt, the Global Information Center for Shi'ism, had already been established by 1998. Under the supervision of Grand Ayatollah Ali al-Sistani's office, the center offers in-depth information in thirty different languages. Its main objective is spreading Shia culture and interpretations via the Internet, creating a direct link between prominent theology scholars in Qom and the public.

In September 2006, Hojjatoleslam Hamid Shahriari, the secretary general of the Information Dissemination Supreme Council (IDSC), under the supervision of Ahmadinejad, also reported the council's plans to expand the presence of religious content on the Web for the public and of intentions to enforce the morality code over blogs. He further remarked that different voices in cyberspace have their audiences, and it is necessary to modify and improve these voices. Therefore, he also stated, the IDSC supports blogs, in particular religious and Quranic ones, and that they "guide" the rest. He defined "guiding" as the provision of certain advice and guidelines.

Accordingly, Ahmadinejad also requested that the Ministry of Communication and Information Technology (MCIT) design a national computer network, as he considered the current network insecure and precarious. During a speech at the thirteenth Press and News Agencies Fair, he stressed that the national press did not include enough analysis and criticism, and that "media personnel should not disregard their major responsibilities."

Three months after this declaration, Ahmadinejad confirmed blogs to be important carriers of ideology and state propaganda, especially in exposure to youth and international public opinion. In early August 2006, Ahmadinejad launched his personal multilingual online journal.

As leading politicians have openly joined Blogistan, the authorities began endorsing religious and Quranic blogs and promoting their public exposure. Quranic blogs are composed by at least three main groups: those who focus on the meanings and interpretations of Quranic verses, those who conduct research on the Quran, and those who study the historical importance of the stories mentioned in the Quran. Religious blogs are dedicated to issues surrounding the daily ritual and moral practices of Islam. Seminary students in Qom are being trained to become active net users, develop Islamic software, and expand Shia clerical transparency online. In March 2006, the First International Quranic Blogging Festival was launched in Iran with the intention of increasing the leading and younger generation's study and contemplation of Quranic and religious issues based on their needs and interests. In recent years, various group blogs have become more transparent online with their vocal support of the Islamic Republic and advancement of its Islamic message against what they refer to as "satanic activism" through computer networking. One notable group is the Muslim Bloggers. Another is Khomeini's Offspring—bloggers dedicated to continuing Khomeini's way and promoting his objectives. Nonetheless, although the leadership directly or indirectly promotes these groups as bastions of the Islamic Republic's future, they also pose an additional challenge to the regime, as they are more versed than other Iranian laymen in the language of religion and Islamic religious texts.

The embrace of the Internet and later of Blogistan by the state's officials and leading clerics has made the Islamic Republic more transparent for the Iranian public and the outside world, displaying some of Iran's complexities and internal contradictions. Clerics or supporters of the Islamic Republic do not necessarily speak with a unanimous voice. In that respect, personal blogs and Web sites are especially revealing of the array of thoughts and perceptions, even in issues of jurisprudence, among the Iranian religious establishment. Blogistan has become a channel through which these different voices can be heard as well. One case in point is a blog calling for the release of Ayatollah Sayed Hossein Kazemeyni Boroujerdi over concerns for his deteriorating health. He was supposedly charged in February 2007 with "acting against state security" by advocating the separation of religion from the political basis of the Iranian state.

The online commemoration of Ayatollah Hussein Ali Montazeri (b. 1922), one of the senior architects of the Islamic Revolution (1979), following his death in December 2009, revived the dissemination of his writings, sermons, memoirs, and religious edicts in Blogistan. Known for his harsh criticism of the post-revolutionary government, the late jurist was considered by many to be an advocate of universal and women's rights and a supporter of the 2009 "green wave" protest. The propagation of his thought via blogs (like a-montazeri.BlogFa.com and amontazeri.BlogFa.com) further revealed fractions among the ruling clerical establishment.

Blogistan and the Paradox for the Islamic Republic

Blogistan, similar to the blogosphere in particular and the global interconnective cybersphere in general, is still a relatively new and highly dynamic phenomenon that has yet to run its full course. Constant growth of Internet accessibility, technological evolution, and changing policies toward the medium have far-reaching effects over patterns of social behavior online, which are difficult to predict.

Nonetheless, blogging has already had a revolutionary effect on the mainstream media and on global interactions. Similar to other Middle Eastern and African countries, such as Egypt, Syria, and Tunisia, Iran aspires to expand its telecommunication services as well as to develop its economy through the use of new technologies. At the same time, all these countries are operating rigorously to respond to the challenges of information and communications technology, such as Blogistan's rapid development.

For a growing number of young Iranians, who comprise the majority of Iran's population, Blogistan became a focal channel for self-expression, interconnectivity, entertainment, and civic empowerment. The relatively free flow of information and growing connectivity and accessibility enabled Iranian bloggers to break through many of the binding social and cultural frontiers employed by the state. The blogosphere also contributed, among other things, to the organization of widespread social and cultural campaigns of NGOs and human rights agencies.

During the past decade the Islamic Republic has implemented various methods and measures to meet these challenges by trying to control local Internet usage, including the Iranian blogosphere. In this regulatory process the executive, legislative, and judicial branches cooperate in issuing and executing state control through at least three interrelated levels, discussed earlier. First, technical measures are implemented in the form of mandatory filtering, including the filtering of certain words (by using algorithms to search for censored words) and blocking of specific domains or users. Second, online surveillance and judicial proceedings are also used against Web site owners, individual bloggers, and online journalists. In November 2009 the Islamic Republic set up a special unit to monitor Web sites as part of its efforts to fight Internet crimes. This unit, headed by Colonel Mehrdad Omidi, operates under the supervision of the chief prosecutor and enjoys a great leeway in determining what constitutes "spreading lies" via the Internet and "insults" against the Islamic system. The third measure is connected with domestic propaganda directed against the negative influences of the Internet. It is coupled with monitoring, surveillance, and legal proceedings by government agencies. Frequent demonizing declarations by state officials, which mean to deter illicit use of blogs especially for political purposes, initiate self-regulatory censorship among indigenous Internet consumers.

Whereas the Islamic Republic operates to limit the virtual frontiers of Blogistan by reducing voices of dissent, it robustly operates to promote its own agenda online and encourages loyal factions to expand their presence in Blogistan. Considering the country's unique demography, consisting of a vast majority of digital-age youth, the future legitimacy of the Islamic Republic depends upon its ability to balance its aspirations for advancement in telecommunications technology on the one hand and forcefully limit its use on the other.

References and Further Reading

Alavi, Nasrin. *We Are Iran: The Persian Blogs.* New York: Soft Skull Press, 2005.

Ashrafologhalaei, Ahmadreza. *E-governance: E-state in Iran: Administrative Reform Plan.* Tehran, Iran: Management and Planning Organization, Bureau for Economic Studies and International Cooperation, 2005.

"The Blog Herald Blog Count February 2006: 200 Million Blogs in Existence." *The Blog Herald.* Available at www.blogherald.com/2006/02/02/the-blog-herald-blog-count-february-2006–200-million-blogs-in -existence/.

The Committee to Protect Journalists (CPJ). *A Worldwide Survey: Attacks on the Press 2005: Iran.* Available at www.cpj.org/attacks05/mideast05/iran_05.html.

Doostdar, Alireza. "The Vulgar Spirit of Blogging: On Language, Culture, and Power in Persian Weblogestan." *American Anthropologist* 106:4 (December 2004): 651.

"The 15 Enemies of the Internet and Other Countries to Watch." Reporters Without Borders, November 17, 2005. Available www.rsf.org/article.php3?id_article=15613.

Fox, Steve. "The New Imagined Community: Identifying and Exploring a Bidirectional Continuum Integrating Virtual and Community Embodiment Model (CEM)." *Journal of Communication Inquiry* 28:1 (January 2004): 47–62.

Freedom House. "Country Report: Iran" (years 2006–2010). Available at www.freedomhouse.org/template.cfm?page=21&year=2006.

———. "Freedom in the World." Available at www.freedomhouse.org/template.cfm?page=15.

Ghaemi, Hadi. "For Iran, the Man Is the Message." *New York Times,* June 29, 2006.

Gillmor, Dan. *We the Media: Grassroots Journalism by the People, for the People.* Sebastopol, CA: O'Reilly Media, 2004.

Hauben, Michael, and Ronda Hauben. *Netizens: On the History and Impact of Usenet and the Internet.* Los Alamitos, CA: IEEE-Computer Society, 1997.

International Quran News Agency (IQNA). "Internet Chat Room for Answering Religious Questions to Be Launched in Grand Ayatollah's Website." September 26, 2006. Available at http://iqna.ir/en/news_detail.php?ProdID=71063.

———. "Quranic Blogging Festival Great Opportunity." March 3, 2006. Available at http://iqna.ir/en/news_detail.php?ProdID=44881.

Internet World Stats. "Internet Usage in the Middle East." Available at www.internetworldstats.com/stats5.htm.

"Iran: Judiciary Should Admit Blogger Abuse." *Payvand's Iran News*. April 5, 2005. Available at www.payvand.com/news/05/apr/1026.html.

Iranian Student's News Agency (ISNA). Interview with Mahdi Boutorabi, November 20, 2006. Available at www.isna.ir/Main/NewsView.aspx?ID=News-828181.

Jones, Quentin. "Virtual-Communities, Virtual Settlements & Cyber-Archaeology: A Theoretical Outline." *Journal of Computer-Mediated Communication* 3:3 (1997). Available at http://jcmc.indiana.edu/.

Khiabany, Gholam, and Annabelle Sreberny. "The Iranian Press and the Continuing Struggle over Civil Society, 1998–2000." *International Communication Gazette* 63:2–3 (2001): 203–223.

Library of Congress, Federal Research Division. *Country Profile: Iran, March 2006*. Available at http://lcweb2.loc.gov/frd/cs/irtoc.html.

Moaveni, Azadeh. *Lipstick Jihad: A Memoir of Growing Up Iranian in America and American in Iran*. New York: Public Affairs, 2005.

National Information and Communication Technology Agenda (TAKFA). www.takfa.ir/.

Persianblog.com. www.faryadebeseda.persianblog.com/.

"Pregnant Blogger Najmeh Omidparvar Freed After 24 Days in Prison." Reporters Without Borders, March 29, 2005. Available at www.rsf.org/article.php3?id_article=12655.

Rahimi, Babak. "Cyberdissident: The Internet in Revolutionary Iran." *Middle East Review of International Affairs (MERIA)* 7:3 (September 2003). Available at www.gloria-center.org/meria/2003/09/rahimi.html.

Samii, Abbas William. "The Contemporary Iranian News Media, 1998–1999." *MERIA* 3:4 (December 1999).

———. "Sisyphus' Newsstand: The Iranian Press Under Khatami." *MERIA* 5:3 (September 2001). Available at www.gloria-center.org/meria/2001/09/samii.html.

Sciolino, Elaine. "Cleric Uses Weapon of Religion Against Iran's Rulers." *New York Times*, September 18, 2000.

Sheykh Esmaili, Kyumars, Mohsen Jamali, Mahmood Neshati, Hassan Abolhassani, and Yasaman Soltan-Zadeh, "Experiments on Persian Weblogs." Tehran: Sharif University of Technology, 2006. Submitted to the WWW2006 Workshop on Weblogging Ecosystem, Edinburgh, May 2006. Available at www.blogpulse.com/www2006-workshop/papers/persian-weblogs.pdf.

Sreberny-Mohammadi, Annabelle, and Ali Mohammadi. *Small Media, Big Revolution*. Minneapolis: University of Minnesota Press, 1994.

Stefanac, Suzanne. *Dispatches from Blogistan: A Travel Guide for the Modern Blogger*. Thousand Oaks, CA: New Riders Press, 2006.

Tait, Robert. "Iran: Mullahs Jump on the 'Weblogestan' Bandwagon." *South China Morning Post*, October 12, 2006. Available at www.asiamedia.ucla.edu/article.asp?parentid=55162.

"Taking Tougher Line on Internet, Authorities Try Cyber-Dissident and Draft Harsh Bill." Reporters Without Borders, August 3, 2004. Available at www.rsf.org.article.php3?id_article=11066.

Villeneuve, Nart. "The Filtering Matrix: Integrated Mechanisms of Information Control and the Demarcation of Borders in Cyberspace." *First Monday* 11:1 (January 2006). Available at www.firstmonday.org/issues/issue11_1/villeneuve/.

How Satellite TV Challenges State Media Monopoly

Al-Jazeera's Coverage of Syria

Najib Ghadbian

The influx of independent satellite TV stations in the Arab world has undermined the ability of governments to control what people watch and consequently to control what they think. Thus, satellite TV stations are subtly challenging the state's monopoly over the means of persuasion and information. Not only is government media rendered less relevant by the new satellite channels, but the introduction of more free and independent sources of information may be an additional tool for civil society in its struggle with states over such issues as the freedom of expression, human rights, and democracy.

Satellite television broadcasts via a signal being bounced off a satellite and going around the world, thus covering huge areas. The first satellite broadcasting came to the Middle East on December 2, 1990, with the launch of the Egyptian satellite channel. This channel transmitted an average of thirteen hours of daily programs including news, entertainment, religious, and health programs to the Middle Eastern, Northern African, and European countries. Later, it increased its broadcast to twenty-four hours. It was followed, in 1991, by the Saudi-owned Middle East Broadcasting Center (MBC). MBC was the first truly pan-Arab TV station transmitting news, family, cultural, and entertainment programs throughout the Arab world and Europe. Both its staff and programming reflected the pan-Arab nature of the channel. MBC introduced communication across the world through its programs, which resembled those of CNN. One successful example was the widely popular show *Hiwar ma'a al-Gharb* (Dialogue with the West). This pioneering program allowed the Arab public to call in and communicate their opinions live and with a certain degree of freedom. Despite its title, the show provided a forum in which Arab political personalities and governments could speak to one another. Unfortunately, the program was discontinued over disagreement about its direction and cost.

Gulf countries launched satellite channels between 1992 and 1994. It is no accident that the Gulf Arab states, along with Egypt, were among the first to transmit through satellite, as they were financially better off than the rest of the Arab countries. Wealthy states were not the only ones to move to satellite broadcasting in order to reach a wider audience. Other Arab countries including Jordan, Tunisia, Morocco, and Algeria entered the competition as early as 1993. In 1994, more TV channels joined the array of government-owned and -controlled stations. These included the privately owned Arab Radio and Television (ART) and Orbit, oriented toward entertainment and owned by Saudi individuals. Both channels operate out of Italy. By early 2000, almost all Arab countries had joined the satellite wave. Iraq inaugurated its satellite TV station with a speech by its former leader, Saddam Hussein, in 1999.

The Qatar-based channel al-Jazeera, launched in 1996, has emerged as the leading source of news and the most candid forum for debating issues throughout the Arab world. The second biggest network is the Middle East Broadcasting Center (MBC), followed by the Arab News Network (ANN), and Abu Dhabi Satellite TV station.

Al-Jazeera's coverage of Syrian politics exemplifies how satellite TV is changing the conditions of communication between citizens and states in the Arab world and increasing the space for civil society, creating more moments in television that are less controlled by states. The significance of the Syrian case lies in the fact that the Syrian regime is highly authoritarian and still maintains total control of information and communication. Examined here is al-Jazeera's reporting of several issues considered highly sensitive according to the censorship policies of Syria's ministries of information, culture, and guidance: political opposition in Syria, succession, and the impact of the peace process on the regime's survival.

Syria's Style of Communication

As in many Arab countries, the media in Syria are controlled and managed by the state. Media workers are considered government employees, and those in higher positions are required to be loyal party members. Media analyst William A. Rugh classifies the press in Syria as a "mobilizing press." The mobilizing role of the media, he says, is to communicate the desires of the leadership in pursuit of its goals of development, industrialization, and enhanced legitimacy. The behavioral characteristics of the mobilizing press, according to Rugh, are no criticism of policy, sanctity of leaders, and nondiversity of views.

Although the Syrian constitution (1973) guarantees the citizens' right to free press and expression, the state has had a virtual monopoly over the press since the Baathist military coup of 1963. After the coup, the military authority closed down all independent newspapers. It passed several restrictive articles under the State of Emergency law, which was instituted during the 1963 military takeover. Article 4b gives the state the right to control newspapers, books, radio and television broadcasting, advertising, and visual arts. It may also confiscate and destroy any work that might be threatening the security of the state. Starting in 1974, the Syrian media became a vehicle to promote President Assad's cult of personality. By 1979, the government tightened its control over the media, increasing censorship in the aftermath of the armed confrontation between the Assad regime and the Muslim Brotherhood. Until 2001, Syria had three major national Arabic newspapers—*al-Baath*, *al-Thawra*, and *al-Tishreen*—as well as one in English, *Syria Times*. All these papers, in addition to the radio and TV, are or were controlled and managed by the Ministry of Information. In 1998, Syria launched its satellite TV station, Syrian Satellite TV.

Over the years, the Syrian government has developed a long list of taboo topics deemed embarrassing or threatening to the regime. For instance, the government prohibits criticism of the president and his family, the ruling Baath Party, the military, the legitimacy of the regime, or the sectarian question. Subjects usually censored by the Ministry of Information include the government's human rights record, Islamist opposition, allegations of involvement of officials in drug trafficking, the activity of Syrian troops in Lebanon, graphic descriptions of sex, and materials depicting the Arab cause in the Arab-Israeli conflict in a negative light.

The government has also prohibited publication of any independent source of information considered threatening or critical of the regime. A case in point was the crackdown on all independent Lebanese newspapers in Lebanon following the Syrian military intervention in that country in 1976–1977, during which the Syrian military closed down seven newspapers and one magazine in Beirut. Amnesty International and Human Rights Watch documented the arrest, expulsion, and even assassination of prominent journalists by the Syrian security forces. One prominent Lebanese journalist, Salim al-Lawzi, the editor of *al-Hawadith*, was abducted, tortured, and killed in 1980. His right hand, the writing hand, was badly mutilated, reportedly to warn others against angering Syrian president Hafez al-Assad.

While the Syrian government has strived to maintain its strict control over the dissemination of information, its efforts have been thwarted by two new sources—satellite TV stations and the Internet. The government's initial reaction to the new technology has oscillated between attempts at control and tolerance. The authorities have been less successful controlling the receiving satellite dishes than restricting the Internet. The proliferation of regional satellite TV stations in the late 1990s has permanently changed the rules of control and censorship.

Al-Jazeera Satellite TV Channel

Al-Jazeera Satellite Channel (JSC) was not the first satellite TV station in the Arab world, but it has become the leading source of political news and programs. Al-Jazeera network was founded in Qatar on November 1, 1996, broadcasting only six hours. By mid-1997, it had increased its broadcasting hours to twelve hours, followed by an increase to twenty-four hours in February 1999. Al-Jazeera employs about 350 editors, anchors, and technicians, and has about 30 correspondents in major capitals around the world. Several factors distinguish al-Jazeera from other satellite TV stations in the region.

First, it is the only twenty-four-hour station dedicated to news, news analysis, talk shows, and documentaries. The only other satellite channel specializing in news coverage and analysis is the Arab News Network (ANN), owned by Sumer al-Assad, a son of Rif'at al-Assad (the brother and sometime rival of Hafez al-Assad), and Saudi individuals; ANN has yet to prove its competence in the competition with al-Jazeera. The second factor in the success of al-Jazeera is its professionalism, including a highly professional staff and crew consisting of many former BBC Arabic news service employees.

The real competition for the new station was not the governmental stations but the two giants, CNN and BBC. Both gained the educated and the well-to-do audiences in the Arab world during the second Gulf war. CNN was a major instrument in the communication/miscommunication between the United States and Iraqi president Saddam Hussein during Desert Shield/Storm in 1991. By the time the United States resumed bombing Iraq in December 1998, al-Jazeera had replaced CNN as the main source of news on the crisis, and it was al-Jazeera—not CNN—that aired the two speeches of the Iraqi dictator during the bombing.

What most Arabs appreciated about al-Jazeera's coverage of the resumed American hostilities against Iraq was the station's condemnatory tone toward the American attack. The channel questioned the timing and rationale for the attack, and highlighted the catastrophic impact of the sanctions on Iraqi citizens, reflecting popular Arab opinion about the U.S. bombing. Al-Jazeera has also presented a very compassionate, yet professional, coverage of the Palestinian intifada that began in September 2000. Several analysts in *Middle East International* have commented on the role of al-Jazeera and other Arab satellite TV stations in spurring "mass action and giving it a pan-Arab nature, by beaming directly into people's homes images of both the horrors experienced by the Palestinians and of solidarity activities elsewhere."

Third, the interactive, provocative programs of al-Jazeera provide Arab audiences with a way to express their views on the airwaves. Most of the talk shows encourage viewers to call in and question guests or comment on the issues under discussion. For example, in a program about the Syrian-Israeli peace talks, Sami Haddad, the host, took a call from Dr. Mansur Abd ad-Da'im of Syria, who said, "I would like to convey to you the voice of the Syrian street. The Syrian people warns the Syrian leadership against this act of betrayal, or they will face the fate of [assassinated Egyptian president Anwar] Sadat." The station has also become a forum for all political sides to debate issues. It has not excluded any political force, from Islamists to Communists, and especially those who are in opposition to their government. One pro-Saudi magazine criticized al-Jazeera for employing Baathists and Muslim Brotherhood members. Second, al-Jazeera engages the Arab public by taking their phone calls.

Fourth, the most important reason for the popularity and success of al-Jazeera is its willingness to discuss sensitive and controversial issues, and its bravery in breaking taboos. Muhammad Jasem al-Ali, al-Jazeera's chief editor, is quoted by Ibn Rushd as saying, "Other TV stations hold too many taboos. We don't have any taboos; our audience has a right to the truth and a right to voice their opinion publicly." The station's news editors have relatively more independence and freedom to report any worthy story. Concurrent topics and themes for its news and programming have included human rights and democracy in the Arab world, political opposition, the peace process and its supporters and opponents, political Islam, the Iraqi question, and Arab unity or disunity.

The frank discussion of these and similar topics has made al-Jazeera the most credible and respected news source for the Arab public. Simultaneously, it has enraged almost every single government in the region. The list of governments that protested or took punitive actions against al-Jazeera or its host country, Qatar, includes Bahrain, Saudi Arabia, Iraq, Kuwait, Jordan, Egypt, Tunisia, Libya, Algeria, and Morocco. But the channel has succeeded in gaining a higher degree of trust among the Arab public than any other source.

Several observers have criticized al-Jazeera for various reasons, including its selectivity in the countries and individuals it criticizes, its use of sensationalism at the expense of informing the public, its heavy management of live programs, and its tacit promotion of normalizing relations with Israel by including Israeli officials and experts among its guests.

Al-Jazeera presents a news summary every hour on the half hour, and four major news hours in the morning, midday, evening, and night. The main programs shown on al-Jazeera are listed in Tables 4 and 5.

Contesting Coverage

Al-Jazeera's coverage of Syrian politics has been wide ranging and has included three features: indirect reference to Syria under topics such as democracy, human rights, and Islamic fundamentalism in the Arab world; direct discussion of the Syrian-Israeli peace talks; and reporting on Syrian domestic developments. In each one of these areas, the coverage challenges the Syrian regime's taboos, which irritates Syria's officials. Over the last three years, major al-Jazeera programs, particularly *al-Itijah al-Mu'akis* (Opposite Directions), *Akthar min Ra'i* (More Than One Opinion), and *Bila Hudud* (Without Bounds), have debated these issues with a tone condemning authoritarianism and human rights violations.

While other TV stations only criticize the Iraqi regime as the archetype of the wicked regime, al-Jazeera has consistently denounced other non-democratic governments—including the Syrian regime—in its shows about democracy and pluralism. On the program *More Than One Opinion*, the pro-Syrian political analyst Zuhair Diyab became a laughingstock among the viewers from several Arab countries when he made excuses for the pervasiveness of authoritarianism in the area.

Another offensive topic for the Syrian regime is the issue of Islamic opposition. Having confronted an armed Islamic movement in the late 1970s and early 1980s, the Syrian government also considers this topic to be taboo. The Syrian regime calls the Muslim Brothers *al-khuwan al-Muslimun* (the Muslim traitors) for having led the opposition to the Assad government, which ended with the regime's killing thousands of civilians in the city of Hama in 1982. During the confrontation, the government issued a law on July 7, 1980, banning the Brothers and making membership in the group, even former membership, a capital offense.

On July 7, 1999, as part of its programming dealing with active Islamic movements, al-Jazeera hosted the leader of the banned Syrian Muslim Brothers for a two-hour interview on the program *Without Bounds*. The format of this program requires the host to take the opposite side of an issue to that of the guest. The Syrian and general Arab audience thus had the opportunity to hear a very moderate voice advocating democracy, demanding an end to marshal law rule, and insisting that his party be legalized. Views were sharply divided between those who repeated the government accusations about the Brothers and their leader, and those who accused the government of committing gross human rights violations and pleaded for an end to the monopoly over power by Assad's sect.

The second category of coverage is the Syrian role in the Arab-Israeli peace process. While overall coverage is somewhat sympathetic to Syria, discussions of the domestic imperatives and implications of the peace process on Syrian society and the regime have not always been appreciated by the Syrian government, which desires all Arab media outlets to repeat its line about the just cause and prudent position of the Syrian regime .

Several programs covered the Syrian-Israeli negotiations, especially during the resumption of talks in late November 1999 and early January 2000. As a guest on *More Than One Opinion*, I raised the issue of the lack of democracy in Syria and how this affects the peace process. Syrians are not permitted to debate their government's policies in the press or in their rubber-stamp parliament, which means that Israel is making peace with an authoritarian state that has little accountability to its own people and is bound to experience a change of leadership soon, thus building peace on precarious footing. Any view that does not celebrate Syria's handling of the peace process is perceived by the government as weakening the position of the Syrian negotiator.

The third contest over the dissemination of information between al-Jazeera and the Syrian

Table 4

Live Programs on al-Jazeera

Program Name	Host	Description
More Than One Opinion (Akthar min Ra'i)	Sami Haddad	Three guests debate the most newsworthy issue of the week
Opposite Directions (al-Ittijah al-Mu'akis)	Faisal al-Qasimi	Two guests take opposing views on an issue
Without Bounds (Bila Hudud)	Ahmad Mansour	Interviews of prominent figures; the host takes a position critical of the guest
Open Dialogue (Hewar Maftuh)	Ghasan Bin Jiddo	Invites Arab intellectuals to discuss a pressing issue
Shari'a and Life (al-Sharia wal Hayat)	Maher Abdullah	Discusses contemporary issues from an Islamic perspective. A regular on the show is Sheikh Youseff al-Qaradawi
The Scene of the Incident (Mawqi' al-Hadath)	Hussein Abdulghani	The host is sent to hot spots to file live reports

Note: All programs are weekly except for *Open Dialogue* (monthly) and *The Scene of the Incident* (occasional).
Source: Al-Jazeera. http://www.aljazeera.net.

Table 5

The Most Watched Recorded Programs on al-Jazeera

Program Name	Host	Description
Under Scrutiny (Taht al-Mijhar)	Various	Investigates a political or social story
Very Confident (Sirri lil Ghaya)	Yousri Foudah	Reexamines sensational stories
Eyewitness to the Era (Shahid ala al-Asr)	Ahmad Mansour	Interviews prominent figures who occupied important roles in the past
A Bit of History (Shay min al-Tarikh)	Ahmad Taha	Examines an event or day in history
Guest & Issue (Dayf wa Qadiya)	Mohamed Kreshan	A conversation with a guest about an issue in the news
The Weekly File (al-Malaf al-Usbu'i)	Jamil 'Azar	Discusses salient news of the week
Al-Jazeera's Correspondents (Murasilu al-Jazeera)	Mohamed al-Bourini	Daily reports from correspondents around the world
Hot Spot (Nuqta Sakhina)	Ahmad Taha	A documentary from hot spots around the world
Private Chat (Ziyara Khassa)	Sami Kulaib	Interviews prominent figures in their places of residence around the world
The Cultural Scene (al-Mashhad al-Thaqafi)	Tawfiq Taha	Discusses cultural news from around the Arab world

Note: All programs are weekly except for *Very Confident* (monthly), *al-Jazeera's Correspondents* (daily), and *Hot Spot* (monthly).
Source: Al-Jazeera. http://www.aljazeera.net.

regime is in the area of reporting and analyzing significant domestic political developments. One such example involved the program *More Than One Opinion* and took place in January 1998, right after President Assad dismissed his brother Rif'at from his position as a vice president for national security affairs. Almost everyone had wondered why Assad kept his brother in this nominal position for so long, while forcing him to stay in exile. The official Syrian media gave no explanation of this decision. It was Sami Haddad, the host of *More Than One Opinion*, who assembled three panelists to discuss the issue. One of them, Zuhair Diyab, supported the Syrian government, the second was Jordanian journalist Salah Qalab, and the third was Syrian dissident Subhi al-Hadidi, a writer living in Paris. Both moderator and guests were very cautious in addressing some of the taboos in Syrian politics, particularly the sectarian question, Assad's strained relations with his brother, and the succession question.

Despite the self-censorship of the participants and actual censorship of the program, reported by some sources, the participants were publicly breaking a taboo by debating such topics. Both the Jordanian journalist and the Syrian dissident disagreed with Syrian commentator Emad Fawzi al-Shu'ibi, who claimed that Syria was a democratic state, governed by institutions and not individuals. The episode was the first to break the tacit agreement between a medium controlled by a Gulf state and the Syrian government, known for its intolerance and dislike of criticism.

With each report, the channel has pushed the limits of taboos. For instance, when Syria's President Assad died, al-Jazeera was a leading medium in its coverage of the domestic and regional implications of his death. It was on this station that several Arab commentators expressed their outrage over the speedy amendment of the constitution in order to move Assad's son, Bashar, into the presidency. Many analysts registered their opposition to the precedent of the bequest of power in republican regimes. Unlike the Syrian TV, which exulted Assad's qualities during the funeral procession, al-Jazeera provided commentary about the future of Syria.

Another recent example of al-Jazeera's distinguished coverage, in comparison with that of the Syrian TV, was the story of Monzer al-Mouseli, an independent member of the Syrian People's Assembly who made headlines by daring to raise an objection to the constitutional amendment that would move Bashar into the presidency. While reading what was supposed to be an endorsement speech, Mouseli reminded his colleagues that they needed to mention the reasons for the amendment, as required by the constitution. His remark, seen as an objection to Bashar's nomination, generated a storm inside the hall. Other members, as well as the speaker of the Assembly, shut Mouseli up before he could finish speaking. And when the Syrian media crew detected a sign of dissent, they ended live coverage of the session and went to the street to show support for the young Assad. Syrian TV resumed its coverage of the Assembly's session to transmit the comments of the speaker who censured Mouseli, stating, "the respected member's sinful part of his soul led him into error, and he just realized his mistake and repented." This sensational story did not escape al-Jazeera, which reported it as the first item on its nightly news. The report recounted what had happened and featured an interview with Mouseli to get his side of the story, which was totally suppressed within Syria. The interview was followed by a discussion with Mustapha Abdul'al, director of the Center for Pluralism, who described the event as "historic" and was very sarcastic about the session and the obvious lack of freedom of expression in the Syrian Assembly.

Response and Effects

Al-Jazeera became a major contending source of news for many Syrians. Like the rest of the Arab public, Syrians are excited about the style and substance of the station, both of which were new for the region. While the number of Syrians who watch al-Jazeera as opposed to the official Syrian channels is unknown, there is ample evidence to suggest that it is more widely watched than the official Syrian channels. One such indication is the proliferation of satellite dishes seen on the roofs of buildings everywhere in the country, especially in major cities. Another sign is the number of callers from Syria who phone to comment on al-Jazeera's programs.

The fact that Syrian audiences are excited by al-Jazeera does not mean they approve of it. Nor does it mean they recognize what it can do for them. To the contrary, some Syrian viewers have complained that al-Jazeera's programs are more confusing than illuminating. During an episode of *Without Bounds,* on which there was a debate about the legitimacy of Bashar al-Assad as successor to his father, a Syrian caller said he felt that the show's host should not be allowed to challenge the guest, Syrian official Riyadh Na'san Agha, because disputing the government version of the issue only causes "confusion" among viewers.

Viewers in Damascus with whom I have spoken say that Syrian audiences are alarmed at hearing vehemently contradictory views about such basic issues, being used to hearing only one correct version of the "truth." This confusion has not prevented Syrians from tuning in to the station's programs, however, and even from expressing satisfaction with its coverage. While Ghasan Bin Jiddo, a correspondent for al-Jazeera, was reporting from Syria during the funeral of Assad, he told of crowds of Syrians coming to greet him and describing their respect for the channel.

As for Syrian officials, the rise of al-Jazeera coincided with the ascendance of Bashar al-Assad to power in Syria. Bashar has been reportedly leading efforts to modernize the country and oversee its entrance into the information age. Bashar was formally head of the Syrian Information Society before he became the president.

Syrian officials have attempted to engage this medium rather than to boycott it. Their engagement with the network is two-pronged. First, like their counterparts in other Arab countries, Syrian officials approve of al-Jazeera as long as it does not step on what they consider sensitive topics or violate what they consider "objective" reporting. On the show *Opposite Directions*, Yasir Nahlawi, a member of the Syrian parliament and a frequent contributor to al-Jazeera, complimented the program but complained that the channel allows "the enemies of Syria and the Arab nation" to communicate their poisonous views on the airwaves.

Second, the participation of Syrian officials on al-Jazeera's programs has revealed their inability to communicate effectively with audiences outside Syria. Here are two examples. In an episode of *Opposite Directions*, on December 16, 1999, devoted to the implications of the Syrian-Israeli peace process, the two guests were Karim al-Shaybani, head of a pro-government party within the National Progressive Front in Syria, and Adli Sadeq, a Palestinian journalist critical of the Syrian government's snubbing of the Palestine Liberation Organization (PLO). Sadeq confronted Shaybani with the lack of democracy in Syria, which Shaybani vehemently denied. Moreover, he was outraged that this challenge to conditions in Syria was raised on the show and was very uncomfortable with the whole topic, wanting it declared irrelevant to the real subject at hand. Sadeq's point, however, was that the peace process will bring greater scrutiny of Syria and hopefully lead to more democracy for its people. The content and style of Shaybani's remarks reflected the propagandist approach used by "official" employees of the Ministry of Information, containing rhetoric that sounded as if it were two decades old.

In another example of Syrian attempts to take advantage of al-Jazeera's reach, Riyadh Na'san Agha appeared on *Without Bounds* right after Assad's death to discuss the future of Syria. He was introduced as the head of the political office of the president, though he is more familiar to Arab audiences as the host of several cultural and literary television programs. What worked for Agha was his eloquence and command of the classic Arabic language, but he immediately clashed with the show's host and lost most Arab viewers when he asserted that the succession of Bashar al-Assad was not a command from above but an overwhelmingly popular choice. He had difficulty communicating with viewers from other Arab countries, who were shocked by his logic, or lack thereof. One viewer from Egypt described Agha's argument as "an insult to the intelligence of the audience."

There has been some evidence that the Syrian government is relaxing its control over media. This retreat could be attributable to two factors. First, Syrian media have lost most of their audiences to other media (e.g., al-Jazeera). In response to the Syrian media's failure, Bashar al-Assad responded in his July 17, 2000, inaugural speech that he wished to lead the country into the information age. A number of measures reflect real efforts by the Syrian government to modify its media policy in response to the competition.

The first was the appointment of the new minister of information, Adnan Umran, in the March 2000 cabinet reshuffle. The new minister, a former Arab League diplomat, is known to be reform-minded. During the ninth congress of the Baath Party (June 15–20, 2000), following the death of Assad, Umran criticized the performance of the Syrian media, using harsh language to describe his predecessor and claiming that Syria did not have a true "media policy," as cited by the London-based *al-Hayat*. He also complained about the decline in sales of Syria's major daily newspapers, almost half of which are returned to distributors.

As a second indication of change, after his inauguration in 2000, Bashar issued two directives regarding development of a "new media discourse." One asked chief editors of print as well as the audiovisual media to embark on a "calm, logical, and balanced" style that should "respect the intelligence of the audience." The other instruction was to stop printing and posting new pictures of him, and to stop the use of the phrase "*al-Ra'is al-Khaled*" (the immortal president). Such immortality, he said, is only for God. Shortly thereafter, the official Syrian TV station removed the caption "the immortal president" from its screen, and the daily *al-Thawra* stopped publishing a giant picture of the president as a regular feature on its first page.

Later, the Ministry of Information reshuffled the heads of its major departments, newspaper editors, and the heads of the Syrian radio and TV agency to reflect the new openness. An article appearing in the daily *al-Thawra* called on Syrian journalists who write for Arab dailies that are a safe distance outside Syria, such as *al-Hayat*, to move the debate about media and information in Syria onto the pages of the local papers.

The third important indication that change is afoot in Syria came from journalists and intellectuals, who demanded more freedom of speech and accountability. Ninety-nine Syrian writers issued a statement in early 2001 demanding freedom of expression, freedom of the press, and an end to one-party rule. The statement was published in two Lebanese dailies, *al-Nahar* and *al-Safir*, on September 26, 2000. Later, a coalition of intellectuals calling themselves "Friends of Civil Society" emerged and began holding "discussion forums." Most of the discussions revolved around the themes advanced in the Manifesto of 99, an open letter by prominent Syrian intellectuals that called for an end to martial law, the release of political prisoners, and the instatement of political freedoms. By early January 2001, the Friends of Civil Society issued a new petition, signed by 1,000 citizens, calling for the restoration of civil society, freedom of speech and the press, political pluralism, and an expanded role for women in public life.

In another response to the poverty of its media, in early 2001, the Syrian government authorized the establishment of the first privately owned newspaper permitted in the country in four decades. The owner and editor in chief of the new paper was well-known political cartoonist Ali Farzat. Hungry readers snatched up the first 75,000-copy edition of *al-Domari* (The Lamplighter) as soon as it appeared. The Syrian government allowed the branch of the Communist Party allied with the government to publish their own newspapers, but issued statements warning that dissent might constitute treason and indicating clear limits to any opening or democratization process.

While al-Jazeera cannot claim full responsibility for all these positive changes, it can be credited with forcing the media inside Syria, as elsewhere in the Arab world, to redefine their discourse so as not to lose what is left of their audiences. Despite the success of channels such as al-Jazeera in expanding the communication and dissemination of information, it is clear that they cannot topple authoritarian regimes.

The Syrian case demonstrates that authoritarian regimes attempt to cope with new technology and the expanded public sphere by incorporating themselves into it, but lack credibility. A case in point is the Syrian regime's crackdown on the activities of dissident groups, starting in March 2001, in which the regime used bureaucratic and legal measures to close down the proliferating discussion forums. All forums are now required to get permission to assemble by providing details about the meeting, the topic to be discussed, the speakers, and the names of all attendees.

Al-Jazeera reported on this news and discussed it on *Opposite Directions*. The program hosted one active member of the Civil Society movement, Aref

Dalilah, with the opposite view presented by Monzer al-Mouseli, who had caused the controversy in parliament the previous summer. The fact that Mouseli was the one willing to rationalize the government's efforts to crack down on Civil Society demonstrates how difficult it is for many Syrians to overcome the decades-long legacy of authoritarian rule.

A second limitation on al-Jazeera's ability to continue its contest with authoritarian media has to do with its ability to maintain its independence. One scholar calls this "the paradox of al-Jazeera." The paradox is that al-Jazeera is relatively independent because it is supported by the government of Qatar, and if it were to be privately owned its relative independence might be curtailed. As author Naomi Sakr has stated, "The problem comes in assessing whether, in the leap from total state control to market-driven programming, Middle East satellite television will ever function as an independent public service providing outlet for investigative journalism and a widened arena of uncensored policy debates." In 2001, there were reports that the managers of al-Jazeera would be moving the channel into the private sector within a five-year period. That proposition ran into two difficulties. One was the challenge of finding enough advertisers. The other was the difficulty of maintaining the network's independent approach without upsetting their sponsors, many of whom were coming from neighboring Gulf states that were not completely enthusiastic about the station. Yet as of now, al-Jazeera became a phenomenon shortly after its launching and owes this as much to its own approach as to the failure of the official Arab media.

References and Further Reading

Alterman, Jon B. "Counting Nodes and Counting Noses: Understanding New Media in the Middle East." *Middle East Journal* 54:3 (Summer 2000).

Amin, Hussein. "The Third Wave: Arab Satellite TV." *Middle East Insight* 14:2 (March–April 1999).

"Arab Reactions." *Middle East International* 635 (October 13, 2000): 13–14.

Belham, Nick. "Seething at Qatar." *Middle East International* 630 (July 28, 2000): 17–18.

Fandy, Mamoun. "Information Technology, Trust, and Social Change in the Arab World." *Middle East Journal* 54:3 (Summer 2000): 378–394.

Ghareeb, Edmond. "New Media and the Information Revolution in the Arab World: An Assessment." *Middle East Journal* 54:3 (Summer 2000): 405–410.

Hamza, Issam. "Syria's First Private Newspaper Is Sell-Off." Reuters, February 27, 2001.

Hasad al-Yawm [Today's Harvest]. Al-Jazeera, June 26, 2000.

Husseini, Nasser. "Beyond CNN: The Proliferation of Satellite Choices." *Middle East Insight* 14:2 (March/April 1999).

"Iraq Protests at al-Jazeera." *Al-Hayat* (London), May 3, 2000.

Middle East Watch. *Syria Unmasked.* New Haven, CT: Yale University Press, 1991.

More Than One Opinion. Al-Jazeera, January 7, 2000.

———. Al-Jazeera, December 13, 1999.

———. Al-Jazeera, October 18, 1999.

———. Al-Jazeera, February 16, 1998.

Moubayad, Sami. "Voices From Damascus." *Washington Report on Middle East Affairs* 20:2 (March 2001).

Opposite Directions. Al-Jazeera, March 13, 2001.

———. Al-Jazeera, May 23, 2000.

Rugh, William A. *The Arab Press.* Syracuse, NY: Syracuse University Press, 1987.

Sakr, Naomi. "State Television and Development in the Middle East." *Middle East Report* (Spring 1999).

"Satellite Excessiveness." *Al-Jadida* (London), May 4, 1998.

"Syria: Volte-Face." *Middle East International* 644 (February 23, 2001).

Wedeen, Lisa. *Ambiguities of Domination.* Chicago: University of Chicago Press, 1999.

Without Bounds. Al-Jazeera, June 14, 2000.

———. Al-Jazeera, July 7, 1999.

European-Based and Satellite Arabic-Language Media

Barry Rubin

Many of the most widely circulated Middle Eastern newspapers, magazines, and television channels are not located in the region at all but have their offices in Europe, mostly in London. This situation owes not to the growing Arabic-speaking immigrant communities in Europe but rather to the greater freedom from censorship and repression enjoyed by the media based there.

This situation developed in two stages. First, Lebanese publishers and journalists fled their country's civil war in the late 1970s, and after settling in Europe, resumed producing newspapers. Second, Arabic-language satellite television broadcasting took off in the 1990s. Being based abroad has given these media substantial freedom from the restrictions of their home countries, yet their dependence on funding from the region, either through direct subsidies or through advertising and subscriptions, leads to self-censorship.

Print Media

The Lebanese publications differed from those emerging from elsewhere in the region. Some of the Europe-based Lebanese publications were simply exiled versions of the ones from Lebanon. In most other cases, though, they were new. The newspaper *al-Sharq al-Awsat*, by contrast, was established in London in 1978 by Saudi Research and Marketing, and it beamed its contents to publishing houses in Saudi Arabia via satellite. This setup had the dual benefits of enhanced access to Western news sources and freedom from the restrictions of the Saudi state. The newspaper was followed in 1988 by *al-Hayat* (which received significant funding from Saudi prince Khalid bin Sultan in 1990) and in 1989 by *al-Quds al-Arabi*, as well as numerous glossy magazines. These publications benefited greatly from the absence of censorship in Europe.

These publications depended on subsidies from Persian Gulf states, as regional businessmen became major investors. The investors saw this as a prestigious and potentially lucrative step, and they also recognized the value of freedom from the publishing restrictions back home. Since Gulf Arabs were more familiar with London, and English had become the international language, they invested there. While many Lebanese had originally settled in France after fleeing the civil war, a lot of other Arab journalists moved to Britain so they could continue their profession.

The dependence on funding from the Middle East led to instances of self-censorship, as editors from various papers softened or edited political commentary in order to avoid being banned, losing advertising revenue, or having personnel replaced. Thus, a publication that depends on Saudi funding must recognize that the country's censors are more open to political commentaries than they are to ones on religious or cultural affairs. The mainstream papers, furthermore, must not criticize the ruling family.

Some of the publications that relocated from Lebanon survived the move to Europe and then returned to Lebanon, while others ceased publication altogether. Smaller dissident publications also took root in Europe.

Saudi Research and Marketing

Saudi Research and Marketing, *al-Sharq al-Awsat*'s parent company, was controlled by Prince Ahmed bin Salman (died in July 2002), son of the company's main financier, Prince Salman bin Abdel Aziz. Two brothers from Saudi Arabia, Hisham Ali Hafiz (died in February 2006) and Muhammad Ali Hafiz, were the newspaper's publishers. Their family had a publishing background, having established *al-Madina* newspaper in 1937, and the two brothers created the English-language *Arab News* in 1974. When Jihad al-Khazen, the editor of *Arab News*, was transferred to London in 1978, he set up *al-Sharq al-Awsat*. The newspaper is printed nationally in Dharan, Jiddah, and Riyadh, regionally in Beirut, Cairo, Casablanca, and Kuwait City, and internationally in Frankfurt, London, Marseilles, and New York.

The weekly *al-Majalla* is the daily's reputable sister publication, and its columnists hold a variety of viewpoints. Saudi Research and Marketing also publishes a weekly sports magazine for young Arabs called *Aalam Alriadah* and a daily sports newspaper called *Arriyadiyah*. Its monthly *Arrajol*, according to the company Web site, is "a magazine for the man of wealth and power . . . born from a desire to create a magazine for the lifestyle of the rich." The monthly *Hia* is for "the discerning affluent Arab lady," and "appeals directly to the decisive Arab lady of taste, style and wealth"; *al-Jamila* is a weekly for women. There are two family magazines, *Al Jadeeda* and *Sayidaty*, and another for children, *Basim*. Specialty publications include *al-Eqtisadiah* (a Saudi national business daily published in London), *Assayarat* (a monthly auto magazine), *Fourousiyah* (a weekly about horses), *al-Muslimoon* (a weekly about Muslim political, social, and cultural issues), and a TV guide.

Saudis make up the bulk of these publications' readership. The Saudi government provides free subscriptions to *al-Majalla* for overseas students. *Al-Sharq al-Awsat* is connected with the Saudi regime and appears to avoid criticism of it, but it also carries a range of perspectives. It is conservative on politics and, according to media analyst William A. Rugh, "very cautious" regarding the internal affairs of Persian Gulf states. The newspaper's editor has acknowledged the limitations that result from the need to respect local laws, but he denies that the Saudi owner interferes with the paper's editorial policy. Staff, on the other hand, say the editors have been pressured by Saudis and others from the Gulf.

Al-Hayat

Published in almost ten locations, *al-Hayat*, in the words of Middle East specialist Jon B. Alterman, has come to be seen as "the leading forum for opinion makers in the Arab world to debate various points of view." The newspaper was originally published in Beirut by Kamal Mroue, starting in 1946. It closed in 1976 and resumed publishing in London some ten years later. Jihad al-Khazen, the founder of *al-Sharq al-Awsat*, was its editor until 1998.

The *al-Wasat* magazine, launched in 1992, is a product of the al-Hayat Publishing Company. It eventually became a supplement of *al-Hayat*. The newspaper itself entered a partnership with the Lebanese Broadcasting Company (LBC) in 2002. The resulting news channel combined the experience and professionalism of the *al-Hayat* staff with the reach and resources of LBC.

Saudi Arabia's Prince Khalid bin Sultan funds *al-Hayat*, and Alterman speculates that he sees it either as a platform for his political views or as a means of playing a personal political role in the region. Rugh asserts that the newspaper runs at a financial loss. Its regionwide circulation necessitates greater awareness of politically sensitive issues since, as Alterman notes, being banned in Saudi Arabia, the daily's biggest market, would lead to a significant loss in revenues. Nevertheless, Alterman argues, the editors view the occasional ban as favorable because it demonstrates the newspaper's independence.

The newspaper has bureaus and reporters in most Arab capitals and focuses on reporting from a pan-Arab perspective. There are differing perceptions of the paper. Some see it as having a Lebanese identity because of its staffing, and others see it as Saudi because of its funding source. The newspaper's editors say its Saudi owners do not exert any editorial pressure.

Al-Quds al-Arabi

The Palestinian Abdel Bari Atwan edits *al-Quds al-Arabi* from London, where it is published. Created in 1989, the newspaper stands out for the quality of its reporting and for its publication of direct translations from the Israeli press, though its circulation is smaller than the others mentioned above. *Al-Quds al-Arabi* has a small staff and uses news agency copy extensively. It is the most outspoken among the major Arabic papers, the most likely to denounce the U.S. position on an issue, and the most closely focused on Israeli-Palestinian news.

Unlike other papers, *al-Quds al-Arabi* is not connected with a major publishing organization and does not carry much advertising. It is not dependent on Saudi funding, and it has a fairly limited circulation. The newspaper's sources of funding have at times included Saddam Hussein's regime, Libya, the Palestine Liberation Organization, Qatar, Sudan, and Syria. Yet the newspaper's occasional criticism of the Syrian regime, as well as the Saudi and Algerian ones, has resulted in short-term bans.

Other Expatriate Newspapers

Al-Arab and *al-Zaman* are two of the smaller Arabic publications from London. The first is published by former Libyan information minister Abdal Munim al-Hawni and generally reflects the official Libyan line. The staff is small and relies on agency materials. The reporting is shallower than that of bigger publications. It has been banned in several countries. *Al-Zaman* is published by Saad al-Bazzaz, who headed Iraqi state television under Saddam Hussein, but became a regime critic after fleeing the country in 1992. After Saddam was overthrown in 2003, the newspaper opened offices in Iraq and is available there. It maintains its London head office, however, and that is where most of its staff are located.

Satellite Television Networks

"Satellite dishes are sprouting up all over the Arab world," Jon Alterman notes in his 1998 study, *New Media, New Politics?* The phenomenon of Arab satellite television can be traced to a 1967 meeting in Tunis of Arab information ministers who, presumably unhappy with the quality of Arabic reporting on the recently concluded war with Israel, decided on the need for a satellite service. The Arab Radio and Television Broadcasting Union was established in 1969, and Arab League members founded the Arab Satellite Communications Organization in 1976 and then created the Arabsat satellite system. Two French-built satellites were put into orbit in 1985, and a third was launched the following year.

Arabic channels have become very popular since then. Out of 155 channels using Arabsat and Nilesat by August 2005, 21 were "free-to-air" news channels. Fifteen of those channels used Arabic, five used English, and one was in French.

Yet there was a limited audience in the 1980s. When Arabsat was launched, satellite reception equipment was prohibitively expensive and also took up lots of space. Technological advances, such as smaller dishes and more affordable equipment, have contributed to satellite television's popularity. With these changes, several households can use one satellite dish at a total cost of just $200.

The 1990–1991 Persian Gulf War appears to have had the most profound impact on regional viewing habits. Television audiences and regional media grew dependent on the U.S. Cable News Network (CNN) for information, according to author Touryaa. The Egyptian Radio and Television Union (ERTU) broadcast more than 800 hours of CNN programming between December 1990 and March 1991, and audiences contrasted the quality of the American programs with those of their national providers.

Also contributing to the popularity of satellite television in the 1990s was the growing number of Arab professionals who had lived in the West for some amount of time, studying, working, or both. According to Alterman, this increase in foreign travel, wealth, and literacy arose from the oil boom of the 1970s. Because this generation was better off than the preceding one, Alterman continues, it was more consumption-oriented. Having gotten used to the entertainment and information options available in the West, this group served as a market for subscription-based satellite services.

According to Naomi Sakr, other reasons for the success of regional satellite television are its geographical spread and its ability to reach a variety of audiences, from educated elites to illiterate villagers. Satellite television was an important form of home-based entertainment, and it connected a Middle Eastern community dispersed by conflict and other traumatic events.

Despite the channels' popularity, in some cases governmental actions make it difficult for them to reach their audience. In Saudi Arabia and Iraq in the 1990s, using, selling, importing, or producing satellite dishes was illegal. In Iraq, after Saddam

Hussein's regime was toppled in 2003 and satellite television was legalized, Iraqis became avid viewers.

Funding Arabic Satellite Television

Production of satellite television programs is costly. In 2003, Rugh cited an estimate of $40 million a year for an Arab satellite TV channel. Alterman breaks this down somewhat, writing that in the late 1990s, renting satellite time cost $4 million a year per channel, and producing or buying programs costs millions of dollars more. Then there are the additional expenses of cameras, computers, and salaries, as well as the expense of operating from Europe. These costs are partially met by collecting subscription fees. The satellite stations send an encrypted signal, and the subscriber must purchase a decoder and "smart card." Subscription fees can be high, according to Alterman, starting at $50 per month for basic service, and this makes the services unaffordable for most Middle Eastern families. Viewers who can afford the expense, however, are the very ones with the disposable income advertisers seek.

The majority of the channels are free-to-air, and they run commercials to generate revenue. Rugh argues that advertising has not met the financial needs of any Arabic channels because the region is not well off; advertisers have little information on the market and tend to prefer regime-friendly channels. The proliferation of channels makes competition for revenues that much more difficult.

Wealthy investors are needed to offset the high cost of satellite television. Rich Saudis with connections to the royal family were among the early investors, and they hoped to use satellite television for commercial and political reasons. Rugh asserts that Saudis control "several leading satellite TV outlets"—with the exception of al-Jazeera—due to their investments. Indeed, the stations' survival would be problematic without subsidies from the investors, because all of them are losing money.

Middle East Broadcasting Center

The Middle East Broadcasting Center (MBC) went on the air in September 1991 and by 1998 was one of the region's most popular channels. MBC has correspondents all over the globe and uses many of the same sources as other international broadcasters. Its news programs are considered the station's preeminent product.

"MBC was the leader in revolutionizing Arab news coverage," Alterman asserts, while Rugh describes MBC as "the pioneer in innovative programming." MBC was the first Arab television channel to open a news bureau in Jerusalem and to report on Palestinian affairs, rather than using third-hand reports or airing polemics. The station reports on issues that make regional governments uncomfortable, and broadcasts documentaries on controversial topics. For example, it ran a seven-part series on Operation Desert Storm featuring interviews with Western officials, Israelis, Iraqis, and Arabs from the anti–Saddam Hussein coalition. In one segment, a Kuwaiti official left the interview because the questioning was more critical than he had expected. Another segment showed "secret footage" of a squabble at an Arab League meeting.

Alterman writes about a five-part MBC series on the Arab-Israeli conflict that upset regional governments. Jordan actually denied one of the program's assertions regarding its contacts with Israel prior to the 1973 war. That the Jordanian government would issue a denial rather than just trying to censor the program led many observers to interpret this as a manifestation of the impact of satellite television on the way governments operate.

Rugh also notes the station is breaking some taboos, but he adds that it avoids traditionally sensitive topics, particularly where Saudi Arabia and the Gulf states are concerned, and its commentaries are "somewhat cautious." As MBC's competitors caught up with quality news coverage of their own, the station turned to providing more entertainment, seeking to attract a bigger audience so as to be more appealing to advertisers.

It is difficult to estimate accurately the size of MBC's audience. Countries have different levels of satellite TV penetration, and only some domestic broadcasters carry MBC news programs. MBC was owned by Sheikh Walid al-Ibrahim, a Saudi related by marriage to King Fahd. Ibrahim's enormous wealth enabled him to operate the station at a loss, buy the best equipment, and pay a staff of Arab and British professionals. According to Alterman, there are allegations that the station is run as King Fahd's personal project, and rumors that the monarch personally dictates the programs to be shown. Rugh adds that it is assumed the Saudi royal family backs MBC in order to have the support of a friendly pan-Arab media outlet.

There were several management shake-ups in MBC's early years, and this coincided with uncertainty about its future. Fluctuations in oil prices after 1998 necessitated cost cutting, and the station moved to Dubai in 2001.

Orbit

Owned by the Mawarid Group, a Saudi Arabian business conglomerate, Orbit went on the air in 1994 and introduced fee-based satellite broadcasting to the region. Prince Khalid bin Abdullah invested more than $2 billion in the station, which was initially based in Italy. It moved to Bahrain in 2000.

Initially, Orbit set out to be a news and documentary service, and it had a contract with the BBC Arabic Service for the production of news. Then Saudi Arabia became upset by several BBC programs—an interview with a Saudi dissident and an exposé on capital punishment in the country. In April 1996, Orbit canceled the BBC contract, its American chief executive officer claiming that the British network had made a "sneering and racist attack on Islamic law and culture."

Orbit then entered a relationship with Star TV, owned by Australian-American media entrepreneur Rupert Murdoch. Orbit shows American sports and entertainment channels, such as ESPN and Disney, as well as channels that play American movies and sit-coms. Rugh writes that viewers see Orbit stylistically as the "most Western" of the Arab satellite channels. Orbit also has two Arabic channels, one of which features Arabic films and the other various Arabic entertainment programs. One of its main shows is a live interview program called *Ala al-Hawa'* (On the Air) that has many regional leaders as guests. The program also has a phone-in segment, which allows people from around the region to ask questions.

Expensive annual subscription fees are one of the factors that has hindered Orbit's success. Alterman also argues that Orbit's offerings might be too Western-oriented for Arab viewers, and that its Arabic programs might find it hard to compete with the greater penetration achieved by al-Jazeera and other channels.

Arab Radio and Television

Another subscription-based satellite television service is Arab Radio and Television (ART), initially based in Italy. The company was created in 1994 by Salah Kamel when he sold his 37.5 percent holding in MBC. Saudi billionaire Prince al-Walid bin Talal was another investor. ART initially went on the air as a free service, but it became subscription-based in 1997 and this is its main source of revenue.

ART set out to be an entertainment network. Its five channels—kids, movies, music, sports, and variety—are mostly Arabic-originated (that is, they are not translated Western programs). Alterman cites Kamel as saying in 1995 that he created the station to counter foreign offerings: "There is a Western media campaign to undermine our Arab culture and traditions. . . . I don't allow anything on ART that I wouldn't want my children to watch."

ART does not focus on the news as much as the other channels do, although Rugh states that it has broken the occasional taboo. In 2000, ART added an Arab Islamic channel.

In its pursuit of appropriate Arabic programs, ART invested a great deal of money in the Media Production City near Cairo and slowly moved its offices to Egypt, where lower production costs were an attraction.

Al-Jazeera

The all-news al-Jazeera, based in Qatar, began broadcasting in November 1996. The station is linked with Qatar's government and received $137 million from it. The channel usually avoids criticizing Qatar, while being outspoken in its reports on other Arab states.

The station's creation came shortly after the June 1995 Qatari coup, when Emir Hamad bin Khalifa al-Thani overthrew his father. Among the motives ascribed to Qatar is a desire to modernize and open up the country, to turn a small, powerless country into a significant international actor, and to compete with (and sometimes bait) Qatar's overshadowing Saudi neighbor. Thus, for example, al-Jazeera's programs on religious topics have been criticized by conservative Saudi Arabians.

In the early days of the station, its staff was dominated by radical Arab nationalists, whose critique of governments was based not only on corruption but on perceived hypocrisy toward political ideals that saw moderation in negative terms. By around 2003, the tone was increasingly set by radical Islamists. A typical interview program would have guests representing two viewpoints on a controversial issue while the host and all the callers would take the radical side.

While al-Jazeera often criticizes Arab governments (other than Qatar's), its critiques are most often based on claiming they are insufficiently militant, insufficiently active in fighting Israel, confrontational toward the United States and the West, or too passive in supporting insurgents in Iraq or other places.

Moreover, while the channel's programs, such as *al-Ray al-Akhar* (The Other Opinion), present panelists with opposing perspectives, the station lets viewers know not so subtly which is the "correct" position. In one case, a deputy prime minister from Jordan debated a frequently imprisoned Islamist leader in a heated argument. The Jordanian government actually rebroadcast the program (indicating its satisfaction with the management and content of the program). This is a relatively rare sign of official tolerance.

Sometimes, however, al-Jazeera has cooperated closely with regimes, notably those of Saddam Hussein in Iraq and the Taliban in Afghanistan. The event that brought the station to international notice was its coverage of the December 1998 Operation Desert Fox—British and U.S. air strikes against Iraq. The absence of international television networks led to Western dependence on al-Jazeera at the time, just as CNN had been the source for coverage of Operation Desert Storm in 1991. Saddam Hussein gave al-Jazeera exclusive coverage of his January 1999 Army Day speech, in which he called for the overthrow of Arab monarchies.

In 1999, al-Jazeera was the only network to accept the Taliban's invitation to open offices in Afghanistan, and in June of that year it interviewed Osama bin Ladin. Al-Jazeera's exclusive broadcasts from Afghanistan after the September 2001 terrorist attacks against the United States were carried globally, because the Taliban had expelled all other correspondents. Its later broadcasts of statements by bin Ladin were used by other networks.

Al-Jazeera's coverage of the March 2003 invasion of Iraq enhanced its reputation among Arab viewers because it was so anti-American and supportive of Saddam's claims that he was winning. A July 2003 analysis from the U.S. government's Open Source Center asserted that al-Jazeera was the most hostile of all Arab media and that it "routinely interjects pejorative and emotive language to present a distorted image of the United States."

Secretary of Defense Donald Rumsfeld said in November 2003 that he had evidence that al-Jazeera (and al-Arabiya) cooperated with Iraqi insurgents, and he pointed to their being on the scene of insurgent attacks before they occurred. The two stations were also temporarily banned by the Iraqi Governing Council for broadcasting statements by former president Saddam Hussein.

Coverage of terrorism by the station's popular *al-Sharia wal-Hayat* (Islamic Law and Life) program (or as the station phrases it, "that which is called terrorism") is instructive. The program's popularity and resultant opinion-making ability, its inclusion of viewers' questions and comments, and its coverage of topics from an Islamic perspective make it representative of "one of the main socio-political currents in Arab society." *Al-Sharia wal-Hayat* addresses subjects on which the average Muslim might need guidance, such as the permissibility of so-called martyrdom operations (suicide bombings). The people who phone in to the program range from the poorly educated man-on-the-street to the engineer with an advanced degree. The program's guests are consistently Muslim scholars and community leaders. Author Ana Belen Soage-Antepazo argues that there is no "real debate" on *al-Sharia wal-Hayat*, because the callers, as well as the host and guests, agree on the basic question. The callers might have less nuanced views than the guests, but the guests consistently praise the callers' perspectives.

There are five recurring themes in *al-Sharia wal-Hayat*. The underlying text of the program is that Islam offers the solution to all of life's problems, and it is also the key to understanding the world. According to the program's host, Mahir Abdallah, "whether we want it or not, everything related to this *umma* [Muslim community] has to do with politics." The Islamic community itself is idealized, and its difficulties are attributed to a variety of factors, ranging from European colonialism to Muslims parting from the faith.

The second theme—that Muslims are always victims—builds on the first one. A frequent guest on the show, religious scholar Yusef al-Qaradawi, claims that there is a real Western policy of weakening the Muslim community. The West fears Islam's potential strength, so it seeks to undermine the community culturally and through evangelical efforts. As victims, Qaradawi adds, Muslims must utilize martyrdom operations and similar unconventional acts. He defends suicide operations by explaining that this is a weapon God gave to the weak.

The third theme is that the West and Islam are enemies, and that the Western representation of Islam is intentionally distorted in order to justify aggression against Muslims. Building on this is the argument that the West is "immoral and materialistic," although the occasional voice of moderation is heard. Muslim leaders from Western countries, for example, have cautioned against generalizing about Western attitudes and policies toward Muslims. This hostile West, according to the fourth theme of *al-Sharia wal-Hayat*, is aided by "treacherous" and "impious" Muslim regimes that collaborate with the West because they are unpopular and illegitimate, and need Western support to survive.

The fifth theme of *al-Sharia wal-Hayat* holds that the extremists are well intentioned even if misguided. The program makes a distinction between the poor who fight corrupt elites and foreigners on the one hand, and the wealthy—such as Osama bin Ladin—on the other. Members of the latter group misinterpret Islam but they mean well, Qaradawi asserts, although this does not excuse their actions. Yet he has agreed with callers who claim Arab regimes use the extremists as a pretext for cracking down on moderates, and furthermore, he has praised extremists' actions, such as the assassination of Egypt's President Anwar Sadat.

While it is often assumed that al-Jazeera is the most popular Arab station, there are no accurate statistics to prove this claim. The very factors that contribute to its popularity detract from its credibility, according to Soage-Antepazo. She refers to its "blatant, populist sentimentalism, with its continuous flow of images showing destroyed homes, mass funerals, and crying mothers in Palestine or Iraq." Soage-Antepazo adds that al-Jazeera's "bias" is yet another problem. She concludes by noting a "certain disregard toward religious minorities." The station mostly tries to appeal to the Muslim, and especially to the Sunni Muslim, majority.

Lebanese Broadcasting Corporation (LBC)

LBC began its terrestrial transmissions in August 1985, and the free LBC SAT was launched in April 1996. Its three encrypted channels—LBC America, LBC Australia, and LBC Europe—began that summer.

LBC concentrates on entertainment more than news, with an offering of music, variety, and gossip. Presenters tend to be comely women in revealing clothes. Typical is a program called *al-Layl Layltak*, which, according to Alterman, describes itself thus: "A program that receives a celebrity not to be interviewed as usual, but to be surrounded by four girls who ask him unusual, funny, and embarrassing questions." *Star Academy*, a reality show in which male and female competitors share a home for three months as audience members vote them off, is also unusually risqué for the Arab world, as are the popular Mexican soap operas the station runs.

That being said, LBC does have its own serious news programs, and it also rebroadcasts ABC News and CNN International. Its programming mix has been successful, and regional media experts have repeatedly cited the station as the only one to make a profit. Given its openness to Western programming and styles, the station chose in 2002 to team with *al-Hayat* newspaper to produce a news program from studios in London.

LBC has done well in attracting advertising from the Gulf, which presumably indicates a substantial viewership in Gulf countries. For this reason, the station strives to avoid offending audiences there. It is owned by Maronite Christian political figures, and its political programming is oriented toward this group. The impact of the relationship with the Maronites is unclear. One observer describes LBC as a Maronite "mouthpiece" that nevertheless is run as a commercial enterprise more than a propaganda instrument.

Arab News Network (ANN)

The London-based ANN went on the air in May 1997 as a twenty-four-hour news channel. Approximately two years later, it added documentaries, movies, and other entertainment in an effort to attract more viewers. It was owned and operated by Sawmar al-Assad, the son of Rifaat al-Assad, political opponent and brother of Syrian president Hafez al-Assad. The station avoided upsetting the regime in Damascus until Hafez's son Bashar came to power in 2000. Rifaat criticized the Syrian succession process, viewing himself as the proper next president. Damascus responded by issuing an arrest warrant.

ANN initially did not carry any advertising and was presumably subsidized by the owner's family, though there was also speculation about Saudi involvement since Rifaat is related by marriage to Crown Prince Abdullah. As of 2002, ANN began carrying advertising from Arab and international businesses, but it appears to have limited resources. It has just a few correspondents in several Arab capitals, its talk shows either host guests in the London studios or have telephone interviews, and the newscasts are often repeats of earlier ones. Unlike most other Arab channels, ANN supported the Iraqi opposition against Saddam Hussein.

Al-Arabiya

This all-news station began broadcasting in February 2003 from Dubai. MBC founder Sheikh Salah Kamel and Kuwaiti, Lebanese, and Saudi businessmen established it. Clearly, the station's goal was to compete with al-Jazeera for the number-one spot among satellite television channels.

The station ran into a number of problems during Operation Iraqi Freedom, according to author Philip Seib. First, it could not get accreditation because it was so new; then, one of its camera crews was captured by the Iraqi army. In November 2003, al-Arabiya was banned for a month by the Iraqi Governing Council after it broadcast an allegedly taped message from Saddam Hussein calling for attacks against Iraqis who cooperated with the coalition. The station was banned again in September 2006 on grounds that it had adopted "a policy that incites sectarianism and promotes violence." A January 2006 survey by Intermedia found that al-Arabiya is more popular than al-Jazeera in Iraq, probably due to the perception that al-Jazeera is pro-Baath.

In 2004, an al-Arabiya correspondent was physically attacked after he reported on a power struggle within the Palestinian Fatah. In January 2006, al-Arabiya angered Fatah and the al-Aqsa Martyrs Brigade by airing what was perceived as criticism of female Palestinian suicide bombers.

Al-Majd

Established in May 2003, the Saudi-financed al-Majd satellite station is based in Dubai, with production studios in Amman, Cairo, and Riyadh, and additional offices in other major Middle East cities. Its collection of channels includes one for children (launched January 2004), three religious ones (Holy Quran, August 2004; Islamic Sciences, March 2005; and Holy Hadith, March 2006); and one each for documentaries (June 2005) and "The World Today" (January 2006). Al-Majd utilizes a pay-per-view smart-card system, and it claims to have hundreds of thousands of subscribers. It also carries some advertising, mostly for food, household goods, and Islamic charities.

The station presents events from a Saudi and Wahhabi perspective, and the guests and speakers tend to be conservative Saudi clerics. On its programs, the grand mufti of Saudi Arabia, Sheikh Abd-al-Aziz al-Sheikh, has condemned extremism and discouraged young people from participating in jihadist training camps. Sheikh Salman al-Awdah, who once opposed the regime, now backs it and has spoken on al-Majd to condemn violence and extremism. During the summer 2006 war between Israel and Lebanon's Hezbollah, several clerics stated on al-Majd that Saudis should not join the conflict, and in a September 2005 program, speakers discouraged Saudis and other Arabs from joining the war in Iraq.

The station's programs reflect the regime's standpoint. Sheikh Dr. Ahmad Nawfal, a lecturer at the Shari'a Faculty of the University of Jordan, said in a November 2005 interview that "pro-Zionist Christians" intend to destroy the al-Aqsa Mosque in Jerusalem and erect a synagogue in its place; he also engages in Holocaust denial. Another guest, al-Imam University scholar Sheikh Abd al-Aziz Fawzan al-Fawzan, said in a January 2006 appearance that Muslims should hate Christians. In a December 2004 appearance, the sheikh described the deadly tsunami that slammed into South Asia as justified because at resorts there, "Fornication and sexual perversion of all kinds are rampant." He went on to call the natural disaster "a sign from Allah. It happened at Christmas, when fornicators and corrupt people from all over the world come to commit fornication and sexual perversion."

In addition to news and talk, the station carries cooking programs, women's issues (although there are no female presenters), and children's shows.

Al-Manar

Al-Manar (The Beacon), the television station associated with Lebanon's Hezbollah organization, began terrestrial broadcasts in June 1991. The station's general manager said in 1992 that its objective is to "express the views of the oppressed . . . and advocate a mass media that respects Islamic morals and Muslim tradition," adding that it will "focus on our hostility and hate toward Israel and its racist government system, whose downfall we see as a fundamental principle of ours."

In late 1994, the Lebanese government passed a law that all television stations must be licensed. Two years later it issued licenses to only five stations, to the exclusion of al-Manar, which continued broadcasting along with several other unlicensed stations. Al-Manar appealed the government decision and was granted a license in July 1997. In March 2000, al-Manar announced its desire to create a satellite station and received Lebanese cabinet approval the next month.

When it went on the air, al-Manar had only old equipment and a weak signal that reached parts of Beirut with difficulty. Today, it utilizes advanced equipment and has a global reach. Whereas the station had few employees in its early days, now al-Manar has bureaus in Egypt, Iran, Jordan, and Dubai, and as well as correspondents in Europe, the Middle East (including Iraq and the Palestinian territories), and the United States. Al-Manar carries advertising, and it also gets support from private investors and donors, but its management claims that the station operates at a loss. Author Avi Jorisch asserts that "Iranian sponsorship" is behind al-Manar's continued activities, although station officials deny this.

Terrestrial broadcasts began at just five hours a day, but had increased to eighteen by 2000. The satellite broadcasts expanded, too, from three hours a day in May 2000 to all day by the end of the year. The programs are not identical, however, with terrestrial programming having a more sectarian angle than the satellite programs, which are intended for a broader pan-Arab and Muslim audience. Initially, therefore, programs focused on the issue of Palestinian sovereignty and what the station portrayed as the Israeli occupation of Arab lands. Hezbollah secretary-general Hassan Nasrallah was shown calling for regional unity. The pattern changed slightly after the March 2003 invasion of Iraq by U.S. and allied forces, and some programming utilized violent imagery to encourage action against U.S. troops.

The station promotes jihad. Martyrdom is a recurring theme, and videotapes made by suicide bombers shortly before they kill themselves are aired. The sacrifices of Hezbollah combatants are emphasized and glorified. Programs also make the point that Hezbollah cares for its combatants. Programs such as these are intended to aid recruitment.

State-Run Satellite Channels

Governments began to establish satellite television networks shortly after the private ones were created. Egypt created the first in 1990, followed by Kuwait (1991), Tunisia and Dubai (1992), Jordan (1993), Morocco (1994), and other Middle Eastern states. Rugh describes governmental involvement in satellite television as "almost universal" and "promoted primarily by political motivations." Even the emirates of the United Arab Emirates (UAE), such as Sharjah and Ajman, have created satellite stations for promotional purposes.

The state-run satellite channels' content was similar to that of the terrestrial channels.

Nevertheless, the state-run channels did increase their news and political programs as a reaction to the competition from private channels. For example, Abu Dhabi Television was launched in 2000, and when Operation Iraqi Freedom began in March 2003, the station adopted a twenty-four-hour-per-day format. Abu Dhabi TV has news bulletins every three hours and also broadcasts culture and entertainment programs, as well as documentaries and political shows. The station is connected with the UAE government—it was originally part of the Ministry of Information and Culture, and when the ministry was dismantled in 2006, the station was made part of Abu Dhabi Media Company. It is managed by Emirates Media, Inc.

Unquestionably, European—mainly London-based—media and satellite television have become major parts of the Arab communications system. Many observers believe that this has opened up discussion of delicate topics and challenged the status quo. At the same time, though, it can be argued that these institutions, especially those related to television, reinforce the status quo.

This is especially true regarding the dominant ideologies of Arab nationalism and Islamism, which are disseminated quite effectively by the overwhelming majority of programs and newspaper articles. These positions are divorced from the interests of specific regimes by the more independent channels and publications but are nevertheless echoed. In a few cases, notably that of *al-Sharq al-Awsat*, liberal democratic ideas are presented, but this is relatively rare. In this context, honest and accurate reporting and truly open debate are equally uncommon.

References and Further Reading

Alterman, Jon B. *New Media, New Politics? From Satellite Television to the Internet in the Arab World.* Washington, DC: Washington Institute for Near East Policy, 1998.

Ayish, Muhammad I. "Arab Television Goes Commercial: A Case Study of the Middle East Broadcasting Center." *Gazette* 59:6 (1997): 473–494.

Boyd, Douglas A. "International Radio Broadcasting in Arabic: A Survey of Broadcasters and Audiences." *Gazette* 59:6 (1997): 445–472.

Ghareeb, Edmund. "New Media and the Information Revolution in the Arab World: An Assessment." *Middle East Journal* 54:3 (Summer 2000): 402–409.

Sakr, Naomi. *Satellite Realms: Transnational Television, Globalization and the Middle East.* London: IB Tauris, 2002.

Seib, Phillip. "Hegemonic No More: Western Media, the Rise of al-Jazeera, and the Influence of Diverse Voices." *International Studies Review* 7 (2005): 601–615.